T0320526

Research Anthology on Applying Social Networking Strategies to Classrooms and Libraries

Information Resources Management Association
USA

Volume III

Published in the United States of America by
IGI Global
Information Science Reference (an imprint of IGI Global)
701 E. Chocolate Avenue
Hershey PA, USA 17033
Tel: 717-533-8845
Fax: 717-533-8661
E-mail: cust@igi-global.com
Web site: http://www.igi-global.com

Library of Congress Cataloging-in-Publication Data

Names: Information Resources Management Association, editor.
Title: Research anthology on applying social networking strategies to
  classrooms and libraries / Information Resources Management Association,
  editor.
Description: Hershey PA : Information Science Reference, 2022. | Includes
  bibliographical references. | Summary: "This reference book presents
  contributed chapters that describe the applications, tools, and
  opportunities provided by the intersection of education and social
  media, considering the ways in which social media encourages learner
  engagement and community participation"-- Provided by publisher.
Identifiers: LCCN 2022030171 (print) | LCCN 2022030172 (ebook) | ISBN
  9781668471234 (hardcover) | ISBN 9781668471241 (ebook)
Subjects: LCSH: Social media in education. | Libraries and social media. |
  Online social networks--Educational applications | Online social
  networks--Library applications.
Classification: LCC LB1044.87 .R46 2022 (print) | LCC LB1044.87 (ebook) |
  DDC 371.33/44678--dc23/eng/20220920
LC record available at https://lccn.loc.gov/2022030171
LC ebook record available at https://lccn.loc.gov/2022030172

British Cataloguing in Publication Data
A Cataloguing in Publication record for this book is available from the British Library.

For electronic access to this publication, please contact: eresources@igi-global.com.

List of Contributors

Table of Contents

Section 2
Development and Design Methodologies

Volume II

Section 3
Tools and Technologies

Volume III

Section 4
Utilization and Applications

Section 5
Organizational and Social Implications

Section 6
Managerial Impact

Section 7
Critical Issues and Challenges

Preface

The introduction of social media has given many communities the opportunity to connect and communicate with each other at a higher level than ever before. Many organizations, from businesses to governments, have taken advantage of this important tool to conduct research and enhance efficiency. Libraries and educational institutions have also made use of social media to enhance educational marketing, engage with learning communities, adapt educational tools, and more.

Staying informed of the most up-to-date research trends and findings is of the utmost importance. That is why IGI Global is pleased to offer this four-volume reference collection of reprinted IGI Global book chapters and journal articles that have been handpicked by senior editorial staff. This collection will shed light on critical issues related to the trends, techniques, and uses of various applications by providing both broad and detailed perspectives on cutting-edge theories and developments. This collection is designed to act as a single reference source on conceptual, methodological, technical, and managerial issues, as well as to provide insight into emerging trends and future opportunities within the field.

The *Research Anthology on Applying Social Networking Strategies to Classrooms and Libraries* is organized into seven distinct sections that provide comprehensive coverage of important topics. The sections are:

1. Fundamental Concepts and Theories;
2. Development and Design Methodologies;
3. Tools and Technologies;
4. Utilization and Applications;
5. Organizational and Social Implications;
6. Managerial Impact; and
7. Critical Issues and Challenges.

The following paragraphs provide a summary of what to expect from this invaluable reference tool.

Section 1, "Fundamental Concepts and Theories," serves as a foundation for this extensive reference tool by addressing crucial theories essential to implementing social networking into classrooms and libraries. The first chapter, "Social Media and the Future of the Instructional Model," by Prof. Soha Abdeljaber of Rising Leaders Academy, USA and Prof. Kathryn Nieves Licwinko of New Jersey City University, USA, provides the latest information on social media and its application in the instructional model. The chapter contains information on how social media enhances learning, especially at times where remote learning is necessary, such as COVID-19. The last chapter, "Facebook in the International Classroom," by Prof. Inna P. Piven of Unitec Institute of Technology, New Zealand, explores international students' learning experiences with Facebook-based activities within the eight-week study term known as the intensive mode of course delivery. By implementing participant observation and two asynchronous Facebook focus groups, the study investigates the potential values of Facebook for learning from international students' perspective.

Section 2, "Development and Design Methodologies," presents in-depth coverage of the design and development of social networking implementation. The first chapter, "Bridging Activities: Social Media for Connecting Language Learners' in-School and Out-of-School Literacy Practices," by Prof. Ellen Yeh of Columbia College Chicago, USA and Prof. Svetlana Mitric of University of Illinois at Chicago, USA, applies pedagogically-focused project design by using Instagram as a platform to investigate how the use of social media such as Instagram in a multimodal digital storytelling model could bridge the skills English language learners (ELLs) learn in the classroom to out-of-school literacy practices. The last chapter, "Social Media, Cyberculture, Blockchains, and Education: A New Strategy for Brazilian Higher Education," by Prof. Matheus Batalha Moreira Nery of Uninassau, Brazil; Prof. Magno Oliveira Macambira of Universidade Estadual de Feira de Santana, Brazil; Prof. Marlton Fontes Mota of Universidade Tiradentes, Brazil; and Prof. Izabella Cristine Oliveira Rezende of Uninassau, Brazil, contributes to the debate of the uses of social media, cyberculture, and blockchain technology for the development of educational strategies. It reviews the existing scientific literature on social networking, social media, cyberculture, and blockchains related to Brazil.

Section 3, "Tools and Technologies," explores the various tools and technologies used in classrooms and libraries for social networking. The first chapter, "Using Social Media in Creating and Implementing Educational Practices," by Profs. Inna P. Piven and Robyn Gandell of Unitec Institute of Technology, New Zealand, examines the use of social media as a couse management tool, the use of social media to enhance student-centered learning and the need for institutional support for using social media in educational contexts. The last chapter, "Is Twitter an Unexploited Potential in Indian Academic Libraries? Case Study Based on Select Academic Library Tweets," by Prof. Swapan Kumar Patra of Tshwane University of Technology, South Africa, maps the Indian libraries' Twitter activities, taking academic libraries as case study.

Section 4, "Utilization and Applications," describes the opportunities and challenges of social networking implementation. The first chapter, "Navigating the Shortcomings of Virtual Learning Environments via Social Media," by Profs. Puvaneswary Murugaiah and Siew Hwa Yen of School of Distance Education, Universiti Sains Malaysia, Penang, Malaysia, uncovers the shortcomings of the use of virtual learning environments (VLEs) for language learning in several Malaysian institutions of higher learning. It also highlights the use of social media in addressing the barriers. The last chapter, "Nexus Between Social Network, Social Media Use, and Loneliness: A Case Study of University Students, Bangladesh," by Prof. Md. Aminul Islam of University of Liberal Arts Bangladesh, Bangladesh and Prof. Bezon Kumar of Rabindra University, Bangladesh, explores how real-life social network and social media use are related to loneliness among university students in Bangladesh.

Section 5, "Organizational and Social Implications," includes chapters discussing the impact of social networking on education and library organizations and beyond. The first chapter, "Identifiable Problems in Social Media: Concerning Legal Awareness Within Academic Libraries," by Prof. Amy D. Dye-Reeves of Murray State University, USA, serves as a primer for academic librarians on helping patrons with disabilities receive, protect, and understand disseminated content on a multitude of popular social media networking platforms. The content of the chapter provides introductory material on the Americans with Disabilities Act (ADA) and the Family Educational Rights and Privacy Act. The last chapter, "Using Twitter to Form Professional Learning Communities: An Analysis of Georgia K-12 School Personnel Discussing Educational Technology on Twitter," by Profs. Charles B. Hodges, Lucas John Jensen, and Mete Akcaoglu of Georgia Southern University, USA, diescusses teacher professional development taking place on Twitter in Georgia, USA.

Section 6, "Managerial Impact," covers the internal and external impacts of social networking within education and library administration. The first chapter, "Social Media in Tertiary Education: Considerations and Potential Issues," by Prof. Ann M. Simpson of Unitec Institute of Technology, New Zealand, addresses some of the considerations and potential issues that impact our use of social media in the higher education classroom. It examines social media as an educational tool in higher education, possible pedagogies for social media use, potential educational contexts, and privacy concerns raised by social media use in educational environments. The last chapter, "Social Media Integration in Educational Administration as Information and Smart Systems: Digital Literacy for Economic, Social, and Political Engagement in Namibia," by Profs. Sadrag Panduleni Shihomeka and Helena N. Amadhila of University of Namibia, Namibia, explains that there are various groups on Facebook where youthful education administrators can use to post educational information and discuss pertinent issues concerning their institutions.

Section 7, "Critical Issues and Challenges," presents coverage of academic and research perspectives on challenges to social networking in education and libraries. The first chapter, "Making Social Media More Social: A Literature Review of Academic Libraries' Engagement and Connections Through Social Media Platforms," by Prof. Elia Trucks of University of Denver, USA, explores how academic libraries have used social media for broadcasting information, responsive communication, and engagement. The last chapter, "Social Media Usage for Informal Learning in Malaysia: Academic Researcher Perspective," by Prof. Mohmed Y. Mohmed Al-Sabaawi of Department of Management Information Systems, College of Administration and Economics, University of Mosul, Iraq; Prof. Halina Mohamed Dahlan of Information Systems Department, Azman Hashim International Business School, Universiti Teknologi Malaysia, Malaysia; and Prof. Hafiz Muhammad Faisal Shehzad of Department of Computer Science and IT, University of Sargodha, Pakistan, explores the use of social media for informal learning, barriers, benefits, and effect of individual factors.

Although the primary organization of the contents in this multi-volume work is based on its seven sections, offering a progression of coverage of the important concepts, methodologies, technologies, applications, social issues, and emerging trends, the reader can also identify specific contents by utilizing the extensive indexing system listed at the end of each volume. As a comprehensive collection of research on the latest findings related to social networking in education and library practices, the *Research Anthology on Applying Social Networking Strategies to Classrooms and Libraries* provides pre-service teachers, teacher educators, faculty and administrators of both K-12 and higher education, librarians, archivists, government officials, researchers, and academicians with a complete understanding of the applications and impacts of social networking. Given the vast number of issues concerning usage, failure, success, strategies, and applications of social networking applied to classrooms and libraries, the *Research Anthology on Applying Social Networking Strategies to Classrooms and Libraries* encompasses the most pertinent research on the applications, impacts, uses, and strategies of social networking.

Chapter 52

The Use of Social Media by Medical Librarians for Inclusive Engagement in the Management of HIV/AIDS in Nigeria University Teaching Hospitals

Wilson Chukwunedum Ochonogor
University of KwaZulu-Natal, South Africa

Stephen Mutula
University of KwaZulu-Natal, South Africa

ABSTRACT

Information and communication technologies (ICTs) have over the years evolved and synthesized to leverage a wide variety of tasks in all fields of human endeavor including library services. This rapid transformation has not only affected information handling procedures but has equally reshaped approach to the work environment in that librarians attached to medical libraries is required to acquire some knowledge of medicine in order to adequately and efficiently make informed decisions that can positively impact on the general medical practice and specifically the management of HIV/AIDS. The use of ICTs such as social media (SM) has further made the work environment a community pivot, a rallying point, rather than the solitary tedium that has retarded learning, communication, advancement, cooperation, and community support in the past.

BACKGROUND

The internet has greatly influenced SM penetration into all aspects of library services especially in the medical library where community of users (CoUs) can converge, confer and proffer simplified work output, better doctor-patient relationship and effective treatment. Hence, for effective implementation

DOI: 10.4018/978-1-6684-7123-4.ch052

of SM in Nigeria university teaching hospitals, there is the need for the following to be put into consideration: formulation of online groups; schedule of regular updating of the site and contact information; simplification of keywords for easy content search and profiling; need to always inform members of current items, creating novel ideas as cleverly and satisfying as possible, need to widen out or reach others with novelties, advancement, activities, current drugs for specific ailments, and resistive drugs.

INTRODUCTION

The success of every establishment depend largely on the availability of information at its disposal. University teaching hospitals are charged with the responsibility of providing useful information to its community and for caring for their patients. They depend on the services of the library to be able to meet with this demand. The library itself in modern times largely depends on information and communication technologies (ICTs) in order to satisfy the information needs of both medical staff, students, and the community. ICT has evolved, diversified, and synthesized to leverage a wide variety of tasks in the medical field as such, the fastest means of communication that can get to the intended public mostly would be sought after. Access to current and useful information is an integral part of national development, whilst ICT such as SM plays a vital role in leveraging university teaching hospital objectives in ensuring that adequate and swift response to healthcare service delivery is practiced (Ochonogor & Okite-Amughoro 2018). To achieve this objective, both the medical practitioners, librarians, students, patients, and the stakeholders must be inclusively engaged and ensure a shared and satisfactory obligations.

The use of SM has however made the work environment a community pivot, or a rallying point, rather than the solitary tedium that has retarded learning, communication, health service delivery and advancement, cooperation or collaboration, and community support in the past. The term social media is broad and constantly evolving (Ventola, 2014) and generally referred to as internet-based tools that allow individuals and communities to gather and communicate; to share information, ideas, personal messages, images and other contents; and, in some cases, to collaborate with other users in real time; (Chauhan, & Coffin, 2012; ASHP, 2012; Duke, Anstey, Carter, Gosse, Hutchens & Marsh, 2017; Lambert, Barry, & Stokes 2012; Von Muhlen & Ohno-Machado, 2012; Ventola 2014) to sustain and ensure inclusivity within the health system. Such prevalent usage of SM has triggered the growing need for a corresponding and enhanced awareness of the field upon which groups forming a social network should be based. Hence, sustaining the group by soliciting information from all its members especially those who are vast in topics of discussion.

As SM use in the field of medical profession gains more ground, it provides tools for the sharing of health information, to debate healthcare policy and practice issues, to promote good health behaviors, to engage with the public, and to educate and interact with patients, caregivers, students, and colleagues (Ventola, 2014) including librarians who source, locate, preserve, and share the required information; and stakeholders responsible for the policy formulation and day-to-day administrative care of man and material items of the teaching hospital. Hence, for a modern UTH librarian or generally, clinical medical librarian (CML) to perform their duty of information provision for the community of medical profession, they require at least some degree of medical training. According to Taggart, Grewe, Conserve, Gliwa, & Isler, (2015) SM, including mobile technologies and social networking sites, are being used increasingly as part of human immunodeficiency virus (HIV) prevention and treatment efforts. They further asserted that SM is an important avenue for communication about HIV, likewise its use may continue to increase and become more widespread. This increase can only arise when librarians attached to teaching hospitals or any other medical library circulate adequate information concerning the use of SM as a tool for HIV/AIDS management and prevention.

According to Hu, Farnham & Monroy-Hernández (2013) SM systems promised powerful opportunities for people to connect to timely, and relevant information at the hyper local level. They also said it has become one of the few sources of local news and life-saving information where traditional media is sometimes censored by governments or even criminal organizations. Social networking media (SNM) affords all the users freedom of expression that no government of criminal organization can censor, and it generates huge information content streams, which leverage, both academia, health profession, developers efforts in providing unbiased, powerful indications of users' opinion and interests (Vakali, Giatsoglou & Antaris (2012). It generally becomes imperative for the health profession under the oversight of seasoned and medical certified librarian to adopt and use SM for their effective medical health service delivery and be able to manage the wide spread of HIV/AIDS.

As the library has the responsibility for the provision of information, to organize and disseminate such information, it becomes interesting for them – librarians to ensure proper search for social media groups (SMGs) that will be of benefit to the medical profession for clinical excellence. Achieving this requires that the librarians become conversant with the profession by acquiring a certificate to position them on how to connect clinicians to various SMGs using their profiles to organize such groups as was done in periodical routine. When the librarian sought and provides the needed information through his online search for groups that the clinicians may form strong tie, they may readily accept to use SM even when they initially would have objected. Bearing in mind that the medical field is time staking, the librarian should work towards saving the time of the health professionals so that they can attend to their duty of saving lives. This unsolicited information delivery will motivate medical practitioners to have a rethink towards SM use in fostering their life saving job. Once they become motivated, they will naturally yearn for more of such services. This is especially important as HIV/AIDS causes stigmatization, depression and shame leading to most affected people in Nigeria not being interested in revealing their status or going for the test all together.

In this chapter, we will look at:

1. The meaning of social media
2. Social media sites
3. What is inclusive engagement?
4. The role of librarian in a medical library
5. Using social media to manage HIV/AIDS
6. Doctors, librarians, students and stakeholders' inclusivity

MEANING OF SOCIAL MEDIA

Having alluded to the varied definitions given by scholars on social media, it would be important to note the several forms of social media. SM are web-based tools that are used for computer-mediated communication and in health care, they have been used to maintain or improve peer-to-peer and clinician-to-patient communication, provide institutional branding, and improve the speed of interaction between and across different healthcare stakeholders (Grajales, Sheps, Ho, Novak-Lauscher & Eysenbach, 2014). SM is internet-based media interface, designed to connect people to each other irrespective of location and facilitate intellectual interaction with user-generated content (Brasg, 2013), for advancement and effective contributions to health care service provision and especially management of HIV/AIDS among members of the same group. SM can be defined to include YouTube, Twitter, and Facebook (Nair, 2011) for the sole aim of communicating amongst a group of people with common objective. Social media technologies (SMTs) have many different forms including blogs, business networks, enterprise social networks, forums, microblogs, photo sharing, products/services review, social bookmarking, social gaming, social networks, video sharing, and virtual worlds (Aichner & Jacob, 2015). The versatility, portability and usefulness of SM in modern workplace permeates compactly with library profession especially those attached to health institutions. With SM, librarians will be able to adequately offer specialized services to the medical library audience (MLA), chiefly the medical professionals and students as they are bound to interact with a wide and varied community of group members, filtering the results of their conversation and making informed recommendations on sources and materials to be consulted by these users to enable them render better and efficient services.

SM refers to software that enables individuals and communities to gather, communicate, share, and in some cases collaborate or play, typically in the context of applications accessible through internet browsers or mobile devices (von Muhlen & Ohno-Machado, 2012). They inferred that it has broadly affected medicine publicly by increasing communication with and among patients who are connected in one social network. Social network applications (e.g., Facebook, Twitter, Foursquare) have gone viral and are dominating the internet today, and they are uniting with conventional applications, such as multimedia streaming, to produce new social media applications, e.g., YouTube-like sites (Wu, Wu, Li, Zhang, Li, & Lau, 2012). It is expected that the future of SM will continue to adopt other versatile technologies for functionalities like streaming to perfect proactive information service and technology demand especially in the field of medicine and particularly for the management of HIV/AIDS and other dreaded diseases.

SM builds on the ideological and technological foundations of the web 2.0 and that allow the creation and exchange of user-generated content (Van Dijck & Poell, 2013). They bolstered this point by inferring that over the past decade, SM platforms have penetrated deeply into the mechanics of everyday life, affecting people's information interactions, as well as institutional structures and professional routines. As such SM can be said to have reshaped the normative face-to-face interaction between family members, friends, workmates, schoolmates and the world in general. Generally, SM has the potentials to transcend its intended membership as each participating members might share the output of their group discussions with others who are none members of the group while the generating source remains normal, unless otherwise negatively affected. The pervasive SMT provides prodigious momentum for a more disruptive mode of information-sharing and relationship building practice and within the space of, a large portion of previously passive information consumers has been transformed into powerful creators, transmitters, and discussants of information (Lee. Oh & Kim, 2013). Hence SM can be said to have broken the ethics of once exclusive reserve of most organizations as debate for a more proactive opinions are solicited from members of an organization before decisions are taken.

The entrant of SMTs in the medical profession must be capitalized on by medical professionals to unprecedentedly accelerate medical public awareness (MPA) especially in relation to management and preventing of the spread of HIV within Nigeria. SMTs are global information infrastructure (GII), where individuals, such as medical doctors and librarians bring their social relations online and share information, photos, videos, songs, as well as ideas (Magno, Comarela, Saez-Trumper Cha, & Almeida, 2012), and these helps to create awareness if properly deployed by medical physicians and MLs in Nigeria. It is clear from all indication that the use of SMN either in the medical field for health care service delivery, or in the library for the dissemination of information within Nigeria is much needed as records shows the effect of HIV/AIDS in Nigeria.

SMTs harnesses the collective knowledge, ignorance, biases, and insights of the active participants (Nair, 2011) thus, informing, awakening a need for an answer, critic others contributions, and or drawing conclusions on generated issues among members of a group. This makes SM use more interesting as important life questions can be anonymously asked, answers sought, thereby making informed decision. SM is much like a continuous learning process whereby new information is constantly created as such Prensky, 2003; Anderson, 2004) postulates that, in SM generally, we socialize and learn:

- Behavior through imitation, feedback, and practice;
- Creativity through playing and socializing;
- Facts through association, drill, memory, and questions;
- Judgement through reviewing cases, asking questions, making choices, and receiving feedback and coaching;
- Language through imitation, practice, and immersion;
- Observation through viewing examples and receiving feedback;
- Procedures through imitation and practice;
- Processes through system analysis, deconstruction, and practice;
- Systems through discovering principles and undertaking graduate tasks;
- Reasoning through puzzles, problems, and examples;
- Skills (physical or mental) through imitation, feedback, continuous practice, and increasing challenge;
- Speeches or performance roles through memorization, practice, and coaching;
- Theories through logic, explanation, and questionings.

It has been observed in recent times that SM creates a great influence on how the work environment functions. As such it becomes critical to measure the influence of social media in areas where it has been applied. Gu & Ye, (2014) averred that with the growing influence of social media, firms increasingly take an active role in interacting with their audience (Gu & Ye, 2014). According to Kami (2013), social media measurement can be as fairly simple or highly complex depending on one's organizational goals or objective.

Social Media Sites

The advent of SM has caused almost every profession around the globe to appraise the features of several networks to adopt and use those that are best suited for their profession. This has adversely affected the number of SMNS with many ascribed to various fields of study and discipline. The following are some of the SMNSs they include both general and specialized sites:

- **Twitter**: This is an online social networking service that enables users to send and receive 140-character messages or tweet (Attai, Cowher, Al-Hamadani, Schoger, Staley, & Landercasper, 2015). It is a space for the informal sharing of health information and advice and may also provide a venue to identify potential dangers, promote positive behavior change and disseminate valid information (Scanfeld, Scanfeld, & Larson, 2010) to facilitate management of HIV/AIDS.

- **Instagram**: Instagram is a social media site that is associated with mobile applications such as iOS and Android. It prompts users to turn their mobile photographs into visually alluring pictures, and these are shared within members of the same network or group. These images can be made public in other social networks, such as Twitter, Facebook, Tumblr, Flickr, and Foursquare. The advent of smartphones with unprecedented high and clear image quality, led to the grand adoption of Instagram where pictures including comments can be posted online. Images posted on the Instagram projects better quality than other social media network/site (SMN/S), hence, its use in the field of medicine can lend credence to better medical images and effective health care service delivery.

- **Pinterest**: This is a photo-only microblogging site where users define themed boards for posting content (e.g., food, art, marine fish including HIV/AIDS images) which can equally be shared via Facebook and Twitter (Bik & Goldstein, 2013). The images are like adverts but can contain warning signs as well, so when used for HIV/AIDS images, group members or the general public after accessing them would be able to know some of the signs or symptoms of the disease. This affords the physician an anonymous posting and patients and the general public benefits from such posts after viewing them.

- **Tumblr**: Tumblr is a microblogging site that can publish any type of media very easily and quickly, such media includes: photos, videos, or short quotes as posted to long written narratives (Bik & Goldstein, 2013). Physicians can take advantage of this kind of site to reach as many persons as possible whenever he makes a post. The librarian can equally ascribe reference on how to reach a physician charged with the management of HIV/AIDS within an hospital or contact information of such physicians.

- **Blackboard VLE**: The blackboard VLE is a learning centered interface or application which allows for mapping of schedules, tracking of activities and achievement, online learning support, online tutor support, peer group support, general communications – through several media, and a connection to other networks both internally and externally. Blackboard facilitating features according to Heaton-Shretha, Gipps, Edirisingha & Linsey, (2007) includes: An 'announcements' area: a type of noticeboard, where message might be uploaded by staff (physicians) ; documents and files area, to which files in a wide variety of formats (word, PowerPoint, Excel, or video and audio creation software) might be uploaded by staff; communication tools: - each department in Blackboard can be allocated its own discussion board, virtual classroom (virtual theatre) or chatroom, and email function; a digital drop-box through which students (patients) might submit assignments (health information query) to physicians electronically; assessment facilities, through which staff (physicians) might create quizzes (health information needs) and tests (health reports) for summative or formative (health requirement) purposes; group features: distinct 'group areas' can be created for groups of students (such as, HIV/AIDS infected persons and those not infected) on a Blackboard module – notice (e.g., students working on a common project – management and or prevention), each with its own discussion board, online file exchange and email function.

- **Facebook**: This is a social media network that is widely used among social network users. it is very popular especially among students and is divided into two opinions: (1) create public profile that may reach a different audience than Twitter or blogs; or (2) they eschew using Facebook for research-related purposes at all, perhaps maintaining private profile for only their closest friends and family (no one should get offended if people do not accept their friend request) (Bik & Goldstein, 2013). Facebook allows users to accept or add friends, send message, and update personal profiles in order to notify friends and peers about themselves, personal activities, current medical procedure, prevention counsel on diseases like HIV/AIDS, HIV/AIDS secure information profiles (Quan-Haase, & Young, 2010). Again, they said, users can also join or form virtual groups, develop applications, host content, and learn about each other's interests, hobbies, and relationship statuses through users' online profiles. In fact, Facebook can help users' widen their range of friendship as they form peer-to-peer, special group, and general group. This implies that while the medical doctors form their medical group, medical librarians also form theirs, HIV/AIDS carriers also form their groups, but does not relinquish members of all these various groups forming a general yet specific group on HIV/AIDS in order to be able to effectively manage the spread and if possible, prevent it altogether.

- **WhatsApp**: This is a cost effective messaging application that allows a user to send and receive messages called chats over internet data plan that is used for emails and web browsing. WhatsApp messenger is applicable with several phone mobile devices such as iPhones, Nokia, Blackberry, Android, and most smart phones that are available in the market today (Mbanaso, Dandaura, Ezeh, & Iwuckukwu, 2015). The WhatsApp application allows only the sender and the receiver of any of the sent content such as: photos, videos, messages, files, or any kind of message will be able to access such chats. Since health especially HIV/AIDS related issue and records are always treated with outmost confidentiality, this use of WhatsApp for medical update and HIV management through this medium becomes considerably an issue of significance.

- **LinkedIn**: This is an SMN that is professionally inclined and emboldens users to build abridged CV in order to institute 'connections'. It makes strict use of individuals' profiles and eliminates other personal details such as favorite music, favorite movies, books, political affiliations, religious affiliations, hobbies, and others. Much like other SM, LinkedIn friendship or membership can be solicited or recommended as stale members notifies others about a members recent achievements in the field. It is increasing its popularity and has become the most used SMN platform for professional activities, even exceeding the popularity of Facebook. While medical librarians can use the LinkedIn to solicit information from other medical librarians across the globe on how to better serve physicians with their information needs, physicians can equally use LinkedIn to get professional information from colleagues who live in a distant location on how to manage HIV/AIDS pandemic. Hence, HIV/AIDS patients can benefit twofold: from the physician and the medical librarian. While the physician handles treatment and advice, the librarian provides the necessary information for the patients' consultation.

- **Flickr**: Flickr is a photo sharing website that aims to provide new ways of organizing photos and other images (Rafferty, & Hidderley, 2007). Flickr adopts author-based indexing but can be done collaboratively if the author allows his family members, friends, and other contacts permission to organize photos – not just to add comments, but also notes and tags (Rafferty, & Hidderley, 2007). It does not only share photos, it also shares videos which can be retrieved in many formats just as photos and videos can be uploaded from a variety of appliances such as mobile devices, the web, and personal computers; and is easy to access from a variety of software as well. This makes its usefulness valid as it will allow physicians to upload photos and videos to educate their patients on how to individually manage HIV/AIDS. On the part of the librarian assisting the physicians becomes even simpler as they can organize site where relevant HIV/AIDS related photos and videos can be found online and forward same to the physician to enable them attend to patients needs on time and with adequate and vivid illustrations on what the patients should do and at what time they should do such things.

- **Google+**: this is an SMN created by google and announced as a new generation of social network and included several new features, such as circles that allow users to share different content with different people and hangouts that lets users to create video chatting session and invite up to nine people from their circle of friends to share the environment (Magno, Comarela, Saez-Trumper Cha, & Almeidda, 2012). They also said since its launch, google+ has been adding new users rapidly as the mere registration of a Gmail account automatically registers such individual google+ account. The good thing about this is that rather than asking An HIV/AIDS patient for registration in order to get updates on new treatments or change of drugs, the mere registration of the patient in the electronic registry of the hospital qualifies such an individual if he or she has a Gmail account. This also helps the librarian to be able to tract and forward relevant health tips on healthy life style that will help HIV carriers remain in stable condition for a long time.

- **YouTube**: This a social media site created in 2005 with the aim of allowing users' to share video, and interact. It can serve the purpose of providing health information for the general public on issues relating to HIV/AIDS drugs, prevention, and other counselling. This network or site facilitates easy access of information that are posted by physicians charged with the responsibility of handling HIV/AIDS cases. Since YouTube has long been in use by many, and it provides an accessible and popular medium for librarians to deliver point of contact and supplementary information and library instruction (Monge, 2007) and also facilitates patients accessibility for their HIV/AIDS counselling, while the physicians can constantly generate or create new videos for their willing patients to access. One very good thing about YouTube is that it does not require any registration, just click and the video or audio is right there on the screen for your viewing or listening. Hence, so, users are not always faced with the challenge of being identified as the sickness in most countries or communities comes with stigmatization.

- **Azure**: This is an enterprise integration solution designed by Microsoft, it combines both computing infrastructure and a platform for developing applications. Although Azure is not a social medial, it is a facilitator as it allows streaming both upstreaming and down-streaming otherwise known as decoupling in real-time. For those who would love to stream or download or upload any content, this application becomes useful.

- **Vlogs**: Vlogs are a form of online publishing, it allows everyone with web access and simple video production tools – such as a computer and a webcam or cell phone with video capabilities – to create and post content (Molyneaux, O'Donnell, Gibson & Singer, 2008). They are generated by individual user members and posted online to solicit comments from members of the group.

- **Wikis**: Wikis used in medical and health care information (MHCI) facilitate information circulation among professionals as it help create and share new knowledge and dialogue collaboratively in virtual terms. It also enable learners engage with others in the same group. Wikis help medical doctors in local or remote locations to collaborate with friends in other parts of the world to share experiences on how they coped with particular disease pandemic. Although wikis has good features, it is prone to hacking and health being a sensitive issue, this makes the use of wikis risky in the health environment.

- **Podcasts**: This is a social networking site that allows the creation of audio and video contents for an audience that would want to listen or view the content when they want, where they want, and how they want ((Buolos, Maramba & Wheeler, 2006) choosing the form that they prefer. They also stated the current educational podcasting applications for medical use to include: recording of lectures for those students unable to attend the lecture in person – this is also applicable to the theatre environment where surgical activities are recorded for future references and display of novelty; audio recordings of textbook content by chapter allowing students to read or view text while walking or driving to class; and downloadable libraries of high resolution heart and respiratory sounds for medical students. Podcast uses really simple syndicate (RSS) which is embedded in Windows Internet Explorer 7. As such, users do not have to depend on devoted "podcatcher-programme" in order to access and download items.

- **Blogs**: Blog is a web site of engages people in knowledge sharing, reflection, and debates, so it often attracts a large and dedicated readership; with main features which include easy posting, archives of previous posts, and standalone Web page for each post to the blog with a unique URL (Buolos, Maramba & Wheeler, 2006). In this way, a clinician can post a photo taken with his digital camera, and make comment on the post for debate.

- **Mashups**: This is a web site that combines information and services from multiple sources on the web; it can be grouped into seven categories, namely: mapping, search, mobile, messaging, sports, shopping, and movies and serves to enhance user interface, value-added information by aggregation and value-added information augmented with and enhanced user interface (Murugesan, 2007).

- **Sermo**: This site is regarded as "virtual doctors' lounge", it's one of the most popular medical site around the globe. Doctors can interact with their peers on issue concerning their patients anonymously and their peers can relate experiences similar to such issue and using discernment to provide care and advice to the patient.

- **Doximity**: This site is United State of America (USA) biased as members are mainly based in the US. Here, journal article are available for members to consult and prepare for their certificate examinations.

- **Orthomind**: This social media site is mainly for orthopedic surgeons and is accessible on smart phones, IPad, and laptops.

- **QuantiaMD**: This site is designed for education and teamwork among medical doctors. If physicians become members and carry their students along, it will lessen the financial burden of materials acquisition in the library.

- **WeMedUp**: This site projects latest medical advancements, generates access to job openings, and keeping abreast with new treatments for diseases. This site enables healthcare service providers to share and compare images like X-ray around the world and can be better use by doctors in isolated areas to function adequately. This sharing of such images and followed by diagnosis and prescription by other doctors equip medical doctors in distant locations the new idea on how some sicknesses are presently treated.

- **Digital Healthcare**: This google+ site is a general site as it welcome both doctor, patients and stakeholders who are involved on healthcare debates.

- **Student Doctors Network**: This is a student support site aimed at helping student attain their goal of becoming a professional. It prepares them by providing assistance needed during training from high or secondary or middle school years of study.

- **Healthcare and Medical Software**: It's a google+ site that provide specific software applications concerning medical profession.

- **DoctorsHangout**: This is a global site for both students and veteran doctors with different groups which allow members to make their choices on which of the groups to join and discuss with.
- **Medical Doctors Medicos Clinical Medicine**: A google+ site for international connections and assistance.
- **MomMD**: This site is gender bias and discusses issues bordering on salaries as women medical practitioners are affected.
- **Medical Doctor**: This google+ site deploys comic reliefs for the entertainment of medical memes as members use their favorite images to.
- **AllNurses**: This is a core professional site designed for advice on topical issues amongst peers.
- **Medical Apps**: This is a google+ site that targets students for assistance on their medical training.
- **NurseZone**: This site deals exclusively on matters bordering on nursing issues ranging from assistance given to newcomer nurse, those already in their carrier path, to seasoned nurses in other to learn a variety of current activities relating to nursing. They also discuss issues on choices of career available in the work of nursing.
- **Ozmosis**: This is a secure site that enable physicians to communicate amid professional groups for the purpose of information sharing devoid of advertisement.
- **Physician's Practice**: This is a LinkedIn professional group that facilitates physicians' day-to-day activities and simplifies discussion.
- **Medical Group Management Association (MGMA)**: This is another professional group from LinkedIn that facilitates skillful track record management practices among health care professionals around the globe for standardization of practice and patient healthcare delivery.
- **Mayo Clinic Social Media Network**: This social media network site (SMNS) is comprehensive, and resourceful for health care professionals as it allows forum discussion, blogging, hence, enabling a user to expand his professional skills.
- **Hootsuite**: this SM tool allows a user to manage several social media profiles at any given time and be able to track increase in followership.

It has become clear then that there are many SMN that is at the disposal of the medical doctors, however, the medical librarian (ML) should be of assistance to these clients to enable them make good choices. They should be aware of the various SMNs available for the profession, join the professionally recognized network; affiliate themselves with those that can facilitate learning, encourage patients to associate with groups that discusses HIV and so on. Through this means therefore, both the librarians, physicians/doctors, and patients can work together to reduce the spread of HIV/AIDS in Nigeria.

WHAT IS INCLUSIVE ENGAGEMENT?

The advent of the internet, chiefly social media, has reshaped the approach to healthcare service delivery and library services as it leverages their access to information. SM have generated tremendous prospects for librarians, students, healthcare professionals, stakeholders and a heterogeneous groups to promote effective communication on healthcare services delivery and wellness. Patients have also tapped from the many benefits of SM, as it leverages anonymous interaction with peers, physicians, librarians and educate others on the peril HIV/aids has caused globally.

The term social inclusion or inclusive engagement is understood as a process by which efforts are made to ensure equal opportunity for all regardless of their background, that is: age, pigmentation, educational background, social status, profession, or otherwise, so that they can achieve their full potentials in life. It is a multi-dimensional process aimed at creating conditions which enable full and active engagement or participation of every member of the society in all aspects of life including civic, social, economic, and political as well as participation in decision making process (Mancinelli, 2008), participating as a full member of society or group and the capacity to realize the conditions of social citizenship (Sinclair, Bramley, Dobbie & Gillespie, 2007). As such, it becomes obvious that social inclusion or engagement exists when people accept and care for each other from the heart regardless of their social class, occupation, sex, and race (Chan, Evans, Ng, Chiu & Huxley, 2014) or on what they stand to benefit from the friendship or group.

According to Moorhead, Hoving, & Sipsma (2015) SM platforms, including mobile technologies and SNSs, are being used increasingly as part of human immunodeficiency virus (HIV) prevention and treatment efforts. They also said that using SM to bridge communication among diverse range of users, in various geographic and social contexts, may be leveraged through pre-existing platforms and with attention to the roles of anonymity and confidentiality in the communication about HIV prevention and treatment. The interesting thing about SM is that any member of the society has equal right of becoming a member, unless otherwise restricted as in the case of medicine where physicians' membership would be screened before they may be allowed to register. In this kind of situation, it is expected that since such site is distinct in nature, only certified or recommended individuals would be granted membership, while the general or open sites can as well serve the general public and they will get as much needed information from such sites as physicians and librarians also are eligible in these networks. The traditional and conventional role of the librarian which is to make information and information materials available to its audience remains paramount especially given the urgency the treatment and prevention HIV demands.

While the medical doctors or physicians are responsible for the treatment and counselling of HIV patients, the librarians' responsibility remains that of providing the needed information in support of any form it may come to satisfy the physicians' information need and quell the information demands of the patients concerning HIV/AIDS treatment and prevention. Although stigma and cultural considerations forms a major prevention for people living with HIV/AIDS and at-risk population from accessing in-person HIV prevention and treatment initiative (Mahajan, Sayles, Patel, Remien, Ortiz Szekeres, & Coates, 2008; Taggart, Grewe, Conserve, Gliwa, & Isler, 2015; Moorhead, Hoving, & Sipsma, 2015; Turan, Cohen, Bukusi, Turan, Stringer, Onono, & Weiser 2014) SM can offer a neutral platform for engagement (Blackstock, Haughton, Garner, Horvath, Norwood, & Cunningham, 2015) in discussions that border on HIVAIDS treatment and prevention. For example, individuals can seek and share information about specific prevention strategies, engage in dialog about HIV research, and leverage support for issues such as medication adherence and emotional coping strategies for HIV research (Taggart, Grewe, Conserve, Gliwa, & Isler, 2015; Muessig, Nekkanti, Bauermeister, Bull, &Hightow-Weidman, 2015; Ko, Hsieh, Wang, Lee, Chen, Chung &Hsu, 2013; DeSouza, & Jyoti Dutta, 2008; Coursaris, & liu, 2009; and Strand, 2012), this is not an exclusive reserve of the physicians or librarians as all renders their separate obligations. According to Taggart, Grewe, Conserve, Gliwa, & Isler, (2015), the increased social support provided by SM has been shown to improve treatment adherence and access to HIV testing and prevention services (León, Cáceres, Fernández, Chausa, Martin, Codina, & Blanco, 2011; Hailey & Arscott, 2013), and also grant HIV patients necessary support to deal with stigmatization associated with the disease as they independently search for information predominantly through SM. The pervasive use of SM has been of great benefit as it help the MLs provide HIV persons with adequate, timely, and relevant information on how to form groups with their peers (people living with HIV-PLHIV), gain emotional backing, and build ties with others suffering from the disease.

Figure 1 show a clear indication of the various categories of individuals that play major roles in inclusivity engagement in the management of HIV/AIDS. Not to be undermined is the significant role information and information providers contribute to satisfy the information needs of these individuals that are engaged for the purpose of providing the needed HIV/AIDS care to patients. Without information, no part of the circle would function because from individual, relationship, community, and policy; all depend on information, and this is the librarians' exclusive reserve as he chooses suitable SMNS for each group and further integrate all in a single network where anonymity facilitates individuals' activities among peers. While individuals are the various members of the group, the relationships simply mean those who are their friends within the group, community refers to the entire group or network, and the policy aspect of the figure is responsible for the rules guiding the entire network for sustainability. No part of the figure is less, as they collaboratively contribute to the general activities of the system.

As the use of SM has crept into all facets of human endeavor, it harmoniously facilitates the way information demand and handling structured. While SM simplifies the work of a librarian, it equally facilitates the physicians' research and leverages patients' mode of communicating with their doctors.

Figure 1. The state of engagement in HIV care in the United States: from cascade to continuum to control (Source: Mugavero, Amico, Horn, & Thompson, 2013)

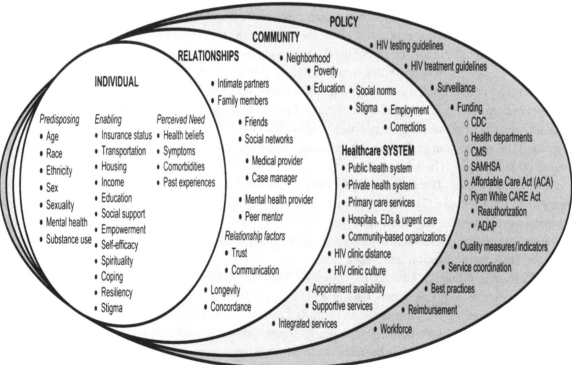

THE ROLE OF LIBRARIAN IN A MEDICAL LIBRARY

According to Veenstra, (1992), the primary role of the clinical medical librarian (CML) is locating and providing quality-filtered, patient-specific information to physicians. As in the past, librarians participated in evidence-based medicine (EBM) which is rooted in past practices, most notably in clinical medical librarianship (Scherrer, &Dorsch, 1999). According to Scherrer, & Dorsch (1999), EBM is defined as the conscientious, explicit, and judicious use of current best evidence in making decisions about the care of individual patients. For a librarian to function, in this capacity, he must be able to search for literature, select what he considers appropriate at the time, and appraise such information by criticizing the source. Since clinicians have their special information needs, and by the librarians' professional training, he must be concise about the information that would be selected to serve health professionals better. Even though the librarians is not trained to go on ward rounds, he must interact with both clinicians and patients to elicit areas of information needed to facilitate his information search and provision. Scherrer & Dorsch (1999) stated that to provide information quickly to physicians and other members of the healthcare team; to influence the information seeking behavior of clinicians and improve their library skills (social media use skills – SMUS); and to establish the medical librarian's role as a valid member of the health care team.

According to Giuse (1997), it is CML responsibility to teach our constituents (physicians and patients) that accurate, up-to-date, quality filtered information provided by CML programs can have a measurable positive impact on the clinical environment. Giuse (1997) also said librarians should engage on rounds and share their findings in the same way the residents do: they should step in front of the group and present what they discovered through their research; by so doing fostering verbal, interactive, eye-to-eye with other members of the team as this is crucial for establishing the librarians credibility not only in terms of understanding the medical issues of the question asked, but also of demonstrating familiarity with and understanding of the information selected and filtered. When CML take up this responsibility, supporting themselves with SM, and certificate in medicine, they make a formidable input in the management of HIV/AIDS.

CML requires background knowledge of clinical activities to prepare for the cultural shift in their role of information provision, and positively discuss with any medical team. As part of their effort to assimilate the new culture, CMLs should seek instructions in the techniques of clinical trials, including randomization and blind techniques; they should study the tenets of evidence-based medicine; they should consult with subject experts and clinicians who can evaluate and support their filtering and interpretation skills; and they should take clinical courses in the medical and nursing schools [(possibly by auditing courses for free; otherwise by drawing on the library professional budget), Giuse, 1997]. This effort will adequately position them with the requisite knowledge that will facilitate their effective interaction with team members and understand clinical professional jargons. Much as this need is important, they do not want to lose sight of the fact that they must be lovers of gadgets for them to be able to effectively use SM in providing information for their clients.

SM has proved to be of crucial significance in harnessing the success of health care service delivery, especially in a debilitating situation such as that created by HIV/AIDS. For clarity on what should be forwarded to the medical professionals, Scherrer, & Dorsch, (1999) pointed out that clinical medical librarians be well-versed in medical terminologies to understand the conversations on round thoroughly. This knowledge will not only be useful in the print arena but will also be relevant searching for SMSs for the clinicians to belong. Once this is done, the librarian also sifts through conversations from such

SMSs and inform the clinicians on what is new especially novel areas that has to do with HIV both for the management and prevention.

USING SOCIAL MEDIA TO MANAGE HIV/AIDS

According to Campbell, Evans, Pumper, & Moreno (2016) research to date on social media and health has largely focused on the patients' experience. They engage in extensive information that most often leads to discussions as a group, using messages, chatrooms and other methods through the internet. They feel critical about the kind of information that will make them get well again and are ready to search and seek it from any available source. They further asserted that not much has been done on the physicians even though physician-generated health information is growing. They pointed out that a growing number of physicians are currently using SM as a professional platform for health communication. Giving the busy nature of medical doctors, it becomes a prerogative responsibility for CMLs to satisfy the information needs of their clients, the doctors, and medical students as well as PLWHA by searching for relevant information using their individual profiles to gather such information and circulate for choices to be made.

The menace brought by HIV/AIDS has been faced with great enthusiasm by doctors around the world, yet its ravaging effect still remains high and challenging as the cure evades science for the time being. Controlling its spread should rather be the focus rather than cure. Hence it has been observed that SM which includes mobile technologies and social networking sites are being used increasingly as part of human immunodeficiency virus (HIV) prevention and treatment (Taggart, Grewe, Conserve, Gliwa & Isler, 2015). This effort will bridge the information divide between those who currently are negative on issues surrounding HIV and adequately inform those whose status have been confirmed positive on how to manage themselves and save members of the public from contracting the deadly virus. Face-to-face discussion between physicians and PLWHA in Nigeria will be a milestone regarding HIV/AIDS as stigmatization is the order of the day. Rather, discussing in anonymous forum where many may create different identity to avoid stigmatization would be of great impact to preventing further spread of this killer disease.

SM according to Young (2012) can be used as an innovative method of HIV prevention. He enunciated that SM enables HIV prevention among at-risk population. This way both those who are currently afflicted with the virus and those that are negative in their status can benefit as information is constantly shared amongst group members. Young also averred that social networking site (SNS) for HIV prevention is an exciting area that combines HIV prevention/public health, engineering/technology, and business. In summary, Young (2012) gave the following guidelines on using social media networking for HIV prevention research which when incorporated into the field of medicine with the cooperation of the librarian can leverage SM in managing HIV/AIDS especially in Nigeria; these guidelines include:

1. Research collaborator experienced in using social networking technologies:

Necessity behooves a progressive and focused system to realize that the future depends on how well today is treated. In the medical profession, life of all must be saved and this calls for adequate and timely information to facilitate prevention of a well-known disease like HIV/AIDS from spreading more than it already has gone. So, at least one of the collaborators should be someone with requisite knowledge of social media network and its technicalities, organization of information, dissemination of information, and observer and listener, and with vision for future as the network system may change with time.

2.   Create a plan for addressing duplicate respondents:

The quality of data/information churned out from a single response to an online query is sometimes amazing and can be confusing if care is not taken. Sequel to this, it becomes critically important for source verification to avoid duplication, and impersonation. Such multiplicity if not checked, can be potentially dangerous hence the need for plans to address them as quickly as they surface. Since HIV is a dreaded disease, sources of data/information on prevention and management must be thoroughly criticized to ensure ingenuity. Young (2012) states: data quality can be improved through the traditional online approaches, as well as method unique to social networking such as Facebook Connect, an application that requests Facebook to verify a Facebook user's identity, can validate that each participant is unique. Facebook user background check on users 'network of friends can also be a great way to avoid duplication. Since health care service delivery is a necessary and sensitive part of human life, members of any social media on health maters should be willing to allow others verify their demographic details, by so doing, lowering the risks associated with misleading information.

3.   A collaborator who understands the social networking business:

The penetration of SM in various aspects of human life over the years has helped to simplify the way humans enjoy entertainment, listen to news, study, conduct research, and work in any field of endeavor. In this regards however, healthcare is not left out for clinicians currently use it to garner data/ information respecting various ailments such as HIV/AIDS. Health researchers must be conversant with policies governing any SNS they choose to join and abide by the norms as so that site owners may not discontinue their use for if their reputation is smeared or image is negatively represented. Young gave this example; that as HIV-related studies can be controversial, Facebook might decide to close an HIV prevention study in the middle if Facebook is negatively represented, so, understanding the business objective of the technology company, as well as gaining support from the business will help to ensure the study progress.

4.   Address participants privacy and confidentiality issues:

In every aspect of medical practice, ethical issue must be observed and individual privacy and discretion must be respected and addressed. Young (2012) opined that

Awareness of the current privacy concerns associated with each technology will help alleviate participants concerns and maintain a confidential study environment. In some parts of the world especially in Nigeria, the stigma associated with HIV/AIDS is too strong and the carriers of this diseases are discriminated against rather than being assisted. Hence, individuals who are sufferers from this disease will be more engaged using SMNSs to their advantage as they interact with others who also have the same disease and with doctors whom for fear of exposure would not been possible on a face-to-face consultation. When the privacy and confidentiality of the sufferers of HIV and image of the social media site (SMS) are observed, the users of such sites experience great joy and would be able to render accelerated information service delivery and effective health care services. All of which will help reposition health industry and instill confidence in the mind of all concerning their health records and privacy.

5.   Internal review boards (IRBs) should include a researcher who is knowledgeable about mobile technologies.

One of the hard challenge medical field has faced in recent times is the management of HIV. Scientific and medical researchers have conducted several researches to discover the cure for this disease but the answer keep alluding humans. Hence it is necessary to look for ways to prevent the disease from further spreading. One of such ways is by getting timely information which can be obtained from the SMN not restricting any who is interested for asking questions or making lucid contributions for the benefit of all. Although it has been on notice that the use of technologies for sexually transmitted diseases are always delayed, focusing on its use at this point where there is no known cure for HIV becomes a universal responsibility and the library cannot shy away from adequately circulating information to curtail this disease spread. Since the use of technologies in the field of medicine are always delayed before deployment, the Internal Review Board, policy makers in the field of medicine must make provisions to persistently conduct research on how to deploy new technologies into clinical practice. Again, it has to be on record that every member of the IRB has the willingness to train and retrain members of the medical community to keep-up with the new trend and technologies like social media. This practice will have both short and long term benefit to the field of medicine by reducing the time lapse on technology deployment to clinical practice and further decrease the spread of HIV especially in Nigeria.

Taggart, Grewe, Converse, Giwa, & Isler, (2015) noted some benefits the use of SM for the management of HIV/AIDS can bring to include:

1.   Access to information,
2.   Enhanced ability to communicate (freedom of expression),
3.   Having an anonymous identity,
4.   A sense of social and emotional support,
5.   Establishing a virtual community, and
6.   Geographical reach.

Access to information is a vital ingredient for survival and most important to those who have a terminal disease like HIV/AIDS which in some cases can be controlled over a long period of time. With the availability of information at the disposal of PLWHA, they would be better informed on how best to sustain their lives after identifying his or her status. People generally are always introverted when it comes to issue related to HIV/AIDS as a result of the stigmatization HIV+ people receive from the community. This is a major reason why most people do not care about checking for their status from time to time, since once an individual is tested positive, he immediately wares a condemned status as well. However, PLWHA demonstrates appreciation for the ease and convenience of accessing information related to HIV care, treatment, management, and prevention through social media (Taggart, Grewe, Converse, Giwa, & Isler, 2015). For example, a single piece of information gained by one HIV person can be circulated among members of a chat group he or she belong which can further spread to non-members of the group depending on the network site the members belong.

Enhanced ability to communicate or freedom of expression comes into play when a HIV+ person has mustered up the boldness to anonymously express himself or herself emotionally and otherwise before the public or with his or her peers. With the use of SM, individuals can easily discuss about HIV person's sexual patterns/attitude and partners, physician or healthcare provider, healthiness/wellbeing, status testing, and or HIV prevention methods. All of these are possible especially as these individuals will not have to be physically present or be face–to-face with whomever they wish to discuss with without living their homes or offices; this includes adolescents who unfortunately would have inherited the disease from their parents, or have been involved in rape of any kind by PLWHA. This kind of information can be generated from the local library after the librarian has sifted relevant ones that are fit for members of group which the medical hospital generated for their clients and community.

Stigmatization, depression, social depravities, and other associated syndromes relating to HIV drives HIV positive persons (HPPs) into anonymity. HPPs are courageous to freely discuss, comment, or ask questions relating to HIV treatments, access to professionals, and prevention plans, as stigmatization and discrimination are leveraged by SM, since they anonymously engage is such acts without being identified. This is further made easy as some of the social media web sites (SMWSs) does not display the actual identity of members who prefer to be anonymous.

Engaging in an online community is a sense of social and emotional support or security for PLWHA since they are always stigmatized and discriminated against. Some who have tested positive to HIV have suffered abandonment by their family and friends creating a void, this situation is being bridged by their group members who either are positive or willing to help through SM discussions.

PLWHA due to stigmatization and discrimination, form virtual communities as a social network base to anonymously interact with others through specific social media, potentially crossing the geographical and political boundaries in order to pursue mutual interests or goals of which some are pervasive virtual communities and online communities operating under social networking services (Rheingold, 1993; & Burger-Helmchen, & Cohendet, 2011). This too can be an efficient way for PLWHA especially embolden themselves as they have been restricted from social life and activities.

PLWHA have been able to get to others outside of their circle of old friends to a larger community for several reasons such as anonymously: getting information related to HIV/AIDS – prevention and treatment efforts, consulting with physicians for counselling, and engaging in social activities, as they communicate with their peers in geographically dispersed arena. For these whole thing to be possible therefore, it means the medical librarian (ML) must be versatile with the various SMS and their membership status.

DOCTORS, LIBRARIANS, STUDENTS, AND STAKEHOLDERS INCLUSIVITY

It is very pertinent to note the value of quick access to information via SM and the extent to which its use can prove efficient for information management within the healthcare environment in Nigeria. In the past, physicians faced enormous challenge in handling HIV persons, for example, a majority of patients did not feel they were properly informed, educated, or given adequate explanation of what to expect throughout the course of their incurable sickness (Valdiserri, Tama & Ho, 1988), this situation after about thirty (30) years, still persist as they fear for the difficulty the patient may face getting his or her scenario/diagnosis. Hence, the advent of the SMN not only benefited the patients, but has also given the physicians an outlet to allow the patient find out some of the necessary information either through the help of a librarian or from SM.

While the medical doctors are responsible for the medical diagnosis, and health care service delivery, they depend on valid sources of information to be able to adequately dialogue and make informed decisions about their patients' health. In this regards, Nair (2011) points out four categories of healthcare on the internet today to include: dialogue, diagnosis, decisions and delivery (4D - for healthcare services on the internet). The 4D are critical to all as librarians, doctors, students, patients, and stakeholders interact before responding to any particular health condition. The librarian requires acceptable knowledge of what is going on around him so that when he makes search for materials to be acquired into the library for use, he will get the best available. Nair further stated that dialogue systems are proliferating as more and more customer (patients) want relevant and timely understanding of medical and health information both directly (from doctors) and from others who share their needs. On the issue of diagnosis, since patients require timely information, they are ready to search for information related to their diagnosed illness via the SM. Regarding this, Nair asserted that patients gain valuable treatment information and insight on social media platforms and online communities. This results when a patient post his diagnosed illness online and allow others to comment on possible treatments and or experience irrespective of the dangers associated with their actions.

In recent times, physicians have been observed using SM either for personal or professional purposes to find, interact, and share health information, communicate/network with colleague's and trainees, disseminate their research, market their practice, or engage in health advocacy (Chretien & Kind, 2013). They added that a growing minority of physicians use SM to directly interact with patients or in other ways that augment clinical care.

Figure 2. Key social media interactions among patients, physicians, (librarians), and the public. Solid line circles denote secure interactions. Dotted line circles denote personal networking interactions. (Source: Chretien & Kind, 2013)

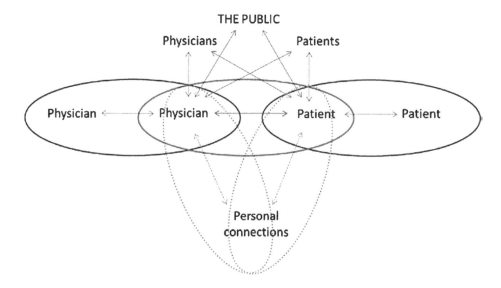

The figure 1 above is a vivid representation of the life circle of a typical SMN. In a clinical setting, individual members of the network have their distinct ideas, experiences or health challenges and personal connections outside the network where some form of behind the scene interaction takes place. These are behind the scene activities and are diffused into the network for analysis and implementation. While the patients trying to understand the health challenge he or a member of his family is facing, the physicians are busy sourcing for solutions by making research and interacting with colleagues one network after another so as to provide and support HIV/AIDS care services delivery. At the same time, the much behind the scene information player - the CML is assembling adequate and timely information to equip the physicians' to be able attend to the health challenge; while the public critically watch and await the outcome.

Succinctly though, the CMLs role in the SM life circle even though invincible stands to facilitate the amount, form, and kind of information available for the physician to sift and come up with an efficient treatment that will be suitable for HIV/AIDS prevention. The public does not require a state of the art infrastructure but competence and confidence in the medical field before they can rely on it. Through social media tool, individual physician markets himself when his contributions in the group is always reliable and clearly understood by both colleagues and the public. This builds the patients confidence and trust as they likely will believe his answers to be more satisfactory. Even as this may seem hard to attain, all members of the group whether a physician, librarian, patient, or in the public group, need to cultivate quality of learning to listen before contributing to the group.

The patients use SM to find HIV/AIDS health information, support through discussion groups and forums, and chronicle their illness (Chretien, & Kind, 2013). The figure 2 shows that patients' discuses with one another and follow through with physicians as they become better equipped after they have searched and gathered view-points from other HIV/AIDS persons that have posted their experiences on the web. At this time, medical librarian (ML) become resourceful as they facilitate patients information needs that are consequently forwarded to the physician in preparation for professional interaction with the patient on later contact. This chain of process continues all through the period as long as the social media group (SMG) is functional.

The general public which often include all the stakeholders, continuously invest time and effort to ensure a more sustainable flow of information among group members. They gather interested individuals who have suffered some form of ailment such as HIV/AIDS to solicit information on how they have been able to cope with their situation in life so that they can use such experiences during their discussions with members of their group. It is expected that physicians and CMLs employ the services of psychologist to properly enlighten PLWHA on how best to sustain their lives and do not be discouraged about the stigmatization that may come with the ailment as this can be done through SMN.

CONCLUSION

Medical librarianship is a special aspect of librarianship that requires proper understanding of medical terminologies before venturing into it. In this era of SM, every unit of an organization need to have good knowledge of what is happening within the establishment to enable them make informed comment in the circle of friends or chat group within the network. This collaborative otherwise called inclusive engagement requires a corresponding obligation by the ML to be equipped with requisite certificate to function efficiently. There has been a growing need for the use of SM by medical doctors for the management of diseases like HIV/AIDS within Nigeria. Nigeria has been adversely affected by the HIV/AIDS scourge as majority of the disease carriers do not have access to antiretroviral drugs for the control of the disease from blowing into a stage where it cannot be managed. Stigmatization has equally left most carriers whit shame as such would not openly go for test on time until the disease has become intensely rooted. Through SMN therefore, it is expected that Nigerians will become well equipped to battle with HIV/AIDS menace, as physicians, librarians, stakeholders and the general public with special focus on HIV persons' will create; circulate; discuss; support socially, emotionally and economically; all forms of information such as pictures, videos, and audio recordings for the purpose of managing this disease.

SM requires effective collaboration among group members. The field of medicine is

RECOMMENDATIONS

The use of social media by medical librarians for inclusive engagement in the management of HIV/AIDS in Nigeria university teaching hospitals, is expected to leverage HIV/AIDS management within Nigeria. Presently, observation shows that physicians argue among themselves and between medical departments about who and which department or unit in the hospital should attend to HIV/AIDS persons. As a result of this, some experienced physicians in the various university teaching hospitals are not given opportunity to PLWHA. This is dichotomous relationship need to be broken in order to realize the objective of provident good health for the public. The entire university teaching hospital should be internally connected and all university teaching hospitals in Nigeria be connected through social media so that they can form a community-based HIV/AIDS initiative and combat the dreaded disease as working as individuals will yield the needed result of preventing and eradicating the disease.

REFERENCES

Aichner, T., & Jacob, F. (2015). Measuring the degree of corporate social media use. *International Journal of Market Research, 57*(2), 257–275. doi:10.2501/IJMR-2015-018

American Society of Health-System Pharmacists (ASHP). (2012). ASHP statement on use of social media by pharmacy professionals: developed through the ASHP pharmacy student forum and the ASHP section of pharmacy informatics and technology and approved by the ASHP Board of Directors on April 13, 2012, and by the ASHP House of Delegates on June 10, 2012. *American Journal of Health-System Pharmacy, 69*(23), 2095.

Anderson, T. (2004). Towards a theory of online learning. *Theory and Practice of Online Learning, 2*, 109-119.

Attai, D. J., Cowher, M. S., Al-Hamadani, M., Schoger, J. M., Staley, A. C., & Landercasper, J. (2015). Twitter social media is an effective tool for breast cancer patient education and support: Patient-reported outcomes by survey. *Journal of Medical Internet Research, 17*(7), e188. doi:10.2196/jmir.4721 PMID:26228234

Bik, H. M., & Goldstein, M. C. (2013). An introduction to social media for scientists. *PLoS Biology, 11*(4), e1001535. doi:10.1371/journal.pbio.1001535 PMID:23630451

Brasg, I. (2013). *CFMS guide to medical professionalism: recommendations for social media.* Ottawa: Canadian Federation of Medical Students.

Campbell, L., Moreno, M. A., Pumper, M., & Evans, Y. (2016). Social media use by physicians: A qualitative study of the new frontier of medicine. *BMC Medical Informatics and Decision Making, 16*(1), 91. doi:10.118612911-016-0327-y PMID:27418201

Chan, K., Evans, S., Ng, Y. L., Chiu, M. Y. L., & Huxley, P. J. (2014). A concept mapping study on social inclusion in Hong Kong. *Social Indicators Research, 119*(1), 121–137. doi:10.100711205-013-0498-1

Chauhan, B., & Janis Coffin, D.O. (2012). Social media and you: what every physician needs to know. *The Journal of Medical Practice Management: MPM, 28*(3), 206.

Chretien, K. C., & Kind, T. (2013). Social Media and Clinical Care. *Circulation, 127*(13), 1413–1421. doi:10.1161/CIRCULATIONAHA.112.128017 PMID:23547180

Coursaris, C. K., & Liu, M. (2009). An analysis of social support exchanges in online HIV/AIDS self-help groups. *Computers in Human Behavior, 25*(4), 911–918. doi:10.1016/j.chb.2009.03.006

DeSouza, R., & Jyoti Dutta, M. (2008). Global and local networking for HIV/AIDS prevention: The case of the Saathii E-forum. *Journal of Health Communication, 13*(4), 326–344. doi:10.1080/10810730802063363 PMID:18569364

Duke, V. J., Anstey, A., Carter, S., Gosse, N., Hutchens, K. M., & Marsh, J. A. (2017). Social media in nurse education: Utilization and E-professionalism. *Nurse Education Today, 57*, 8–13. doi:10.1016/j.nedt.2017.06.009 PMID:28683342

Giuse, N. B. (1997). Advancing the practice of clinical medical librarianship. *Bulletin of the Medical Library Association, 85*(4), 437. PMID:9431437

Grajales, F. J. III, Sheps, S., Ho, K., Novak-Lauscher, H., & Eysenbach, G. (2014). Social Media: A of Applications in Medicine and Health Care. *Journal of Medical Internet Research, 16*(2). PMID:24518354

Gu, B., & Ye, Q. (2014). First step in social media: Measuring the influence of online management responses on customer satisfaction. *Production and Operations Management, 23*(4), 570–582. doi:10.1111/poms.12043

Hailey, J. H., & Arscott, J. (2013). Using technology to effectively engage adolescents and young adults into care: STAR TRACK Adherence Program. *The Journal of the Association of Nurses in AIDS Care, 24*(6), 582–586. doi:10.1016/j.jana.2013.03.001 PMID:23809658

Heaton-Shrestha, C., Gipps, C., Edirisingha, P., & Linsey, T. (2007). Learning and e-learning in HE: The relationship between student learning style and VLE use. *Research Papers in Education, 22*(4), 443–464. doi:10.1080/02671520701651797

Hu, Y., Farnham, S. D., & Monroy-Hernández, A. (2013, April). Whoo. ly: facilitating information seeking for hyperlocal communities using social media. In *Proceedings of the SIGCHI Conference on Human Factors in Computing Systems* (pp. 3481-3490). ACM. 10.1145/2470654.2466478

Johnson, H. A. (2017). Trello. *Journal of the Medical Library Association: JMLA, 105*(2), 209. doi:10.5195/jmla.2017.49

Kami Huyse, A. P. R. (2013). *Social Media Measurement: A Step-by-Step Approach.* Academic Press.

Ko, N. Y., Hsieh, C. H., Wang, M. C., Lee, C., Chen, C. L., Chung, A. C., & Hsu, S. T. (2013). Effects of Internet popular opinion leaders (iPOL) among Internet-using men who have sex with men. *Journal of Medical Internet Research, 15*(2), e40. doi:10.2196/jmir.2264 PMID:23439583

Lambert, K. M., Barry, P., & Stokes, G. (2012). Risk management and legal issues with the use of social media in the healthcare setting. *Journal of Healthcare Risk Management, 31*(4), 41–47. doi:10.1002/jhrm.20103 PMID:22528403

Lee, K., Oh, W. Y., & Kim, N. (2013). Social media for socially responsible firms: Analysis of Fortune 500's Twitter profiles and their CSR/CSIR ratings. *Journal of Business Ethics, 118*(4), 791–806. doi:10.100710551-013-1961-2

León, A., Cáceres, C., Fernández, E., Chausa, P., Martin, M., Codina, C., ... Blanco, J. L. (2011). A new multidisciplinary home care telemedicine system to monitor stable chronic human immunodeficiency virus-infected patients: A randomized study. *PLoS One, 6*(1), e14515. doi:10.1371/journal.pone.0014515 PMID:21283736

Magno, G., Comarela, G., Saez-Trumper, D., Cha, M., & Almeida, V. (2012, November). New kid on the block: Exploring the google+ social graph. In *Proceedings of the 2012 ACM conference on Internet measurement conference*(pp. 159-170). ACM. 10.1145/2398776.2398794

Mahajan, A. P., Sayles, J. N., Patel, V. A., Remien, R. H., Ortiz, D., Szekeres, G., & Coates, T. J. (2008). Stigma in the HIV/AIDS epidemic: A review of the literature and recommendations for the way forward. *AIDS (London, England), 22*(Suppl 2), S67. doi:10.1097/01.aids.0000327438.13291.62 PMID:18641472

Mancinelli, E. (2008). e-Inclusion in the Information Society. *Information Society. From theory to political practice. Coursebook*, 171-182.

Molyneaux, H., O'Donnell, S., Gibson, K., & Singer, J. (2008). Exploring the gender divide on YouTube: An analysis of the creation and reception of vlogs. *American Communication Journal, 10*(2), 1–14.

Monge, R. (2007, November). Designing YouTube instructional videos to enhance information literacy. In *Brick and Click Libraries: An Academic Library Symposium.* Northwest Missouri State University.

Muessig, K. E., Nekkanti, M., Bauermeister, J., Bull, S., & Hightow-Weidman, L. B. (2015). A systematic review of recent smartphone, Internet and Web 2.0 interventions to address the HIV continuum of care. *Current HIV/AIDS Reports, 12*(1), 173–190. doi:10.100711904-014-0239-3 PMID:25626718

Mugavero, M. J., Amico, K. R., Horn, T., & Thompson, M. A. (2013). The state of engagement in HIV care in the United States: From cascade to continuum to control. *Clinical Infectious Diseases, 57*(8), 1164–1171. doi:10.1093/cid/cit420 PMID:23797289

Murugesan, S. (2007). Understanding Web 2.0. *IT Professional, 9*(4).

Nair, M. (2011). Understanding and measuring the value of social media. *Journal of Corporate Accounting & Finance*, *22*(3), 45–51.

Ochonogor, W. C., & Okite-Amughoro, F. A. (2018). Building an Effective Digital Library in a University Teaching Hospital (UTH) in Nigeria. In Handbook of Research on Managing Intellectual Property in Digital Libraries (pp. 184-204). IGI Global.

Prensky, M. (2003). Digital game-based learning. *Computers in Entertainment*, *1*(1), 21–21. doi:10.1145/950566.950596

Quan-Haase, A., & Young, A. L. (2010). Uses and gratifications of social media: A comparison of Facebook and instant messaging. *Bulletin of Science, Technology & Society*, *30*(5), 350–361. doi:10.1177/0270467610380009

Rafferty, P., & Hidderley, R. (2007, July). Flickr and democratic indexing: Dialogic approaches to indexing. *Aslib Proceedings*, *59*(4/5), 397–410. doi:10.1108/00012530710817591

Rheingold, H. (1993). *The virtual community: Finding commection in a computerized world*. Addison-Wesley Longman Publishing Co., Inc.

Scanfeld, D., Scanfeld, V., & Larson, E. L. (2010). Dissemination of health information through social networks: Twitter and antibiotics. *American Journal of Infection Control*, *38*(3), 182–188. doi:10.1016/j.ajic.2009.11.004 PMID:20347636

Scherrer, C. S., & Dorsch, J. L. (1999). The evolving role of the librarian in evidence-based medicine. *Bulletin of the Medical Library Association*, *87*(3), 322. PMID:10427434

Sinclair, S., Bramley, G., Dobbie, L., & Gillespie, M. (2007). *Social inclusion and communications: a review of the literature*. Communications Consumer Panel.

Strand, C. (2012). Blogging: a new tool for coping and accessing psycho-social support for people living with HIV? In E-Health communities and online self-help groups: Applications and usage (pp. 106-120). IGI Global. doi:10.4018/978-1-60960-866-8.ch007

Taggart, T., Grewe, M. E., Conserve, D. F., Gliwa, C., & Isler, M. R. (2015). Social media and HIV: A systematic review of uses of social media in HIV communication. *Journal of Medical Internet Research*, *17*(11), e248. doi:10.2196/jmir.4387 PMID:26525289

Turan, B., Cohen, C. R., Bukusi, E. A., Turan, J. M., Stringer, K. L., Onono, M., & Weiser, S. D. (2014). Linkage to HIV care, postpartum depression, and HIV-related stigma in newly diagnosed pregnant women living with HIV in Kenya: A longitudinal observational study. *BMC Pregnancy and Childbirth*, *14*(1), 400. doi:10.118612884-014-0400-4 PMID:25467187

Valdiserri, R. O., Tama, G. M., & Ho, M. (1988). A survey of AIDS patients regarding their experiences with physicians. *Academic Medicine*, *63*(9), 726–728. doi:10.1097/00001888-198809000-00011 PMID:3418679

Van Dijck, J., &Poell, T. (2013). *Understanding social media logic*. Academic Press.

Veenstra, R. J. (1992). Clinical medical librarian impact on patient care: A one-year analysis. *Bulletin of the Medical Library Association, 80*(1), 19. PMID:1537012

Ventola, C. L. (2014). Social media and health care professionals: Benefits, risks, and best practices. *P&T, 39*(7), 491. PMID:25083128

Von Muhlen, M., & Ohno-Machado, L. (2012). Reviewing social media use by clinicians. *Journal of the American Medical Informatics Association, 19*(5), 777–781. doi:10.1136/amiajnl-2012-000990 PMID:22759618

Von Muhlen, M., & Ohno-Machado, L. (2012). Reviewing social media use by clinicians. *Journal of the American Medical Informatics Association, 19*(5), 777–781. doi:10.1136/amiajnl-2012-000990 PMID:22759618

Wu, Y., Wu, C., Li, B., Zhang, L., Li, Z., & Lau, F. (2015). Scaling social media applications into geo-distributed clouds. *IEEE/ACM Transactions on Networking, 23*(3), 689–702. doi:10.1109/TNET.2014.2308254

Young, S. D. (2012). Recommended guidelines on using social networking technologies for HIV prevention research. *AIDS and Behavior, 16*(7), 1743–1745. doi:10.100710461-012-0251-9 PMID:22821067

ADDITIONAL READING

World Health Organization. (2016). *Consolidated guidelines on the use of antiretroviral drugs for treating and preventing HIV infection: recommendations for a public health approach*. World Health Organization.

Haider, M., & Subramanian, A. (2004). *Analysis of Experience: The Role of Public-private Partnerships in HIV/AIDS Prevention, Control and Treatment Programming*. University Press of America.

Schiavo, R. (2013). *Health communication: From theory to practice*. John Wiley & Sons.

KEY TERMS AND DEFINITIONS

Inclusive Engagement: The action of involving every individual in an establishment by granting all equal opportunities in the decision-making process towards achieving a common purpose.

Management of HIV/AIDS: Acts involving the prevention, control, education, support, and adherence to treatment.

Medical Librarians: Librarians with knowledge of medical profession by training and certification.

Social Media: Online tools that facilitates sharing of information, photos, and videos that is available in smartphones.

This research was previously published in the Handbook of Research on Digital Devices for Inclusivity and Engagement in Libraries; pages 1-24, copyright year 2020 by Information Science Reference (an imprint of IGI Global).

Chapter 53
A Kaupapa Māori Facebook Group for Māori and Indigenous Doctoral Scholars:
Maryann Lee in Conversation With Dr. Mera Lee-Penehira, Dr. Hinekura Smith, and Dr. Jennifer Martin

Maryann Lee
Unitec Institute of Technology, New Zealand

ABSTRACT

This chapter examines the use of Facebook to support Māori and Indigenous doctoral scholars who are enrolled in the MAI ki Tāmaki Makaurau doctoral programme in Auckland, New Zealand. The programme is part of a National Māori and Indigenous (MAI) Network aimed to increase doctoral participation and completion rates of Māori scholars. Drawing on three Kaupapa Māori principles introduced in chapter three: tino rangatiratanga (self-determination principle), taonga tuku iho (cultural aspirations principle), whānau (extended family structure principle), the author explores some of the key considerations in creating a Kaupapa Māori digital learning space with the use of social media. Through conversations with three Māori academics who adminisiter the MAI ki Tāmaki Facebook group, this chapter captuers their unique perspectives and provide rich insights into the ways in which the Facebook group can provide a strong network of support for Māori and Indigenous scholars.

INTRODUCTION

In 2012, the MAI ki Tāmaki Makaurau doctoral programme was led by Dr Jenny Lee-Morgan and Dr Mera Lee-Penehira at Te Puna Wānanga, School of Māori and Indigenous Education, the University of Auckland. The programme is part of a National Māori and Indigenous (MAI) Network, supported by Ngā Pae o te Maramatanga (Māori Centre of Research Excellence) primarily made up of Māori and

DOI: 10.4018/978-1-6684-7123-4.ch053

Indigenous doctoral students and emerging academics enrolled in tertiary organisations throughout Aotearoa, New Zealand. Established in 2002, the Network aims to increase doctoral participation and completion rates of Māori scholars (Te Kupenga o MAI, n.d.). The MAI ki Tāmaki Makaurau doctoral programme was innovative in its approach, bringing Māori and Indigenous academics together through a range of cultural, social and academic events.

Alongside the MAI ki Tāmaki Makaurau programme a MAI ki Tāmaki Facebook Group was created to provide additional support and guidance for Māori scholars between events. Over the last six years the Facebook group's membership has steadily increased, with a total of 85 members in 2018. It has also extended its membership to include postgraduate Māori and Indigenous students, as well as senior Māori and Indigenous academics. The inclusion of Masters and Honors students is an important part of the recruitment or encouragement pathway into doctoral study, supporting a tuakana-teina approach (older and younger sibling relationship). Additionally, inviting senior academics to the Facebook group enables students to interact with a greater pool of Māori and Indigenous academic knowledge. The Facebook members are diverse in their research disciplines and research experiences, with a much higher ratio of Māori women (90%) to Māori men (10%).

This research examines how the MAI ki Tāmaki Facebook Group reflects a Kaupapa Māori online learning space to support Māori scholars on their doctoral journey. Through gaining perspectives from three senior Māori academics who administer the site - Dr Mera Lee-Penehira, Dr Jen Martin and Dr Hinekura Smith - this research seeks to identify key Kaupapa Māori elements that underpin the Facebook group, and highlight ways in which members engage with each other as Māori Indigenous academics.

This chapter is designed to be read in conjunction with chapter three, which provides a context for the use of social media for Indigenous communities in general. Chapter three highlights how Māori and Indigenous groups are engaging in social media in ways that reflect the cultural aspirations for their communities, as well as outlining the risks associated with social media. This chapter focuses on a case-study that examines the use of Facebook to support Māori and Indigenous students and academics within the New Zealand tertiary environment. Both chapters draw on three Kaupapa Māori principles to frame similar themes that were identified in the literature review and examples provided in chapter three, and in the case-study in this chapter.

A KAUPAPA MĀORI APPROACH

This research is underpinned by a Kaupapa Māori methodological approach outlined in chapter 3. Here, it is importan for the purpose of analyzing discussions about the Māori online space to reiterate key features of the approach, particular with regard to the role of the Kaupapa Māori researcher.

A Kaupapa Māori approach enables Māori researchers to engage from a local theoretical position and that encompasses a Māori worldview at a spiritual, cultural and political level (Smith, 2003). Kaupapa Māori seeks to legitimize cultural aspirations and identity and create a space for Māori to be Māori. Linda Smith (2003) describes Kaupapa Māori methodology as, "centering our concepts and world-views and then coming to know and understand theory and research from our own perspectives and for our own purposes" (p. 39).

Whilst Kaupapa Māori is intimately connected to the sustainability of Māori cultural identity and Māori knowledge, it has come from a political and strategic move to provide a powerful space for Māori researchers, and aligns with a critical theory paradigm that asserts a transformative praxis (Smith,

2012). Kaupapa Māori is considered to be a living response to the historical events of colonisation, and a resistance to the dominant power relationships that exist today (Walker, 1996). The term 'research' for Indigenous peoples can be a reminder of the historical colonisation practices carried out that saw Indigenous groups as the 'researched' (Waziyatawin & Yellow Bird, 2012).

With this in mind, Linda Smith (2003) argues that a critique of one's intention to conduct Kaupapa Māori research is essential. She proposes a series of questions that researchers must be mindful of: "Whose research is this? Who owns it? Whose interests does it serve? Who will benefit from it? Who has designed its questions and framed its scope? Who will write it up? How will the results be disseminated?" (p. 10). These questions assist Māori and Indigenous researchers to reflect upon their own research agenda, the responsibilities of being a researcher, and how their research may contribute directly to their communities, whānau, hapū and iwi (L. Smith, 2003).

RESEARCH METHOD

My research is a case-study on the MAI ki Tāmaki Facebook Group. I chose a case-study method as it enables the researcher to focus on, and capture in-depth perspectives of the three Māori academics who play an integral role in maintaining a digital space that supports Kaupapa Māori principles. This research is one example of a Māori and Indigenous Facebook group, and therefore is not intended to reflect and represent all Māori and Indigenous Facebook groups. However, the research does highlight some central principles that can be considered when using social media to develop a culturally safe digital learning space for Indigenous peoples.

My interest in this research stems back to an e-learning role I held at the Faculty of Education at the University of Auckland, New Zealand, where I supported teacher education lecturers to design online courses and integrate learning technologies in their teaching. I was fortunate to have the opportunity to work alongside Māori staff and doctoral students, and this work included supporting the MAI ki Tāmaki Programme in 2012. At the same time, I was undergoing my post-graduate studies in Māori education and developing an awareness of Kaupapa Māori theory and methodology. Through my studies I began to reflect more deeply on my identity as an Indigenous Māori Chinese woman growing up in a predominantly western world. In the process of applying a Kaupapa Māori lens to my research, I began to consider the impact of colonization on Indigenous communities, and how the Internet and digital technologies can play a role in perpetuating colonized ideologies and frameworks. I completed my Masters of Professional Studies in Education in 2015, focusing my research on how Māori tertiary students engage in digital learning spaces.

As a Kaupapa Māori researcher, developing relationships with the research participants and identifying with them is an important Kaupapa Māori principle. Indigenous researchers take on a 'participatory mode' whereby they, too, contribute their personal knowledge and understandings as part of the research process (Denzin & Lincoln, 2008). I am fortunate to have established relationships with all three participants over a number of years through various connections both within a whānau (family) and a professional context. At the time of interviewing, all participants worked at the University of Auckland in Māori academic positions. In this section, I introduce each of the participants.

Dr Mera Lee-Penehira (Iwi: Ngati Raukawa and Rangitaane) works as a senior Māori lecturer and Supervisor at Te Puna Wānanga, School of Māori and Indigenous Education at the Faculty of Education. Mera is also the Director of Research and Postgraduate Studies, offering support to Māori postgraduate and doctoral students. She is the academic leader for MAI ki Tāmaki Makaurau programme and established the MAI ki Tāmaki Facebook Group. Mera's research interests are on Māori and Indigenous women, identity and wellbeing. They include Māori sexual health and reproductive health, and she developed a Kaupapa Māori model of resistance and wellbeing in this context. Mera's doctoral research centred on traditional knowledge and healing practices case studying Māori women with hepatitis C. In particular, she examined the process of moko (traditional Māori skin carving) and notions of mouri as legitimate components of Māori wellbeing.

Dr Hinekura Smith (Iwi: Te Rarawa) is currently working at the Centre for Learning and Research in Higher Education, as a Māori Academic Developer. Previously, she taught as a Te Reo Māori teacher for many years in mainstream secondary schools, working with a wide range of youth, their whānau and communities. Hinekura has recently completed her Ph.D. and has been an active member of the Facebook group, initially as a doctoral student and now as an administrator. Hinekura's research explores Māori aspirations to live 'as Māori', through the stories of eight Māori women and the aspirations they hold for their children and grandchildren to live 'as Māori'.

Dr Jen Martin (Iwi: Te Rarawa) has a background in Māori immersion education. Jen is currently working as a lecturer of Te Reo Māori in Māori Studies, in the Faculty of Arts. Jen has also been an active member of the Facebook group and continues to support it as an administrator. Jen's research interests include Māori language revitalization and development, academic writing in Te Reo Māori (Māori language), and Māori achievement and advancement through education. Her doctoral thesis awarded in 2014, written in Te Reo, uses a Kaupapa Māori narrative research approach to consider the notion of educational success in the context of Kura Kaupapa Māori (Māori schooling).

All three participants bring a wealth of knowledge and experience as Kaupapa Māori academics, alongside the many other roles they play within their whanau (family), hapū (sub-tribe) and Iwi (tribe). During my interviews, I was mindful of my role and responsibilities as researcher, and that my engagement with each of the participants was underpinned by the following values:

- Aroha ki te tangata (a respect for people),
- Kanohi kitea ('the seen face', which refers to presenting yourself to people face to face),
- Titiro, whakarongo ... korero (look, listen ... speak),
- Manaaki ki te tangata (share and host people, be generous),
- Kia tupato (be cautious),
- Kaua e takahi te mana o te tangata (do not trample over the mana of people),
- Kaua e mahaki (don't flaunt your knowledge). (L. Smith, 2003, p. 120)

Ethics approval was sought and approved by Unitec Institute of Technology in 2017. In accordance with ethical requirements, participants were provided with information outlining the aims of the research along with individual consent forms.

MAI DOCTORAL PROGRAMME

Under the leadership of Professors Graham and Linda Smith, the initiative for a doctoral network originally began in the 1990s during their time teaching and mentoring Māori postgraduate students at the University of Auckland. Graham and Linda had a vision for a national Māori network for postgraduate students that transitioned and supported Māori and Indigenous scholars in their doctoral studies. The conscious move to increase the number of Māori doctoral students and develop a national network was supported by Ngā Pae o te Māramatanga (Māori Centre of Research Excellence). In 2002, the MAI programme across six regions was funded, and included ten MAI networks groups throughout New Zealand.

The key objectives for the MAI programme aim to: increase Māori doctoral participation and completion rates; grow a strong network of Māori researchers across New Zealand; support pathways from postgraduate to doctoral studies; and to build Māori leadership and research capability from doctoral study to post-doctoral research and to future career pathways (Te Kupenga o MAI, n.d.). Each network offers different activities, such as academic seminars, Indigenous conferences, writing retreats and workshops and social gatherings. Despite such a highly regarded programme, recent restructuring of funding has meant that programs are now having to severely limit the activities being offered.

The MAI programme has been instrumental in building a strong network for Māori scholars to regularly come together in both a culturally and academic supportive forum. Between 2005 and 2015 the number of doctoral students have almost doubled, with 275 doctoral students enrolled in 2005, and 515 enrolled in 2015. While these figures highlight the success of the support provided by MAI, Māori-awarded doctorates are still underrepresented, making up only 6% of all New Zealand doctorates awarded between 2006 and 2013 (Pihama, et al., 2017, p. 29).

Research highlights a number of challenges for Māori and Indigenous scholars during their doctoral journey. These include: lack of institutional support, limited access to Māori academics and supervisors, and feelings of isolation within their disciplines (Hohepa, 2010; McKinley, Grant, Middleton, Irwin, & Williams, 2007). A recent report titled Te Tātua o Kahukura (2017) identifies similar challenges that include both systemic issues and financial constraints. The report highlights how doctoral Māori students felt that mainstream activities were often not appropriate, and that "institutional racism and white privilege were identified as a fundamental issue for Māori and Indigenous doctoral scholars engaging in western university structures" (Pihama et al., 2017, p. 8).

MAI KI TĀMAKI FACEBOOK GROUP

The following section highlights some of the key themes identified from the interviews with three Māori academics who administer the MAI ki Tāmaki Facebook group. Their perspectives provide a rich insight into the ways in which the Facebook group can support Māori and Indigenous scholars, as well highlighting the considerations in creating a Kaupapa Māori digital learning space. I have drawn on three of the Kaupapa Māori principles by G. Smith (1991), to reflect a range of research themes; Tino rangatiratanga (self-determination principle), Taonga tuku iho (cultural aspirations principle), Whānau (extended family structure principle). Each of these principles have been explored in chapter three and provide a cultural context for the following section.

Tino Rangatiratanga: Self-Determination Principle

'Tino rangatiratanga' represents sovereignty and self-determination for Māori whānau, hapū and iwi. It can also be viewed as a direct protest to the Crown that acknowledges the struggles over Māori sovereignty and the loss of control by tangata whenua. Tino rangatiratanga is reflected within the Facebook group in a number ways. Mera highlights how members are given the power to equally contribute in ways that supports the collective group which supports the principle of tino rangatiratanga. She discusses how the Facebook group has been intentionally set up without an approval or editing function by the administrators to control the space:

Anyone can post up what they like - there is no approval function on that page ... that's an important underpinning of the page - I think this is something that is connected to a Kaupapa Māori way of doing things in social media. Because it takes away that power relationship between the administrator and participant. We all have equal value and opportunity and power to put things up there.

Additionally, Mera discusses how the Facebook group reflects a strong political element supporting the Kaupapa Māori principle of tino rangatiratanga. Raising the political awareness of Māori scholars is something that Mera sees as one of her roles as the MAI programme leader and a senior Māori academic:

I think that one of our jobs in the MAI programme is to build and maintain a sound level of political awareness and consciousness. Part of the underpinning of the MAI programme is that you can't really be a successful Māori or Indigenous scholar without a clear understanding of politics and without strong politics to your academic work. The MAI ki Tāmaki Makaurau programme encourages and helps people develop that, and the Facebook page certainly reflects this - we have some pretty political posts that happen in our group.... Scrolling through the page, I can see that it is really highly political. And I don't think postgraduate pakeha sites are highly political. I'm on one of them here at the university and they are more about informing events, academic workshops and things happening. We do all of that - but we also politicize quite strongly through this medium.

For Mera, the Facebook group is an effective forum for raising the political conscientization of Māori scholars at both a local and global scale. It also connects students, particulary who may be experiencing isolation in their doctoral journey, to a wider Indigenous community, and a greater awareness of Indigenous political movements throughout the world.

It's all about political conscientization, doing research that is necessarily transformative for whānau, hapū and iwi. When we see things that are happening in the wider Aotearoa or the wider world that are transformative, that reflect those kinds of values we are trying to promote in the MAI programme, then we pop those up in the Facebook group. And it's a good way of beginning to connect people with other Indigenous and native scholars throughout the world, which really excites people......Our politics can be quite burdensome, and to see the work that other people are doing like in Canada Hawaii or in Australia is sometimes quite heartening and strengthening of our own work that we need to do here. It can be just a matter of seeing a Facebook post that pushes you through the next part of the chapter and your work, and it reminds you that your work is absolutely and fundamentally linked to bigger things than this piece of study. That it is linked to global Indigenous and Native activism. It just gives people that wider lens outside of the supervision relationship, where you are quite focused on that chapter.

Mera's comments provide insight into how significant the principle of tino rangatiratanga is in the lives and work of Māori academics, and how this is also strongly reflected within the Facebook group. The MAI ki Tāmaki Facebook Group provides a powerful space to raise the level of political conscientization of Māori academics, to demonstrate political activism and to connect them to a wider Indigenous community.

Taonga Tuku Iho: Cultural Aspirations Principle

'Taonga tuku iho' is a key Kaupapa Māori principle that validates Māori ways of being and creates a space for Māori to 'be Māori', whereby cultural aspirations and identity are legitimized. In chapter three, the section on taonga tuku iho highlighted ways in which Indigenous people engage in social media to support their cultural aspirations. This section discusses the online tikanga of the Facebook group and the creation of a culturally safe space for Māori academics within which to engage.

My discussion with Hinekura led us to explore the online tikanga (protocols) of the Facebook group. For Māori, tikanga is about ways of conducting oneself that is considered tika or correct in ways that draw upon on Māori principles and values. Hinekura begins by discussing the online tikanga for accepting members into the group and draws on the principle of whanaungatanga (maintaining relationships) that places emphasis on people's established connections and relationships.

At the moment, someone will request to join, and they might sit there for a while, whilst we find out who they are and how they were invited into the Facebook group. Our process is inclusive - but we also need to understand that whanaungatanga comes about through connections - and if we've got requests from people we don't know, then we need to establish where the relationship lies within the group.

Hinekura emphasizes the importance of knowing where the connection lies with new members, so that there is a shared responsibility and obligation in inviting members into the group.

When I think of whakapapa in that digital space - it goes back to who brought that person in, and so where is that connection. It hasn't happened as far as I can recall, but if there was something really inappropriate put up on the Facebook group - it would be a matter of tracing back to who brought that person here. That's the responsibility of introducing someone into that whakapapa, which I think is a very Māori thing.

Hinekura reflects on how the tikanga of the group is not explicitly outlined anywhere on the Facebook group. However, there is an assumption that members should know how to conduct themselves within a Kaupapa Māori framework. She conceptualizes the Facebook group as a space that supports Māori values and principles, and draws parallels with a physical Māori space.

When you go into a Māori space, you sit back and watch what's happening and what's the norm. Is it ok to do this? and can I sit here? Perhaps that is a similar way of operating in this digital space. When I am invited into the Facebook group, I sit back and I read and watch how others operate first before posting. So just like when we go into the marae ... there's not a written set of guidelines ..... If there was an occasion where there was something not right, like at a marae when someone sits in the wrong place, or if someone wears their shoes in the whare, then we have a conversation, and a bit of leaning in and support of that person.

When asking Hinekura whether Māori values could be expressed and experienced within an online space, she felt that they were present within the MAI ki Tāmaki Facebook Group.

The idea of whanaungatanga (relationships) and manaakitanga (caring for each othe) are important to how we support each other. Whether it's sitting here like we are now, or whether it's an online discussion on Facebook. Would somebody mind reading this chapter and giving feedback? So koha-atu-koha mai (reciprocity) is also important. And just a whole lot of aroha (love).

The values expressed by Hinekura contribute to a Kaupapa Māori space where being Māori is 'normalized'. Additionally Jen highlights the importance of incorporating the Māori language in her posts, and describes how it validates students as Māori within the online learning space.

On a Māori Facebook page, things Māori are much more normal. You are not going to be looked upon as holding extreme views, nor are you expected to clarify or explain certain things further..... because it is much more accepted and it's much more normal. And you can share things in a Māori group and not question yourself about how are non-Māori going to respond to these comments? ....Posting in Te Reo (Māori language) is a big deal for me, we are a predominantly Māori group, we are a Kaupapa Māori group - so why not post in both languages. I do always try and post bilingually. As someone who wrote in Māori for my PHD, I think it is important to continue promoting the use of te reo Māori in academic spaces as it is becoming more common for people to engage in academic writing in te reo Māori. However, I do keep the posts bilingual knowing that there are also many of our people who wouldn't necessarily understand if I just post in Māori.

Mera also talks about how the MAI ki Tāmaki Facebook Group provides members with a culturally safe space to express themselves. She discusses how members will often share their challenges and demands that reflect their doctoral journeys. Mera highlights how these are not limited just to research challenges that students face, but the wider issues that impact on their lives:

I think they see MAI Ki Tāmaki group is a space where they can discuss not just the academic challenges they are facing but the broader challenges in terms of - managing doctoral life, whānau life, hapū life, iwi life, the whole socio economic political environment that we are all living. I think that as a cohort the programme provides for that and that is reflected on the Facebook page and in the posts..... People will post things like a picture of themselves balancing a baby in one hand and the other hand on the keyboard laptop. They are commenting, "Here I am up till mid-night typing up the last draft of chapter 3, wouldn't have it any other way holding my baby." Those sorts of posts serve to strengthen the cohort - people are sharing the realities of being a mum or dad, and having children, doing a doctorate and working.

The principle of taonga tuku iho was highlighted at the beginning of this section by discussing the tikanga of the Facebook group that is supported by Māori values and principles. The notion of whanaungatanga provided a premise for the group membership, and ensured a strong sense of obligation and expectation in relation to how members conducted themselves online. Creating a space that felt culturally safe and that normalized 'being Māori' was another key component of this section. Supporting Te Reo Māori use in the site, and encouraging members to share their doctoral experiences all contributed to a Facebook group that underpins a Kaupapa Māori approach.

Whānau: Extended Family Structure Principle

The term 'whānau' is often used as way to describe a group of people who share the same kaupapa or are working together to a shared outcome. The practice of whanaungatanga comes from whānau, which places emphasis on strong relationships amongst members, and the roles and obligations of all members.

The MAI ki Tāmaki Makaurau programme operates as a whānau and, as highlighted in the first section, whanaungatanga underpins both the programme and the Facebook group. Jen discusses how the administrators manage the group in an inclusive way, and how it has extended its membership to include post-graduate students and other Māori and Indigenous academics. One of the aims of the MAI ki Tāmaki Makaurau programme is to encourage postgraduate students to transition to doctoral studies, and Jen sees the Facebook group as an effective platform for this:

In the past couple of years, we've tried to extend our reach …. One of the things we are trying to do is not only support those that are currently doing their PhDs, but to try and show those who are at honors or masters level that there is a pathway. For many of them it is a massive decision for them to go into a PhD…. It's a good way for them to be able to engage and interact with others that might already be on that journey and to get a feel for the sorts of things people are going through.

Jen describes how, within the Facebook group, various members will take on different roles to support other members, so that it is not always left to the administrators and senior academics to provide assistance. She discusses the concept of 'tuakana-teina' within the Facebook group, where members within the group, particularly those who are closer to the completion of their doctorate, are providing greater guidance to those starting their academic journey:

Whether we are finished our PHDs, whether we are just starting - we all have something to learn from everybody else in the group. Whether it's people posting about their research or sharing an opinion about something - we can learn from each other - so just being part of the group, and being in that collegial and scholarly environment is an opportunity to learn constantly, even if some are more active than others …… We have whanaungatanga as a core principle in everything that we do. Trying to include everybody, trying to encourage participation from everybody. But also, the tuakana-teina approach, where there are those who may be finished or closer to the end who may be able to support those coming through.

The Facebook group has a number of senior Māori academics, professors and supervisors as members. All administrators discuss the value of having senior academics joining the group to extend their support to doctoral scholars, as well as members providing support to each other. Mera states:

If you think about the underpinning of ako being that notion of reciprocity and people contributing and sharing to each other's growth, it's very much a part of what MAI programme is about, and you can see that evident on the Facebook page as well ….. It's great opportunity for students to engage with professors in an environment that is less threatening. They are getting lots of mentorship from people like myself Jenny and Leonie who are senior academics who engage on that page, but also there's peer mentoring that goes on. Particularly between the third, fourth, fifth year doctoral candidates and those that just come in.

Another key concept that was discussed by all administrators was the significance of 'kanohi-ki-te-kanohi', the ability for members to engage face-to-face. All administrators felt that the Facebook group complemented the face-to-face space, and that it was the physical engagement amongst members that was critical to the success of the Facebook group. Mera states:

The real growth for our doctoral students are those who engage in both the face-to-face end of the programme and the social media scene. People don't see the Facebook page as an alternative to the face-to-face engagement- they see it as an entry into the face-to-face, or backing up the face-to-face stuff. So, we have opportunities to meet monthly and Facebook is used in the between times.

Jen reflects on the MAI ki Tāmaki Makaurau writing retreats that she has attended with other Māori doctoral students, and feels that many of the conversations shared could not have occurred in the online space.

The online group helped us maintain relationships outside of those face-to-face meetings. But if we didn't have any face-to face interaction then we are just not going to interact in the same manner as on the Facebook group. The two spaces complement each other.

Hinekura also reflects on the physical engagement with another person compared to engaging in the Facebook group. She highlights how the online space cannot replicate the physical space, particularly in relation to the wairua and the spiritual breath of a person:

In a physical connection, you have the wairua there. That is the risk of the online space - how does the wairua of our korero come through? Ko te Ha - the spiritual breath of the person - that you can't just send through the keyboard and Te Ao Hurihuri.

When further considering the online space, Hinekura suggests that wairua (spirit of a person) can potentially be felt within the site, but this is dependent on whether or not you have met that person in the physical sense before:

There is some wairua in the site - I wonder if the key to that is that the fact that we have real live relationships with these people. When we know that person, how they operate and how they talk - we are better able to interpret and feel their wairua. If I didn't know a person in a physical way - would I understand and feel what they are posting? I don't think so.

This section discusses ways in which the Facebook group operates as a whānau in terms of supporting a collective kaupapa. The notion of ako is fundamental to the Facebook group, where reciprocity is central to how members support each other and take on roles and responsibilities for the good of the group. The Kaupapa Māori learning environment draws from the principle of kanohi-ki-te-kanohi principles that enables students to connect, in ways that are not able to be replicated online.

CONCLUSION

This chapter provides a case-study on the MAI ki Tāmaki Facebook Group and highlights key themes that were discussed by the administrators. A strong emphasis in the research was to examine the Kaupapa Māori elements that underpin the Facebook group, which enable Māori doctoral scholars and academics to engage in ways that support their cultural values and practices.

For administrators, it is critical to create a space where being Māori is 'normalized', and where principles, such as whanaungatanga, manaakitanga, and aroha contribute to this. Additionally, a strong sense of reciprocity amongst the group is expected, ensuring that there is a responsibility to the collective by all members. While the Facebook group was clearly not a substitute or a replication of a Māori physical space, some aspects of the online space could be conceptualized in the same way, particularly when it came to tikanga and ways of engaging within the group.

Emphasis on establishing relationships in a physical space through kanohi-ki-te-kanohi was of high importance. Administrators felt that without this face-to-face engagement the relationships within the online forum would lack a sense of whanaungatanga, as well as wairua that could be felt only between members with a prior physical connection. The Facebook group was a valuable place to continue and extend conversations that were had during MAI-ki- Tāmaki programme events. It also provided a space to raise political conscientization amongst scholars and opportunities to be more connected to Indigenous communities at a global level.

A central aspiration for the MAI ki Tāmaki Makaurau programme is for Māori and Indigenous scholars to remain grounded and connected to whānau, hapū, iwi and communities, and to engage in research that purposefully seeks to contribute to the positive development and transformation of their communities. This research indicates that the MAI ki Tāmaki Facebook Group provides a new platform to support this aspiration in ways that align with a Kaupapa Māori framework. The use of social media sites, if managed by and for Māori, can become culturally safe places for learning in ways that reflects their cultural practices and values.

REFERENCES

Denzin, N. K., & Lincoln, Y. S. (2008). Critical methodologies and Indigenous inquiry. In *Handbook of critical methodologies and Indigenous inquiry* (pp. 1–20). Sage Publications.

Hohepa, M. (2010). 'Doctoring' our own: Confessions of a Māori doctoral supervisor. In J. Jesson, V.M. Carpenter, M. McLean, M. Stephenson & Airini (Eds.), University teaching reconsidered: justice, practice, inquiry (pp. 129-138). Wellington, New Zealand: Dunmore Publishing Ltd.

McKinley, E., Grant, B., Middleton, S., Irwin, K., & Williams, L. R. T. (2007). Teaching and learning in the supervision of Māori Doctoral Students: Project outline. *MAI Review LW, 1*(3), 6.

Pihama, L., Lee-Morgan, J., Tiakiwai, S., Tauroa, T., Mahuika, R., & Lonebear, D. (2017). *Te Tātua o Kahukura*. Te Kotahi Research Institute.

Smith, G. (2012). Interview: Kaupapa Māori: The dangers of domestication. *New Zealand Journal of Educational Studies*, 47, 10–20.

Smith, G. H. (1991). *Reform & Māori educational crisis: A grand illusion*. The University of Auckland.

Smith, L. T. (2003). *Decolonising methodologies: Research and Indigenous peoples* (6th ed.). Dunedin, New Zealand: University Otago Press.

Te Kupenga o MAI. (n.d.). *Te Kupenga o MAI Māori and Indigenous Scholar Support*. Retrieved November 6, 2017, http://mai.ac.nz/about

Walker, S. (1996). *Kia tau te rangimarie: Kaupapa Māori theory as a resistance against the construction of Māori as the other* (Unpublished master's thesis). The University of Auckland, New Zealand.

Waziyatawin, & Yellow Bird, M. (Eds.). (2012). *For indigenous minds only: A decolonization handbook*. School for Advanced Research Press.

This research was previously published in Global Perspectives on Social Media in Tertiary Learning and Teaching; pages 72-90, copyright year 2018 by Information Science Reference (an imprint of IGI Global).

APPENDIX

Please note, some of following Māori words are not direct translations, but explanations as they relate specifically to the context in which they are used in this chapter.

Ako: Culturally preferred pedagogy principle.
Aotearoa: New Zealand.
Aroha: Love.
Aroha ki te Tangata: A respect for people.
Hapū: Subtribe.
Iwi: Tribe.
Kanohi Kitea: "The seen face," which refers to presenting yourself to people face to face.
Kanohi-ki-te-Kanohi: Face-to-face.
Kaua e Mahaki: Do not flaunt your knowledge.
Kaua e Takahi te Mana o te Tangata: Do not trample over the mana of people.
Kaupapa: Collective philosophy.
Kaupapa Māori: Māori principles.
Kia Piki Ake i Ngā Raruraru o te Kainga: The mediation of socio-economic factors principle.
Kia Tupato: Be cautious.
Ko te Ha: The essence of life.
Koha-Atu-Koha Mai: Reciprocity.
MAI Ki Tāmaki Makaurau: Auckalnd Māori and Indigenous doctoral program.
Manaaki Ki Te Tangata: Share and host people, be generous.
Manaakitanga: Kindness and caring.
Rangatahi: Youth.
Tamariki: Children.
Tangata Whenua: Local people.
Taonga Tuku Iho: The treasure and values that are inherited by us (cultural aspirations principle).
Te Ao Hurihuri: The changing world.
Te Reo Māori: Māori language.
Tikanga: Protocols.
Tika: Correct.
Tino Rangatiratanga: Self determination principle.
Titiro, Whakarongo ... Korero: Look, listen ... speak.
Tuakana-Teina: Older younger sibling relationship.
Wairua: Spirit.
Whakapapa: Genealogy.
Whānau: Extended family.
Whanaungatanga: Relationship, kinship.

Chapter 54

Is Twitter an Unexploited Potential in Indian Academic Libraries?
Case Study Based on Select Academic Library Tweets

Swapan Kumar Patra

(iD) https://orcid.org/0000-0002-0825-7973

Tshwane University of Technology, South Africa

ABSTRACT

Social media have revolutionized today's globalized world including all spheres of modern human being. Among many social networking sites (SNSs), Twitter is one of the most popular. Librarians all over the globe are increasingly using Twitter in their daily routine activities as well as promotion of their systems and services. This study is an attempt to map the Indian libraries' Twitter activity, taking academic libraries as case study. Selected Indian academic library tweets have collected form the Twitter using R programming language. The study further compares few develop countries' academic library tweets. The study observed that Indian academic libraries are very limited activities in Twitter. The sentiment analysis shows that library Tweets are more positive. The study recommends more Twitter activity for Indian academic libraries to attract their users. With the more Twitter activities, library's image will be more friendly and acceptable to the young users particularly the college and university students.

INTRODUCTION

In the present day, with the development of latest Information and Communication Technology (ICT), particularly with the advancement of many Web Technologies, the human life has been transformed in an unprecedent way. Today, social media and its effects are all pervasive. There are many Social Networking Sites (SNSs) which have become inseparable for modern human being. Libraries are not immune to this

DOI: 10.4018/978-1-6684-7123-4.ch054

recent ICT effect, rather libraries all over the globe are the primary adopter of ICT systems and services. The use of social media tools like microblogs (e.g. Twitter) has gained wide acceptance in libraries and among librarians globally (Munigal 2014). Library and Information Science (LIS) professionals are always forerunners in adoption and utilization of the latest ICT tools and techniques for disseminating information to their users. Libraries have adopted various ICT tools in their routine housekeeping activities, marketing their systems and services. In the recent years, many of the routine library activities are getting new dimensions with the popular social media. For example, the networking sites, like Facebook and Twitter are getting popularity in libraries and librarians for promoting their library services. Among all the SNS, Twitter is the most popular microblog where anyone can open an account and post textual, video, images and other contents. However, its users can post very limited text. It is freely available and become common in all strata of public life.

Librarians have struggled hard to dispel their stereotype image in information processing and management. The people's perception of libraries and librarians is gradually changing with the ICT tools to deliver services innovatively. Twitter is one of those innovative ways that librarians have added to existing communication channels (Patra 2019). Many big and famous libraries around the world use Twitter for their various services for example, content alerts, Selective Dissemination of Information (SDI), Current Awareness Service (CAS) and so on services (Munigal 2014).

Because of its handy and inexpensive characters, librarians worldwide are using it as an effective communication tool. The greatest advantage of Twitter is its direct and two-way communication with its users. In Twitter librarians can interact with their users and can get direct feedback.

In this context, it is an exploratory study of Indian academic libraries' activities in Twitter. Indian Libraries are one of the early adapters of ICT tools in their libraries among the developing Asian countries. However, how the Indian libraries are in social media network is the main objectives of this study. To fulfil this objective this study has selected academic libraries as case study. Some selected libraries are chosen and their Tweets are collected from the Twitter handle. The study will further examine the most frequently occurring keywords and the sentiments are derived from the tweets.

Literature Review

Information and Communication Technology (ICT) have revolutionized every aspect of modern human being. Along with the ICT revolution, the emergence of social media has added a new dimension to the modern human life. Today, Social networking sites (SNSs) have gradually acquired important share of time and space in people's daily routines. Several SNS have emerged in the last decade, such as Twitter, Facebook, LinkedIn and so on (Vassilakaki & Garoufallou 2015).

Among all these social media, Twitter is one of the most important as well as popular instant messaging platform (Sakas & Sarlis 2016). It is a microblogging social networking service where a user can post very limited text. With this limited text, it can offer news services, share information, and can interact with their users. Moreover, it also offers additional functions, for example, sharing of pictures, audio and videos messages. Beside this, Twitter's Application Programming Interface (API), gives users the opportunity to build various applications for different devices and diverse platforms (Stuart 2010).

Twitter provides 140-character microblogging service, is very popular among the LIS professionals (Stuart 2010). It is popular among LIS professional because of it inexpensive and quick means of reaching users (Shulman, Yep and Tomé 2015; Fields, 2010). It is an important tool for promoting their services (Vassilakaki and Garoufallou 2015). Twitter can also act as a marketing tool for librarians (Carscaddon and Chapman 2013). As a continuous stream of user's post in various different format, it generates a constant stream of unstructured data. This massive source of data is considered a huge source of information. These unstructured data can generate very meaningful information, if it is processed in ordered way (Thelwall, Buckley and Paltoglou 2011). An analysis of Twitter may therefore, give insights into the peoples' opinion in a particular subject or events. It may be used as a strong feedback mechanism of any event or organisation. Hence, Twitter offers an unprecedented opportunity to public utility or benefit organizations like libraries to promote their services and build a powerful digital information exchange community (Sakas and Sarlis 2016). So, it is very interesting to examine this phenomenon in different kinds of Indian libraries (Aharony 2010).

Twitter and Libraries

As it is already discussed in the previous section, that Twitter is becoming increasingly popular since the last few years. Microblogging SNSs like Twitter is a relatively a recent development in online social networking. Libraries all over the globe use the potential of Twitter in their daily routine activities. Along with the growth and popularity of this SNSs its various facets have been investigated from different developed countries perspective (Verishagen and Hank 2014; Del Bosque, Leif and Skarl 2012; Palmer 2014).

Empirical studies have observed that, librarians use of Twitter is context dependent. Its use depends on the nature of the library, for example, there are differences of Tweets between public and academic libraries. The variations may include the number of Tweets, linguistic differences, and content. However, the library and librarian's use of twitter is mainly to disseminate and share information about their activities, opinions, status, and professional interests (Aharony 2010).

There is no general trend of who control twitter handle of an academic institution's library. However, it is observed that academic libraries' Twitter accounts associated directly with the institutions get more attention. In many cases it is found that some of the individual related to library activity, university faculty, staff, or students, are regulating or maintaining Twitter accounts. However, that types of accounts get less attention (followers). So, according to this observation academic library's Twitter networks must be directly handled by the responsible persons of the library rather than the other individuals. Furthermore, the library, as an institutional account itself, is also influential entity to the broader Twitter community of its parent institution. So, it can be said that library is a vital organization and in a key position to propagate information from the parent institute's accounts (Shulman, Yep and Tomé 2015).

Academic libraries use Twitter as a multifaceted tool. Academic libraries and librarians are using Twitter more efficiently and effectively (Al-Daihani and AlAwadhi, 2015). Academic libraries have posted a variety of information for their patrons on Twitter. The trends indicate that the primary groups for disseminating the tweets of academic libraries are within the university community and students (Kim, Abels and Yang 2012). From the users' trend analysis, it is observed that the general "News and announcements" related Tweets receives the maximum attention among the followers. The second most important and popular posting is the "library collections" and "library services". Beside these two categories the following postings are popular; "library marketing and news", "answers and referrals" and "books" and so on. Moreover, there is a global trend that shows that academic libraries have the tendency of posting links more often than other types of contents. Other results show different patterns of communication and interaction between libraries and their Twitter followers (Al-Daihani and AlAwadhi 2015).

Twitter and Indian Libraries

It is now globally recognised that SNSs are very powerful tool today to provide library services. Many libraries are now using online social networking services to make their services popular and user friendly (Vassilakaki and Garoufallou, 2015). Various SNSs for example, Facebook, YouTube, twitter, LinkedIn, Instagram have many applications that could be utilised by the libraries to provide number of services in libraries (Deepthi, Tadasad & Patil 2017). Along with the services provided by the libraries, the SNSs has also changed the nature of library users (Chakravarty and Kiran 2013). Indian libraries have understood the importance of SNS and other Web 2.0 phenomenon of social networking. These kinds of latest and handy tools could enable Indian libraries to engage with their users in the virtual environment for the promotion of the library services. Moreover, SNSs are improving the professional relationships among the LIS profession. More professional contact may result in an increase of information sharing. In this way librarians can meet the demands and needs of their students (Chakravarty and Kiran 2013).

The libraries' use of Twitter and its different pros and cons are quite adequately investigated from developed country's context. A proper investigation of Indian Libraries and their use of Twitter is significantly lacking. This is not only the case of India but valid from the other developed country's context also. The case of developing countries for example in Nigeria's case, it is observed that majority of the library and information professionals have Facebook profiles but the LIS professionals are comparatively less active in Twitter. Findings revealed further that younger librarians showed more positive attitude towards the use of SNSs (Fasola 2015).

As it is mentioned above, Indian libraries are quite interested to adopt ICT tools and techniques in their library services. Contrary to this, they are not that much receptive towards SNSs. It is observed from many empirical evidences that Indian librarian are yet to adopt the popular SNS tools as their daily functioning. For example, based on a study of 54 university websites in Karnataka state showed that 53 of 54 universities (98.14 percent) have their own websites. About 29.62 percent State/Central universities are connected to Facebook, 18.51 percent are connected to YouTube. There are very few universities connected to Twitter and LinkedIn. The study further observed that the university libraries in the study area are lagging behind and trying to catch up with the SNSs. Some of the university libraries are in social network domain. However, their networking services are very limited and used for very basic or elementary purposes. (Deepthi, Tadasad and Patil 2017).

The study on the use of SNS by the students of Tamil Nadu, India shows that university students are quite well versed with the latest SNSs. However, if students require information, they prefer 'Google' search for data (Balamurugan and Thanuskodi 2019). The study observed that Google search engine is the most preferred search engine. Majority of the respondents (about 69 percent) are aware of Google scholar for scholarly literature search. Students have very limited awareness about Research gate, Twitter, SlideShare, Academic.edu. and LinkedIn and so on (Krishnamurthy and Shettappanavar 2019). However, beyond Google, there is a developing pattern of utilizing social media for specific data among students. According to that findings, Social Media is emerging as an alternate source of information from different group. Students find Social Media as a platform for one to one or one-to many ways of communication for subject specific questions or queries. Further the study by Balamurugan and Thanuskodi (2019) found that students are the primary user of social media (Balamurugan and Thanuskodi 2019). So, there are enormous opportunity if the student's community is targeted using these social media platforms. Students can be more attracted towards the respective university of college libraries if they are tapped through the social medias.

Although Twitter is being used by people in various spheres of life. These empirical evidences observed that the use of Twitter by Indian libraries is very limited. Scholarly research in this domain is also very limited (Patra 2019). In this context, this study is an attempt to investigate the Indian libraries' use of Twitter for their various services. This study selects Indian academic libraries as case study to find the following research question:

Research Questions

- How Indian academic libraries Tweets?
- How Indian libraries differs in Tweets in comparison of academic libraries of other developed countries?
- What are the keyword trends in their Tweets?
- What kind of sentiments (positive, negative or neutral and so on) the Tweets carry?

Methodology

For this study, tweets from 10 Indian academic libraries are collected through R interface. These libraries are, Learning Resource Centre, *Silvassa College*, Silvassa, Union Territory of Dadra and Nagar Haveli, *Institute of Hotel Management Catering Technology and Applied Nutrition*, Bhubaneswar, Odisa, Department of Library and Information Science, *Gauhati University*, Guwahati, Library Learning Center, *Indian Institute of Management Raipur*, Vikram Sarabhai Library, *Indian Institute of Management, Ahmedabad*; Central Library of *Indian Institute of Technology Bombay*; MACFAST Library and Information Centre (MLIC) of *Mar Athanasios College for Advanced Studies* Tiruvalla; College library of *Maharshi Dayanand College of Arts, Science and Commerce*; The Central Library of *Amrita Vishwa Vidyapeetham*; Central Library of *Kalinga Institute of Industrial Technology* (Deemed to be University).

These sample libraries are selected because they have minimum 100 Tweets. The sample is a fair representation of academic libraries from different states in India. Also, in the sample, there are public and private educational institutions including college, universities and technical institutes.

This study further makes a comparison of the Indian academic libraries' Tweets with that of other library Tweets of top ranked global institutes' libraries around the world. For the comparison purpose, the Tweets from the following libraries are downloaded. These libraries are *Trinity College Library*, UK; *National University of Singapore, Cornell Library*, USA, *University of Adelaide*, Australia, *York University*, Canada and *Nanyang Technological University Library* Singapore. The Tweets from these different libraries around the globe will act as a comparator to map the position of Indian libraries' activity in Twitter.

The Tweets are collected form Twitter using the R programming languages. The further analysis is done based on the strong statistical and text mining capabilities of the software R. The figure 1 below shows the step by step methodology for generating word cloud and sentiments

Limitations: this study has the following limitations. *Firstly*, it is based on only one social media, i.e. Twitter. *Secondly*, the study is limited to academic libraries only. Inclusion of other libraries for example; public libraries, school libraries, research libraries, special libraries and other social media like Facebook, LinkedIn will perhaps give a better and holistic picture of Indian libraries' activities on social media. *Thirdly*, the research scope is narrow and only studied the selected libraries activities in microblog Twitter. *Finally*, the Tweets are collected from the library Twitter handle in the particular time of a year. As the field is very dynamic the number of tweets may vary. Future research should focus on the data collection and sorting, make comparative studies from the data of different times including different social network platforms in libraries.

Figure 1. Methodology flow chart

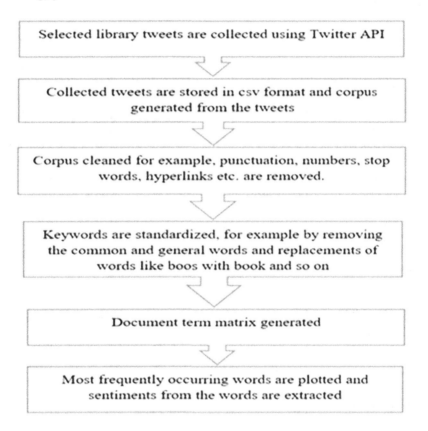

Results

There are altogether about 8,512 Tweets of the 10 different libraries from different parts of India are harvested for this analysis to answer the research questions raised above. It is mentioned in the literature review section that Indian libraries are the early adopter of ICT tools and techniques but their presence in SNSs are not prominent. With the extensive search on the Internet while collecting the Tweets from different library Twitter handles, it is observed that Indian Libraries are generally not that active in Twitter. Many of the famous Indian academic libraries do not even have Twitter account. Many of the library's Twitter handles are inactive and many of them have very limited activities.

The libraries with more than 100 Tweets are selected for this study. The study has taken into account the following 10 libraries. Table 1 shows the profile of different library Tweets harvested from different Indian libraries in the month of August 2019. The table describes different library Tweets and their Twitter handles, their number of Tweets, whom they are following, their followers, the year the Twitter account has been created and from the Indian state or provinces the library or institute is belong to. From the table 1 it is observed that Central Library of Kalinga Institute of Industrial Technology (KIIT) has the maximum number of Tweets followed by Department of Library and Information Science, Guwahati University, Guwahati. Tweets of the rest other libraries are shown in the Table 1 as decreasing order.

Table 1. Indian Libraries and their Tweets

Sl. No	Name of the Library	Twitter Handle	Number of Tweets	Following	Followers	Year of join in Twitter	State
1.	Central Library of Kalinga Institute of Industrial Technology (Deemed to be University)	@Library_KIIT	3384	79	781	Apr- 2016	Orissa
2.	Department of Library and Information Science, Guwahati University, Guwahati	@DLISGU	2876	29	66	Oct- 2012	Assam
3.	The official Twitter account of Vikram Sarabhai Library, Indian Institute of Management, Ahmedabad	@VSLIIMA	594	648	1225	Dec- 2016	Gujarat
4.	Central Library of Indian Institute of Technology Bombay	@centrallibraryb	520	104	148	Mar-2010	Maharashtra
5.	Institute of Hotel Management Catering Technology and Applied Nutrition, Bhubaneswar	@dash1983	312	52	72	Sep-2013	Orissa
6.	Library Learning Center, Indian Institute of Management Raipur	@IimLibrary	230	19	39	Jul-2018	Chhattisgarh
7.	Learning Resource Centre, Silvassa College, Silvassa, UT of DNH	@SIHL_Library	166	63	52	Mar-2012	Dadra and Nagar Haveli (Indian union territory)
8.	College library of Maharshi Dayanand College is Arts, Science & Commerce	@MDCLibrary	165	70	86	Sep-2011	Mumbai
9.	The Central Library of Amrita Vishwa Vidyapeetham	@ASASLibrary	158	21	51	Jun-2009	Karnataka
10.	MACFAST Library and Information Centre (MLIC) of Mar Athanasios College for Advanced Studies Tiruvalla	@Macfast_Library	107	86	55	Mar-2011	Kerala

For a comparative purpose the following (Table 2) library Tweets from different global academic libraries are chosen. Because of certain limitations, the Twitter API allows to download only 3,500 Tweets at a time. So, the Twitter handles of the following libraries are chosen. In the month of August / September 2019 there were altogether 15,724 Tweets collected form these selected foreign academic libraries. These Tweets are stored in Microsoft Excel comma delimited format for further analysis.

It is evident from the Table 2 that all these libraries have quite significant number of followers. The number of followers shows that these libraries are quite popular among its user. The number of Tweets shows the activity of these libraries and apparently it shows that these libraries are quite active than the Indian academic libraries.

This study has further observed that there are very few Indian libraries that have separate Twitter accounts (different from their parent institute). It is also not clear who handles these accounts. Moreover, Libraries with Twitter account are very less active. Contrary to this, the libraries from the other developed countries are comparatively more active in Twitter. Those libraries Tweet various information, including new material arrival in the library, seminar announcements and so on.

Table 2. Select foreign libraries and their Tweets

Sl. No.	Name of the Library	Twitter Handle	Number of Tweets	Following	Followers	Joined	Country
1.	The Trinity College Library in Cambridge.	@TrinCollLibCam	1423	217	1958	Oct- 2014	UK
2.	Cornell University Library	@Cornell_Library	1723	903	2790	Jul- 2017	USA
3.	The University of Adelaide Library	@uofalib	1860	96	1004	Mar- 2011	Australia
4.	York University Libraries	@yorkulibraries	3295	825	2569	Dec- 2008	Canada
5.	Princeton University Library	@PULibrary	1642	166	1505	Dec- 2012	USA
6.	Nanyang Technological University Library	@NTUsgLibrary	2724	140	6013	Aug- 2011	Singapore

Topic Modelling

Word frequency analysis or Topic modelling is the concept to extract themes from the textual data. Documents naturally contain words which can represent topics. Hence, Topic modelling can be described as a distribution of concepts over the terms in a corpus of documents. Topic models are applicable in a variety of scientific fields to identify hidden structures in otherwise unstructured text collections (Buckley 2016).

The collected Tweets are further processed by removing the punctuation marks, stop words, space and hyperlinks for word cloud formation and sentiment analysis. From the selected 8,512 Tweets the word corpus is generated. The word cloud shows that 'need' is the most frequently occurring keyword in these words cluster followed by 'delhi.' These words are the most frequently occurred because of the job vacancy announcements. For example, library Tweets, library needs library professionals, librarian and so on. Figure 2 shows the word cloud form the library Tweets.

Figure 3 shows the top 20 most frequently occurring keyword form the Indian academic library's Tweets. The word like assam, kissfoundation kitt, kiss are the prominent keywords. These institutes are the most active in Tweet their contents in Twitter. Hence, it is obvious that these institutes' name will appear and come in priority. Hence it is evident from the Tweet's trends of Indian academic libraries that libraries are more concern about the job-related advertisements and also more towards the contents of their parent institutes in their Tweets rather than their own contents.

Figure 2. Word cloud from Indian academic library tweets

Figure 3. The top 20 Tweets collected from the Indian Library Tweets

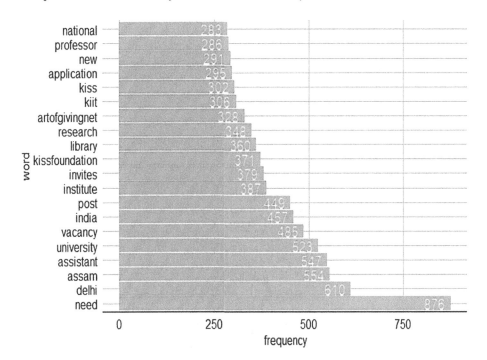

Moreover, the word frequency analysis shows that, Indian academic libraries mainly 'Retweet' their parent institute's Tweets with very little contents or value edition of their own. So, it can be concluded that, Indian academic libraries are quite poor in generating content on the Twitter.

Similar to the Tweets collected for the Indian academic libraries, the Tweets from foreign academic libraries are also collected and processed. There are altogether 12,667 Tweets collected form those selected libraries. These tweets are collected as comma delimited format and word corpus created. The figure 4 shows the word cloud generated from the different library Tweets of selected foreign academic libraries. In this case, library is the most prominent keyword, followed by new, book, today and so on. The trends in keywords shows that these libraries are giving more emphasis on library's activities in that day and so on. The words like books and new etc shows the new arrival in the library.

The figure 5 shows the most frequently occurring keywords from the foreign library Tweets. Library is the most frequently occurred keyword with 2,317 occurrences, followed by new, book, today and so on. The word youku is in the fifth position with 741 occurrence represents. The word 'youku' represents York University Libraries is the library system. The topic also shows more towards libraries or library related activities among these libraries. It includes the words like research, students, university and so on.

Sentiment Analysis

This section deals with the sentiment analysis of Tweets collected form the selected library's Twitter handles. The objective of this section is to analyse the trends among the library Tweets. By analysing the words in the Twitter, it is trying to identity the sentiments associate with the words.

Figure 4. Word cloud of different foreign academic library Tweets

Figure 5. Top 20 most frequently occurring words from selected foreign library Tweets

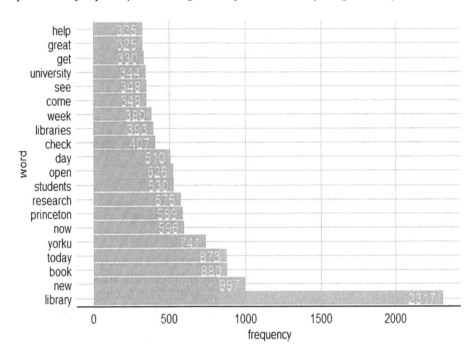

Sentiment analysis (SA) is about the extraction of sentiment, opinion from the text through the computational treatment of structured or unstructured text (Pang and Lee 2008). With the social media boom in recent years, a vast amount of unstructured data with opinions from various topics are available. With proper treatment of these text many valuable and meaningful information can be extracted (Thelwall, Buckley, and Paltoglou 2011). With the increasing computational power these types of analysis are inexpensive source for opinion analysis of organizations and individuals. Sentiment can be of various categories. For example, a sentiment extracted from the word can be positive, negative, or neutral. Sentiment analysis has widespread applications in various institutes or organization for example in sales prediction, stock management, ad placements, products and so on (Oliveira, Cortez and Areal 2016).

For this study the sentiments extracted from the Tweets are of 10 types. The different types of Tweets are; Positive, Trust, Anticipation, Joy, Negative, Surprise, Fear, Sadness, Anger and Disgust. Figure 6 shows the different types of sentiments extracted from two different type of libraries.

Although the number of Tweets form two different types of libraries varies, the tweets of both types of libraries have similar trends (figure 6). These two different types of Tweets have similar types of sentiment. From the foreign libraries among the 20,808 words 13,674 are positives words (65.72 percent). Similarly, in Indian libraries among 15,401 words 9,960 are positive (64.67 percent) sentiments. However, in case of India libraries 42 percent are trust and in case of foreign libraries are 27 percent trust. Rest other sentiments follow the similar trends. Hence, it is quite optimistic scenario that Indian academic libraries Tweets carry more optimistic and positive sentiment.

Figure 6. Comparison of sentiments from the words of Indian and Foreign Library Tweets

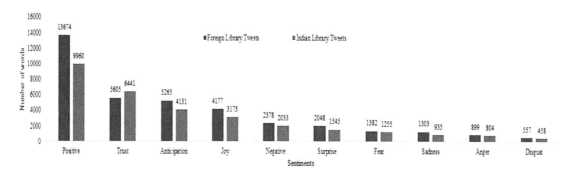

CONCLUDING REMARKS AND POLICY IMPLICATIONS

With the increasing availability, popularity and accessibility of SNSs many new opportunities and challenged are opened for the academic libraries. The SNSs are quite popular among the university and college students. In this context, SNSs could be very important platform for Indian academic libraries for self-promotion and marketing of their systemS and services (Liu, Zhang and Ye 2018). Students (both university and college) are the main user of the academic libraries. Students of these age group are quite well versed of using different ICT tools and techniques in their daily routine. With the recent mobile and smartphone penetration among the general population, most of the young people are tech savvy and have Facebook and Twitter accounts. So, Twitter is very helpful to reach these young users. If libraries can be active in social media like Twitter, they can reach these users quite easily and efficiently. The more active twitter handle will certainly be useful to reach the more users.

In comparison to many academic libraries of developed world, Indian academic libraries are not that active in Twitter. Also, it is not evident from the present Twitter handle, who maintains the Twitter account of academic libraries. In this context, it is advisable that, Indian academic libraries should assign an expert LIS professional to maintain their library's Twitter account. A separate division of work with defined job responsibility must be there to look after and coordinate the library Twitter activity regularly. In this way libraries can Tweet their activities to the user or interested patrons. This will in the long run attract more users, particularly the youths in the college and universities who are the primary users of the library.

Indian libraries are early adapter of ICT Tools and services. However, in the case of social media uses, Indian academic libraries are lagging behind in comparison to academic libraries of developed countries. Although, there are difference in social and economic conditions, for example, the financial resources in the libraries, however, Twitter and library Tweeting activity is not an expensive affair. So, Indian libraries could maintain regular Twitter handle to promote their activities. Academic library professional in India must be active in social media include Twitter. More activities on the social media will give a positive picture to the libraries and the librarians as a whole. This will also help to reach their library patrons and other target audience.

The study presented above have used quite simple tools. LIS professionals should use or apply these types of exercises in their libraries regularly. Librarians can adopt this technique to get immediate feedback about their library services and opinions about other things in the library.

REFERENCES

Aharony, N. (2010). Twitter Use in Libraries: An Exploratory Analysis. *Journal of Web Librarianship*, *4*(4), 333–350. doi:10.1080/19322909.2010.487766

Al-Daihani, S. M., & AlAwadhi, S. A. (2015). Exploring academic libraries' use of Twitter: A content analysis. *The Electronic Library*, *33*(6), 1002–1015. doi:10.1108/EL-05-2014-0084

Balamurugan, T., & Thanuskodi, S. (2019). Use of social networking sites among the college students in Tamil Nadu, India. *Library Philosophy and Practice*, *2301*, 1–12.

Buckley, P. (2016). Topic Modelling. In M. Hofmann & A. Chisholm (Eds.), *Text Mining and Visualization Case Studies Using Open-Source Tools*. CRC Press, Taylor and Francis Group.

Carscaddon, L., & Chapman, K. (2013). Twitter as a marketing tool for libraries. *Marketing with social media: A LITA guide*, 147-163.

Chakravarty, R., & Kiran, A. (2013). Social Networking in Libraries: A Case Study of Post Graduate Students and Research Scholars of Panjab University Library, India. In S. Thanuskodi (Ed.), *Challenges of Academic Library Management in Developing Countries*. IGI Global. doi:10.4018/978-1-4666-4070-2.ch009

Deepthi, T. (2017). Use of online social networking services in university libraries: A Study of university libraries of Karnataka, India. *DESIDOC Journal of Library and Information Technology*, *37*(4), 249–258. doi:10.14429/djlit.37.4.10498

Del Bosque, D., Leif, S. A., & Skarl, S. (2012). Libraries atwitter: Trends in academic library tweeting. *RSR. Reference Services Review*, *40*(2), 199–213. doi:10.1108/00907321211228246

Fasola, O. S. (2015). Perceptions and acceptance of librarians towards using Facebook and Twitter to promote library services in Oyo State, Nigeria. *The Electronic Library*, *33*(5), 870–882. doi:10.1108/EL-04-2014-0066

Fields, E. (2010). A unique Twitter use for reference services. *Library Hi Tech News*, *27*(6/7), 14–15. doi:10.1108/07419051011095863

Kim, H. M., Abels, E. G., & Yang, C. C. (2012). Who disseminates academic library information on Twitter? *Proceedings of the ASIST Annual Meeting*, *49*(1), 1-4. 10.1002/meet.14504901317

Krishnamurthy, C., & Shettappanavar, L. (2019). Digital literacy among female postgraduate students of Karnatak University, Dharwad, Karnataka, India: A study. *Library Philosophy and Practice*, *2934*, 1–16.

Liu, L., Zhang, L., & Ye, P. (2018). Research on the application of SNS in university libraries. *The Electronic Library*, *36*(2), 369–386. doi:10.1108/EL-05-2016-0120

Munigal, A. (2014). Use of Microblogs in India: A Study of Twitter Usage by Librarians and in Libraries. *Journal of Library Administration*, *54*(7), 590–608. doi:10.1080/01930826.2014.964021

Oliveira, N., Cortez, P., & Areal, N. (2016). Sentiment Analysis of Stock Market Behavior from Twitter Using the R Tool. In M. Hofmann & A. Chisholm (Eds.), *Text Mining and Visualization Case Studies Using Open-Source Tools*. CRC Press, Taylor and Francis Group.

Palmer, S. (2014). Characterizing university library use of social media: A case study of Twitter and Facebook from Australia. *Journal of Academic Librarianship, 40*(6), 611–619. doi:10.1016/j.acalib.2014.08.007

Pang, B., & Lee, L. (2008). Opinion mining and sentiment analysis. *Foundations and Trends® in Information Retrieval, 2*(1–2), 1-135.

Patra, S. K. (2019). How Indian libraries tweet? Word frequency and sentiment analysis of library tweets. *Annals of Library and Information Studies, 66*, 131–139.

Sakas, D. P., & Sarlis, A. S. (2016). Library promotion methods and tools modeling and simulation on Twitter. *Library Review, 65*(6-7), 479–499. doi:10.1108/LR-06-2015-0068

Shulman, J., Yep, J., & Tomé, D. (2015). Leveraging the power of a Twitter network for library promotion. *Journal of Academic Librarianship, 41*(2), 178–185. doi:10.1016/j.acalib.2014.12.004

Stuart, D. (2010). What are libraries doing on twitter? *Online (Wilton, Connecticut), 34*(1), 45–47.

Thelwall, M., Buckley, K., & Paltoglou, G. (2011). Sentiment in Twitter Events. *Journal of the American Society for Information Science and Technology, 62*(2), 406–418. doi:10.1002/asi.21462

Vassilakaki, E., & Garoufallou, E. (2015). The impact of Twitter on libraries: A critical review of the literature. *The Electronic Library, 33*(4), 795–809. doi:10.1108/EL-03-2014-0051

Verishagen, N., & Hank, C. (2014). Are there birds in the library? The extent of Twitter adoption and use by Canadian academic libraries. *First Monday, 19*(11). Advance online publication. doi:10.5210/fm.v19i11.4945

This research was previously published in Big Data Applications for Improving Library Services; pages 123-141, copyright year 2021 by Information Science Reference (an imprint of IGI Global).

Section 4
Utilization and Applications

Chapter 55

Navigating the Shortcomings of Virtual Learning Environments Via Social Media

Puvaneswary Murugaiah

School of Distance Education, Universiti Sains Malaysia, Penang, Malaysia

Siew Hwa Yen

School of Distance Education, Universiti Sains Malaysia, Penang, Malaysia

ABSTRACT

It is undeniable that the higher education landscape worldwide has changed with the emergence of virtual learning environments (VLEs). These systems offer learning space and resources for teachers and students regardless of time and place. Although they significantly contribute to the achievement of learning objectives and outcomes, their usage is generally limited. This article uncovers the shortcomings of the use of VLEs for language learning in several Malaysian institutions of higher learning. It also aims to highlight the use of social media in addressing the barriers. Adopting a qualitative approach, data were gathered via in-depth interviews. Employing the dimensions proposed by Chun, Kern and Smith, the hindrances related to VLEs were examined. The findings revealed that instructors faced obstacles linked to the technology, students' experience and expectations as well as language learning environment. Social media helped them in addressing these obstacles.

1. INTRODUCTION

Educational technology within higher education has greatly impacted the teaching and learning landscape, challenging institutions to change their models of pedagogical practices. With the emergence of web technologies for instance, students participate, collaborate and interact with one another; actively engaging in co-creating knowledge. Instructors on the other hand, promote networked social activities and provide broader opportunities for more independent and cooperative learning for their students.

DOI: 10.4018/978-1-6684-7123-4.ch055

The adoption of such progressive technology creates more fluid learning spaces making learning more distributed; thus blurring the lines between online and offline teaching and learning practices.

The call for increased and efficient adoption of technologies has prompted higher institutions of learning to design their own virtual learning environment (VLE). Its features include the creation and sharing of learning resources; facilitation of interactions among students as well as between students and instructors; administration of learning tasks and assessments as well as management of course and students (Cavus, 2015; Dobre, 2015). Despite its benefits, the VLE is not fully utilized by academics for instructional purposes. Although factors related to the behaviour and attitude of users are key contributors to this problem, in many instances it is the position of VLE in the pedagogical context that determines its use.

Due in part to this, the employment of social media by the academic community is fast growing. Social technologies such as Facebook, Twitter and WhatsApp have especially become an integral part of students' lives. In fact, the demands for and the potency of these social technologies have played a role in the shift towards a participatory and collaborative learning model in higher education (delaat & Prinsen, 2014). However, the use of social media is yet to be readily embraced by the academic community.

Building on the discussion so far, identifying and understanding the barriers for effective instructional practices using VLEs as well as the use of social media to check them is critical. The present study therefore, probes not only the technology but also the environment in which the system is set. Additionally, it examines the role of social media in circumventing issues hindering the effective use of VLEs. Although research on VLEs and the various uses of different social media tools in instruction is abundant, there is paucity in research on how the limitations of VLEs are checked by the use of social media especially in language teaching. Very few studies focussed on both VLEs and social media. In one, the potential of Facebook to complement an LMS was explored (Wang, Woo, Quek, yang and Liu, 2011) while in the other the possibility of replacing LMS with Facebook as a course communication tool was examined (Shroeder and Greenbowe, 2009).

This paper describes a segment of the data gathered from a larger study on the use of web technologies in English language teaching at Malaysian universities. Using a qualitative approach, the current study examines the shortcomings faced by language instructors in using VLEs in four Malaysian public universities. It also investigates how they used social media to check these barriers. It is anticipated that the findings of the study will help not only instructors but also institution administrators to understand the constraints faced by instructors and the role of social media in mitigating them. Additionally, they can evaluate and upgrade the effectiveness of the VLE systems. Furthermore, the study will contribute to literature on the emerging debate of social media adoption by HEIs. It can shed more light on the position of social media as an addition to VLEs or as a course management tool.

2. VIRTUAL LEARNING ENVIRONMENTS

Over the years, the advent of web tools namely interactive tools has driven HEIs to provide a single institutionalized online system for e-learning. Also known as learning management system (LMS), web-based learning system (WBLS) or course management system (CMS), virtual learning environment (VLE) is generally defined as 'a centralized system that gives a consistent user experience to everyone' (Weller, 2010 p. 3). More specifically, the system enables learners and teachers to have access to varied learning tools at any time and place (Raaij & Schepers, 2008). As it is a centralized system integrating several web tools, it is user-friendly (single sign-on), flexible and easily available. VLEs help students access learning resources, interact with content, peers and instructor. In learning English, for example, it not only aids students in locating a myriad of resources but also in providing vast opportunities for them to communicate in English with their peers and instructors such as discussion forums, wiki and blogs (Kalayci & Humiston, 2015; Lin, 2012). As de Laat and Prinsen (2014) point out, the social practice produced by VLEs offers a dynamic space for learning. Instructors on the other hand, can use VLEs to enhance learning by uploading additional resources and activities. Moreover, the system enables them to conduct course assessments and offer feedback during collaboration in quizzes and forums. By providing learning resources and assessment activities, there is centralized support for student learning (Weller, 2010; Omar et al., 2012). Moreover, by integrating various tools, instructors and administrators can monitor students' use of the VLE. They can for instance, track students' resource accessibility and collaboration patterns (Weller, 2010). As a centrally-hosted system, it helps instructors monitor student participation and progress in learning.

According to Motaghian et al. (2013), although various VLE systems are in place to facilitate teaching and learning, they are not commonly used by academics. Research has revealed that such a trend is glaring in developing countries. In Turkey for example, Kalayci and Humiston (2015) reported the inactive and ineffective use of the Moodle. In sub-Saharan countries like Tanzania and Sudan, Mtebe and Raisamo (2014) contended that there is an increased adoption of LMS in their universities. However, its use is reported to be dismal. Similarly, Wichadee (2015), in her study on VLE adoption among 62 language instructors of a university in Thailand, declared that the system was hardly used although the instructors were given ample training. The LMS is also not optimally utilized in Malaysia. A study on e-learning in Malaysian institutions of higher learning conducted by Al-rahmi, Othman and Yusuf (2015) revealed that the LMS is found to be only moderately viable as far as accessibilty (61.5%), ease of use (57.7%) and flexibility (53.8%) are concerned.

3. SOCIAL MEDIA TECHNOLOGY

Social media are fast emerging as educational tools namely in universities. They are changing the way students communicate, collaborate and learn (Tess, 2013). Literature has shown that social media have led to increased student-student, student-content and student-instructor interactions (Manca & Ranieri, 2017; Odom, 2010; McCarthy, 2010, Ajjan & Hartshone, 2008), which promote active learning in students through varied educational activities such as content generation tasks, collaborative problem solving assignments and active participation in discussion forums (McLoughlin & Lee, 2007; Osman & Koh 2013; Gray, Annabell & Kennedy, 2010). In language teaching for example, Liu, Evans, Horwitz, Lee, McCrory, Park and Parrish (2013) reported that the use of social networking sites such as Buusu, Live Mocha and English Café brought about learner satisfaction because of factors such as comfort level, language proficiency level, preferred communication modes and the design of the sites. These valuable educational resources enable instructors to select compatible activities for their teaching purposes. Kharbach (2014) for example, used Facebook to involve students in writing workshops while Manan, Alias and Pandian (2012) used it as a space for students to connect with each other and chat in English. Students' meaningful engagement in language learning using social media can create a sense of belonging and community (Blattner & Fiori, 2011). Thus, instructors are prompted to use the media to boost student engagement in learning inside and outside the language classroom (Arshad & Akram, 2018).

4. LINKING VIRTUAL LEARNING ENVIRONMENTS AND SOCIAL MEDIA IN HIGHER EDUCATION

A VLE is developed by an institution to foster pedagogical practices it deems important and practical. As a *managed* system (Selwyn, 2012), the content provided and interaction of both learners and instructors are structured. Both learners and instructors are confined to work in an environment determined by the institution. The options for independent learning, collaboration and sharing knowledge for example, are limited. Although the VLE functionalities are enhanced by including Web 2.0 features, these features appear within the context of a protected environment provided by the institution (Selwyn, 2012). Furthermore, in most cases a VLE resembles a traditional classroom model (Tess, 2013) that enshrines content acquisition and transmission with little room for innovation. On the other hand, a social media tool is an embodiment of democracy, openness and individual expression. As the use of Web 2.0 features is outside institutional control, users are inspired to share and co-create knowledge through collaboration and working independently. This generative nature promotes novelty in learning. Thus, instead of being consumers of content, users of social media are co-producers of knowledge (Simoes, 2011).

It is widely accepted that the millennial generation literally live in a digital environment. Having exposed to technology since young, they use it optimally in their daily lives. They search, consume and share content as well as contribute and participate in discussions, especially when using social media (Bolton et al., 2013). Therefore, it is crucial that technology enables easy accessibility of materials, downloading of multiple files at any one time, accessibility from mobile applications as well as smooth operation of its functions. A study by Chaw and Tang (2017) on LMS use by students in a Malaysian university revealed that due to the lack of these features, the use of VLEs is impacted. Adding to this, institutions are normally slow to react to the fast-paced technological developments (Simoes, 2011), which contributes to the lack of advanced features that appeal to the technology-savvy students in the VLE. Social media, on the other hand, allow students to interact, collaborate and share information in an open rather than closed, bottom-up rather than top-down manner (Tess, 2013; Hamid et al., 2015).

Moreover, Kula (2010) argued that institutional VLEs are rigidly structured, which does not allow room for instructors to manoeuvre their functions to suit their teaching objective. In a similar vein, Wichadee (2015), Montaghian et al. (2013) and Manca and Ranieri (2017) demonstrated that one major limitation of LMS is the inconvenience of using some of its features. Social media, on the other hand, provide instructors opportunities to select activities in line with their teaching objectives. Facebook, for example has been found to enhance communication and motivate students to learn and improve their English (Kabilan, Ahmad & Bidin, 2010; Ng & Wong, 2013; Mitchell, 2012). However, concerns related to privacy (Huffman, 2013), formal language use (Manan et al, 2012; Fewkes & McCabe, 2012) as well as the tools' affordances in promoting higher cognitive skills (Friesen & Lowe, 2011) seem to hinder instructors from using social media extensively with their students.

5. CHALLENGES RELATED TO INSTRUCTIONAL TECHNOLOGY ADOPTION IN HIGHER EDUCATION

Studies pertaining to the adoption of digital resources have revealed various challenges that hinder its acceptance. According to McLoughlin et al. (2008), the barriers can be broadly categorized as:

- Internal (lack of infrastructure, time or training)
- External (beliefs and attitudes)

Selim (2007) on the other hand, grouped them into four categories:

- Instructor
- Students
- Technology
- Support

Recently, Reid (2014) further classed the obstacles for higher education instructional technology adoption into five categories:

- Technology
- Process
- Faculty
- Environment
- Administration

Few studies such as that by Weller (2010) centre on the tool itself. He reported that concerns of higher education instructors regarding VLE adoption are linked to its pedagogic suitability, relevance as well as instructor control and personalization of it.

6. EVALUATING THE SUITABILITY OF VLEs IN LANGUAGE TEACHING AND LEARNING

Adopting Weller's (2010) argument, for the current study the use of VLE was evaluated based on instructors' view of its affordances. Chun, Kern and Smith's (2016) in-depth meta-analysis of technology-enhanced language teaching and learning is of particular relevance in the current study as it scrutinizes technological tools from instructors' standpoint. It must be noted that although their study did not examine VLEs specifically, it covers the ambit of technological tools in ESL pedagogical practices. Their guideline is used here to identify the shortcomings of VLEs that can contribute to its underutilization for the teaching and learning of English in universities.

The three dimensions identified by Chun, Kern and Smith (2016) that would impede the effective use of VLEs are the tool's affordances, students' experience and expectations and the language learning environment (see Table 1). Tools affordances actually shape the activities and tasks that can be performed by both instructors and students. These include temporality, which refers to the immediacy of message transmission; modality, that is; the availability of features such as text, audio, video and graphics; and spatiality, which is the capacity to manipulate the spatial distance during communication. The second element, students' experiences and expectations relate to learner variables such as age, proficiency level, interest and technological prowess. As Hubbard (2011) reiterated that 'learner fit' influences the adoption of a tool that is; the extent to which a tool is compatible with learner variables. The last aspect is the language learning environment that encompasses issues that include Internet accessibility, pedagogic suitability as well as administrative support and control.

Table 1. Themes for data analysis

Dimensions	Themes
VLE's affordances	Temporality Modality Spatiality
Student experience and expectations	Student attitude Student interest
Language learning environment	Pedagogic suitability Internet accessibility Compulsory use of VLEs Lack of teaching resources

7. METHODOLOGY

This research is part of a larger study being conducted to explore the acceptance and adoption of web technology by English language instructors in four public universities. The selected universities represent Malaysian public universities in general as they fall under the three categories of public universities established by the Ministry of Higher Education (Public Institutions of Higher Education, 2016). According to the classification, public universities can be grouped as research universities (focus on research), comprehensive universities (emphasis on diverse courses and fields of study) and focused universities (concentration on specific fields). Participants from a comprehensive university, a focused university and two research universities were involved in this study. Moreover, in accordance with the National Higher Education Action Plan (NHEAP) 2007–2010 (Ministry of Higher Education, 2007) and the recent Malaysian Education Blueprint 2015-2025 (Ministry of Higher Education, 2015), all Malaysian public universities have their own e-learning policies and strategies. The integration of VLEs and other digital resources in pedagogical practices including language teaching and learning is common in all public universities (Al-rahmi et al., 2015), including those in the present study.

The purpose of this phenomenological study is to understand and illuminate the phenomenon of digital resources' adoption in language teaching and learning. It specifically aims to determine the challenges faced in using VLEs for effective instructional practice and the technological measures taken to check them. In line with this, a qualitative approach is employed. In the larger study conducted prior to the current study, it was found that most of them used both VLEs and social media to a certain extent and for varied purposes (Murugaiah and Yen, in press). Following this, sixteen of the instructors who used these resources were selected using a purposive convenience sampling method. It must be noted that the number is in tandem with Creswell's (1998) recommendation of between 5 and 25 participants in phenomenological studies. Since instructors from four universities were involved, those who were available during the researchers' visit were interviewed. As shown in Table 2, the participants were predominantly women (87.5%) with an age range of 30 - 40 years (50%). Most of them teach between 3 to 4 courses (50%) and their teaching experience at the university level varied between 6-15 years (62.5%).

Table 2. Demographic profile

	Number	Percentage
GENDER		
Male	2	12.5
Female	14	87.5
AGE		
20-30 years	3	18.8
31-40 years	8	50.0
41-50 years	5	31.5
TEACHING EXPERIENCE		
< 5 years	3	18.8
6-10 years	4	25.0
11-15 years	6	37.5
16-20 years	3	18.8
NO. OF COURSES TAUGHT		
3	4	25.0
4	8	50.0
> than 5	4	25.0

An in-depth interview lasting about one hour was conducted to gather data. The questions were formulated based on the quantitative analyses of the questionnaire data used in the larger study. The questions were checked by two qualitative educational technology experts in the researchers' university. Their comments were used to improve on the tool and interview protocol. Employing a semi-structured format, the interview questions ranged from the types and uses of web technologies in language teaching to the factors that impact on their use. The interview was conducted by both researchers. During the interview, care was taken to guard researcher biasness, assumptions and beliefs from marring the responses. Interview notes were taken down to ensure there in no misinterpretation of meaning. Queries regarding the responses were clarified with the participants. Furthermore, after conducting interviews in each university, a running account of the interview process was discussed between the researchers. Every interview was audio-taped and transcribed for analysis. The data were analysed by two independent coders who were experienced researchers. They each identified emerging themes related to types, uses and reasons for use of the technologies and later they compared their coding with the other coder. In the event of any disgreement, the questionable data set was examined until an agreement was reached. To ensure confidentiality, in this paper the universities were labelled as A, B, C and D while the participants from university 'A' were labelled as A1 to A4, those from university 'B' as B1 –B4, university 'C' from C1 to C4 and university 'D' from D1 to D4.

8. FINDINGS

Data analysis was guided by the themes formulated using Chun, Kern and Smith's (2016) evaluation dimensions. In this section, interview responses that matched the themes related to challenges in using VLEs in language teaching and learning as well as measures taken to overcome them are presented.

8.1. Affordances of VLEs

It can be gleaned from the transcripts that all the instructors faced challenges with the VLEs regardless of the universities they were from. The issue of temporality is a common one. For example, both A4 and C1 had to resort to social media to overcome this problem:

A4: ...if they post it on e-learn (VLE) I have to go online to check if there is something there...WhatsApp ... I get a notification immediately... find it easier to communicate with them using WhatsApp. Response is immediate

C1: I post it basically on Facebook ...because the students get the information faster...

Furthermore, it is not user friendly, as attested by A3:

A3: ...to use the portal (e-learn)... they (students) have to go in and subscribe...they don't really do all this...they find it troublesome. So it's really quite difficult for me to reach them... via e-learn but with Facebook and WhatsApp... it's faster and the students can respond better

Another challenge in utilizing VLEs fully is the element of spatiality. This is a fundamental issue in university 'D' which has a distributed campus. Due to the varied degrees of Internet accessibility in the region, instructors like D2 and D4 find that the VLE is not capable to overcome the spatial distance during communication with their students in different locations:

D2: We have MyLinE (VLE)... it is compulsory but it's not effective. You see if we go to the main campus I sometimes can access it but in other places like this rural place... the internet there is so bad. So every time I want to use MyLinE to communicate with them (students), it's impossible. It's crazy...

D4: ... is not effective because we just meet the students once a week and for that once a week we have only two hours. So within two hours we have to make sure that we cover the syllabus... so we need to upload materials, communicate with students, have discussions etc. But if I cannot interact with all my students effectively... I mean some students can access it (MyLinE), others cannot... it's difficult

However, some instructors like B3 and D2 have circumvented this challenge using social media in an innovative way:

B3: I use Facebook and WhatsApp a lot...we have WhatsApp groups. Any problems, they can contact me through Facebook. If they don't understand something I will discuss in their WhatsApp group. I even upload materials, games etc. in Facebook

D2: I do have one website, a forum actually. So every Friday night… they have to log into that particular website… using their Smartphones normally… into that forum, and I will give them one topic, so they will talk about it… for example I have three classes… so for example this week on Thursday it will be class A… so Friday will be class B… on Saturday night it will be… class C… something like that… We have to do that… if not the students will not practise using English…

Apart from these issues, the VLE is also deemed unsuitable as it does not cater for personalized communication with students, as claimed by C2 and A3:

C2: For example… we have WhatsApp group, which allows me to personally approach my students should…if they have anything regarding the course. I cannot do that in the portal

A3: … I prefer using app Moodle compared to e-learn because I want to have separate groups … like I need to give some notes to these two groups and the other two haven't learnt it yet. So I need separate groups … cannot use e-learn. So I choose app Moodle

8.2. Students' Experience and Expectations

Students' attitude in not wanting to use VLE also influences these instructors, as put forward by C4 and B1:

C4: …sometimes I can see that half of the class haven't accessed learning zone (VLE) for one semester! So… I decided this semester maybe I can take another alternative to use maybe WhatsApp or Facebook… the students took their own initiative to create their own group and invited me as well… so teachers prefer posting announcement through Facebook, WhatsApp because they find it very useful and also reachable to all the students

B1: …like my I-class (VLE), some of them… their participation is very minimum…in one month, not even once

A probable reason for this is they have other preferences with regards to instructional technology, as mentioned by B2 and D2:

B2: Students nowadays … 24/7 (all the time) with their gadgets and they know more than us actually. So I think why not I join them and use this technology to teach them, to help them, to communicate with them… so I thought the in thing right now is mobile phone … for example last week I asked them 'Where do you see yourself after graduation?' and then they posted the answers in WhatsApp group … so everybody can see their answer … So everyone participates …

D2: …they prefer something that is familiar to them that they can access from their smartphone … so I found out that Facebook is more interesting …effective

8.3. Language Learning Environment

The language learning environment has the highest impact on instructors' usage of the VLEs. In fact, all the instructors faced various challenges with regards to it. A key determinant of VLE usage is whether it suits their teaching aims. They assert that the VLE is not suitable for certain language activities, as claimed by C4, D2 and A3, especially in classroom teaching:

C4: In 'process writing'...this one activity called summary ...they have to paraphrase sentence or sentences and also sometimes they have to find synonyms ... so in class how to use learning zone? It is difficult ... since they have smartphones I ask them to go to online dictionary so that they can not only look at the words but they can also listen ... how the words are pronounced

D2: one time I asked students to post their reflection on something. They took pictures from their phones ... and posted their reflection in WhatsApp

A3: I use twitter too ... there are some accounts I would like my students to follow... some academicians who share ... notes on grammar...on twitter. Better than explaining in e-learn

A major issue in the learning environment is Internet connectivity and accessibility. As mentioned earlier, a huge obstacle for the instructors in university 'D' is Internet accessibility. However, problems related to the Internet are present in other universities too. For example, instructors C2 and A1 lament about the availability, accessibility and connectivity issues:

C2: the internet is quite slow. And then, some of the classes, they don't have direct access to internet. It's only limited to a ...few classes

A1: ...the connection ... even students complain ... I think students don't want to use it (e-learn) because of the connection ... They always complain that the connection is very poor

As for two instructors, the environment inhibits their use of the VLE because they are forced to use it. In universities 'B' and 'C', it is compulsory for both instructors and students to use the VLEs. As a result, they are not motivated to use it as revealed by B2 and C4:

B2: They are forcing all the staff to use online learning website...but if you do not use ... They will ask you, 'why are you not using it?'. For certain classrooms the lecturers can no longer use their USB when they do their presentation. They have to use their notes ... upload online to that online learning website. ...the computer there (in some classes) will block all the USB connection ... very frustrating. So I just upload one or two materials, that's all. I use Facebook because it's more user friendly...my students also like it.

C4: Here it's compulsory...but I find it difficult. Not motivating at all. My students don't access it frequently...so how? As my colleague says, just upload something and continue using other tools

Apart from this, one instructor finds the VLE does not contain features that would enable her not only to upload materials for students but also share resources with other instructors, as cited by A3:

A3: In e-learn, there's no support for us...I mean to interact or share activities between teachers. You know at app Moodle there's a network between teachers...so I will use some materials from the teachers on their Moodle and watch some videos that they have prepared... use a little bit from this one, a little bit from that one...it's interesting. I learn a lot

9. DISCUSSION AND IMPLICATIONS

It is apparent from the findings that instructors involved in the study faced several challenges, which might have actually contributed to their reluctance to use VLEs for their instructional practice. It appeared that all the dimensions postulated by Chun et al. (2016) were present. The findings related to VLEs affordances such as temporality, modality and spatiality are congruent with those by Chaw and Tang (2017), Kula (2010) and Simoes (2011). They argued that VLEs are rigidly structured and lack dynamic features such as those in social media that showcase an open environment full of novelty. Moreover, they provide more space for 'learner voice' (Selwyn, 2012) through their interactions and sharing of resources with peers and instructors.

Students' experience and expectations are also viewed as affecting the use of VLEs. It is natural for students to insist that any technological tool should provide them fast and easy access to information as stated by Bolton et al. (2013) and demonstrated in the study,. According to Reid (2014), when students' demands regarding a tool's traits such as accessibility, usability and flexibility are not met, they get frustrated. They are not motivated as the VLE lacks the kind of features that are important to them (Simoes, 2011). On the other hand, social media tend to satisfy their expectations as they can check course related material and information at any time and place. They can also access instructors instantly, in an informal and relaxed manner unlike in VLEs (Manca and Ranieri, 2017).

A conducive language learning environment is pivotal to the success of any pedagogical practice. The current study revealed that issues related to the suitability of the technology for instruction, the Internet and culture of an institution impact upon the effective use of the VLEs. That pedagogic suitability of technologies is a major factor is in tandem with the findings of Wichadee (2015), Montaghian et al. (2013) and Manca and Ranieri (2017) which revealed that low perceived usefulness and compatibility influenced instructors' adoption of VLEs in their instruction. Furthermore, problems with the Internet influence VLE use as demonstrated in many studies (Embi, 2011; Kula, 2010; Abdelrahman et al., 2016; Tyagi, 2012). In situations where Internet connectivity is a problem, students and instructors tend to resort to using social media like Facebook and WhatsApp. Another facet of the learning environment that was highlighted was the 'institutional grammar' (Cuban, 2001, p. 129) that influences an institution to adopt certain stands regarding their practices. In the present study, for example it was revealed that in two universities the use of VLEs was compulsory. This 'situationally constrained choice' (Manca and Ranieri, 2017, p. 614) impedes students' and instructors' freedom; leading to frustration, anxiety and resistance towards the systems (Manca and Ranieri, 2017).

Higher education institutions today are challenged by not only the rapid advancement in technology, but the changing nature of students entering university. Students do not seem to prioritize the use of VLEs in their learning. Instead they find it more meaningful and valuable to use social media. The rigid communication and learning structure placed by most universities is not in tandem with students' expectations of open and easy access to knowledge. This 'digital disconnect' (Selwyn, 2012) need to be addressed. To begin with, the effectiveness of VLEs must regularly be evaluated and upgraded. It is the role of system administrators to ensure they are user-friendly, flexible and compatible for both students and instructors. Secondly, instructional technologies are continuously and rapidly changing. Institutions too must continually improve and upgrade their VLEs to be on par with these changes. Introducing 3D environments with avatars and incorporating Second Life virtual worlds in institutions could be the way forward (Lim and Kim, 2015).

10. LIMITATIONS AND FUTURE RESEARCH

The study examined language instructors' perceptions regarding challenges related to the use of VLEs in language pedagogical practices and how social media helped check these barriers. However, it did not specifically compare instructors' and students' use of VLEs for universities to make informed decisions on the systems. Moreover, it did not examine their perceptions regarding the formal use of social media as an addition to VLEs. Further research on these would shed more light on the adoption of technological tools to effectively facilitate and enhance pedagogical practices in higher learning institutions. Besides this, the study did not focus on any specific social media tool but rather on social media in general. The impact of employing a particular tool is important because the adoption levels of different users may vary according to their diverse characteristics and backgrounds. It would be interesting to explore the use of specific social media tools by different instructors with varied backgrounds and on assorted platforms. Moreover, the study was conducted in four universities. The findings of a larger sample may portray other challenges related to VLE and social media adoption among the academic community. Furthermore, convenience sampling was used in the study. The issue of biasness related to this method could be checked by employing other techniques such as cluster sampling in future research.

11. CONCLUSION

The current research highlights the barriers related to VLE use in Malaysian universities. It also demonstrates the impact of social media in checking these hindrances. It is inevitable for institutions to acknowledge the growing presence of social media in higher education. It is transforming education from institutionalized practices into open learning spaces (deLaat & Prinsen, 2014). Participatory and collaborative learning, the very tenet of student-centred learning, is vastly promoted via networked social activities which have become the pedagogical norm. In many institutions, social-media-supported learning is still positioned outside and not part of the formal pedagogical system set by the university. It is therefore, timely for institutions to embrace social media as pedagogical strategies complementing VLEs. Merging the affordances provided by VLEs and social media will greatly benefit learners, instructors and the institution at large.

ACKNOWLEDGMENT

The authors would like to thank Universiti Sains Malaysia for funding this work through the grant (304/PJJAUH/6313067).

REFERENCES

Abdelrahman, M. A., Abdelmuniem, A., & Almabhouh, A. A. (2016). The current use of web 2.0 tools in university teaching from the perspective of faculty members at the college of education. *International Journal of Instruction*, *9*(1), 179–193. doi:10.12973/iji.2016.9114a

Ajjan, H., & Hartshorne, R. (2008). Investigating faculty decisions to adopt web 2.0 technologies: Theory and empirical tests. *The Internet and Higher Education*, *11*(2), 71–80. doi:10.1016/j.iheduc.2008.05.002

Al-rahmi, W. M., Othman, M. S., & Yusuf, L. (2015). The effectiveness of using e-learning in Malaysian higher education: A case study of Universiti Teknologi Malaysia. *Mediterranean Journal of Social Sciences*, *6*(5), 625–637. doi:10.5901/mjss.2015.v6n5s2p625

Arshad, M., & Akram, M. S. (2018). Social media adoption by the academic community: Theoretical insights and empirical evidence from developing countries. *International Review of Research in Open and Distributed Learning*, *19*(3), 243–261. doi:10.19173/irrodl.v19i3.3500

Blattner, G., & Fiori, M. (2011). Virtual social network communities: An investigation of language learners' development of socio-pragmatic awareness and multiliteracy skills. *CALICO Journal*, *29*(1), 24–43. doi:10.11139/cj.29.1.24-43

Bolton, R. N., Parasuraman, A., Hoefnagels, A., Migchels, N., Kabadayi, S., Gruber, T., ... Solnet, D. (2013). Understanding Gen Y and their use of social media: A review and research agenda. *Journal of Service Management*, *24*(3), 245–267. doi:10.1108/09564231311326987

Cavus, N. (2015). Distance learning and Learning Management Systems. *Procedia: Social and Behavioral Sciences*, *191*, 872–877. doi:10.1016/j.sbspro.2015.04.611

Chaw, L. Y., & Tang, C. M. (2017). The voice of the students: Needs and expectations from learning management systems. *Paper presented at the European Conference on e-learning* (pp. 116-123). Retrieved from https://search.proquest.com/docview/1968935606?accountid=14645

Chun, D., Smith, B. & Kern, R. (2016). Technology in language use, language teaching, and language learning. *The Modern Language Journal, 100*, 64-80.

Creswell, J. W. (1998). *Qualitative inquiry and research design: Choosing among five traditions*. Thousand Oaks, CA: Sage Publications.

Cuban, L. (2001). *Oversold and underused. Computers in the classroom*. Cambridge: Harvard University Press.

de Laat, M., & Prinsen, F. (2014). Social leaning analytics: Navigating the changing settings in higher education. *Research and Practice in Assessment*, *9*, 51–60.

Dobre, I. (2015). Learning management systems for higher education - an overview of available options for higher education organizations. *Procedia: Social and Behavioral Sciences*, *180*, 313–320. doi:10.1016/j.sbspro.2015.02.122

Embi, M. A. (Ed.). (2011). e-Learning in Malaysian Higher Education Institutions. Klang: Ministry of Higher Education, Malaysia.

Fewkes, A., & McCabe, M. (2012). Facebook: Learning tool or distraction? *Journal of Digital Learning in Teacher Education*, *28*(3), 92–98. doi:10.1080/21532974.2012.10784686

Friesen, N., & Lowe, S. (2011). The questionable promise of social media for education: Connective learning and the commercial imperative. *Journal of Computer Assisted Learning*, *28*(3), 183–194. doi:10.1111/j.1365-2729.2011.00426.x

Gray, K., Annabell, L., & Kennedy, G. (2010). Medical students' use of Facebook to support learning: Insights from four case studies. *Medical Teacher*, *32*(12), 971–976. doi:10.3109/0142159X.2010.497826 PMID:21090950

Hamid, S., Waycott, J., Kurnia, S., & Chang, S. (2015). Understanding students' perceptions of the benefits of online social networking use for teaching and learning. *Internet and Higher education*, *26*, 1–9. doi:10.1016/j.iheduc.2015.02.004

Hubbard, P. (2011). Evaluation of courseware and websites. In L. Ducate & N. Arnold (Eds.), *Present and future perspectives of CALL: From theory and research to new directions in foreign language teaching* (pp. 407–440). San Marcos, TX: CALICO.

Huffman, S. (2013). Benefits and pitfalls: Simple guidelines for the use of social networking tools in K-12 education. *Education*, *134*(2), 154–160.

Kabilan, M., Ahmad, N., & Abidin, M. (2010). Facebook: An online environment for learning of English in institutions of higher education? *The Internet and Higher Education*, *13*(4), 179–187. doi:10.1016/j.iheduc.2010.07.003

Kalayci, S., & Humiston, K. R. (2015). Students' attitudes towards collaborative tools in a virtual learning environment. *Educational Process: International Journal*, *4*(1-2), 71–86. doi:10.12973/edupij.2015.412.6

Kharbach, M. (2014). The ultimate guide to the use of Facebook in education. *Educatorstechnology*. Retrieved from http://www.educatorstechnology.com/2012/06/ultimate-guide-to-use-of-facebook-in.html

Kula. (2010). Barriers for ICT integration, strategies developed against them and cases in Turkey. Retrieved from http://edu.rsei.umk.pl/weee2013/publications/v1/V1.3_100-Angudi-fullR-FPR.pdf

Lim, K., & Kim, M. H. (2015). A case study of the experiences of instructors and students in a virtual learning environment (VLE) with different cultural backgrounds. *Asia Pacific Education Review*, *16*(4), 613–626. doi:10.100712564-015-9400-y

Lin, W. S. (2012). Perceived fit and satisfaction on web learning performance: IS continuance intention and task-technology fit perspectives. *International Journal of Human-Computer Studies*, *70*(7), 498–507. doi:10.1016/j.ijhcs.2012.01.006

Liu, M., Evans, M., Horwitz, E., Lee, S., McCrory, M., Park, J. B., & Parrish, C. (2013). A study of the use of language learning websites with social network features by university ESL students. In M. N. Lamy & K. Zourou (Eds.), *Social Networking for Language Education* (pp. 137–157). Basingstoke, UK: Palgrave Macmillan. doi:10.1057/9781137023384_8

Manan, N., Alias, A., & Pandian, A. (2012). Utilizing a social networking website as an ESL pedagogical tool in a blended learning environment: An exploratory study. *International Journal of Social Sciences & Education*, 2(1), 1–9.

Manca, S., & Ranieri, M. (2017). Implications of social network sites for teaching and learning. Where we are and where we want to go. *Education and Information Technologies*, 2(2), 605–622. doi:10.100710639-015-9429-x

McCarthy, J. (2010). Blended learning environments: Using social networking sites to enhance the first year experience. *Australasian Journal of Educational Technology*, 26(6), 729–740. doi:10.14742/ajet.1039

McLoughlin, C., Black-Hawkins, K., McIntyre, D., & Townsend, A. (2008). *Networking practitioner research*. New York: Routledge Taylor & Francis Group.

Ministry of Education Malaysia. (2012). *Malaysian Education Blueprint 2013-2025*.

Ministry of Education Malaysia. (2016). *Public Institutions of Higher Education*. Retrieved from http://www.moe.gov.my/en/ipta

Ministry of Higher Education Malaysia. (2007). *National Higher Education Action Plan 2007-2010: Triggering higher education transformation*.

Mitchell, K. (2012). A social tool: Why and how ESOL students use Facebook. *CALICO Journal*, 29(3), 471–493. doi:10.11139/cj.29.3.471-493

Motaghian, H., Hassanzadeh, A., & Moghadam, D. K. (2013). Factors affecting university instructors' adoption of web-based learning systems: Case study of Iran. *Computers & Education*, 61, 158–167. doi:10.1016/j.compedu.2012.09.016

Mtebe, J. S., & Raisamo, R. (2014). A model for assessing learning management system success in higher education in Sub-Saharan countries. *The Electronic Journal on Information Systems in Developing Countries*, 61(7), 1–17. doi:10.1002/j.1681-4835.2014.tb00436.x

Murugaiah, P., & Yen, S. H. (in press). Profiling web technology adoption of English language instructors in Malaysian universities. *Malaysian Online Journal of Educational Technology*.

Ng, E. M. W., & Wong, H. C. H. (2013). Facebook: More than social networking for at-risk students. *Procedia: Social and Behavioral Sciences*, 73, 22–29. doi:10.1016/j.sbspro.2013.02.014

Odom, L. (2010). Mapping Web 2.0 benefits to known best practices in distance education. *University of Maryland University College Faculty Center for Support of Instruction*. Retrieved from https://blackhawkinstructorsupport.files.wordpress.com/2013/06/mapping_web_2-0_benefits_laddieodom.pdf

Omar, L. M., Platteaux, H., & Gillet, D. (2012). An institutional personal learning environment enabler. In *12th IEEE International Conference on Advanced Learning Technologies*.

Osman, G., & Koh, J. H. L. (2013). Understanding management students' reflective practice through blogging. *The Internet and Higher Education*, *16*, 23–31. doi:10.1016/j.iheduc.2012.07.001

Raaij, E. M., & Schepers, J. J. L. (2008). The acceptance and use of a virtual learning environment in China. *Computers & Education*, *50*(3), 838–852. doi:10.1016/j.compedu.2006.09.001

Reid, P. (2014). Categories for barriers to adoption of instructional technologies. *Education and Information Technologies*, *19*(2), 383–407. doi:10.100710639-012-9222-z

Selim, H. M. (2007). Critical success factors for e-learning acceptance: Confirmatory factor Models. *Computers & Education*, *49*(2), 396–413. doi:10.1016/j.compedu.2005.09.004

Selwyn, N. (2012). Social media and higher education. In *The Europa World of Learning*. London, UK: Routledge.

Simoes, L., & Gouveia, B. (2011). Social technology appropriation in higher education. *Romanian Journal of Social Informatics*, *3*(16), 21–34.

Tess, P. (2013). The role of social media in higher *education* classes (real and virtual) – A literature review. *Computers in Human Behavior*, *29*(5), A60–A68. doi:10.1016/j.chb.2012.12.032

Tyagi, S. (2012). Adoption of Web 2.0 technology in higher education: A case study of universities in National Capital region, India. *International Journal of Education And Development*, *2*, 40–46.

Weller, M. (2010). The Centralisation Dilemma in Educational IT. *International Journal of Virtual and Personal Learning Environments*, *1*(1), 1–9. doi:10.4018/jvple.2010091701

Wichadee, S. (2015). Factors related to faculty members' attitude and adoption of a Learning Management System. *Turkish Online Journal of Education*, *14*(4), 53–61.

This research was previously published in the International Journal of Virtual and Personal Learning Environments (IJVPLE), 9(2); pages 1-14, copyright year 2019 by IGI Publishing (an imprint of IGI Global).

Chapter 56
Academic Dishonesty:
Does Social Media Allow for Increased and More Sophisticated Levels of Student Cheating?

Linda M. Best

Edinboro University of Pennsylvania, Edinboro, USA

Daniel J. Shelley

Robert Morris University, Pittsburgh, USA

ABSTRACT

This article examines the effects of the social media applications Facebook, Twitter, Snap Chat/Instagram, Texting and various smartphone applications on academic dishonesty in higher education. The study employed a mixed-methods approach conducted through an emailed question-pro student survey consisting of 20 questions. The results of the study indicated that the majority of students in higher education utilize the social media applications Facebook, Twitter, Snap Chat/Instagram and Smart Phones to assist with their academic studies. Although students report utilizing these forms of social media to assist with their studies most do not use these applications for cheating or any form of academic dishonesty. There was an increased willingness to use texting, screenshots, video and audio recordings to cheat on exams and other academic requirements. In addition, the majority of participants indicated they felt any form of cheating or academic dishonesty was wrong. However, most indicated they would do little or nothing to intervene or prevent it in their particular classroom situations.

INTRODUCTION

Early on in education, cheating and academic honestly has been a concern. Whether writing notes on a sleeve, desktop, using a mobile phone, or creating a "cheat sheet," some students have creatively found ways to get assistance. As teachers and professors become more aware of the various cheating procedures and plans they may counteract with new sets of rules and various classroom techniques, forcing

DOI: 10.4018/978-1-6684-7123-4.ch056

the perpetrators into new and more improved cheating scenarios. With the introduction of social media devices and applications, academic dishonesty has moved to a new "High-Tech" level. Professors could react to this new, enhance level of dishonesty with numerous strategies including; collecting all smart phones during testing, going back to the old paper and pencil methods of testing and asking students to sign honesty pacts.

Howard Gardner (2012) from the Harvard Graduate School of Education, studied professional and academic integrity for over 20 years. He believes that the students' ethical muscles have atrophied in part because of a culture that exalts success, however it is attained. A 2011 study of 14,000 undergraduate students over a four-year span found that over two-thirds of the students admitted to cheating on tests, homework, and other assignments (Novotney, 2011). There have been many studies that attempted to understand why students cheat at any academic level. Many point out the need for an academic edge with all the pressure on Grade Point Average and building up the most impressive resume. Various research studies on cheating indicate the same trends; students cheat because it has become the campus norm, the penalties not really that severe, little chance of getting caught and the faculty don't really make efforts to stop current forms of academic dishonesty.

REVIEW OF LITERATURE

It was not the intent of this research to examine the reasons or the "why" of student cheating, as much has been written on this subject over the years. A study of several midsized private and public universities by Shelley (2014) found, while most students understand the rules, most look to peers for cues as to what is acceptable behavior. The first large-scale study of academic cheating in higher education was conducted by Bill Bowers in 1964 with 5,000 students from 99 institutions were surveyed. This study found that over 75% of the participants admitted to some level of cheating or academic dishonesty. This study was replicated 33 years later (McCabe, Trevino, 1993) using many of the same institutions for the sample population. They reported only a modest increase in the percentage of academic cheating with the greatest increases being among females. Academic dishonesty among college students is now recognized as a serious problem in institutions of higher education. In fact, as many as eight out of every ten students admitted engaging is some form of cheating in their collegiate courses (Gabriel, 2010).

What is Considered Cheating?

Lipson (2004) also offered three principles that apply to academic dishonesty in higher education:

1. Tell you have done the work if it has actually been done by you;
2. Cite someone's works if you have used it;
3. Present research materials fairly and truthfully.

In the 1990's, Pavela (1997) developed what has become a widely accepted framework that defines the types of academic dishonesty; 1) cheating, 2) plagiarism, 3) fabrication, and 4) facilitation. He also broke down academic dishonesty into two realms, analog (traditional) and digital (cyber cheating).

Large scale cheating has been reported recently at some of the nation's most competitive schools like the Air Force Academy and Harvard (Peres-Pena, 2012). A survey of 14,000 undergraduate students conducted by Donald McCabe (2011) at Rutgers University reported about two-thirds of the students admitted to cheating on tests, homework and other assignments. A total of 273 alumni reported on their prevalence and perceived severity of 19 cheating behaviors. According to Yardley, et. al. (2009), the vast majority of participants (81.7%) report having engaged in some form of cheating during their undergraduate career.

In recent years, more and more cases of academic dishonesty are now of the digital\cyber formats. These cases of digital cheating are usually through devices like smartphones, emails, or various social networks (Stogner, Miller & Marcum, 2012).

Why do Students Cheat?

Most of the existing literature attempts to gauge the complex reasons as to why students revert to various levels of cheating in academia. However, this study examined the newer technologies and social media and how they have affected the level of student dishonesty in the classroom. Hensley (2013) reported that the rapid advances in technology has simply made it easier for students to plagiarize papers, exchange answers or purchase a prewritten paper and is too easy to pass up. Two of the most consistent reasons given for cheating is that the students need to obtain higher grades to satisfy family members and\or maintain certain beneficial opportunities for themselves. In addition, students with low self-esteem and little confidence in their academic abilities are more likely to cheat than confident students (Moeck, 2002). Additionally, when the views of students are considered, Crews and Butterfield (2014) found certain constraints and ongoing factors exist including; frequent, multiple, large classes; evolving social norms; objections to what some may regard as self-righteous moralizing; even the intrinsic impersonality and benign anonymity that commonly marks online education.

Research indicates that cheating can also be contagious. According to a study of 158 undergraduates, Rettinger (2009) found that direct knowledge of others' cheating is the best predictor of individual's willingness to also engage in cheating. Additional research indicates that most of the dishonest behaviors in academia are motivated by grade-related achievement, lack of student efficacy, or academic stressors such as time constraints (Davis et al., 1992; McCabe, Butterfield & Trevino, 2006). A study by O'Rourke, et. al. (2010), indicated that one factor influencing cheating or academic dishonesty is the student's perception or experience with others, or peers, cheating. This study suggested that, when viewed as a social behavior, the knowledge, suspicion, or direct observation of peers cheating may have an important effect on student's behavior.

Will Students Report Cheating?

A study by Desalegn & Berhan (2014) indicated that approximately 78% of the students attending a medical school would not report observed cheating to instructors or others in charge of the classroom. In contrast, a study by Rennie and Crosby (2002) put the percentage of students willing to report cheating peers at only about 13%. The author also found that students indicated that they would not report cheating classmates because of the feeling of camaraderie, fear of retaliation, lack of clear academic guidelines. Additionally students indicated that they did not believe that it was their responsibility to monitor others' cheating. It was also found that many students admit to cheating because they feel the need to satisfy family members and others who are supporting their educational endeavors (Moeck, 2002).

In summary, the temptations for university students to cheat will always exist and will likely intensify as the newer technologies further simplify the process. This study intended to examine four important aspects of the use of social media and academic dishonesty.

RESEARCH QUESTIONS

This research project examined the following research questions:

RQ#1: Does the prevalence of social media in society allow for greater levels of academic dishonesty in intuitions of higher education?

RQ#2: Do students have a preference among the selected forms of social media including, Face Book, Twitter, Instagram/Snap Chat and texting when it comes to academic dishonesty?

RQ#3: Are university students concerned about academic dishonesty among their peers?

RQ#4: Will university students report and\or otherwise act upon evidence that one or more of their classmates are cheating?

METHODOLOGY AND SAMPLE

To examine the various social media applications and academic dishonesty, the researchers designed a 20-question survey using Question-Pro. This survey was designed in five sections; 1) Demographics, 2) Student use of selected social media, 3) Student use of selected social media for academic dishonesty or cheating, 4) Student views on academic dishonesty and cheating and, 5) Opened ended questions and responses. After a small pilot study with two graduate research classes, the survey was revised and adjusted to more clearly focus on the intent and design of this research study. The Question-Pro survey creates an easily accessible online link to share with participants. The sample for this study (N=195) was drawn from four institutions of higher education; a mid-sized private school, a large state supported university, a small religious affiliated college and a mid-sized state university. It was hoped that this population would give the best representation of students in various academic situations in higher education. The basic design of the survey, beyond the demographic section, allowed for five possible responses from the student participants. The survey was administered in the spring 2017 term. The completion rate was encouraging with 205 participants starting the survey and 195 (N=195) completing the survey for a 95% completion rate.

SURVEY RESULTS

When the demographics of the study are examined; the majority (88%) were full-time students. The male-female breakdown was almost even; Male=48% and female=52%.

Of the 195 respondents, the majority, 58% were freshman and sophomores. About 20% of the respondents were at the graduate level leaving only 26% shared equally between juniors and seniors (see Figure 1).

Figure 1. Present academic level

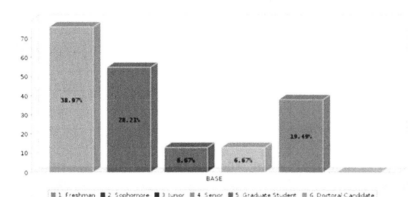

Answer	Count	Percent
1. Freshman	76	38.97%
2. Sophomore	55	28.21%
3. Junior	13	6.67%
4. Senior	13	6.67%
5. Graduate Student	38	19.49%
6. Doctoral Candidate	0	0.00%
Total	195	100%

Mean : 2.395	Confidence Interval @ 95% : [2.180 - 2.609]	Standard Deviation : 1.527	Standard Error : 0.109

Student Utilization of Social Media in Higher Education

Questions 4-6 of the survey asked the participants if they used FaceBook, Twitter, SnapChat and\or Instagram to enhance and\or support their current academic college program. The results for all three were similar and indicated that: 77% used FaceBook somewhat or now and then, 61% used Twitter somewhat or now and then and, 77% indicated that they used SnapChat and\or InstaGram somewhat or now and then (see Figure 2).

Student Use of Social Media to Cheat or Engage in Academic Dishonesty

Survey questions 7-10 asked the participants to indicate if they ever used any of the social media applications to embellish, gain an advantage, cheat or otherwise engage in an activity that would be considered academically dishonest. Figure 3 displays the results of FaceBook with an overwhelming majority (94%) indicating that they have never used the application in a way that would be considered academically dishonest.

Figure 4 displays the results of Question #8 on Twitter, with again, an overwhelming majority (94%) indicating that they have never used the application in a way that would be considered academically dishonest.

Question #9 asked the participants to indicate if they ever used SnapChat and\or InstaGram in a way that would be considered academically dishonest. Figure 5 displays the results of this question with again, an overwhelming majority (92%) indicating that they have never used the application(s) in a way that would be considered dishonest.

Figure 2. Facebook, Twitter and SnapChat\InstaGram usage

Face Book

	Answer	Count	Percent
	1. I never use Facebook	55	28.21%
	2. I use FaceBook but not for any college related activity	91	46.67%
	3. Somewhat	42	21.54%
	4. A lot, I use Facebook in a number of my college courses	3	1.54%
	5. Extensively	4	2.05%
	Total	195	100%

Mean : 2.026	Confidence Interval @ 95% : [1.904 - 2.147]	Standard Deviation : 0.864	Standard Error : 0.062

Twitter

	Answer	Count	Percent
	1. I never use Twitter	45	34.62%
	2. I use Twitter but not for any College related activities	62	47.69%
	3. Somewhat, now and then	18	13.85%
	4. A lot, in many of my courses	2	1.54%
	5. Extensively	3	2.31%
	Total	130	100%

Mean : 1.892	Confidence Interval @ 95% : [1.744 - 2.041]	Standard Deviation : 0.865	Standard Error : 0.076

InstaGram or Snap Chat

	Answer	Count	Percent
	1. I never use either program	25	19.23%
	2. I use them but not for any College related activity	83	63.85%
	3. Somewhat	17	13.08%
	4. A lot, I use them in a number of my College Courses	3	2.31%
	5. Extensively	2	1.54%
	Total	130	100%

Mean : 2.031	Confidence Interval @ 95% : [1.902 - 2.159]	Standard Deviation : 0.746	Standard Error : 0.065

Figure 3. Have you ever used Facebook to embellish, gain an advantage, cheat or otherwise engage in an activity that would be considered dishonest?

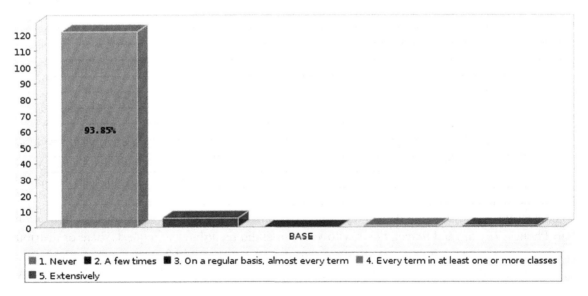

93.85%

BASE

■ 1. Never ■ 2. A few times ■ 3. On a regular basis, almost every term ■ 4. Every term in at least one or more classes
■ 5. Extensively

Figure 4. Have you ever used Twitter to embellish, gain an advantage, cheat or otherwise engage in an activity that would be considered dishonest?

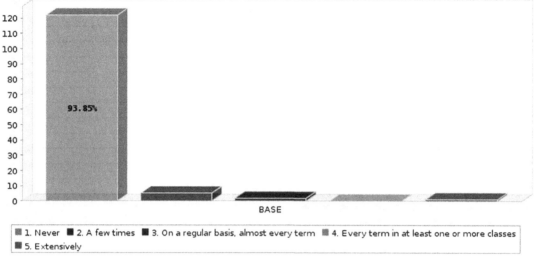

Figure 5. Have you ever used SnapChat and\or InstaGram to embellish, gain an advantage, cheat or otherwise engage in an activity that would be considered dishonest?

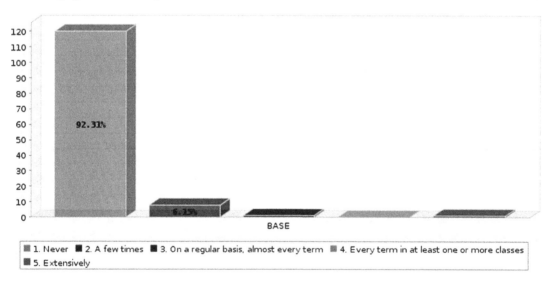

In all cases, the students indicated that they rarely use any of these applications to cheat or be in any way academically dishonest. There was only one participant that consistently indicated that they used these applications extensively in an inappropriate way. For the purpose of this study, that set of responses was considered in question and an outlier.

The next three questions on the survey, 10-12 examined other popular social media applications; Smart Phones, Texting and Screen Shots with video or audio recordings to request, share or distribute answers and\or information during a class exam or other graded activity? Question #10 asked if they ever used a SmartPhone or an iPhone to engage in these activities, about 25% responded that they have, at least a few times. Only about 3% indicated that they do this activity on a regular or extensive basis. The majority (73%) of the students indicated that they never engage in any of these dishonest activities with SmartPhones or iPhones. Figure 6 displays the graphic results of this question.

Figure 6. Have you ever used a SmartPhone or iPhone to request, share or distribute answers and\or information during a class exam or other graded activity?

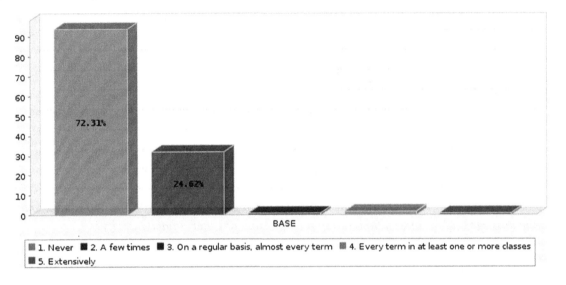

Question #11 examined the improper usage of texting to share or distribute answers and\or information during a class exam or other graded activity? The results were close to the previous Smart Phone and\or iPhone responses. When asked if they ever used texting to engage in these activities, about 25% responded that they have, at least a few times. Only about 3% indicated that they do this activity on a regular or extensive basis. The majority (71%) of the students indicated that they never engage in any of these dishonest activities through texting. Figure 7 displays the graphic results of this question.

Question #12 examined the improper usage of features like screen shots, video recording and audio recording to share or distribute answers and\or information during a class exam or other graded activity? The results were close to the previous Smart Phone\iPhone and Texting responses. When asked if they ever used screen shots, video recording and audio recording to engage in these activities, about 22% responded that they have, at least a few times. About 5% indicated that they do this activity on a regular or extensive basis, the highest in this group of questions. Again, the large majority (74%) of the students indicated that they never engage in any of these dishonest activities through screen shots, video recording and audio recording. Figure 8 displays the graphic results of this question #12.

The results of this group of questions, that directly questioned the students level of involvement in academically dishonest activities using various forms and applications of social media, indicated a strong, positive pattern that they rarely do not engage is such activities. However, it should be noted and of obvious concern that approximately 25-30% of the students surveyed indicated that they engaged in dishonest academic usage of social media at least a few times or on a regular basis.

Figure 7. Have you ever used Texting to request, share or distribute answers and\or information during a class exam or other graded activity?

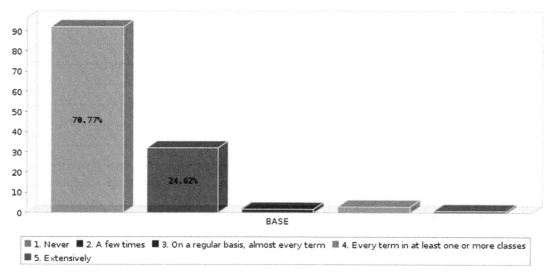

Figure 8. Have you ever used screen shots, video recording and audio recording to request, share or distribute answers and\or information during a class exam or other graded activity?

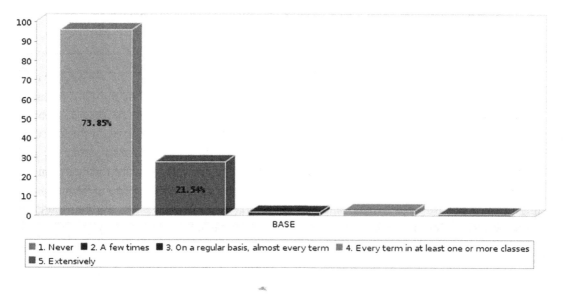

The next two questions on the survey looked at the students' attitudes toward academic dishonesty and cheating. Question #13 asks the question, "My personal feelings toward any type of cheating or academic dishonesty is ..." The students had the following five possible responses: 1) It's always wrong and unethical, 2) I don't really care, others do it but I don't, 3) No Opinion, 4) It's okay if you don't get caught and, 5) It is okay sometimes, the academic requirements are too stressful. The results here were interesting and more dispersed over the five options. The majority (46%) felt that it is always wrong. However, almost one-third of the students (31%) indicated that they didn't really care, others do it but I don't. Thirteen percent had no opinion. Only 11% of the students indicated that it is okay sometimes,

the academic requirements are too stressful. Figure 9 displays the percentage breakdown of the participants' responses.

Figure 9. My personal feelings toward any type of cheating or academic dishonesty is

	Answer	Count	Percent
1.	It's always wrong and unethical	60	46.15%
2.	I don't really care, others do it but I don't	40	30.77%
3.	No opinion	16	12.31%
4.	It's okay if you don't get caught	0	0.00%
5.	It is okay sometimes, the academic requirements are too stressful	14	10.77%
	Total	130	100%

Mean : 1.985	Confidence Interval @ 95% : [1.770 - 2.200]	Standard Deviation : 1.251	Standard Error : 0.110

Question #14 asks the participants if you saw one or more of you classmates cheating you would: 1)
do nothing, ignore it, 2) let them know I saw it and disapprove, 3) no opinion, 4) threaten them but do
nothing, 5) inform the professor or instructor. The majority (47%) indicated option #1, do nothing, ignore
it. About 12% indicated that they would let the cheater know and that they disapproved. Less than 23%
had no opinion and less than 1% said they would threaten the cheater but do nothing. Only 18.46% of
the student participants said they would inform the professor or instructor (see Figure 10).

Figure 10. If you saw one or more of your classmates cheating you would

	Answer	Count	Percent
1.	do nothing, ignore it	61	46.92%
2.	let them know I saw it and disapprove	15	11.54%
3.	No opinion	29	22.31%
4.	threaten them but do nothing	1	0.77%
5.	inform the professor or instructor	24	18.46%
	Total	130	100%

Mean : 2.323	Confidence Interval @ 95% : [2.062 - 2.584]	Standard Deviation : 1.516	Standard Error : 0.133

These findings are consistent with those of Rennie and Crosby (2002) that indicated the percentages
of students willing to report peers cheating at only 13%. This study suggested the some of the reasons
for not reporting peers included; camaraderie, fear of retaliation, cheating is the accepted norm, and the
perception that it is not their responsibility to police classmates cheating.

SUMMARY AND LISTING OF OPEN-ENDED RESPONSES: DIRECT QUOTES

1. Use this space to make any additional comments on your experiences with Social Media and
Academic Dishonesty in your college program or specific course(s)!

I have heard about cheating but never seen it on any social media.

I personally haven't used social media for any gain through schooling however I have seen some do it. And with that I told them if I saw it again then they would be reported.

I haven't seen any cheating yet.

I think this is a more difficult subject for online students where they can get help from others or the internet/their phones without it being noticed by anyone. I am much more willing to seek outside help during an online exam than I am in a classroom.

Depending on the type of cheating I would report my classmate cheating, it depends on whether it was an assignment or exam and the weight of the both the activity and action. I would give them the opportunity to turn themselves in.

I have never used social media for help or answers in any classes. I would not of even thought of doing that.

I think that social media is used more for simply being social with friends and family, not for cheating related reasons.

I've seen people cheating and tell them when I do. I don't usually tell the professor if I have a good grade in the class because I don't feel like it will make a difference for me to tell them.

I personally do not think that many college students use social media to compromise their academic integrity.

I don't think a lot of students use social media to cheat, but I know 99% of students Google answers to quizzes and exams that are online. There's nothing stopping them.

It's morally wrong, and it proves that student doesn't have the ambition to research and find the answer.

I don't use social media very often, so I have never really had any experience with it and academic dishonesty.

I only use things like texting for homework, not exams.

2. Is there any other aspect of this topic and research project that you would like to make a comment?

Social media is something to be aware of moving forward with education, I think for better more than for worse.

Some of these questions are too direct, cheating is a tough subject to discuss, maybe ask questions about considering to cheat or if the participant was ever tempted to cheat. Most of the time, people don't want to admit to cheating, even if it is anonymous, so I would add some questions that address consideration or temptation of cheating. Overall, the survey was good, it could just use a couple additions.

Since my classes are all online, I do my work independently so a lot of this does not apply to me.

I think that more college students share answers to exams through the use of screen shots, text messages, and Google.

Ask if they have ever used websites or apps for help.

The students that I see cheating from phones the most are usually engineering students.

ANALYSIS AND RECOMMENDATIONS

Although the responses were somewhat limited for both questions, considering that 195 students took the survey, there are some themes and suggestions to consider. The participants that responded in this section seemed to be more of the "non-cheating" students. They did indicate that it is easier to cheat in an online course as opposed to traditional classes. Several comments indicated that, for themselves, and probably a lot of students, these questions were difficult to answer. Even though the Question-Pro survey indicated in the introduction that all answers were confidential and anonymous, some students did not fully believe or trust that they could not be identified. A few responses indicated that there are applications (apps) that are available that were not considered in this study that allows for students to engage in academic dishonesty if desired. Some of these listed responses from the students taking the survey provide some possible directions for continued research and further studies.

SUMMARY AND CONCLUSION

The participants' responses indicate a high level of usage (70%+) of the various social media applications in education that were the focus of this study; Facebook, Twitter, Snap Chat/Instagram and Smart Phones\iPhones. However, the 30% that indicated they are not using the social media applications to assist in their academic programs did probably affect the numbers of responses on questions to questions 7-13 that focused on using these applications to cheat. The responses to this group of questions dropped somewhat compared to the rest of the survey.

The results indicate that Facebook, Twitter and Snap Chat\Instagram are not widely used to cheat or in any way enhance the academic requirements in higher education. The general response to these three social media applications was mostly Never (over 70%). However, when texting, and the use of iPhones and Smart Phones were discussed, the numbers increased somewhat. The general results of these responses indicate that 22-25% of the students admit to using these applications for cheating on exams and\or other class requirements. The largest reported usage of an application for cheating on exams or other class requirements was Texting with 25% indicating that they cheated a few times and 4% indicating that they cheated on a regular basis.

Although it is a small percentage and could be considered minimal, about 2-3% of the participants reported they use all the examined social media applications to cheat almost every term or extensively. However, even this small percentage would mean a professor with a class of 30 students would have two or three students that are willing to engage in some form of academic dishonesty. There will obviously always be the temptations to cheat during a student's college program. The findings of this study were consistent with other studies. The temptation to engage in some form of academic cheating may actually intensify as emerging technologies continue to further simplify the process. The temptation may also be compounded by pressure to succeed in academics within high stakes testing environments.

RECOMMENDATIONS FOR FURTHER STUDY

The greatest challenge to any study that focuses on academic dishonesty and\or cheating is to, 1) get a sufficient response level on any survey to make meaningful conclusions and, 2) to get the participants to answer honestly and freely. Any replication or follow-up to this study must take these facts into consideration. In addition, as indicated in the Open-Ended responses, just looking at the most popular forms of social media and newest technologies may not be sufficient to answer the research questions. With new apps coming out on a regular basis, as indicated by some students, there are those specifically designed for academic cheating.

REFERENCES

Crews, T., & Butterfield, J. (2014). Improving the learning environment in beginning programming classes: An experiment in gender equity. *Journal of Information Systems Education, 14*(1).

Desalegn, A. A., & Berhan, A. (2014). Cheating on examinations and its predictors among undergraduate students at Hawassa University college of Medicine and Sealth Services, Hawassa, Ethiopia. *BMC Medical Education, 14*(1), 89. doi:10.1186/1472-6920-14-89 PMID:24885973

Davis, S. F., Grover, C. A., Becker, A. H., & McGregor, L. N. (1992). Academic dishonesty: Prevalence, determinants, techniques, and punishments. *Teaching of Psychology, 19*(1), 16–20. doi:10.120715328023top1901_3

Gabriel, T. (2010). Plagiarism lines blur for students in digital age. *New York Times*, August, retrieved from www.nytimes.com/2010/education

Gardner, H. (2012). The ethical muscles have atrophied, *New York Times*, September. retrieved from www.nytimes.com/(2012)/education

MaCabe, D.L. (2005). Cheating among college and university students: A North American perspective. International Journal for Educational Integrity, 1(1).

McCabe, D. L., & Trevino, L. K. (1993). Academic dishonesty: Honor codes and other contextual influences. *The Journal of Higher Education, 64*(5), 522–538.

McCabe, D. L., Butterfield, K. D., & Trevino, L. K. (2006). Academic dishonesty in graduate business programs: Prevalence, causes, and proposed action. *Academy of Management Learning & Education, 5*(3), 294–305. doi:10.5465/AMLE.2006.22697018

McCabe, D. L., Trevino, L. K., & Butterfield, K. D. (2001). Cheating in academic institutions: A decade of research on ethics and behavior. *Ethics & Behavior, 11*(3), 219–232. doi:10.1207/S15327019EB1103_2

Moeck, P. (2002). Academic dishonesty: Cheating among community college students. *Community College Journal of Research and Practice*, *26*(6), 479–491. doi:10.1080/02776770290041846

Novotney, A. (2011). Beat the cheat! *Monitor on Psychology*, *2*(6), 54–60.

O'Rourke, J., Barnes, J., Deaton, A., Fulks, K., Ryan, K., & Rettinger, D. A. (2010). Imitation is the sincerest form of cheating: The influence of direct knowledge and attitudes on academic dishonesty. *Ethics & Behavior*, *20*(1), 47–64. doi:10.1080/10508420903482616

Pavela, G. (1997). Applying the power of association on campus: A model code for academic integrity. *Journal of Business Ethics*, *16*(1), 97–118.

Peres-Pena, R. (2012, September 7). Studies find more students cheating, with high achievers no exception, *New York Times*.

Rennie, S. C., & Crosby, J. R. (2002). Students' perceptions of whistle blowing: Implications for self-regulation. A questionnaire and focus group survey. *Medical Education*, *36*(2), 173–179. doi:10.1046/j.1365-2923.2002.01137.x PMID:11869446

Rettinger, D. A., & Kramer, Y. (2009). Situational and personal causes for cheating. *Research in Higher Education*, *50*(3), 293–313. doi:10.100711162-008-9116-5

Shelley, D. J. (2014). University faculty and students use of social media in higher education (3rd ed.). Hershey, PA: IGI Global.

Stogner, J. M., Miller, B. L., & Marcum, C. D. (2012). Learning to E-Cheat: A criminological test of internet facilitated academic cheating. *Journal of Criminal Justice Education*, *1*(25). doi:10.1080/10511253.2012.693516

Yardley, J., Rodriguez, M. D., Bates, B. C., & Nelson, J. (2009). True confessions: Alumni's retrospective reports on undergraduate cheating behaviors. *Ethics & Behavior*, *19*(1).

This research was previously published in the International Journal of Information and Communication Technology Education (IJICTE), 14(3); pages 1-14, copyright year 2018 by IGI Publishing (an imprint of IGI Global).

Chapter 57
Usage of Social Networking Sites Among Post Graduate Students

S. Thanuskodi

(iD) https://orcid.org/0000-0001-8471-5799

Department of Library and Information Science, Alagappa University, India

ABSTRACT

Social networking sites over the years have changed from a few user-based sites into a phenomena that has become a platform for a huge number of users. However, the growth and development of social networking sites have brought great concerns on parents and educational authorities with respect to potential risks that are facing the university students as they use online social networking frequently for gathering information. The risk associated with social networking sites when used for oral communication rather than face-to-face communication results in damaging interpersonal communication among the users. The results obtained from this study have shown that a reasonable number of university students use the social networking sites. Therefore, the popularity of the social networking usage by university students of Tamil Nadu and the benefits it has on the student-users have been confirmed from the findings of this study. There are also various purposes for which the students use the social networking sites to achieve and that have been investigated. Technology is a double-edged sword. Its power for bad and good resides in the users. Based on this, it is instructive to note that the relevant government authorities have to take good measures to ensure that they (student) are made to be aware of how and why they use the social networking sites.

INTRODUCTION

Social Networking Sites are integrated into everyone's life. Man cannot live without society. Family is the primary spot for figuring out how to be in the gathering. Gatherings likewise stretch out to class, college, work place, playground and so forth. In ongoing year's new relationship began with the entry of artificial machines called PC and web. Individuals talk, offer and trade their delights, distresses,

DOI: 10.4018/978-1-6684-7123-4.ch057

everyday happenings, instruction, relationship and so on, with the assistance of desktop through online Social Networking Sites.

The innovative progression had made an extraordinary and huge effect in the general public and particularly on the more youthful age. This logical headway is helping from basic assignment in making the work and occupation simpler. Computer turned into an unimaginable device in the realm of correspondence. The creative progression of the PC and web in the age enables the general population to impart even they are of million miles from one another. Once we were very much aware of pen-companions from different parts of the world. Without knowing one another, individuals had contact abroad. Clearly, by and by the history rehashes as Social Networking Sites. Today the friendship ratios among the young genes have broadened across the sea.

BACKGROUND OF THE STUDY

In the most recent years of the twentieth century, the world and particularly India saw a wonderful and quick headway in data and correspondence advancements. In this time, "correspondence" has developed as the most well-known term. Today the correspondence upset has united individuals paying little heed to geological limits. The need to convey is a piece of an individual's inborn being. Since the very beginning mankind has imparted utilizing distinctive procedures and strategies. Conditions and accessible innovation have directed the technique and methods for correspondences. Subsequently, every once in a while new communication technologies have been developed for better individual and also for mass correspondence. With the approach of the printing innovation the new time of mass correspondence started. At that point the innovation of wireless communication came into existence – Radio was found. Afterward, the creation of Television had an enormous effect around the world.

SOCIAL NETWORKING SITES (SNS)

A social networking site can be characterized as online administrations that enable people to: a. Build a public or semi-public profile inside a limited framework b. Explain a rundown of different clients with whom they share an association c. View and cross their rundown of associations and those made by others inside the framework. Christian Fuchs characterizes Integrated social networking sites (ISNS) as an electronic stages that coordinate distinctive media, data and correspondence advancements, that permit at any rate the age of profiles that show data that depicts the clients, the presentation of associations (association list), the foundation of associations between clients that are shown on their association records, and the communication between clients. Online social networking sites permits the multimodal client produced substance to be shared Social networking sites are applications that empower clients to interface by making individual data profiles, welcoming companions and associates to approach those profiles, and sending messages and texts between one another. These individual profiles can incorporate any kind of data, including photographs, video, sound records, and web journals.

An online social networking site can be formally characterized as an online social network which has limited arrangement of on-screen characters and ties between the on-screen character. Every actor is characterized by ID. Each ID has a corresponding client's profile. This client profile gives some data about the genuine performer. A social networking site utilized to keep up a current disconnected tie between on-screen characters, (changing over a disconnected to online tie). It can likewise be utilized to make online tie between the performing artists where no disconnected tie exists. Social networking site may join highlights of other online social networks like web journals, email, gatherings. The performing artist speaks with one another sharing multimodal digital content.

A social networking site is utilized for keeping up solid and in addition weak ties. The quality of weak is likewise appropriate on online social networking sites. Online social networking sites (OSNS) is a subset of online social network and which thusly is a subset of social network, every one of the properties of social network and online social network are acquired by OSNS. Alternate properties might be the social networks that are vast scale network: - The span of online social networking sites (OSNS) is high. For example social networking site Facebook has progressively 1550 Million enlisted dynamic clients. A few on-screen characters in online social networking sites has high degree (in-degree and out degree in the event of bi-directional network).

Growth of Social Networking Sites

The quantity of social networking sites is expanding step by step and quantities of clients of the well-known sites is likewise developing. In 2007, social networking as a class had fewer than 500 million clients speaking to 58% of World online Population. In 2011 it had developed to 1.2 billion clients speaking to 82 percent of World online Population. From that point forward social networking is most well-known online action worldwide. The clients of age group 15 to 24 were most exceedingly engaged group of individuals spending about 8 hours of time each day on these sites. More seasoned clients bunch was additionally quickest developing fragment. Popularity of smart phones has brought about the development of versatile social network clients. In 2011, India's online gathering of people was 45.9 million and 94.8% of the online clients visit social networking sites. The normal time spent on these sites was 3.4 hours. By 2013 India has turned out to be third biggest purchaser of web beside US and china achieving 73.9 million clients. Social network was still most number one online action. 75% of the clients of web clients where between the age gathering of 15 to 35 years and 86% of Indian web client visit social networking sites. As indicated by the report of Internet and Mobile Association of India (IAMAI) about 74% of all Active Internet clients in Urban India utilize social media, most noteworthy extent of social media usage was seen among the statistic portions of Young Men and College Going Students, with 84% and 82% entrance levels separately.

Benefits of Social Networking Sites for Students

Being included with a Social Networking Site gives students numerous advantages. Following are some of the operations in which students get engaged with social networking sites:

- **Create Profile:** Social Networking Sites give highlights to make new profiles which are filled by true to life subtleties, photographs or recordings, and their zones of intrigue.
- **Upload Videos/Photos:** These sites encourage transferring of photographs, recordings and imparting to other people. The clients can advance their very own recordings by utilizing this medium.
- **Creating and Advertising Events:** The occasions making or joining highlights of SNS allow the client to advance gatherings, workshops, meetings or social events that will be facilitated. For

example, various clients make occasions on lislinks.com in regards to participation of a specific meeting or class by the individuals.

- **Group Searching/Joining:** People can seek different sorts of bunches identified with various fields and join these that are identified with their fields of intrigue. There are different kinds of gatherings accessible on Social Networking Sites, for example, proficient related, social based, form related, innovation, news, library related, social affiliations, human rights, shopping, showcasing, training, sports and the travel industry.

- **Friend Searching/Adding:** It likewise encourages the inquiry for specific kinds of companions and sends friend requests to be part of friends' list.

- **Message Post:** This is the most advantageous approach to communicate with companions through post hostile to send messages over.

- **Chatting:** Social Networking Sites offer the office of messaging and video based talking with their companions.

- **Games:** They give various sorts of gaming offices. Anybody can turn into a part and access office on their particular page.

- **Appearance and Layout:** Users can make their decision based appearances of individual pages on these sites. They can likewise modify their substance on sites before showing it to other people.

- **Tagging:** It is the way toward giving a catchphrase to specific substance to portray it as indicated by possess capacities and offer it with others. The clients can label explicit data to their companions.

- **Download applications:** It is a little program which is made by the clients for different purposes.

Statement of the Problem

Social networking sites, over the years have changed from few user based sites into a phenomena that has become a platform for huge number of users. However, the growth and development of social networking sites have brought great concerns on parents and educational authorities with respect to potential risks that are facing the university students as they use online social networking frequently for gathering information.

The risk associated with social networking sites when used for oral communication rather than face-to-face communication results in damaging interpersonal communication among the users. Although social networking brings convenience in connecting with people far away, it causes addiction and establishes a feeling of loneliness, insensitivity and disconnection with the real world. It is significant to choose the social networking site prior creating our profile and entering personal details for the risk of privacy. Hence, the present study discusses the usage of social networking sites and its prospects and challenges for university students of Tamil Nadu.

Need for the Study

The use of social networking sites among the university students requires much attention with increasing number of students creating profile and feeding their personal information into the sites. The increasing activity on the sites by student community can negatively impact the normal activity of students' life. This can also become a hindrance to the academic development as well as social engagement of students. Therefore, there is a need to study, assess and evaluate the issues revolving the usage of social networking sites among the student community.

REVIEW OF LITERATURE

Singh and Kumar (2013) from Punjab University directed an investigation to gauge the use of social networking among their research students. The discoveries of the investigation demonstrates that larger part of the respondents were observed to know and making utilization of social media in their exploration work. Their examination additionally uncovers that Facebook is the most well known social networking locales among the exploration researchers. American young people go through normal 3.8 hours daily on social networking from a PC, cell phone as well as tablet.

Walsh et al. (2013) found that female first-year college students go through almost 12 hours daily utilizing social media by and large. Also they found a relationship between lower GPAs and higher social media use. The researchers additionally found the utilization of a few sorts of social media has gainful impacts, such as helping students recognize a sense of identity and establish networking skills.

Manjunatha (2013) explained 80% of the students investing impressive measure of energy in utilizing social networking sites routinely. Dominant part of Indian students (62.6%) spent up to 10 hours out of every week of their time on utilizing social networking sites and apparently 17.5% of students went through over 10 hours a week

Stollak et al. (2011) revealed that 78.3% of students spent major time on Facebook networking site while 77.2% among them spent over 30 minutes per day browsing the site. It was also demonstrated that over 75% of web clients in India are school and college going students. Among them, 89% of students use it for email and social networking.

Su, (2011) cites in his articles that Professor Christine Greenhow has discovered that students assemble essential bonds when they interface with school companions on Social Networking Sites. "At the point when students feel associated and have a solid feeling of having a place with the instruction network, they improve the situation in the instructive establishments," said Greenhow, a training teacher. "They endure in training at higher rates and accomplish at higher rates. It's really encouraging that taking part in Social Networking Sites could assist them with developing and extend their bonds after some time." Greenhow recognizes there are potential entanglements, yet says it's limited to overlook the positive angles. She has contemplated youthful Internet propensities since 2007, and found that secondary school students are boosting their inventiveness and specialized abilities through the sites.

Hargittia's (2008) investigation of undergrads SNS utilization recognizes the distinction of the individuals who are SNS clients, and all the more explicitly are Facebook clients. The examples from the University of Illinois demonstrated that 88% of them were SNS clients, with 78.8% of that rate being Facebook clients

Dwyer et al., (2007) contemplated how trust in a specific site and different individuals can influence client's readiness to share data and grow new connections. The connection between web protection concerns and readiness to share data and grow new connections was examined. The investigation led with an examination of Facebook and MySpace. The outcomes demonstrated that online kinships can create in sites where trust perceived is low and security of protection is insignificant. The comparative study uncovered fascinating similitude and contrasts between the two sites.

Dwyer, Hilts and Widmeyer (2008) discovered that dynamic investment in contemporary society is winding up progressively dependent on computerized advances, a pattern that demonstrates that Social Networking Sites, an innovation installed in the everyday lives of a great many individuals around the world.

Hargittai (2007) says that the decision of social networking site utilized may increment both advanced and social disparity. In which she says that there is an advanced gap among the relatives, relatives and companions circle. The imbalance is extremely distinctive that individuals who use PC for web and different facilities. .

Acar and Sheldon (2008) reported that as a normal Facebook client has a few times a larger number of companions on Facebook than, all things considered, in light of an apparent lower danger of tolerating new individuals, simplicity of asking for an enrolment, social attractive quality (positive sentiment of online ubiquity) and inability to reject individuals who are never again reached.

Lenhart and Madden (2007) have led a study for Pew Internet and American Life Project among the US youth and found that half of the considerable numbers of young people who approach the web utilize Social Networking Sites. Among this 66% say that their site is limited or private. 48 percent of them visit the site once in multi day

Telwall and Halser (2007) directed an investigation on the weblog. The center goal of the examination was to explore the abilities and constraints of weblog search engines. Evaluative examination was embraced for this specific investigation. From the discoveries it was reasoned that in spite of the fact that blog seeking was a helpful new method, looking the consequences of discoveries were sensitive to the decision of internet searcher. The outcome demonstrates that from individual to individual. The utilization of parameter, search engine and amount of spam varies with one another.

Acquisti and Gross (2006) carried out a study, titled "Imagined communities Awareness, information Sharing and Privacy on Facebook", to comprehend hidden statistic or social contrasts between the networks of the system's individuals and non-individuals and effect of privacy concerns on behaviour of the member. In this examination, the specialists discovered that age and status of students are the most essential factors in deciding the Facebook participation, however the security concerns likewise play a role, yet just for non-graduate students. Majority of the individuals know about the perceivability of their profiles and they depend without anyone else capacity to control the data they scatter. In any case, they archive huge divisions between explicit protection concerns and revelation behaviour with actual information.

Boyd's (2006) reports Friendster's popularity get under way on an influx of advancement here. Friendster ought to have ruled the market, yet what it picked up by being the first to accomplish sensible achievement, it lost through a progression of specialized and social stumbles, most strikingly the organization's assurance to arrange how its initial adopters drew in with the site.

El-Badawy & Hashem (2015), as they would like to think the more youthful age examined in this exploration paper are school students between the ages of 12 to 19 years of age. A couple of the stages they use are Facebook, YouTube, Google, and numerous others that will be talked about in the discoveries of this exploration. The more youthful age is the people that will lead our reality later on, they should be accomplished to have the capacity to affect this world and improve Egypt a nation making a course for progress. The investigation directed about the diverse things they are presented to, that may influence them adversely or emphatically. Their examination means to evaluate the recurrence at which the students are social networking, and whether it has any impact on their scholastic execution

Piotrowski (2015) intended to examine the measure the extent of the exploration space of instruction typology by directing a substance investigation of exposition inquire about around there. A watchword hunt of the term (Social Media) yielded 662 studies spoke to in ProQuest's Dissertations and Theses database. The creator condensed the real result discoveries of 29 expositions that had an explicit spotlight on SM-Education issues. Of these, just 2 thinks about revealed any negative perspectives by either students or personnel on the execution of SM stages for scholastic purposes. Educators' absence of adequacy in Web 2.0 technology, security issues, and information over-burden were the real concerns noted. As these outcomes depend on territories of investigatory enthusiasm of youthful scientists, the flow discoveries give an indicator of developing patterns with respect to basic issues in Social Media-Education research.

Subramani (2015) analyzed the scholastic utilization of social media applications by college students, and to contemplate the use of different scholarly uses of social media by the college students. The number of inhabitants in the investigation comprised of thirteen noteworthy order of students in Doctoral, M Phil and Master Branches. The sample size of the examination included 482 students chose through helpful inspecting method. The organized survey was utilized for data collection.

Helou and Mahamat (2014) endeavoured to get students' discernments on how their utilization of social networking sites impacts their scholarly execution and led a primer review of a gathering of Malaysian college student to accumulate beginning discoveries on their utilization of social networking sites and its effect on their scholastic execution. This investigation found that the majority of respondents concurred that social networking sites positively affect their performance academic wise.

Nee and Ken (2014) examined the effects of fusing Edmodo as educational system, into a classroom setting on the scholastic accomplishment of Biology students dependent on three sorts of reasonable dimension contains immediate, basic, and complex idea. The outcomes showed that students that were told by the guidance with mediation played out a bigger on the gain scores of all the three psychological dimensions; than those taught by the customary methodologies. This instructive system will saturate all aspects of the educational modules as another worldview of educating devices.

Kulandairaj (2014) said that social media underpins communication among individuals in which they make offer or trade data and thoughts in virtual networks and networks; it relies upon portable and online advancements to make very intuitive stages. They acquaint generous and inescapable changes with correspondence between associations, networks, and people, the expanded utilization of the Internet as another device in correspondence has changed the manner in which individuals interface. As of late, another method for online communication has risen with its own arrangement of quirks. This new communication style occur using social networking site.

Steiner (2012) stated that heap of existing stages for social media fluctuate in reason, target group and prominence. Habitually referenced among them in this investigation are Facebook, Twitter, LinkedIn, YouTube and Tumblr. For example, a composition concentrated course incorporated an address on the significance of social media stages, similar to Twitter. It was joined by an activity where we were required to compose tweets in a breaking news style. In another course, the educator set up a Facebook page used to share recordings and additionally give refreshes about the class. Being in classes and tuning in to boards and meetings that fused social media or that supported this sort of joining made her think about how different schools moved toward the contraption and how it was being coordinated into their projects, educational module and online presence.

Thanuskodi (2013) academic libraries cater to the diverse needs of scholars, scientists, technocrats, researchers, students, and others personally and professionally invested in higher education. Due to advancements in information and communication technologies (ICT), the vision and mission of academic libraries are changing in developing countries.

Dutta (2011) "Social Responsibility of Media and Indian Democracy" expresses that broad communications have affected human life in the present century in various structures. They have given data and diversion to individuals crosswise over nations. Print media, being the pioneer over an extensive timeframe has now got solid rivalry from Television media, which is in charge of a considerable lot of the social changes. The principle open intrigue rules that the media need to consider incorporate opportunity of distribution, majority in media proprietorship, decent variety in data, culture and feeling, bolster for the law based political framework, bolster for open request and security of the state, all inclusive achieve, nature of data and culture spread to the general population, regard for human rights and keeping away from mischief to people and the general public. Advising the subjects about the improvements in the general public and helping them to settle on educated decisions, media helps majority rules system to work in its actual spirit.

Yoo and Gretzel (2010) accentuated that it is important to look at the ramifications of identity with regards to social media since it has been observed to be an imperative factor affecting a wide assortment of human practices and decisions.

Kaplan and Haenlein (2010) characterized social media as "a gathering of Internet-put together applications that work with respect to the ideological and innovative establishments of Web 2.0, and that permit the creation and trade of User Generated Content". Kaplan and Haenlein then ordered social media into six noteworthy sorts dependent on a lot of hypotheses, which are media explore (media extravagance hypothesis and social presence), and social procedures (self-introduction and self-revelation), in particular cooperative activities, sites, content networks, social networking sites, virtual amusement universes and virtual social universes. Kaplan and Haenlein even recognized social media from Web 2.0 and user-generated content

Taylor and Kent (2010) opined that social media instruments incorporate intelligent social networking sites, and also blogs, digital recordings, message boards, online recordings and picture albums, and cell phone cautions. In addition, social media are viewed as easy to use, modest, adaptable web and versatile based advances that take into consideration the sharing of user-generated materials.

Thanuskodi (2013) this chapter reports the result of a survey conducted at Annamalai University to determine the extent to which users are aware and make use of e-journals. The study also examines the search pattern of e-journals. A questionnaire was distributed among the faculty members, research scholars, and post-graduate students to collect desired data. A total of 200 questionnaires were distributed to the selected sample of Faculty of Engineering and Technology; 180 valid samples were collected. The result reveals that 46.67% of respondents want to access only electronic version of journals, whereas only 23.88% of users want to read the printed journals, but 29.45% of respondents want to use both electronic and printed journals. The study found that most of the respondents 73.33% use e-journals for writing papers. 68.33% of respondents use e-journals for studying their course work, and 51.11% of respondents use them for research work. The analysis reveals that most of the respondents, 73.33%, use e-journals for writing papers.

Curtis et al. (2010) considered the selection of social media by PR professionals in the non-profit organizations by utilizing the Unified Theory of Acceptance and Use of Technology (UTAUT). Their survey estimated social media reception with relations to execution anticipation, exertion hope, social impact, encouraging conditions, and wilfulness of utilization, self-viability and anxiety. They found that social media apparatuses are getting to be gainful techniques for correspondence for PR experts and associations with characterized PR divisions are bound to receive social media advancements and use them to accomplish their authoritative objectives. Nevertheless, PR professionals are bound to utilize social media devices on the off chance that they discover them realistic.

Mahajan (2009) in the paper entitled Use of social networking in a linguistically and literally rich India' investigated the use, effect and issues identified with Social Networking sites and their effect on the social and cultural ethics of India. It also described the top most social networking websites of India alongside their awful and great elements.

RESEARCH OBJECTIVES

- To know the significance of social networking sites among the students generation
- To study the impact of social networking sites on university students
- To determine the benefits obtained from using the social media
- To ascertain the threats involved in using social media platform by the students

Research Question

1. Research Question 1 (RQ1): Does the dimensions viz. Interactive, Socialization, Information Sharing, Social Awareness and Facilitation have an impact on Knowledge management?
2. Research Question 2 (RQ2): Does the dimensions viz. Interactive, Socialization, Information Sharing, Social Awareness and Facilitation have an impact on SNS Threat?
3. Research Question 3 (RQ3): Does the dimensions viz. Knowledge management and SNS Threat have an impact on Students' Achievement?

Hypotheses

$H_{01:}$ There is no significant difference between age groups with regards to the Interactive, Socialization, Information Sharing, Social Awareness, Facilitation, Knowledge Management, SNS Threat and Students Achievement.

$H_{02:}$ There is no significant difference between degree pursuing groups with regards to the Interactive, Socialization, Information Sharing, Social Awareness, Facilitation, Knowledge Management, SNS Threat and Students Achievement.

Analysis and Discussion

It can be seen from Table 1 that "Gender" obtained the following ratings: 70.2% respondents are male and 29.8% respondents are female.

It can be seen from Table 2 that "Age" obtained the following ratings: 14.4% respondents are below 20 years, 33.7% respondents are between 20 – 22 years, 48.9% respondents are between 23 – 25 years and 3.1% respondents are above 25 years.

It can be seen from Table 3 that "Degree Pursuing" obtained the following ratings: 39.6% respondents are UG, 51.1% respondents are PG and 9.2% respondents are others.

Table 1. Gender – wise distribution of respondents

Particulars	Number of Respondents	Percentage (%)
Male	342	70.2
Female	145	29.8
Total	**487**	**100.0**

Source: Primary Data

Table 2. Age- wise distribution of respondents

Particulars	Number of Respondents	Percentage (%)
Below 20 years	70	14.4
20 – 22 years	164	33.7
23 – 25 years	238	48.9
Above 25 years	15	3.1
Total	**487**	**100**

Source: Primary Data

Table 3. Education-wise distributions of respondents

Particulars	Number of Respondents	Percentage (%)
UG	193	39.6
PG	249	51.1
Others	45	9.2
Total	**487**	**100**

Source: Primary Data

Table 4. Memberships of social networking sites

Particulars	Number of Respondents	Percentage (%)
Yes	460	94.5
No	27	5.5
Total	**487**	**100**

Source: Primary Data

It can be seen from Table 4 that "Are you member of any social networking sites" obtained the following ratings: 94.5% respondents are yes and 5.5% respondents are no.

It can be seen from Table 5 that "Which of the following Social Networking Sites do you use" obtained the following ratings: 34.9% respondents says Facebook, 7.4% respondents says twitter, 5.5% respondents says Linked in, 1.8% respondents says Pinterest, 3.7% respondents says Google+, 9.2% respondents says Instagram, 24.4% respondents says WhatsApp and 12.9% respondents says You tube.

Table 5. Most preferred use of social networking sites

Particulars	Number of Respondents	Percentage (%)
Face book	170	34.9
Twitter	36	7.4
Linked in	27	5.5
Pinterest	9	1.8
Google+	18	3.7
Instagram	45	9.2
WhatsApp	119	24.4
You tube	63	12.9
Total	**487**	**100.0**

Source: Primary Data

Table 6. Reasons for using social media

Particulars	Number of Respondents	Percentage (%)
Learning	135	27.7
Events	36	7.4
Networking	37	7.6
Entertainment	13	2.7
Chatting With Friends	33	6.8
Obtaining Information	51	10.5
Sharing Information	110	22.6
Killing Time	59	12.1
Others	13	2.7
Total	**487**	**100.0**

Source: Primary Data

It can be seen from Table 6 that "Reasons for using social media by university students" obtained the following ratings: 27.7% respondents says Learning, 7.4% respondents says Events, 7.6% respondents says Networking, 2.7% respondents says Entertainment, 6.8% respondents says Chatting With Friends, 10.5% respondents says Obtaining Information, 22.6% respondents says Sharing Information, 12.1% respondents says killing time and 2.7% respondents says others.

Table 7. Problems faced while using social media sites

Particulars	Number of Respondents	Percentage (%)
Electricity	90	18.5
Bandwidth	120	24.6
Time management	150	30.8
Infrastructure	55	11.3
Privacy	36	7.4
Bullying	9	1.8
Physical Problems	27	5.5
Total	**487**	**100.0**

Source: Primary Data

It can be seen from Table 7 that "Problems faced by students using Social Media Sites" obtained the following ratings: 18.5% respondents says Electricity, 24.6% respondents says Bandwidth, 30.8% respondents says Time management, 11.3% respondents says Infrastructure, 7.4% respondents says Privacy, 1.8% respondents says Bullying, and 5.5% respondents says Physical Problems.

Table 8. Time spent for using SNS by university students

Particulars	Number of Respondents	Percentage (%)
Less than 30 minutes	63	12.9
30 min to 2 hrs	144	29.6
Above 2 hrs	280	57.5
Total	**487**	**100.0**

Source: Primary Data

It can be seen from Table 8 that "Number of hours spent using SNS by university students" obtained the following ratings: 12.9% respondents says Less than 30 minutes, 29.6% respondents says 30 min to 2 hours and 57.5% respondents says Above 2 hrs.

Inference: "Above 2 hours" dominates the rating for "Number of hours spent using SNS by university students".

Table 9. Nativity -wise distribution of respondents

Particulars	Number of Respondents	Percentage (%)
Urban	164	33.7
Semi-urban	260	53.4
Rural	63	12.9
Total	**487**	**100**

Source: Primary Data

It can be seen from Table 9 that "Location" obtained the following ratings: 33.7% respondents are in Urban, 53.4% respondents are in Semi-urban and 12.9% respondents are in Rural.

It can be seen from Table 10 that "Students interact about the society through SNS" obtained the following ratings: 5.5% respondents rated strongly disagree, 4.3% respondents rated disagree, 12.7% respondents rated neutral, 50.9% respondents rated agree and 26.5% respondents rated strongly agree.

It can be seen from Table 11 that "Virtual interactions for sharing research findings by the university students" obtained the following ratings: 7.2% respondents rated strongly disagree, 6.8% respondents rated disagree, 15.2% respondents rated neutral, 42.3% respondents rated agree and 28.5% respondents rated strongly agree.

It can be seen from Table 12 that "There is convergence of personal and professional network through SNS" obtained the following ratings: 10.9% respondents rated strongly disagree, 16.2% respondents rated disagree, 26.9% respondents rated neutral, 29% respondents rated agree and 17% respondents rated strongly agree.

It can be seen from Table 13 that "Many SNS are competing to give the best features in terms of socialization, interaction, privacy and entertainment" obtained the following ratings: 6.4% respondents rated strongly disagree, 8% respondents rated disagree, 17.7% respondents rated neutral, 45% respondents rated agree and 23% respondents rated strongly agree.

Table 10. Students interaction with society through SNS

Particulars	Number of Respondents	Percentage (%)
Strongly Disagree	27	5.5
Disagree	21	4.3
Neutral	62	12.7
Agree	248	50.9
Strongly Agree	129	26.5
Total	**487**	**100.0**

Source: Primary Data

Table 11. Virtual interactions for sharing research findings

Particulars	Number of Respondents	Percentage (%)
Strongly Disagree	35	7.2
Disagree	33	6.8
Neutral	74	15.2
Agree	206	42.3
Strongly Agree	139	28.5
Total	**487**	**100.0**

Source: Primary Data

Table 12. Convergence of personal and professional network through SNS

Particulars	Number of Respondents	Percentage (%)
Strongly Disagree	53	10.9
Disagree	79	16.2
Neutral	131	26.9
Agree	141	29.0
Strongly Agree	83	17.0
Total	**487**	**100.0**

Source: Primary Data

Table 13. SNS Features in terms of socialization, interaction, privacy and entertainment

Particulars	Number of Respondents	Percentage (%)
Strongly Disagree	31	6.4
Disagree	39	8.0
Neutral	86	17.7
Agree	219	45.0
Strongly Agree	112	23.0
Total	**487**	**100.0**

Source: Primary Data

It can be seen from Table 14 that "SNS is largely used for socializing with friends as well as interacting with lecturers" obtained the following ratings: 16.6% respondents rated strongly disagree, 9% respondents rated disagree, 21.1% respondents rated neutral, 42.1% respondents rated agree and 11.1% respondents rated strongly agree.

It can be seen from Table 15 that "Helping you to maintain friendships" obtained the following ratings: 11.1% respondents rated strongly disagree, 14% respondents rated disagree, 10.5% respondents rated neutral, 44.6% respondents rated agree and 19.9% respondents rated strongly agree.

It can be seen from Table 16 that "Social media usage should not be blocked in educational institution" obtained the following ratings: 4.5% respondents rated strongly disagree, 4.7% respondents rated disagree, 14.4% respondents rated neutral, 52% respondents rated agree and 24.4% respondents rated strongly agree.

It can be seen from Table 17 that "Improving communication skills" obtained the following ratings: 18.5% respondents rated strongly disagree, 18.3% respondents rated disagree, 15.2% respondents rated neutral, 30% respondents rated agree and 18.1% respondents rated strongly agree.

It can be seen from Table 18 that "SNS has impacted your social life" obtained the following ratings: 16% respondents rated strongly disagree, 20.9% respondents rated disagree, 15.4% respondents rated neutral, 29.8% respondents rated agree and 17.9% respondents rated strongly agree.

Table 14. SNS is largely used for socializing with friends as well as interacting with lecturers

Particulars	Number of Respondents	Percentage (%)
Strongly Disagree	81	16.6
Disagree	44	9.0
Neutral	103	21.1
Agree	205	42.1
Strongly Agree	54	11.1
Total	**487**	**100.0**

Source: Primary Data

Table 15. Helping to maintain friendships

Particulars	Number of Respondents	Percentage (%)
Strongly Disagree	54	11.1
Disagree	68	14.0
Neutral	51	10.5
Agree	217	44.6
Strongly Agree	97	19.9
Total	**487**	**100.0**

Source: Primary Data

Table 16. Social media usage should not be blocked in educational institution

Particulars	Number of Respondents	Percentage (%)
Strongly Disagree	22	4.5
Disagree	23	4.7
Neutral	70	14.4
Agree	253	52.0
Strongly Agree	119	24.4
Total	**487**	**100.0**

Source: Primary Data

Table 17. Improving communication skills

Particulars	Number of Respondents	Percentage (%)
Strongly Disagree	90	18.5
Disagree	89	18.3
Neutral	74	15.2
Agree	146	30.0
Strongly Agree	88	18.1
Total	**487**	**100.0**

Source: Primary Data

Table 18. Impact of SNS with social life

Particulars	Number of Respondents	Percentage (%)
Strongly Disagree	78	16.0
Disagree	102	20.9
Neutral	75	15.4
Agree	145	29.8
Strongly Agree	87	17.9
Total	**487**	**100.0**

Source: Primary Data

It can be seen from Table 19 that "SNS helps in participating political parties, volunteering with civil society and students organizations" obtained the following ratings: 7.8% respondents rated strongly disagree, 9.4% respondents rated disagree, 13.3% respondents rated neutral, 52.2% respondents rated agree and 17.2% respondents rated strongly agree.

Table 19. SNS helps in participating political parties, volunteering with civil society and students organizations

Particulars	Number of Respondents	Percentage (%)
Strongly Disagree	38	7.8
Disagree	46	9.4
Neutral	65	13.3
Agree	254	52.2
Strongly Agree	84	17.2
Total	**487**	**100.0**

Source: Primary Data

Table 20. Students develop virtual interpersonal relationships through SNS

Particulars	Number of Respondents	Percentage (%)
Strongly Disagree	48	9.9
Disagree	74	15.2
Neutral	64	13.1
Agree	199	40.9
Strongly Agree	102	20.9
Total	**487**	**100.0**

Source: Primary Data

It can be seen from Table 20 that "Students develop virtual interpersonal relationships through SNS" obtained the following ratings: 9.9% respondents rated strongly disagree, 15.2% respondents rated disagree, 13.1% respondents rated neutral, 40.9% respondents rated agree and 20.9% respondents rated strongly agree.

Suggestions

University students should involve themselves in forming a group or community which would focus on their studies in helping them to learn and acquire new information. The students should be taught enough to limit the time spent on social networking sites. Parents can likewise provide guidance and screen their adolescent children to constrain the time they spent on social networking. They should rather utilize those hours to peruse other scholarly books that will enhance their insight.

Most of the students make utilization of smart phones with internet facilities to get to social networking sites. Along these lines such students should be urged to utilize a similar facility to enhance their learning as opposed to utilizing such facility to chat with companions for a long time in social applications such as WhatsApp. Teachers should assist the students with making significant utilization of social networking sites by joining them into their activities.

This should be possible by acquainting the students with the social networking sites that are entirely for scholarly work and research. Both the parents and teachers should attempt endeavors to urge the students to invest more energy studying their books than on social networking sites.

Students should be informed about the threats regarding getting dependent on social networking. Parents of students, teachers, management of the universities and direction advisors must urge the students to stop utilizing Social Networking Sites since it misleads the young children. It must be ensured that university students utilize Social Networking Sites appropriately for the sake of limited entertainment as well as for communicating with their families, friends and educators.

Creators of Social Networking Sites and organizations must enhance the security and protection that they are providing for their clients to advance a sheltered situation particularly for children of adolescent age. Since the majority of the users do not know about the need for changing the default protection settings, it is fundamental to set the default setting as sheltered as could be expected under the circumstances.

The SNS creators additionally needs to offer easy to understand rules that assist the users to change the security settings effectively.

CONCLUSION

People are naturally inquisitive and have the penchant to be constantly forward looking; choosing not to move on is not worthy to him. Thus, people have the tendency to advance in different perspectives among which innovative improvement shapes part. Internet is the latest and one of a kind innovation ever of. Absolutely Internet has encouraged the lives of people colossally through the plenty of points of interest it gives. Internet has empowered social association through Social Networking Sites. The most famous Social Networking Sites are Facebook, Twitter, Google Plus and numerous others. Through these networking sites an individual can take part in multitudinous exercises, for example, sharing videos and pictures, approaching national and in addition worldwide contacts, etc.

Social networking sites have turned into a standard mode for a huge number of youngsters and grown-ups from all around the globe including India. These sites urge and empower individuals to trade data about themselves, share pictures or videos, and use online journals and private information to speak with companions, other people who share interests and now and again even the world at large. Networking websites work like an online network of internet clients. Contingent upon the site being referred to, a considerable lot of these online network individuals share a typical intrigue, for example, leisure activities, religion, or legislative issues.

The greater part of current students assemble have approached the Internet and PCs for a huge level of their lives and time. Students take a gander at these logical advancements as a coherent expansion of customary specialized strategies (letter, telephone calls and wire, and so forth.) and watch the Social Networking Sites as regularly an a lot snappier and increasingly appropriate approach to connect with companions and gatherings. They are even mindful of the peril and dangers associated with these Social sites which are a positive marker that Indian youth are not just techno-keen and socially dynamic through social networking sites yet they likewise have social awareness.

It is explored that the vast majority of the adolescents are turning towards this pit hole of spending most of the time and money on Social Networking Sites because of peer pressure. They need to keep up their status in the present aggressive condition among their companions. This empowers them for quick selection of Social Networking Sites for keeping up their companions, having a great time sharing of information and amusement, and etc.

In managing the instructive effect on students, Social Networking Sites has made its impact on the present youth which was apparent through the investigation that school youth select Social Networking Sites for instructive related issues and additionally for stimulation, fun and training. The investigation likewise demonstrates that the entire idea of Social Networking Sites depends just on Facebook overwhelming over alternate sites like Twitter and My Space.

In general, Social Networking Sites are imperative instruments of correspondence, amusement and partaking in this period. Thusly there has been extensive ascent in its use particularly in the Indian Society. Actually, the youths are progressively inclined to be associated with Social Networking sites than some other group. Social Networking Sites encourage sharing of data, expanding contacts, etc. However an exceptional change has been seen relating to the use of Social Networking Sites in connection to relational connections among the university students.

The study on the use of Social Networking sites by the University students' of Tamil Nadu conveys the existing pattern that there exists a held demeanor in the utilizing academic contents through Social Media for academic perfection. While 'Google' is an all around acknowledged medium for looking through all or any sort of data through Internet, there is a developing pattern of utilizing Social Media for specific data. Today, Social Media is the new Google where one can make separate group for detailed exchanges identifying with all fields of study. Social Media constructs a platform for one-on-one and one-to-many for pointed insights concerning the subject and to improve dominance over a subject. The prime consumers of the Social Media are students who approach boundless utilization for they have additional time and psyche to concentrate on their quest for knowledge.

ACKNOWLEDGMENT

This article has been written with the financial support of RUSA – Phase 2.0 grant sanctioned vide Letter No. F.24-51 / 2014-U, Policy (TNMulti-Gen), Dept. of Edn. Govt. of India, Dt.09.10.2018

REFERENCES

Acar, A. (2008). Antecedents and consequences of online social networking behavior, the case of Facebook. *Journal of Website Promotion*, *3*(1-2), 62–83. doi:10.1080/15533610802052654

Boyd, D. (2006). Friends, Friendsters, and Myspace top 8, Writing community into being on social network sites. *First Monday*, *11*(12).

Curtis, L., Edwards, C., Fraser, K. L., Gudelsky, S., Holmquist, J., & Thornton, K. (2010). Adoption of social media for public relations by nonprofit organizations. *Public Relations Review*, *36*(1), 90–92.

Dutta, S. (2011, June). Social Responsibility of Media And Indian Democracy. Global Media Journal – Indian Edition.

Dwyer, C., Hiltz, S., & Passerini, K. (2007). Trust and privacy concern within social networking sites: A comparison of Facebook and MySpace. *Proceedings of the Thirteenth Americas Conference on Information Systems*, 339.

Eleanor, Y. S. (2011). Retrieved from http://californiawatch.org/dailyreport/social-networkinghelpsstudents-perform-better-professor-says-12292.

Hargittaii, E. (2007). Whose space? Differences among users and non-users of social network sites. *Journal of Computer-Mediated Communication*, *13*(1), 14. doi:10.1111/j.1083-6101.2007.00396.x

Helou, A. M. (2014). The Influence Of Social Networking Sites On Students' Academic Performance In Malaysia. *International Journal of Electronic Commerce Studies*, *5*(2), 247–254. doi:10.7903/ijecs.1114

Jesu Kulandairaj, A. (2014). Impact of Social Media on The Lifestyle of Youth. *International Journal of Technical Research and Applications*, *2*(8), 22-28. Retrieved from www.ijtra.com

Kalplan, A. M., & Haenlein, M. (2010). Users of the World, Unite. The Challenges and Opportunities of Social Media. *Business Horizons*, *53*(1), 59–68. doi:10.1016/j.bushor.2009.09.003

Kumar, A., & Thanuskodi, S. (2015). Using social network sites for library services in public libraries: Possibilities and challenges. In Handbook of Research on Inventive Digital Tools for Collection Management and Development in Modern Libraries (pp. 53–68). Academic Press. doi:10.4018/978-1-4666-8178-1.ch004

Lenhart, A., Madden, M., Macgill, A.R., & Smith, A. (2007). *Teens and social media*. Pew internet American life project.

Mahajan, P. (2009). Use of social networking sites in a linguistically and culturally rich India. *The International Information & Library Review*, *41*(3), 129–136. doi:10.1080/10572317.2009.10762807

Manjunatha, S. (2013). The Usage of Social Networking Sites among the College Students in India. *International Research Journal of Social Sciences*, *2*(5), 15–21.

Nee, C. K. (2014). The Effect Of Educational Networking On Students' Performance In Biology. *International Journal on Integrating Technology in Education*, *3*(1), 21–41. doi:10.5121/ijite.2014.3102

Nielit, S. G., & Thanuskodi, S. (2016). E-discovery components of E-teaching and M-learning: An overview. In E-Discovery Tools and Applications in Modern Libraries (pp. 240–248). Academic Press. doi:10.4018/978-1-5225-0474-0.ch013

Piotrowski, C. (2015, January). Emerging research on social media use in education: A study of Dissertations. *Research in Higher Education*, *27*, 1–12.

Subramani, R. (2015). The Academic Usage of Social Networking Sites by the University Students of Tamil Nadu. *Online Journal of Communication and Media Technologies*, *5*(3), 162–175. doi:10.29333/ojcmt/2522

Tarek, A. (2015). The Impact of Social Media on the Academic Development of School Students. *International Journal of Business Administration*, *6*(1).

Telwall, M., & Helser, L. (2007). *Blog Search Engine: Online Information Review*. Emerald Group Publishing Ltd.

Thanuskodi, S. (2013). *Challenges of academic library management in developing countries*. Academic Press. doi:10.4018/978-1-4666-4070-2

Thanuskodi, S. (2016). Awareness and use of e-resources among social scientists of alagappa university and its affiliated colleges. *Library Philosophy and Practice*, *2016*, 1–28.

Thanuskodi, S., & Meena, M. (2013). Use of e-journals by the faculty members, researchers, and students in the faculty of engineering and technology, annamalai university: A survey. In Challenges of Academic Library Management in Developing Countries (pp. 218–225). Academic Press. doi:10.4018/978-1-4666-4070-2.ch016

Yoo, K.-H., & Gretzel, U. (2010). Influence of personality on travel-related consumer generated media creation. *Computers in Human Behavior*, *27*(2), 609–621. doi:10.1016/j.chb.2010.05.002

ADDITIONAL READING

Alagu, A., & Thanuskodi, S. (2018b). *Awareness and use of ICT among undergraduate students of rural areas in Dindigul district: A study. Library Philosophy and Practice, 2018.* Retrieved from Scopus.

Muthuvennila, S., & Thanuskodi, S. (2018). *Impact of open access resources on library and information science students in India. Library Philosophy and Practice, 2018.* Retrieved from Scopus.

Singh, H., & Kumar, A. (2013). Use of social networking sites (SNSs) by the research scholars of Panjab University, Chandigarh: A study. In *58th International Conference on: Next Generation Libraries: New insights and Universal Access to Knowledge* (pp. 682-691).

Stollak, M. J., Vandenberg, A., Burklund, A., & Weiss, S. (2011). Getting Social: The Impact of Social Networking Usage on grades Among College Students. *ASBBS, 18*(1), 859–865.

Taylor, M., & Kent, M. L. (2010). Anticipatory socialization in the use of social media in public relations: A content analysis of PRSA's Public Relations Tactics. *Public Relations Review, 36*(3), 207–214. doi:10.1016/j.pubrev.2010.04.012

Thanuskodi, S. (2013). Students' attitudes towards library facilities and information resources of university libraries in Tamil Nadu: A survey. In Challenges of Academic Library Management in Developing Countries (pp. 1–15). doi:10.4018/978-1-4666-4070-2.ch001

Thanuskodi, S. (2015). *Handbook of research on inventive digital tools for collection management and development in modern libraries.*, doi:10.4018/978-1-4666-8178-1

Thanuskodi, S. (2015). ICT skills among library professionals: A case study of universities in Tamilnadu, India. In Handbook of Research on Inventive Digital Tools for Collection Management and Development in Modern Libraries (pp. 1–20). doi:10.4018/978-1-4666-8178-1.ch001

Walsh, J. L., Fielder, R. L., Carey, K. B., & Carey, M. P. (2013). Female College Students' Media Use and Academic Outcomes Results From a Longitudinal Cohort Study. *Emerging Adulthood, 1*(3), 219–232. doi:10.1177/2167696813479780 PMID:24505554

This research was previously published in the Handbook of Research on Digital Content Management and Development in Modern Libraries; pages 148-168, copyright year 2020 by Information Science Reference (an imprint of IGI Global).

Chapter 58
Utilizing Social Networking Sites for Communication in Higher Education

Jodi Whitehurst
Arkansas State University--Beebe, USA

Jim Vander Putten
ⓘ https://orcid.org/0000-0003-0098-3791
University of Arkansas at Little Rock, USA

ABSTRACT

This chapter first analyzes the need for communication and collaboration tools to connect units of higher education. It then examines a popular social networking site, Facebook, as a possible platform of communication. This chapter also discusses findings from a phenomenological study that explored rhetorical roles employed by participants on Facebook and then connects findings to current research concerning communication and collaboration in higher education. Data indicated that messages on Facebook were used for cooperation and coordination, but not necessarily collaboration. It also indicated that while participants were audience-minded, they were not necessarily audience-aware, and participants used audience shaping as a coping mechanism. Finally, composers' inclinations to exercise authority over their personal, representational space (Facebook wall) led the researchers to conclude that use of Facebook in higher education may best be achieved by creating a Facebook page or group for specific communicative purposes.

INTRODUCTION

Over the past decade institutions of higher education have encountered various internal and external challenges. From a decline in completion rates, to a decline in funding, to a decline in trust and support, the American university has confronted (and continues to confront) multiple crises. One indicator of an institution's resilience while managing challenges is the quality of its communication (Boyer, 2016). At

DOI: 10.4018/978-1-6684-7123-4.ch058

the same time, colleges and universities have become complex webs of administrators, faculty members, support staff, and students. Such organizational structures hinder communication and ultimately the flow of ideas. Now, more than ever, it is integral for professionals in higher education to find creative ways to foster a culture of communication and collaboration in order to withstand the challenges ahead.

In the last decade, professionals have studied social networking sites as possible platforms for communication and collaboration in higher education. However, these studies have often been narrow in scope, typically focusing on specific course disciplines, such as Cain and Policastri's (2011) study of Facebook use in a pharmacy management, leadership, and business course; LaRue's (2011) study using Facebook as course management software in a nursing informatics course; and Estus' (2010) study utilizing Facebook in a geriatrics pharmacotherapy class. Studies like these are useful for understanding the use of a particular social networking site within a specific discipline. However, they do not indicate how these platforms might be used on a broader scale. To understand the nature of communication on social networking sites and how they might be utilized in higher education, it is useful to study the rhetorical situation on these platforms (Olson, 2001).

To illustrate the differences in the rhetorical situation while using a social networking platform, first consider communication and collaboration as it occurs in a face-to-face setting. Typically, the number of participants is limited to a physical space—in a room and in a geographic region. They are limited by time since collaboration must take place synchronously. They are limited by the visual tools available (i.e. pictures, videos, and links). In face-to-face situations, the audience members often listen passively until his or her turn to speak. In contrast, communication through a social networking site imposes no restrictions through physical space, time, or time zones since collaboration can take place asynchronously. Also, numerous tools are available for illustration and reference for all collaborators. The audience is rarely passively reading; they are responding in multiple rhetorical forms.

This illustration demonstrates some of the ways in which roles of composers and audience members in collaboration naturally change in a social networking platform, like Facebook. The roles re-shape the context of the communication act (Olson, 2001). Gaining a better understanding of rhetorical roles of communicators and collaborators on social networking sites could offer insights into how these digital platforms might be used effectively across units of higher education.

For the last decade colleges and universities have been utilizing social media. For example, Barnes and Lescault's (2012) edition of their annual national study of college and university social media adoption included interviews with 456 institutional representatives at an array of different institutional types. Data analyses indicated that nearly 100% of colleges and universities surveyed used some form of social media in 2010-2011, and this increased from 61% in 2007-2008. Findings from longitudinal data analyses suggested that institutional usage continues to rise for the most popular tools, but adoption of others has leveled off or fallen. Ninety-eight percent of colleges and universities reported having a Facebook page in 2010-2011. This is more than a 10% increase from the previous year, and it is more than a 60% increase since 2008-2009. While digital platforms like Facebook are being utilized in higher education, they are typically only used to recruit and research prospective students (Barnes & Lescault, 2012).

For many years, Facebook has been one of the most commonly used social networking sites for American internet users. In a Pew Research Center survey by Smith and Anderson (2018) involving 2,002 American adults, Facebook and YouTube were the most commonly used social networking sites. Sixty-eight percent of respondents used Facebook, more than Twitter (45%), Instagram (35%), Pinterest (29%), and Snapchat (27%). However, the number of Facebook users is leveling off while other social networking sites continue to rise, and Facebook, which has dominated social media usage, has now been surpassed by YouTube (73%).

There is evidence that professionals in higher education are participating on Facebook. Data from a Pew Research Center survey by Parker, Lenhart, and Moore (2011) including college presidents at 1,055 two-year and four-year institutions indicated that college presidents were "major adopters" of technology (p. 7). It also indicated that 50% of those college presidents surveyed used Facebook. In addition to this, survey data from a Faculty Focus (2011) study of faculty Facebook use including nearly 900 faculty members indicated that the majority were utilizing Facebook. Of those respondents, nearly 85% of faculty members had Facebook accounts. Almost all respondents to a 2015 Educause survey of more than 13,000 faculty reported owning laptops, tablets, and/or smartphones. This can facilitate the adoption of instructional technology for the purposes of using Facebook. However, about half of survey respondents believed additional technology training was necessary, including training on social media, to increase instructional effectiveness. These studies and others like them have indicated that increasing numbers of professionals in higher education are selecting to participate on Facebook. Some have even incorporated Facebook into the higher education classroom, and while it remains a contentious subject, there is evidence that it could increase student engagement and learning. In a study conducted by Akcaoglu and Bowman (2016) involving 87 students from 15 institutions, students who used Facebook for class perceived greater value in the course content and experienced higher levels of student engagement. Most recently, Sheeran and Cummings (2018) investigated levels of student engagement in courses with official and unofficial Facebook groups. The study used within and between group analyses of 471 participants to study levels of student engagement (in terms of relationships with faculty members, relationships with peers, behavioral engagement, cognitive engagement, and sense of belonging). Those students in the courses with official Facebook groups reported significantly higher levels of relationships with peers compared to those in the unofficial Facebook group. Furthermore, both groups reported having a higher sense of belonging. There is clear evidence that administrators and faculty are utilizing Facebook in higher education.

Studying Communication in Digital Environments Using Rhetoric

Every type of communication—including the messages composed on Facebook—takes place in the context of a rhetorical situation. A rhetorical situation is traditionally understood to include interactions between an author, an audience, and a message (Welch, 1990). Historically, rhetoric implied oral communication, but when focus shifted from oral communication to written communication, the rhetoric was reshaped (Ede & Lunsford, 1984). A similar re-creation of rhetoric is taking place as interfaces have shifted from paper to screen (Lunsford, 2006).

Contemporary rhetoric has focused less on the simple, traditional concepts of author, audience, and message and more on a rhetoric that is disciplinary in nature; that is to say that contemporary rhetoric is thought to construct and regulate within specific discourse communities or platforms. Some examples of this splintering of rhetoric include You's (2005) rhetorical analysis of Chinese textbooks to understand ideologies in the People's Republic of China, Hoang's (2009) identification of a "rhetoric of injury" in the 2002 interracial conflict at a public California university, Cushman's (2008) analysis of political identities among Native scholars, and Trabold's (2009) analysis of a resistance rhetoric of South African anti-apartheid journalists. Each of these rhetorical analyses examined communication within separate contexts to gain insight into the rhetorical situations.

One field of particular interest to many contemporary rhetoricians is that of digital rhetoric, which represents a convergence of multiple disciplines (Yancey, 2009). Digital rhetoric is concerned with examining how rhetoric functions within digital environments, like the popular social networking site, Facebook.

In This Chapter

In this chapter the authors will begin by discussing the major expansions in higher education which have led to a greater need for digital spaces to aid in communication and collaboration; the growth of digital platforms (including Facebook) as a means of connecting; the justification for studying Facebook communication through the rhetorical lens; the methods, analyses, and findings of a qualitative study of the rhetorical situation on Facebook; and conclusions concerning Facebook as a platform for communication and collaboration in higher education.

BACKGROUND

The "Multiversity" and the "Metaversity"

It is difficult to unravel and roll out the details of what led to the complex, multi-functional American university. As E. D. Duryea (2000) observed, "…complex institutions such as universities do not appear full-blown at a particular point in time. They evolve through that complicated process by which men and cultures mingle over a history fraught with traditions and happenstance" (p. 3). The modern research university grew into a multi-purposed, multi-governed, multi-structured entity. No one articulated this better than Kerr (1963), former University of California president, who described the contemporary American university at an unprecedented time of growth. He described the American university as a "multiversity," needing to balance teaching and research roles, create a curriculum of generalization and specialization, attend to individual students in an immense student body, and, most relevant to this book chapter, generate contact "broader than the one-way route across the lectern or through the television screen" (Kerr, 1963, p. 119).

Institutions of higher education have continued to expand in the 21st century and have precipitated an even greater need for channels of communication. One indication of expansion is student enrollment. The National Center for Education Statistics (NCES, 2018), the primary federal entity for collecting and analyzing education data in the United States, reported a 41% increase in enrollment at degree-granting institutions between 2000 and 2016. In Fall 2016, total undergraduate enrollment in degree-granting postsecondary institutions was 16.9 million students, which is an increase of 28% from 2000. According to a 2011 NCES report, colleges have also become more diverse. Between 2000 and 2010, the enrollment of students ages 25 and older increased 42%, and the number of women increased by sixty-two percent (NCES, 2011). In addition, Hispanic, Asian/Pacific Islander, and Black minority groups all increased in enrollment growth (NCES, 2011). Colleges and universities in the United States have not only been serving increasing numbers of students but increasingly diverse populations. This growth in enrollment has produced a need for greater numbers of faculty, staff, and administrators. Furthermore, it has necessitated a platform for communication to connect them.

Another indication of expansion in higher education can be found in the increased number of campuses. Many institutions support some form of extended campus networks (Fonseca & Bird, 2007). These intended supplements or complements to the primary institutions vary in purposes, but the primary reasons are often to generate additional revenue or to reach underserved populations (Fonseca & Bird, 2007). Extended campuses also vary in distances from their main campuses (Baron-Nixon, 2007). For example, Drexel University, based in Pennsylvania, also has campuses in New Jersey and California. Duke University, with multiple schools and institutes in North Carolina, also opened a campus in China. While this trend has served important purposes, the physical spreading of campuses has created another hindrance to open communication in higher education.

Those examples of higher education expansion mentioned up to this point still bear a resemblance—albeit to a greater degree— to the complex features of Kerr's (1963) depictions of the multiversity. However, over the last decade the expansion of higher education has stretched in new directions— passed what can be recognized through Kerr's descriptions of the growing complexities of the university— toward digital spaces. While complications that resemble the multiversity continue, there now also exists a digital dimension of higher education expansion. This digital expansion involves people interacting in virtual digital environments, a phenomenon referred to by Collins (2008) as a "metaverse." The metaverse term—or perhaps it should be "metaversity" for the purposes of this discussion—was used by Collins (2008) to refer mostly to Second Life, a virtual 3-D digital world. However, the term, defined as the "convergence of virtually-enhanced physical reality and physically persistent virtual space," could easily apply to many digital spaces now utilized by institutions of higher education (Collins, 2008, p. 52).

Higher learning in online environments is a prime example of the metaversity. The number of classes taking place completely online has increased exponentially in the last decade. A study by Seaman, Allen, and Seaman (2018) of Babson Survey Research Group based on data from more than 4,700 colleges and universities indicated that in the 2016 Fall semester, 31.6% of college students took at least one online class. The Babson Survey Research Group has studied online learning for fourteen consecutive years and has reported growth every year (2018). Sloan Consortium (2012), a professional leadership organization in online learning, conducted a 10-year study based on responses from chief academic officers at more than 2,800 colleges and universities in the United States from 2002 to 2012. In this time, the number of online learners increased from 570,000 to 6.7 million. In the same report, a survey of chief academic officers indicated that 69.1% of chief academic officers stated that online learning was critical to their long-term strategy.

In addition to creating a virtual learning place for more students, learning in digital spaces creates a virtual work environment for more faculty members. Professionals in higher education are becoming more geographically dispersed. In these situations, there is no longer a "water cooler effect," where employees build relationships through chance encounters; there is no shared physical space to collaborate on joint projects; and there is no communication to organize and coordinate day-to-day operations. Studies on collaboration suggest that collaborators experience increased and more meaningful knowledge production, improved learning outcomes, and an overall improved environment (Kezar & Lester, 2009). There is also evidence that the Generation X faculty (those born between 1965 and 1981) thrive in environments with continuous opportunities for feedback (Bova & Kroth, 2001); professional relationships; and webs of support that are non-hierarchical, collaborative, and cross-cultural (Sorcinelli & Yun, 2007). As higher education culture changes, it is necessary to locate new channels of communication and collaboration, like digital spaces that allow for connectivity between geographically dispersed administrators, faculty, staff, and students.

The Growth of Digital Networks as Communication Platforms

The term "Web 2.0" was conceived by Dale Dougherty—author, editor, publisher, and co-founder of O'Reilly Media— in 2004 and popularized by MediaLive International and O'Reilly Media (Madden & Fox, 2006). It was a comprehensive term to be used by marketers, analysts, and other professionals in the field of technology to refer to emerging features of the participatory web (Madden & Fox, 2006). Since its inception, Web 2.0 has had multiple definitions. The majority of these definitions involve a listing of interactive capabilities, such as O'Reilly's definition, which includes "utilizing collective intelligence, providing network-enabled interactive services, giving users control over their own data" (Madden & Fox, 2006, p. 1). Concept words that aptly encompass these multiple definitions include: interactivity, networked, and user-generated.

O'Reilly Media sponsored a conference back in 2005 to characterize the paradigm shift taking place since the initiation of Web 2.0. They characterized the transformation as being a shift from static, isolated repositories of information (Web 1.0) to dynamic, user-driven, participatory sites (Web 2.0) (Singel, 2005). Ross Mayfield, CEO of a California-based company that creates Wiki software, portrayed the transformation as Web 1.0 being commerce-focused and Web 2.0 being people-focused (Singel, 2005). However it is defined, Web 2.0 is a socially networked digital space that brings people together in user-driven participatory forums.

In discussing Web 2.0, it is also necessary to consider the mobile computing devices that have enabled this pervasive connectivity. Mobile computing systems include devices that can be moved without inhibiting their computing capabilities. Distinguishing features of mobile computing devices includes their small size, wireless networked connectivity, and power sources that enable mobility (B'Far, 2005). Some popular examples of mobile computing devices include laptops, smartphones, tablets, and e-readers.

Data from a 2018 survey conducted by researchers at the Educause Center for Applied Research including 64,536 undergraduate students at 130 institutions indicated that 95% of students owned smartphones and 91% of students owned laptop computers (Galanek, Gierdowski, & Brooks, 2018). The report indicated that "practically every student has access to at least one of the technologies students identify as among the most important for their academic success" (Galanek, Gierdowski, & Brooks, 2018, p. 7). Laptops, hybrids, desktops, and smartphones were rated as "very important" or "extremely important" to student success. However, the importance of these devices differs considerably by student demographics. Women, students of color, students with disabilities, first-generation students, students who are independent (with or without dependents of their own), and students who reported being from disadvantaged socioeconomic backgrounds see their devices as significantly more important to their success than their peers. While demographics do impact the perceived academic need for these devices, nearly all students rated them as important to their academic success (Galanek, Gierdowski, & Brooks, 2018). It is clear that mobile devices are already an important part of communication in higher education.

The development of Web 2.0 along with the advances in mobile computing devices has caused an unprecedented degree of connectivity. One of the most popular facets of Web 2.0 is social networking sites. Boyd and Ellison (2006) defined social networking sites as "web-based services that allow individuals to (1) construct a public or semi-public profile within a bounded system, (2) articulate a list of other users with whom they share a connection, and (3) view and traverse their list of connections and those made by others within the system" (p. 211). Since their introduction, social networking sites (SNSs) have attracted millions of users. After joining, these users are typically prompted to design personal profiles and to locate others with whom they share some association. Common terms used to identify these connections include "contacts," "fans," "followers," or "friends." This public display of connections has been a distinguishing characteristic of SNSs. Acknowledging these connections enables users to link to other personal profiles and navigate through connections of connections (Boyd & Ellison, 2006). The majority of SNSs also have some form of messaging tool that enables users to leave private messages for people with whom they have an established connection. Other than creating personal profiles, establishing connections within the network, and private messaging, features for SNSs vary greatly (Boyd & Ellison, 2006).

Studies have indicated a steady increase in social media use by adults. A Pew Research Center survey reported by Smith and Anderson (2018) of 2,002 adult internet users indicated that 69% of online adults use some type of social networking site. A comparison of past data analyses suggested a trend of increasing social media usage among online adults from 8% in 2005 to 29% in 2008 to 65% in 2011, and finally 69% in 2018 (Madden & Zickuhr, 2011; Smith & Anderson, 2018). Data further indicated that the majority of SNS users—roughly two-thirds— reported that they make social media platforms a part of their everyday lives.

Social networking sites gained real popularity in 2002 and 2003 with the launch of sites like Friendster, LinkedIn, and MySpace. While MySpace attracted significant media attention in the United States and around the world, many other social networking sites developed in niche communities (Boyd & Ellison, 2008). Friendster gained users in the Pacific Islands. Orkut became the premier social networking site in Brazil and India. Mixi was widely adopted in Japan, and Bebo became common in the United Kingdom, New Zealand, and Australia (Boyd & Ellison, 2008). However, no social networking site matched the number of users participating on the social networking site, Facebook.

Facebook launched in 2004 as a Harvard-only social networking site. It quickly expanded to include all interested users (Cassidy, 2006). In 2012, Facebook was the second most accessed website in the United States, and it was the most accessed social networking website in the world (Most Popular Websites, 2011). As of 2011, there were 500 million active Facebook users, and 48% of those checked Facebook every morning (Hepburn, 2011). In 2010, a 20-minute span of time meant that 1,000,000 links were shared; 1,323,000 photos were tagged; 1,484,000 invitations were sent out; 1,587,000 walls were posted; 2,716,000 photos were uploaded; 4,632,000 messages were sent; and 10,208,000 comments were made (Hepburn, 2010). More recently, a Pew Research Center survey reported by Smith and Anderson (2018) of 2,002 adult internet users indicated that 68% of adults in America use Facebook. With the exception of YouTube (73%), Facebook is the most widely-used social networking site.

Facebook is also a commonly used social networking site on college campuses. For example, evidence suggests that more and more administrators are using Facebook. Data from a Pew Research Center survey by Parker, Lenhart, and Moore (2011) of college presidents at 1,055 two-year and four-year institutions indicated that college presidents were "major adopters" of technology (p. 7). It also indicated that 50% of those college presidents surveyed used Facebook (Parker, Lenhart, & Moore, 2011). In addition to this, survey data from a Faculty Focus (2011) study of faculty Facebook use including nearly 900 faculty members indicated that the majority were utilizing Facebook as well. Of those respondents, nearly 85% of faculty members had Facebook accounts (Faculty Focus, 2011). Also, Sapkota and Vander Putten (2018) completed a qualitative study to investigate business communications faculty members' perceptions of using social media in the college classroom. Faculty accepted social media as an important business tool, but curricular adoption was inconsistent because of varying levels of faculty knowledge of social media.

The development of Web 2.0 in conjunction with mobile computing devices has produced widespread digital interconnectivity. At the hub of this phenomenon are hundreds of social networking sites that the majority of American online adults access daily. One of the most commonly used SNS in the United States and on college campuses is Facebook.

Studying Facebook Communication Through the Rhetorical Lens

As a part of the old Trivium, rhetoric has had a long and celebrated history. Through the course of time, it has been defined in numerous ways. For this reason, rhetoric has been somewhat perplexing to those outside of the discipline. For the purposes of this study, rhetoric will be defined very broadly, as Lunsford (as cited in Howard, 2010) defined it, as "the art, practice, and theory of human communication" (p. 172). Because the purpose of this study was to gain an understanding of communication as it occurs on Facebook, rhetoric was the selected means of analysis.

Another rationale for selecting rhetoric to analyze communication on Facebook is its inherent relationship with technology. *Techne*, a key concept in classical rhetoric, refers to the art of bringing form to material in order to achieve some purpose. *Techne* rhetoric, like digital technologies, combines technical knowledge with an artistic awareness in order to achieve a desired rhetorical purpose (Porter, 2009). As Yancey stated in an interview with D. A. Hart (personal communication, March 19, 2011) and other professionals have echoed, "…the technology that you use is rhetorical—it's appropriate to the purpose…" Since Facebook is a digital platform that involves technical knowledge to integrate digital technologies (for example, video and text) to achieve a purpose, it was appropriate to use the rhetorical lens to study communication.

While this study examines the communication situation through rhetoric, traditional rhetorical heuristics were not used in data analysis. Rhetoric has typically relied on traditional heuristics, such as the five cannons of rhetoric—invention, arrangement, style, memory, and delivery—or the rhetorical appeals—logos (message logic), pathos (reader emotion), and ethos (writer credibility). However, since the focus of discourse shifted from oral speech to written communication, from written communication to static screens, and from static screens to interactive digital communication interfaces; scholars within the field of rhetoric and composition have questioned whether these traditional heuristics still apply to 21st century digital discourse (Lunsford, 2006).

The evolution of the canons of rhetoric from oral communication to interactive digital communication can best be illustrated by discussing delivery. Delivery, the fifth of the five canons of rhetoric, traditionally involved *how* something was said whether than *what* was said. It was concerned with voice and gestures during oral speaking. However, delivery—historically associated with the human body—took a subordinate (if any) position when discourse moved from oral communication to written communication (Lunsford, 2006). As discourse then shifted to static screens and again to interactive digital technologies, rhetoricians recovered the canon of delivery for digital rhetoric. As Kathleen Welch (1990) argued, "The fifth canon is now the most powerful canon of the five" (p.26). While digital delivery is still concerned with *how* something is said, it has evolved into a consideration of how composers select interactive technologies to deliver their messages.

This evolution of rhetoric has sparked the creation of new loosely-bound heuristics to describe the canons in digital situations. For example, Porter (2009) framed five contexts for digital delivery, including body/identity, which involved online representations of the body; distribution/circulation, which was concerned with technological options for circulating digital information; access/accessibility, which represented audience connectedness to information on the Web; interaction, which referred to the range of types of interactions; and economics, which involved copyright and ethical use of information. Porter

(2009) described these topics as "categories that operate heuristically and productively across multiple situations to prompt rhetorical decisions" (p. 208). While Porter and others caused professionals to consider how the canons of rhetoric could be redefined in new digitally-defined systems, these heuristics have not typically been developed or tested through research. It is also unknown whether one heuristic could classify any one canon across multiple digital platforms.

Most relevant to this study, it has been recognized that digital rhetoric could also alter the traditional discursive roles in communication. Lunsford (2006) recognized this when she stated, "It is as though our old reliable rhetorical triangle of writer, reader, and message is transforming itself before our eyes, moving from three discrete angles to a shimmering, humming, dynamic set of performative relationships" (p. 170). It is obvious that professionals in rhetoric and composition are probing the traditional rhetorical constructs to determine whether they apply when transplanted to digital communication. For this reason, this study employed a phenomenological approach, resisting the tendency to classify data into traditional rhetorical heuristics.

MAIN FOCUS OF THE CHAPTER

Methods

In the spring of 2011, a phenomenological study was conducted to explore the rhetorical roles that Facebook users employ as composers and audience members while communicating through this digital platform. The goal was to gain a broad understanding of the communication acts taking place on Facebook. The central research question guiding this study was: what is the essence of the rhetorical situation in communication on Facebook? Issue sub-questions included:

1. What types of messages are being composed on Facebook?
2. What considerations are made when shaping content on Facebook?
3. In what ways do audience members respond to messages on Facebook, and what considerations do they make when responding?

Participants

Six face-to-face interviews were conducted to explore themes involving the rhetorical composer and audience roles on Facebook. The interviewees were divided into three age groups with one male and one female represented in each group. Group one consisted of two participants in the 18 to 24-year-old bracket; group two contained two participants falling in the 25-35 year span; and group three consisted of two participants in the 36 and older grouping. Previous studies support differences in the ways men and women and various age groups utilize Facebook. For example, a Pew Research Center study by Hampton, Goulet, Rainie, and Purcell (2011) involving 1,787 internet users indicated that Facebook participation varied based on age and gender. More specifically, data suggested that "women and the young drive Facebook usage" (p. 14). This data indicated that 18% of women reported updating their status daily compared to only 11% of men, suggesting that women participate on Facebook more frequently than men. Furthermore, those Facebook users over the age of 35 who participated in the survey were least likely to have updated their statuses, indicating that older age groups participated less than younger age groups. Therefore, for the purposes of this study, maximal variation sampling (for age and gender) was used so that a full range of acts of various composers and audience members could be included in the data. The goal was not to further study the characteristics of these age and gender groups but to obtain a typical sampling, to use a broad scope, and to include an open range of composer and audience activities.

At the onset of the study, one priority was to obtain participants who were not acquaintances since it is arguable that interviewees could alter their answers based on their relationship and knowledge of the interviewer. The majority of the interviewees—two in group one and two in group three—were obtained through a gatekeeper. This gatekeeper provided e-mail addresses for her acquaintances and co-workers, and invitations to participate in the study were sent out through this medium. Of the eight invitations sent out, four agreed to become participants in the study.

All six interviewees were asked the same questions pertaining to their Facebook use, and all responses were audio recorded. The interviews ranged from about 20 to 30 minutes long, depending upon the length of answers. No interviews were limited by outside time constraints, and the interview protocol was comprised of five questions:

1. Describe the kinds of posts or messages you generally put on Facebook. Feel free to use examples if it is helpful.
2. How do you decide whether to post something on Facebook? Describe an example of a time when you chose to put something on Facebook and a time when you chose not to put something on Facebook (maybe you even deleted it) and why.
3. When you are composing on Facebook, how do you usually decide whether to use pictures, symbols, or text? Again, please describe examples.
4. How do you decide to respond to some posts and not to respond to others? You can use examples if it is helpful.
5. In what ways do you think that using Facebook has benefitted you? What evidence do you have of this benefit? Give an example of how it has benefitted you.

Data Analysis

The data analysis procedure followed the five-phase cycle as described by Yin (2011). The first phase involved compiling verbatim transcripts of all answers to interview questions that pertained to composer and audience. The second phase, disassembling, included uploading the data into NVivo9 qualitative data analysis software and coding emerging constructs. During the third phase, reassembling, the themes were organized, and a table was generated. Interpretation of the data was the fourth phase, which will be reported in the "Results and Discussion" section of this chapter. Finally, Yin's (2011) fifth phase of data analysis, concluding, will address the application of these results to communication and collaboration in higher education.

During the second phase of data analysis, two initial themes emerged. Interview data was coded in two categories: (a) composer considering audience and (b) audience considering message. To better understand these initial category codes, consider the following quote from the male in group two:

I don't use symbols like the smiley face. That seems too immature, like something a teenager would do. I don't use LOL. I just spell out 'I'm laughing out loud.' I also know that everyone does not know all the symbols. I don't know the symbols. I just found out what OMG means. Sometimes I get confused when they write in code or symbols.

The first half of this quote— "I don't use symbols like the smiley face. That seems too immature, like something a teenager would do. I don't use LOL. I just spell out 'I'm laughing out loud.' I also know that everyone does not know all the symbols."—was coded as (a) composer considering audience because the participant was discussing ways he considered his audience while composing. The second part of the quote— "I don't know the symbols. I just found out what OMG means. Sometimes I get confused when they write in code or symbols."—was coded as (b) audience considering message since the participant was referring to his response to messages he read on Facebook.

During this initial coding, it became obvious that at times the line between composer and audience roles blurred. This often occurred during real-time chat. To account for this additional theme, a third category was then created for (c) composer-audience role. To better understand this category, consider a statement from the male in group two: "Other times, like when a sports game is on, you get on there and everybody is talking about what they're seeing while it's going on." In this instance, the participant is not clearly defined as composer or audience; he is both.

During the coding of these primary categories— (a) composer considering audience, (b) audience considering message, and (c) composer-audience—varying characteristics in each category emerged. For example, when participants mentioned "liking" certain posts (referring to the action of clicking the "like" option under Facebook posts), it was coded as (b) audience considering message. At the same time, when participants discussed reading and viewing messages as audience members, it was also coded (b) audience considering message. However, these are very different actions. Therefore, sub-categories were developed for each of the three categories to account for these differences. For the purpose of clarification, these differing characteristics within each major category will be referred to as "characters." All categories were further delineated into the emerging characters under each major category.

Therefore, the data analysis unfolded, beginning from two broad categories— (a) composer considering audience and (b) audience considering message. The inability to separate some acts into these two initial categories formed a third category—(c) composer-audience role. Then distinct sub-categories or "characters" emerged within each of the three categories.

Composer Considering Audience Category

The (a) composer considering audience category was divided into three characters: linear posts, wall design, and audience shaping. The linear posts character included all composing that proceeded down the page in a linear direction. This type of composing involved all text, pictures, media, etc. Two typical examples of linear posts mentioned during interviews were status updates and picture posting. The second character, wall design, included more multi-dimensional, recursive composing, such as photo albums, reported interests, and other representational information that stayed attached to the composer's wall or profile. The final character under (a) composer considering audience that was also the most unexpected was audience shaping. Due to the large pool of readers on Facebook, composers often shaped or specified their audiences using tools like messaging and groups. To understand the type of comment coded as audience shaping, consider the following comment from the male in the age 18-24 group: "Anything that I think should be private, I do direct messaging or chatting." Comments like this one implied a different sort of audience mindfulness, one in which the composer shaped the audience to fit the message as opposed to the traditional shaping of a message to fit the audience.

Audience Considering Message Category

The second category was (b) audience considering message. The characters that surfaced during coding included: passive audience and active audience. The passive audience role included only reading and viewing composing done by others. In other words, this was the undetected audience. A quote from the female in group one, the 18-24 age group, that was coded in this category was, "Facebook provides the opportunity to see what everybody is doing without getting involved. So, indirectly you can know what people are doing, but you don't have to communicate with them about it." This audience role differed from the active audience role. The active audience was detected by answers to posts, replies to messages, and similar feedback activities. The active audience role involved responses that could be detected by other users while the passive audience role only involved comments that referred to viewing and reading.

Composer-Audience Category

The final category was (c) composer-audience role, and it had two characters, which were titled real-time communication and space keeping. The first character, real-time communication, involved activities, like the chat tool, that did not obviously shift between composer and audience roles. One previously mentioned quote from the male in the 25-35 age group best characterizes this role: "Other times, like when a sports game is on, you get on there and everybody is talking about what they're seeing while it's going on." In this instance, the participant assumed the audience and composer roles during real-time conversation. Not only was he a member of a community audience, he was also a member of a sports audience. At the time he was receiving text and viewing a game, he was also composing. Reading, viewing, and composing was all happening simultaneously.

The second character involved in the (c) composer-audience role was space keeping. Space keeping involved activity concerned with protecting a participant's personal wall from unwanted composing. The following quote from the male in the 25-35 age group provides an example of space keeping:

I have received inappropriate posts from people. I took them off my friends list because they were posting inappropriate pictures. I decided that I didn't want my wife, pastor, or employer to see it… Companies and employers now look at your Facebook page…One lady at work got fired for inappropriate pictures of herself. They are really patrolling that to see what lifestyle their employees really live and how they're being represented. Sometimes personal lifestyle affects your work. Everyone can see how you're representing the company.

This Facebook user (and others) viewed the inappropriate composing from others on his wall as a negative representation of him. He, therefore, became the audience (reader and viewer) and composer (editor) of his space. Hence, the role of composer and audience was filled relatively at the same time.

RESULTS AND DISCUSSION

Coding through NVivo9 revealed that the (a) composer considering audience role was the role most discussed by participants when asked about their Facebook use. The unexpected category—(c) composer-audience role—was only mentioned two percent of the time. Linear post references accounted for the majority of the (a) composer considering audience category while the active audience character accounted for most of the (b) audience considering message category. The space keeper character accounted for most of the (c) composer-audience category references. It is important to note that the number of references to these roles does not necessarily imply a connection to the importance of the roles or the frequency of the roles used on Facebook. It is merely another way to describe the data. A thorough description of data is an important means of interpreting qualitative data (Yin, 2011). The remainder of this section will address the three issue sub-questions contributing to the main research question for this study and connect the results to a discussion of communication and collaboration on Facebook.

Types of Messages Being Composed on Facebook

The comments concerning messages composed on Facebook were primarily in the (a) composer considering audience category. The linear posts character accounted for the majority of the types of messages in this category. The term "linear posts" could be misleading, because the term seems to imply messages involving simple text that moves down the screen (like a page), involving a simple top-to-bottom and left-to-right message. This could not be further from the truth. Consider the following quote from the male in group one that was coded as a linear post:

Most of my wall posts are links. I'll copy and paste and comment about the link. I sometimes comment on somebody's wall just to add humor. I put links though if I find items someone may like—music, funny videos—I put it on my wall.

Eleven of the thirty-seven references in the linear posts character involved non-text composing. However, these were coded "linear composing" because the text, links, pictures, videos, and other multimedia were positioned in a linear direction moving down the user's Facebook wall.

Many of the references to messages on Facebook involved simple text composed by the participants or personal photos with text. For example, the male in group three stated, "I mostly just use text. My wife and daughter use a lot of pictures though. She [wife] even adds on my Facebook, but I mostly just use text." The type of message referred to by this participant is read on the screen in a traditional way, top-to-bottom and left-to-right. However, some of the references to messages on Facebook involved a sort of multimedia arrangement that included arranging pictures, videos, and links designed by other people and text composed by the participants. For example, the quote mentioned earlier from the male in group one referred to the action of copying and pasting in a link and adding his own composing with the link. In instances such as these, messages were more like multimedia collages that reflected arrangements of collective composing.

Most relevant to this book chapter, comments from participants suggested that many Facebook messages were used for cooperation and coordination but not necessarily for collaboration. As Kezar and Lester (2009) noted, collaboration must involve joint goals and a reliance on others to accomplish those goals. They also added that for collaboration to take place, participants must have shared rules, norms, and structures (Kezar & Lester, 2009). Bailey and Koney (2000) defined collaboration as parties who "work collectively through common strategies" and "relinquish some degree of autonomy toward the realization of a jointly determined purpose" (p. 6). Data in this study did not indicate this degree of alliance between participants. This does not necessarily imply that Facebook cannot be used as a tool for structured collaboration, but analyses did not indicate that it was a part of the unstructured communication naturally taking place on Facebook among the participants in this study.

While interview data concerning messages on Facebook did not suggest that collaboration was a major part of communication acts, it did suggest that messages on Facebook were commonly used for cooperation and coordination. Cooperation, which involves shared information and joint support, is particularly evident in the interview data (Bailey & Koney, 2000). For example, the male in group three stated, "I had a friend looking for information on a flower shop in [city name]. I responded and provided all [of the] information for a flower shop." The male in group one stated, "Facebook is a benefit if I need some immediate information about a paper or a test or dates. I can go online now and just have 80 friends sitting there on Facebook…" Likewise, the male in group two commented, "Posts I respond to are often questions to give information." Comments like these indicated that messages on Facebook were often used for cooperation.

Data also indicated that messages involving information sharing were often simple self-reporting. For example, the male in group two stated, "I'm remodeling my kitchen, and I posted pictures to share my work to show the difference." He also stated, "I've put a picture of my kid sitting on our dog and funny comments about my kid." The female in group one said, "Last night I was bored at work, and I just updated my status with 'Cleaned up my apartment a little bit today. Now I'm at work trying to be productive." Likewise, the female in group two stated, "My posts are about my day…or if there was a major event or vacation going on." Five of the six participants indicated that Facebook had benefitted them by keeping them connected through information sharing messages like these.

Messages involving coordination, which involves shared tasks and compatible goals, was also evident in the interview data (Bailey & Koney, 2000). For example, the male in group three stated, "I have a long-distant friend whose son was in town. We got in contact through Facebook, and when his son came to town, I was able to help him." Likewise, the male in group two stated, "I use it [Facebook] sometimes with certain people when I draw house prints for work. They'll send me their information on Facebook. Then I send back plans through e-mail." This comment indicated a shared task and a shared goal. However, it was not necessarily collaborative action, which would require a reliance on collaborators, shared power, and shared responsibility (Kezar & Lester, 2009; Bailey & Koney, 2000).

Considerations by Composers When Shaping Content on Facebook

Of the three main categories—(a) composer considering audience, (b) audience considering message, and (c) composer-audience—the (a) composer considering audience had the most references. Data from this study indicated that although composers were very audience-minded, they were not necessarily audience aware. The vast audience on Facebook made it very difficult and almost impossible to craft audience-aware messages. All participants at some point in the interview indicated extreme caution when composing. For example, the female in group three stated, "On special events I put pictures up. I don't put up exclusive pictures that don't include all friends. I don't want other people to feel excluded…I don't like to offend people." The male in group two stated, "It is usually humor that offends people… There are a lot of my friends who are not offended by that type of humor, but there are some who might get offended by it so I don't even post." Some participants, like the male in group one, chose to deal with challenges in determining audience through audience shaping. He stated, "I'm careful about what I post and what others' pictures and comments are posted on my wall as well. Anything that I think should be private, I do direct messaging or chatting." As illustrated in this quote, instead of shaping his message to fit the audience, this participant used Facebook tools to shape or limit the audience receiving the message. This type of audience shaping defies the traditional dynamics of a rhetorical situation by giving the composer unprecedented control over the audience.

Another character that involved composers shaping content was space keeping, which was classified in the (c) composer-audience category. Space keeping involved all activity concerned with protecting a participant's personal wall from unwanted composing. Several comments by participants referred to the Facebook wall as being a space that represented them, although much of the composing was done by other people. For example, consider a quote by the male participant in group two: "I have received inappropriate posts from people. I took them off my friends list because they were posting inappropriate pictures. I decided that I didn't want my wife, pastor, or employer to see it." Quotes like this one suggested that composers viewed their wall as a representational space, and they exercised authority over the composing there. It also indicated the degree to which the composer and audience roles can become blurred.

To illustrate this connectivity, think of this in terms of writing on paper. Consider a group of composers writing on their own papers. Every time the composers write on their own papers, they must also go to the papers of every other participant to write the same thing. In this situation, which of the participants is the audience and which of the participants is the composer? When participants look at their papers, are they the composers of the document or the audience members? The answer is both. In the case of composing on Facebook, data suggested that the participants in this study redeemed that personal space by editing or deleting the composing of others.

The space keeping character illustrates the extent in which Facebook is a collectively constructed space. Data indicated that composing was often a shared act, and in personal spaces (like the Facebook wall) the composing of others was viewed as a collective representation of the owner of that space. However, it also demonstrated study participants' unwillingness to completely give authority of their space (Facebook wall) to the group.

Many scholars in the field of rhetoric and writing have contended that digital writing shifts the authority of writing from single composers to collective composers. Data from this study indicated that while participants did not exercise a great degree of power over their personal composing, they did exercise power over their personal spaces. When composers did exercise power over their composing, they did this through audience shaping—selecting which audience members received their messages. This finding is relevant to the discussion of utilizing Facebook for communication and collaboration. It is possible that composers may not feel the same responsibility to protect their representational space if a shared space was established, like a Facebook group or a Facebook page designed for specific communicative or collaborative purposes.

Types of Responses and Considerations by Audience Members

Data concerning responses by audience members mainly occurred in the (b) audience considering message category. The majority of these comments pertained to the active audience character. Participant statements were coded in the active audience character when they referred to responding in ways that could be detected by other Facebook users. However, it is important to note that the responses were active in more than one way. Active responding involved "liking" a post, responding with text, or responding with multi-media. Consider this quote from the male in group two: "I sent information to a friend who asked a question about how to watch a sports game on a website. I sent a link to give her the information, and she was really grateful." This quote implied a very active style of responding in which the audience member was able to produce real results for the composer. Another way audience members actively responded to composing was to "like" a comment. This type of response operated as simple affirmation for the composer. For example, the female in group one stated, "There are some times I will 'like' an inspirational quote. I won't comment on them, but I will 'like' them." In this instance, this Facebook participant viewed the "like" option as a lesser form of audience feedback than commenting. This is another Facebook option that very obviously altered the rhetorical audience role. Audience members were able to provide feedback that required very minimal effort.

The passive audience character, or the undetected audience, allowed participants to read and view without interference. Take into account this quote by the female in group one: "I do go Facebook creeping. It's profile creeping. You look at other status updates. If you're a creeper that means you look at other profiles." This same participant later stated, "Facebook provides the opportunity to see what everyone is doing without getting involved. So, indirectly you can know what people are doing, but you don't have to communicate with them about it."

This type of passive audience role has also been referred to as surveillance. This term was first used by Lampe, Ellison, and Steinfield (2006). In a very influential study, Lampe, Ellison, and Steinfeld (2006) conducted two surveys of first-year students at Michigan State University. Data from this study indicated that Facebook allowed members to maintain relationships just by "allowing users to track other members of their community" (Lampe, Ellison, & Steinfeld, 2006, p. 167). While most discussions concerning surveillance tend to be negative, data from this study of rhetorical roles on Facebook indicated that surveillance offered a relationship maintenance component that participants viewed as valuable. For example, consider the quote from the female in group two: "It [Facebook] keeps me in the loop more than I can be. I'm able to see photos and growth without being directly in the vicinity." The male in group three stated, "I use it [Facebook] for a long-distance brother... I learned information—that he got married—on Facebook. We were able to meet his wife on Facebook." Likewise, the male in group two said, "I have [a] long distance family [member] that I didn't speak to. Now we're in constant contact. I get to see pictures of his kids or family." Comments like these suggested that being audience members on Facebook allowed participants to maintain relationships by reading and viewing information about members of their community.

A point particularly notable to this discussion of communication and collaboration on Facebook is that relationship maintenance is an integral part of collaboration. As Gajda (2004) noted, "Collaboration depends upon positive personal relations and effective emotional connections between partners" (p. 69). The literature concerning collaboration indicates that the foundation for partnerships is an ongoing interpersonal connection (Gajda, 2004; Bailey & Koney, 2000; Austin, 2000). It is possible that Facebook might be used to reinforce relationships that could lead to collaborations.

FUTURE RESEARCH DIRECTIONS

This chapter adds to the objectives of this book by providing stakeholders in higher education information concerning the types of communication taking place on Facebook. Data from this study indicated that Facebook was already being utilized for cooperation and coordination, two features that could have strong positive impacts on units of higher education. For example, this could be used to better serve students by eliminating the need to go between multiple offices to obtain solutions to problems. Coordinating efforts could also lead to greater efficiency through sharing information resources. Future research specifically addressing the uses of Facebook to aid in cooperation and coordination between units of higher education is needed.

This study explored the communication situations naturally taking place on Facebook. While data did not indicate that collaboration took place, more research is needed to address collaboration using Facebook in a formalized collaborative situation. Collaborators managed by external structures could greatly affect the potential for collaboration using this digital platform. Finally, a conceptual model reflecting the rhetorical situation on Facebook could be a useful tool to guide future research across multiple units and disciplines in higher education.

CONCLUSION

It is important to understand that most of the collaboration literature is conceptualized as developing through various degrees or strengths of partnerships. For example, Bailey and Koney (2000) conceptualized alliances as developing through a four-level continuum: cooperation, coordination, collaboration, and coadunation. At the beginning of the continuum, cooperation involves shared information and joint support, and at the end of the continuum, coadunation involves an integrated structure in which individual members surrender their autonomy. These varying degrees of partnerships are often referred to as alliances (Gajda, 2004). Therefore, it is important when considering platforms for collaboration not to dismiss those that support a lesser degree of alliance, which could progress into collaboration.

This point is particularly relevant in the context of this study, which indicated that messages on Facebook did not suggest collaborative alliances but did suggest cooperation and coordination. As alliances increase from cooperation toward collaboration, they increase in their extent of interdependence and in their need for formalization (Gajda, 2004; Bailey & Koney, 2000). Formalization is the extent in which members are managed by external structures, like policies or procedures (Bailey & Koney, 2000). This study focused on understanding the essence of the unstructured communication acts already taking place on Facebook and how stakeholders in higher education might utilize this to improve communication and collaboration in higher education. Therefore, the absence of formalization within the design of this study possibly limited the likelihood of locating collaborative alliances.

This study also suggested that composers on Facebook took part in collective composing but still exercised power or control over their personal representational spaces (Facebook wall). Literature concerning alliances suggests that as alliances progress through the continuum toward collaboration, collaborators must also relinquish greater degrees of autonomy or individual power (Bailey & Koney, 2000). For this reason, the personal space on Facebook could prove to be a hindrance to collaboration. This might be avoided by creating a shared space, like a Facebook page or group for particular collaborative purposes.

Finally, this study indicated that audience members on Facebook used this platform for maintaining relationships. This could pose a threat to professionals who desire to separate their public and private lives. However, the literature concerning alliances suggests that maintaining relationships is integral for sustaining partnerships (Austin, 2000; Gajda, 2004). As Austin (2000) noted, collaborators must "connect personally and emotionally" to maintain successful alliances (p. 173). Findings from this study indicated that Facebook could be a valuable communication tool to navigate the growing complexities of American colleges and universities.

REFERENCES

Airey, J. (2011). The disciplinary literacy discussion matrix: A heuristic tool for initiating collaboration in higher education. *Across the Disciplines: A Journal of Language, Learning, and Academic Writing*. Retrieved from http://wac.colostate.edu/atd/ clil/airey.cfm

Akcaoglu, M., & Bowman, N. D. (2016). Using instructor-led Facebook groups to enhance students perceptions of course content. *Computers in Human Behavior, 65*, 582–590. doi:10.1016/j.chb.2016.05.029

Austen, J. (2000). *The collaboration challenge: How nonprofits and business succeed through strategic alliances.* San Francisco, CA: Jossey-Bass.

B'Far, R. (2005). Mobile computing principles: Designing and developing mobile applications with UML and XML. Cambridge, UK: Cambridge University Press.

Bailey, D., & Koney, K. M. (2000). *Strategic alliances among health and human services organizations: From affiliations to consolidations* [ABRIDGED]. Thousand Oaks, CA: Sage. doi:10.4135/9781483328546

Barnes, N., & Lescault, A. (2012). Social media adoption soars as higher-ed experiments and reevaluates its use of new communications tools. Retrieved from http://www.umassd.edu/cmr/studiesandresearch/socialmediaadoptionsoars/

Baron-Nixon, L. (2007). *Connecting non full-time faculty to institutional mission.* Sterling, VA: Stylus.

Bova, B., & Kroth, M. (2001). Workplace learning and generation X. *Journal of Workplace Learning, 13*(2), 57–65. doi:10.1108/13665620110383645

Boyd, D. M., & Ellison, N. B. (2008). Social networking sites: Definition, history, and scholarship. *Journal of Computer-Mediated Communication, 13*(1), 210–230. doi:10.1111/j.1083-6101.2007.00393.x

Boyer, R. (2016, July 16). Great colleges to work for 2016. *The Chronicle of Higher Education.* Retrieved from https://www.chronicle.com/specialreport/Great-Colleges-to-Work-For/47

Cain, J., & Policastri, A. (2011). Using Facebook as an informal learning environment. *American Journal of Pharmaceutical Education, 75*(10), 1–8. doi:10.5688/ajpe7510207 PMID:22345726

Cassidy, J. (2006). Me media: How hanging out on the internet became big business. *The New Yorker, 82*(13), 50.

Collins, C. (2008, Sept. 15). Looking to the future: Higher education in the metaverse. *Educause Review.* Retrieved from http://www.educause.edu/ero/article/looking-futurehigher-education-metaverse

Cushman, E. (2008). Toward a rhetoric of self-representation: Identity politics in Indian country and rhetoric and composition. *College Composition and Communication, 60*(2), 321–365.

Dahlstrom, E. (2012). *ECAR study of undergraduate students and Information technology, 2012.* Retrieved from http://net.educause.edu/ir/library/pdf/ERS1208/ERS1208.pdf

Duggan, M., & Brenner, J. (2012). *The demographics of social media users-2012.* Retrieved from http://pewinternet.org/~/media//Files/Reports/2013/ PIP_SocialMediaUsers.pdf

Duryea, E. D. (2000). Evolution of the university. In M. C. Brown (Ed.), *Organization and governance in higher education* (5th ed.). Boston, MA: Pearson Custom Publishing.

Ede, L., & Lunsford, A. (1984). Audience addressed/Audience invoked. In V. Villanueva (Ed.), *Cross talk in comp theory: A reader* (2nd ed., pp. 77–95). Urbana, IL: NCTE.

Estus, E. L. (2010). Using Facebook within a geriatric pharmacotherapy course. *American Journal of Pharmaceutical Education, 74*(8), 145. doi:10.5688/aj7408145 PMID:21179256

Faculty Focus. (2011). *Social media usage trends among higher education faculty.* Retrieved from http:// www.facultyfocus.com/free-reports/social-media-usage-trends-among-higher education-faculty/

Fonseca, J. W., & Bird, C. P. (2007, October). Under the radar: Branch campuses take off. *University Business Solutions for Higher Education Management.* Retrieved from http://www.universitybusiness. com/article/under-radar-branch-campuses-take

Gajda, R. (2004). Utilizing collaboration theory to evaluate strategic alliances. *The American Journal of Evaluation, 25*(1), 65–77. doi:10.1177/109821400402500105

Galanek, J., Gierdowski, D. C., & Brooks, D. C. (2018). *ECAR Study of Undergraduate Students and Information Technology, 2018.* Retrieved from https://library.educause.edu/ resources/2018/10/2018-students-and-technology-research-study

Hampton, K., Goulet, L., Rainie, L., & Purcell, K. (2011). *Social networking sites and our lives: How people's trust, personal relationships, and civic and political involvement are connected to their use of social networking sites and other technologies.* Retrieved from http://pewinternet.org/Reports/2011/ Technology-and-social-networks.aspx

Hepburn, A. (2010, March 22). Facebook: Facts and figures for 2010 [Web log post]. *Digital Buzz.* Retrieved from http://digitalbuzzblog.com/facebook-facts-figures-2010

Hepburn, A. (2011, Jan. 18). Facebook statistics: Stats and facts for 2011 [Web log post]. *Digital Buzz.* Retrieved from http://digitalbuzzblog.com/facebook-statistics-stats-facts-2011

Hoang, H. (2009). Campus racial politics and a "rhetoric of injury.". *College Composition and Communication, 61*(1), 188.

Howard, G. T. (2010). *Dictionary of rhetorical terms.* Bloomington, IN: Xlibrus Publishing.

Kerr, C. (1963). *The uses of the university.* Cambridge, MA: Harvard University Press.

Kezar, A., & Lester, J. (2009). *Organizing higher education for collaboration.* San Francisco, CA: Jossey-Bass.

Lampe, C., Ellison, N., & Steinfeld, C. (2006). In P. Hinds, & D. Martin (Eds.), A Face(book) in the crowd: Social searching vs. social browsing. *Proceedings of the 2006 20th anniversary conference on Computer supported cooperative work* (pp. 167-170). New York, NY: Association for Computing Machinery.

LaRue, E. M. (2012). Using Facebook as a course management software: A case study. *Teaching and Learning in Nursing, 7*(1), 17–22. doi:10.1016/j.teln.2011.07.004

Lunsford, A. (2006). Writing, technologies, and the fifth canon. *Computers and Composition, 23*(2), 169–177. doi:10.1016/j.compcom.2006.02.002

Madden, M., & Fox, S. (2006). Riding the waves of "Web 2.0:" More than a buzzword but still not easily defined. Retrieved from http://www.pewinternet.org/ Reports/2006/Riding-theWaves-of-Web-20.aspx

Madden, M., & Zickuhr, K. (2011). *65% of online adults use social networking sites.* Retrieved from http://pewinternet.org/~/media//Files/Reports/2011/PIP SNSUpdate-2011.pdf

Most Popular Websites. (2011). *Most popular websites on the internet.* Retrieved from http://mostpopularwebsites.net/

National Center for Education Statistics, Institution of Education Sciences. (2011). *Digest of education statistics, 2011.* Retrieved from http://nces.ed.gov/fastfacts/display.asp?id=98

National Center for Education Statistics, Institution of Education Sciences. (2018). *The Condition of Education, 2018.* Retrieved from https://nces.ed.gov/pubs2018/2018144.pdf

Olson, D. (2001). *The world on paper.* New York, NY: Cambridge University Press.

Parker, K., Lenhart, A., & Moore, K. (2011). *The digital revolution and higher education: College presidents, public differ on value of online learning.* Retrieved from http://www.pewinternet.org/~/ media//Files/Reports/2011/PIP-Online Learning.pdf

Porter, J. (2009). Recovering delivery for digital rhetoric. *Computers and Composition, 26*(4), 207–224. doi:10.1016/j.compcom.2009.09.004

Richardson, J. T. (1999). Centralizing governance isn't simply wrong; it's bad business, too. *Chronicle of Higher Education.* Retrieved from http://chronicle.com/article/Centralizing Governance-Isnt/8672

Sapkota, K., & Vander Putten, J. (2018). Social media acceptance and usage by business communications faculty. *Business and Professional Communication Quarterly, 81*(3), 328–350. doi:10.1177/2329490618777818

Seaman, J. E., Allen, I. E., & Seaman, J. (2018). *Grade Increase: Tracking Distance Education in the United States.* Retrieved from https://www.onlinelearningsurvey.com/highered.html

Sexton, J., & Bollinger, L. C. (2002). Fostering collaboration in higher education. *Bulletin - American Academy of Arts and Sciences, 55*(3), 59–68. doi:10.2307/3824212

Sheeran, N., & Cummings, D. J. (2018). An examination of the relationship between Facebook groups attached to the university courses and student engagement. *Higher Education, 76*(6), 937–955. doi:10.100710734-018-0253-2

Singel, R. (2005, Oct. 6) Are you ready for Web 2.0? *Wired.* Retrieved from http://www. wired.com/science/discoveries/news/2005/10/69114

Sloan Consortium. (2012). *Changing course: Ten years of tracking online education in the United States.* Retrieved from http://sloanconsortium.org/publications/survey /changing_course_2012

Smith, A., & Anderson, M. (2018). *Social Media Use in 2018: A majority of Americans use Facebook and YouTube, but young adults are especially heavy users of Snapchat and Instagram.* Retrieved from http://www.pewinternet.org/2018/ 03/01/social-media-use-in2018/

Sorcinelli, M. D., & Yun, J. (2007). From mentor to mentoring networks: Mentoring in the new academy. *Change, 39*(6), 58–61. doi:10.3200/CHNG.39.6.58-C4

Thelin, J. (2004). *A history of American higher education*. Baltimore, MD: The Johns Hopkins University Press.

Trabold, B. (2009). Walking the cliff's edge: The new nation's rhetoric of resistance in apartheid South Africa [Excerpt]. *College Composition and Communication, 61*(2), 372.

Welch, K. (1990). Electrifying classical rhetoric: Ancient media, modern technology, and contemporary composition. *Journal of Advanced Composition, 10*(1), 22–38.

Yancey, K. B. (2009). *Writing in the 21ˢᵗ Century*. Urbana, IL: National Council of Teachers of English.

Yin, R. K. (2011). *Qualitative research from start to finish*. New York, NY: Guilford Press.

You, X. (2005). Ideology, textbooks, and the rhetoric of production in China. *College Composition and Communication, 56*(4), 632–653.

This research was previously published in Enriching Collaboration and Communication in Online Learning Communities; pages 186-206, copyright year 2020 by Information Science Reference (an imprint of IGI Global).

Chapter 59

The Effectiveness of Self–Directed English Learning through SNS:
Adopting Facebook based on Gamification

Eun-Sok Won
Mokwon University, Daejeon, South Korea

Jeong-Ryeol Kim
Korea National University of Education, Cheongju, South Korea

ABSTRACT

This article suggests an efficient self-directed learning method that will help improve students' actual English ability by adopting Facebook, which is one of the most represented social networking services (SNS). The purpose of this article is to present a practical way in which to implement SNS-based, self-directed English learning by applying useful concepts from gamification and to ascertain the effectiveness of this method.

INTRODUCTION

As social network services (SNS) such as Facebook, Twitter, and smartphones have emerged, they have affected various fields including economics, industry, culture, and even education (Koo, Yoo, & Choi, 2010). In the English educational field, teaching and learning via smart technologies and services have spread widely, covering drawbacks in traditional methods. As a result of these changes, it has become important to consider how to practically and efficiently adopt SNS in the design of English classes.

SNS are the most appropriate representations of Web 2.0 technology and emphasize the value of openness, participation, and sharing. They provide users with the ability to communicate, participate, collaborate, and cooperate anytime and anywhere. In education, by utilizing Facebook to learn, students

DOI: 10.4018/978-1-6684-7123-4.ch059

are able to study without being restricted by time and space and to connect various media such as photos, videos, and texts as well as hypertext.

Since 2000, the Ministry of Education has established "Guidelines for the Operation of Information and Communication Technology Education for Elementary and Secondary Schools" (2005) to establish and propel various policies meant to strengthen information and communication technology (ICT) education. The most important concept of the guide was the recommended use of ICT in all subjects for more than 10% of the course materials. This means that students, who already live in a smart technology environment, will be able to effectively utilize smart technologies in their learning activities and concurrently improve their ability to naturally do so in solving the problems they face in their daily lives.

In this study, Facebook was selected as the main material in an English class of 52 adult learners. To propel their self-directed English education, the learning and teaching procedures were designed by utilizing useful elements of gamification. The class was implemented for six weeks, during which we collected data such as the participants' opinions, which were gathered through interviews and emails, and reviews in the form of Facebook replies. We also analyzed survey responses.

LITERATURE REVIEW

Facebook in Education

An SNS is a communication channel that emphasizes the values of openness, participation, and sharing. It provides users with the ability to communicate, participate, and collaborate at anytime and anywhere (Park & Park, 2014). Boyd and Ellison (2008) suggested that SNS could be used to (1) allow individuals to build their own personal information publicly or semi-publicly within a particular system, (2) provide a list of other users with whom they are affiliated, and (3) serve as a web-based service that allows you to browse a list of networks that other users have as well as a list of networks that others have in the system (Kang & Chang, 2015).

The most widely used SNS in the world is Facebook, which was founded by Mark Zucherberg and initiated on February 4, 2004. Anyone aged 13 years or over can easily join by providing their name, e-mail address, date of birth, and gender. Therefore, when using Facebook as a teaching and learning material, there are advantages such as ease of use, ease of securing the participants, and creating less burden on the system's utilization capability (Kang & Chang, 2015; Hasan, Ozlem, & Mehmet, 2017).

The basic functions of Facebook consist of one's "Profile," which shows their personal details and preferences; "Wall," where users can post diverse digital contents such as text messages, pictures, video clips, etc.; "Status," which informs the user's friends of his or her current location and activities; "Message," where users write and send private messages to each other; "News Feed," which shows the user's profile and new posts from his or her friends; "Like" button, which allows the user to indicate preference to someone else's post; and various content management functions.

Based on the concept of converting offline human networks to online relationships, Facebook has expanded continuously in the forms of information sharing, knowledge creation, and collective intelligence, beyond the mere strengthening of its original concept (Kim & Lee, 2011; Boyd & Ellison, 2007). The functions and features of Facebook have influenced the field of education by increasing the possibility of creating new types of learning and teaching activities.

If learning and teaching has until now been conducted only through restricted methods and limited educational environments, new open structures like Facebook will allow learners with various interests and needs to experience the most suitable learning contents and instructions delivered via the network (Um, 2011).

The changes caused by the appearance of SNS in the learning and teaching environment are emphasizing Social Learning, which utilizes SNS as a learning platform and changes teaching and learning methods and activities (Hasan, Ozlem, & Mehmet, 2017; Um, 2011; Cho, 2011). Social Learning refers to the learning of information sharing and interaction among learners by utilizing various SNS, such as Facebook, Twitter, Instagram, and so on. TED and iTunes U, which present world-famous and excellent university lectures free of charge on the internet, are early models of Social Learning. Social Learning in the face-to-face learning environment is also considered positive because of the possibility of enhancing social interactions and communications in the class (Park & Lim, 2012).

Gamification

Gamification means complementing or reinforcing an existing system by adapting the strong attributes (immersion, fun, and sustainability) of games to other fields (Huh, Kim, & Seo, 2016).

Figure 1. Concept of gamification

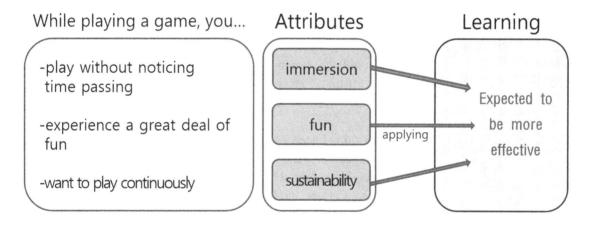

Figure 1 illustrates the concept of gamification. Looking at the picture, one can see that if a user playing a game experiences fun, he or she will be so immersed in the game that the passage of time goes unnoticed. Here, the keywords "fun," "immersion," and "sustainability" can be elicited, and the application of these attributes to learning is defined as gamification. Therefore, gamification focuses on devising and planning specific ways to enhance effectiveness and efficiency by adapting the users' powerful experiences during game play (Won, 2015).

Although gamification is based on game play, it focuses on experiences that can be encountered during game play process rather than focusing on game content itself. In other words, the identity of the precise game is not important but rather what is experienced through playing a game. Consequently, identifying how to utilize the experiences from playing interesting games is the core of gamification (see Figure 2).

Figure 2. Main approaches of gamification

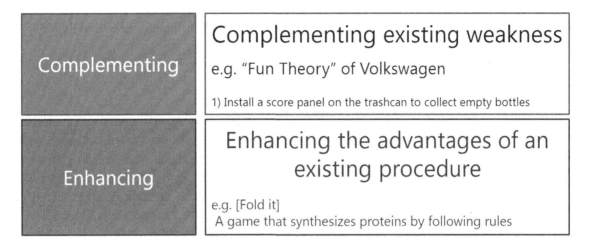

Self-Directed Learning

Self-directed learning is the process in which learners diagnose their needs, set their own goals, and meet these goals by selecting the materials and resources required to achieve them and self-evaluating their own performances (Seoul Education Training Institute, 1998).

Self-directed learning has been defined differently according to the viewpoints of scholars. Knowles used self-directed learning as a learning process in which a learner has authority in diagnosing his or her own needs, setting goals, identifying material and learning resources, and selecting and implementing appropriate learning strategies (1975). Smith argues that self-directed learning is a process by which learners perform learning tasks in their own ways in an environment where they control their overall education (1982).

In other words, success in self-directed learning requires the ability to choose one's learning contents, time, method, and place, to set realistic goals, to discover learning resources, and to select and execute learning strategies. In addition, as learners concentrate on their own education, it becomes possible to overcome individual disabilities, maintain motivation, predict progress, and evaluate results.

Self-directed learning does not simply mean learning individually but rather in cooperation with various helpers, such as teachers, tutors, human resources, peers, textbooks, and educational institutions. Learners are primarily responsible for planning, executing, and evaluating the entirety of their learning. In other words, it is the essence of self-directed learning that students are granted autonomy and initiative in the entire learning process, from design to evaluation.

METHODS

Participants

Because one of main focuses in this study is the maintenance of learners' autonomy, 52 adults who use Facebook regularly were selected as research participants. They were selected from among the researchers' 1,431 Facebook friends. The purpose of this study is to examine how much the English abilities of the participants had increased in the domain of four skills (speaking, listening, reading, and writing) while they conducted the allotted learning tasks by themselves. The research can be roughly divided into three stages: preparation, research, and summarization.

Research Design

The first step was research design preparation. Through a literature review, data on the characteristics of Facebook, its usages in educational purposes, and its educational priorities were collected. Along with these, the goals of the research and practical implementation methods were drawn. The second stage was the research itself. First, examples and questions based on English reading and listening skills were collected, which were closely related to the needs of the participants. In addition, by gathering the opinions of the participants who were asked to conduct pilot tasks, the examples and questions were revised and supplemented to secure their reliability and validity (Won & Shin, 2013).

Through the aforementioned process, it was possible to grasp the needs of the participants, and finally, the main purpose of the tasks was set to enhance the ability to deal with the Test of English for International Communication (TOEIC). To collect meaningful data through this research, all of the comments and replies from the participants were gathered. An online survey was also conducted, and 47 participants answered the questionnaires. All of the data were integrated and analyzed.

Activities

In order to evaluate the English competence and preference of the participants, the participants were presented with 20 TOEIC examples that the researchers had selected after twice cross-checking that they contained the four English skills. We chose TOEIC examples because most of the participants wanted to take lessons based on the TOEIC.

Reading Activities

The preliminary reading materials used in the beginning stage of the course were elicited from newspaper articles related to travel in order to pique the students' interest. All of the articles were composed of three paragraphs, and the participants were asked to summarize what they read in a few sentences, and to make a list of those words that they did not understand (see Figure 3).

After two weeks, when the participants became accustomed to the routine of the lesson, reading passages from TOEIC Part 7 were presented instead of news articles. In this stage, learners were asked to solve the examples attached to the reading passages. After that, the participants checked the answer key for each example and then asked the instructor about anything that they did not understand or examples that they failed to correctly solve. The instructor responded to the learners' questions via "Reply," and if the instructor thought that it was necessary to communicate with the inquirer personally, they sent messages through "Direct Message."

Figure 3. Example of the reading activity

Listening Activities

The listening practice material used during the first and second weeks was a video clip from TED-Ed, "Who is Alexander von Humboldt?" by George Mehler. It was a 4-minute and 22-second video introducing the accomplishments of von Humboldt, and it depicts his achievements via images and video to help viewers understand the contents. All of the participants were asked to summarize what von Humboldt achieved in three sentences. After that, the participants check other learners' answers and compared them with each other's. This activity was intended to encourage learners to write and listen together (Figure 4).

Figure 4. Example of a Listening Activity

Two weeks later, the participants were presented with questions from TOEIC Parts 3 and 4. The sample structure of Part 3 is a dialogue between two or three speakers with three questions. The sample structure of Part 4 is a monologue of one speaker dealing with various themes (notifications, speeches, advertisements, events, etc.) with three questions. The learner was to solve the presented listening questions, confirm the correct answers, and then ask the instructor questions.

Survey

To understand the participants' interest and confidence in using Facebook in the study of English, a survey was carried out before and after the instruction was given. The questionnaires consisted of 12 questions. Through a factor analysis, all of the questions were classified into one of two categories: "Efficacy of using Facebook in an English class" and "Effect of using Facebook in an English class." (see Table 1 and Table 2)

Table 1. Questionnaires on the efficacy of using Facebook in an English class

No.	Efficacy of using Facebook in an English class	α values if deleted
1	I like studying English.	.756
2	I know how to study English well.	.764
3	I can understand what the teacher says during the lesson.	.755
4	I can understand the reading passages of the TOEIC well.	.712
5	I can understand well when listening to the dialogues and monologues of the TOEIC.	.745
	Overall reliability	.778

Note: Test of English for International Communication (TOEIC)

Table 2. Questionnaires on the effect of using Facebook in an English class

No	Effect of using Facebook in an English class	α values if deleted
6	English lessons using Facebook will help improve my English competence.	.899
7	English lessons using Facebook will improve my English reading skill.	.910
8	English lessons using Facebook will improve my English listening skill.	.902
9	I will become interested in English reading through this instruction.	.892
10	Compared to other methods, English instruction using Facebook will help improve my English reading competence.	.904
11	Compared to other methods, English instruction using Facebook will help improve my English listening competence.	.908
12	I can understand the learning contents provided in this instruction.	.899
	Overall reliability	.912

As a result of the factor analysis, the efficacy of English learning could be determined by using all five items. In the reliability verification that was conducted to understand the consistency among the questions, the alpha value was .801, showing a high consistency.

This category was composed of seven items in total, and the alpha value was .933, indicating a high consistency. All of the responses were converted into analytical data after coding. To compare the results from before and after survey objectively, a paired sample t test was conducted to verify the differences between the two categories: the efficacy of using Facebook in an English class and the effect of using Facebook in an English class.

By utilizing the statistical analysis program SPSS 13.0, the aforementioned comparison was implemented. Based on the fiducial significance judgment point of 0.05, the significance was divided into three levels.

RESULTS AND DISCUSSION

Opinions from Interviews

At the conclusion of the research, the researchers conducted interviews with 15 participants who were selected through random sampling. An overall analysis of the opinions from the interviews revealed two topics: "The advantages of self-directed English learning using Facebook," and "The difficulties of self-directed English learning using Facebook." Detailed results were as follows.

First, most of the participants thought that it was good to be exposed to English (TOEIC) study every day. In addition, solving the questions in a short amount of time was more efficient than studying for a long period of time. As for the amount of learning, the students were able to adjust the amount according to their environments and circumstances, and they found this helpful. For example, they could control the amount of learning, such as doing three or four days' worth of tasks in a single day if they had failed to do them regularly. The main feature of self-directed learning using Facebook that was mentioned the most was that learners were able to confirm the answers and explanations in real time while studying the items according to their own levels (see Figure 5).

Figure 5. Students' opinions on the advantages of self-directed learning

"When I get up every morning, I check for news and updates on Facebook on my phone. I begin my day with solving tasks" (Yang, male).

"It is not easy to study because I work, but after lunch I was able to do the learning task. It is good that I can check the answer and explanation immediately" (Won, female).

"I tried to solve the questions one by one, but I always forget it again. It was nice to be able to solve it again and again" (Goo, female).

By summarizing the students' opinions on the difficulties of self-directed English learning, it was possible to categorize them into two domains. The first was study difficulties caused by a lack of further information while learning. They required clear explanations regarding their questions, but the answers they received were not sufficient for them to understand by only checking the reply; the replies often failed to fully explain why the answer was correct. When this occurred, they tended to end the self-directed learning in the form of simply asking for help in order to obtain accurate answers rather than try to solve the problems themselves (see Figure 6).

Figure 6. Students' opinions about the drawbacks of self-directed learning

"I want the teacher to explain the correct answer and explanation in detail" (Go, female).

"I could not be assured that my answer was correct" (Yang, male).

"When many other posts come up, the comments about learning tasks go down. So, it was difficult for me to find them and to solve the questions by myself" (Han, female).

Finally, self-directed learning involves studying with self-awareness of one's goals. However, the participants sometimes delaying their learning due to how busy they were, and it was difficult for them to make decisions in this situation. Some of them mentioned that if there was no alarm from the researchers, they would fail to catch up on the curriculum properly. This can be regarded as a deficient self-directed learning state, which shows that they did not completely deviate from the control of the teacher.

Results of the Survey

The efficacy of self-directed English learning using SNS increased from 3.47 in the pre-survey to 3.70 in the post survey, which was statistically significant. Therefore, it can be concluded that the efficacy of self-directed English learning increased after the participants had conducted learning tasks through Facebook. In other words, it can be stated that the students' opinions about studying English on their own were enhanced (see Table 3).

Table 3. Efficacy of self-directed English learning using a social network service

Categories	Pre/Post	N	Mean	Std. deviation	Mean difference	t-Value	Sig.
Efficacy	Pre	51	3.47	.599	-.23	-2.72*	.011
	Post	47	3.70	.632			
Effectiveness	Pre	51	3.41	.599	-.36	-2.18*	.038
	Post	47	3.77	.632			

The response regarding the effectiveness of self-directed English learning using SNS felt by the learners rose from 2.13 to 3.81, which shows statistical significance. Therefore, it can be suggested that the learners' belief in the effectiveness of using SNS in an English class increased. In other words, it can be stated that conducting English learning tasks using Facebook positively affected the learners' attitudes about the effectiveness of doing so.

CONCLUSION

In order to enhance English learning ability through SNS, this study examined how the self-directed English learning ability of adult students using Facebook can be changed through six weeks of activities. By conducting online interviews, detailed opinions on the advantages and drawbacks of self-directed English learning with SNS were presented.

One of the greatest advantages was that learners were able to study as much as they wanted, to check the results of their activities, and to interact not only with other learners but with the instructor, as well, in real time. On the other hand, the difficulties drawn from this research were that learners should participate of their own volition and that it was difficult for them to participate continuously.

As for the results of the survey, opinions about both the efficacy and effectiveness of the use of SNS in an English class were enhanced significantly through the implementation of the research instruction. The results of the survey about studying English on their own were enhanced, and conducting English learning tasks using Facebook positively affected the learners' attitudes.

This study has significance in proving that English learning can be easily conducted at any time through Facebook by using a portable device or computer. To accelerate the usage of SNS in English learning, it is also necessary to adapt self-directed learning in a way that makes it possible for learners to use their time efficiently and makes their study more meaningful and influential.

Further, it is important that learning contents and notifications are provided continuously in order to maintain the students' attention and motivation. Even if the students are all adults, it is easy for them to fail to consistently stay abreast of their course work in self-directed learning. Therefore, it is recommended that they create their own archives of learning materials and information when making decisions and setting learning goals.

ACKNOWLEDGMENT

This research was supported by the Ministry of Education of the Republic of Korea and the National Research Foundation of Korea [NRF-2016S1A5A8019764].

REFERENCES

Boyd, D. M., & Ellison, N. B. (2008). Social Network Sites: Definition, History, and Scholarship. *Journal of Computer-Mediated Communication*, *13*(1), 210–230. doi:10.1111/j.1083-6101.2007.00393.x

Cho, Y. K. (2011). *Social Learning Platform Design on Facebook* [MA Dissertation]. Ewha Womans University, Seoul.

Hasan, K., Ozlem, C., & Mehmet, K. (2017). Impact of the educational use of Facebook group on the high school students' proper usage of language. *Education and Information Technologies, 22*(2), 677–695. doi:10.100710639-015-9428-y

Huh, J. H., Kim, H. B., & Seo, K. R. (2016). A Design of Smart-based Education Gamification Platform Using Mobile Devices for Digital Content. *International Journal of Multimedia and Ubiquitous Engineering, 11*(12), 101–114. doi:10.14257/ijmue.2016.11.12.10

Kang, S. Y., & Chang, J. H. (2015). A Study of the Effects of Writing Instruction Using EBSe and SNS on Students' Writing Ability, *Secondary. English Education, 8*(1), 3–27.

Kim, K. S., & Lee, S. Y. (2011). A Case Study of Informal Learning on Office Workers Utilize SNS. *HRD Research., 13*(4), 1–31.

Knowles, M. S. (1975). Self-directed Learning: A Guide for Learners. Chicago: Follett Publishing Co.

Koo, C. H., Yoo, Y. S., & Choi, K. M. (2010). *Facebook What it is and How to use.* Seoul: The Soop.

Ministry of Education. (2005). *Guidelines for the Operation of Information and Communication Technology Education for Elementary and Secondary Schools.* KERIS.

Park, S., & Park, S. H. (2014). A Study on the Effects of the UCCs-producing Activity through SNS in Primary English Class, *Primary. English Education, 20*(2), 105–135.

Park, S. Y., & Lim, G. (2012). Suggestions for Building 'Smart Campus' Based on Case Studies on the Effectiveness of Instructions with Smart-Pads. *Journal of Digital Convergence, 10*(3), 1–12.

Seoul Education Training Institute. (1998). *Theory and Practice of Self-directed Learning for Open Education.* Seoul: MunSung Publishing.

Smith, R. M. (1982). *Learning how to learn: Applied theory for Adults.* Chicago: Follett Publishing Co.

Um, D. J. (2011). *Analysis of the 3 major factors of social learning platform* [MA Dissertation]. Han-Yang University, Seoul.

Won, E. S. & Shin, S. J. (2013). Suggesting a developmental direction of Smart-learning English education based on a survey toward the use of mobile devices by university students. *The Mirae Journal of English Language and Literature, 18*(2), 225-249.

Won, E. S. (2015). Analyzing Game Interfaces for Adapting Games in English Learning and Teaching, *Journal of Korea Game society, 15*(2), 131-144.

This research was previously published in the International Journal of Mobile and Blended Learning (IJMBL), 10(3); pages 1-10, copyright year 2018 by IGI Publishing (an imprint of IGI Global).

Chapter 60
Diversifying Content Across Social Media Platforms

Maggie Clarke
California State University, Dominguez Hills, USA

Jillian Eslami
California State University, Dominguez Hills, USA

ABSTRACT

In this chapter, the authors describe how a committee of librarians' project to revamp the social media presence at a public comprehensive university library has helped foster deeper student engagement. By temporarily restructuring the library social media committee into subcommittees and assigning each one a single social media platform, librarians were able to develop stronger understanding of the content, norms, and audience of each platform and create more diverse and targeted content for each. This change has resulted in increased interaction with students across all platforms leading to higher attendance at library events. Preliminary findings also suggest that increased student engagement has the potential to illuminate opportunities for partnership across campus.

INTRODUCTION

Social media has a huge presence in students' lives. With students increasingly invested in an ever-changing social media landscape, librarians concerned with meeting students at their point of need cannot ignore the importance of social media. This constantly evolving mode of communication is now an essential way for academic libraries to connect with their students, faculty, and the larger academic community. At the same time the need for academic libraries to demonstrate their value, often by quantifying their impact on student success, makes it increasingly important that libraries take measures to maintain their visibility in the campus community and in students' academic lives.

As Clark and Melancon observed, social media has changed marketing into an interactive media which encourages "two-way conversations (Clark & Melancon, 2013, p. 132). Social media allows academic libraries to both tell students about events and resources and invite student response at various levels.

DOI: 10.4018/978-1-6684-7123-4.ch060

This chapter will describe how the University Library at California State University Dominguez Hills (CSUDH) is using social media to more effectively facilitate these interactions in support of the library's Vision. CSUDH University Library defines its Vision as the desire to:

- Be the center of intellectual and creative life at CSUDH, facilitating teaching, learning, research, intellectual inquiry, and curiosity.
- Be an innovative, collaborative, inclusive, and flexible organization that provides responsive, learner-centered services and technologies that meet the evolving information, curricular, and research needs of CSUDH students, faculty, and staff and the surrounding community.
- Provide vibrant, welcoming, and engaging learner-centered physical **and virtual spaces** [emphasis ours] that facilitate innovation, collaboration, and boundary-free access to information. (CSUDH, 2018)

In the spirit of innovation, flexibility, and centering learners embedded in this Vision, the University Library makes it a priority to meet students where they are. Students who cannot come to campus and visit the library in person, who are enrolled in distance education programs, or who suffer from library anxiety, all have the option of accessing help from a librarian online via chat reference, virtual research consultation meetings, or library email. It is the authors' hope that the library's social media presence will function not only as a marketing tool but as an extension of the library's virtual spaces. Social media includes all students who follow-- regardless of if they are on campus students can read a tweet or see a post on Instagram. Students can access the library and its various social platforms at their leisure, and decide whether they want to utilize a resource or attend an event. They can also learn more about the library's resources and services without having to visit in person or consciously choose to seek out that information on our website. Using social media in this way has the potential to bridge the gap between feeling comfortable in the library and avoiding it due to library anxiety. A student may be less inclined to talk to other students in person about a library event, a book, or a resource, but have no qualms about posting or replying to a comment on Twitter or Facebook. The usage of social media goes beyond advertisement and promotion of the library to engage and support the students as well (Mellon, 2015).

In this chapter, the authors will describe how a project to revamp the social media presence by a committee of librarians at a public comprehensive university library beginning in January 2018 has helped increase attendance at library related events and fostered deeper student engagement. By restructuring the library social media committee into smaller groups and assigning each one a single social media platform, the different accounts have evolved unique voices suited to the content, norms, and audience of each platform. The decision to offer different information across each, or the same information in a variety of ways, allows the committee to better tailor the content on each platform to its audience based on students' feedback and engagement.

BACKGROUND

In considering social media as a tool for promoting student engagement, the natural question to begin with is whether students are willing to interact with library social media accounts at all. In 2015, roughly two-thirds of adults reported using social media, up from just 7% in 2005. Though this increase can be seen across all demographics, it is most marked among the demographic associated with the majority of college students: young adults. Participation in social media for this demographic has risen from 12% in 2005 to over 90% in 2015 (Perrin, 2015). Among young adults, surveys indicate that Instagram and Snapchat are the most used social media platforms, followed by Facebook and Twitter (Alhabash & Ma, 2017; Anderson & Smith, 2018). Despite this variance in popularity, 71% of young adults use more than one social media platform suggesting that an effective social media plan will need to keep in mind the needs of multi-modal users (Lenhart, 2017).

As for how and why students (and others) use social media, research suggests that, depending on the platform, what users hope to find on social media (as opposed to what they hope to communicate to others) can be distilled into three primary categories: entertainment, social interaction, and information seeking (Whiting & Williams, 2013; Brookbank, 2015) . Though entertainment and social interaction may fall somewhat out of the scope of an academic librarian's area of expertise, recognizing our social media feeds as an information source for university students, faculty, staff, and outside stakeholders makes developing a strong social media presence integral to meeting students at their point of information need. As early as 2001, the American Library Association was reporting on the perceived benefits of an effective social media presence for libraries (ALA, 2001). Since then research on libraries and social media has illustrated that academic libraries have used their social media feeds as tools to share announcements about library events, photos, and resources (Chen, Chu, & Xu, 2012; Hendrix et al., 2009; Jacobson, 2011; Lihn, 2008), to define their brand and encourage positive perceptions of the library (Harrison, et al., 2017), and as a means to communicate directly with students (Ntaka, 2017).

Of course, just because both students and libraries use social media does not guarantee they are engaging with one another. Huber, et al. (2018) address this question in their study using a recent study from Purdue University in which students were surveyed electronically about their perceptions and preferences related to academic libraries on social media. They found 40% of students responded that they were either "very likely "or "somewhat likely" to follow the library on Instagram and Twitter. The specific information needs students' bring to library social media are addressed by Stivilia and Gibradze (2017) who note that students find "postings related to operations updates, study support services, and events as the most useful." These findings demonstrate general agreement between what students consider to be the most useful content available from library social media platforms and the content being prioritized by libraries themselves. However, it is worth noting that the studies above utilize students' self-reported data to predict the potential for student engagement with library social media accounts. In considering the efficacy of academic library social media analytic data is also an essential component to assessing impact (King, 2015). Furthermore, though the demographic and qualitative data presented above has been foundational for our team in forming a more robust and effective social media plan, it is essential to recognize that social media is defined by its mutability. There can be no doubt that these numbers will change as platforms evolve and new social media networks arise. Frequently revisiting the available literature on both academic libraries in social media, and broader trends in social media use, is recommended to maintain librarians' facility with social media technology and trends, and develop responsive strategies to inevitable changes.

MAIN FOCUS OF THE CHAPTER

Issues, Controversies and Problems

A close examination of the previous social media policy revealed that, though well-intentioned, encouraging ad hoc posting by all members of the social media committee across all platforms resulted in inconsistency in terms of frequency and content of posts as well as excessive repetition- all of which negatively impacted student engagement. While the overall idea was to promote the library by ensuring the same information was presented on all platforms, frequent cross posting does not account for each platform being better suited for certain types of information and promotion. Twitter, though known for its brevity, did increase its character count from 140 characters to 280 characters in late 2017 (Rosen & Ihara, 2017). While having the character count doubled did help in creating longer posts, Twitter remains best suited to short and incisive posts, usually accompanied by hashtags that help circulate the information by making it easier for other users to find. Facebook, on the other hand, has a huge character limit (over 60,000 characters for a text post with no images or video), making it more appropriate for longer, text-heavy information such as events with more details. Additionally, while hashtags can be used on Facebook, our experience suggests that they are not as effective as they are on Twitter for making information accessible. These two platforms are a good example of how cross-posting identical material to both accounts ultimately ignores the affordances and weakness of each platform, as well as users' expectations for the content they will find there. What can be said on Twitter, can be expanded on Facebook. Unfortunately, in the past, the committee would schedule the same content, verbatim, across both, under utilizing both platforms.

Additionally, changes to the sorting and display algorithms of Facebook and Instagram in 2018 (Gollin, 2018a; Gollin, 2018b) seriously impact the number of impressions being generated by our social media content. As a public institution, the University Library welcomes community engagement in our physical and virtual spaces, however much of what appears on our social media platforms is naturally of limited interest to those not affiliated with our university. Even before developing documentation surrounding committee goals and outcomes, general consensus in the group was that communicating with the campus community was our primary mandate rather than merely gathering large numbers of followers. With no budget for proprietary tools to gather rich data on engagement with our social media platforms the committee had never made a consistent practice of documenting changes in our social media account analytics beyond discussion of number of followers for each account. However, after a noticeable drop in engagement with our Facebook page, illustrated in Figure 1, we began monitoring our page's reach.

Facebook defines reach as "the number of people who had any content from your Page or about your Page enter their screen" ("What's the difference between Page views and Page reach on Facebook?", 2018). We discovered that between October 1, 2017 and March 31, 2018 our page Reach had plummeted by 80.5%. In order to adapt to these changes (and changes which will certainly arise in the future), a revitalized social media strategy was necessary.

Figure 1. Weekly Facebook reaches

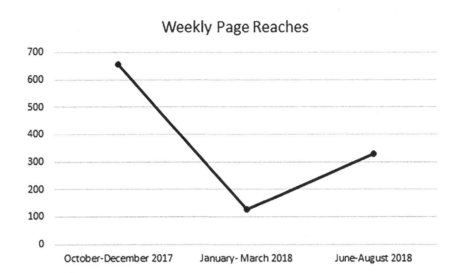

SOLUTIONS AND RECOMMENDATIONS

The first step towards redeveloping the social media team was to look at the existing committee and how it had been structured in the previous academic year, 2016-17. The committee was relatively new and most of the social media platforms for the institution had only been created only in the previous three years. Furthermore, the committee itself had experienced numerous changes in membership with librarian involvement fluctuating from semester to semester. The only criteria to be a part of the committee was the desire to be on it and no specializations or explicit time commitments were required. The social media committee for the 2017-18 academic year was ultimately a team of six librarians, each with full time-appointments in Reference, Outreach, and Instruction Services (RIOS) or Circulation, Acquisitions and Processing Services (CAPS), as well as campus service and scholarship responsibilities.

Once the new team was formed, the next step to revitalizing our social media presence was a thorough review and revision of committee goals including creating schedules for posting and documenting the type of content desirable to create and promote. No previous documentation surrounding outcomes for engaging with students via social media, goals for the social media committee, or responsibilities of its members was available and the lack of clear vision as to the purpose of the library's social media presence was immediately identified as a key issue in need of redress. In order to provide necessary guidance in creating committee policy the following goals were adopted:

- Reach out and engage the students, staff and faculty of CSUDH
- Cultivate an open, professional and responsive dialogue with our users in order to meet them at their point of need
- Promote the value and importance of services offered by the faculty and staff of the CSUDH Library
- Advertise library and campus events to increase student attendance
- Promote research tips and useful tools for scholarship to aid student and faculty research

In light of these clarified goals, a strategic plan of how to enact them while respecting the already full schedules of our committee members was essential. A decision was made to create subcommittees for each of our active social media platforms: Facebook, Twitter, Instagram, and our institutional student engagement network, Torolink. This structure would allow each subcommittee to develop a unique voice for their platform rather than merely cross posting, as well as to assess and respond to student engagement with that specific platform. This policy was documented in a departmental social media style guide created using Springshare's LibGuides, which also outlines the mission, goals, and vision of our social media presence. This social media guide also includes best practices, styles guidelines for creating posts across different platforms, and university-wide social media policies. The social media guide was also a resource for finding successful hashtags and peak times for posting which all committee members' reference when planning their social media posts.

In creating the subcommittees, the hope was that each team would then create the content with the platforms unique features in mind. Some examples of this would be short, brief tweets with eye-catching images and relevant hashtags on Twitter. For Facebook, similar content could be used, but expanded in description and maybe with multiple images or links could be included to highlight and promote the library. Instagram is very image driven, so more emphasis might be placed on creating visual information, with shorter captions to accompany. The committee would get a list of upcoming library events that could be included as posts, compiled by the head of the committee. It would be up to the head to signify which events needed to be included, such as upcoming hour changes/holidays/events, and each team would then create the content as they saw fit.

As noted above, no requirements were imposed for committee members' experience with social media technology in order for them to join. In the midst of creating the smaller teams within the committee, some valuable professional development opportunities arose. Though committee members were enthusiastic about joining subcommittees, experience with using the platforms themselves was varied. As such, it became necessary to train the team in the different platforms. The value of having the small teams was so the content would vary, and that the individuals on the teams would feel most comfortable on the platform they signed up for. This presented the committee with a chance to delve into each platform and discuss not only what content would be best for each, but the most effective ways to employ each platform to maximize engagement. Though Twitter, Facebook, and Instagram are similar in many ways, each has its own nuances when it comes to creating and scheduling content as well as interacting with followers. In order to ensure all committee members were comfortable with the basics of their assigned platform, librarians worked together in informal peer training groups to address gaps in knowledge. This included a range of activities, such as signing up for an individual Instagram account to link to the library's account and the adding of members to the Facebook page administration page so everyone could approve or edit posts. There are opportunities here, depending on your institution and the committee's overall experience with social media, to offer workshops on the various platforms. Our committee also utilized Lynda.com, a proprietary platform for training and skill development videos subscribed to by University Library, as a training resource for more experienced librarians.

In order to remain aware of what content was being shared across platforms and to ease some of the time burden of creating and posting new content frequently, we began using a social media management system, Hootsuite, to schedule posts for each platform, as well as to manage cross posting of content. All committee members can access Hootsuite and schedule content. Using this service has made it easier for more events and programs to be advertised as it gives the members of the social media committee autonomy over posting.

Like many academic librarians, those on our social media committee were keenly aware of the discrepancy between services offered and student awareness of them. Reflected in the revised goals for our committee was the desire to increase student engagement not just online, but in the physical library. These changes to our social media activity coincided with (and were likely influenced by) an expansion of the University Library programming schedule to include multiple new workshops and events during the year and more Stress Relief Weeks programming, an ongoing, two week-long event hosted by the University Library to help students practice self-care during a possibly stressful time leading up to and during final exams. As such, we planned to assess our success not only by analytic changes related to our social media accounts (increased followers and interactions), but through increased student engagement with services and events like Finals Stress Relief Week and Open Access Week, program attendance, and participation in passive programming activities. Passive programming includes aspects of the event/program that does not need to be monitored or led by a librarian/library staff. An example would be a table stocked with coloring pages, markers/crayons/pencils, a table with an in progress puzzle, etc. These are programs where students, faculty and staff can participate in with no start or stop time.

Once committee members felt that they had develop sufficient proficiency with their platforms, the social media committee revised the subcommittee structure to allow more flexibility for members to post across all platforms if they chose. The social media committee for the 2018-19 academic year was also expanded to include full-time staff members who were interested in joining. The committee began blending the content, meeting once a month to create most or all of the content for the month and schedule it all out together. This approach helped the keep the committee accountable for their content and it also allowed them to address their social media commitment in full, for the month. This provided a solution for a lack of consistency of posting as well as enabled more content to be shared more efficiently. In scheduling out content as a team, the group is able to create a month's worth of content in just an hour. Consistency and efficiency, as well as accountability were the overall improvements the committee noticed.

Content

Though a voice which is in line with an individual library's goals, audience, and institutional requirements will of course be highly individual and largely dependent on the creativity of the librarians involved, here we will break down some of the content strategies which have proven useful for us. Due partly to limitations of the available analytics, these strategies were developed out of trial and error as well as our own observations of how users responded to differences in content across platforms.

In considering the library's "voice" across platforms, it is essential to consider the form content takes as this will necessarily affect how users communicate. It should also be noted that, though the content of each platform as a whole is tailored to that platform and audience, there are some instances of cross posting identical or very similar content across platforms. This is both for efficiency and because some content works well for all or most platforms. Figure 2 describes the types of content we have found to be most appropriate for each platform based on the the platforms' features and user engagement.

The library focuses primarily on original content across all platforms (not reposts or retweets), using free, online design applications such as Canva and Piktochart, as well as utilizing Creative Common licensed images whenever possible. The library also makes use of popular "days", such as "National Coffee Day", "International High Five Day", etc., as material for content creation. Promotion of library events, hours, holidays, research tools, or a highlight of the print collection are other examples of content that can be created. The library might make three different posts, all promoting the same service, but in different ways that suit the platform the best. For example, if we are highlighting a new online tutorial, we might make a Facebook post that describes the tutorial and who might find it useful. The post would also include videos as well as provide a direct link. For Twitter, we might include a simpler description and a direct link, along with appropriate hashtags to make the tweet more findable between users. Since Instagram does not allow for links in individual posts it would not be the best platform for this type of post, but if we were to include it we might create a screen grab of the tutorial or create a different image to accompany a caption with information on where students can find the video.

Figure 2. Types of content posted by platform. Note: AMA stands for Ask Me Anything, an invitation for followers to ask direct questions to an account

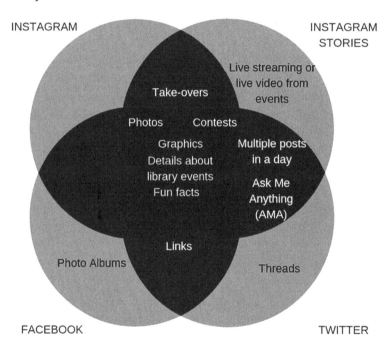

The library also attempts to utilize the unique features of each social media platform. For example, InstaStories allows users to create short-term post(s) that will only be available for 24 hours or stream live video which appears only on this platform. Facebook also has a "Stories" feature that can be used in the same way although we have seen significantly more engagement with InstaStories. This feature is a great tool for "live streaming" an event as it is happening or using it to engage with students directly by asking questions or creating a poll. The stories function can include live, in the moment content, and then filters, stickers, gifs, etc., can be added to them, or previously created content can be added and altered. Stories can also be added to a "highlights" reel, where your followers can view the stories indefinitely.

Below are examples of posts pertaining to passive Stress Relief Week programming from the end of the spring 2018 semester which illustrate how a single event can be represented differently across platforms.

Figure 3. A Facebook post from May 1, 2018 describing some of the passive programming being offered in the library for Stress Relief Weeks

Figure 4. A screen capture of an InstaStory about puzzles in the library from Stress Relief Weeks

Figure 5. A tweet from May 1, 2018 about passive programming in the library for Stress Relief Weeks

Though each of these posts has the same basic purpose- to inform students of some of the stress relieving activities that will be available to them in the library throughout their finals- the way the content is present on each platform is unique. Figure 3 includes a photograph from right after the table was set up. This static image is a visual representation of what is described in the text-- a table full of coloring sheets, crossword puzzles, and craft supplies. Since Facebook has no limits on the amount of text the description can be longer than on other platforms and the image can serve to illustrate what is found in the text and let students know what to look for if they want to make use of this service.

The same space is presented very differently in our InstaStory. As seen in Figure 4 the table is presented as a hub of collaborative activity giving students a sense of the experience of being there with other students. In addition to the screengrab shown here, our InstaStory included videos of students coloring and working on puzzles at the table. Rather than detailing the specific amenities available these images and videos speak for themselves (at times literally) rather than relying on significant amounts of text.

The tweet shown in Figure 5 includes a graphic rather than a photograph as well as briefer text than what is seen in the post from Figure 3. Because of Twitter's text limits some information, in this case, the location of the event, is provided in the image itself. Creating graphics which blend text and images allows more information to be shared without encountering character limits.

The library's voice across all the platforms aims to be professional, friendly and helpful, just as the librarians themselves. We want our students to not only become more aware of the events and resources the library has to offer, but also feel comfortable engaging and responding to the social media accounts.

Results

Since making the above changes to the library's social media strategy, student engagement across platforms has made significant increases in spite of algorithmic changes. As noted, our committee does not have a budget for advanced third-party analytics tools and has been reliant on Facebook and Instagram's "Insights" tools and Twitter's "Analytics" tool to gather data. In analyzing the available data our focus is on metrics which are most reflective of how many users are actually seeing and engaging with our content. However, engagement does not mean the same thing across platforms. For example, while Facebook Reach measures, "The number of people who had any content from your Page or about your Page enter their screen" Twitter Impressions measures the, "Number of times users are served your Tweet in timeline, search results, or from your profile" (emphasis ours) ("What's the difference between Page views and Page reach on Facebook?", 2018; "About account home," 2018). Facebook defines their Engagement metric as the number of post clicks, reactions, comments, and shares while Twitter measures engagement by, "Total number of times a user interacted with a Tweet. Clicks anywhere on the Tweet, including Retweets, replies, follows, likes, links, cards, hashtags, embedded media, username, profile photo, or Tweet expansion," ("Insights," 2018; "About your activity dashboard," 2018). Instagram likes and comments may be more transparent metrics to an average user but do not map easily to the metrics which are freely available from Twitter and Facebook. Because of these variances, as well as the subcommittee structure which encourages the librarians responsible for each platform to monitor and respond to the analytics for that platform, we have chosen to assess each platform's performance separately.

As seen in Figure 6, thus far Facebook has shown the greatest growth in engagement, which subverted the committee's initial belief that Instagram would be the most popular platform among students. Though continued algorithmic changes, evolving audiences, and the vagaries of the academic calendar all impact the reach of the library's social media presence, consistent growth can be seen on all platforms.

Figure 6. Average engagements per Facebook post

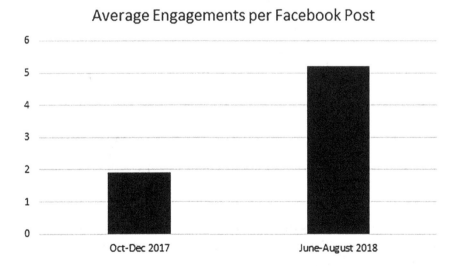

As indicated in Figure 7, average likes per Instagram post have increased by over 500% in the past year. Though growth in the average number of comments on Instagram posts has been less robust, Figure 8 also illustrates a clear upward trend.

Figure 7. Average likes per Instagram post

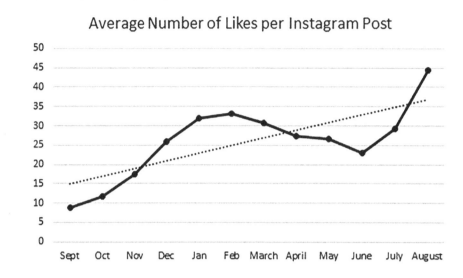

Figure 8. Average number of comments per Instagram post

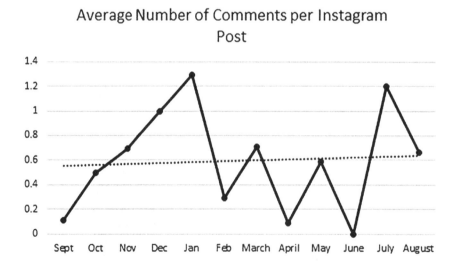

Though Figure 9 indicates significant fluctuation in average Tweet Impressions despite overall growth, Figure 10 illustrates that the overall percentage of users who see our content and engage with it is rising. This potentially indicates an improvement in the relevance and quality of content to our followers related to more frequent posting and close monitoring direct and indirect user feedback by the Twitter subcommittee.

Figure 9. Average impressions per Tweet

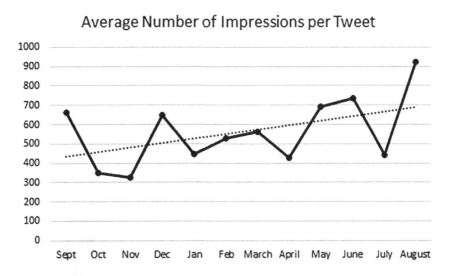

Figure 10. Average % engagement per Tweet

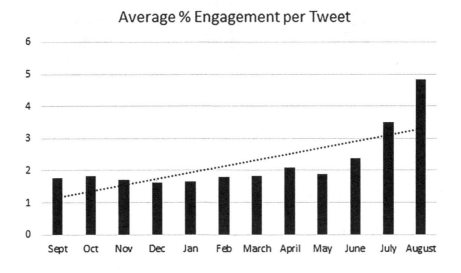

As previously discussed, though a useful tool, analytics are not the primary means by which our committee assesses success. Perhaps the most compelling area of growth affected by adopting a more structured approach to social media has been student participation in library events and programming. As indicated in Figure 11, between the Fall 2017 and Spring 2018 semesters, we have seen a 60% increase in attendance for active programming held within the library for Finals Stress Relief Week. Prior to our social media intervention, the library had minimal promotion of the events surrounding Finals Stress Relief Week, and student participation mirrored those efforts. Once a concerted effort was made towards engaging the students across multiple platforms, marketing events sufficiently resulted in a quick return on investment regarding student engagement and involvement. Part of the efforts made in breaking out the social media platforms into teams also involved the planning and scheduling of content, which made the promoting and marketing of events easier to manage. Increase of participation from students in the Fall of 2017 provided useful information as to what types of events students seemed most interested in and as a result, the events for the Spring 2018 semester were more tailored to what the students wanted, including more therapy dog visits and free drinks and snacks. Feedback was collected both in person with anonymous evaluations as well as online via the platforms polling and messaging features.

Figure 11. Participants in active programming during Stress Relief Week: 2017-2018

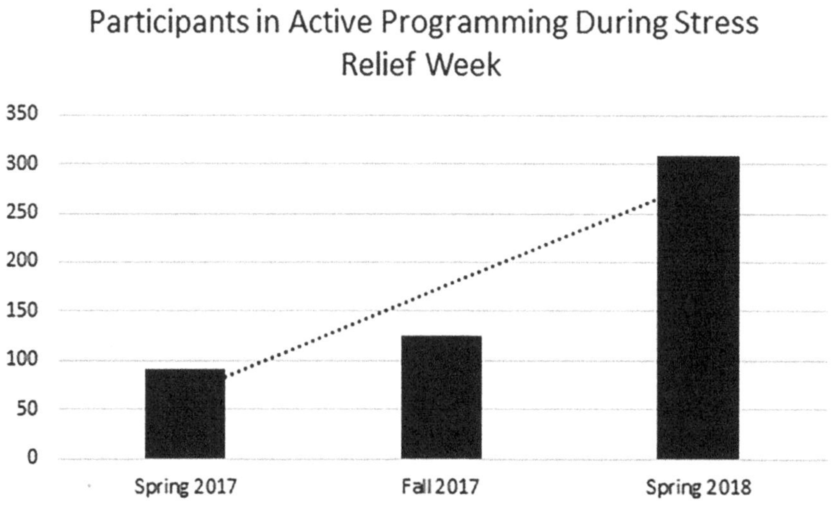

Participants in Active Programming During Stress Relief Week

While the committee currently does not have a structured schedule for posting content, studies have shown that because of current algorithms, posting consistently several times per week, rather than post-ing multiple times per day (sometimes characterized as spamming) to the accounts, not only increases visibility and engagement, but keep the pages relevant. Depending on the type of account you are rep-resenting, such as a brand page or a media page, posting once per day seemed to be the ideal number ("How often should you post on your Facebook pages?", 2011).

As much as consistency matters regarding engagement with the campus as a whole, content matters too. According to Harrison et al (2017), there has been little research done on the content that libraries choose to post, and with that the overall impact using social media libraries has in regards to the institution. In our case, the social media committee approaches content by aligning the medium with the purpose, using a design method similar to our instructional material design. The library attempts to create content in a variety of ways so that it can be viewed and comprehended in the variety of ways students learn. Facebook is great for promoting events and eliciting student engagement, as there is no real character limit, and pictures, as well as text, can be used. Twitter is better for smaller pieces of information, ac-companied with a picture/infographic in which students can digest the information in a more visual way. Instagram is the similar, in that it is more visually driven, even more so than Twitter, relying more on the graphic than the text. However, both Twitter and Instagram are better vehicles for promotion through hashtags(#), making the content easier to find to users who may not already be following the accounts.

Analysis of Perceived Content Effectiveness

One unanticipated boon to the reach of University Library's social media not reflected in these analytics has been expanded collaboration and engagement with other campus affiliates. These collaborations have included event cross-promotion with our campus student government, resource centers, student groups, and individual faculty to raise awareness about library resources and collections. For example, the library collaborated with the University Veterans' Resource Center to curate a book display, promoting not only the library's military collection, but a student center housed in the library that serves students in an entirely different way. The collaboration resulted in multiple Instagram posts where each departments were tagged, cross promoting the material in very different ways, to two different student audiences. This was only one such example that illustrates how, by collaborating and promoting through the various social media, the library has increased student engagement.

As more collaborations develop, the more the campus at large acknowledges and appreciates the library as more than just a building. As Harrison, et al said, "Social media, which empowers libraries to connect with and engage its diverse stakeholder groups, has a vital role to play in moving academic libraries beyond their traditional borders."(Harrison, et al, 2017, p. 248). Social media has allowed the library to improve not only its resources and services, but also to expand its presence as a main hub on campus for students and faculty alike, with the increased engagement and collaboration across multiple departments. Social media has been a vital addition to the library's marketing strategy which shows growing success when it comes to connecting not only with students, but staff, faculty, and campus stakeholders. In expanding the library to beyond the physical walls, the collaborations that have resulted have helped increase the libraries identity and recognition throughout the campus.

Another unexpected benefit from our subcommittee structure has been facilitating faster responses to questions and concerns shared by users via our social media platforms. While the librarians are accessible through an online reference chat service, some students have taken to messaging the library through Twitter or Facebook and, to a lesser extent, Instagram, particularly during hours when chat reference isn't available. These messages mostly consist of noise complaints or questions about library hours. With fewer platforms for individual librarians to monitor, student messages have been received and answered in a more timely manner, while in the past these messages might have been unanswered for weeks, even months. By having more people involved with a specific platform, faster response times have resulted in more positive student experiences, hopefully encouraging them to continue the use of the social media as a way to reach out to the library.

FUTURE RESEARCH DIRECTIONS

As a new semester starts, the library's social media committee will continue to meet and assess the data that the various social media platforms produce. While the overall transition into smaller teams to represent each account was a step in a new direction, the library realized that there were definite flaws in the original concept. In addressing those flaws, the social media committee was able to improve not only the consistency overall, but the content as well. As the committee works together and make continuous changes, they acknowledge that the library is ready and willing to adapt to new and more progressive forms of social media to meet users' needs for a social media presence from the library. Based on our success in increasing student engagement since moving aways from platform based subcommittees, the social media committee plans to continue with the structure of shared creation and scheduling with a few refinements. Now that we have had a chance to review the results of our strategic changes the committee has a benchmark from which to assess future performance and implement evidence-based practices. To facilitate this assessment we have added the following Outcomes to our committee guide to supplement the committee's Strategic Goals:

- Increase average reach/engagement on Instagram, Facebook, and Twitter by 10% each semester
- Produce 4-6 weekly posts per platform
- Increase overall attendance at/ participation in in-person programs within the library by 10% each semester

Another area for future research is to solicit direct feedback from users. There are a multitude of ways social media can be used to enhance library services outside of student engagement. Since students are using these platforms already, reaching out to them in this way makes sense. All three platforms most used by the library have polling features, which we can use to ask students questions and use those results to implement new ideas or programs based on student-driven feedback. There could even be an opportunity to invite users of the library to share what they look for in an organization's social media, what their likes and dislikes are so the library or organization might have a better understanding of their users, their campus, and the overall drivers of the library, the students.

Furthermore, though our initial changes have focused on increasing student engagement, the social media committee acknowledges the importance of staff, faculty, and other campus stakeholders in our campus community. In the coming year we hope to solicit direct feedback from faculty and staff with the aim to initiate more collaborations and foster opportunities to cross-promote and represent the library and campus through a wider lens.

Beyond developing expertise with the social media platforms themselves, we have also found that members of the social media committee are seeking additional support in managing and creating content through a variety of third party services for example: using a management system like Hootsuite and creating content in using various digital design applications like Canva, Piktochart, or Adobe Photoshop. This presents further opportunities for professional development to support our committee in creating and sharing impactful content. A series of peer lead workshops has been suggested with the potential to include staff and faculty outside the library who may also wish to develop these skills.

CONCLUSION

As communication increasingly takes place in digital spaces, developing a well-curated, impactful social media presence is essential for academic libraries to meet users at their point of need and maintain the library's visibility in their campus community. Creating and maintaining relevant and engaging social media pages requires dedicated time and consideration from the librarians tasked with this responsibility and, as such, should be approached with clear goals and expectations. Our research suggests that dividing social media responsibilities by platform could allow librarians the space to develop their mastery of one platform, rather than splitting their focus. This can improve content quality and, as a result, inter-est in and engagement with the library's social media posts, while minimizing workload for librarians. However, as was in the case of the University Library, the subcommittee approach did evolve into the more collaborative direction that is now being used. We further recommend that libraries interested in adapting either model for their own use make a practice of frequent assessment in order to effectively align with the needs and expectations of their campus community.

ACKNOWLEDGMENT

The authors thank our colleague, Carolyn Caffrey Gardner, at the California State University Dominguez Hills University Library whose insight and generous comments greatly improved the quality of this research.

This research received no specific grant from any funding agency in the public, commercial, or not-for-profit sectors.

REFERENCES

About account home. (n.d.). Retrieved August 29, 2018, from https://help.twitter.com/en/managing-your-account/twitter-account-home

About your activity dashboard. (n.d.). Retrieved August 29, 2018, from https://help.twitter.com/en/managing-your-account/using-the-tweet-activity-dashboard

ALA. (2001). *Libraries making good use of social media and Web 2.0 applications*. Retrieved August 21, 2018, from http://www.ala.org/news/mediapresscenter/americaslibraries/socialnetworking

Alhabash, S., & Ma, M. (2017). A tale of four platforms: Motivations and uses of Facebook, Twitter, Instagram, and Snapchat among college students? *Social Media Society*, *3*(1). doi:10.1177/2056305117691544

Anderson, M., & Smith, A. (2015) Social Media Use 2018. *Pew Research Center*. Available at: http://www.pewinternet.org/2018/03/01/social-media-use-in-2018/

Brookbank, E. (2015). So much social media, so little time: Using student feedback to guide academic library social media strategy. *Journal of Electronic Resources Librarianship*, *27*(4), 232–247. doi:10.1080/1941126X.2015.1092344

Chen, D. Y., Chu, S. K., & Xu, S. (2012). How do libraries use social networking sites to interact with users. *Proceedings of the American Society for Information Science and Technology*, *49*(1), 1–10. doi:10.1002/meet.14504901286

Clark, M., & Melancon, J. (2013). The influence of social media investment on relational outcomes: A relationship marketing perspective. *International Journal of Marketing Studies*, *5*(4), 132–142. doi:10.5539/ijms.v5n4p132

Gollin, M. (2018a). *The 2018 Instagram algorithm change: what it means for marketers*. Retrieved August 13, 2018, from https://www.falcon.io/insights-hub/topics/social-media-strategy/the-2018-instagram-algorithm-change-what-it-means-for-marketers/#/GEN

Gollin, M. (2018b). *How will the 2018 Facebook algorithm change affect marketers?* Retrieved August 13, 2018, from https://www.falcon.io/insights-hub/industry-updates/social-media-updates/facebook-algorithm-change/#/GEN

Harrison, A., Burress, R., Velasquez, S., & Schreiner, L. (2017). Social media use in academic libraries: A phenomenological study. *Journal of Academic Librarianship, 43*(3), 248–256. doi:10.1016/j.acalib.2017.02.014

Hendrix, D., Chiarella, D., Hasman, L., Murphy, S., & Zafron, M. L. (2009). Use of Facebook in academic health sciences libraries. *Journal of the Medical Library Association: JMLA, 97*(1), 43–46. doi:10.3163/1536-5050.97.1.008 PMID:19159005

Howard, H., Huber, S., Carter, L., & Moore, E. (2018, March). Academic libraries on social media: Finding the students and the information they want. *Information Technology and Libraries, 37*(1), 8–18. doi:10.6017/ital.v37i1.10160

Insights I Facebook Help Center I Facebook. (n.d.). Retrieved August 29, 2018, from https://www.facebook.com/help/794890670645072/?helpref=hc_fnav

Jacobson, T. B. (2011). Facebook as a library tool: Perceived vs. actual use. *College & Research Libraries, 72*(1), 79–90. doi:10.5860/crl-88r1

King, D. L. (2015). Chapter 5: Analytics, goals, and strategy for social media. *Library Technology Reports, 51*(1), 26–32.

Lenhart, A. (2015). Teens, social media & technology overview 2015. *Pew Research Center*. Retrieved from http://www.pewinternet.org/2015/04/09/teens-social-media-technology-2015/

Linh, N. C. 2008. A survey of the application of Web 2.0 in Australasian academic libraries. *Library Hi Tech, 26*(4), 630–53.

Mellon, C. (2015). Library anxiety: A grounded theory and its development. *College & Research Libraries, 76*(3), 276–282. doi:10.5860/crl.76.3.276

Ntaka, A. (2017). *The use of social media sites by university library staff to facilitate undergraduate students* (Dissertation). Retrieved from http://urn.kb.se/resolve?urn=urn:nbn:se:lnu:diva-68483

Perrin, A. (2015) Social networking usage: 2005-2015. *Pew Research Center*. Available at: http://www.pewinternet.org/2015/10/08/2015/Social-Networking-Usage-2005-2015/

Rosen, A., & Ihara, I. (2017, September 26). *Giving you more characters to express yourself*. Retrieved from https://blog.twitter.com/official/en_us/topics/product/2017/Giving-you-more-characters-to-express-yourself.html

Socialbakers. (2011, April 19). *How often should you post on your Facebook pages?* Retrieved from https://www.socialbakers.com/blog/147-how-often-should-you-post-on-your-facebook-pages

Stvilia, B., & Gibradze, L. (2017). Examining undergraduate students priorities for academic library services and social media communication. *Journal of Academic Librarianship, 43*(3), 257–262. doi:10.1016/j.acalib.2017.02.013

What's the difference between page views and page reach on Facebook? | Facebook Help Center | Facebook. (n.d.). Retrieved August 29, 2018, from https://www.facebook.com/help/274400362581037

Whiting, A., & Williams, D. (2013). Why people use social media: A uses and gratifications approach. *Qualitative Market Research*, *16*(4), 362–369. doi:10.1108/QMR-06-2013-0041

ADDITIONAL READING

Al-Daihani, S. M., & Abrahams, A. (2018). Analysis of academic libraries' facebook posts: Text and data analytics. *Journal of Academic Librarianship*, *44*(2), 216–225. doi:10.1016/j.acalib.2018.02.004

Ballard, T. 2012. Google this!: putting Google and other social media sites to work for your library. Oxford [England]: Chandos Pub, Chandos Publishing.

Collins, G., & Quan-Haase, A. (2012). Social media and academic libraries: Current trends and future challenges. *Proceedings of the American Society for Information Science and Technology*, *49*(1), 1–4. doi:10.1002/meet.14504901272

Dale, P., Beard, J., & Holland, M. (2011). *University libraries and digital learning environments*. Farnham, Surrey, England; Burlington, Vt.: Ashgate.

Ezumah, B. A. (2013). College students' use of social media: Site preferences, uses and gratifications theory revisited. *International Journal of Business and Social Science*, *4*(5).

Garofalo, D. A. (2013). *Building communities: Social networking for academic libraries*. Philadelphia, PA: Chandos Publishing. doi:10.1533/9781780634012

Nicholas, W., Watkinson, A., Rowlands, I., & Jubb, M. (2011). Social media, academic research and the role of university libraries. *Journal of Academic Librarianship*, *37*(5), 373–375. doi:10.1016/j.acalib.2011.06.023

Sahu, M. K. (2016). Best practices of social media in academic libraries: A case study of selected engineering college libraries of Odisha. *DESIDOC Journal of Library and Information Technology*, *36*(5), 302–308. doi:10.14429/djlit.36.5.10445

Valenza, J. K. (2014). *Social media curation*. Chicago, IL: ALA TechSource.

This research was previously published in Social Media for Communication and Instruction in Academic Libraries; pages 55-73, copyright year 2019 by Information Science Reference (an imprint of IGI Global).

Chapter 61
Use of Social Media in Libraries and Impact on Undergraduates

Jane Igie Aba
Ambrose Alli University, Nigeria

Theresa Osasu Makinde
Ambrose Alli University, Nigeria

ABSTRACT

This chapter examined the use of social media in libraries and impact on undergraduates. The study covers concepts of utilization of social media: benefits, impact, and challenges that affect the use of social media and academic performance of undergraduate students. The concepts generally implied that social media is the use of technology as the best medium to explore wide area of knowledge to produce positive impact on academic performance of students. There is a direct relationship between social media usage and the academic performance of students. It was recommended among others that awareness programs of use of social media platforms should be provided by the university and library to students; access to use of social media resources and services by librarians should be provided to students; educational forums that will facilitate group collaboration and discussion on academic performance should be promoted in universities; connectivity to social media network sites and internet should be improved to facilitate instant information search by students.

INTRODUCTION

Modern communication technology has transformed the entire world into a "Global village". Technology is like two sides of a coin with negative and positive sides. It helps people to be better informed, enlightened and keeping abreast with world developments. Technology exposes mankind to a better way of doing things (Osharive, 2015). Currently, there is a growing awareness and increase in the use of Social Media (SM). Social network is a social structure made up of individuals or organizations called "nodes", which are tied (connected) by one or more specific types of interdependency, such as friendship, kinship, common interest, financial exchange, dislike, sexual relationships or relationships

DOI: 10.4018/978-1-6684-7123-4.ch061

of beliefs, knowledge or prestige (Adeboye, 2012, cited in Asemah and Edegoh, 2012). Social network can also be referred to as a map of specified ties, such as friendship, between the nodes being studied. The nodes, to which an individual is connected are the social contacts of that individual. Social networking sites include: Yahoo Messenger, Facebook Messenger, Blackberry Messenger (BBM), Google talk, Google+Messenger, iPhone, Androids. These networking sites are used by most people to interact with old and new friends, physical or internet friends (Adeboye, 2012, cited in Asemah and Edegoh, 2012). Martn, (2008) & Lusk, (2010) also stated that social media is the use of Facebook, Blogs, Twitter, My Space and LinkedIn for the purpose of communication, sharing photos as well as videos.

The growth of social media over the years has changed the way users communicate, collaborate and exchange knowledge through the various platforms (Wasko, Teigland and Faray, 2009). Similarly, the World Wide Web has been radically transformed, shifting from an information repository to a more social environment where users are not only passive receivers or active harvesters of information but creators of content (Bruns, 2008). Social media is built on the idea of how people know and interact with each other. It gives people the power to share, making the world more open and connected with each other. Social networking has a vital influence on our lives. Social media provides data easy and quick information within a fraction of seconds. Social media applications therefore allow users to converse and interact, create, edit and share textual, visual and audio content. Social media applications are open rather than closed. Social networking websites provide tools by which librarians communicate, share information and create relationships among users. The popularity of social networking websites has affected social interaction due to technological changes. The way library users interact and talk to each other has changed. These users now socialize through the internet. Social networking websites have also affected our social interaction by changing the way we interact face-to-face, receive information, and the dynamics of social groups and friendships have equally change (Asur and Huberman, 2010).

CONCEPT OF SOCIAL MEDIA

Social media and library services are intervening concepts. Thus, social media is a term that encompasses that internet forums, weblogs, social blogs, micro blogging, wikis, podcasts, pictures, video, rating and social bookmarking (Sanusi *et al*., 2014). It involves the use of technology as the best medium to explore and share information resources. According to Andreas and Michael (2010) social media is a group of internet based application that builds on the ideological foundation and allows the creation and exchange of users-generated content. Thus, social media comprise online applications for social networking sites, social bookmarking and sharing tools, social citation tools, blogging and microblogging tools, virtual worlds, e-conference presentation sharing tools, audio and video tools, e-project management tools, and research and writing collaboration tools; primarily developed to foster user-centered social interaction. Social media is the relationships that exist between network of people such as library users (Qingya, Wei & Yu, 2011). It is used to describe different types of electronic communication platforms. The availability of high speed internet broadband connection with massive use of desktop computers, laptops, e-readers, tablets and smart phones enable millions of library users to actively engage in social networking, text messaging, blogging, content sharing, online learning, and much more. Social media are technologies that facilitate social interaction, collaboration and enable deliberation across stakeholders. These technologies now include blogs, wikis, media (audio, photo, video, text) sharing tools, networking platforms, and virtual worlds (Bryer and Zavatarro, 2011). There is a direct relationship between Social media usage and library services in universities. Kyoshaba (2009) stated that academic institutions are established with the aim of imparting knowledge and skills to those who go through them with the use of social media. Therefore, libraries measured their services

TYPES OF SOCIAL MEDIA

Kanelechi, Nwangwa, Ebun, and Omotere (2014) identified the categories and functions of social media (Table 1).

Table 1.

S/N	Category of Social Media	Functions
1	Social Networking Sites (SNS)	*Facebook* - www.facebook.com (Facebook is a social utility that connects people with friends and others who work, study and live around them, even if they are in other countries). *LinkedIn* - www.linkedin.com (LinkedIn is a social networking website for people in professional occupations.) *Research Gate* - www.researchgate.net (This is a social networking site for scientists and researchers to share papers, ask and answer questions, and find collaborators) *Academia* - www.academia.edu (Academics use the platform to share their research, monitor deep analytics around the impact of their research, and track the research of academics they
2.	Social Bookmarking and Sharing Tools	*CiteULike* - www.citeulike.com (This social bookmarking site allows users to save and share citations of academic papers amongst researchers). *Delicious* - www.delicious.com (This is a social bookmarking web service for storing, sharing, and discovering web bookmarks). *Digg* – www.digg.com (This is a news aggregator site that share the most interesting and talked about stories, videos and pictures on the web). *Reddit* - www.reddit.com (Reddit, stylized as reddit, is a social news and entertainment website where registered users submit content in the form of either a link or a text post of either a link or a text post).
3	Blogging and Microblogging Tools	*Blogger* - www.blogger.com (This is a weblog publishing service from Google, for sharing text, photos and video). *Wordpress* - www.wordpress.org (It's an open source blogging tool and a content-management system (CMS) based on PHP and MySQL, which runs on a web hosting service). *Tumblr* - www.tumblr.com (This is a microblogging platform and social networking service that allow users to post multimedia and other content to a short-form blog) *Twitter* - www.twitter.com (This is an online social networking site and microblogging service that enables users to send and read "tweets", which are text messages limited to 140 characters. Registered users can read and post tweets but unregistered users can only read them)
4	Virtual Worlds	*Second Life* - www.secondlife.com (This is a free 3D virtual world where users can socialize, connect and create using free voice and text chat) *OpenSim* – www.opensimulator.org (This is an open source multi-platform, multi-user 3D application server. It can be used to create a virtual environment (or world) which can be accessed through a variety of clients, on multiple protocols. It allows virtual world developers to customize their worlds using the technologies they feel work best).
5	Presentation Sharing Tools	*Scribd* - www.scribd.com (This is a digital documents library that allows users to publish, discover and discuss original writings and documents in various languages using their iPhone, iPad, Kindle Fire and Nook tablet). *SlideShare* - www.slideshare.net (This platform allow the sharing of information in PowerPoint, OpenOffice presentations, Keynote, PDF and infographics). *Sliderocket* - www.sliderocket.com (SlideRocket is an online presentation platform that let users create, manage, share and measure presentations).
6.	Audio and Video Sharing Tools	*YouTube* - www.youtube.com (YouTube is a video-sharing website which allow users to share their videos with friends, family, and the world. *Flickr* - www.flickr.com (This is an image and video hosting website with large pool of picture galleries available with social networking, chat, groups, and photo ratings). *Livestream* - www.livestream.com (This is a live streaming video platform that allows users to view and broadcast video content using a camera and a computer through the internet).
7.	Research and Writing Collaboration Tools	*PBworks* – www.pbworks.com/education (PBworks is a commercial real-time collaborative editing system that allow users to capture knowledge, share files, and manage projects within a secure, reliable virtual environment). *Wikispaces* - www.wikispaces.com (The section of this social site allow teachers to create a classroom workspace where the teacher and students can communicate and work on writing projects alone or in teams). *Wikipedia:* www.en.wikipedia.org Wikipedia is a free online encyclopedia, written collaboratively by the people who use it. It is a special type of website designed to make collaboration easy, called a wiki. Jimmy Wales and Larry Sanger launched Wikipedia on January 15, 2001, the latter creating its name, wiki (quick) and encyclopedia.
8.	Project Management, Meeting and Collaboration Tools	*BigBlueButton* – www.bigbluebutton.org (It is built for online learning. BigBlueButton enables universities and colleges to deliver a high-quality learning experience to remote students). *Skype* - www.skype.com (The service allows users to communicate with peers by voice using a microphone, video by using a webcam, and instant messaging over the Internet. Phone calls may be placed to recipients on the traditional telephone networks)

Social media can be used to enhance library services in the followings areas:

1. *Social Bookmarking:* Interact by tagging website and searching through website book marked by others (Blink List, Simple); (Anjugu,2013)
2. *Social News:* Interact by voting for articles and commenting on them (Digg, Propello).
3. *Social Networking:* Interact by adding friends, commenting on photo and profiles, sharing groups for discussions (Facebook, Imo, Whatsapp, Snapshat, Instagram, Blackberry Messenger chat);
4. *Social Photo and Video Sharing:* Interact by sharing photos or videos and commenting on the user submission (YouTube and Flicker, Instagram); and
5. *Wikis:* Interact by adding articles and editing existing articles (Wikipedia).

Similarly, Social media can include blogs, wikis, media (audio, photo, video, text), sharing tools, networking platforms, and virtual worlds (Boyd & Ellison, 2008). Kaplan and Haenlein (2010) also classified social media into six distinct categories for library services such as:

Collaborative Projects

This enable the joint and simultaneous creation of knowledge related content by many end-users. Whereas blog content is authored by a single person or a few editors and may later be commented on by others, collaborative projects are different in that they allow all users to equally post, add, or change content. They are probably the most democratic form of social media. Collaborative projects allow library users to add and edit content in a community-based data base. There are different types of collaborative projects and they include:

- **Wikis**: Wiki means "quick" in the Hawaiian language and its originator, Microsoft Encarta described a wiki as a type of server software that enables users to create or alter content on a Web page. Wikis are interlinked web pages based on the hypertext system of storing and modifying information. Each page can store information and is easily viewed, edited, and commented on by other people using a web browser. Functionally, a wiki is meant to engage individuals to regularly update wiki pages in a collaborative fashion, to add new information, and to create links between pages. This can be beneficial to library users when a wiki is employed as part of a blended learning approach (Neumann & Hood, 2009). For instance, Wikipedia, a free online encyclopedia ransform the web into a collaborative environment as it enables library users to create and edit encyclopaedia articles (Desilets et al., 2005).
- **Social Bookmarking Sites or Collaborative Tagging Services:** This allow library users to organize and share links to websites; interact by tagging website and searching through website bookmarked by others that can subsequently be organized in the form of tag clouds: visual representations of tags, this could be indicated by font size or colours.
- **Online forums or message boards:** The enable library users to hold conversations in form of posted messages. As opposed to wikis, forums usually do not allow library users to edit content posted by others, but rather only respond to or discuss content within their own postings. The right of editing is limited to the librarian who is the forum administrators or moderators. Also, forums only count as collaborative projects when their focus is on the joint creation of knowledge (Kaplan & Haenlein, 2014).

- **Review Sites:** This focuses on exchanging feedback on all areas of knowlegde. The interaction of library users is by voting for articles and commenting on them. These include Propello, TripAdvisor and Epinions.com. The review sites use reputation system to allow library users compute reliability scores based on ratings received within user reviews. These systems are designed to avoid strategic manipulation of the content posted (Kaplan & Haenlein, 2014).

- **Blogs:** These are Web information sharing technology (Boulos, Maramba, & Wheeler, 2006). According to Kaplan and Haenlein (2010), blogs are the social media equivalent of personal web pages with multitude of variations, from personal diaries describing the author's life to summaries of all relevant information on specific content area. Blogs also functions as an online journal with unique date entries about an issue with current comments that shown first in reverse chronological order (Mayfield, 2008). This consists of text, image, videos, commentary, and links to other Web sites, the contents are contributed by library users, professionals and amateurs. Boyd (2006) distinguished blogs from generic Websites in that blogs capture ongoing expressions, not the edits of a static creation and because the expressions are captured locally, not in a shared common space. Moreover, blogs are easily subscribed through RSS technology. Popular blogs include Wordpress, Blogger, Movable, LiveJournal, and Xanga. Although blogs did not originate in education sectors such as the library but have become useful as an authoring tool. According to Kist (2013) Blogs offer library users the opportunity of accessing multimedia records, incorporating video and sound files, as well as images into written record. The ability for library users to comment on each blogs allows collaborative studies and discussions. Åkerlund (2011) states that engaging in dialogues in form of blog comments are associated with positive attitudes towards online peer interaction which motivate library users.

- **Content Communities:** Allow library users to share photos or videos and commenting on other users' submission. It also enable library users to organize, share and comment on different types of contents such as images, videos(Dewing, 2012). The main objective of content communities according to Kaplan and Haenlein (2010) is the sharing of media contents between users. Content communities exist for a wide range of different media types, including text (e.g., BookCrossing), photos (e.g., Flickr), videos (e.g., YouTube), and PowerPoint presentations (e.g., Slideshare). YouTube footages enable direct access to a vast array of performance techniques, interpretative decisions and visual cues that can be replayed and reviewed at will, thus, this enhance the dissemination of information as a learning tool (Jones & Cuthrell, 2011). The YouTube as a tool of communication is very useful in the development of critical awareness and the use of audio-visual resource as a tool for self directional learning in the library (Monkhouse & Forbes, 2015). YouTube was established primarily to enable library users to share personal objects, experiences and observations with colleagues (Kietzmann, Hermkens, McCarthy & Silvestre, 2011).

- **Social Networking Sites:** This allow library users to connect by creating personal information profiles, inviting friends and colleagues to have access to their profiles and sending messages (Kaplan & Haenlein, 2010). SNSs have achieved phenomenal success since the launch of six-degrees.com in 1997 (Kent, 2008). According to Statista 1.4 billion people used social networking sites around the globe in 2012; by 2016, this number will grow to an estimated 2.13 billion. While Facebook remains the dominant platform with just over 1.5 billion registered users many other platforms and apps have considerable audiences. Created in 2004, Facebook according to NOIPolls (2016) is the most popular SNS in Nigeria. To join Facebook, a user had to have a harvard.edu email address. Beginning in September 2005, Facebook expanded to include high school students, professionals inside corporate networks, and, eventually, everyone. The change to open signup did not mean that new users could easily access users in closed networks—gaining access to corporate networks still required the appropriate dotcom address, while gaining access to high school networks required administrator approval (Boyd and Ellison, 2007). Facebook allows each user to create a profile, updating it with personal information such as home address, mobile phone number, interests, religious views, and even data like relationship status. In addition to creating individual profiles, Facebook users can also "designate other users as friends, send private messages," join groups, post and/or tag pictures and leave comments on these pictures as well as on either a group's or an individual's wall (Grossecka et al., 2011). Other SNSs include Pinterest (a site where the user can "pin" the things he/she likes in a particular category to create a "board" to group them all together, for example, future research ideas) and Instagram (a site dedicated to taking pictures and allowing them to tell an entire story) allow members to instantly see the creativity of a friend and can help the user to brainstorm new ideas.

- **Virtual Game Worlds:** This enable the library to fulfill its role of providing relaxation to users. In virtual game worlds users are usually required to follow strict rules that govern their behaviour (Kaplan & Haenlein, 2009). Many multi-player worlds are intrinsically associated with the role-playing game genre, inspired in its computerised format by the tabletop role-playing games; "you" as player inhabit the body of a character, your avatar, through whose eyes you see the world (Klastrup, 2003; Kaplan & Haenlein, 2009) .The primary goal of virtual game worlds users is to improve the "stats" (statistics of health, stamina) and skills (dexterity, intelligence, fighting skills with sword, arrow) of library users.

USE SOCIAL MEDIA IN LIBRARIES BY UNDERGRADUATES

Utilization of social media is the extent to which social media are utilized in different formats to obtain vital information that will satisfy specific information needs of users (Makinde et al, 2017). Social media allows users to create personal profiles, while connecting with other users of the sites. Users can upload photographs and post what they are doing at any given time (Pempek, Yermolayeva, and Calvert, 2008). Social media is generally used on a regular basis by millions of people across the globe for different reasons. In February 2017, Statistica.com publish a statistic of information on the most popular social media sites used by teenage and young adult users in the united states. During the survey period, it was found that 79% of the respondents mostly use snapshot, 76% use facebook, 73% use Instagram, 40% use Twitter, 31% use Pinterest, 16% use Tumbir, 15% use Whatsapp, 11% use Musical.ly, and 9% use LinkedIn.

Currently, studies revealed that young people especially university/college students' use social media. McLoughlin and Lee (2008) asserted that online social networks allowed learners to access peers, experts, and the wider community in ways that enable reflective, self-directed learning. Joinson (2008) provided a list of factors that motivate people to join online social networks that included social connection, shared identities, content, social investigating, social network surfing, and status updating. Similarly, Kimberly, Charles, Nicole, Sittie, Gemeile and Ikka (2009) argued that the involvement of a student in activities such as making friends on online social networks should be seen as a way of having access to up-to-date information that can be channeled towards improving academic performance which they described as how students cope with or accomplish different tasks given to them by their teachers.

Santos, Hammond, Durli and Chou (2009) studied students in Singapore and Brazil and discovered that most Brazilian students used online social networks to socialize and discuss their studies while the Singaporean students used them for social interactions only.

Kanelechi, Nwangwa, Ebun and Omotere (2014) found that undergraduates are often referred to as "Net Generation" students (those born between 1980 and 1989) consumed approximately 9 hours of social media per day with most of them using social network sites (SNS) with Blogging and Microblogging tools (Rosen, 2011, Cabral, 2011). Prensky (2001) describes them as heavily involved in computer games, email, the Internet, cell phones and instant messaging as parts of their lives. This group of students functions best when networked and they prefer games to "serious" work. The "I Generation" (those born between 1990 and 1999) even consume more time on social media particularly on chatting platforms such as Facebook Chat, 2GO and Google Chat than they do with their friends Face-to-Face. These two 'generations' spend more time on social media than the "Generation X" (those born between 1965 and 1979) who spend approximately from 20 minutes to 3 hours on social media (Rosen, 2011). This implied that, most undergraduates running full time programmes in Nigerian universities spend more time on social media than any other activity of the day, including academic work. Besides, several web statistics testify that large proportion of young people check their Facebook when they first wake up even before going to the bathroom (www.qbeemedia.com/facts). In order words, as students become addicted to social media, it split their attention, causing massive decrease in knowledge retention (Junco & Cotten, 2012).

Mehmood and Taswir (2013) found that students use social media for: downloading/uploading music/video, posting photos, chatting, blogging, creating polls/quizzes, submitting articles to website and communication with teachers/class. Thus, while the first three are basically for entertainment purposes, the last three however, are for academic purposes. This shows that students use social media for entertainment mostly and less for educational purposes; while most students used social networks for entertainment purposes. Helou and Ab.rahim (2014) also found that students use social networking sites for making friends, receiving and sending messages, chatting with friends, playing games, sharing files, and communicating with supervisors or lecturers. Onyeka *et al* (2013) found that students use social networking sites so as to: keep in touch with others; while away time; maintain a sense of belonging; and to solve social problems. Similarly, Ezeah *et al* (2013) found that Nigerian students use social media to watch movies, pornography and for discussion of serious national issues like politics, economy and religion. Eke *et al* (2014) found that students use SNSs for communicating and interacting with friends; online learning; finding friends online; leisure and personal socialization; searching for job; academic discussion and getting study partners online; watching movies; connecting and interacting with business partners; communicating, mobilizing and organizing national issues like politics, economy and religious matters; updating profile information. Rosen (2009) confirmed that social media is part and parcel of youth life today. Lin (2010) found that majority of college students in the United States used SNSs at least one hour a day. Ahamed and Qazi (2011) in a study of 6 universities in Pakistan, found that majority of the students spent 1-3 hours daily on social networking sites. Tham (2011) in a study conducted at St. Cloud State University in Minnesota found that, while both males and females spent time spent on SNSs, the said time however, decreased as the age of the respondents increased and the results revealed that female college students spent more time on SNSs than male students. Jagero and Muriithi (2013) in the context of students in private universities in Dar Es Salaam, Tanzania, found that a majority of the students spent 30 minutes to 1 hr daily on social networking sites. In Nigeria, Onyeka *et al* (2013) found that majority of university students in Adamawa State spent 2-4 hours daily on social networking sites, while Anjugu (2013) in a study of students of the University of Abuja found that: "92 respondents (70.8%) spend 6 hours online, 30 respondents (23.1%) spend 4 hours online, 6 respondents (4.6%) spend 2 hours online, and 2 respondents (1.5%) spend 1 hour online". Akubugwo and Burke (2013) found that many students use social media especially Facebook, Myspace, and Twitter during academic classes. Social media negatively impact on the students' academic performance. Asemah *et al* (2013) found that social media has a negative effect on the academic performance of Nigerian students in that students: spend more time on social media than reading their books; rely on social media to do their assignments without consulting other sources; who spend more time on social media are likely to perform poorly in their academic activities than those who do not. Iorliam and Ode (2014) found that the time spent on social media, the frequency of visit and the total number of online friends has a statistically significant relationship with a student's academic performance. Ahmed & Qazi (2011) found a *positive* relationship between use of internet/social media and the academic performance of student users. Thus, students using internet were found to score higher on reading skills test and had higher grades. Pasek, Kenski, Romer and Jamieson (2006) found that Facebook users score higher grades. Social networking sites have even been found to provide a rich mean of interaction between teachers and students (Roblyer, McDaniel, Webb,Herman & Witty, 2010). Mehmood and Taswir (2013) found positive effects of social media on the academics of students.

Eke, Omekwu and Odoh (2014) surveyed 150 students and found that the students use the SNSs to communicate with friends; watch movies; discuss national issues like politics, economy and religious matters; and for academic purposes which particularly is relevant to their academic pursuit. Lamanaus-kas et al (2013) found that the most important function of social media use by respondents from all countries they surveyed were communication, learning and exchanging information. A similar study by Mehmood and Taswir (2013) revealed that of the 80 percent students who reported that they used a social networking site on phone and that the smart features available on social networks like reading RSS feeds, location tagging and status updates were popular uses of social network on mobile phone. However these were not directly related to their educational pursuit. Alhazmi and Rahman (2013) found that the student's use social media to keep in touch with friends, to let others know what is happening in their life, communicate with friends on classwork, sharing of news and other issues and these do not relate to their academic goals. Ebele and Oghentega (2014) found that undergraduates do not use social media for academic purposes but mainly for general information that are not relevant to academics.

Similarly, Ezeah, Asogwa and Edogor (2013) found that students in South-East Nigeria use social media partly because of the pleasure and fun they derive from the pornographic contents and watching movies using the social media. Okundia (2016) found that students use social media in pursuing activities that do not have bearing with their academics. In a similar study to ascertain the purpose students use social media. Al-Sharqi, Hashim, and Kutbi (2015) found that students use social media tools for a blend of academic and non-academic purposes. And that a significant number of students use social media for entertainment, information searching and learning. Owusu-Acheaw and Larson (2015) found that student use social media to chat than academic purpose. Buhari and Ashara (2014) found that social media is used to connect; interact; share information and chat with friends.

BENEFITS OF SOCIAL MEDIA TO UNDERGRADUATE STUDENTS

Oghenetega and Ejedafiru (2014) stated that social media have affected communication between people in educational community positively since the past decades. Life is made easy by media in different areas such as academically, socially, and politically for any that is connected to it. Social media not only helps to acquire knowledge but also establishing enduring relationships with real people, connecting with fellow dorm residents through Facebook, Twitter and various social sites can help a student overcome the kind of isolation that otherwise might lead her to leave school. What makes social networking websites unique is not that they allow individuals to meet strangers, but rather that they enable users to articulate and make visible their social networks. While Social media have implemented a wide variety of technical features, their backbone consists of visible profiles that display an articulated list of Friends who are also users of the system. Profiles are unique pages where one can "type oneself into being" . A Twitter account can provide a shy student with information about events that facilitates face-to-face encounters with other students. Such personal interactions are vital to creating and sustaining a sense of belonging.

The strength of social media applications is that they offer an assortment of tools that learners can mix and match to best suit their individual learning styles and increase their academic success. The social networking sites focus heavily on building online communities with common interests or activities. Social networking sites also can help students develop leadership skills, from low-level planning and organizing to activities that promote social change and democratic engagement. social media tools and networking sites encourage students to engage with each other and to express and share their creativity. Courtney (2007) enumerated the following as the beneficial impact of Social Media to students:

1. Google and education: Google has helped over 20 million student in their education using their tools. The internet (Google) is a valuable source of information for students looking for ideas for projects and assignments. With over 50 million web sites on the net the chances are that any information however obscure can be found. The only tools required to find this information would be some patience and a decent search engine (Ehrmann, 1995; Adebiyi et al., 2015). Furthermore it has been widely acknowledged that Google has been at the apex and fore at providing resource to information needs.
2. By spending so much time working with new technologies: students develop more familiarity with computers and other electronic devices.
3. With the increased focus on technology in education and business, this will help students build skills that will aid them throughout their lives.
4. Talents got discovered faster, students who were good at programming got their name out their easily, student who were good in music, got their videos out and shared leading them to their dreams.
5. A lot of the students were able to inform public about their issues – using social media which brought awareness and helped solve a lot of problems.
6. The ease with which a student can customize their profile makes them more aware of basic aspects of design and layout that are not often taught in schools.
7. The ease and speed with which users can upload pictures, videos or stories has resulted in a greater amount of sharing of creative works. Being able to get instant feedback from friends and family on their creative outlets helps students refine and develop their artistic abilities and can provide much needed confidence or help them decide what career path they may want to pursue.

Oyeboade (2017) asserted that social media affect academic performance of undergraduates because academic successes greatly influence student's self-esteem, motivation, and perseverance in higher education. Social networking sites (facebook) have transformed the ways users interact socially and have shaped communication, research, assignments, and relationships in unique ways. Furthermore, this redefinition has fostered the creation of ''virtual society''(Adebiyi et al., 2015). Courtney (2007) enumerated the consequences of social media to includes popularity of social media, and the speed at which information is published, has created a lax attitude towards proper spelling and grammar. The social media reduces a student's ability to effectively write without relying on a computer's spell check feature.

- Many students rely on the accessibility of information on social media and the web to provide answers. This reduces focus on learning and retaining information.
- ability to retain information has decreased, and the willingness to spend more time researching and looking up good information has reduced, due the fact we got used to the ease of accessibility to information on social media.
- The more time students spend on social sites, the less time they spend socializing in person. Because of the lack of body signals and other nonverbal cues, like tone and inflection, social networking sites are not an adequate replacement for face-to-face communication. Students who spend a great deal of time on social networking are less able to effectively communicate in person.
- The degree to which private information is available online and the anonymity the internet seems to provide has made students forget the need to filter the information they post. Many colleges and potential employers investigate an applicant's social networking profiles before granting acceptance or interviews. Most students don't constantly evaluate the content they're publishing online, which can bring about negative consequences months or years down the road.
- Students are having a harder time getting to communicate face to face with people, and are losing their people skills, due to that they are spending more and more time talking from behind a screen.

According to (Blogger, 2012) the negative effects of these social media networking site seem to apparently overweigh the positive ones. Researchers indicate that these sites have caused some potential harm to the society. The students become victims of social networks more often than anyone else. This is because when Blogger, further explained that other negative effects of social networking websites include: Reduced learning and research capabilities- Students seem to rely more on the information accessible easily on these Social Media Networking Site and the web. This reduces their learning and research capabilities because some of them smuggle their phone into the exam hall to get answers to exam questions which sometimes becomes impossible and leads to exam failure. Multitasking- Students who get involved in activities on social media sites while studying, get their focus of attention reduced, this results in lack of concentration to study well and consequently poor academic performance. Moreover, the more time the students spend on these social media sites, the less time they spend socializing personally with others. This reduces their communication skills or lack of the ability to communicate and socialize effectively in person with others. The effective communication skills are key to success in the real world. Reduces command over language usage and creative writing skills. Students mostly use slang words or shortened forms of words on social networking sites. They start relying on the computer grammar and spelling check features. This reduces their command over the language and their creative writing skills. Many Nigerian students lost interest in reading because they are addicted to social media networking site, while some hardworking students became lazy as a result of bad company on social media networking site, these Nigerian students were introduced to Examination malpractice (exam runz) at social media networking site. This has however, contributed to lowering of Nigeria education standard in the form of numerous certified illiterates in Nigeria (Penkraft, 2015). A research carried out by Oyewumi, Isaiah and Adigun (2015) revealed that excessive and uncontrolled or compulsive social networking use has been known to have negative effects on psychological well-being of adolescents, such as loneliness.

The value of interactive social media technologies in high institutions of learning is now recognized in the way that teaching and learning strategies is in an increasingly globalized process (Gray, Chang & Kennedy, 2010). One of the most commonly cited benefits of social media by scholars is their ability to facilitate collaborative learning and communication among peers and with people outside academia (Collins & Hide, 2010; Rowlands, Nicholas, Russell, Canty & Watkinson, 2011). Other than communication, scholarly Twitter users cite information distribution among the primary advantages of social networking and have proven to become popular especially in academic conferences (Letierce, Passant, Breslin & Decker, 2010; Ross, Terras, Warwick & Welsh, 2011). Another frequently reported advantage of social networking is its remarkable ability to facilitate information distribution. Among the examples include blogging tools which are used by many students to disseminate information within their area, their peers and also to everyone globally (Bukvova, Kalb & Schoop, 2010; Luzon, 2009). The basic advantage of using social media to aid learning and teaching and this can be achieved with the existence of rules and regulations (Rutherford, 2010).

Impact of Social Media on Undergraduate Academic Performance

The term impact can be either negative or positive. It is generally agreed that social media has both positive and negative effects on the academic performance of students globally:

- Positive effects: Eke *et al* (2014) has noted the following positive impacts of social media on the academics of students:
  - *Web Engagement*: In a word where online engagement is important for businesses, students are becoming experts at developing a sense of internet presence. Not only do they know how to interact with others on the internet, they know how to use basic and even complex functions in order to do so. Thus, students use social networking sites to interact with their peers and even teachers about class-related subjects.
  - *Informal Knowledge and Skill*: Social Networking sites can facilitate learning and skill development outside formal learning environments by supporting peer- to peer learning, skills collaboration and diverse cultural expression. The knowledge and skill young people are learning through SNSs are directly relevant to the 'participatory web' in which 'user generated content is now integral in a rapidly developing online business model that capitalizes on the social networks, creativity and knowledge of its users; and this means that new business models are expected to emerge.
  - *Education*: Social networking sites help in schools and universities programmes. Such social networking sites for example, blogs help to leverage or complement formal educational activities and enhancing outcomes. SNSs are also used to extend opportunities for formal learning across geographical contexts. Thus, social media can enhance the interactions of

marginalized young people with their teacher and increase their confidence in educational activities.

- ○ *Individual Identify and Self-Expression*: Because SNSs are essentially flexible and designed to promote individual customization, they are used to experiment as well as find legitimacy for their political, cultural or sexual identity. Social networking sites can provide users with a space to work out identity and status, make sense of cultural cues, negotiate public life and increase user's sense of personal belonging. This sense of personal belonging and identity has been positively correlated with academic performance.
- ○ *Strengthening Interpersonal Relationships*: generally, studies have found that having positive interpersonal relationships is an important predictor of wellbeing. Social media by and large, has been found to strengthen individual interpersonal relationships. Email, instant messaging and social networking can address new barriers people may face to forming and maintaining public places together, limited transport to get there, and time free of structured activities such as school and sport.
- Negative effects: Social media has been noted to have some negative effects on students' academics:
  - ○ *Displacement effect on academic activities*: since majority of students use social networking sites socializing purposes, they therefore tend to spend more time for socializing rather than learning. Thus, excessive use of SNSs reduces student's academic performance since time meant for studies is used on non-academic issues like chatting and making friends (Salvation &Adzharuddin 2014).
  - ○ *Psychological disorders and health problems*: anxiety, depression, poor eating habits, and lack of physical exercise; increasingly short attention spans and subverted higher-order reasoning skills such as concentration, persistence, and analytical reasoning among frequent users of social media; a tendency to overestimate one's ability to multi-task and manage projects; and technology being seen as a substitute for the analytical reasoning process. Collectively, these play roles in a student's educational process to various degrees and at various times (Blogger, 2012).

Academic performance is used interchangeably with academic achievement which refers to "a successful accomplishment or performance in a particular subject area. It is indicated as by grades, marks and scores of descriptive commentaries. It includes how pupils deal with their studies and how they cope with or accomplish different tasks given to them by their teachers in a fixed time or academic year" (Adane, 2013). According to Adimora (2016) achievement is accomplishing whatever goals one set for oneself. Academic achievement is the overall academic performance of a student in the school which could be assessed by the use of tests and examinations. It is the attainment of standard of academic excellence. Students' academic achievement plays an important role in producing the best quality graduates who will become great leaders and manpower for the country thus responsible for the country's economic and social development (Ali, Jusoff, Ali, Mokhtar & Salamt, 2009). Ask (2015) explained academic achievement as student's success in meeting short- or long-term goals in education. In the big picture, academic achievement means completing high school or earning a college degree. In a given semester, high academic achievement places a student on the honor roll. Teachers and school administrators can measure students' academic achievement through school-wide standardized tests, state-specific achievement tests and classroom assessment. Standardized and state tests enable educational professionals to see how students in a school are achieving in a variety of subjects compared to those at other schools and geographic locations. Classroom assessments enable teachers to see how well students are learning concepts for a specific class (Ask, 2015). This study would look at academic performance as measured from the angle of grades or Cumulative Grade Point Average (CGPA).

Social media is one of the fastest ways information been send and receive timely but it has cause some negative impact to those addicted to it. According to Oyeboade, J.A (2017) postulated that social media by their nature have the capabilities of educating, informing, entertaining and inflaming the audience above all, they possess a contagious and outreaching influence which the conventional media lack. Social media use by undergraduate students reflect more on their academic grades, a study released by Ohio State University reveals that college students who utilize Facebook spend less time on studying and have lower grades than students who do not use the popular social media (Kalpidou, Costin, and Morris, 2011). Cao & Hong, (2011) and Dahlstrom (2012) are of the opinion that Integrating social media for both entertainment and learning is common among students in higher level of education. College students use various social media applications to the extent that it is now an indispensable part of their everyday life for personal and learning purposes. Studies have proved that most students invest time and efforts on social networks in building relationships around on shared interests and on same grounds (Maloney, 2007).

In a study conducted on Social Network Addiction among Youths in Nigeria, Ajewole, Olowu, and Fasola (2012), concluded that majority of the respondents spend more time on social media, which affects their academic productivity negatively. According to Penkraft (2015) Social Media Networking Sites were not aimed to decrease the academic performance of students, but rather to be used for academic purposes. The enthusiasm of Nigerian students for Social Media Networking Site is one of the causes of their poor academic performance. Most Nigerian students prefer to exhaust all their time online chatting at their lesson period, they do not even have time to do their home work as well as read for examinations. These activities have a negatively tremendous influence on their academic achievement. Adimora et al (2016) revealed that students engage more in distracting social networking than to academic activities. To affirm this assertion, Blogger (2012) pointed out that when students are searching for their course material online; in order to kill the boredom in their study time, they get attracted to these sites which divert their attention from their study, such distraction makes them forget their major reason of using internet. As the case may be, the waste of time sometimes makes them unable to deliver their work in the specified time frame and consequently leads to their low grades in their school work.

Adimora's et al (2016) study revealed that a negative and weak relationship between students' social networking and their academic achievement. Blogger (2012) stated that students who get involved in activities on social media networking site while studying, get their focus of attention reduced, this results in lack of concentration to study well and reduction in their academic performance. The study of Adimora et al (2016) also found that neither students' masculinity nor femininity on the use of social networking predicts their academic achievement. Issa, Isaias and Kommers (2016) found that social media networking site such as facebook, Pinterest and instagram as popular with females, and that overall females subscribe to online social network platforms to a greater extent than men, and that Nigerian males were more likely to use online social media for academic pursuits as compared to females who prefer using it for pleasure. Ebele & Oghenetega (2014) found that undergraduates in the four universities perform poorly in academic because of addiction with social media activities. These findings showed that social media cause low performance among Nigeria students. The direct link between social media usage and students' academic performance has been the focus of extensive literature during the last two decades (Aghaunor & Ekuobase, 2015). Results of available studies indicate that while some students use social media for socializing, others might use it for learning activities thus enhancing academic performance. Although social media is a very helpful tool in students' hands, it was found by many studies that a negative impact of social media usage on academic performance could occur (Maqableh, Rajab, Quteshat, Masa'deh, Khatib & Karajeh, *2015*). Social media users devote lesser time to their studies in comparison to nonusers do and subsequently get lower GPAs (Kirschner & Karpinski, 2010). Results of a study by Hasnain, Nasreen and Ijaz (2015) indicated that the usage of social media has an inverse relationship with academic performance of students. This implies that the more students spend time on social media, the more their GPA is affected. According to Khan and Balasubramanian (2009), social media users often time experience poor performance academically. In a study to find out the direct consequences of ICT in Nigeria Universities, Enikuomehin (2011) surveyed 1,860 Facebook users from the Lagos State University and found that 90 percent of the students could not get up to cumulative grade point. average (CGPA) above 3.50 because they had spent a large part of their time on social media than on their homework and study time that could have contributed to the attainment of higher grade. Similarly, Englander, Terregrossa & Wang (2010) posit that social media is negatively associated with academic performance of student and is a lot more momentous than its advantages.

Griffith and Liyanage, (2008) found that support from instant messaging, wikis, blogs, discussion boards, and other Web 2.0 facilities can complement what is taught in a traditional classroom setting. Also, Boyd and Ellison, (2007) assert that the copy and paste practices on MySpace serves as a form of literacy involving social and technical skills. Whereas according to Pasek, More and Hargittai (2009) the use of Facebook has a positive relationship with academic performance. In another study, Haseena and Rasith (2016) conducted a survey of 200 students among the students of Eastern University, Sri Lanka. Their findings concluded that there is a significant positive relationship between social media usage and academic performance. Indicating that if the students spend more time on social media it will help the students to easily discuss about the study task, assignment and exams. When the time spending on social media is increasing it will also increase the performance of the students. Findings from a survey of 932 students of Kaduna Polytechnic by Buhari and Ashara (2014) revealed that students perceived social media usage as something interesting that they can use to improve their academic performances.

However, the overuse of these sites on a daily basis seems to have many negative effects on the physical and psychological health of students, because it makes them lethargic and unmotivated to create contact with the people in person. An excessive use of these sites could be detrimental to these students' psychological health (Blogger, 2012). According to About.com (2006) psychological health is a mental state of someone who is functioning at a satisfactory level of emotional and behavioural adjustment. It may also include an individual's ability to enjoy life, and create a balance between life activities and efforts to achieve psychological resilience. World Health Organization (WHO) explained mental health as subjective well-being, perceived self-efficacy, autonomy, competence, intergenerational dependence, and self-actualization of one's intellectual and emotional potential (World health report, 2001). WHO further states that the well-being of an individual is encompassed in the realization of their abilities, coping with normal stresses of life, productive work and contribution to their community (Mental health, 2014).

Adane (2013) noted four groups of factors that influence the academic achievement of students: home-related factors, school-related factors, student characteristics and teacher-side factors. Similarly, Salvation and Adzharuddin (2014), while conceding that students' "academic performance is multi-dimensional construct", however opined that it consists of three dimensions: student's characteristics, teacher/lecturer's competencies and academic environment.

CHALLENGES THAT AFFECT THE USE OF SOCIAL MEDIA BY UNDERGRADUATE STUDENTS IN THE LIBRARIES

There are challenges that affect the use of social media for educational purposes. It has been reported that one of the problems associated with using social networking sites for scientific studies is the possibility of students spending a lot of time on them and denying other important aspects the time they deserve (Rowlands et al., 2011). Rithika and Selvarag (2013) stated that social media can increase student learning through student interactions, challenges arise when social media are incorporated into an academic course.

The assumption that students are familiar with and agreeable to using certain types of social media can cause educators to inadvertently fail to provide the resources or encouragement necessary to support student usage and learning. When social media is used for an educational purpose, students incorporate the technology into their lives in a way that may differ from the intentions of the course instructor. For example, off-topic or non-academic discussions occur on social media because of its primary design as a social networking tool. Further, as a student's age increases, the frequency of off-topic discussions also increases (Rowlands et al., 2011). This indicates that while social media may encourage broader discussions of course content, older students may spend more time than younger students engaging in unrelated discussions.

Conn and Brady (2008) and Griffith and Liyanage (2008) highlighted the reasons for students use of social networking sites in educational environments to include preconceptions associated with exposing students to inappropriate online content, fears of online sexual predators, and student-based cyber bullying, or online student harassment. Lederer (2012) stated that the challenges of social media included distraction that divert learner's attention from classroom participation and finally are disruptive to the learning process. The second challenge is that cyber bullying can be used as a weapon for malicious behaviour. Lastly, social media discourages face-to-face communication. Jones et al (2012) found that five challenges of social software for learning included separation of life and studying; originality and copyright issues; sense of information flooded; time constraint and lecturers are not up-to-date and may not know how to integrate and make use of social software.

Farkus, George, et al. (2012) asserted that the challenges associated with use of Social Networking Sites stem from the risks inherent in student internet usage. Internet exposes students to inappropriate material, unwanted adult interactions, and bullying from peers. Keen (2007) also affirms that the quality of content is also a major concern. Ngonidzashe (2013) indicated that the major challenges or concerns relating to social networking technologies are loss of control as one can receive unsolicited negative comments, time commitment and information overload.

Scholars have conducted several studies on the use of social media in libraries and impact on undergraduates both within and outside Nigeria. Most of these studies concentrated on the types, purpose; utilization and effect of social networking sites on academic achievements, of students. In a related study, Hasnain, Nasreen and Ijaz (2015) studied impact of social media usage on academic performance of university students. The study adopted survey research design using stratified random sampling to select 191 students from four private universities. Questionnaire was used to collect data and data was analyzed using frequency counts and simple percentage while the hypothesis was tested using linear regression analysis. Findings revealed that usage of social media has an inverse relationship with academic performance of students.

Similarly, Owusu-Acheaw and Larson (2015) studied students' use of social media and its effect on academic performance of tertiary institutions students in Ghana with a focus on Koforidua Polytechnic students. The study adopted survey research design using stratified random sampling technique to sample a total number of 1508 students. Questionnaire was used as the data collection instrument and the results were analyzed with the use of the Statistical Package for Social Science (SPSS) and the result shown in tables with corresponding frequencies and percentage. The study revealed that majority of the respondents had mobile phones which also had Internet facility on them and had knowledge of the existence of many media sites. The study further confirmed that most of the respondents visit their social media sites using their phones and spend between thirty minutes to three hours per day. In addition the study revealed that the use of social media sites had affected academic performance of the respondents negatively and that there was direct relationship between the use of social media sites and academic performance

Youssef and Alobaidy (2016) investigated the impact of social networking sites on student academic performance: The Case of University of Bahrain. Survey research method was adopted and a structured questionnaire was used to collect data. A total of six hundred twenty eight (628) students were sampled. Data was analyzed using Statistical Package for Social Sciences (SPSS). The result revealed that SNS have positive and negative impacts on student academic performance. At the end, the authors came up with fruitful recommendations on how to get benefit from the SNS to improve the learning process.

Irshad (2012) evaluated the Social Media trends among University Students in Islamia University of Bahawalpur, Pakistan. Survey research method was adopted and a structured questionnaire was used to collect data. A total of six hundred (600) students were sampled using convenient sampling technique. Data was analyzed using MS-Excel Programme. The result revealed that students used face-book for exchanging academic activities and developing social networks throughout the world. Social media was also used for sharing learning experiences with colleagues and international community. Social media was used to promote collaboration and linkage in developing Virtual Community across the world. The problems of social media included bandwidth of internet and electricity break down/ load shedding.

In a related study, Knight-McCord, Cleary, Grant, Herron, Jumbo, Lacey, Livingston, Robinson, Smith and Emanuel (2016) studied social media sites that college students use most in co-educational university in southeastern, Alabama State, United State of America. Survey research method was adopted and a structured questionnaire was used to collect data. A total of three hundred and sixty three (363) college students were sampled. Data was analyzed using descriptive statistics and mean statistics. The result revealed that Instagram was the most used social networking site followed by Snapchat and Facebook. Students used social networking sites that enable them to post pictures and videos. They least use social networking sites that enable them to develop a professional network or post media content into organized categories. Social media sites are increasingly tailored to meet the needs of specific target markets. Understanding this evolutionary pattern is the key that unlocks which social media platforms college students will continue to use most.

In a similar study Omekwu, Eke and Odoh studied the Use of Social Networking Sites among Undergraduate Students of University of Nigeria, Nsukka. Survey research method was adopted and a structured questionnaire was used to collect data. A total of one hundred and fifty (150) undergraduate students were sampled using convenient sampling technique. Data was analyzed using random sampling techniques. The result revealed that student were using the social networking sites in interaction with friends, connecting to their class mates for online study and for discussing serious national issues and watching movies etc. There are also laudable benefits of using social networking sites and dangers associated with social networking and such dangers can be ameliorated using the strategies available in the work. Drawn from the findings, it was recommended that university Authorities should organize seminars to enlighten students on the not-so good aspects of social networking sites etc. In addition useful suggestions for further research were equally made.

Kanelechi, Nwangwa, Yonlonfoun and Omotere (2014) examined undergraduates and use of Social Media: Assessing Influence on Research Skills in six different universities randomly selected from six geo-political zones in Nigeria. Survey research method was adopted and a structured questionnaire was used to collect data. A total of six hundred (600) students were sampled using purposive sampling technique. Data was analysed using descriptive analysis and frequency and Chi-square (X^2) was used to test null hypothesis in the study. The result revealed that undergraduates frequently copy from Wikipedia as their major source of information; uses Facebook to generate ideas from colleagues about their research focus; and make use of Wordpress or Blogger to develop their creative writing skills. However, students' reliance on these social media tools alone has resulted in their dwindling research skills to produce quality research works. Recommendations were made on how to improve students' research skills.

Osharive (2015) studied the influence of Social Media and Academic Performance Of students in University of Lagos, Nigeria. Survey research method was adopted and a structured questionnaire was used to collect data. A total of three hundred and seventy eight (378) students were sampled using random sampling technique. Data was analyzed using descriptive analysis and frequency and Chi-square (X^2) was used to test null hypothesis in the study. The result revealed that students were addicted to social media. Recommendations were made on the use of social media for educational purposes as well; Social Networking Sites should be expanded and new pages should be created to enhance academic activities and avoid setbacks in the students' academic performance; and Students should be monitored by teachers and parents on how they use these sites This is to create a balance between social media and academic activities of students to avoid setbacks in the academic performance of the students

In a similar study, Onuoha and Shaeed (2011) studied perceived influence of online social networks on academic performance: a study of undergraduates in selected universities in Ogun State, Nigeria. Descriptive survey research method was adopted and a structured questionnaire was used to collect data. A total of four hundred and two (402) students were sampled. Data was analyzed using descriptive analysis and frequency and percentage counts. The result revealed that majority of the respondents used online social networks was used for social interaction than academic purposes. Most of the respondents, however, agreed that the use of online social networks have positive influence on their academic performance.

Olajide and Oyenira (2014) studied the knowledge and use of social media among Nigerian Librarians in twenty-six different tertiary institutions (Universities, Polytechnics, Colleges of Education, school of nursing in south west Nigeria. Descriptive research design was adopted and a structured questionnaire was used to collect data. A total of Two hundred (200) librarians were sampled using random sampling technique. Data was analyzed using descriptive analysis and frequency and Statistical Package for Social Sciences (SPSS) version 20. The result revealed that about half of the Librarians are yet to have in-depth knowledge of SM; Facebook is the still the most common while Skype, Twitter, and LinkedIn were not very popular among them. Facebook is also the mostly used SM, the duration spent on SM weekly is small and the major hardware used is phone and personal laptops. The usual place of accessing SM address is the Library/office. Majority of the Librarians have 2 SM account and the major uses are chatting and gisting. Uploading, reading of blogs or posting of other people and asking of questions have a low response. Recommendations were made as to improve on the knowledge and use of SM among Librarians in Nigeria.

CONCLUSION

Social media have a positive impact on academic performance of undergraduates and there is a direct relationship between Social media usage and academic performance of students. Therefore, Undergraduate students should be enlightened and encouraged to develop habits of using social media platforms for positive academic purposes and to complement their studies. The review presented a general overview of social media where the types of social media in various formats were highlighted. Literatures on the following concepts were also reviewed: concepts of utilization of social media; benefits, impact and challenges that affect the use of social media and academic performance of undergraduate students. The concepts generally implied that social media is the use of technology as the best medium to explore wide area of knowledge to produce positive impact on academic performance of students.

RECOMMENDATION

The following recommendations are made as follows:

1. awareness programmes of use of social media platforms should be provided by the university and library to students.
2. access to use of social media resources and services by librarians should be provided to students.
3. educational forums that will facilitate group collaboration and discussion on academic performance should be promoted in universities.
4. connectivity to social media network sites and internet should be improved to facilitate instant information search by students.
5. provision of equipments such as computers, printers, scanners and photocopiers should be made available to students.
6. training on information search skills should be given to students by librarians to ensure properly utilized of social media resources.
7. adequate funding should be provided by parent institutions for subscription to social media sites

REFERENCES

Adane, L. O. (2013). *Factors affecting low academic achievement of pupils in Kemp Methodist Junior High School in Aburi, Eastern Region* (Master's thesis). University of Ghana, Legon. Retrieved from http://ugspace.ug.edu.gh

Adenubi, O. S., Olalekan, Y. S., Afolabi, A. A., & Opeoluwa, A. S. (2013). Online Social Networking and the Academic Achievement of University Students – The experience of selected Nigerian Universities. *Information and Knowledge Management, 3*(5). Retrieved from: www.iiste.org

Adimora, D. E., Ngwuchukwu, M. N., & Onuoha, J. C. (2016). Prevalence of social media networking on academic achievement and psychological health of undergraduate students in Federal Universities in Nigeria. *Global Journal of Psychology Research: New Trends and Issues, 6*(3), 135–147.

Aghaunor, C. T., & Ekuobase, G. O. (2015). ICT social services and students' academic performance. A Multidisciplinary Journal Publication of the Faculty of Science, Adeleke University, Ede, Nigeria, 2, 29-46.

Ahmed, I., & Qazi, T. F. (2011). A look out for academic impacts of Social networking sites (SNSs): A student based perspective. *African Journal of Business Management*, 5(12), 5022–5031.

Boyd, D. (2006). A Blogger's Blog: Exploring the Definition of a Medium. *Reconstruction, 6*(4). Retrieved from http://reconstruction.eserver.org/064/boyd.shtml

Boyd, D. M., & Ellison, N. B. (2007). *Social network sites: definition, history, and scholarship*. Academic Press.

Bruns, A. (2008). *Blogs, Wikipedia, Second life, and Beyond: from production to produsage*. Academic Press.

Bryer, T., & Zavattaro, S. (2011). Social media and public administration: Theoretical dimensions and introduction to symposium. *Administrative Theory & Praxis*, 33(3), 327.

Buhari, S. R., & Ashara, B. H. (2014). Use of social media among students of Nigerian polytechnic. *International Conference on Communication, Media, Technology and Design*, 302-305.

Cao, Y., & Hong, P. (2011). Antecedents and consequences of social media utilization in college teaching: A proposed model with mixed-methods investigation. *On the Horizon*, 19(4), 297–306. doi:10.1108/10748121111179420

Choney, S. (2010). *Facebook Use Can Lower Grades by 20 Percent, Study Says*. Retrieved from http://www.msnbc.com/id/39038581/ns.technology_and_science-tech_and_gadgets/.Retrieved

Chukwuemeka, O. (2013). Environmental influence on academic performance of secondary school students in Port Harcourt Local Government Area of Rivers State. *Journal of Economics and Sustainable Development*, 4(12), 34–38.

Conn, K., & Brady, K. P. (2008). Myspace and its relatives: The cyberbullying dilemma. *West's Education Law Reporter*, 1-7. Available at http://www.webcitation.org/5hGReihs

Courtney, N. (2007). *Library 2.0 and beyond: Innovative technologies and tomorrow's user*. Westport, CT: Libraries Unlimited.

Dahlstrom, E. (2012). *ECAR study of undergraduate students and information technology*. Louisville, CO: EDUCAUSE Center for Applied Research.

Daluba, N. E., & Maxwell, C.E.O. (2013). *Effect of social media on the use of academic library by undergraduate*. Academic Press.

Kanelechi,, C.K., Nwangwa, E. Y., & Omotere, T. (2014). Undergraduates and Their Use of Social Media: Assessing Influence on Research Skills. *Universal Journal of Educational Research*, 2(6), 446–453.

Owusu-Acheaw, M., & Larson, A. G. (2015). Use of Social Media and its Impact on Academic Performance ofTertiary Institution Students: A Study of Students of Koforidua Polytechnic, Ghana. *Journal of Education and Practice*, 6(6). Available at www.iiste.org

Oyeboade, J. A. (2017). Socio-economic status, peer pressure and use of social media by undergraduate students in university of Ibadan, Ibadan, Oyo State, Nigeria. *Library Philosophy and Practice,* 1495. Retrieved http://digitalcommons.unl.edu/libphilprac/1495

Pasek, J., More, E., & Hargittai, E. (2009). Facebook and academic performance: Reconciling a media sensation with data. *First Monday, 14*(5). doi:10.5210/fm.v14i5.2498

Peluchette, J., & Karl, K. (2008). Social networking profiles: An examination of student attitudes regarding use and appropriateness of content. *Cyberpsychology & Behavior.*

Peter, O. (2015). *Social Media and Academic Performance of Students in University of Lagos. Being a research project submitted to the department of educational administration, faculty of education.* University of Lagos.

Pew Research Centre. (2017). Which social media platforms are most popular. *Internet, Science Computer-Mediated Communication, 13*(1). Retrieved http:jcin.indiana.edu/vol13/issue1/boyd.ellison.html

Rithika, M., & Selvaraj, S. (2013). Impact of social media on student's academic performance. *International Journal of Logistics & Supply Chain Management Perspectives, 2*(4), 636–640.

Rowlands, I., Nicholas, D., Russell, B., Canty, N., & Watkinson, A. (2011). Social media use in the research workflow. *Learned Publishing, 24*(3), 183–195. doi:10.1087/20110306

Salvation, M., & Adzharuddin, N. A. (2014, August). The influence of social network sites (SNS) upon academic performance of Malaysian students. *International Journal of Humanities and Social Science, 4*(10[1]), 131–137.

Santos, I., Hammond, M., Durli, Z., & Chou, S. Y. (2009). Is there a role for social networking sites in education? In A. Tatnall & A. Jones (Eds.), *Education and technology for a better world. Proceedings of the 9th IFIP TC 3 World Conference on Computers in Education* (pp. 321–330). Berlin, Germany: Springer. 10.1007/978-3-642-03115-1_34

Statista. (2017). *World report on social media usage.* Retrieved from http://www.statista.com/statistics/272014/global-social-networks-ranked-by-number-of-users/

The World Health Report. (2001). *Mental Health: New Understanding, New Hope.* Retrieved from: https://en.wikipedia.org/wiki/Mental_health

Wang, Chen, & Liang. (2011). *The Effects of Social Media on College Students.* The Alan Shawn Feinstein Graduate School. Providence, RI: Johnson & Wales University.

Wasko, M. M. L., Teigland, R., & Faray, S. (2009). The Provision of Online Public Goods: Examining Social Structure in an Electronic Network of Practice. *Decision Support Systems, 47*(3), 254–265. doi:10.1016/j.dss.2009.02.012

KEY TERMS AND DEFINITIONS

Academic Performance: In this study, it refers to level of performance in written works and exams. How students deal with their studies and how they cope with or accomplish different tasks given to them by their teachers, within this work measured from the standpoint of academic grades.

ICT: In this study, it refers to information and communications technology (or technologies) that is the infrastructure and components that enable modern computing.

Internet: In this study, it refers to global computer network providing a variety of information and communication facilities, consisting of interconnected networks using standardized communication protocols.

Social Media: In this study it refers to different types of communication technologies that facilitate social interaction and collaboration between people. This includes Facebook, blog, Twitter, wiki, instant messaging, etc.

Social Media Usage: In this study, it refers to the amount of time spent on social media.

Undergraduates: In this study, it refers to students who are studying for first degree (usually entitled Bachelor of Arts [BA] or Bachelor of Science [Bsc] in a university).

This research was previously published in the Handbook of Research on Digital Devices for Inclusivity and Engagement in Libraries; pages 350-370, copyright year 2020 by Information Science Reference (an imprint of IGI Global).

Chapter 62

How Students are Using Social Networks?
Emotional Intelligence as a Determinant

Sobuh Abu-Shanab
University of Jordan, Amman, Jordan

Emad Ahmed Abu-Shanab
Qatar University, Doha, Qatar

ABSTRACT

Social networks are now being used by the majority of Internet users and are becoming an important part of social life. This exploratory study utilized a sample of 254 high school students to explore their social networks' use and its relationship to emotional intelligence dimensions. The study used a newly developed survey to explore the area, understand student's use level/pattern, and answer the research question. Results indicated that only the motivational dimension and social emotional management were significant in predicting the use of social networks. Further conclusions and analysis are described in this paper.

1. INTRODUCTION

Social media is influencing our lives and even how we conduct business. Individuals are using social media for all purposes like socializing, education, entertainment, and many other purposes (Alquraan, Abu-Shanab, Banitaan & Al-Tarawneh, 2017). One of the major applications of social media is social networks (SNs), where millions of people are connected for the purpose of utilizing an open domain for interacting with others and socializing with all types of media (text, voice, images, or videos). This phenomenon has influenced student's behavior and even student's academic performance (Abu-Shanab & Al-Tarawneh, 2015). The influence of social networks on students' performance is based on formal interactions with instructors, acquiring help from their social network, and acquiring extra resources for educational purposes.

DOI: 10.4018/978-1-6684-7123-4.ch062

Social networks are "web-based services that allow individuals to construct a public or semi-public profile within a bounded system, articulate a list of other users with whom they share a connection, and view and traverse their list of connections and those made by others within the system" (Boyd & El-lison, 2007, p. 211). The use of social networks is open for all users (if they have an account on certain platforms). Facebook, Twitter, WhatsApp, and other platforms are opening doors for all categories of society to participate and build their network. This is also valid for students. Students are building net-works of colleagues: networks managed by instructors or by student society members. The society (or network) aims at exchanging information, helping in educational task, reminding and directing mem-bers to specific tasks, and other options. Research indicated that social networks have crucial influence on students' education if utilized in the proper direction (Tuan & Tu, 2013). On the other hand, social networks might cause harm for students like addiction and information overload (Haq & Chand, 2012).

As mentioned previously, social networks are open for all categories of students. Still, students' gains from social networks are dependent on their personalities and demographic factors. Based on that, if formal channels of education need to utilize social networks, they need to be aware of issues related to personal differences. The major reason behind this argument is the equity and fairness of educational system. Some researchers relate this to the efficiency of such systems.

This study focuses on a major personal ability: emotional intelligence. Emotional intelligence (EI) influences how people cope with stress and would influence their satisfaction with the job, emotional intelligence represents a personality trait that distinguish personal behaviors towards others (Jordan et al., 2002; Salovey & Mayer, 1997). Research indicated that individuals with managed emotional intelligence abilities are expected to socialize more and have more interactions on social media (Lopes, Salovey & Straus, 2003; Rossen & Kranzler, 2009). Based on that, this study will try to answer the following research questions: 1) Do the managed abilities of emotional intelligence influence social network use? 2) What are the EI dimensions that predict social networks' use?

The following sections will summarize the available literature in this area and try to understand what previous work has accomplished. Section three will describe the research method including the instru-ment used and the sampling process. The fourth section summarizes the data analysis and discussion of results. Finally, section five reports our conclusions, limitations, and future work.

2. BACKGROUND

Social networks (Like Facebook, Twitter and WhatsApp) are being used extensively in the educational sector. They form societies that can exceed country's size. The society within social networks includes all categories of people; people with special needs, elderly, youngsters, and males/females. This study tries to identify the influence of emotional intelligence (EI) dimensions on the use levels of social networks (SN). Following is a brief introduction on EI.

2.1. Emotional Intelligence

Being intelligent does not mean only knowing things, but also mean how you interact with others. The concept of intelligence evolved over time, but became more complicated and categorized. One of the major milestones in research was what Gardner proposes as the multiple intelligences theory (Gardner, 1997). In his theory, Gardner brought attention to the existence of more than one type of intelligence.

The following are the major types proposed by Gardner and in more than one publication: Logical-mathematical, linguistic, musical, spatial, bodily kinesthetic, interpersonal, and intrapersonal (Gardner & Hatch, 1989). The interpersonal intelligence evolved in later publications into what we know now as emotional intelligence, where research defined it as the ability to identify, assess, and control one's own emotions, the emotions of others, and that of groups (Goleman, 1996).

Emotional intelligence (EI) represents a personality trait that distinguish personal behaviors towards others. More than one framework described this dimension and grounded research proposed instruments for it. Salovey and Mayer (1997) posit in their proposed framework four abilities that could be acquired through learning: perceiving, using, understanding, and managing emotions. Their framework is applicable in social and emotional adaptation. The second version of the scale proposed by Salovey and Mayer was modified and included 141 items measuring EI and its subcomponents (Rossen & Kranzler, 2009). Emotional intelligence (EI) influences how people cope with stress and would influence their satisfaction with the job (Jordan et al., 2002).

EI is used as a predictor or as a classifier of behaviors in most research studies. Many studies focused on EI and reflected certain conclusions based on the famous instruments measuring it. On the contrary, the following study tried to measure how an educational program influences EI levels. The researchers utilized 5 groups of MBA students during their study and how their emotional intelligence capabilities improved over time (Boyatzis, Stubbs & Taylor, 2002). The study also investigated the relationships between problem solving skills, self-confidence, and EI.

2.2. Social Networks Influence

The concept of social media included many types of platforms like social networks, video sharing, wikis and blogs. It is convenient to focus on one type of platform in order to better understand the boundaries of our research. Social networks (SNs) are platforms that allow users to build their own network of friends, share and exchange information with them and extend their communication with their networks of friends. Examples of the major platforms of social media are the following: Facebook, Twitter, WhatsApp, and Google+.

The influence of social networks on students' performance varied. Having both a negative and positive influence, social networks are becoming more important for students and an integral part of their lives. A study be Abu-Shanab and A-Tarwaneh (2015) indicated a negative correlation between students' GPA and time spent on Facebook. Some researchers reported that SNs can cause addiction (Andreassen, Torshem, Brunborg & Pallesen, 2012), waste of time (Gafni & Deri, 2012; Paul, Baker & Cochran, 2012), and risk-taking behavior (Burak, 2012). Other studies correlated the use of SNs against students' performance and concluded that they have negative influence on students' performance (Haq & Chand, 2012; Paul et al., 2012).

On the other hand, other studies reported important benefits from using SNs within the educational system. Contradicting with the previously reported research, Tuan and Tu (2013) reported an improvement in students' performance. Other studies indicated that SNs influence extracurricular activities and how students perform their assignments and tasks ((Junco, 2012). Such benefits come from the exchange of information and guidance through an open communication channel (Gafni & Deri, 2012). Studies indicated a relationship between culture and social network activities (Facebook in this case), where Saudi students showed more inclination to expose their personal information to others (Aljasir, Bajnaid, Elyas & Alnawasrah, 2017).

The vast use of social networks made it an integral part of educational domain. A study tried to investigate the differences in Facebook use between American and Jordanian students and concluded that significant differences are attributed to culture of the country (Alquraan et al., 2017). Our interest in the previously mentioned study is the dimensions used by the authors in classifying the use of Facebook by students. The authors classified the various uses of students into four major directions: entertainment, personal, educational, and social. Based on their results, educational purposes ranked second after entertainment in predicting the intention to continue using social networks. It is also important to know that all four dimensions were significant, which supports the importance of using Facebook for all directions.

Similar studies explored the relationship between social networks (like Facebook) and the educational sector and concluded that the use of social media is growing and witnessing a substantial contribution toward more effective and efficient learning process. A study by Moran and his colleagues claimed that social media tools helped students in collaborative learning (Moran, Seaman & Tinti-Kane, 2011). Another study asserted that Facebook helped students find more friends to help them in their assignments (Madge, Meek, Wellens & Hooley, 2009). Such link supports the importance of Facebook as a domain that might bridge the face-to-face interaction and improve students' performance.

2.3. Related Social Network Behavior

Many studies tried to investigate the relationship between EI and personality traits. Research found conflicting results with respect to the relative strength of relationship between such measures (Petrides et al., 2010). Still, the significance of relationship or its existence is highly supported. In the previously mentioned study, two samples were used to test the relationship between EI and the big five dimensions and concluded to significant relationships and trends.

Another study concluded that couples who are rated high on emotional intelligence were most likely to be open in discussing their problems with their partners. The study utilized a sample of 82 couples (i.e. total sample size 164) who completed three surveys pertaining to measures of communication patterns, emotional intelligence, and relationship quality components (Smith, Heaven & Ciarrochi, 2008). One final conclusion by the study indicated that partners who perceived themselves to be equal on the emotional intelligence scale where more satisfied than others.

On the other hand, it is expected that social interaction be related to emotional intelligence abilities. In an organizational context, EI abilities are assumed to influence people's interactions within social networks (internal and external). A study in healthcare sector concluded to such relationship, where internal networks benefit teamwork and the effectiveness of work. On the other hand, the influence on external networks can benefit managers' interactions with accreditation personnel and partner's relationship (Freshman & Rubino, 2004).

A group of researchers conducted two studies and concluded that individuals with high ability to manage their emotions showed quality interactions. The two studies used the previously mentioned Mayer-Salovey-Caruso Emotional Intelligence Test. The first study included 118 students, and the second study utilized 103 German students (Lopes et al., 2004). Another conclusion was related to the social interactions between males and females, where it was influenced by subjects' emotional intelligence ability. Similar studies concluded that people with managed EI abilities have self-perceived quality of interpersonal relationships (Lopes et al., 2003). People who managed their emotional intelligence, showed higher quality of social interactions.

An experiment conducted on 103 university students revealed that students with high emotional management reported higher positive relationships with friends (Lopes, Salovey & Straus, 2003). Another study aimed at exploring how EI can explain certain behaviors concluded that the study of EI significantly explain the variation in social outcomes of users behaviors (Rossen & Kranzler, 2009). The context of the study focused more on the social/emotional relation of EI levels and utilized 150 undergraduate students. Furthermore, a study in a Swedish university concluded that using Facebook by students with extraverted personalities will result into poor academic performance (Rouis, 2011). The study used a sample of 239 students who filled a survey measuring the personality big five instrument and reported their Facebook use.

Based on the literature mentioned in this section and the conflicting results regarding the personality type and how it affects educational performance when using Facebook (or other types of social media), the researchers believe that this study fills a gap in research. The previous section supported the role of social networks in educational sector (Moran et al., 2011; Madge et al., 2009; Abu-Shanab & A-Tarwaneh, 2015), where many students used Facebook for educational purposes, and many ranked it before personal and social. If Facebook can be used for educational purposes, which category of students (based on EI classifications) will be more reinforced or hindered by this use. The following section will describe the research method.

3. RESEARCH METHOD

Our previous literature review concluded to a gap in the literature regarding the link between educational performance, emotional intelligence, and using social media. The conflicting results related to such triangle made it necessary to conduct this study. In an educational environment, it is assumed that students use social networks for many reasons (as described in the previous section). Still, would they be using it to improve their educational performance? Would their personality type (Based on EI factor) influence such use of social media? Figure 1 depicts our research context.

The first question will be forwarded to future research. Our focus in this study is the second question. The tests implemented will also associate students' use of social media to their EI index. This study postulates a relationship between certain categories of people (based on their EI abilities) and their social networks use. Based on such relationship and students' sample used, it is assumed that such context can explain much in our study. Based on the previous discussion, the following major questions are formulated:

RQ1: Do the managed abilities of emotional intelligence influence social network use? RQ2: What are the EI dimensions that predict social networks' use?

It is assumed that people have certain levels of EI dimensions regardless of the differential weight of each dimension. Based on this we can associate (using multiple regression) the four known dimensions of EI to the use of social media. This exploratory study aims at understanding the relationship between EI dimensions and social networks use in an educational context. The sample can infer such context. Following is a description of the instrument development process followed by the sample and sampling process.

Figure 1. Research context

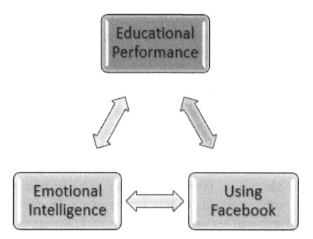

3.2. Research Instrument

The survey items used in this study were adopted from previously mentioned studies and few Arabic studies. As we are conducting this study in Jordanian schools and we assume that student's language skills would influence the results (Abu-Shanab & Md Nor, 2013), we built the survey using Arabic language to make it easier to students to assimilate the items and respond more accurately to them. The survey used included two sections and an introduction. The introduction included a short description of research objectives, sections, and the guidelines for filling the survey. The survey items for the EI dimensions were adopted from Arabic instruments used by previous research in Arabic countries (Abu-Ajaj, 2014). The study was conducted on in Palestine and on high school students to measure their social networks use. The instrument used a 5-point Likert scale also with similar scaling categories.

The first section included few demographic factors and social media use. The survey required respondents to check the correct corresponding box regarding their age, class (year in school), gender, and if they use any of social networks applications. This section also included a table with four types of applications that we deemed popular in Jordan (Facebook, WhatsApp, Twitter, and Snapchat), where students are required to fill their use rate per day. Finally, this section included some questions about their use of social media.

The second section included 26 items measuring four dimensions of EI and they are emotional awareness (EA, 6 items), emotional management (EM, 7 items), social emotional management (SEM, 7 items), and motivational dimension (MD, 6 items). The items used in the study were adopted from more than one study, where the authors tried to come up with a short list of unique items that measure the four commonly used dimensions of EI. The items used utilized more than one source to build the survey items (Thainat, 2015; Abu-Ajaj, 2014; MHS, 2002).

The survey used a 5-point Likert scale with one representing a total disagreement, and five representing a total agreement with the statement of item. As we explained earlier, we can assume that each person carries certain value of each dimension, but might express differential presence of one or more of the four major dimension of EI. When using such scale, a mean between 1 and 2.333 will be considered low, a mean between 2.333-3.666 will be considered moderate, and a mean between 3.666-5 will be considered high (Abu-Shanab & Md Nor, 2013).

3.3. Sample and Sampling Process

This study was conducted in Jordanian schools in the capital city of Amman and in Zarqa city. The environment of the schools and the two cities are considered similar and no differences can be accounted for the school location or city. This study utilized a sample of 254 surveys for analysis, where one survey was excluded from analysis. The research team distributed 160 surveys in female schools, and 100 surveys in male schools. The study distributed surveys in four schools in total, with two male schools and two female schools. The sample included the 10th and 11th grades only as the sampling time missed the 12th grade students based on the exam preparation period for the national exam in Jordan. The sampling also was voluntary among sections, where the research team called for teachers to allow for distributing the survey and did not force them to do it. In addition, students were free to fill the survey or not without any restrictions or motivation (like extra grade).

The total collected surveys from all four schools were 255 surveys. The researchers collected the surveys (paper copies), coded them into a spreadsheet application, then transferred the data to SPSS for analysis. The total entered surveys were 254, and were all used for analysis. The demographics of data collected are listed in Table 1.

Table 1. Sample demographics

Gender	Freq.	%	Grade	Freq.	%
Male	96	37.8	10th grade	183	72.0
Female	157	61.8	11th grade	68	26.8
Not reported	1	0.4	Not reported	3	1.2
Total	254	100	Total	254	100

4. DATA ANALYSIS AND DISCUSSION

This study utilized two types of analysis: descriptive analysis and ANOVA tests. The first tests aimed at exploring the sample demographics and their use levels of social networks. It also tries to investigate the reasons behind their use. The second set of tests investigated the research question directly by comparing the means of certain categories.

4.1. Descriptive Analysis

The first step in the analysis is to inspect the use level of social networks. The survey included a table with four types of social networks (SN): Facebook, WhatsApp, Twitter, and Snapchat. The table also enabled respondents to state the use level based on time, where four options are open: 1 hour per day, 2-4 hours per day, 406 hours per day, and more than 6 hours. The frequencies and percentages of such use are shown in Table 2.

The data depicted in Table 2 indicates a popularity of Facebook among Jordanian students, followed by WhatsApp and Snapchat. The use of Twitter is severely lower than the other three applications, which makes it the last used application. The use of the four apps showed different trends with respect to the level. Still, the last two use levels were similar in frequencies and the majority of our sample used one or more of the social apps 1 hour per day as the highest use level followed by 2-4 hours per day.

Table 2. The use levels of social networks

Social Network	No Use		1 hr./day		2-4 hrs./day		4-6 hrs./day		>6 hours		Used
	Freq.	%	Freq.	%	Freq.	%	Freq.	%	Freq.	%	Freq.
Facebook	43	16.9	112	44.1	58	22.8	25	9.8	16	6.3	211
WhatsApp	59	23.2	118	46.5	46	18.1	14	6.7	17	6.7	195
Twitter	183	72.0	49	19.3	15	5.9	5	2.0	2	0.8	71
Snapchat	84	33.1	96	37.8	44	17.3	11	4.3	19	7.5	170
Other apps	171	67.3	21	8.3	23	9.1	14	5.5	25	9.8	83
Total checks	540		396		186		69		79		730

The survey allowed our students to fill other apps they used, where a short-list of applications were mentioned like Instagram, LinkedIn, and YouTube. We also asked students to indicate the level of use of this category and yielded the following figures (Data for all other applications): 1 hour per day (21 ⇒ 8.3%), 2-4 hours per day (23 ⇒ 9.1%), 4-6 hours per day (14 ⇒ 5.5%) and finally more than 6 hours (25 ⇒ 9.8%). This category also included 171 surveys with no data (i.e. did not report other apps that they used). This row included all other networks and were all nearly equivalent to Twitter use. Such result indicates our accurate use of the four categories for the Jordanian environment. Figure 2 shows a histogram with the relative use of each application.

Figure 2. The relative use of social networks

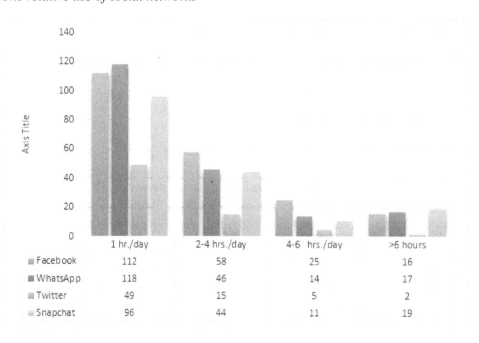

The second test is to explore the reason for using social networks. The survey included a blind question with respect to social network type. Based on this the answers we generated in the data represents the sample's perceptions on diverse types. The responses of this question are shown in Table 3 below. Subjects responded to this question by ticking one or more of our listed options. Based on this, our data does not sum to the sample size, even though the total is not far from the sample size.

Table 3. Reasons for using SN

Reason for Use	Freq.
Academic	23
Entertainment	191
General knowledge	83
For News	27
Other	27
Not reported	5

The results shown in Table 3 indicates that the common use of social media is entertainment (191) followed by general knowledge (83). Only five surveys did not report any type of use. The surveys reporting one or more type of use were as follows: one type of usage (181), two types of use (42), three types (12), four types (2), all types of uses with others (11). It is obvious that the two categories that are popular and commonly used together are entertainment and general knowledge.

We also asked students about the location they usually use social media. Their responses also opened the floor for multiple selections. The responses frequencies are depicted in Table 3. Based on this condition the total responses will exceed the sample size. The majority of SN use by students is concentrated on home (242), school (26), and other locations (28). It is obvious that this result is affected by the Ministry of Education's policy to keep using mobile phones as restricted as possible, which prevents students from using them in schools. The survey also could not propose other common places (like Coffees or shopping malls), which also supports our premise as the other category included low percentage (9%) (Table 4).

The survey also included a question about using social media during social events and gatherings. The responses open for them were Yes/No. this question was followed by another question about the type of social meeting (options were three: family gatherings, with friends, and other). Table 5 depicts the results of the two questions.

Results indicate that students use SN in social events and gatherings. The percentage of who use SN reached 146 (57%), and those who claim they do not use SN in social events accounted for 103 (41%). On the other hand, when asked about using SN in certain types of events, responses were distributed between family gathering (102 responses) and with friends (121 responses). The slight difference towards friends might be attributed to the lose environment and the restrictions families impose on their kids.

Table 4. The location where students use SN

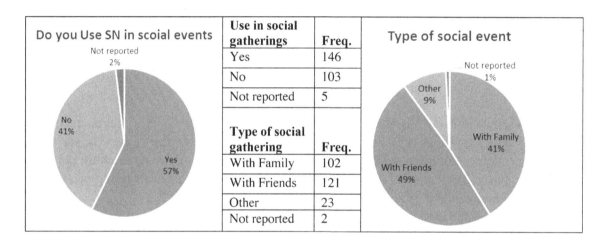

Location of use	Freq.
Home	242
School	26
Other	28
Not reported	4

Table 5. The use of social networks in social events

Use in social gatherings	Freq.
Yes	146
No	103
Not reported	5

Type of social gathering	Freq.
With Family	102
With Friends	121
Other	23
Not reported	2

Finally, we asked if students use SN to better express their feelings and emotions. The question included two options: Yes or No. The responses were distributed between the two options with two responses not reported. Students who used Sn to express their feeling and emotions more accounted for 134 (52.8%) and those who claim that they do not use SN for expressing their emotions and feelings accounted for 118 (46.6%) (Table 6).

When exploring emotional intelligence (EI) items, we estimated the item means and the total dimension mean. The sample showed a moderate to high mean values. All item means were more than 2.43, and reached as high as 4.18. When estimating the total dimension mean, we can see that the means and standard deviations of dimensions were as follows: EA (3.51, 0.699), EM (3.26, 0.751), SEM (3.70, 0.746), and MD (3.78, 0.682). Appendix A depicts all item means and standard deviations and the total dimension estimates.

The sample used in this research totaled 254, which satisfies the generalizability of results (Hair et al., 1998). The same source lists the different sample sizes and their associated power effect. The sample size needed to reflect a large power effect (= 0.8) with 4 variables used in the study is 145 (Olbricht & Wang, 2018). Thus, the sample size is satisfactory to what statistical resources require (Hair et. al., 1998).

Table 6. The use of SN for expressing feelings and emotions

Using SN for Expressing Feelings and Emotions	Freq.	
Yes	134	
No	118	
Not reported	2	

Finally, factor analysis was conducted to estimate the factor loadings of various items on the four dimensions used for EI variable. Results are shown in Appendix B, where all items loaded with more than0.5 (as the minimum recommended value by Hair et al. (1998)), except the following three cases: EM3, SEM7 & MD3. As noticed, one has loaded on a different dimension (SEM7), and two loaded partially (value less than 0.4 and on two dimensions). Such result is not satisfactory but addresses the minimum requirements.

4.2. Regression Analysis

The major research question of this study can be answered by using multiple regression technique. As we assume that each person will express certain portion of the four dimensions of EI, and thus based on such distribution will use social networks. we can predict the use of social network based on multiple regression using the following mathematical expression:

$$SN\ use = a + b_1\ EA + b_2\ EM + b_3\ SEM + b_4\ MD + e$$

To test this equation, we used the summative measure of each dimension by estimating the mean of the items constituting it. Therefore, for the value used in the test for emotional awareness, we used the mean of the first 6 items. The same for the other three EI dimensions. For the SN use, we converted all codded values of the use data to their hours value and summed all into one measure. As an example, if a respondent reported in his survey the following consecutive values for his use: 2 (Facebook), 3 for WhatsApp, 0 for Twitter, 1 for Snapchat, and 1 for other, then his total use of SN will be $= 2*1 + 3*5 + 0 + 1*1 + 1*1 = 19$ hours. We assumed a mean of each interval for the categories used in the survey.

Based on that we regressed the four dimensions on the SN use using an error rate $= 0.05$. The Model passed the test after we excluded three outliers (based on their extreme value; > 3 sigma). The model was significant with an $F_{4,249} = 4.98$, $p = 0.001$. The coefficient of determination value of the model R $= 0.274$, $R_2 = 0.75$, which explained only 7.5% of the variance of SN use. Table 7 represents the coefficient table of regression.

Table 7. The coefficients table of regression

Predictors	Unstand. Coeff.		Stand. Coeff. Beta	t	Sig.
	B	Std. Error			
(Constant)	9.005	2.274		3.959	0.000
Emotional Awareness (EA)	0.481	0.568	0.061	0.847	0.398
Emotional Management (EM)	-1.774	0.472	-0.252	-3.754	0.000
Social Emotional Management (SEM)	1.175	0.495	0.166	2.372	0.018
Motivational Dimension (MD)	-0.577	0.607	-0.075	-.952	0.342

Dependent Variable: SN Use

The results of this study depict a significant prediction of SN use based on two major emotional intelligence dimensions: emotional management and social emotional management. Such results might be expected by readers based on the close relationship between the social aspect of the third dimension on one hand, and the ability of managing emotions on the other. Still, being aware of your emotions, and the motivational dimension are not significant in influencing social network use. This means that being aware of your emotions would not influence your SN use. The same with your motivations, which might mean that it is a prerequisite for such step. On the other hand, the SEM results supports previous expectations of research where the ability to manage others' emotions can encourage people to use social media (Freshman & Rubino, 2004). On the other hand, managing emotions was reported to yield better quality interactions only (Lopes et al., 2004).

The second issue related to the results of Table 7 is the negative sign associated with the emotional management beta. Such sign means that individuals with high ability to manage their emotions will use social networks less. This result poses an important question as to the use of SN by such individuals as a replacement (or an escape from) to face-to-face interaction. It is important to recall and relate the low use of SN for motivational objectives (for study and life guidance) with the insignificant relationship with use. Previous research commended the role of Facebook in reforming youth (with a sample in Jordan) and helping them in their study (Abu-Shanab & Frehat, 2015). The other beta represents a positive relationship between the use of social network and individuals who are successful in managing other interactions and emotional ques. Such result supports previous research reported in similar studies (Thainat, 2015).

4.3. Differences in Gender, Age and Class

The final step in Analysis included a comparison in EI dimensions based on three demographic factors. The surprising result included no significant ANOVA tests on all four dimensions. Such result is partially in alignment with previous research (Haq & Chand, 2012; Abu-Shanab & Al-Tarawneh, 2015) (Table 8).

5. CONCLUSION AND FUTURE WORK

This study aimed at exploring the relationship between emotional intelligence (EI) and the use of social networks. This exploratory study utilized a questionnaire with items measuring four EI dimensions. The aim was to explore the influence of EI on social networks' use. We collected data from a sample of 254 school students from the 10th and 11th grade. The responses were analyzed to come up with a regression equation to predict the use of SN. The results supported only two out of four dimensions and the regression equation is the following:

SN use = 9.005 – 1.774 EM + 1.175 SEM + e

Table 8. ANOVA Factor

ANOVA Factor	Gender		Age		Class	
Dimension	F	Sig.	F	Sig.	F	Sig.
Emotional Awareness (EA)	1.636	0.202	0.932	0.395	0.952	0.330
Emotional Management (EM)	0.008	0.928	1.861	0.158	0.001	0.979
Social Emotional Management (SEM)	1.150	0.285	0.150	0.861	1.368	0.243
Motivational Dimension (MD)	1.565	0.212	1.173	0.311	0.741	0.390

Our results did not fully support the results of previous research, where EM and EA are crucial in identifying individuals with active status on social networks (Lopes, Salovey & Straus, 2003; Rossen & Kranzler, 2009). Such conflict (or partial support) calls for more research to identify individuals and customize their offered treatments.

The EI measures also reported moderate to high values which might not explain much, but our sample represented individuals with high ability to manage their life and be guided by their emotional intelligence characteristics (Mean = 3.78). The other factor that scored high (mean = 3.70) is the third one, which represents individuals with high ability to manage other feelings and interactions. On the other hand, individuals who are characterized by being aware of their emotions and manage them well, scored moderate on their factors (EA = 3.51 & EM = 3.26).

The significant relationship between social media and EI is important for efficiency and effectiveness of educational system (Tuan & Tu, 2013). Such results imply that teachers need to understand the personality of their students before imposing social media use on them. Teachers can measure their students' EI index and setup the stage for a customized curriculum or course structure. This can be done at the start of the semester only (or academic year). In business domain, if firms want to hire people who are aware of their emotions and can manage them, they might not find them active on social media. On the other hand, individuals who are active on social media will be successful in groups and dealing with others' emotional issues. The second implication is to try to attract a diverse workforce based on their ability on all four dimensions. Using social networks by high school students does not mean they are using it for entertainment, but as a way to interact with others.

More than one side limits this study. The first is the language of survey. This study utilized a new survey that might need further replications to see how it can yield reliable results. Future research is needed to replicate this study and validate the survey in Arabic language. The second limitation is the sample size. Future studies might increase the sample size to improve the coefficient of determination and support the study findings. Other limitations might be attributed to the period of sampling, where it was done period to exam period in Jordan, which excluded the 12th grade students and also influenced the results based on exam anxiety. Finally, we paved the road for other researchers to explore this topic, but postponed the other research question which relates to the relationship between students' performance and the context of this study.

REFERENCES

Abu-Ajaj, M. (2014). *The Relationship between the Level of Emotional Intelligence and the Level of Use of Social Communication Network among High School Students in the Area of Beersheba* [master thesis]. Amman Arab University, Amman, Jordan.

Abu-Shanab, E., & Al-Tarawneh, H. (2015, April-June). The influence of social networks on high school students' performance. *International Journal of Web-Based Learning and Teaching Technologies*, *10*(2), 44–52. doi:10.4018/IJWLTT.2015040104

Abu-Shanab, E., & Frehat, M. (2015, January-March). The role of social networking in the social reform of young society. *International Journal of Technology Diffusion*, *6*(1), 62–77. doi:10.4018/IJTD.2015010104

Abu-Shanab, E., & Md Nor, K. (2013). The influence of language on research results. *Management Research and Practice Journal*, *4*(2), 37–48.

Aljasir, S., Bajnaid, A., Elyas, T., & Alnawasrah, M. (2017). Facebook's compatibility, reasons for disclosure, and discussion of social and political issues: The case of university students using Facebook. *Journal of Management and Strategy*, *8*(5), 1–17. doi:10.5430/jms.v8n5p1

Alquraan, H., Abu-Shanab, E., Banitaan, S., & Al-Tarawneh, H. (2017). Motivations for using social media: comparative study based on cultural differences between American and Jordanian students. *International Journal of Social Media and Interactive Learning Environments*, *5*(1), 48–61. doi:10.1504/IJSMILE.2017.086093

Andreassen, C., Torshem, T., Brunborg, G., & Pallesen, S. (2012). Development of a Facebook addiction scale. *Psychological Reports*, *110*(2), 501–517. doi:10.2466/02.09.18.PR0.110.2.501-517 PMID:22662404

Boyatzis, R., Stubbs, E., & Taylor, S. (2002). Learning cognitive and emotional intelligence competencies through graduate management education. *Academy of Management Learning & Education*, *1*(2), 150–162. doi:10.5465/amle.2002.8509345

Boyd, D., & Ellison, N. B. (2007). Social network sites: Definition, history, and scholarship. *Journal of Computer-Mediated Communication*, *13*(1), 210–230. doi:10.1111/j.1083-6101.2007.00393.x

Burak, L. (2012). Multitasking in the university classroom. *International Journal for the Scholarship of Teaching and Learning*, *6*(2), 1–12. doi:10.20429/ijsotl.2012.060208

Das, B., & Sahoo, J. (2011). Social networking sites, a critical analysis of its impact on personal and social life. *International Journal of Business and Social Science*, *2*(14), 222–228.

Freshman, B., & Rubino, L. (2004). Emotional Intelligence Skills for Maintaining Social Networks in Healthcare Organizations. *Hospital Topics*, *82*(3), 2–9. doi:10.3200/HTPS.82.3.2-9 PMID:15754856

Gardner, H. (1983). Frames of Mind: The Theory of Multiple Intelligences (2nd ed.). Basic books Publishers.

Gardner, H., & Hatch, T. (1989). Multiple intelligences go to school: Educational implications of the theory of multiple intelligences. *Educational Researcher, 18*(8), 4–10.

Goleman, D. (1996). Emotional intelligence. Why it can matter more than IQ. *Learning, 24*(6), 49–50.

Hair, J., Anderson, R., Tatham, R., & Black, W. (1998). *Multivariate data analysis.* Upper Saddle River, NJ: Prentice Hall, Inc.

Haq, A., & Chand, S. (2012). Pattern of Facebook usage and its impact on academic performance of university students: A gender based comparison. *Bulletin of Education and Research, 34*(2), 19–28.

Jordan, P., Ashkanasy, N., & Hartel, C. (2002). Emotional intelligence as a moderator of emotional and behavioral reactions to job insecurity. *Academy of Management Review, 27*(3), 361–372. doi:10.5465/amr.2002.7389905

Junco, R. (2012). Too much face and not enough books: The relationship between multiple indices of Facebook use and academic performance. *Computers & Education, 58*, 187–198.

Lopes, P., Bracket, M., Nezlek, J., Schurtz, A., Sellin, I., & Salovey, P. (2004, August). Emotional Intelligence and Social Interaction. *Personality and Social Psychology Bulletin, 30*(8), 1018–1034. doi:10.1177/0146167204264762 PMID:15257786

Lopes, P., Salovey, P., & Straus, R. (2003). Emotional intelligence, personality, and the perceived quality of social relationships. *Personality and Individual Differences, 35*(3), 641–658. doi:10.1016/S0191-8869(02)00242-8

Madge, C., Meek, J., Wellens, J., & Hooley, T. (2009). Facebook, social integration and informal learning at university: 'It is more for socialising and talking to friends about work than for actually doing work.' *Learning, Media and Technology, 34*(2), 141–155. doi:10.1080/17439880902923606

Multi-Health Systems Inc. (MHS). (2002). MSCEIT Resource Report, for the Mayer-Salovey-Caruso Emotional Intelligence Test. Retrieved from https://www.mhs.com/MHS-Talent?prodname=msceit

Moran, M., Seaman, J., & Tinti-Kane, H. (2011). *Teaching, Learning, and Sharing: How Today's Higher Education Faculty Use Social Media.* Boston, MA: Babson Survey Research Group.

Olbricht, G., & Wang, Y. (2018). Power and Sample Size Calculation. Retrieved from http://www.stat.purdue.edu/~bacraig/SCS/Power%20and%20Sample%20Size%20Calculation.doc

Paul, J., Baker, H., & Cochran, J. (2012). Effect of online social networking on student academic performance. *Computers in Human Behavior, 28*(6), 2117–2127. doi:10.1016/j.chb.2012.06.016

Petrides, K., Vernon, P., Schermer, J., Ligthart, L., Boomsma, D., & Veselka, L. (2010). Relationships between trait emotional intelligence and the Big Five in the Netherlands. *Personality and Individual Differences, 48*(8), 906–910. doi:10.1016/j.paid.2010.02.019

Petrides, K., Vernon, P. A., Schermer, J. A., Ligthart, L., Boomsma, D. I., & Veselka, L. (2010). Relationships between trait emotional intelligence and the Big Five in the Netherlands. *Personality and Individual Differences*, *48*(8), 906–910. doi:10.1016/j.paid.2010.02.019

Rossen, E., & Kranzler, J. (2009). Incremental validity of the Mayer–Salovey–Caruso Emotional Intelligence Test. *Journal of Research in Personality*, *43*(1), 60–65. doi:10.1016/j.jrp.2008.12.002

Rouis, S. (2012). Impact of Cognitive Absorption on Facebook on Students' Achievement. *Cyberpsychology, Behavior, and Social Networking*, *15*(6), 296–303. doi:10.1089/cyber.2011.0390 PMID:22703035

Salovey, P., & Mayer, J. D. (1990). Emotional intelligence. *Imagination, Cognition and Personality*, *9*(3), 185–211. doi:10.2190/DUGG-P24E-52WK-6CDG

Smith, L., Heaven, P., & Ciarrochi, J. (2008). Trait emotional intelligence, conflict communication patterns, and relationship satisfaction. *Personality and Individual Differences*, *44*(6), 1314–1325. doi:10.1016/j.paid.2007.11.024

Thainat, O. (2015). The relationship between Procrastination and Emotional Intelligence among Yarmouk University Students [master thesis]. Yarmouk University, Irbid, Jordan.

Tuan, N., & Tu, N. (2013). The Impact of Online Social Networking on Students' Study. *NU Journal of Education Research*, *29*(1), 1–13.

This research was previously published in the International Journal of Cyber Behavior, Psychology and Learning (IJCBPL), 9(1); pages 49-64, copyright year 2019 by IGI Publishing (an imprint of IGI Global).

APPENDIX A: SHORT DESCRIPTION OF ITEMS AND THEIR MEANS AND STANDARD DEVIATIONS

Table 9. Short description of items and their means and standard deviations

Code	Description	Mean	Std. Dev.
EA1	I find it difficult to understand others' nonverbal messages	2.43	1.149
EA2	I am aware of my emotions that I live and experience	3.76	1.091
EA3	I am aware of the nonverbal messages that I send to others	3.82	1.142
EA4	I am aware of the nonverbal messages sent by others	3.63	1.080
EA5	I can distinguish my negative and positive feelings and their impact on me	4.03	1.071
EA6	I can express and talk about my emotions easily	3.49	1.324
Emotional Awareness (EA)		**3.51**	**0.699**
EM1	I can control myself when I'm angry	2.83	1.350
EM2	I can easily forget my negative feelings	2.83	1.361
EM3	I feel that I can accomplish my work with patience	3.58	1.147
EM4	I can shift my negative feelings to positive ones when necessary	3.76	1.066
EM5	I can control my feelings under all circumstances	3.21	1.237
EM6	I can be calm under any circumstances I am exposed to	3.10	1.286
EM7	I am calm when I do any work	3.64	1.168
Emotional Management (EM)		**3.26**	**0.751**
SEM1	I try not to hurt the feelings of others	4.04	1.126
SEM2	I feel the needs of others	3.97	1.072
SEM3	I feel bad when I hurt others	4.01	1.169
SEM4	Others see that I am sensitive to their emotional needs	3.10	1.211
SEM5	I sympathize with people because I feel their feelings	3.85	1.074
SEM6	People feel that I am sensitive to their feelings and what happens to them	3.26	1.246
SEM7	I can solve problems and conflicts between others	3.66	1.014
Social Emotional Management (SEM)		**3.70**	**0.746**
MD1	My feelings guide me to how to deal with others	3.68	1.148
MD2	When I am in a positive mood, I can come up with new ideas	4.18	1.041
MD3	When I feel a change in my emotions, I tend to come up with new ideas	3.56	1.088
MD4	I use my positive emotions to guide my life	3.79	1.065
MD5	I can change my emotions depending on the situation	3.60	1.160
MD6	I use my good mood to keep going and face obstacles	3.90	1.080
Motivational Dimension (MD)		**3.78**	**0.682**

APPENDIX B: ROTATED COMPONENT MATRIX[A]

Table 10. Rotated component matrix

Items	Dimensions			
	1	2	3	4
EA1	0.654			
EA2	0.701			
EA3	0.660			
EA4	0.529			
EA5	0.654			
EA6	0.586			0.332
EM1			0.694	
EM2			0.589	
EM3			0.355	0.344
EM4			0.562	
EM5			0.719	
EM6			0.711	
EM7			0.575	0.383
SEM1	0.326	0.646		
SEM2		0.718		
SEM3		0.813		
SEM4		0.542		0.515
SEM5		0.819		
SEM6		0.575		0.529
SEM7				0.583
MD1	0.514	0.335		
MD2	0.696			
MD3	0.378			0.370
MD4	0.484			
MD5	0.434		0.358	
MD6	0.430			

Extraction Method: Principal Component Analysis; Rotation Method: Varimax with Kaiser Normalization; a. Rotation converged in 11 iterations

Chapter 63
Student and Faculty Perceptions of Social Media Use and Relationships Inside and Outside the Higher Education Classroom

Julie A. Delello
https://orcid.org/0000-0002-4326-8096
The University of Texas at Tyler, USA

Kouider Mokhtari
https://orcid.org/0000-0002-0794-6697
The University of Texas at Tyler, USA

ABSTRACT

This study examined student and faculty perceptions of social media use inside and outside the classroom. Three hundred and ninety-six students and fifty faculty members at a regional university campus in the south central United States voluntarily completed an online survey soliciting quantitative and qualitative data about their perceptions of social media use. Results revealed important findings highlighting similarities, differences, and insights among student and faculty perceptions of social media use in the classroom, their views about whether social media use constitutes a distraction, and how each group views social media relationships in and out of the classroom. These findings are quite consistent with prior and emerging research about social media use and have implications for how institutions of higher education can explore meaningful ways of incorporating social media in the classroom with the goal of strengthening teaching and learning.

DOI: 10.4018/978-1-6684-7123-4.ch063

INTRODUCTION

New and emerging advances in social media and mobile technologies have allowed us to communicate with others almost anywhere and at any time. In fact, the New Media Consortium predicted that social media will be used as a platform for continuous sharing of information and collaboration in education over the next five years (Adams Becker, Cummins, Davis, Freeman, Hall Giesinger, & Ananthanarayanan, 2017). According to a survey by the Pew Research Center, Americans build connections and share information with one another through the social media technologies Facebook, Youtube, and Twitter (Smith & Anderson, 2018). In 2019, there are predicted to be approximately 221 million Facebook, 200 million You Tube, and 69 million Twitter users in the United States (Clement, 2019). According to Clement (2019), there were also 203 million daily Snapchat users. These social media consumers are predicted to spend an average of 2 hours and 22 minutes per day networking socially (GlobalWebIndex, 2019).

Social media have also permeated institutions of higher education. According to the *NMC Horizon Report: 2015 Higher Education*, the use of social media by faculty members and students on campuses is expanding (Johnson, Adams Becker, Estrada, & Freeman, 2015). Research has suggested that more than half of college students are continuously connected to popular social networking sites (SNS) such as Facebook, YouTube, Snapchat, Instagram, and Twitter (Smith & Anderson, 2018). Mirroring the general population, researchers reported that 70% of faculty utilized SNS and of those, 55% used social media for managing their professional image (Seaman & Tinti-Kane, 2013). In another study, almost 85% of faculty noted having a Facebook account, two-thirds (67%) were on LinkedIn, and 50% used Twitter (Faculty Focus, 2011). However, other research has highlighted much lower percentages of faculty (50%) utilizing social media for instruction especially among those over age 55 (Kumi-Yeboah & Blankson, 2018).

Heiberger & Junco (2015) suggested that in order to improve educational outcomes, faculty should be using social media like Facebook and Twitter to engage students. But to what extent are faculty and students actually using social media in the classroom? The purpose of this study was to examine student and faculty perceptions regarding the potential benefits or detriments in the classroom. Do they view social media as beneficial for instruction? Or do they see them as a mere distraction? A related purpose of this research was to highlight how faculty and students felt about extending social media relationships outside the classroom. To date, little is known about the effects of teacher-student social media relationships in the higher education setting (Metzger, Finley, Ulbrich, McAuley, 2010; Hershkovitz & Forkosh-Baruch, 2013).

BACKGROUND

Social media technologies have the capability to change "the nature of the way we communicate, access information, connect with peers and colleagues, learn, and even socialize" (Johnson, Adams Becker, & Cummins, 2012, p. 6). The term social media is defined as "a group of Internet-based applications that build on the ideological and technological foundations of Web 2.0 and that allow the creation and exchange of user-generated content" (Kaplan & Haenlein, 2010, p.61). Web 2.0 refers to the second generation of the World Wide Web which promotes greater collaboration and sharing across the Internet through social media platforms such as Facebook, Pinterest, and Instagram which integrate visual tools with digital technologies (Delello & McWhorter, 2014). The evolution from Web 1.0 to 2.0 has allowed for more user participation and improved interaction and socialization (Eteokleous-Grigoriou & Ktoridou, 2014). Moreover, Web 3.0, combining the features of Web 1.0 and 2.0, will continue to evolve as a more intelligent web poised to allow users to co-construct and share additional information with one another.

Use of Social Media Among Young Adults

The Keiser Foundation (2013) reported that, "The continued expansion of high-speed home Internet access, the proliferation of television content available online, and the development of compelling new applications such as social networking and YouTube, have all contributed to the increase in the amount of media young people consume each day" (p. 3). Sites such as YouTube, Facebook, Instagram, Snapchat, Twitter, and Pinterest have continued to be most popular for adults 18 to 29 years of age (Perrin & Anderson, 2019). In fact, 80% of users, ages 18-29, use Snapchat and 76% of these users reported using Instagram daily with most using the SNS multiple times per day (Perrin & Anderson, 2019). More than half (51%) of the 18-24 year olds also reported that they would have a difficult time if they were unable to use social media (Smith & Anderson, 2018).

Use of Social Media among College Students

According to the New Media Consortium [NMC], the use of social media is positioned to change the face of education (Adams Becker, Cummins, Davis, Freeman, Hall Giesinger, &, Ananthanarayanan, 2017). Students will use SNS to embark on collaborative learning and "seamless sharing and communication" (Adams Becker, et al, 2017, p. 20). The Institute of Politics at Harvard Kennedy School (2017), reported that "Facebook (87%), Twitter (47%), Instagram (45%), Pinterest (37%), Snapchat (34%) and Tumblr (19%) are all more popular among college students than among young Americans who are not in, or never have attended, college" (para. 5). Quan-Haase and Young (2010) noted that majority of college students visited multiple social media sites daily to stay connected with their family and friends. This may be correlated to the upsurge in the use of Internet ready mobile devices as 97% of college students own a Smartphone (Neilson, 2016) and are connected to a digital device more than 141 hours per week (Refuel Agency, 2015).

In the United States, young adults spend close to 200 minutes per day on their mobile device and much of this time is devoted to using SNS (Clement, 2019). In fact, Wang, Chen, and Liang (2011) reported that college students post or respond to social media 6-8 hours per day and much of this takes place during school hours. Moreover, Junco & Cotton (2011) noted the typical college student sends an average of 96 text messages and receives nearly 104 text messages per day, and spends an average of 1.4 hours on Facebook.

Use of Social Media among College Faculty

A Pearson report, *How Today's Higher Education Faculty Use Social Media* suggested that almost 65% of faculty use social media for personal use while 45% of faculty used social media for their professional careers outside of teaching. Most of this use was with the social media platform Facebook with over half of faculty surveyed reporting using it monthly (Moran, Seaman, & Tinti-Kate, 2012). Additonally, some studies have shown that more than 80 percent of professors may be using social media as part of their teaching (Moran, Seaman, & Tinti-Kate, 2011). Research supports the notion that younger faculty use social media 10% more than those with more than 20 years of teaching experience; 30% of faculty have used social media to post content for students outside class, and 20% have asked students to comment or add additional posts online (Moran, et al., 2011). It is not surprising to also note that research has shown that faculty who teach online are somewhat more likely to visit social media sites than those who only teach face-to-face (F2F) courses (Tinti-Kane & Seaman, 2010). Additionally, an additional 30% of faculty do not use social media at all (Moran, et. al, 2011).

Use of Social Media in Teaching and Learning

Social media may be leveraged by faculty to create learning opportunities within the classroom (Delello, McWhorter, & Camp, 2015; Helvie-Mason, 2011; Junco, Hemberger, & Loken, 2010). For example, Irwin, Ball, Desbrow, and Leveritt (2012) reported that 78% of the students they surveyed felt that Facebook could be an effective tool for classroom instruction. More recently, another study reported that 75% of education students and 68% of business students noted that Facebook enhanced their course learning experience (Hall, McWhorter, & Delello, 2017). Additonally, Thalluri and Penman (2015) suggested that creating content specific discussions and reflections on Facebook are valuable approaches to using SNS for teaching and learning. Delello, McWhorter, & Camp (2015) conveyed that Facebook, used as part of a course, was beneficial in terms of engaging students and building community and personal meaning. Some researchers also reported that students perceived that using Pinterest supported both course engagement and motivation (Delello & McWhorter, 2014). Additionally, the use of Twitter has also been shown to promote active participation of educator communities, develop social presence, and reshape the way students learned (Delello and Consalvo, 2019; Baisley-Nodine, Ritzhaupt, & Antonenko, 2018).

Visual Social Media

Delello and McWhorter (2014) found that "A powerful social media trend is the blending of visual tools with innovative digital technologies such as Facebook, Twitter, Pinterest, and Instagram" (p. 371). This is consistent with prior reseach indicating that students spend 1-5 hours per day networking and even more on the weekends posting pictures and videos across social media sites (Knight-McCord, Cleary, Grant, Herron, Jumbo, Lacey... Emanuel, 2015). Videos, emojis, Bitmojis, GIFs, and memes are also quickly becoming part of a college students' social media landscape. Colleges are transforming their social media use to reach students. According to the New York Times, students coming to campus are from "a generation that rarely reads books or emails, breathes through social media, feels isolated and stressed but is crazy driven and wants to solve the world's problems (not just volunteer)" (Pappano, 2018, para. 4). These Generation Z students, ages 14 to 23, spend three hours or more a day using YouTube (Pearson, 2018). Moreover, Zmikly (2016) reported that the SNS Snapchat has become "impossible to ignore" as it has "a rapidly growing user base and content reaching 41 percent of all 18-to-34-year-olds in the United States" (para. 3).

In a survey conducted by the Harris Poll and commissioned by Tenor (2017), 36% of millennials ages 18-34 prefer to use visual expressions such as emojis and GIFs. In 2015, the word emoji, defined as an icon used to express an idea or emotion in electronic communication, was added to the Oxford Dictionary as word of the year (Oxford University Press, 2019). Billions of emojis have been shared across SNS and the 'face with tears of joy' emoji has been shared over two million times (Rothenberg, 2019; see Figure 1). Similar to an emoji, Bitmoji, owned by Snapchat, is an avatar that can be created, personalized, and shared across SNS (see Figure 2). A GIF (Graphical Interchange Format) is a short animated video or series of images that consistently loop. For example, Microsoft created a GIF of an angler fish to accompany their phrase "empowering every student and educator to achieve more" (see https://gph.is/2zzwhJa); it was uploaded into giphy (giphy.com) to allow users to share across SNS. Similar to a GIF, a meme is a virally transmitted photograph or image. Facebook, Twitter, and Tumblr have all incorporated GIFs or memes within their social media pages.

Students have reported that the use of such visuals communicate their feelings better than words (Tenor, 2017). Moreover, some educators are finding the use of visual social media tools like Bitmojis and GIFs are positively reinforcing to their students (King, 2019). Additionally, 37% of educators surveyed incorporated visual images like memes, emojis, and GIFs to help facilitate a lesson noting that the use of social media allowed them to better relate to their students (Will, 2017).

According to Educause (2006), "Any technology that is able to captivate so many students for so much time not only carries implications for how those students view the world but also offers an opportunity for educators to understand the elements of social networking that students find so compelling and to incorporate those elements into teaching and learning" (p. 2).

Figure 1. Face with Tears of Joy Emoji

Figure 2. Example of a Bitmoji

CHALLENGES TO A LACK OF SOCIAL MEDIA PRESENCE

College students who do not have mobile devices such as cell phones may feel disconnected, feel anxious and/or have a fear of missing out (FoMO) if not connected (Alt, 2018). Studies have shown that students may even develop nomophobia or "the fear of being out of mobile phone contact" (SecurEnvoy, 2012, para. 1). Researchers at The University of Buffalo reported that smartphones are reinforcing to students and students would rather be deprived of food than give up their phone (O'Donnell & Epstein, 2019). Other researchers found that females who were common users of Pinterest and Instagram and males who spent time using Facebook were more likely to have cell phone addictions (Roberts, Yaya, & Manolis, 2014).

Even though faculty may be increasing their use of social media in the classroom, concerns over student privacy and the integrity of student work exist (Seaman & Tinti-Kane, 2013; Waycott, Thompson, Sheard, & Clerehan, 2017). Garrison (2017) suggested that social media has not been purposed for education but rather used as a means to share personal "selfies and titillating bits of information" (p. 153). Some researchers have suggested that "distractions, stress, anxiety, and social media plague the college classroom making it tough for faculty to teach" (Myatt & Kennette, 2017, para. 2). In fact, over 75% of faculty surveyed noted that digital media has increased communication but also added additional stress and work hours to their loads (Seaman & Tinti-Kate, 2013). And, a large proportion of faculty say Facebook (53%) and Twitter (46%) have "negative" value for use in class (Moran, et al., 2011). For example, researchers found that Facebook use was negatively correlated to both grade and study habits (Junco & Cotton, 2012; Kirschner & Karpinski, 2010). Sanger (2010) noted that "There is no reason to think that repurposing social media for education will magically make students more inspired and engaged" (p. 18). Others have also suggested that undergraduate students may have difficulties in judging the legitimacy of the validity of content shared on social media (Adams Becker, et al., 2017). According to Hall, Delello, & McWhorter (2017) students may also have personal reasons against using sites such as Facebook which must be considered by instructors before making SNSs mandatory.

Social Media Relationships Outside the Classroom

Previous studies have reported that informal or out-of-classroom communication between students and teachers results in positive outcomes, including greater academic achievements (Pascarella, 1985) and a greater sense of well-being of both teachers and students (Roorda, Koomen, Spilt, & Oort, 2011). Helvie-Mason (2011) conveyed that students may use social media for mentoring or to stay connected to their instructors after the course has ended. In one study, almost 40% of students reported being friends with faculty outside of class (Sheldon, 2015). Students suggested that befriending faculty outside of class allowed them to see their instructors as real persons (DiVerniero & Hosek, 2011). Sturgeon and Walker (2009) found that students were more willing to communicate with their instructors if they were already friends on a social media site. Another study reported that faculty members who posted personal tweets on Twitter were more credible to students than those who only posted scholarly ones (Johnson, 2011).

However, the notion of faculty-student social media relationships remains somewhat controversial. Due to the pervasive nature of social media, many times, the boundaries between the professional and personal lives of faculty and students may become blurred. Cain and Fink (2010) noted that even though faculty may want to use social media for instruction, negative results may occur when knowing too much about one's private life outside of the classroom. When it comes to connecting with students personally, research indicates that only 32% of faculty have friended undergraduate students and about half (55%) connected with some students after graduation; Many students reported that they would terminate their social media connection with their instructor at the end of the semester (DiVerniero & Hosek, 2011). Furthermore, because social media policies are non-existent or "gray" at almost 25% of institutions of higher education, the potential risk of crossing personal-professional boundaries may be high (Pomerantz, Hank, & Sugimoto, 2015).

Social Presence Theory

Researchers have suggested that learning through social media may create a sense of "social presence" between faculty-student and student-student (Delello & Consalvo, 2019). Garrison, Anderson and Archer (2000) defined *social presence* as the "the ability of participants in a community of inquiry to project themselves socially and emotionally, as 'real' people (i.e., their full personality), through the medium of communication being used" (p. 94). Gunawardena and Zittle (1997) argued that social presence is really about the degree to which a person is perceived as real within the mode of communication. Akyol, Garrison, and Ozden (2009) noted that students value social presence as a means to "share ideas, to express views, and to collaborate" (p. 76). Kawachi (2013) reported that social media can strengthen social presence by creating a sense of trust between individuals. And, according to Aragon (2003), "Social presence is one of the most significant factors in improving instructional effectiveness and building a sense of community" (Aragon, 2003, p. 57). However, research by Kaplan (2010) suggested that there are degrees of social presence within SNSs, which range from low to high. For example, the use of blogs would be considered low, social media like Facebook were ranked in the mid-range, and virtual worlds such as Second Life are considered high in terms of social presence.

Garrison (2017) questioned whether social media can move beyond a superficial role and promote an effective educational learning experience. Rather than a human-machine interaction, students and faculty must view the social media experience as a human-human relationship (Kerhwald, 2007). Researchers also noted that many times, when social media is integrated into the classroom, students may use it differently than it was assigned for such as non-academic discussions (Arnold & Paulus, 2010). It is evident that additional research is needed to better understand the challenges associated with the use of social media within the classroom (Delello & McWhorter, 2015) and the nature of the relationships of social presence and social media use in the classroom (Dunlap and Lowenthal, 2009).

FOCUS OF THE CURRENT CHAPTER

This chapter presents findings from a descriptive study, in which the authors explored faculty and student perceptions regarding the use of social media in the higher education classroom. A standard mixed-methods survey design was used to gather data pertaining to faculty and student perceptions of social media inside and outside the classroom. The online survey consisted of closed and open-ended questions allowing us to uncover as well as to more fully describe faculty and student views and opinions about social media use in the classroom and explore perceived personal and social media relationships between faculty and students outside of the classroom. The following two overarching research questions guided the study.

1.   What are students and faculty perceptions of social media use in the classroom?
2.   What are students and faculty views of social media relationships outside the classroom?

Study Participants

Participants in this study consisted of 396 students and 50 faculty members from a mid-size, regional four-year university in the Southwestern United States. Table 1 presents a description of student demographic characteristics. Of the 396 students participating, 120 (30%) were male and 272 (69%) were female. Four students (1%) reported their gender as other. Two hundred-forty five (62%) were White, 66 (17%) Hispanic, 40 (10%) Black, 33 (8%) Asian, 2 (.5%) Native American, and 9 (2%) were reported as other. There were almost as many graduate students as undergraduates participating in the study. Additionally, the students represented all seven of the university's colleges: Nursing (81/21%); Education and Psychology (74/19%); Business and Technology (105/26%); Pharmacy (14/4%); Engineering (37/9%); Arts and Sciences (70/18%); and the University College (7/2%). Seven (2%) stated other.

Table 1. Student demographic profiles (N=396)

	Count	Percent
Gender		
Male	120	30%
Female	272	69%
Other	4	1%
Ethnicity		
African-American	40	10%
Asian-American	33	8%
White	245	66%
Hispanic	66	17%
Native-American	2	.5%
Other	9	2%
Year in College		
Freshmen	7	1.77%
Sophomore	36	9.09%
Junior	83	20.96%
Senior	89	22.47%
Graduate	181	45.71
College Affiliation		
Arts & Sciences	70	17.72%
Business	105	26.58%
Education & Psychology	74	18.73%
Engineering	37	9.37%
Nursing & Health Sciences	81	20.51%
Pharmacy	14	3.54%
University College	7	1.77%
Other	7	1.77%

Table 2 presents a description of faculty demographic characteristics. of the 50 faculty members participating in the study, 22 (44%) were male and 28 (56%) were female. Forty (80%) of the faculty who responded were White, 4 (8%) were Hispanic, 2 (4%) were Black, and 4 (8%) were Asian. Respondents included all faculty ranks with the majority representing Assistant Professors (38%), followed by Non-Tenure Track Faculty consisting of lecturers and other (28%), Associate Professors (20%), and Full Professors (14%). Additionally, faculty members reported from one to 38 years of teaching experience (Mean=13.78; SD=36.1). The majority of faculty reported teaching face-to-face (62%) as compared to online classes (38%). It is worth noting that Non-Tenure Track (71.7%), Assistant (66.1%) and Associate Professors (68.5%) reported teaching more face-to-face than online classes. Inversely, Full Professors reported teaching more online (60.7%) than face-to face classes (39.3%).

Table 2. Faculty demographic profiles (N=50)

	Count	Percent
Gender		
Male	22	44%
Female	28	56%
Ethnicity		
African-American	2	4%
Asian-American	4	8%
White	40	80%
Hispanic	4	8%
Academic Rank		
Lecturer	7	18%
Assistant Professor	19	38%
Associate Professor	10	20%
Full Professor	7	14%
Other	5	10%
Percent Classes Taught		
Face-to-Face	59.71%	
Online	16.0%	
Hybrid	21.6%	
Years Teaching Experience		
Mean	13.78	
Standard Deviation	9.17	

Survey Instruments

Data was gathered using two versions of an online survey in order to examine student and faculty perceptions of social media use and relationships inside and outside the classroom. The student survey contained four demographic questions regarding gender, ethnicity, classification, and major. Additionally, four open-ended questions on the survey asked students whether they were allowed to use social media during class time, whether social media was required as a part of any course they were taking, whether using social media in the classroom was viewed as a distraction, and if they were "friends" with their instructor on any social media platform outside of school. Furthermore, each question had an open-ended comment box to allow participants the opportunity to provide additional feedback.

The faculty survey closely mirrored the student survey and asked demographic questions regarding gender, ethnicity, years of teaching experience, and rank. Additionally, faculty members were asked four questions regarding whether students were permitted to use social media in class, the types of social media they used as part of a course requirement, whether they viewed social media as a distraction, and if students had access to their personal social networks (e.g. Facebook, Twitter) outside of school. Faculty were also given the opportunity to provide additional feedback on the open-response items.

Students and faculty participants received an email invitation with a follow-up reminder at two weeks, four weeks, and six weeks to complete an anonymous online Qualtrics survey, which was approved by the university's Institutional Review Board (IRB). For purposes of survey quality design considerations as well as data triangulation and trustworthiness, the survey was piloted with five students and three faculty members and subsequently revised prior to administration.

DATA ANALYSIS

Three types of analyses were conducted when exploring faculty and student perceptions social media use and connections in and outside the classroom. Descriptive statistics such as frequencies, means, and standard deviations were used to analyze participant responses to quantitative questions. A Pearson Chi Square was utilized, where appropriate, to determine if differences exist among participants by independent variables such as gender, ethnicity, faculty rank, years of teaching experience. To complement these analyses, a constant-comparative method was used to analyze participant responses to open-ended questions. Following qualitative research guidelines, the open-ended responses, the authors individually compared and contrasted the data, creating codes and developing meaningful themes, and discussed the themes emerging from the data (Miles & Huberman, 1994).

RESULTS

Student and Faculty Perceptions of Social Media Use in The Classroom

Social Media Use in Courses

When students were asked specifically if they were allowed to use social media in class, 34% reported yes and 66% said no. When asked if their instructors used social media as part of a course, 29% reported using no social media. However, students reported that 71% of their instructors used some type of social media for instruction. Specifically, students noted that You Tube (23%), LinkedIn (8.1%); Google (6.6%), Facebook (6%), Skype (5.7%), Twitter (5.6%), Pinterest (5.4%), Instagram (2.4%), and My Space (.9%) were incorporated into their courses.

In the open-ended comment boxes provided in the survey, students reported using other social media such as Tumblr, Zoom, FaceTime, Blackboard, electronic portfolios, and the Internet. Some students also noted they used various websites related to course content.

Similarly, when faculty were asked whether they allowed students to use social media in the classroom, 28% stated yes and 72% reported no. Male (16%) faculty allowed students to use more social media than female (12%) faculty. Assistant Professors (38%) reported the most use, followed by Non-Tenure track (28%), Associate Professors (20%), and Full Professors (14%). Of those social media sites reported, faculty members noted they used YouTube (29%), Google+ (13%), Twitter (8.4%); Facebook (6%); LinkedIn (3.6%), Skype (3.6%); Pinterest (2.4%), and other online sites such as Tumblr or Zoom (9%). However, when stratified by gender, female faculty (56%) reported higher uses of all social media in their classrooms than male faculty (44%). In fact, female faculty used all types of social media more than their male counterparts.

Regarding the role social media plays in course instruction, only the use of Google produced a statistically significant difference across gender ($\chi^2 = 3.18$, p > .05). Moreover, for female faculty who used social media, the majority used just one site for instruction in a course (16%) while male faculty used two or more (10%).

Social Media as a Distraction

When faculty and students were asked whether they felt distracted when students use electronic devices (e.g. iPhone, iPad, laptop, tablet) during class and why, slightly more than half (52%) of faculty stated yes but only 23% of students thought the use of devices were a distraction. For the students who freported feeling distracted, 22% of the responses were related to the use of social media. For faculty who reported feeling distracted, females (29.8%) were more distracted by their students' use of social media than males (17%).

In response to this question, students reported 167 open-ended statements regarding the use of social media as a distraction in the open-ended comment boxes. A qualitative analysis of these data yielded six themes, which were categorized as: Disengagement, sound media, light media, location, privacy, and irrelevance. Subthemes included texting, talking, chatting, surfing, in-class, and online (see Table 3).

Furthermore, among students who did not think the use of social media was a distraction, some reported that social media use was *irrelevant* and "just a part of everyday life". Other students noted a need to respect other students' privacy. For example, one student stated, "I respect others privacy, no matter if they are taking notes on their device or texting someone, it's not my place to be in their business".

Similarly, the themes emerging from faculty comments focused on policies, strategies, disrespect, and distraction. For the first theme of distraction, faculty responses ranged from "Actually it bothers me" to "YES! and I think all the other students do too" to "It does not distract my ability to teach at all, as taking notes and looking at the internet appear the same to me." When faculty were asked whether they felt distracted when students used electronic devices such as cell phones, iPads, laptops, and tablets, 52.08% reported not being distracted while 47% reported feeling distracted. One faculty stated that they were unsure whether devices in class were a distraction to students noting, "I can't speculate on student's reactions." Another theme that emerged was that of disrespect as one faculty member reported that even though they were not distracted, they felt disrespected and felt the students "were missing out by not participating."

The third theme that emerged was related to policies guiding socia media use in the classroom. Some faculty felt that it was important to have a policy in place. In fact, one faculty member even cited a particular business school that changed its policy to not allow electronic devices in class.

Table 3. Themes related to using social media devices in the classroom

Themes	Subthemes	YES	NO
Disengaged		• Because somethings might be more interesting than the class. • They are not on task • I am easily distracted by just about anything, to be honest - but, if they are doing something other than course work, I am curious/nosy, and wish to see what it is. • Concentration is affected • Usually it's for something social and not school related. • Yes, because it demonstrates the student is not fully present with the class.	• Not as much as the professors get distracted or annoyed by it. It's not a bad distraction. Sometimes it keeps me awake. • I don't feel distracted all of the time, but there are some moments when it can get that way. As a student, when you see someone doing something other than listening to the lecture, it can be distracting to know what they're doing.
Sound Media	• Texting • Chatting • Talking • Surfing	• Because seeing someone texting or messing around on social media on their phone can take my attention away from what the professor is saying. • If they are taking notes it is fine, but if they are on social websites or chatting it is distracting and aggravating. • I get distracted when people talk about what they see on Facebook or other social media sites. • Yes, at times because students will be surfing the web, using social media and other things.	
Light Media		• I tend to watch their screen or get distracted with the noise from typing.	
Location	• In Class • Online	• If they're right in front of me, it can be distracting if they're not using it for the class. • Sometimes yes. If someone is sitting in front of me and they're playing a video game or on Pinterest it distracts me.	• I sit close up front or am writing notes. • I don't pay attention to other students. I sit in the front and don't see what is on their computers. • I'm doing everything online, so I am not distracted by other students.
Privacy			• …It's not my place to be in their business.
Irrelevance			• It doesn't really matter if they do. • It's part of everyday life.

Finally, faculty noted they were working on strategies to integrate more social media devices in the classroom. Two faculty members reported allowing devices for class assignments and one noted, "I have been working on strategies to use the smartphone as part of class activities. This seems to diminish usage during regular lecture, which I view as a distraction." Another member wrote, "But it depends on what they are doing. I let them use devices as writing or research tools when we are writing in class".

Student and Faculty Perceptions of Social Media Relationships Outside The Classroom

When students were asked whether they were connected to any of their instructors' personal social networks outside of school (e.g. "friend or tweet" them?)", 16% reported doing so while an overwhelming majority reported not doing so. For those stating yes, three specific social media were mentioned which included LinkedIn, Facebook, and Twitter. For example, one student commented, "Yup, I'm friends with several of my professors on Facebook. We're cool." Another student noted, "Friends of FB and following on Twitter."

Similarly, when faculty were asked whether they allowed students to access their personal social networks. 29% stated yes while 71% reported no. In terms of gender, female (16.3%) faculty friended students slightly more than male faculty (12.2%). Of those faculty who reported yes, a few stated that they only allow students to "friend" them personally after they have "finished the course" or "graduated". One faculty noted, "Only on LinkedIn" while another stated, "I have a professional Facebook page for students". For those faculty who conveyed they did not allow students personal access to their social media, some stated it was "unprofessional" or that departmental policies did not allow for it. Faculty who taught F2F courses (52.5%) stated they would allow personal friendships as compared to just 47.5% of those teaching in online environments.

While social media relationships are occurring inside and outside the classroom between faculty and students, it is unclear whether these relationships truly create a sense of social presence and if so, to what degree. Thus, the role that social media play in the academic performance of students should be further investigated.

IMPLICATIONS FOR PRACTICE

This study revealed important findings. One key findings pertains to a significant discrepancy among faculty (52%) and students (23%) with respect to whether social media use is or is not a distraction inside the classroom. A second key finding relates to how the participants view social media relationships both inside and outside the classroom. Current research (e.g., Moran et al. 2012), suggest that a little over one-third of faculty use social media in the higher education classroom. The findings of our survey reveled a slightly lower percentage of faculty (28%) using social media for instruction. Moran et al. (2011) found that less experienced faculty use social media 10% more than faculty with more than 20 years of experience. In this study, more experienced faculty (M=13.77; SD=9.26) or those who were full professors were less likely to use social media than any other faculty ranking (non-tenure track, assistant professors, associate professors). It is interesting to note that those faculty who used the least social media and who had been employed in higher education the longest taught the most online courses. This is somewhat inconsistent with earlier research noting that faculty who teach online tend to visit social media sites more often (Tinti-Kane, et al., 2010).

Social media use was reported as the primary distraction in college classrooms. Papacharissi and Mendelson (2011) noted that "online media serve as functional alternatives to interpersonal and mediated communication, providing options or complements for aspects of an individuals' environment that are not as fulfilling" (p. 214). It is important to educate students on how to be responsible with their social media use (e.g. silencing devices, limiting use). However, it is just as important to create engaging classrooms which hold a student's attention. Delello & McWhorter (2015) noted that we must find ways to use social media in class as a tool for engagement as well as instruction. Hall, Delello, & McWhorter (2017) and Leder (2012) suggested that social media use over other learning management systems (LMS) such as discussion boards can enhance student communication and engagement leading to greater social presence. However, the lack of social presence may lead to lower levels of student satisfaction and perceived learning (Richardson, Maeda, Lv, Caskurlu, 2017) as well as higher levels of frustration (Wei, Chen, and Kinshuk, 2012). In this study, most of the social media (e.g. Facebook,

Twitter, YouTube) reported by students to be utilized for instruction would be classified as having a medium degree of social presence (Kaplan, 2010). It would be valuable to instructors to make sure they are matching the appropriate social media with the task in order to creates higher degrees of satisfaction.

Contrary to prior research indicating that interpersonal boundaries between faculty and student are shifting as we become more connected via social media; only 17% of students and 29% of faculty noted forming social media friendships outside of the classroom. In 2012, Wakefield found that 32% of faculty connect with undergraduates and almost 55% connect with graduate students. However, research has shown that interpersonal boundaries between faculty and student are shifting as we become more connected to one another and the world at large (Schwartz, 2012). Faculty need to set clear expectations for use in class but also boundaries—including their policies on friending students on personal social media pages. These should correlate to the college/department policies which should be created if they are not already in place.

CONCLUSION AND RECOMMENDATIONS

Because technological devices and the use of social media have become an integral part of college students' everyday life, there is value in finding new ways to incorporate information communication technologies into the classroom, which may encourage students to collaborate and communicate better with fellow students and faculty. On the other hand, faculty need to find ways to limit distractions these media can potentially create while promoting student learning and engagement. Additionally, while social media relationships are occurring both inside and outside the classroom between faculty and students, it is unclear whether these relationships truly create a sense of social presence and if so, to what degree. Thus, the role that social media play in the academic performance of students should be further investigated.

The findings of this study have important implications for faculty professional development opportunities where faculty work together to discuss and explore new and innovative ways of incorporating social media in the classroom. Questions examined in this study could form a basis for faculty professional development. For instance, should socia media be systematically incroprated in teaching and inside the higher education classroom? What is the role of students and faculty in determining which social media to inrporate in the classroom? In what ways can research, policy, and best practices help in developing a campus-wide vision for incorporating social media inside and outside the classroom? What curricular changes need to be made so that social media can be meaqnigfully incorporated in teaching and learning? What data should be collected to help ensure the impact of social media use in and outside of the classroom is systematically documented? Exploring these questions, and others, can be used to develop a research-informed strategy for socia media use that could potentially strengthen instruction and increase student and faculty engagement in teaching and learning. Suggestions for a start of such a professional development program could begin with having junior faculty team with more experienced faculty members to collaborate on how they use technology and further foster opportunities for teaching and scholarship between the group members. Groups of faculty could offer workshops or share examples of using technology at faculty meetings. Additionally, incentives could be offered such as academic innovation or teaching awards for those faculty members that use technology in their classrooms in new ways to promote student engagement and learning.

Limitations

Although this study has achieved its aims, it has unavoidable limitations, which must be taken into consideration when interpreting its findings. First, because of resource and access constraints, the study was conducted in only one, relatively small, public university setting. Thus, it is conceivable that different findings could be attained if the study were replicated in another university setting, at a different time, or with a different target group of students and faculty.

Second, the survey is a self-report instrument, which generates perceptual data about respondents use of social media inside and outside the classroom. These data reflect what respondents think they do and not what they actually do. For purposes of this study, student and faculty responses were viewed at face value. In addition, it is likely that some respondents may have had difficulty understanding some of the questions despite efforts to field-test the survey to evaluate administration procedures and survey items to identify potential issues prior to fullscale data collection. Some students may have alternative views and arguably different definitions of social media. A few noted that social media included the Internet, electronic portfolios, and video conferencing tools such as Zoom. In addition, students and faculty may not have been totally forthright regarding the personal nature of their online relationships with one another. Thus, there is a need in future research to take these liniting factors into consideration when exploring student and faculty perceptions aboit social media use inside and outside the classroom.

Finally, while the student sample size was adequate, the faculty sample size was much smaller. This makes it difficult to examine potential associations across variables within the faculty dataset, as statistical tests generally require larger sample sizes to ensure a representative distribution of the population. On the other hand, it is worth noting that this faculty sample represented approximately 20% of all faculty surveyed at the university and closely reflected the total faculty population in terms of age, gender, ethnicity, and other related characteristics. All faculty who responded to the surveys completed 100% of the survey questions. However, the response rate for female faculty members was 69%, compared to a response rate for male faculty members of 31%. Additionally, the majority of the faculty participants were White and thus the experiences of other faculty respondents may be underrepresented. Faculty respondents reflect the demographics of the institution as there are more females than men and only 17% of the full-time faculty are members of minority groups. These aspects of the study, and perhaps others, can potentially limit the generalizability of the study and should be interpreted with caution.

REFERENCES

Adams Becker, S., Cummins, M., Davis, A., Freeman, A., Hall Giesinger, C., & Ananthanarayanan, V. (2017). *NMC Horizon Report: 2017 Higher Education Edition*. Austin, TX: The New Media Consortium.

Akyol, Z., Garrison, D. R., & Ozden, M. Y. (2009). Online and blended communities of inquiry: Exploring the developmental and perceptional differences. *International Review of Research in Open and Distance Learning, 10*(6), 65–83. doi:10.19173/irrodl.v10i6.765

Alt, D. (2018). Students' wellbeing, fear of missing out, and social media engagement for leisure in higher education learning environments: Research and reviews. *Current Psychology, 37*(1), 128-138. http://dx.doi.org.ezproxy.uttyler.edu:2048/10.1007/s12144-016-9496-1

Aragon, S. R. (2003). Creating social presence in online environments. *New Directions for Adult and Continuing Education, 100*(100), 57–68. doi:10.1002/ace.119

Arnold, N., & Paulus, T. (2010). Using a social networking site for experiential learning: Appropriating, lurking, modeling and community building. *Internet and Higher Education, 13*(4), 188–196. doi:10.1016/j.iheduc.2010.04.002

Baisley-Nodine, E., Ritzhaupt, A., & Antonenko, P. (2018). Exploring social presence within an online course using Twitter. *E-Learning and Digital Media, 15*(5), 235–253. doi:10.1177/2042753018786004

Cain, J., & Fink, J. L. III. (2010). Legal and ethical issues regarding social media and pharmacy education. *American Journal of Pharmaceutical Education, 74*(10), 1–8. doi:10.5688/aj7410184 PMID:21436925

Clement, J. (2019, July). *Reach of leading social media and networking sites used by teenagers and young adults in the United States as of February 2017*. Retrieved from https://www.statista.com/statistics/199242/social-media-and-networking-sites-used-by-us-teenagers/

Delello, J. A., & Consalvo, A. L. (2019). "I Found Myself Retweeting": Using Twitter Chats to Build Professional Learning Networks. In J. Yoon & P. Semingson (Eds.), *Educational Technology and Resources for Synchronous Learning in Higher Education* (pp. 88–108). Hershey, PA: IGI Global. doi:10.4018/978-1-5225-7567-2.ch005

Delello, J. A., & McWhorter, R. R. (2014). New visual social media for the higher education classroom. In G. Mallia (Ed.), *The social classroom: Integrating social network use in education* (pp. 368–393). Hershey, PA: IGI Global. doi:10.4018/978-1-4666-4904-0.ch019

Delello, J. A., & McWhorter, R. R. (2014). Creating virtual communities of practice with the visual social media platform Pinterest. *International Journal of Social Media and Interactive Learning Environments, 2*(3), 216–236. doi:10.1504/IJSMILE.2014.064205

Delello, J. A., McWhorter, R. R., & Camp, K. M. (2015). Using social media as a tool for learning: A multi-disciplinary study. *International Journal on E-Learning, 14*(2), 163–180.

DiVerniero, R. A., & Hosek, A. M. (2011). Students' perceptions and communicative management of instructors' online self-disclosure. *Communication Quarterly, 59*(4), 428–449. doi:10.1080/01463373.2011.597275

Dunlap, J. C., & Lowenthal, P. R. (2009). Tweeting the night away: Using Twitter to enhance social presence. *Journal of Information Systems Education, 20*(2).

Educause. (2006). *7 things you should know about Facebook*. Retrieved from https://net.educause.edu/ir/library/pdf/ELI7017.pdf

Eteokleous-Grigoriou, N., & Ktoridou, D. (2014). Social networking for educational purposes: The development of social-cultural skills through special interest groups. In G. Mallia (Ed.), *The social classroom: Integrating social network use in education* (pp. 394–416). Hershey, PA: IGI Global. doi:10.4018/978-1-4666-4904-0.ch020

Faculty Focus. (2011). *Social media usage trends among higher education faculty*. Faculty Focus Special Report. Retrieved from http://cdn.facultyfocus.com/wp-content/uploads/2011/09/2011-social-media-report.pdf

Garrison, D. R., Anderson, T., & Archer, W. (2000). Critical inquiry in a text based environment: Computer conferencing in higher education. *The Internet and Higher Education, 2*(2/3), 87–105.

Garrison, R. D. (2017). *21ˢᵗ century e-learning*. Routledge.

Globalwebindex. (2019). *The latest social media trends to know in 2019*. Retrieved from https://www.globalwebindex.com/reports/social

Gunawardena, C. N., & Zittle, F. J. (1997). Social presence as a predictor of satisfaction within a computer-mediated conferencing environment. *American Journal of Distance Education, 11*(3), 8–26. doi:10.1080/08923649709526970

Hall, A. A., Delello, J. A., & McWhorter, R. R. (2017). Using Facebook to supplement instruction in online and hybrid courses. *Journal of Innovation and Learning, 22*(1), 87–104. doi:10.1504/IJIL.2017.085250

Heiberger, G., & Junco, R. (2015). *Meet your students where they are: Social media*. National Education Association. Retrieved from http://www.nea.org/assets/docs/HE/HigherEdSocialMediaGuide.pdf

Helvie-Mason, L. (2011). Facebook, friending, and faculty–student communication. In C. Wankel (Ed.), Teaching Arts and Science with the New Social Media. Emerald Group Publishing Limited. doi:10.1108/S2044-9968(2011)0000003007

Hershkovitz, A., & Forkosh-Baruch, A. (2013). Student-teacher relationship in the Facebook era: The student perspective. *International Journal of Continuing Engineering Education and Lifelong Learning, 23*(1), 33–52. doi:10.1504/IJCEELL.2013.051765

Irwin, C., Ball, L., Desbrow, B., & Leveritt, M. (2012). Students' perceptions of using Facebook as an interactive learning resource at university. *Australasian Journal of Educational Technology, 28*(7), 1221–1232. doi:10.14742/ajet.798

Johnson, K. (2011). The effect of Twitter posts on students' perceptions of instructor credibility. *Learning, Media and Technology, 36*(1), 21–38. doi:10.1080/17439884.2010.534798

Johnson, L., Adams Becker, S., & Cummins, M. (2012). *The NMC horizon report: 2012 higher education edition*. Austin, TX: The New Media Consortium.

Johnson, L., Adams Becker, S., Estrada, V., & Freeman, A. (2015). *NMC horizon report: 2015 K-12 edition*. Retrieved from http://cdn.nmc.org/media/2015-nmc-horizon-report-HE-EN.pdf

Junco, R. (2012). Too much face and not enough books: The relationship between multiple indices of Facebook use and academic performance. *Computers in Human Behavior, 28*(1), 187–198. doi:10.1016/j.chb.2011.08.026

Junco, R., & Cotton, S. (2011). *A decade of distraction? How multitasking affects student outcomes*. Paper presented at A Decade in Internet Time Symposium on the Dynamics of the Internet and Society, Oxford Internet Institute, University of Oxford, Oxford, UK. 10.2139srn.1927049

Junco, R., & Cotton, S. (2012). The relationship between multitasking and academic performance. *Computers & Education, 59*(4), 1–10. doi:10.1016/j.compedu.2011.12.023

Junco, R., Heiberger, G., & Loken, E. (2010). The effect of Twitter on college student engagement and grades. *Journal of Computer Assisted Learning, 27*(2), 119–132. doi:10.1111/j.1365-2729.2010.00387.x

Kaplan, A. M., & Haenlein, M. (2010). Users of the world, unite! The challenges and opportunities of Social Media. *Business Horizons, 53*(1), 59–68. doi:10.1016/j.bushor.2009.09.003

Kawachi, P. (2013). Online social presence and its correlation with learning. *International Journal of Social Media and Interactive Learning Environments, 1*(1), 19–31. doi:10.1504/IJSMILE.2013.051653

Keiser Foundation. (2013). *Generation M²: Media in the lives of 8-to-18-year-olds.* Retrieved from https://kaiserfamilyfoundation.files.wordpress.com/2013/04/8010.pdf

King, T. (2019, July). Bitmojis, GIFs, and Snaps in the Classroom? Oh My! *Faculty Focus.* Retrieved from https://www.facultyfocus.com/articles/effective-classroom-management/bitmojis-GIFs-and-snaps-in-the-classroom/

Kirschner, P. A., & Karpinski, A. C. (2010). Facebook and academic performance. *Computers in Human Behavior, 26*(6), 1237–1245. doi:10.1016/j.chb.2010.03.024

Knight-McCord, J., Cleary, D., Grant, N., Herron, A., Jumbo, S., Lacey, T., ... Smith, R. (2016). What social media sites do college students use most? *Journal of Undergraduate Ethnic Minority Psychology, 2*(21), 21–26.

Kumi-Yeboah, A., & Blankson, H. (2018). Social media and use of technology in higher education. In M. Khosrow-Pour (Ed.), *Teacher Training and Professional Development: Concepts, Methodologies, Tools, and Applications, 4* (Vol. 41, pp. 932–952). Information Resources Management Association. doi:10.4018/978-1-5225-5631-2.ch041

Metzger, A. H., Finley, K. N., Ulbrich, T. R., & McAuley, J. W. (2010). Pharmacy faculty members' perspectives on the student/faculty relationship in online social networks. *American Journal of Pharmaceutical Education, 74*(10), 188. doi:10.5688/aj7410188 PMID:21436929

Miles, M. B., & Huberman, A. M. (1984). *Qualitative data analysis* (Vol. 16). Newbury Park, CA: Sage.

Moran, M., Seaman, J., & Tinti-Kane, H. (2011). *Teaching, learning, and sharing: How Today's Higher Education Faculty Use Social Media.* Pearson Learning Solutions and Babson Survey Research Group.

Moran, M., Seaman, J., & Tinti-Kane, H. (2012). *Social Media in Higher Education.* Pearson Learning Solutions and Babson Survey Research Group.

Myatt, B. M., & Kennette, L. N. (2017, Jan.). *Towards a positive u.* Faculty Focus. Retrieved from http://www.facultyfocus.com/articles/effective-classroom-management/towards-positive-u/

Nielson. (2016). *2016 Nielson social media report. Social studies: A look at the social landscape.* Retrieved from https://www.nielsen.com/content/dam/corporate/us/en/reports downloads/2017-reports/2016-nielsen-social-media-report.pdf

O'Donnell, S., & Epstein, L. H. (2019). Smartphones are more reinforcing than food for students. *Addictive Behaviors*, *90*, 124–133. doi:10.1016/j.addbeh.2018.10.018 PMID:30390436

Oxford University Press. (2015). *Word of the year 2015*. Retrieved from https://languages.oup.com/word-of-the-year/word-of-the-year-2015

Pappano, L. (2018). The iGen shift: Colleges must change to reach the next generation. *New York Times*. Retrieved from https://www.nytimes.com/2018/08/02/education/learning/generationz-igen-students-colleges.html

Pascarella, E. (1985). College environmental influences on learning and cognitive development: A 32 2g critical review and synthesis. In J. Smart (Ed.), *Higher education: Handbook of theory and research* (Vol. I). New York: Agathon.

Pearson. (2018). *Beyond millennials: The next generation of learners*. Retrieved from https://www.pearson.com/content/dam/one-dot-com/one-dot-com/global/Files/news/news-annoucements/2018/The-Next-Generation-of-Learners_final.pdf

Perrin, A., & Anderson, M. (2019). *Share of U.S. adults using social media, including Facebook, is mostly unchanged since 2018*. Retrieved from https://www.pewresearch.org/fact-tank/2019/04/10/share-of-u-s-adults-using-social-media-including-facebook-is-mostly-unchanged-since-2018/

Pomerantz, J., Hank, C., & Sugimoto, C. R. (2015). The state of social media policies in higher education. *Plos*. Retrieved from http://journals.plos.org/plosone/article?id=10.1371/journal.pone.0127485

Quan-Haase, A., & Young, A. L. (2010). Uses and gratifications of social media: A comparison of facebook and instant messaging. *Bulletin of Science, Technology & Society*, *30*(5), 350–361. doi:10.1177/0270467610380009

Refuel Agency. (2015). *College explorer '15*. Retrieved from http://research.refuelagency.com/wp-content/uploads/2016/01/College%20Explorer%202015%20Final.pdf

Richardson, J. C., Maeda, Y., Lv, J., & Caskurlu, S. (2017). Social presence in relation to students' satisfaction and learning in the online environment. *Computers in Human Behavior*, *71*(C), 402–417. doi:10.1016/j.chb.2017.02.001

Roberts, J. A., Yaya, L. H., & Manolis, C. (2014). The invisible addiction: Cell-phone activities and addiction among male and female college students. *Journal of Behavioral Addictions*, *3*(4), 254–265. doi:10.1556/JBA.3.2014.015 PMID:25595966

Roorda, D. L., Koomen, H. M. Y., Spilt, J. L., & Oort, F. J. (2011). The influence of affective teacher–student relationships on students' school engagement and achievement. *The Journal of Educational Research*, *81*(4), 493–529.

Rothenberg, M. (2019). *Emoji tracker*. Retrieved from http://emojitracker.com/

Sanger, L. (2010). Individual knowledge in the Internet age. *EDUCAUSE Review*, *45*(2), 14–24.

Schwartz, H. L. (2012). From the classroom to the coffee shop: Graduate students and professors effectively navigate interpersonal boundaries. *International Journal on Teaching and Learning in Higher Education, 23*(3), 363–372.

Seaman, J., & Tinti-Kane, H. (2013). *Social media for teaching and learning.* Pearson Learning Solutions and Babson Survey Research Group. Retrieved from http://www.pearsonlearningsolutions.com/assets/downloads/reports/social-media-for-teaching-and-learning-2013-report.pdf#view=FitH,0

SecurEnvoy. (2012). *66% of the population suffer from Nomophobia the fear of being without their phone.* Retrieved from http://www.securenvoy.com/blog/2012/02/16/66-of-the-population-suffer-fromnomophobia-the-fear-of-being-without-their-phone/

Sheldon, P. (2015). Understanding students' reasons and gender differences in adding faculty as Facebook friends. *Computers in Human Behavior, 53*, 58–62. doi:10.1016/j.chb.2015.06.043

Smith & Anderson. (2018). *Social Media Use in 2018.* Retrieved from https://www.pewinternet.org/2018/03/01/social-media-use-in-2018/

Sturgeon, C. M., & Walker, C. (2009). *Faculty on Facebook: Confirm or deny.* Paper presented at the Annual Instructional Technology Conference, Murfreesboro, TN.

Tenor. (2017). *10 Years with the iPhone: Communication is now visual.* Retrieved from https://blog.tenor.com/10-years-with-the-iphone-communication-is-now-visual-c2b7dae6cf07

Thalluri, J., & Penman, J. (2015). Social media for learning and teaching undergraduate sciences: Good practices guidelines from intervention. *Electronic Journal of E-Learning, 13*(6), 455–465.

The Institute of Politics at Harvard Kennedy School. (2017). *Use of social networking technology.* Retrieved from https://iop.harvard.edu/use-social-networking-technology

Wakefield, K. (2012). Should professors use facebook to communicate with students? *Faculty Focus.* Retrieved from http://www.facultyfocus.com/articles/edtech-news-and-trends/should-professors-use-facebook-to-communicate-with-students/

Wang, Q., Chen, W., & Liang, Y. (2011). The effects of social media on college student (Paper 5). *MBA Student Scholarship.* Retrieved from https://scholarsarchive.jwu.edu/mba_student/5

Waycott, J., Thompson, C., Sheard, J., & Clerehan, R. (2017). A virtual panopticon in the community of practice: Students' experiences of being visible on social media. *The Internet and Higher Education, 35*, 12–20. doi:10.1016/j.iheduc.2017.07.001

Wei, C., Chen, N., & Kinshuk. (2012). A model for social presence in online classrooms. *Educational Technology Research and Development, 60*(3), 529–545. doi:10.100711423-012-9234-9

Will, M. (2017). Memes, emojis, and GIFs, oh my! Teachers tell how they use social media. *Education Week.* Retrieved from http://blogs.edweek.org/teachers/teaching_now/2017/08/most_teachers_think_social_media_are_bad_for_grammar_and_spelling_but_still_use_it_in_class.html

Zmikly, J. (2016). Remix: How to use Snapchat in the classroom. *Mediashift.* Retrieved from http://mediashift.org/2016/09/remix-snapchat-classroom/

ADDITIONAL READING

Barnes, N. G., & Lescault, A. M. (2012). *Social media adoption soars as higher-ed experiments and reevaluates its use of new communications Tools.* University of Massachusetts Dartmouth. Retrieved from https://www.umassd.edu/cmr/studiesandresearch/socialmediaadoptionsoars/

Greenwood, S., Perrin, A., & Duggan, M. (2016). *Social media update 2016: Facebook usage and engagement is on the rise, while adoption of other platforms holds steady.* Pew Research Center. Retrieved from https://www.pewinternet.org/2016/11/11/social-media-update-2016/

Kehrwald, B. (2007). The ties that bind: Social presence, relations and productive collaboration in online learning environments. In ICT: *Providing choices for learners and learning.* Proceedings Ascilite Singapore 2007. Retrieved from http://www.ascilite.org.au/conferences/singapore07/procs/kehrwald.pdf

Lenhart, A., Purcell, K., Smith, A., & Zickuhr, K. (2010). *Social media and young adults.* Washington, DC: Pew Internet and American Life Project.

Pew Research Center. (2017). *Social media fact sheet.* Retrieved from https://www.pewinternet.org/fact-sheet/social-media/

Rifkind, L. J. (1992). Immediacy as a predictor of teacher effectiveness in the instructional television. *Journal of Interactive Television, 1*(1), 31–38.

KEY TERMS AND DEFINITIONS

Distraction: Something that divides one's attention.
Emerging Technology: Technologies that are currently being developed or refined.
Social Media: Interactive Web 2.0 application that allows for sharing of information across the Web.
Social Presence: Ones ability to feel connected or present in their environment.
Visual Social Media: The use and sharing of visual images across social media.
Web 2.0: Second generation of the world-wide web that allows for more collaboration and interaction.

This research was previously published in Innovative Perspectives on Interactive Communication Systems and Technologies; pages 23-44, copyright year 2020 by Information Science Reference (an imprint of IGI Global).

Chapter 64
Hybrid Ensemble Learning With Feature Selection for Sentiment Classification in Social Media

Sanur Sharma
Guru Gobind Singh Indraprastha University, Delhi, India

Anurag Jain
Guru Gobind Singh Indraprastha University, Delhi, India

ABSTRACT

This article presents a study on ensemble learning and an empirical evaluation of various ensemble classifiers and ensemble features for sentiment classification of social media data. The data was collected from Twitter in real-time using Twitter API and text pre-processing and ranking-based feature selection is applied to textual data. A framework for a hybrid ensemble learning model is presented where a combination of ensemble features (Information Gain and CHI-Squared) and ensemble classifier that includes Ada Boost with SMO-SVM and Logistic Regression has been implemented. The classification of Twitter data is performed where sentiment analysis is used as a feature. The proposed model has shown improvements as compared to the state-of-the-art methods with an accuracy of 88.2% with a low error rate.

INTRODUCTION

In the ongoing surge of social media, user opinions have an incredible reach to the world through the internet. The posts and tweets that user share and the level of interactions that are possible on social media have an immense potential in influencing people. Twitter is one such medium where the user opinions and views build their social profile and present them online. This has made the twitter data-rich and an authoritative source of sharing views which is why twitter data has been used very extensively for study and for making predictions at large. Sentiment analysis is one technique where the text is analysed, and

DOI: 10.4018/978-1-6684-7123-4.ch064

predictions are made based on the user opinions which are derived from the text that has been posted on the medium. Sentiment analysis, in general, classifies the text into positive, negative and neutral and performs evaluation and prediction of events. Various techniques for sentiment classification include machine learning techniques where supervised learning, semi-supervised, unsupervised and ensemble techniques have been applied on the social media dataset. Lexicon based techniques include dictionary-based, corpus-based and Lexicon with Natural Language Processing NLP and hybrid techniques (Medhat et al. 2014; Goyal and Bhatnagar 2016; Hussein, 2018). The various social media data includes Twitter data, social network data, movie and product review data and more.

Social media data is heterogeneous, and data dimensionality is one of the significant factors that make its processing and analysis difficult. The textual nature of the data makes its processing difficult, and to understand the emotions behind the text becomes challenging. The varied number of attributes in social media data causes intractability towards the classification of data. The various challenges that arise in the analysis of such data are domain dependence which includes topic-oriented features, negation handling which alters the meaning of the word, lexicon-based features that characterise the linguistic features of the text, parts of speech tagging, bag of words, term presence and frequency. Another challenge that arises is to identify opinionated words and phrases to understand the contextual meaning of the text. There is also a vast set of lexicons that are present in textual data which makes the extraction process challenging to identify and time-consuming. In consideration to this, feature selection techniques are used to overcome these challenges and perform dimensionality reduction where redundant and irrelevant features of the text are removed to improve the classification of the text. This article considers these challenges that arise in the analysis of textual data and presents feature extraction techniques combined with ensemble learning to make the sentiment classification process efficient (classification accuracy, f-score, etc.) and less complex. The proposed model combines various feature selection techniques and finds the best combination of feature selection methods and further incorporates the best set of ensemble classifiers. The proposed method outperforms various state of the art methods.

This paper contributes in several ways:

- The proposed approach incorporates different compound feature set using string to word vectorisation, n-gram model and tf-idf (term frequency and inverse document frequency) which performs better than other simple features;
- The proposed Hybrid Ensemble Learning Method (HELM) incorporates ensemble features in place of using a single set of features which performs repeated feature extraction process to obtain the best set of features;
- The proposed approach has integrated features like Information Gain (IG) and Chi-Squared (CHI) feature selection algorithms which selects relevant features by evaluating the importance of the features. The performance results of ensemble features are compared to a single set of feature selection methods;
- The proposed HELM incorporates ensemble classifiers instead of single base classifiers. The performance of proposed HELM classifier (ADA boost + SMO-SVM+Logistics Regression) has been compared with various machine learning classifiers and state of the art ensemble classifiers. It was found that HELM outperforms state of the art classifiers like Naïve Bayes, SVM, LR, SGD, RF and SMO.

The remaining paper is organised as follows: Section 2 presents the related work in the field of twitter sentiment analysis and ensemble learning. Section 3 introduces the evaluation framework for sentiment classification. Section 4 presents the proposed hybrid ensemble learning model with section 5 discussing the experimental results on the implementation of the evaluation framework. Section 6 presents the discussion, conclusion and future scope of the research.

RELATED WORK

Recent work in the field of social media analysis includes twitter sentiment analysis where twitter data is analysed to understand the sentiments and emotions of social media users (Jansen et al., 2009; Pak and Paroubek, 2010; Ardehaly and Culotta, 2017). The time-evolving nature of social media makes its analysis complex and time-consuming. Therefore, an intelligent system is required to search the relevant information using intelligent retrieval via web mining for dynamic social network (Sonkar et al., 2015). A framework for dynamic social network analysis is presented where social network measures are used to extract structural information before applying any security measure (Sharma and Bhatnagar, 2013). Sharma and Jain, (2019a) presents performance evaluation of dynamic social network and incorporates an evolutionary approach to timestamp the network data. A distant supervision approach for sentiment classification has been applied using machine learning algorithms like Naïve Bayes, maximum entropy and SVM with accuracy of greater than 80% (Go et al., 2009). Another method that uses linguistics features for evaluating tweet sentiments by using supervised approach on hashtagged twitter data is presented in (Kouloumpis et al., 2011). Sarlan et al. (2014) reports twitter sentiment analysis to find customer perceptions via classifying tweets as positive and negative. A unified framework-based hybrid classification scheme for twitter sentiment analysis incorporates four classifiers (Slang classifier, emotion classifier, senti word net classifier and a domain-specific classifier) that provide better accuracy than other existing models (Asghar et al., 2018). Another unified framework for tourism sector is presented where tweets are extracted and multi-label Naïve Bayes classifier is used for identification of top destinations (Sinha et al., 2018). Bhatnagar et al., (2018) have proposed a framework for aspect-based opinion mining on hotel reviews form trip advisor. The opinion score is calculated by ranking of aspects using Senti-WordNet dictionary. Abu-Salih et al., (2018) have proposed a time-aware framework for the Twittersphere platform that incorporates machine learning tools to perform classification at the user and message level. It uses semantic analysis to analyse the historical content of users'. Abu-Salih et al. (2019a, 2019b) proposed credSat, a credibility analysis framework that evaluates the credibility of users on social media to detect anomalous behaviour. The feature set is constructed by extracting the domain-based features (tweet similarity and user content score), social features (user matrix, sentiment matrix, and friend relation matrix), temporal factors and credibility level. The various feature selection methods are based on two aspects: first is the attribute evaluator, and second is the evaluation heuristics. The task of feature selection is performed based on three methods: Wrapper method, filter method and embedded method (Zareapoor & Seeja, 2015; Singh & Jain, 2019). Sharma and Jain (2019b) have presented a comparative analysis of correlation-based feature selection methods on twitter data. More recently, ensemble learning has been used for feature selection where more than one set of features are used to perform dimensionality reduction (Guan et al., 2014; Latif & Qamar, 2019). Here the feature selection process is repeated several times to produce varied feature selectors, and the outputs are aggregated together to get an optimum feature set. Ensemble Learning has also been used for generating multiple classifiers where supervised learning has been used, and the resulting classifier is the aggregation of the classification results that presents higher accuracy levels (Guan et al., 2014).

Ensemble learning methods combine a set of base classifier models in order to obtain a model that achieves better classification results. The methods that are used for construction of ensemble classifiers are based on two approaches: first is the meta-learning model, and second are the rule-based models. Guan et al. (2014) present a review on ensemble feature selection and discusses various approaches used and stability measurement issues with other methods. In (Araque et al, 2017), two ensemble techniques are proposed which combines the deep learning classifier and CEM (ensemble of classifiers) with surface vectors and genetic word vectors. In (Randhawa et al., 2018) hybrid models based on ADA Boost and majority voting is proposed for credit card fraud detection. Their results show that majority voting gives better accuracy in detecting credit card fraud cases. Lin et al. (2019) have constructed ensemble classifiers with feature selection techniques. The constructed combined classifier (GA, Naïve Bayes and SVM) gives lowest prediction error rates than the bagging and boosting ensemble classifiers. Ubing et al. (2019) have integrated feature selection algorithm with majority voting ensemble classifier for phishing website detection that gives improved accuracy over other phishing detection models. The various works in the field of ensemble learning used for sentiment analysis in social media are presented in Table 1. It also compares the proposed method (HELM) with the other state of art methods. It can be noted that the proposed method has used both ensemble features and ensemble classifiers which is not used in other methods and also gives a high classification accuracy when compared with other methods listed below.

METHODOLOGY

The evaluation framework constructed in this research is presented in Figure 1. The various levels at which the proposed model will work are dataset preparation, pre-processing and vectorisation, feature selection that includes ensemble features and finally sentiment classification that is built on ensemble classifiers.

Dataset Description

The data was collected through a Twitter API where tweets were fetched in real time. The 'Cambridge Analytica' dataset was constructed by searching the keyword and gathering the tweets related to the key word. The total tweets that were extracted were 7116 for 42 users.

The following are the features of the tweet:

- Tweet created
- Tweet ID
- Retweet
- Location
- Profile image URL
- Retweet count
- Status score
- Text
- Screen name

Table 1. A comparison of existing methods based on ensemble learning used for sentiment analysis in social media

Author/Year	Feature	Classifier	Evaluation Matrix	Dataset	Ensemble Learning
Xia et al. (2011)	Uni-gram, Bi-gram	Meta Classifier NB, Max Entropy, SVM	Accuracy 85.6%	Movie Review E-Product Review	Ensemble Classifier
Agarwal & Mittal. (2013)	IG + RSAR	SVM NB	F-Measure 87.7 80.9	IMDB Product Review	Ensemble Features
Wang et al. (2013)	Unigram – Tf-Idf	RS-SVM Bagging-SVM Boosting-NB	Accuracy 75.6 75 74	10 Public SA dataset [one Movie Review & nine Whitehead & Yaeger data]	Ensemble Classifier
	Bigram – Tf-Idf	RS –SVM Bagging SVM Boosting NB	75.3 74 73		Ensemble Classifier
Al-Moslmi et al. 2015	IG, CHI, Gini	SVM NB	F-Measure 85.33 80.88	Movie Reviews	Ensemble Features
Koutanaei et al. (2015)	PCA Relief GA IG	ANN-Bagging	Accuracy 88.4 88.3 87.4 87.1	Credit Data	Ensemble Classifier
Fattah, 2015	Unigram, Tf-df, CHI	Voting SVM, NN, Gaussian Mixture Model	Accuracy 91.8%	Movie Review E-Product Review	Ensemble Classifier
Xia et al., 2016	Uni-gram, Bi-gram	Stacking SVM, LR, NB	Accuracy 86.6%	Movie Review E-Product Review	Ensemble Classifier
Ghosh and Sanyal (2018)	(IG, CHI, GI)	LR MNB RF	F-Score 87.3 88.18 87.73	Movie Review & e-product Review	Ensemble Features
Khurshid et al. (2019)	CHI Squared	DMMB J48 TLR SVM	F-Measure 0.841 0.817 0.761	Yelp Ott Pos Ott Neg	Ensemble Classifier
Latif and Qamar, 2019	Lexicon Uni-gram, Phrase, IG+GI	SVM	Accuracy 92.7%	Movie Review & e-product Review	Ensemble Features
Proposed Method (HELM)	STWV Tf-idf Ngram IG+CHI	Ada Boost+SMO-SVM + LR	Accuracy 88.27%	Twitter Data	Ensemble Features + Ensemble Classifier

Lexicon Dictionary: An opinion lexicon of 6789 words is used, out of which 4783 words are negative and 2006 words are positive (Hu and Liu, 2004). Table 2 presents the sentiment tweet data summary for 'Cambridge Analytica' where the tweets were categorised as positive, negative and neutral.

Pre-Processing and Vectorisation

Pre-processing includes stemming, POS tagging, stop word removal and tokenisation. Vectorisation includes string to word vectorisation which is a predictive model for creating word embedding from the text. It includes various models like word2vec (continuous bag of words, skip gram model) and doc2vec approach (Distributed memory version, Distributed Bag of words).

Table 2. Sentiment Tweet data set summary

Dataset	Sentiment Class	Tweets	Time Span
Cambrige Analytica	Positive	1332	May 2018-June 2018
	Negative	2454	
	Neutral	3330	

Figure 1. Evaluation framework for sentiment classification

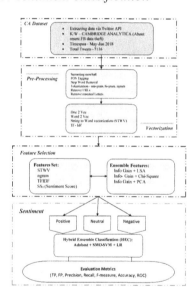

Feature Selection

This section presents feature selection methods used in the evaluation framework.

Text Categorisation: N-Gram and Tf-Idf as a Feature

In the evaluation framework, for text categorisation n-gram vectorisation is used where trigram features are formed based on the text data and a dictionary of trigrams is maintained. The scores are evaluated for the sentiment polarity and are used to model the classification results. Another feature for text categorisation that is evaluated is term presence and frequency which is based on document term matrix that performs vectorisation based on vocabulary. Tf-Idf is evaluated as follows:

$$TF - IDF = TF(w) * IDF(w) \tag{1}$$

where:

$$TF\left(w\right) = \frac{\text{no. of times word } 'w' \text{ appears}}{\text{total no. of words}} \tag{2}$$

$$IDF\left(w\right) = log\left(\frac{\text{total no. of docs}}{\text{no. of docs with word } 'w'}\right) \tag{3}$$

Sentiment Feature

Sentiment Analysis on the data is performed to evaluate the polarity of the text. For the proposed hybrid model, we have evaluated the sentiment polarity based on the lexicon approach by matching the words from the lexicon dictionary and evaluating the sentiment score as follows:

$$SS_t = \rho\{\sum(PP_i - NP_i)\} \tag{4}$$

where:

$$\rho_t = \begin{cases} 1, & if\, t > 0 \\ -1, & if\, t < 0 \\ 0, & if\, t = 0 \end{cases} \tag{5}$$

Information Gain

IG evaluates the information a feature gives about the class. The features that are not relevant or unrelated produce no information. It is a measure of the change in the entropy (Ghosh and Sanyal, 2018; Sarkar and Goswami, 2013):

$$Entropy\, H = -\sum_{i=1}^{n} p_n log_2 p_n \tag{6}$$

$$IG = \Delta H = H - \frac{m_k}{m} H_k - \frac{m_l}{m} H_l \tag{7}$$

where:

- m is the total number of instances;
- m_n are the instances that belongs to class n, and n= 1,2, ..., n.

The information gain for a feature is evaluated as follows (Ghosh and Sanyal, 2018; Sarkar and Goswami, 2013):

$$IG(f) = \left(\sum_{i=1}^{n} \frac{p_i}{p} \log \frac{p_i}{p}\right) + \left(\sum_{i=1}^{n} \frac{X_i}{p}\right)\left[\sum_{i=1}^{n} \frac{X_i}{X_i + A_i} \log \frac{X_i}{X_i + A_i}\right] + \left(\sum_{i=1}^{n} \frac{p_i - X_i}{p}\right)\left[\sum_{i=1}^{n} \frac{p_i - X_i}{p_i - X_i + B_i} \log \frac{p_i - X_i}{p_i - X_i + B_i}\right]$$

(8)

Here, p- total no. of documents:

- P_i- no of doc in i^{th} class;
- X_i -no of doc in i^{th} class that contain feature f';
- A_i- no of doc not in the ith class that contain feature 'f';
- B_i= p-p_i-A_i- no of doc not in the ith class that do not contain feature f.

IG Score of each term is evaluated by calculating the no of bits of information that defines the presence of the term in the ith class.

Chi-Square

Chi square is a statistical measure to test the lack of independence between feature and a class. So, if there is dependence, then the occurrence of the feature is used to predict the presence of a class. A high value of χ^2 depicts the hypothesis of independence is not correct and there exists a close relationship between feature F and class (Ghosh and Sanyal, 2018; Sarkar and Goswami, 2013):

$$\chi^2 = \frac{p\left\{X_i\left(p - p_i - A_i\right) - \left(p_i - X_i\right)A_i\right\}^2}{p_{i\left(p-p_i\right)\left(X_i + A_i\right)\left\{p - \left(X_i + A_i\right)\right\}}}$$

(9)

Latent Semantic Analysis

Latent Semantic Analysis is a feature selection technique for text classification problems where it evaluates relationship between the terms and the semantics contained in the text. It is based on the SVD (Singular Value Decomposition) that evaluates the relative distances in the vector space model and correlates to the semantic space model for dimensionality reduction. LSA basically extracts the contextual meaning from the text by establishing relationship between terms that have similar context (L'Huillier et al., 2010; Süzek, 2013; Zareapoor and Seeja, 2015).

X_{ij} is the input sparse matrix of terms that occur in the document presents the term weights for the entire corpora. SVD decomposes the input matrix X into 3 matrices:

$$X = R\sum S^t \tag{10}$$

- R is the vector matrix constructed from the concepts of the terms (rows) of the input matrix;
- $\sum$ is diagonal matrix presenting singular values;
- S is an orthogonal matrix constructed from concepts of documents (columns) of the input matrix.

Principal Component Analysis (PCA)

PCA is a dimensionality reduction technique which uses eigen vectors to interpret variance in the original data. It then removes the worst values of eigen vectors and then transforms it back to original space and thus reduces the dimensionality (Song et al., 2010). The covariance is evaluated as:

$$C = \frac{A^T A}{N} \tag{11}$$

Let m be the eigen vector of covariance matrix C of PCA and N is the dimensionality of sample vector, then feature extraction would result in:

$$X = a^T m = \sum_{i=1}^{N} a_i m_i \tag{11}$$

Ensemble Feature

Ensemble features uses the combination of the various feature selection methods in order to obtain the common features that give the best results. It combines different feature subsets to construct an ensemble of features that can be applied on the data and then finally perform classification with the help of various classifiers.

Classification Algorithm

The various classifiers or the classification algorithms used in the evaluation framework are discussed below (Sharma and Jain 2019c).

Support Vector Machine (SVM)

SVM uses linear separators for classification of the data into various classes. In general, it is difficult to find linear separators for textual data. So SVM classifier identifies the best separator between the positive and negative data samples by considering the minimisation error. It constructs hyperplane for identifying sentiment polarity for classification in high dimensional feature space. SVM minimises misclassification errors in the prediction process of its implementation (Huang et al., 2017):

$$y = \begin{bmatrix} 1, & if & xi\varphi - a > 0; \\ -1, & otherwise \end{bmatrix} \tag{12}$$

$$argmin\varphi = \sum_{i}^{n} \delta\left(yi\left(xi\varphi - a\right) \leq 0\right) \tag{13}$$

Naïve Bayes

Naïve Bayes Classifier is works on the concept of Bayes Theeorem (i.e. independent assumption theory) that evaluates the posterior probabilities of a class. The probability of a text belonging to a feature is evaluated based on the maximum posterior value of a class (Vo and Collier, 2013). It is evaluated as follows:

$$P\left(l \,/\, f\right) = \frac{P\left(l\right)^* \prod_{i=1}^{m} P\left(f_i \,/\, l\right)}{P\left(f\right)} \tag{14}$$

Sequential Minimal Optimisation (SMO)

Sequential minimal optimisation is a learning algorithm that trains the SVM and uses analytical quadratic programming and evaluates the smallest optimisation problem at each step and finally returns global optimum solution and updates the SVM model. SMO can handle large sizes of training data and is scalable as it requires linear memory. Its computation time is better than SVM and therefore is fastest for linear SVM's. It does not require any extra matrix storage and is less vulnerable to problems related to numerical precision [Platt, 1998].

Logistic Regression

Logistic Regression defines a set of classification rules that constructs set of weighted features from the input data and computes correlation between a feature and the class to which it belongs. It makes use of logistics function that classifies an observation into one of the predefined classes. The generalised linear model is as follows (Huang et al., 2017):

$$F\left(x\right) = \frac{e^x}{1 + e^x} \tag{15}$$

$$Ai \,/\, Bi = bi\bar{\ }binary(p(bi)) \tag{16}$$

$$p\left(bi\right) = P\left(Ai = 1 \,/\, Bi = bi\right) = \frac{e^{b^i} * \beta}{1 + e^{b^i} * \beta} \tag{17}$$

Random Forest

Random forest is a classification problem that is based on ensemble approach that generates multiple random decision trees. It uses random feature selection based on bootstrapping of the training data. The RF model is built on majority voting of the most popular class. The class prediction with n number of trees can be defined as follows (Ghosh and Sanyal, 2018):

$$\widehat{C} = majority\,voting\left\{\widehat{C}^n\right\}_1^n \tag{18}$$

where C_n be the prediction of tree T_n

Ensemble Classifiers

Ensemble classifiers train multiple models to predict and perform classification on the training data. It aggregates the results of all the classifiers and the final result is generally more accurate than the individual classifiers (Ghosh and Sanyal, 2018). Following are the three types of ensemble classifiers that are used in the evaluation framework.

Ada Boost

Ada Boost is based on bootstrapping method that combines the weak classifiers to form a strong classifier that gives better prediction results. T works in a sequential fashion and the model that is built tries to fit in the observations that are complex in order to reduce the bias. Ada Boost in general is sensitive to noisy data and outliers.

Bagging

Bagging is also a bootstrapping method that combines weak learners, but the classifiers work independently. The prediction results are obtained by averaging the results of the various classifiers. The final ensemble model produced has a low variance. The averaging function that is used is again based on majority voting.

Stacking

In stacking the heterogeneous classifiers that work in parallel are considered and are combined by a meta-learning model which predicts the classification results based on the weak set of classifiers. Stacking increases the predictive force of the classifiers as the stacking of classifiers can be done at various levels. Due to multi-level, stacking can be time and data expensive, which is a major factor that needs to be considered while using this technique.

PROPOSED HYBRID ENSEMBLE LEARNING MODEL

The proposed HELM works at two levels where level 1 has Ensemble feature Information Gain and Chi-Squared. These ensemble features have been applied to the input data. The output of the first level of ensemble features has been fed into the level 2 as input. Level 2 has Ensemble classifiers Ada Boost, SMO-SVM and Logistic Regression as the meta classifier. Figure 2 presents the proposed HELM model. To validate the proposed model, a comparison of the proposed model with the state of art classifiers like SVM, Naïve Bayes, Logistic Regression and Random Forest has been presented.

Figure 2. Hybrid Ensemble Learning Model (HELM)

Table 3 presents the scheme of the proposed Ensemble Learning based on ensemble features and ensemble classifier where first the data is loaded into the system after it is pre-processed and vectorised. In the first step, a List of features selection algorithms have been applied, and the best set of feature selection technique is selected. Next, a list of classifiers is applied and the best set of classifiers called the ensemble classifier is applied on the reduced dataset. The resultant classifier gives the best performance results.

Table 3. Scheme of hybrid ensemble learning based on ensemble feature selection and ensemble classification

Algorithm HELM
Input: T→ Training Data, F→ Feature Selection, C→ Classification Algorithm
Parameter: X (no. of feature selectors), Y (no. of classifier)
Output: HEL (Hybrid Ensemble Learning)
1. From the training data (T_1, T_2 ...... T_n)
2. For i= 1 to X
3. For k= 1 to m
4. Select the best Feature Set $FS_i = F_{i,m}(T)$
5. Let FS_k = Best feature (BF) of size 'm'
6. BF= Min{Prediction Error}
7. FS ← Union (FS_1, FS_2, ... FS_X)
8. For j= 1 to Y
9. Select the best Classifier Set $CS_j = C[FS(T)]$
10. Let CS_j = Best Classifier (BC) of size 'n'
11. BC= Max {Classification Score}
12. HEL= CS← Union (CS_1, CS_2, ... CS_Y)

EXPERIMENTAL RESULTS

The experimental setting includes the dataset preparation and modelling that performs the tokenisation and vectorisation of data, as discussed in the previous section. The feature selection methods used in the evaluation model presenting the search method, no of features and their statistics are shown in Table 4.

Table 4. Feature subset selection statistics

Subset Evaluator	Search Method	Number of Features	Statistics			
			Min	max	mean	StdDev
IG	Ranker	1490	0	2.588	0.156	0.481
LSA	Ranker	478	-0.064	0	-0.005	0.016
PCA	Ranker	511	-11.297	47.22	0	2.699
Chi Square	Ranker	1490	0	3.045	0.123	0.482

The total number of features that were present when no feature selection was applied was 1925. These features were reduced to 1490, 478, 511 when feature selection techniques- information gain, LSA and PCA were applied. Table 5 presents a comparison of various algorithms when no feature reduction was applied. The dataset was vectorised on String to word vectorisation with n-gram text categorisation with term frequency and inverse document frequency (tf-idf).

Table 5. Comparison between various classifiers for sentiment modelling without using attribute selection methods

Classifier	Performance Measures			ROC	Accuracy
	Precision	Recall	F-Measure		
Naïve Bayes	0.797	0.721	0.726	0.854	72.08
SVM	0.824	0.763	0.722	0.664	76.28
LR	0.853	0.851	0.852	0.889	85.13
SGD	0.866	0.867	0.865	0.842	**86.66**
SMO	0.865	0.866	0.864	0.841	**86.63**
Simple Logistic	0.868	0.866	0.864	0.944	**86.58**
Random Forest	0.861	0.861	0.858	0.941	86.04
Multinominal Naïve Bayes	0.851	0.844	0.846	0.937	84.39

The results show that the accuracy of the eight classifiers when compared over text categorisation as a feature gives the highest accuracy of 86.6% for SGD and SMO classifier. Simple Logistic and Random forest classifier results are also in the same range. The lowest performance measure was given by the Naive Bayes classifier and showed it to be unsuitable for this dataset. Further, when feature selection techniques were applied, it was seen that the performance of the various classifiers was improved and is shown in Table 6.

Table 6. Performance evaluation of various classifiers based on the ranking based feature selection methods in terms of their Precision (P), Recall (R), F-measure (F), Accuracy (ACC) and ROC

| Classifier | Metric | IG | Features Selection | | | | IG+LSA | IG+PCA |
			CHI	LSA	PCA	IG+CHI		
Naïve Bayes	F	0.728	0.728	0.703	0.724	0.728	0.782	0.77
	Acc	72.32	72.32	69.65	71.87	72.32	**78.13**	77.31
	ROC	0.855	0.855	0.787	0.774	0.855	0.86	0.795
SVM	F	0.731	0.731		0.858	0.731		0.868
	Acc	76.92	76.92	64.82	86.24	76.92	64.82	**87.29**
	ROC	0.673	0.673	0.5	0.827	0.673	0.5	0.834
LR	F	0.87	0.872	0.857	0.856	0.871	0.865	
	Acc	87.27	**87.43**	85.76	85.6	87.35	86.77	
	ROC	0.946	0.946	0.92	0.901	0.946	0.926	
SGD	F	0.876	0.876	0.841	0.835	0.876	0.856	0.849
	Acc	**87.9**	**87.9**	84.31	83.73	**87.9**	85.74	85.15
	ROC	0.845	0.845	0.818	0.809	0.845	0.834	0.821
SMO	F	0.874	0.874	0.853	0.849	0.874	0.855	0.836
	Acc	**87.87**	**87.87**	85.55	85.29	**87.87**	86.13	84.57
	ROC	0.841	0.841	0.828	0.816	0.841	0.814	0.789
Random Forest	F	0.855	0.856	0.838	0.842	0.857	0.866	0.869
	Acc	85.81	85.87	84.44	84.68	85.95	86.74	**87.06**
	ROC	0.935	0.936	0.929	0.928	0.936	0.933	0.936
Simple Logistic	F	0.873	0.873	0.832	0.83	0.873	0.879	0.877
	Acc	87.72	87.72	83.57	83.46	87.72	88.22	**88**
	ROC	0.95	0.95	0.923	0.921	0.95	0.953	0.953

From Table 6 it is clear that after applying feature selection techniques, the classifier's performance has been improved. It should be noted that ensemble features have further improved the classification accuracy and IG+LSA has given the highest accuracy (88%) when used with simple Logistic regression. In addition, the other ensemble classifiers IG+CHI gives the best accuracy for SGD (87.9) and SMO (87.87) classifiers and IG+PCA give best accuracy for SVM (87.29), and Random Forest (87.06). Figure 3 presents the performance of various classifiers based on ranking based feature selection showing the plot for F-measure and ROC.

In consideration to this Figure 4 presents the average accuracy results of the various classifiers based on the three categorisation: first when no feature selection technique is applied and full features set is used for the classification of the data. Second, when the ranking based four feature selection methods (IG, CHI, LSA & PCA) are applied for classification and finally third is the ensemble feature selection where the combination of features is used. In this framework, three ensemble feature selection methods (IG+CHI, IG+LSA, IG+PCA) have been used.

Figure 3. Performance of various classifiers based on ranking based feature selection showing the plot for F-measure and ROC

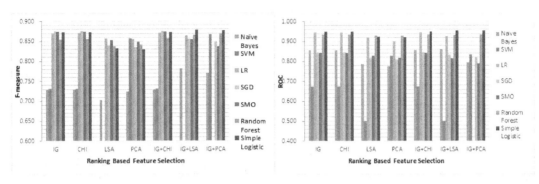

Figure 4. Average accuracy performance of classifiers considering Full Features (FF), Feature Selection (FS) and Ensemble Features (EF)

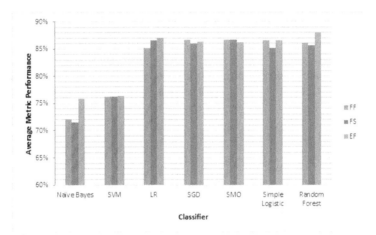

From Figure 4, it is clear that in general ensemble feature selection methods is an improvement over FF and FS methods and the best classifier accuracy is given by Random Forest classifier when used with ensemble feature selection. In this setup, the proposed HELM uses the ensemble features and ensemble classifiers one by one to further improve the classification of the model. Table 7 presents the various ensemble classifiers that are used in combination with the feature selection method that improves the performance results of the base classifiers. The ensemble classifiers used in the setup are Adaboost, Bagging and Stacking and among them, Adaboost gives best performance with 88% when used with IG feature selection. Therefore, in the proposed model, the authors have used Adaboost classifier and IG feature selection in combination with other features and classifiers. The HELM model presented in this paper uses the ensemble features – IG+CHI with the ensemble classifiers- Ada Boost, SMO-SVM, Logistic Regression together. The comparison of the model is shown with the other ensemble classifiers, and it can be seen that the performance measures of the HELM are the best when compared with other models. It gives the highest accuracy in classification with 88.3%, F-measure 0.88 and ROC of 0.952, as shown in Figure 5.

Table 7. Performance Evaluation of various ensemble classifiers with feature selection in terms of their Precision (P), Recall (R), F-measure (F), Accuracy (ACC) and ROC

Ensemble Classifier	Feature Selection		Performance Metrics				
	Feature	No. of Features	P	R	F	Acc	ROC
AdaBoost	IG	1490	0.883	0.881	0.878	**88.14**	0.951
Bagging	IG	1490	0.879	0.872	0.867	87.24	0.869
Stacking	IG	1490	0.884	0.879	0.874	87.8	0.836
Adaboost	CHI	1490	0.864	0.864	0.864	86.42	0.934
Bagging	CHI	1490	0.88	0.873	0.868	87.29	0.868
Stacking	CHI	1490	0.884	0.879	0.875	**87.9**	0.837
AdaBoost	PCA	511	0.856	0.857	0.855	**85.71**	0.927
Bagging	PCA	511	0.849	0.847	0.842	84.71	0.879
Stacking	PCA	511	0.854	0.853	0.849	85.29	0.812
HELM (AdaBoost +SMO-SVM+ LR)	**IG+CHI**	**1490**	**0.885**	**0.883**	**0.88**	**88.27**	**0.952**

Figure 5. Performance of various ensemble classifier with feature selection and the Hybrid Ensemble Learning Model (HELM)

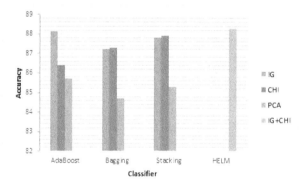

LIMITATIONS OF THE STUDY

The study was aimed at the implementation of ensemble learning for sentiment classification of social media data, which incorporates ensemble features and classifiers together to improve the classification accuracy. Although the proposed approach provides some considerable advantages for sentiment classification, there are some limitations of this work which are addressed below:

1. The proposed model has not been applied on other datasets and therefore the performance of the proposed model on other datasets may vary and in future the implementation can be extended on other datasets;

2. The proposed method did not focus much on the neutral sentiments and required to analyse neutral emotions further to find more contextual meanings from them which might include anger, sad, happy, excited etc. This work can be extended to incorporate more linguistic traits of the text to evaluate hidden and more emotions from the text data, which is currently not covered in this study;

3. The selection of feature selection methods was based only on the ranking based methods and therefore more parameters can be studied and applied to other datasets for classifying sentiments. The method can be improved by integrating more advanced algorithms which will further increase the scope of this study.

DISCUSSION AND CONCLUSION

This study presents the performance evaluation of ensemble learning with feature selection techniques for twitter sentiment analysis. The tweets were extracted in real-time using the twitter api, and R tool was used for pre-processing and evaluation of sentiments. The dataset was prepared by collecting tweets on Facebook data theft by Cambridge Analytica in 2018. There were 7116 tweets that were collected via the Twitter API out of which 1332 tweets were classified as positive, 2452 as Negative and 3300 as negative. The sentiment classification was done based on the sentiment score evaluated by using lexicon-based techniques which uses a lexicon of words for classification.

The experiments were carried out in three settings, wherein the first setting full feature set was used, i.e. no feature reduction is performed on the data. It was observed that the efficiency of the classifiers on the textual data was marginal, although the correctness of the feature set was not disturbed the prediction accuracy was average. In the second setting feature selection techniques have been employed for dimensionality reduction, removal of redundant feature, and evaluating the importance of features with respect to the class. The investigation showed that feature selection techniques based on ranking based features preserved the correctness of feature set and improved the prediction accuracy. Feature selection techniques like IG, CHI, LSA and PCA have been studied, and a combination of these features were used in the proposed HELM. The ensemble feature used combined the IG feature selection, and CHI Squared feature selection techniques one after the other that performed ranking based prediction. The results showed a prediction accuracy of 87.9%, which was an improvement over single feature selection methods. In the third setting, for sentiment classification ensemble classifiers like AdaBoost, Bagging and stacking were investigated and were compared with the base classifiers. It was observed that ensemble classifiers further improved the classification accuracy when compared with the base classifiers when used together with an ensemble feature set. The maximum accuracy with ensemble classifiers that was achieved was 88.1% with Ada Boost. The proposed Hybrid Ensemble Learning Method (HELM) incorporates hybrid ensemble classifier composed of AdaBoost + AMO-SVM + Logistic Regression and uses 10-fold cross-validation (with proper split of training and testing data). Together these set of classifiers, when combined with ensemble features, outperforms the various state of the art methods Naïve Bayes, SVM, LR, SGD, RF and SMO with a classification accuracy of 88.23%.

The future scope of this study will be the implementation of more classifiers on various other standard dataset. More recently, deep learning has also gained importance in the field of sentiment analysis. Therefore, in future deep learning algorithms will be implemented to evaluate the performance on the given dataset.

ACKNOWLEDGMENT

This publication is an outcome of the R & D work undertaken project under the Visvesvaraya Ph.D. Scheme of Ministry of Electronics & Information Technology, Government of India, being implemented by Digital India Corporation and with the cooperation of GGSIP University.

REFERENCES

Doaa, M. E., & Mohamed, H. (2018). A survey on sentiment analysis challenges. *Journal of King Saud University-Engineering Sciences*, *30*(4), 330–338. doi:10.1016/j.jksues.2016.04.002

Abu-Salih, B., Bremie, B., Wongthongtham, P., Duan, K., Issa, T., Chan, K. Y., & Alahmari, M. (2019b, March). Social Credibility Incorporating Semantic Analysis and Machine Learning: A Survey of the State-of-the-Art and Future Research Directions. In *Workshops of the International Conference on Advanced Information Networking and Applications* (pp. 887-896). Cham: Springer. 10.1007/978-3-030-15035-8_87

Abu-Salih, B., Wongthongtham, P., & Chan, K. Y. (2018). Twitter mining for ontology-based domain discovery incorporating machine learning. *Journal of Knowledge Management*, *22*(5), 949–981. doi:10.1108/JKM-11-2016-0489

Abu-Salih, B., Wongthongtham, P., Chan, K. Y., & Zhu, D. (2019a). CredSaT: Credibility ranking of users in big social data incorporating semantic analysis and temporal factor. *Journal of Information Science*, *45*(2), 259–280. doi:10.1177/0165551518790424

Agarwal, B., & Mittal, N. (2013). Sentiment classification using rough set based hybrid feature selection. *Proceedings of the 4th Workshop on Computational Approaches to Subjectivity, Sentiment and Social Media Analysis* (pp. 115-119). Academic Press.

Al-Moslmi, T., Gaber, S., Al-Shabi, A., Albared, M., & Omar, N. (2015). Feature selection methods effects on machine learning approaches in malay sentiment analysis. *Proc. 1st ICRIL-Int. Conf. Inno. Sci. Technol.(IICIST)* (pp. 1-2). Academic Press.

Araque, O., Corcuera-Platas, I., Sanchez-Rada, J. F., & Iglesias, C. A. (2017). Enhancing deep learning sentiment analysis with ensemble techniques in social applications. *Expert Systems with Applications*, *77*, 236–246. doi:10.1016/j.eswa.2017.02.002

Ardehaly, E. M., & Culotta, A. (2017, November). Mining the demographics of political sentiment from twitter using learning from label proportions. *Proceedings of the 2017 IEEE International Conference on Data Mining (ICDM)* (pp. 733-738). IEEE. 10.1109/ICDM.2017.84

Asghar, M. Z., Kundi, F. M., Ahmad, S., Khan, A., & Khan, F. (2018). T-SAF: Twitter sentiment analysis framework using a hybrid classification scheme. *Expert Systems: International Journal of Knowledge Engineering and Neural Networks*, *35*(1), e12233. doi:10.1111/exsy.12233

Bhatnagar, V., Goyal, M., & Hussain, M. A. (2018). A novel aspect based framework for tourism sector with improvised aspect and opinion mining algorithm. *International Journal of Rough Sets and Data Analysis*, *5*(2), 119–130. doi:10.4018/IJRSDA.2018040106

Fattah, M. A. (2015). New term weighting schemes with combination of multiple classifiers. *International Journal of. Neurocomputing, 167*, 434–442. doi:10.1016/j.neucom.2015.04.051

Ghosh, M., & Sanyal, G. (2018). An ensemble approach to stabilize the features for multi-domain sentiment analysis using supervised machine learning. *Journal of Big Data, 5*(1), 44. doi:10.118640537-018-0152-5

Go, A., Bhayani, R., & Huang, L. (2009). Twitter sentiment classification using distant supervision. CS224N Project Report.

Goyal, M., & Bhatnagar, V. (2016). Classification of Polarity of Opinions Using Unsupervised Approach in Tourism Domain. *International Journal of Rough Sets and Data Analysis, 3*(4), 68–78. doi:10.4018/IJRSDA.2016100105

Guan, D., Yuan, W., Lee, Y. K., Najeebullah, K., & Rasel, M. K. (2014). A review of ensemble learning based feature selection. *IETE Technical Review, 31*(3), 190–198. doi:10.1080/02564602.2014.906859

Hu, M., & Liu, B. (2004, August). Mining and summarizing customer reviews. *Proceedings of the tenth ACM SIGKDD international conference on Knowledge discovery and data mining* (pp. 168-177). ACM.

Huang, C. L., Hu, Y.-C., & Lin, C. H. (2017). Twitter sentiment analysis. Retrieved from https://cseweb.ucsd.edu/classes/wi17/cse258-a/reports/a080.pdf

Jansen, B. J., Zhang, M., Sobel, K., & Chowdury, A. (2009). Twitter power: Tweets as electronic word of mouth. *Journal of the American Society for Information Science and Technology, 60*(11), 2169–2188. doi:10.1002/asi.21149

Khurshid, F., Zhu, Y., Xu, Z., Ahmad, M., & Ahmad, M. (2019). Enactment of Ensemble Learning for Review Spam Detection on Selected Features. *International Journal of Computational Intelligence Systems, 12*(1), 387–394. doi:10.2991/ijcis.2019.125905655

Kouloumpis, E., Wilson, T., & Moore, J. (2011, July). Twitter sentiment analysis: The good the bad and the omg! *Proceedings of the Fifth International AAAI conference on weblogs and social media.* AAAI Press.

Koutanaei, F. N., Sajedi, H., & Khanbabaei, M. (2015). A hybrid data mining model of feature selection algorithms and ensemble learning classifiers for credit scoring. *Journal of Retailing and Consumer Services, 27*, 11–23. doi:10.1016/j.jretconser.2015.07.003

L'Huillier, G., Hevia, A., Weber, R., & Rios, S. (2010, May). *Latent semantic analysis and keyword extraction for phishing classification. Proceedings of the 2010 IEEE international conference on intelligence and security informatics* (pp. 129–131). IEEE.

Latif, M., & Qamar, U. (2019, July). A Novel Ensemble Approach for Feature Selection to Improve and Simplify the Sentimental Analysis. In *Intelligent Computing-Proceedings of the Computing Conference* (pp. 573-592). Springer, Cham. 10.1007/978-3-030-22871-2_39

Lin, W. C., Lu, Y. H., & Tsai, C. F. (2019). Feature selection in single and ensemble learning-based bankruptcy prediction models. *Expert Systems: International Journal of Knowledge Engineering and Neural Networks, 36*(1), e12335. doi:10.1111/exsy.12335

Medhat, W., Hassan, A., & Korashy, H. (2014). Sentiment analysis algorithms and applications: A survey. Ain Shams Engineering Journal. doi:10.1016/j.asej.2014.04.011

Pak, A., & Paroubek, P. (2010, May). Twitter as a corpus for sentiment analysis and opinion mining. In LREc (Vol. 10, pp. 1320-1326). Academic Press.

Randhawa, K., Loo, C. K., Seera, M., Lim, C. P., & Nandi, A. K. (2018). Credit card fraud detection using AdaBoost and majority voting. *IEEE Access*, *6*, 14277–14284. doi:10.1109/ACCESS.2018.2806420

Sarkar, S. D., & Goswami, S. (2013). Empirical study on filter based feature selection methods for text classification. *International Journal of Computers and Applications*, *81*(6).

Sarlan, A., Nadam, C., & Basri, S. (2014, November). Twitter sentiment analysis. *Proceedings of the 6th International Conference on Information Technology and Multimedia* (pp. 212-216). IEEE. 10.1109/ICIMU.2014.7066632

Sharma, S., & Bhatnagar, V. (2013). A Conceptual Framework for Social Network Data Security: The Role of Social Network Analysis and Data Mining Techniques. In Data Mining in Dynamic Social Networks and Fuzzy Systems (pp. 58–86). Hershey, PA: IGI Global. doi:10.4018/978-1-4666-4213-3.ch004

Sharma, S., & Jain, A. (2019a). Dynamic social network analysis and performance evaluation. *International Journal of Intelligent Engineering Informatics*, *7*(2-3), 180–202. doi:10.1504/IJIEI.2019.099088

Sharma, S., & Jain, A. (2019b). An Empirical Evaluation of Correlation based Feature Selection for Tweet Sentiment Classification. *Proceedings of the International Conference on Cybernetics, Cognition, and Machine Learning Approaches 2019*. Springer India.

Sharma, S., & Jain, A. (2019c). Cyber Social Media Analytics and Issues: A Pragmatic Approach for Twitter Sentiment Analysis. In *Advances in Computer Communication and Computational Sciences* (pp. 473–484). Thailand: Springer. doi:10.1007/978-981-13-6861-5_41

Singh, A., & Jain, A. (2019). Adaptive Credit Card Fraud Detection Techniques Based on Feature Selection Method. In *Advances in Computer Communication and Computational Sciences* (pp. 167–178). Singapore: Springer. doi:10.1007/978-981-13-6861-5_15

Sinha, S., Bhatnagar, V., & Bansal, A. (2018). Multi-label Naïve Bayes classifier for identification of top destination and issues to accost by tourism sector. *Journal of Global Information Management*, *26*(3), 37–53. doi:10.4018/JGIM.2018070104

Song, F., Guo, Z., & Mei, D. (2010, November). *Feature selection using principal component analysis. Proceedings of the 2010 international conference on system science, engineering design and manufacturing informatization* (Vol. 1, pp. 27–30). IEEE.

Sonkar, S. K., Bhatnagar, V., & Challa, R. K. (2015). Need of Intelligent Search in Dynamic Social Network. *Information Resources Management Journal*, *28*(2), 46–61. doi:10.4018/IRMJ.2015040104

Süzek, T.Ö. (2017). Using latent semantic analysis for automated keyword extraction from large document corpora. *Turkish Journal of Electrical Engineering and Computer Sciences*, *25*(3), 1784–1794.

Ubing, A. A., Jasmi, S. K. B., Abdullah, A., Jhanjhi, N. Z., & Supramaniam, M. (2019). Phishing website detection: an improved accuracy through feature selection and ensemble learning. *International Journal Of Advanced Computer Science And Applications*, *10*(1), 252–257. doi:10.14569/IJACSA.2019.0100133

Vo, B.K.H., & Collier, N. (2013). Twitter emotion analysis in earthquake situations. *International Journal of Computational Linguistics and Applications*, *4*(1), 159–173.

Wang, G., Sun, J., Ma, J., Xu, K., & Gu, J. (2014). Sentiment classification: The contribution of ensemble learning. *Decision Support Systems*, *57*, 77–93. doi:10.1016/j.dss.2013.08.002

Xia, R., Xu, F., Yu, J., Qi, Y., & Cambria, E. (2016). Polarity shift detection, elimination and ensemble: A three-stage model for document-level sentiment analysis. *Journal of Information Processing and Management*, *52*(1), 36–45. doi:10.1016/j.ipm.2015.04.003

Xia, R., Zong, C., & Li, S. (2011). Ensemble of feature sets and classification algorithms for sentiment classification. Information Sciences, *181*(6), 1138–1152. doi:10.1016/j.ins.2010.11.023

Zareapoor, M., & Seeja, K. R. (2015). Feature extraction or feature selection for text classification: A case study on phishing email detection. *International Journal of Information Engineering and Electronic Business*, *7*(2), 60. doi:10.5815/ijieeb.2015.02.08

This research was previously published in the International Journal of Information Retrieval Research (IJIRR), 10(2); pages 40-58, copyright year 2020 by IGI Publishing (an imprint of IGI Global).

Chapter 65
Users' Distribution and Behavior in Academic Social Networking Sites

Omar Saad Almousa

Jordan University of Science and Technology, Irbid, Jordan

ABSTRACT

Academic social networking sites (SNSs) are growing rapidly. Worldwide, academicians use academic SNSs for many reasons regardless of their nation, gender, position, and discipline. In this paper, the authors extend their previous work in exploring the distribution and behavior of a particular academic SNS (academia.edu) on a large scale. The authors classify users into different groups based on their position, discipline, and continent. This study gives a better understanding of usage patterns in academic SNS, especially in the lack of large-scale studies about different classes of users on academic SNSs.

1. INTRODUCTION

Academic social networking sites (SNSs) are growing rapidly. This growth is driven mainly by the continuous demand from academic people to exploit different aspects of the Internet. Similar to general-purpose SNSs, Academic SNSs offer several functionalities such as the management of profiles, posts, connections, and private messaging. However, in academic SNSs these features have more emphasis on academic metaphors. Several reasons motivate people to join academic SNSs, especially communicating peers and thus collaborating with them. Academic SNSs users vary on different levels, such as their academic position, discipline, country, experience, and motivation. This wide diversity is reflected on their behavior and usage patterns. It is obvious that studying users' distribution and behavior is essential in providing a better understanding their needs and thus improving academic SNSs.

This paper aims to find whether different groups of academic users have behavioral patterns on academic SNSs (specifically on academia.edu). The significance of this study originates from the need for large scale studies about academic SNS; especially with different user classes/categories. Moreover, understanding academic users' behavior and distribution is vital not only in improving existing systems for them, but also for designing new services and systems for their ease. To achieve this, we directly collected data of more than 30 thousand user profile from academia.edu website. We looked after users

DOI: 10.4018/978-1-6684-7123-4.ch065

from four different academic disciplines, namely: Anthropology, Chemistry, Computer science, and Philosophy. We categorized our data set into four groups on basis of the academic position of each user: faculty members, graduate students, independent researchers, and post-doctoral researchers. After that, we analyzed our data set on basis of seven variables that we defined according to different elements of a user profile on academia.edu. Our analysis indicates that each of the four groups of users generally has a regular behavior regardless of the science discipline it originates from. However, there we found obvious behavior division in some aspects; especially in the behavior of independent researchers. Although these irregularities, independent researchers have distinct behavior pattern most of the time.

The rest of the paper is structured as follows: In Section 2, we give a discussion of related research in order to put this study in its context. Section 3 gives an overview of the academic social network site that we target in our study, namely: academia.edu. In Section 4, we present our research methodology in order to show processes, data, sampling, and variable definitions. Section 5 shows our main results followed by a discussion for our findings. Finally, we conclude with a set of findings and future work in Section 7.

2. RELATED RESEARCH

In this section, we try to navigate through some related literature. We start with general concepts about social networks, then we narrow our review to academic SNS. In general, a social network (SN) is found when a computer network connects people or organizations as in Schleyer et al. (2008). According to Cooke (2006), it is defined as a group of people and connections among them. Since the World Wide Web (WWW) is shifting to Web 2.0, the Internet become more of a social network serving people with information resources, creating ties among them, and allowing them to create their own content easily, cf. DiMicco et al. (2008). The use of collaborative technologies such SNSs invoked people to create on-line communities to facilitate their communication and collaboration effortlessly, Fu et al. (2008). An SNS is defined in Kumar et al. (2013) as a web-based service that allows users to construct a profile, articulate a list of other users, and traverse their list of connections and those made by others within a bounded system. The nature of these connections may vary from site to site. In light of Boyd and Ellison (2007); Boyd (2006) and the previous definition, an SNS can be defined is website that offers the ability for people of common interest to manage profiles, posts, comments, relations, feelings, and messaging. By management we mean the ability to create, edit, delete, and constraint a specific feature or artifact, e.g., SNSs users can create their own profiles, edit them, delete posts, block a friend (constraint a relation), etc. Again, the nature of constructed relations within an SNS along with the common interest articulate the type of SNSs creating specialized SNSs, e.g., professional, academic, etc. Before specialized SNSs, people of common interest started using general-purpose SNS to achieve the aforementioned goals of communicating and collaboration. However, it was obvious that general-purpose SNS cannot cope with certain needs of such groups. The emergence of specialized SNSs, according to Vascellaro (2007), is targeted toward specific user groups of specific common interest and provide added value to several kinds of users in different ways in comparison to general purpose SNS, Li (2011). Specialized users can gather and meet new or previously known people remotely, and thus achieve shared goals with them, McCarthy (2007). Therefore, professionals use SNSs in order to extend their professional networks, learn about colleagues and their colleagues, locate experts, solve problems, and find potential collaborators as to Joinson (2008). According to McCarthy (2007) SNSs can play a critical role in specifying ways to solve problems, run organizations, and increase the success level of goal achievement for individuals. Thus, SNSs are increasingly attracting the attention of professionals motivated by its availability and reach. cf. Lampe et al. (2008). One of those specific user groups targeted by SNSs is the scientific or the academic body; providing academic people with a computer-supported cooperative work (CSCW) tools. Moreover, SNSs help scientists find appropriate collaborators more quickly and efficiently than other methods especially as science has become more collaborative in over past several decades, Joinson (2008).

Academic and scientific SNS offer several social neworking services that are on-line services that help in constructing scholarly SNs by focusing in providing on-line research-oriented activities, Oh and Jeng (2011). Academic SNS such as academia.edu[1], LinkedIn[2], ResearchGate[3], and some others are becoming increasingly popular recently. According to Alexa[4], their global ranking was 7982, 16, and 16324 respectively (as in June, 18th 2011). Note that this work extends our previous work (Almousa (2011)) by asking/answering a third question about users' behavior in accordance to their geographical location worldwide (the study questions are a paragraph away from here). Since that, several related work was produced such as in Thelwall and Kousha (2014) in which authors investigated profile views on academia.edu for faculty and students in philosophy, computer science, law and history. Unlike our work, they classified users according to their gender, and introduced a method to handle time delays in joining academia.edu. In Elsayed (2016), the researcher designed an on-line questionnaire and invited more than 3000 Arab researchers in order to find out their motives in joining academic SNSs. She received 315 answered questionnaires, and her analysis found that the majority of Arab researchers tend to prefer ResearchGate and their main motive was to share their publications. The authors of Jordan and Weller (2018) used an on-line survey to find a disciplinary divide on the selection of an academic SNS, they also find a position divide on the purposes of usage of academic SNSs. With a reasonably large data set, Manca and Ranieri (2017) investigated over 6,000 Italian scholars in quest for their motivations and use frequencies. The authors tried to find correlations in light of different factors such as gender, academic title, and years of experience. However, the novelty of this research is still persistent being amongst the first ones to address the particularity of academic SNSs on a large scale (+30,000 profiles). In fact, several of the previous works cited the conference version of this paper Almousa (2011) that we extend here on basis of study questions, discipline coverage, and continent distribution. Although academic SNSs are gaining more popularity among academic people, and they are extremely important in determining how scientific collaborations are formed, SNs have not yet been studied comprehensively, although usage patterns in SNSs were studied as in Stutzman (2011) and Lampe et al. (2008). Yet, a little is known about academic SNSs and how academic people use academic SNSs, so there is a lack of knowledge on users' groups and usage behaviors. This study aims to explore users' groups and behavior in academia.edu by different groups of academic users. To that end, we try to answer the following three questions:

1. Do people from different disciplines use academic SNSs differently?
2. Do people with different academic positions use academic SNSs differently?
3. Do people from different places use academic SNSs differently?

To answer this question, we classified users according to their continents. More specifically, the classification is made on basis of the continent of their affiliated university not their citizenship continent; since academia.edu does not offer citizenship information of users. The next section gives an overview of academia.edu SNS.

3. ACADEMIA.EDU

Now we give an overview about academia.edu SNS. In October 2008, academia.edu was first introduced, and within 30 months it reached more than 300,000 profiles with one million hits daily. We selected academia.edu in this research because of its academic nature of profiles including university, department, primary research interest and many others. Additionally, academia.edu has a wide users' diversity on basis of their academic position, i.e., department members, students (graduate and undergraduate), post doctoral, independent researchers, etc.. Moreover, we consider Alexa ranking for similar SNSs, as other SNSs with better ranking are not as academic oriented as academia.edu, for instance LinkedIn can be considered as more professional-oriented than academic-oriented SNSs. Like most of SNSs, a user profile in academia.edu acts as a personal image of the user by which she can express her academic personality. It is a crucial component for establishing connections (Tufekci, 2008), and according to Boyd and Ellison (2007) user profiles are the "backbone" of any SNS. In academia.edu a user profile contains personal information, contact information, position information, and academic related information such as research interests. The complete list of information found in a user profile on academia.edu is as follows:

1. Personal information that includes: Name, Picture, Status, Position, Position title, Department, University, About.
2. Contact details that includes: Email, Homepage, Address, Phone, Skype, and Recent updates.
3. Research Interests that includes: Primary Research interests and Secondary Research interests.
4. Uploaded Materials that includes: Papers, Books, Talks, Teaching Documents, Blogs, CV, Websites, and Others.
5. Relationships that includes: Colleagues, Follows, and Followed by.
6. Questions that includes: Asked Questions, and Answered Questions.
7. Following that includes: Following Papers, Following Questions, and Following (updates).

Academia.edu motivates its users to build connections by following researchers and research; this is reflected in many ways. For example, it enables users to follow other users, papers, questions, and updates. Moreover, it has a logo that says: "Follow Research". Users are informed about others following them or their work. "Recent updates" feature dynamically report activities a user may perform. This feature reports not only the type of a recent activity, but also it reports the users involved in that activity, as well as the date or the time elapse of that activity.

4. METHODOLOGY

After reviewing some of related literature and introducing academia.edu, we now describe our research methodology. We start with our research questions, then we discuss the data collection process followed by presenting users' distributions.

4.1. Research Questions

In this research, we try to answer the following questions:

1. Do people from different academic disciplines use SNSs differently?. In other words, we wonder if a user behavior is affected by the user academic discipline. In order to answer this question, we consider four different academic disciplines trying to cover different specificities from different natures. The four academic disciplines are as follows:

   (a) Anthropology from humanities disciplines.

   (b) Philosophy from arts disciplines.

   (c) Chemistry from natural sciences disciplines.

   (d) Computer science from technical sciences.

2. Do people with different academic positions use SNSs differently?. By this question we try to know if the academic position of a user affects the behavior of that user. In order to answer this question, we consider four different academic positions, namely:

   (a) Faculty members.

   (b) Graduate students.

   (c) Independent researchers.

   (d) Post-doctoral.

We selected these positions since we noticed during primary navigation of academia.edu that they cover a majority of users. Moreover, the four academic positions cover most of people working in academia.

3. Do people from different places use SNSs differently?. By this question we aim to know if a user place affects her behavior on academia.edu. To answer this, we divided users into their continents. More specifically, the continent of the university they belong to, not their citizenship continent; since academia.edu do not offer citizenship information as we discuss later.

As we pointed our previously, our different classification is mainly motivated by its wide coverage of the population. This coverage has two levels: data set coverage and academic discipline coverage, i.e., we believe that the four academic disciplines are a good representative for academic disciplines in general. Moreover, they formed a majority in our primary exploration. Among each of the four disciplines, we found that the dominant academic position categories were faculty members, graduate students, independent researchers, and post-doctoral researchers.

4.2. Data Collection

In this section, we describe the process of our data set construction. We collected our data directly from academia.edu website using C# code in the period from March 15th 2011 to June 1st 2011. (We performed recent attempts to update our data set, but we failed mainly because of countermeasures taken by websites against data harvesting, e.g., CAPTCHA). The total number of harvested profiles exceeded 30,000 records in our data set. After that, we performed a data cleaning step to filter out problematic records that contain for example spelling mistakes, or spurious records. We also made a data unification step to gather records that are supposed to belong to the same set. For example, a user with post-doc position should belong to the same set of another user with post-doctoral position. Another example, a user from USA should belong to the same set of another user with United Stated of America in country field. After that, we performed a step to classify our data set in three different ways:

1. Academic discipline: Anthropology and Philosophy from art disciplines, Chemistry from natural sciences, and Computer science as technical science discipline.
2. Academic position: Faculty members, Graduate students, Independent research, and Post-doctoral researchers.
3. University country.

The reason behind the selection of theses specific four classes or groups is due to the fact that they have the widest coverage of total users with nearly 70% from the total data set as illustrated by Figure 1. Finally, we codified our data set and specified its variables as a preparation for further analysis. Codification and variables are shown in Table 1.

After the process of data gathering, codification, and variable definitions is done, the results are shown in Table 1.

Figure 1. Academic disciplines coverage

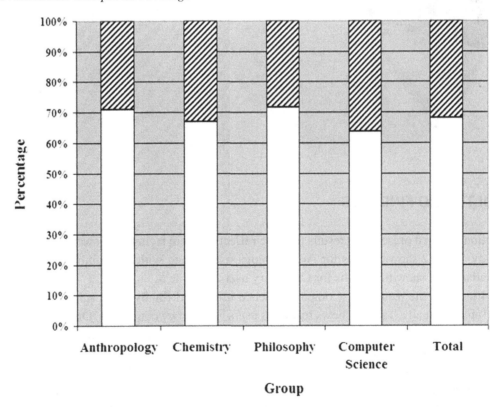

4.3. User Distribution

Concerning continents, continent-groups are: Africa, Asia, Australia, Europe, North America, and South America. The distribution of users in our data set over continents is given in Figure 2. Figure 2 shows that users from North America and Europe have the largest share amongst others with a percentage of 71%. This is clearly due to many reasons. First, the number of universities in the two continents is larger than in the rest of continents. Second, English language is the interface language of academia.edu, and users from the two continents have English language as either a native language or widely used and practiced. Lastly, academia.edu is an American website, and thus it is widely diffused there. For the rest of continents, users from Asia present 19% with the third share. South America, Australia, and Africa are all behind with less than 10%.

Figure 2. Continent distribution

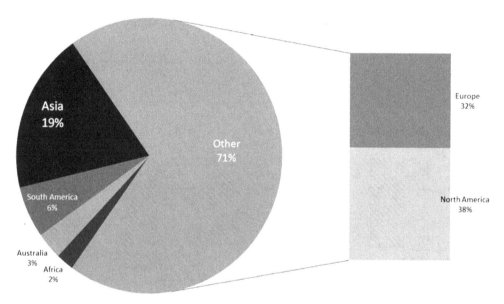

5. RESULTS AND FINDINGS

In this section, we first present our results then we reflect on them trying to answer the three questions of this study. Table 2 shows results for Anthropology users along with the number of people in each group. Similarly, we show the results for Chemistry users in Table 3.

Table 4 presents the results for Computer science users, and finally the results of Philosophy are shown in Table 5. Finally, Table 6 shows results of users grouped by continents. One can notice that the total users distributed over continents is larger than the total of users in all disciplines; this is mainly due to the fact that Independent researchers have no institutions, and thus we cannot associate any of them to a country. Moreover, for some of the institutions, we cannot associate them to a country; since a user on academia.edu can make up any name for his institution and associate it to any country!.

Now we present the first two questions jointly, then we finish with the third question. We first address each variable separately for a better presentation.

Table 1. Variables and codification

Variable name and description	Computation method	Items	
		Item name	*Data type and codification method*
Profile completeness: expresses personal information and contact details provided by the user, and it is shown in his profile.	Computed by finding the mean of the following (right) data items (after being codified) as we explain, and then finding the average for all users in each group (class).	Picture	Binary: 1: picture uploaded, 0: otherwise
		Status	Binary: 1: status mentioned, 0: otherwise
		Position title	Binary: 1: Position title mentioned, 0: otherwise
		About	Binary: 1: About mentioned, 0: otherwise
		Email	Binary: 1: Email mentioned, 0: otherwise
		Homepage	Binary: 1: Homepage mentioned, 0: otherwise
		Address	Binary: 1: Address mentioned, 0: otherwise
		Phone	Binary: 1: Phone mentioned, 0: otherwise
		Skype	Binary: 1: Skype mentioned, 0: otherwise
Uploaded Material: Expresses the uploaded materials of a uses.	Same as above	Papers	Discrete: number of papers
		Books	Discrete: number of books
		Talks	Discrete: number of talks
		Teaching Documents	Discrete: number of teaching documents
		Blogs	Discrete: number of blogs
		CV	Binary: 1: CV uploaded, 0: otherwise
		Websites	Discrete: number of websites
		Others	Discrete: number of other materials
Research Interest: Expresses the research interests a user adds into his profile.	Same as above	Primary Research interests	Discrete: number of primary research interests
		Secondary Research interests	Discrete: number of secondary research interests
Relationships: Expresses number of users that a user is connected to in somehow.	Same as above	Colleagues	Discrete: number of department colleagues
		Follows	Discrete: number of other users that the user follows.
		Followed by	Discrete: number of other users following the user.
Questions: Expresses the questions a user asked or answered.	Same as above	Asked Questions	Discrete: number of asked questions by the user.
		Answered Questions	Discrete: number of answered questions by the user.
Following: Expresses the activities that a user follows.	Same as above	Following Papers	Discrete: number of papers followed questions by the user.
		Following Questions	Discrete: number of questions followed by the user.
		Following (updates)	Discrete: number of updates followed by the user.
Activity Frequency: Expresses the frequency of activity for a user.	Derived by dividing #Updates by Delta Days	Delta Days	Discrete: derived from "Recent updates" by finding the difference in days between first update and last update
		#Updates	Discrete: derived directly from "Recent updates" by counting number of updates

Table 2. Anthropology results

	Faculty Members	Graduate students	Independent Researchers	Post Doctoral
Number	2481	3539	804	391
Profile Completeness	0.303	0.236	0.185	0.306
Research Interest	6.958	6.924	10.989	6.703
Relationships	16.128	16.777	6.208	18.046
Following	1.426	1.367	0.970	1.769
Activity Frequency	0.033	0.036	0.057	0.039
Questions	0.036	0.028	0.015	0.049
Uploaded Material	1.004	0.428	0.424	1.009

Table 3. Chemistry results

	Faculty Members	Graduate students	Independent Researchers	Post Doctoral
Number	1113	1658	221	458
Profile Completeness	0.245	0.178	0.154	0.208
Research Interest	2.837	2.794	5.217	2.571
Relationships	6.633	6.000	2.863	7.218
Following	0.328	0.406	0.860	0.414
Activity Frequency	0.028	0.026	0.068	0.025
Questions	0.007	0.003	0.059	0.001
Uploaded Material	0.755	0.272	0.307	0.686

5.1. First Two Questions

- **Profile Completeness:** Both of faculty members and post-doctoral researchers have close values for this factor that exceeds other two groups; this can be attributed to the demanding career of them. Graduate students have recorded more incomplete profiles, but independent researchers are the least. The latter case is somehow not much typical for the case as they are looking for "marketing" themselves through such SNSs.
- **Research Interest:** One can easily notice that independent researchers group has the highest values compared to other groups; we attribute this to the willingness to find as many collaborators as they can. Another reason can be their openness to target new research areas, especially as they are not restricted to research groups within institutions.
- **Relationships:** Independent researchers have the very least score in relationships (a third of the next 4.412 to 12.047 for graduate students); this may probably account for the lack of institutional body that supports their connections with others. Other groups have very close results; since they exist within academic institutions. Among them, post-doctoral group has the highest score; possibly since their early academic career that may need stronger ties with others.

- **Following:** Post-doctoral researchers have the largest result for this variable/ Other groups have close values. This applies to Anthropology, Computer science and Philosophy. In Chemistry However, independent researchers have the highest score. They even two-folded the next greatest (0.860 to 0.414). This indicates that Chemistry independent researchers are interested in following updates, papers and questions much more than their colleagues in other disciplines.

- **Activity Frequency:** The group of independent researches score the highest value. We think that it is due to their willingness to stay "connected" to peers. Another reason for that can be the fact that they have fewer duties than other.

- **Questions:** Unlike previous result of variable, here we have an evident difference amongst disciplines. This is the case especially for independent researchers. More specifically, independent researchers in Anthropology have the least value, while independent researchers of computer science and chemistry have the highest value. This result indicates their high activity in asking and answering questions. On the other hand, post-doctoral researcher of Philosophy and Anthropology are the most active in questioning and answering. This can be because for their time freedom that they have in comparison to faculty members. Faculty members and graduate students share a moderate level in all disciplines.

- **Uploaded Material:** faculty members and post-doctoral researchers are the first in uploading materials in comparison to other groups. Obviously this is because both groups have teaching responsibilities and therefore upload teaching materials on academia.edu. Another reason is that they are generally more research productive than students and independent researchers, and they tend to upload their research materials.

Table 4. Computer science results

	Faculty Members	**Graduate students**	**Independent Researchers**	**Post Doctoral**
Number	3177	5026	757	619
Profile Completeness	0.262	0.202	0.148	0.268
Research Interest	4.293	3.483	7.077	3.645
Relationships	10.079	10.794	3.592	10.812
Following	0.595	0.514	0.569	0.647
Activity Frequency	0.023	0.027	0.068	0.023
Questions	0.006	0.004	0.011	0.008
Uploaded Material	0.852	0.323	0.296	0.768

5.2. Third Question

- Profile Completeness: As shown in Table 6, users can be divided into three groups, the highest from Europe and Australia, followed by users from America (North and South), and the lowest were from Asia and Africa. However, there is no evident difference in profile completeness among users from different continents.

Table 5. Philosophy results

	Faculty Members	Graduate students	Independent Researchers	Post Doctoral
Number	3718	3673	1043	455
Profile Completeness	0.309	0.240	0.168	0.314
Research Interest	6.337	6.676	8.364	6.512
Relationships	15.554	14.617	4.986	17.771
Following	1.195	1.238	0.810	1.668
Activity Frequency	0.032	0.035	0.063	0.035
Questions	0.031	0.035	0.011	0.053
Uploaded Material	0.975	0.448	0.392	0.963

- Research Interest: Users from Europe have the highest values amongst others, whereas Asians have the lowest score in this.
- Relationships: Differences among continent groups are obvious in relationships. Users from South America and Africa are the least in relations, while Europeans are the highest. After the European come North Americans, then Australians and Asians.
- Following: The same as the results of the previous one.
- Activity Frequency: No evident difference holds in this criterion.
- Questions: The least active users are the ones from Africa, Asia and South America. On the other hand, Australians, North Americans and Europeans score the highest.
- Uploaded Material: The same order of groups remains as in the previous variable, but with Europeans group having the highest score instead of Australians.

Table 6. Continents results

	Africa	Asia	Australia	Europe	North America	South America
Number						
Profile Completeness	0.198	0.205	0.278	0.282	0.250	0.229
Research Interest	4.691	3.780	5.425	6.021	5.328	5.743
Relationships	6.064	10.378	11.592	16.460	14.285	8.772
Following	0.544	0.572	0.898	1.223	0.981	0.843
Activity Frequency	0.030	0.032	0.030	0.031	0.030	0.033
Questions	0.004	0.003	0.049	0.027	0.028	0.006
Uploaded Material	0.380	0.393	0.774	0.778	0.647	0.544

6. DISCUSSION

Now we present our reflections on the results and findings of the previous section. In concern to the first question, users from arts and humanities are more active than users from the other two disciplines. We attribute this to the type of research activities they carry out that needs an involvement of bigger groups. Additionally, the "humanity" nature of these disciplines encourages higher communication skills, and therefore stronger relationships with peers. In the least active part, users of computer science are more active than chemistry, we think that the more "technical" a discipline is, the less its people have connections or seeking for.

Moving to the second question, one can notice that Post-docs are the most active disregarding the originating discipline. We think that this is due to their efforts are focused mainly on research, i.e., they have less administration and teaching duties. Faculty members have similar levels of activity with Post-doctoral researchers. However, they have lower levels of activity in relationships. This is so since they have extra non-research duties, and also because they are more likely to have more experience and thus wider relationship circles. Moreover, the set of prospective collaborators for Faculty members is mostly known to them because of their career maturity. The behavior of Graduate students is not far from the two previous groups. This behavioral similarity is caused by the existence of an institutional frame for the three groups. Nevertheless, graduates are less active because they have less research experience, and premature career.

Independent researchers are the least active in comparison to others. However, but they show some behavioral irregularities that we think that they are worth mentioning; e.g., they have a wide set of research interests. Moreover, they have more frequent updates. This probably reflects their willingness to increase their prospective collaborators. On the other hand, independent researcher are the least in having relationships, following updates, and providing materials, but with the exception of Chemistry independent researchers who are the most active "followers"!. Another irregularity is revealed in asking and answering Questions; i.e., they have the highest activity in Anthropology and Philosophy, but the lowest in Chemistry and Computer science. We think that the openness of discussions in arts and humanities disciplines cause longer conversations, i.e., more questions and answers.

Finally, in reference to the third question, we noticed slight differences among different groups from different continents. European researchers tend to be the most active in almost all aspects. On the other hand, researchers from Africa and South America tend to be the least active. Users from Australia and North America have shown a high level of activity in most of the criteria studied. Note that we have a brief discussion on the results of the third question because we think that this needs to delve into cultural differences among users. In fact, we have some primary results in our previous work: Almousa (2012).

7. CONCLUSION AND FUTURE WORK

This study aims to find distinct users' behaviors and groups in academia.edu being an representative example of academic SNSs. To that end, we directly collected a data set of 30 thousands user profiles distributed over four academic disciplines, four job positions, and all continents. The academic disciplines are: Anthropology, Chemistry, Computer science, and Philosophy. We also classify our data set based on their job position: Graduate students, Faculty members, Post-doctoral researchers, and Independent researchers. A third classification we perform is based on the continent of users depending on the country of their university of affiliation. The study tries to answer three questions that concern the existence of behavior difference among users grouped by discipline, position, and continent respectively to the questions. We analyze our data set in reference to a number of variables that we define according to academia.edu profile elements.

Our analysis indicates that each of the academic position groups has generally a distinct behavior despite of the discipline the group belongs to, with some irregularities that we pointed out in the Discussion (Section 6). We find that independent researchers have most of the time a divergent behavior. We also noticed that Faculty members and post-doctoral researchers almost share a unique behavior. Moreover, graduate students behave in a similar way to the previous two groups, but they are less active in general.

As expected, this investigation was subject to several limitations. First one is its limitation to a single academic SNS, we believe that considering several SNSs will give better understanding and finer results. Another limitation is considering four disciplines of science only. Although we think that they are a good representative for other disciplines, but having more disciplines can surely support our results and enhance our findings. Finally, the continent based grouping is not very accurate. This is because we consider the citizenship of universities instead of the citizenship of users. In fact, the citizenship of users is not available on academia.edu. These limitations can be addressed in future works that target more academic SNSs, more science disciplines, finer country associations, and the effect of cultural factor in the behavior of users.

This study may be improved in many directions. Thanks for to constructive feedback from the reviewers. For example, this research can be improved by rerunning the study with recent data, and compare how behavior patterns changed since then. Another way to improve the findings is performing more sophisticated statistical tests such as t-test or ANOVA. It will be also very interesting to look at the data from different perspectives, e.g., examine the items within the variables in Table 1 as individual variables. Investigating the relationship between the research quality/quantity produced by a user and her behavior on academic SNSs is also another very interesting future work.

REFERENCES

Almousa, O. S. (2011). Users' classification and usage-pattern identification in academic social networks. In *Applied Electrical Engineering and Computing Technologies (AEECT), 2011 IEEE Jordan Conference on*. IEEE.

Almousa, O. S. (2012). *Cross-Cultural Analysis of Academic Social Network Sites* (Master's thesis). University of Ternto.

Boyd, D. (2006). *Friends, friendsters, and myspace top 8: Writing community into being on social network sites*. Academic Press.

Boyd, D. M., & Ellison, N. B. (2007). Social network sites: Definition, history, and scholarship. *Journal of Computer-Mediated Communication, 13*(1), 210–230. doi:10.1111/j.1083-6101.2007.00393.x

Cooke, R. J. E. (2006). *Link Prediction and Link Detection in Sequences of Large Social Networks Using Temporal and Local Metrics* (Ph.D. thesis). University of Cape Town.

DiMicco, J., Millen, D. R., Geyer, W., Dugan, C., Brownholtz, B., & Muller, M. (2008). Motivations for social networking at work. In *Proceedings of the 2008 ACM conference on Computer supported cooperative work*. ACM.

Elsayed, A. M. (2016). The use of academic social networks among arab researchers: A survey. *Social Science Computer Review*, *34*(3), 378–391. doi:10.1177/0894439315589146

Fu, F., Liu, L., & Wang, L. (2008). Empirical analysis of online social networks in the age of web 2.0. *Physica A*, *387*(2-3), 675–684. doi:10.1016/j.physa.2007.10.006

Joinson, A. N. 2008. Looking at, looking up or keeping up with people? Motives and use of facebook. In *Proceedings of the SIGCHI conference on Human Factors in Computing Systems*. ACM. 10.1145/1357054.1357213

Jordan, K., & Weller, M. (2018). Communication, collaboration and identity: Factor analysis of academics' perceptions of online networking. *Research in Learning Technology*, 26.

Kumar, N. S., KarthikChandran, U., ArunKumar, N., & Karnavel, K. (2013). *Social networking site for self portfolio*. arXiv preprint arXiv:1307.3399

Lampe, C., Ellison, N. B., & Steinfield, C. (2008). Changes in use and perception of Facebook. In *Proceedings of the 2008 ACM conference on Computer supported cooperative work*. ACM. 10.1145/1460563.1460675

Li, X. (2011). Factors influencing the willingness to contribute information to online communities. *New Media & Society*, *13*(2), 279–296. doi:10.1177/1461444810372164

Manca, S., & Ranieri, M. (2017). Networked scholarship and motivations for social media use in scholarly communication. *The International Review of Research in Open and Distributed Learning*, 18.

McCarthy, J. F. (2007). The challenges of recommending digital selves in physical spaces. In *Proceedings of the 2007 ACM conference on Recommender systems*. ACM. 10.1145/1297231.1297269

Oh, J. S., & Jeng, W. (2011). Groups in academic social networking services–an exploration of their potential as a platform for multi-disciplinary collaboration. In *Privacy, Security, Risk and Trust (PASSAT) and 2011 IEEE Third International Conference on Social Computing (SocialCom), 2011 IEEE Third International Conference on*. IEEE. 10.1109/PASSAT/SocialCom.2011.202

Schleyer, T., Spallek, H., Butler, B. S., Subramanian, S., Weiss, D., Poythress, M. L., ... Mueller, G. (2008). Facebook for scientists: Requirements and services for optimizing how scientific collaborations are established. *Journal of Medical Internet Research*, 10. PMID:18701421

Stutzman, F. D. (2011). *Networked Information Behavior in Life Transition* (Ph.D. thesis). The University of North Carolina at Chapel Hill.

Thelwall, M., & Kousha, K. (2014). Academia. edu: Social network or academic network? *Journal of the Association for Information Science and Technology*, *65*(4), 721–731. doi:10.1002/asi.23038

Tufekci, Z. (2008). Can you see me now? audience and disclosure regulation in online social network sites. *Bulletin of Science, Technology & Society*, *28*(1), 20–36. doi:10.1177/0270467607311484

Vascellaro, J.E. (2007). Social networking goes professional: Doctors, salesmen, executives turn to new sites to consult, commiserate with peers; weeding out impostors. *Wall Street Journal*.

Omar Saad Almousa is an Assistant professor at Jordan University of Science & Technology holding a PhD in Computer Science from Technical University of Denmark.

ENDNOTES

[1]   http://www.academia.edu, Last accessed: 22-7-2018.
[2]   http://www.linkedin.com, Last accessed: 22-7-2018.
[3]   http://www.researchgate.net, Last accessed: 22-7-2018.
[4]   http://www.alexa.com, Last accessed: 15-6-2012.

This research was previously published in the International Journal of e-Collaboration (IJeC), 14(3); pages 49-65, copyright year 2018 by IGI Publishing (an imprint of IGI Global).

Chapter 66

Peripheral Vision:
Engaging Multimodal Social Media Datasets to Differentiate MOOC Platforms by Course Offerings and Us

Shalin Hai-Jew

ⓘ https://orcid.org/0000-0002-8863-0175
Kansas State University, USA

ABSTRACT

In the dozen years since massive open online courses (MOOCs) have been a part of open-source online learning, the related platforms and technologies have settled out to some degree. This chapter indirectly explores 10 of the most well-known MOOC platforms based on social data from the following sources: large-scale web search data (via Google Correlate), academic research indexing (Google Scholar), social imagery and related image tagging (Google Image Search), crowd-sourced articles from a crowd-sourced encyclopedia (Wikipedia), microblogging data (Twitter), and posts and comments from social networking data (Facebook). This analysis is multimodal, to include text and imagery, and the analyses are enabled by various forms of "distant reading," including topic modeling, sentiment analysis, and computational text analysis, and manual coding of social imagery. This chapter aims to define MOOC platforms indirectly by their course contents and the user bases (and their social media-based discourses) that have grown up around each.

INTRODUCTION

Taking a massive open online course (or "MOOC") is a fairly simple endeavor. One registers with a validated email, selects from a range of courses, and chooses how much to participate. For a majority of learners, the cost is free because the learners are not taking a course for credit or digital badging or some other formal acknowledgment. In the MOOCs that this author has experienced, the co-learners tend to be friendly and mutually supportive. While the MOOC platforms include some friendly invitations to

DOI: 10.4018/978-1-6684-7123-4.ch066

do homework assignments, learners who lurk are supported. The author has experienced several MOOC platforms over the years. The experiences have been edifying and positive, on the whole. For research, though, there are strengths and limits to *sousveillance* (or monitoring from within).

The first massive open online course ("In/Formation Year") was offered in 2006 (Davidson, Sept. 27, 2013), even though it was not known by that name at that time and did not apparently use any unique platform. The term "massive open online course" or "MOOC" was coined in 2008 by Dave Cormier (of the University of Prince Edward Island) and Bryan Alexander (of the National Institute for Technology in Liberal Education), in reference to a course by George Siemens and Stephen Downes of the University of Manitoba (Connectivism and Connective Knowledge), which attracted approximately 2,300 learners (McAuley, Stewart, Siemens, & Cormier, 2010, as cited in Yang, 2014, p. 325).

MOOCs became a "thing" in 2012 (Pappano, 2012; Massive open online course, Jan. 12, 2018). An authoring team writes of the importance of Peter Norvig and Sebastian Thrun's "Introduction to Artificial Intelligence" class, which brought out 160,000 enrollees, and sparked interest by investors to fund several MOOC platforms:

Following this massive success, several private initiatives started to establish online platforms to organize these courses. Sebastian Thrun went on to create Udacity, a website that could provide other courses than his own. Andrew Ng and Daphne Koller, two other Stanford professors, founded Coursera, while MIT and Harvard University jointly created edX. The success was almost immediate, and MOOCs quickly became a buzzword in the sector of online distance education, which was not used to be in the spotlights. For example, as of early 2015, Coursera partnered with 119 institutions from all over the world, the vast majority of which being traditional higher education institutions, to provide more than 1000 courses, which have attracted more than 13 million single users. In less than 3 years, Coursera also succeeded in attracting more than $85 million in venture capital investment. (Belleflamme & Jacqmin, Mar. 2016, pp. 148-149)

MOOCs are hosted mostly on private platforms, without or with minimal funding (Belleflamme & Jacqmin, Mar. 2016, pp. 149 - 150). This fact is heightened given the high costs to create a successful MOOC and the high risks to reputation (Dennen & Chauhan, 2013). A range of methods have been explored to make MOOCs financially viable and sustainable, and the most common model seems to be the so-called "freemium model" (a portmanteau word created from "free" and "premium," with a majority of learners taking courses for free and some "premium" learners taking courses under a paid tuition model for credit or badging or other acknowledgment (Belleflamme & Jacqmin, Mar. 2016, p. 159).

Over the years, the MOOC platforms have settled out to dedicated MOOC sites, learning management systems (LMSes), and other technologies. There are different typologies of MOOCs—such as the differentiation between connectivist MOOCs (cMOOCs) and more classic university-teaching-based xMOOCs. Adaptive MOOCs or "aMOOCs" involve the uses of adaptive customization designs and technologies like software agents (Daradoumis, Bassi, Xhafa, & Caballé, 2013) to provide more unique MOOC experiences based on learner needs. Many MOOCs also have built-in recommender systems to help learners identify learning tracks and courses of potential interest. Various public listings of MOOC platforms show over three dozen common ones globally today.

Researchers have been collecting basic metrics about the various MOOC platforms: their numbers of learners and their locations, their funding sources, course focuses, technological features, and others. The three top MOOC providers based on numbers of students, courses/courseware, and institutional alliances are Coursera (over 7 million learners, over 640 courses, and over 100 institutions); edX (over 2 million learners, 175 courses, and over 45 institutions), and Udacity (1.5 million learners, over 35 courses, and over 10 institutions) in 2014 (Taneja & Goel, May 2014, p. 223), based on volume measures. There are some professional assessments of top MOOC platforms based on features, such as usefulness, consistency, and credibility…and core metrics (credentialing, course diversity, course features, social features, and partner institutions) ("The Best MOOC Platforms of 2018," 2018). Based on one organization's analysis, the best MOOC platforms are (in descending order): Coursera, edX, Udacity, FutureLearn, iversity, and Cognitive Class. In the academic research literature are more formalized classifications of MOOC quality criteria, such as one that focuses on two tracks based on the design and development of MOOC learning: pedagogical criteria (including instructional design and assessment) and technical criteria (including user interfaces, video content, learning and social tools, and learning analytics) (Yousef, Chatti, Schroeder, & Wosnitza, 2014). A study of learners' experiences on MOOCs identified various MOOC aspects that provide a quality experience: interactivity, collaboration, pedagogy, motivation, network of opportunities/ future directions, assessment, learner support, technology, usability and content (Gamage, Fernando, & Perera, 2015, p. 2).

While one of the most highly vaunted features of MOOCs is their scale and ability to accommodate a large number of simultaneous learners (Pappano, Nov. 2, 2012), MOOCs have been harnessed on a small scale, for so-called "SPOCs" or "small private online courses" (Fox, Patterson, Ilson, Joseph, Walcott-Justice, & Williams, 2014). These new uses show the transferability of such technologies and fresh ways to harness technology tool features.

To seed the research, ten MOOC platforms listed in a journalistic article were selected, including: Coursera, edX, Udacity, FutureLearn, NovoEd, Iversity, Canvas, Open2Study, OpenLearning, and Udemy. The basic approach was to see how these ten platforms stacked up based on indirect somewhat-decentralized and multimodal information (text, tags, image, maps, and others). This data sources include large-scale Web Search data (via Google Correlate), Google Scholar, social imagery and related image tagging (Google Image Search), crowd-sourced articles from a crowd-sourced encyclopedia (Wikipedia), microblogging data (Twitter), and posts and comments from social networking data (Facebook).

This analyses are enabled by various forms of "distant reading," including topic modeling, sentiment analysis, and computational text analysis…and manual coding of social imagery.

This work aims to define MOOC platforms not on their technological features but indirectly by their course contents and the user bases (and their social media-based discourses) that have grown up around each, to see how these technologies vary. This effort is built off the concept of "peripheral vision" or "side vision"—without the direct focus of focal vision…but observations from the blurry edges, which are informative in their own way. The basic hypothesis is that indirect or peripheral research may surface insights that may not be observable otherwise.

REVIEW OF THE LITERATURE

The study of massive open online courses (MOOCs) include a range of topical foci. One of the main areas focuses on methods for enhancing learning. As many had predicted, MOOCs saw the critical emergence of different definitions of "teaching"—as the "charismatic celebrity professor, the co-learner or facilitator, or the automated responses" (Ross, Sinclair, Knox, Bayne, & Macleod, March 2014, p. 57). To improve learning, augmentary informal learning activities around MOOCs are encouraged (Fidalgo-

Blanco, Sein-Echaluce Lacleta, García-Peñalvo, & Esteban-Escaño, 2014). Various technology integrations, such as virtual technologies with MOOCs, enable broadened learning experiences (Stathakarou, Zary, & Kononowicz, 2014).

The broad popularization of MOOCs in the online learning space has meant that those who host MOOCs have access to large amounts of learner data, which enables a broad range of research, including the mass-scale automated analysis of learner discourse in MOOCs (Ezen-Can, Boyer, Kellogg, & Booth, 2015). One endeavor involves the creation of the MOOCdb data model, to standardize learner data from MOOCs, in order to enable easier harnessing of their informational value (O'Reilly & Veeramachaneni, Winter 2014).

The mass-scale narratives around MOOCs are not only about their net positives in making learning available to individuals who would not have access otherwise in the developing world (Escher, Noukakis, & Aebischer, 2014). Some see signs of neocolonial implications and control over information, with attendant political implications (Altbach, Spring 2014).

UNDERSTANDING MOOC PLATFORMS BY AVAILABLE COURSES AND USER BASES…FROM SOCIAL MEDIA DATA

To achieve the "peripheral vision" about the MOOC platforms, their basic facts (their histories, their metrics) have not been included. These details are widely available online. This section includes data from the following sources: large-scale web search data, academic scholarship indexing, social imagery, crowd-sourced articles, microblogging data, and social networking data.

Large-Scale Web Search Data (via Google Correlate)

The Google Search engine is the most widely used one in the world, capturing 64% of searches ("comScore releases February 2016 U.S. desktop search engine rankings," Mar. 16, 2016). Using Google Correlate (https://www.google.com/trends/correlate), it is possible to identify web search terms that are correlated with a target term, and these sometimes may provide insights about people's mass-scale ideas. For example in Tables 1 and 2, the first table shows the top 20 search term correlations with "MOOC" over a monthly time series over extended time (2004 – 2017), and the latter over weekly time series over the same time period. These tables show some ties between "mooc" and various computer technologies but not any of the MOOC platforms or directly related technologies.

Figure 1 shows a line chart of "mooc" and "moocs" based on monthly correlations in Google Search web search engine queries. Figure 2 shows the same data in a scattergraph. Both are from Google Correlate.

Academic Research Indexing (Google Scholar)

In this section, a search in Google Scholar (https://scholar.google.com/) provides a sense of the research popularity and potential of the respective ten MOOC platforms. The top three seem to align with other measures of popularity in the mainstream MOOC literature (Figure 3).

Table 1. Top search terms correlated with "mooc" search on Google search in Google Correlate (based on monthly time series over extended time)

Correlation Coefficient	Correlating Search Term
0.9904	moocs
0.9902	what is a mooc
0.9872	6570b
0.9845	hp probook 6570b
0.9823	probook 6570b
0.9819	centrino advanced-n 6235
0.9817	server 2012 core
0.9812	intel centrino advanced-n 6235
0.9811	hp probook 4440s
0.9806	server 2012 standard
0.9805	probook 4440s
0.9800	what is mooc
0.9800	zoey nixon
0.9798	putting me together
0.9798	best adc
0.9796	aquamail
0.9789	lenovo t430
0.9789	best trap music
0.9788	league of legends memes
0.9788	vcenter sso

Table 2. Top search terms correlated with "mooc" search on Google search in Google Correlate (based on weekly time series over extended time)

Correlation Coefficient	Correlating Search Term
0.9860	moocs
0.9766	6570b
0.9702	server 2012 standard
0.9701	hp probook 6570b
0.9700	probook 6570b
0.9694	lenovo t430
0.9690	e6430
0.9673	office 2013
0.9673	8470p
0.9666	dell e6430
0.9656	server 2012 core
0.9656	putting me together
0.9656	dell latitude e5530
0.9655	8570p
0.9649	latitude e6430
0.9648	best adc
0.9647	league of legends memes
0.9646	elitebook 8570p
0.9646	office 2013 download
0.9646	server 2013

Figure 1. "MOOC" and "moocs" monthly time series search on Google search (Google Correlate)

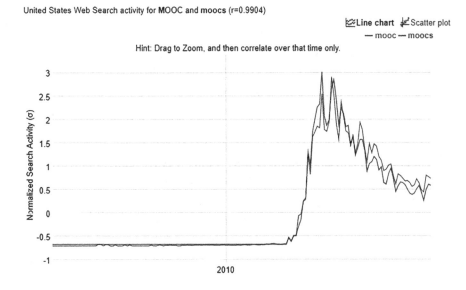

Figure 2. "MOOC" and "moocs" monthly time series search on Google search (Google Correlate)

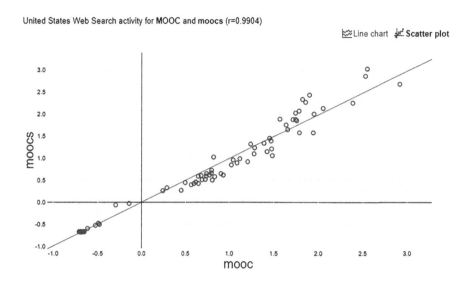

Figure 3. MOOC platform-related articles on Google Scholar (in descending order)

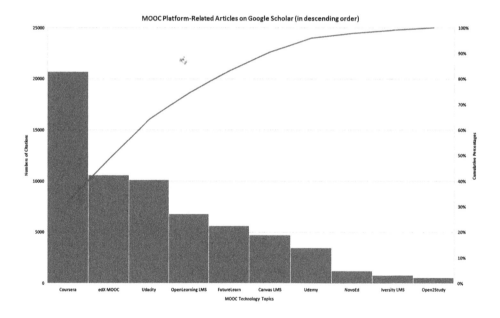

The popular literature may differ. For comparison, the same queries were run with the terms in quotation marks to enable some disambiguation. The results may be seen in the Pareto chart in Figure 4. Notice that both "canvas lms" and "instructure" were run separately to try to get at a more accurate sense of the Canvas LMS's search results. "Canvas" by itself is a generic and non-disambiguated term, but adding "lms" to the search delimits the search fairly extensively.

Figure 4. MOOC platform-related pages on Google search (in descending order)

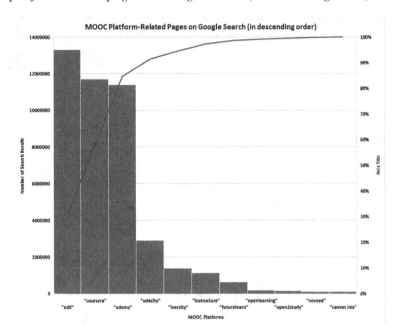

Social Image Sets (Google Image Search)

An exploration of social imagery related to each of the MOOC socio-technical spaces was also captured (all on the same day, for the same "slice in time"). Social imagery refers to the digital images shared on people's social media accounts. Figure 5 shows a collection of imagery from the Flickr image- and video-sharing site as captured by Flickr Downloadr. This screenshots a wide range of imagery, with only some related to MOOCs.

Most social imagery is tagged in a "folk" (amateur, non-professional) way by the users who generated the contents. Some tags are auto-generated based on algorithms using machine vision. Even though the Flickr collection showed hundreds of images tagged with "MOOC," multiple attempts to capture related tags networks from Flickr for "mooc" or "moocs" did not result in any such networks. There were insufficient amounts of imagery on the network to meet the threshold for the capture of co-occurring tags (using the Network Overview, Discovery and Exploration for Excel or "NodeXL" tool). Figure 6 shows a 1.5-degree related tags network on Flickr, with related representational images to the respective tags depicted as well. The respective groups of co-occurring tags provide a sense of how "online" may be conceptualized as a tag.

Respective image sets based on text searches in Google Search resulted in 400 – 600 images per set. In Table 3, the respective tags to the sets may be seen. Tags were categorized for some of the search terms because of the breadth and diversity of the tag terms (such as with Coursera); here, the tag sets are separated by semi-colon, and the tags themselves are separated by commas. In terms of the coding, each image was coded once based on a simple formula. Note that not all the images in any of the sets could be coded because some of the collected data was not openable.

The coding was simple and rough-cut. The images were coded by type: digital drawings and logos, screenshots, data visualizations, photos, and animated GIFs (Table 4 and Figure 7)

Figure 5. A mish-mash of "MOOC"-tagged social imagery from the Flickr downloadr

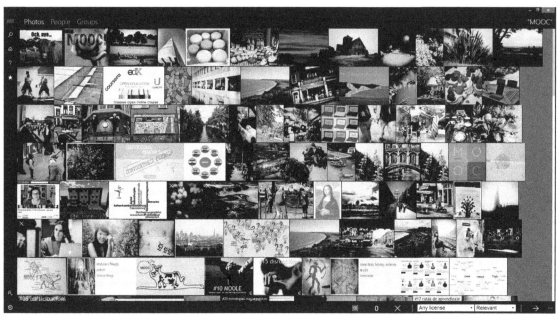

Figure 6. "Online" related tags network on Flickr (1.5 Deg.)

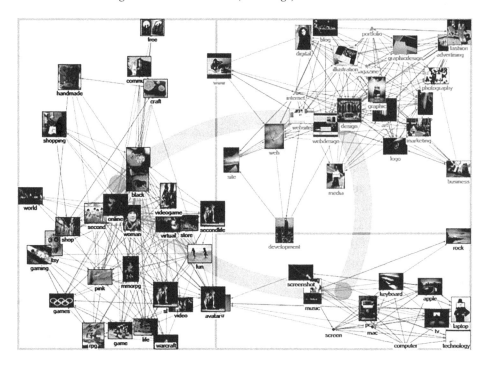

Table 3. Basic data of the social image sets from Google images

MOOC Platform	Tags on Google Images	Number of Images in the Image Set	Number of Images Coded
Coursera	business, linkedin, video; refugee; india; svg; edx; yale; r programming; linkedin profile	479	470
edX	coursera, certificate, micromasters, university, logo, harvard, edx certificate, edx logo, courses, edx svg, online, twitter, online courses, google, harvardx, open edx	552	552
Udacity	data, udacity logo, google, nanodegree, png, twitter, science, courses, android, udacity blitz, analyst, business, vector, logo png, robotics, demand	446	423
FutureLearn	certificate, future learn, courses, open university, participation, sample, statement, digital, logo, moocs, online courses, program, icon, achievement, reading, mooc provider	538	493
NovoEd	release, press, logo, statement, accomplishment, philanthropy, office, linkedin, learning, thinking, university, glassdoor, design, social, update, working	553	545
Iversity	hannes klöpper, learning, certificate, logo iversity, business, Europe, round, managing, director, twitter, inside, statement, iversity participation, introduces, funding, tracks	608	603
CanvasLMS	logo; instructure; transparent; panda; mobile, education, facebook, college, school; sjsu; open source; bridge; instructure ap; canva	487	446
Open2Study	achievement; iversity; futurelearn; courser; edx; mooc; khan academy; swinburne university, Macquarie university; honor code; diploma, graduate; sample; accounting; honour code; yale, harvard; saylor org	520	508
OpenLearning	act, dead, engine, write, integrated, https, wikipedia, authoring, nercomppdo4, rendering, play, org, environment, purchase, network, services	661	653
Udemy	free, logo, new, coupon, udemy courses, guitar, $10, udemy coupons, udemy course, icon, excel, affiliate, cryptocurrency, starting, money, marketing	514	521

Table 4. MOOC platform-based social image set features from rough coding

MOOC-based Image Set	Digital Drawings / Logos	Screenshots	Data Visualizations	Photos	Animated GIFs
Coursera	93	345	14	16	2
edX	154	276	74	46	2
Udacity	164	166	10	76	7
FutureLearn	146	179	22	140	6
NovoEd	128	166	36	214	1
Iversity	186	134	69	212	2
Canvas LMS	115	286	23	21	1
Open2Study	163	96	41	207	1
OpenLearning	250	180	121	100	2
Udemy	282	203	7	26	3

Figure 7. MOOC platform-based social image set features from rough coding

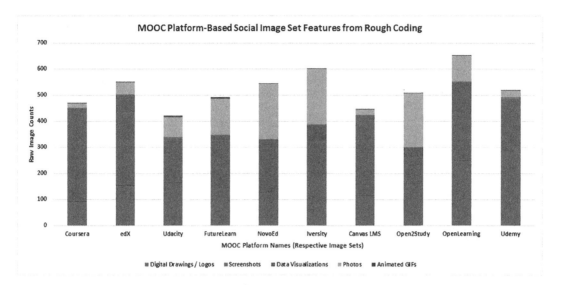

Using this simple approach, it is possible to compare image sets across the ten sets. Most of the images across the sets were only lightly informative. One of the image sets had a large amount of advertising and coupons for itself and its course offerings. Multiple image sets had logos from various universities and colleges included.

- Most digital drawings and logos were used for branding, meme creation, logos, avatars, and political statements.
- Most screenshots were of the MOOC platform and learning contents (with a lot of video stills and PowerPoint slideshow slides).
- Most data visualizations seemed to be learning contents (articles, maps, data visualizations, table data, diagrams, letters, posters, word clouds, and others), and data dashboards from MOOC platforms.
- Most photos were of conferences, events with speakers, learners with paper certificates, some stock imagery of computer technologies, and physical classrooms.
- Animated GIFs were few and showed a spinning spiral (indicating computational process), a smiling person, slide sequences, and a visual gag (showing a person being pumped up full of helium like a balloon and floating).

From an exploration of the image sets, it was clear that the MOOC providers had some shared interests: branding, public relations, teaching and learning, publicity, commemoration (of live events, of technological processes), and information sharing. While these social images are diffuse and from distributed sources, the makers of the MOOC platforms have an interest in sharing information, and many do have a fairly central and dominant role in the image creations and sharing. Figure 8 shows some of the captured images for the Canvas LMS image set; these were downloaded using the Picture Downloader Professional add-on to the Google Chrome web browser). User-generated contents were built off of (or derived from) the MOOC platforms (such as through screenshots). Many of the images are self-referential, with the MOOC name and logo appearing many times in the image sets.

Figure 8. Screenshot of some of the scraped images (as thumbnails) from the canvas LMS image set

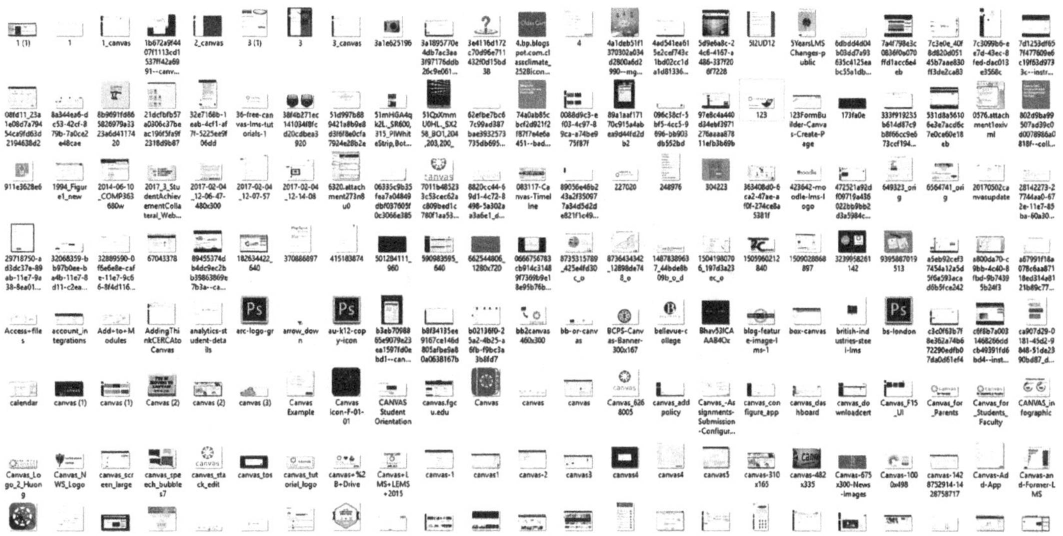

Data From a Crowd-Sourced Encyclopedia (Wikipedia)

Another approach for sideways views of MOOCs was to explore crowd-sourced encyclopedias. For example, a page/article was collected for each of the target MOOC platforms on Wikipedia. The auto-extracted topics from the entire text set may be seen in Figure 9, and the respective topical representations of the individual articles may be seen in Figures 10 and 11 (which contain the same data but are different visualizations). Figure 9 shows more of a general summary, and Figures 10 and 11 show the emphases in topics in the respective articles.

Figure 9. Auto-extracted themes from the whole Wikipedia text set

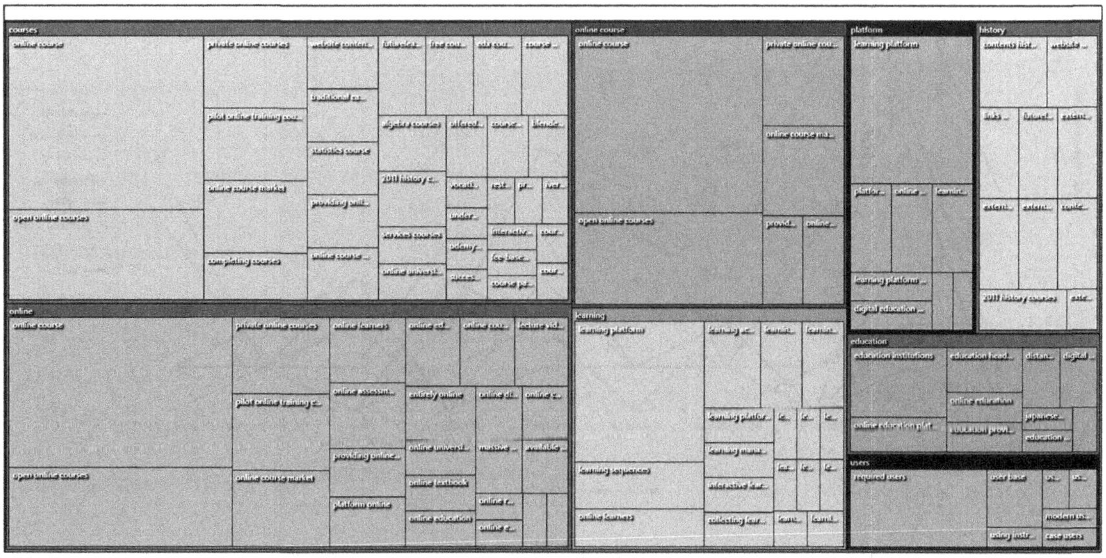

Figure 10. Auto-extracted themes from the Wikipedia text set (3d linegraph)

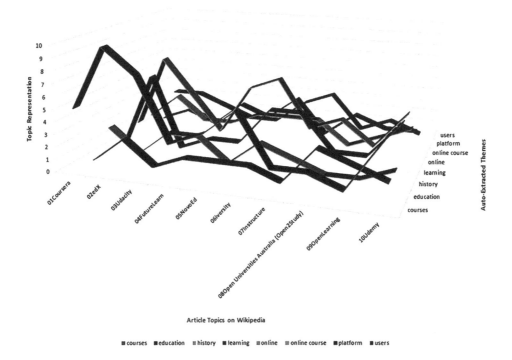

Figure 11. Auto-extracted themes from the Wikipedia text set (linegraph)

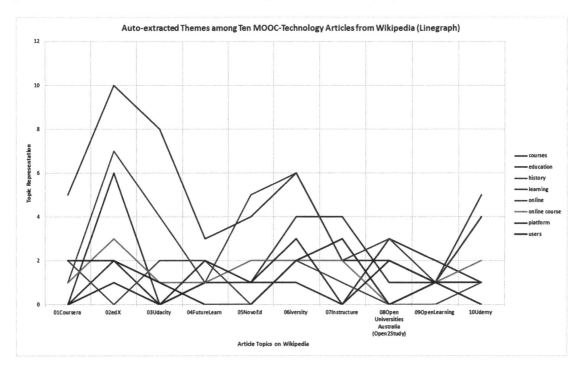

An auto-coded sentiment chart shows the Wikipedia text sets have different sentiment focuses (Figure 12).

Figure 12. Sentiment analysis from the Wikipedia text set

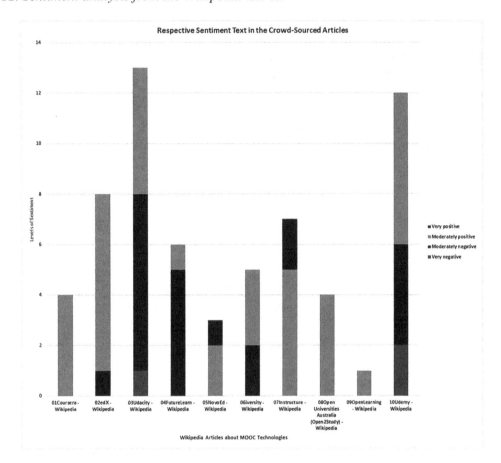

This same data may be seen in a word frequency count as a word cloud in Figure 13. The words added to the stopwords list were the following: com, http, https, and www.

Through computational text analysis, the 10 MOOC platform articles on Wikipedia may be seen as generally highly analytic, fairly high in language indicating clout, low in authenticity (self-revelation to create warmth), and more negative in terms of tone (sentiment), based on the LIWC 2015 tool (Figure 14).

Data From Social User Account Tweetstreams (Twitter)

Microblogging enables people to share snippets of information, imagery, URLs (uniform resource locators), video snippets, and other data with audiences of various sizes (narrowcasting or broadcasting). Exploring the various Twitter accounts related to the respective platforms [@coursera, @edXOnline, @udacity, @FutureLearn, @GoNovoEd, @iversity, @CanvasLMS, @Open2Study, @openlrning, and @udemy] may shed light on what is being discussed and the main areas of communication interest—at a particular moment in time. Interesting, all ten of the sites enabled public data collection. The Twitter Application Programming Interface (API) does engage in rate-limiting, so most of the data are from a week-long period just prior to the data extraction, and the data is considered incomplete (no N of all unless the researcher goes with a commercial company to access that data). In this case, NCapture was used to collect the microblogging messages (including retweets) from the account for a week period. The Tweets are the collected microblogging messages; the Following are those whom the account "follows" and whose messages are being subscribed to; the Followers are those who "follow" or subscribe to the particular target account; the "likes" show affirmation expressed for particular messages; the "lists" show curated Twitter accounts; "Moments" show linked Tweets that together create a sequential sense of stories (Figure 15).

Figure 13. Word frequency count word cloud from the Wikipedia text set

The accounts show variances between when they were started on the platform, and only some mentioned locations (Table 5).

The respective landing pages show the above data at the moment of capture (Figure 16).

The respective Tweetstreams of the accounts showcase different auto-extracted themes (Figure 17).

In terms of auto-extracted themes (from topic-modeling), there are not just English terms enabled through UTF-8. For example, the @iversity account has some German terms (Figure 18).

In the Open2Study account on Twitter, there seems to be a much wider range of topics being discussed (Figure 19).

Figure 14. Text characteristics of 10 MOOC platform articles on Wikipedia

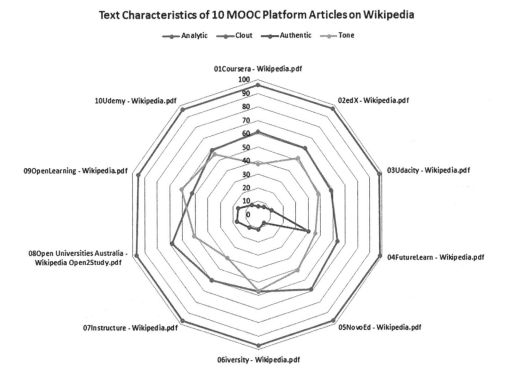

Figure 15. Comparative microblogging account stats across ten MOOC LMS accounts on Twitter

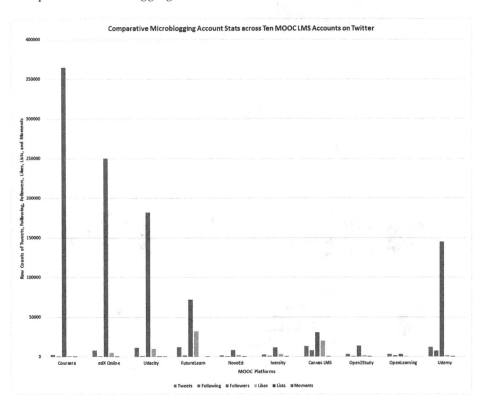

Table 5. Comparative join dates and location information

	Joined Date	Location Listed
Coursera	8/1/2011	N/A
edX Online	4/1/2012	Cambridge, Massachusetts
Udacity	6/1/2011	Mountain View, California
FutureLearn	12/1/2012	N/A
NovoEd	4/1/2013	San Francisco, California
Iversity	5/1/2009	Berlin, Germany
Canvas LMS	5/1/2009	Salt Lake City, Utah
Open2Study	2/1/2013	N/A
OpenLearning	6/1/2017	Sydney, Australia
Udemy	8/1/2009	San Francisco, California

Figure 16. Screenshots of landing pages of the MOOC platforms on Twitter

Figure 17. Auto-extracted topics across the MOOC platforms on Twitter

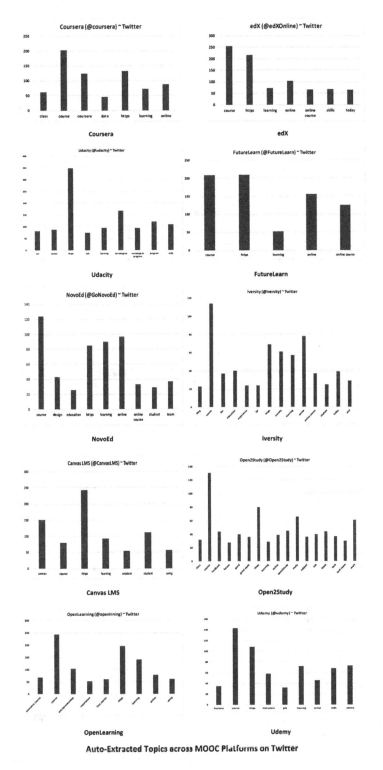

Figure 18. Auto-extracted topics for @Iversity on Twitter as a treemap diagram

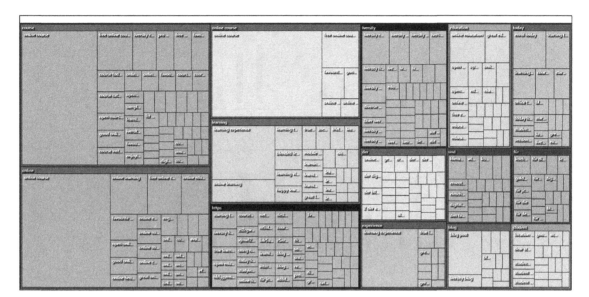

Figure 19. Wider range of topics in Open2Study

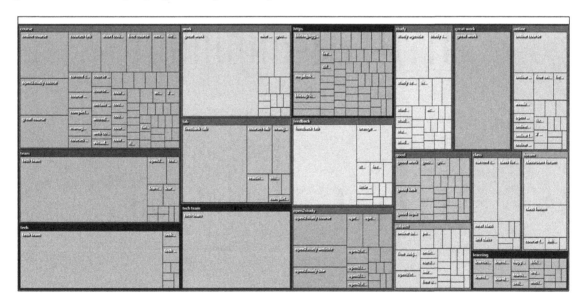

A generalized treemap diagram of the collective topics from the ten MOOC social accounts may be seen in Figure 20.

Where the respective members of the social networks interacting with the target Twitter accounts are based may be seen in the collected maps in Figure 21. Note that there are different levels of zoom here.

Figure 22 shows stacked bar charts of respective topics addressed in the social accounts' Tweetstreams.

In terms of the sentiments expressed in the Tweetstreams, the results may be seen in the intensity matrix in Figure 23.

Figure 20. Auto-extracted topics about MOOCs on Twitter

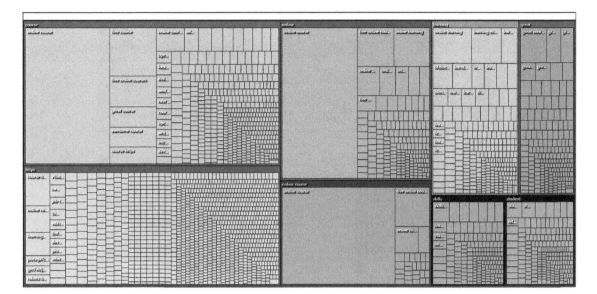

Finally, it is possible to place the topics from the MOOC Accounts on Twitter in a cluster diagram to show the interrelatedness of the discussed topics (Figure 24). In this visual, proximity and color show relatedness, and the respective sizes of the nodes show the frequency count of the reference. The @ symbol comes before account names, and # (hashtags) indicate social media campaigns and / or discussions of particular topic labeling.

Word clouds show basic frequency counts of semantic terms. These are not formal theme extractions, but simple counts. Each of the accounts on Twitter were mapped to attain a sense of the subjects of interest (Figure 25). For @coursera, "http" and "https" were added to the stopwords list before the final word cloud was created, but no other terms were put on the stopwords for any of the other social user accounts on Twitter.

Data From User Accounts on Social Networking Pages

The next data extraction came from Facebook. Again, all the accounts here were publicly accessible. Table 6 shows the amount of data captured from each respective Facebook page. As with other social media platforms, only some data is available for public capture. The data is the most recent available posts and comments.

Figure 26 provides a view of what the respective Facebook pages looked like at the time of the data collection.

Figure 27 shows the auto-extracted topics from the respective Facebook accounts' posts and comments.

The Udacity Facebook page's posts and comments show a depth of themes and subthemes (Figure 28).

The respective locales of those participating on the Facebook pages show some overlap with the Twitter networks but also some differences (Figure 29). The sense of location shows something about geography and populations and cultures…but also something about the respective social media platforms.

Figure 30 shows some topics of common interest across all ten of the MOOC social account posts and comments on Facebook.

Figure 21. Geographic-based regionalisms of MOOC social networks on Twitter

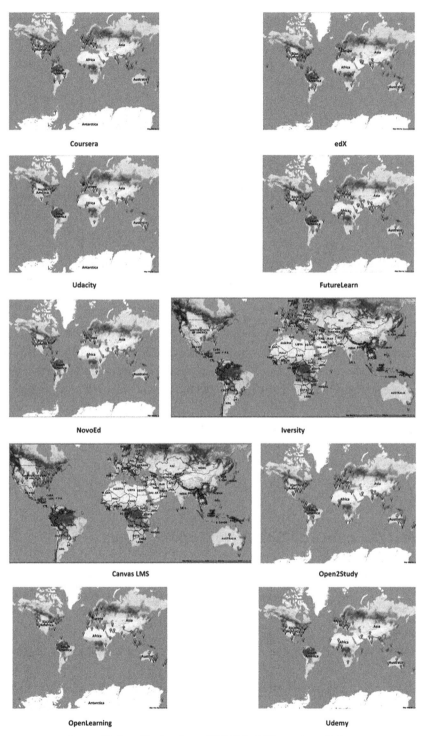

Geographic-Based Regionalisms of MOOC Social Networks on Twitter

Figure 22. Main topics in recent tweet discussions as auto-extracted onegrams and bigrams across ten MOOC platform social accounts (on Twitter)

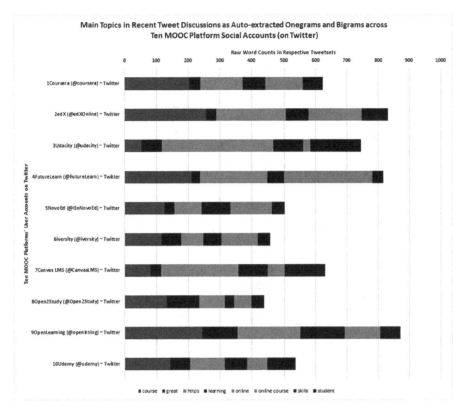

Figure 23. Auto-extracted sentiment in recent tweet discussions from ten MOOC platform social accounts (on Twitter)

	Very negative	Moderately negative	Moderately positive	Very positive
1Coursera (@coursera) ~ Twitter	62	81	337	357
2edX (@edXOnline) ~ Twitter	40	49	351	263
3Udacity (@udacity) ~ Twitter	60	71	274	503
4FutureLearn (@FutureLearn) ~ Twitter	60	107	232	111
5NovoEd (@GoNovoEd) ~ Twitter	15	30	143	174
6iversity (@iversity) ~ Twitter	54	77	235	316
7Canvas LMS (@CanvasLMS) ~ Twitter	47	43	279	353
8Open2Study (@Open2Study) ~ Twitter	78	126	304	551
9OpenLearning (@openlrning) ~ Twitter	60	44	327	600
10Udemy (@udemy) ~ Twitter	71	77	344	496

#HASHTAG NETWORKS AROUND THE MOOC PLATFORMS

Another way to approach microblogging sites is to eavesdrop on #hashtag conversations to find out who is communicating with others publicly and to hear what they are saying. Oftentimes, there may be multiple #hashtags applied to a MOOC platform. In this case, only the most generic ones were used: #coursera, #edX, #udacity, #futurelearn, #gonovoed, #iversity, #canvasLMS, #open2study, #openlrning, and #udemy. NodeXL (Network Overview, Discovery and Exploration for Excel) was used for the data extraction, with an 18,000 Tweet limit for the software and rate-limiting from the Twitter API.

Figure 24. A 2D cluster diagram of recent microblogging topics in the 10 MOOC accounts

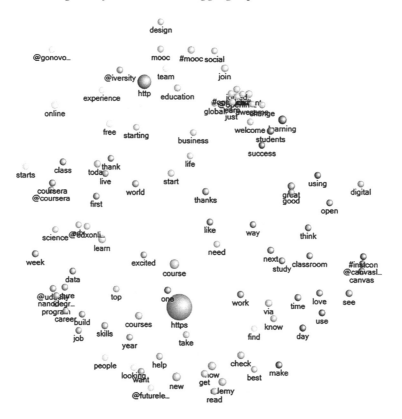

The #coursera hashtag network on Twitter had 123 vertices, with 235 unique edges. Its geodesic distance was 7. (Table 7) An extraction of clustering using the Clauset-Newman-Moore algorithm found 36 groups.

Some of the members of the #coursera hashtag network may be seen in Figure 31.

The #edX hashtag network on Twitter identified a network with 63 nodes (Table 8). From this network, 18 groups were identified.

Figure 32 shows some of the Tweets shared among the #edX hashtag network on Twitter at the moment of data capture.

The #udacity hashtag network had a graph with 253 vertices and 871 unique edges; the maximum geodesic distance was 7 (Table 9 and Figure 33). A total of 37 groups was identified in this network, interacting among themselves on issues of mutual interest. The data extraction includes more information than is shown on Figure 33; for example, the respective shared messages are collected in a data table as well as some locational data.

The #futurelearn hashtag network had a smaller graph, of only 32 nodes, and a graph diameter of 4 (Table 10 and Figure 34). Of this network, 11 groups were extracted.

The hashtag network for #gonovoed and #novoed showed no members in either network.

The hashtag network for #iversity on Twitter captured a sparse network of 8 members, with 13 unique edges, and a graph diameter of only 2. There was only one group or cluster in this network. (The more accurate term may be that this had limited motifs.) (Table 11 and Figure 35)

Figure 25. Word clouds (frequency counts) of Tweetstreams of the MOOC entities

Word Clouds (Frequency Counts) of Tweetstreams of the MOOC Entities

Figure 26. Screenshots of landing pages of the MOOC platforms on Facebook

Figure 27. Auto-extracted themes from Facebook posts and comments related to official MOOC platforms

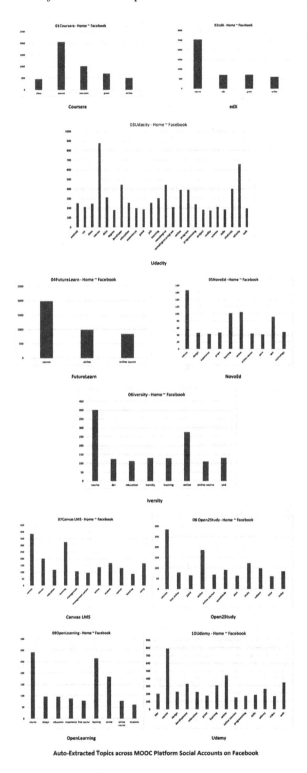

Auto-Extracted Topics across MOOC Platform Social Accounts on Facebook

Table 6. Data captures from MOOC-based social media accounts on Facebook

Name of MOOC Platform	Posts and Comments	URL on Facebook
Coursera	1248 posts, 23007 comments	https://www.facebook.com/Coursera/
edX	2383 posts, 31626 comments	https://www.facebook.com/edX/
Udacity	3455 posts, 9253 comments	https://www.facebook.com/Udacity/
FutureLearn	1809 posts, 8245 comments	https://www.facebook.com/FutureLearn/
NovoEd Team	375 posts, 940 comments	https://www.facebook.com/NovoEdTeam/
Iversity	1449 posts, 3150 comments	https://www.facebook.com/iversity.org/
CanvasLMS	1814 posts, 1052 comments	https://www.facebook.com/CanvasLMS/
Open2Study Education	871 posts, 5039 comments	https://www.facebook.com/Open2StudyEducation/
OpenLearning	1049 posts, 236 comments	https://www.facebook.com/OpenLearning/
Udemy	1307 posts, 11953 comments	https://www.facebook.com/udemy/

Figure 28. Autoextracted themes and subthemes from Udacity Facebook posts and comments (in a treemap diagram)

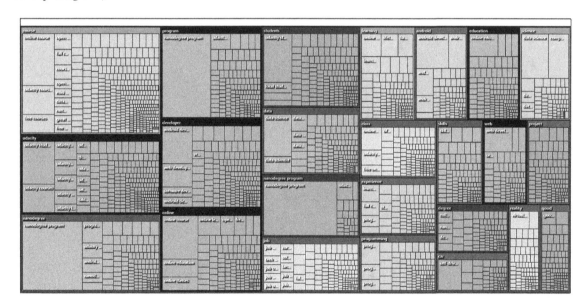

The #canvasLMS hashtag network is represented by 72 vertices and 296 unique edges. The maximum geodesic distance was 5 (Table 12 and Figure 36). Nine groups were identified.

For the #open2study hashtag network, this only consisted of two nodes formulating one group (a motif). There was only one connected component, and the graph diameter was one (each member is only one hop away from the only other member). See Table 13 and Figure 37 for more. The message itself seems promotional.

For the #openlrning hashtag network, this also only had two vertices (Table 14 and Figure 38).

Finally, the #udemy hashtag network had a graph consisting of 12 nodes and 11 unique links. Six groups were identified. (Table 15 and Figure 39)

Figure 29. Geographic-based regionalisms of MOOC social networks on Facebook

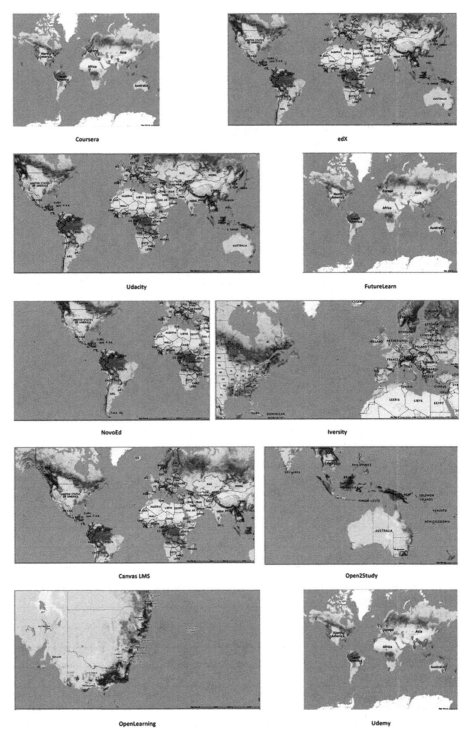

Geographic-Based Regionalisms of MOOC Social Networks on Facebook

Figure 30. Word cloud of the 10 MOOC social accounts on Facebook

Table 7. Graph metrics for #coursera hashtag network on Twitter

Graph Type	Directed
Vertices	123
Unique Edges	235
Edges With Duplicates	143
Total Edges	378
Self-Loops	129
Reciprocated Vertex Pair Ratio	0.085106383
Reciprocated Edge Ratio	0.156862745
Connected Components	29
Single-Vertex Connected Components	24
Maximum Vertices in a Connected Component	91
Maximum Edges in a Connected Component	346
Maximum Geodesic Distance (Diameter)	7
Average Geodesic Distance	2.816969
Graph Density	0.013594562
Modularity	Not Applicable
NodeXL Version	1.0.1.336

Figure 31. #Coursera hashtag network on Twitter

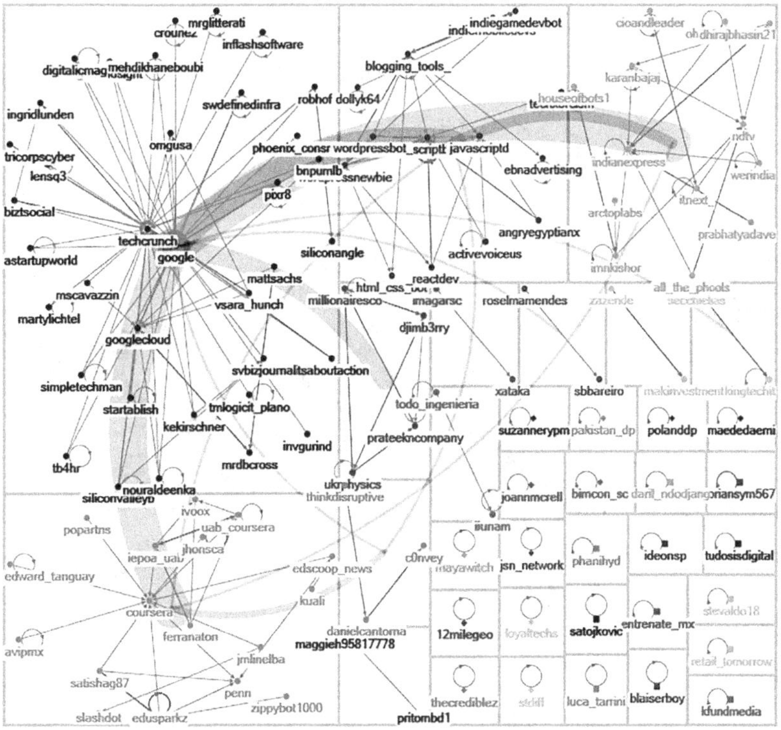

Table 8. Graph metrics for #edX hashtag network on Twitter

Graph Metric	Value
Graph Type	Directed
Vertices	63
Unique Edges	215
Edges With Duplicates	83
Total Edges	298
Self-Loops	22
Reciprocated Vertex Pair Ratio	0.532467532
Reciprocated Edge Ratio	0.694915254
Connected Components	16
Single-Vertex Connected Components	12
Maximum Vertices in a Connected Component	31
Maximum Edges in a Connected Component	244
Maximum Geodesic Distance (Diameter)	4
Average Geodesic Distance	1.78658
Graph Density	0.060419867
Modularity	Not Applicable
NodeXL Version	1.0.1.336

Figure 32. #edX hashtag network on Twitter

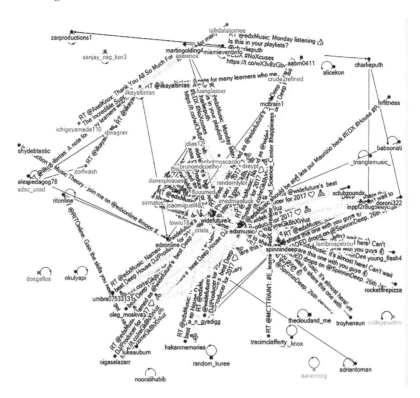

Table 9. Graph metrics for #udacity hashtag network on Twitter

Graph Metric	Value
Graph Type	Directed
Vertices	253
Unique Edges	871
Edges With Duplicates	189
Total Edges	1060
Self-Loops	203
Reciprocated Vertex Pair Ratio	0.090534979
Reciprocated Edge Ratio	0.166037736
Connected Components	29
Single-Vertex Connected Components	27
Maximum Vertices in a Connected Component	224
Maximum Edges in a Connected Component	1028
Maximum Geodesic Distance (Diameter)	7
Average Geodesic Distance	2.701297
Graph Density	0.012469415
Modularity	Not Applicable
NodeXL Version	1.0.1.336

Figure 33. Members of the groups discussing #udacity on Twitter in a week-long period

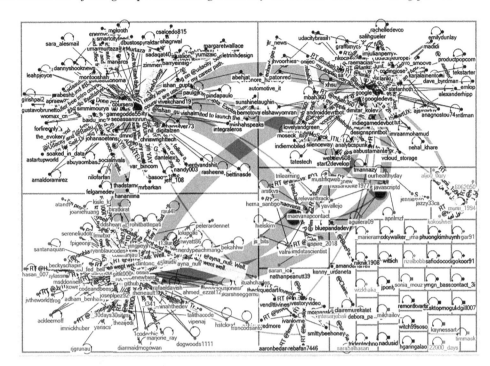

Table 10. Graph metrics for #futurelearn hashtag network on Twitter

Graph Metric	Value
Graph Type	Directed
Vertices	32
Unique Edges	67
Edges With Duplicates	62
Total Edges	129
Self-Loops	10
Reciprocated Vertex Pair Ratio	0.462962963
Reciprocated Edge Ratio	0.632911392
Connected Components	8
Single-Vertex Connected Components	7
Maximum Vertices in a Connected Component	25
Maximum Edges in a Connected Component	122
Maximum Geodesic Distance (Diameter)	4
Average Geodesic Distance	2.357595
Graph Density	0.079637097
Modularity	Not Applicable
NodeXL Version	1.0.1.336

Figure 34. Members of the groups discussing #FutureLearn on Twitter (and some Tweets) in a week-long period

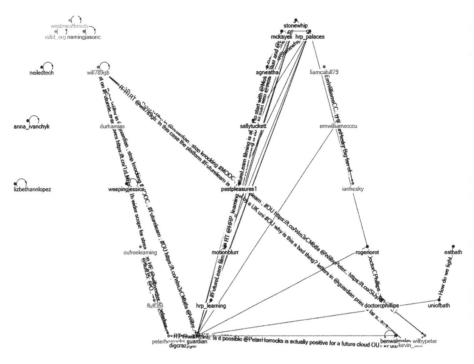

Table 11. Graph metrics for #iversity hashtag network on Twitter

Graph Metric	Value
Graph Type	Directed
Vertices	8
Unique Edges	13
Edges With Duplicates	2
Total Edges	15
Self-Loops	1
Reciprocated Vertex Pair Ratio	0
Reciprocated Edge Ratio	0
Connected Components	1
Single-Vertex Connected Components	0
Maximum Vertices in a Connected Component	8
Maximum Edges in a Connected Component	15
Maximum Geodesic Distance (Diameter)	2
Average Geodesic Distance	1.34375
Graph Density	0.232142857
Modularity	Not Applicable
NodeXL Version	1.0.1.336

Figure 35. Members of the groups discussing #iversity on Twitter in a week-long period

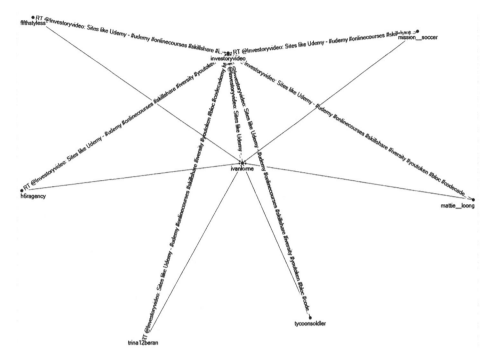

Table 13. Graph metrics for #canvasLMS hashtag network on Twitter

Graph Metric	Value
Graph Type	Directed
Vertices	72
Unique Edges	296
Edges With Duplicates	93
Total Edges	389
Self-Loops	29
Reciprocated Vertex Pair Ratio	0.423423423
Reciprocated Edge Ratio	0.594936709
Connected Components	4
Single-Vertex Connected Components	1
Maximum Vertices in a Connected Component	64
Maximum Edges in a Connected Component	372
Maximum Geodesic Distance (Diameter)	5
Average Geodesic Distance	2.459486
Graph Density	0.061815336
Modularity	Not Applicable
NodeXL Version	1.0.1.336

Figure 36. Members of the groups discussing #canvasLMS on Twitter in a week-long period

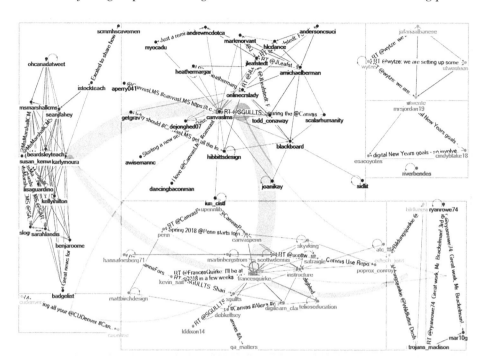

Table 13. Graph Metrics for #open2study Hashtag Network on Twitter

Graph Metric	Value
Graph Type	Directed
Vertices	2
Unique Edges	0
Edges With Duplicates	2
Total Edges	2
Self-Loops	0
Reciprocated Vertex Pair Ratio	0
Reciprocated Edge Ratio	0
Connected Components	1
Single-Vertex Connected Components	0
Maximum Vertices in a Connected Component	2
Maximum Edges in a Connected Component	2
Maximum Geodesic Distance (Diameter)	1
Average Geodesic Distance	0.5
Graph Density	0.5
Modularity	Not Applicable
NodeXL Version	1.0.1.336

Figure 37. Members of the groups discussing #open2study on Twitter in a week-long period

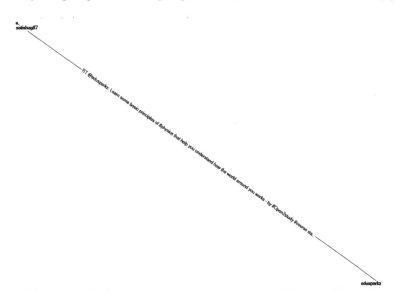

Table 14. Graph metrics for #openlrning hashtag network on Twitter

Graph Type	Directed
Vertices	2
Unique Edges	1
Edges With Duplicates	0
Total Edges	1
Self-Loops	0
Reciprocated Vertex Pair Ratio	0
Reciprocated Edge Ratio	0
Connected Components	1
Single-Vertex Connected Components	0
Maximum Vertices in a Connected Component	2
Maximum Edges in a Connected Component	1
Maximum Geodesic Distance (Diameter)	1
Average Geodesic Distance	0.5
Graph Density	0.5
Modularity	Not Applicable
NodeXL Version	1.0.1.336

Figure 38. Members of the groups discussing #openlrning on Twitter in a week-long period

Table 15. Graph metrics for #udemy hashtag network on Twitter

Graph Metric	Value
Graph Type	Directed
Vertices	12
Unique Edges	11
Edges With Duplicates	33
Total Edges	44
Self-Loops	34
Reciprocated Vertex Pair Ratio	0.125
Reciprocated Edge Ratio	0.222222222
Connected Components	5
Single-Vertex Connected Components	3
Maximum Vertices in a Connected Component	7
Maximum Edges in a Connected Component	20
Maximum Geodesic Distance (Diameter)	3
Average Geodesic Distance	1.5
Graph Density	0.068181818
Modularity	Not Applicable
NodeXL Version	1.0.1.336

Figure 39. Members of the groups discussing #udemy on Twitter in a week-long period

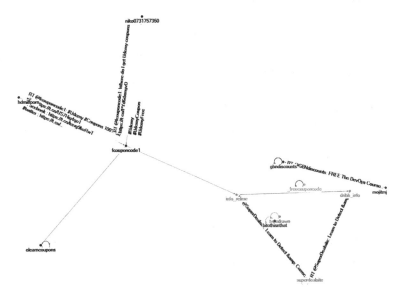

DISCUSSION

This work began with the supposition that taking a sideways view of massive open online courses by using a range of technologies and methods may shed light on the respective technologies as socio-technical spaces. Indeed, this work does provide a sense of the respective platforms, some of the course holdings, the interests of some of its more social learners, and other insights. In a sense, this reads like a back-of-the-napkin approach, but it is possible to build on empirical data and to use that data for inferences. It is possible to capture a sense of the public opinions and "mass mind" of some of the platforms. It is possible to identify some of the personalities related to the MOOC technologies. The uses of computational means to analyze text—like distant reading—does enable major speed efficiencies.

Another benefit is to understand MOOC providers beyond the public relations messages and advertising to see what those in the general public is discussing.

Also, for those looking to take a MOOC, there is a general assumed sequence. The learners have a topic of interest and learn of a MOOC's availability. Or they hear positive electronic word-of-mouth (eWOM). They decide to give the MOOC a try. These methods provide a sense of a MOOC that would not be as directly available.

Technologies Used

The technologies used for the computational analytics include NVivo 11 Plus and NCapture, Linguistic Inquiry and Word Count (LIWC), Network Overview, Discover and Exploration for Excel (NodeXL), and Excel. A number of social media platforms were used as well, along with various cloud-based analytics tools and web browser add-ons.

FUTURE RESEARCH DIRECTIONS

Certainly, there are a number of different other sideways ways to achieve understandings about massive open online courses, the technologies, the personalities, the courses, and the experiences. To these ends, it would help to engage other technologies to explore data about online learning. Also, with the speed of change, it is likely that the culled information is valuable for a short time but may not be that informative in the long run. Updating such knowledge may be helpful.

Also, those who provide MOOCs may benefit from seeing how their brand portrays online and how they may improve on the look-and-feel and messaging, by engaging more with their various publics.

CONCLUSION

This work sheds some light on the respective 10 targeted MOOC providers profiled through a peripheral vision approach. There were some leads and impressions that could be followed up on for further research (to validate or invalidate the sense).

REFERENCES

Altbach, P. G. (2014, Spring). MOOCs as neocolonialism: Who controls knowledge? *Industry and Higher Education, 75*(75), 5–7. doi:10.6017/ihe.2014.75.5426

Belleflamme, P., & Jacqmin, J. (2016, March). An economic appraisal of MOOC platforms: Business models and impacts on higher education. *CESifo Economic Studies, 62*(1), 148–169. doi:10.1093/cesifo/ifv016

comScore releases February 2016 U.S. desktop search engine rankings. (2016, Mar. 16). Retrieved from https://www.comscore.com/Insights/Rankings/comScore-Releases-February-2016-US-Desktop-Search-Engine-Rankings

Daradoumis, T., Bassi, R., Xhafa, F., & Caballé, S. (2013). A review on massive e-learning (MOOC) design, delivery and assessment. *Eighth International Conference on P2P, Parallel, Grid, Cloud and Internet Computing*, 208 – 213.

Davidson, C. (2013, Sept. 27). *What was the First MOOC?* Humanities, Arts, Science and Technology Alliance and Collaboratory (HASTAC). Retrieved from https://www.hastac.org/blogs/cathy-davidson/2013/09/27/what-was-first-mooc

Dennen, V. P., & Chauhan, A. (2013). Shall we MOOC? A SWOT analysis at the program level. *MOOCs Forum, 1*, 17 – 21. Retrieved from http://online.liebertpub.com/doi/abs/10.1089/mooc.2013.0008

Escher, G., Noukakis, D., & Aebischer, P. (2014). Boosting higher education in Africa through Shared Massive Open Online Courses (MOOCs). In G. Carbonnier, M. Carton, & K. King (Eds.), *Education, Learning, Training: Critical Issues for Development*. Leiden: Brill Nijhoff. doi:10.1163/9789004281158_011

Ezen-Can, A., Boyer, K. E., Kellogg, S., & Booth, S. (2015). Unsupervised modeling for understanding MOOC discussion forums: A learning analytics approach. *Proceedings of the Fifth International Conference on Learning Analytics and Knowledge (LAK '15)*. Retrieved from https://dl.acm.org/citation.cfm?id=2723589

Fidalgo-Blanco, Á., Sein-Echaluce Lacleta, M. L., García-Peñalvo, F. J., & Esteban-Escaño, J. (2014). Improving the MOOC learning outcomes throughout informal learning activities. In F. J. García-Peñalvo (Ed.), *Proceedings of the Second International Conference on Technological Ecosystems for Enhancing Multiculturality (TEEM 2014)* (pp. 611-617). New York: ACM. 10.1145/2669711.2669963

Fox, A., Patterson, D. A., Ilson, R., Joseph, S., Walcott-Justice, K., & Williams, R. (2014). *Software engineering curriculum technology transfer: Lessons learned from MOOCs and SPOCs*. Technical Report No. UCB/EECS-2014-17. Electrical Engineering and Computer Sciences, University of California at Berkeley.

Gamage, D., Fernando, S., & Perera, I. (2015). Factors leading to an effective MOOC from participants' perspective. In *Proceedings of 2015 8th International Conference on Ubi-Media Computing (UMEDIA)*. Colombo, Sri Lanka: IEEE Xplore Digital Library.

Google Correlate. (2011). Retrieved from https://www.google.com/trends/correlate

Massive Open Online Course. (2018, Jan. 12). In *Wikipedia*. Retrieved from https://en.wikipedia.org/wiki/Massive_open_online_course

O'Reilly, U.-M., & Veeramachaneni, K. (2014, Winter). Technology for mining the big data of MOOCs. *Research & Practice in Assessment*, *9*, 29–37.

Pappano, L. (2012, Nov. 2). The Year of the MOOC. *The New York Times*. Retrieved from http://www.nytimes.com/2012/11/04/education/edlife/massive-open-online-courses-are-multiplying-at-a-rapid-pace.html

Ross, J., Sinclair, C., Knox, J., Bayne, S., & Macleod, H. (2014, March). Teacher experiences and academic identity: The missing components of MOOC pedagogy. *MERLOT Journal of Online Learning and Teaching*, *10*(1), 57–69.

Stathakarou, N., Zary, N., & Kononowicz, A.A. (2014). *Beyond xMOOCs in healthcare education: Study of the feasibility in integrating virtual patient systems and MOOC platforms*. Academic Press.

Taneja, S., & Goel, A. (2014, May). MOOC providers and their strategies. *International Journal of Computer Science and Mobile Computing*, *3*(5), 222–228.

(The) Best MOOC Platforms of 2018. (2018). Retrieved from https://www.reviews.com/mooc-platforms/

Yang, Q. (2014). Students' motivation in asynchronous online discussions with MOOC mode. *American Journal of Educational Research*, *2*(5), 325–330. doi:10.12691/education-2-5-13

Yousef, A. M. F., Chatti, M. A., Schroeder, U., & Wosnitza, M. (2014). What drives a successful MOOC? An empirical examination of criteria to assure design quality of MOOCs. *IEEE 14th International Conference on Advanced Learning Technologies*, 44 – 48. 10.1109/ICALT.2014.23

KEY TERMS AND DEFINITIONS

Affordance: A capability, an enablement.

Feature: An aspect, a dimension.

Folk Tagging: Amateur labeling of digital contents like imagery.

Functionality: A range of capabilities for a tool.

Integration: The combining of software systems and mixed capabilities.

Massive Open Online Course (MOOC): Online courses that enable large-scale enrollments of learners (tens of thousands) from around the world for tuition costs for some learners and free for others.

Related Tags Network: A network graph of tag labels on digital artifacts showing relatedness and co-occurrence.

Social Imagery: User-generated digital imagery shared on social media platforms.

Social Media: Web-based platforms that enable people to create persistent profiles, interact and communicate with others, and share informational contents.

Sousveillance: Recording of an event or activity by a participant usually through mobile technologies.

Tagging: The applying of descriptive labels to digital contents.

User Base: The typical population of people who have used and continue to use a particular software or platform.

Web Search Data: Data about topical, locational, time, and other related data about people's uses of web search engines.

This research was previously published in Methods for Analyzing and Leveraging Online Learning Data; pages 168-210, copyright year 2019 by Information Science Reference (an imprint of IGI Global).

Chapter 67

A Feminist Autoethography of Academic Performance on Twitter:
Community, Creativity, and Comedy

Sharon Lauricella

University of Ontario Institute of Technology, Canada

ABSTRACT

The online arena is rife with mansplaining, harassment, and intimidation of women. Similarly, women in academia operate in a traditionally patriarchal, misogynistic environment. What happens when a female academic creates a vibrant online presence? This chapter is an autoethnographic account of the author's experiences managing the public, online performance of a female scholar (@AcademicBatgirl) with the objective to create and cultivate community. She argues that in the online landscape, prosocial behaviour is essential in creating community and sustaining cohesion. She addresses the prosocial effects of humour, including examples of memes that she created and posted on Twitter. She also addresses pitfalls relative to student shaming that she recommends academics avoid in any online or offline forum.

INTRODUCTION

The best-known iteration of Gotham City's Batgirl was played by iconic ballerina Yvonne Craig in the final season of the campy television series *Batman*. While parents in the sixties objected to what they feared was a homoerotic subtext of the program by means of the partnership between Batman and Robin, the introduction of Batgirl was an attempt to add a feminine presence (certainly the purple and gold sparkly costume was of significant assistance in achieving this goal). By day, bespectacled and demure, the most recognized version of Batgirl possessed a doctoral degree and spent her days as a librarian in Gotham City's Public Library. As evening set in and crimes abound, Batgirl donned her batsuit and, alongside her comrades Batman and Robin, served justice in the community. Void of any superpowers, Batgirl was a superhero solely by means of her physical and intellectual skills.

DOI: 10.4018/978-1-6684-7123-4.ch067

Batgirl is therefore not unlike many academic women – most hold a Ph.D. and by day work in a publicly visible job, are surrounded by books, and (we expect) serve as morally upstanding examples in our society. After exiting classrooms and scholarly labs, academic women become the superheroes of their own families and their own personal lives; there are friends to support, partners to either collaborate with or defend themselves against, batlings to protect, and shrewd decisions to be made.

For many women, not only their presence but also their embodied performance of womanhood (Butler, 1988) simply doesn't fit in the academy. A recent debate about what female professors should (and should not) wear to teach and research was highly visible in social media (Flaherty, 2015). Dress up? Dress down? Lab coat or tweedy blazer with elbow patches? The academy is a longstanding example of a traditionally patriarchal and misogynistic culture for both faculty (Meyers, 2013) and students (National Union of Students, 2015).

Similarly, the online landscape is also a treacherous one. There is lively debate in popular culture about the misogynistic, critical nature of women's online behaviour such as the practice of taking "selfie" photographs (Tiidenberg, 2014; Tiidenberg & Gomez Cruz, 2015), the potential issues with taking and sending nudes (Ringrose, Harvey, Gill, and Livingstone, 2013) and a largely hostile culture for females in online gaming (Consalvo, 2012; Jenson & DeCastell, 2013). Not surprisingly, women are about twice as likely than men to report that they have been harassed online (Duggan, 2017). Where the academic and the online meet is arguably a loaded minefield for women.

Yet still, in May, 2014, I threw open the saloon doors of social media and joined the potentially wild, wild landscape of Twitter via the avatar @AcademicBatgirl. Today, Dr. Academic Batgirl has nearly 30,000 followers and is one of the most significant voices in the academic social media community. Why Twitter? And why would I even contemplate doing this to myself? This chapter is an autoethnographic account of how social media provided me with the community I so deeply desired, and how online communities, particularly amongst academics, offer the opportunity for scholars to identify with a supportive group and engage in an encouraging, prosocial community.

WHAT DOES IT MEAN TO PERFORM AS AN ACADEMIC ONLINE?

Any professional seeking recommendations for best practices and tips for incorporating the Twitter experience into their social media presence will find a vast array of advice (Morris, 2010; Schaefer, 2014). Academics looking to add more papers to their ever-growing stack of refereed journal articles to read will find a neverending list by means of following fellow scholars. Specific advice for using social media – and in particular, how Twitter can be used in the academic experience – is readily available (for example, Gulliver, 2012; Scoble, n.d.).

The debate about what makes a "serious academic" (Gannon, 2016) aside, the perception of social media in academia is steadily moving from that of a mindless online time-waster to a professionally meaningful activity. Academics are coming to view social media as having the potential to build community (Baym, 1999; Veletsianos & Kimmons, 2012), facilitate contact between/amongst professionals, and build trust, collaboration, and mentorship (Murthy, Hastings, & Mawrie, 2014). Academics, ever the seekers of information, know better than to limit their academic presence to books and peer-reviewed journals, and have therefore embraced social media, and in particular Twitter, into the scholarly process (Green, 2015). This microblogging platform has shown to be helpful in communicating at academic conferences (Parra, Trattner, Gomez, Hurtado, Wen & Lin, 2016), and is an integral part of fostering a sense of community and support, particularly amongst graduate students (Bennett & Folley, 2014) and early career academics (Ferguson & Wheat, 2015). Studies have shown that activity on Twitter can build affect-based trust and meaningful collaboration even in traditionally conservative academic and professional areas dismissive toward the value of social media such as science (Murthy & Lewis, 2015; Murthy, Hastings, & Mawrie, 2014).

Figure 1.

For many academics, engagement with social media means that online and offline scholarly realities are not mutually exclusive. Scholarship indicates that there is a deserved focus on the interrelationship between online and offline worlds (Hine, 2008). urgenson (2011) argues that the online and offline "worlds" are not two different, distinct places. Rather, the two coexist in order to create what Jurgenson calls an "augmented reality" (2009). In other words, one's participation and very presence in online and offline arenas allows for each to influence the other. This phenomenon was perhaps first observable in the online gaming arena (Dibbell, 1999; Pearce, 2009) and has been more recently observable in the building of online communities via social media such as Twitter (Himelboim, McCreery & Smith, 2013). As a member of an active Twitter community (in my case, the academic camaraderie and sometimes complainers, also known as #AcademicTwitter) I have the unique benefit of being a member of the community under investigation (Markham, 1998) and am able to reflect upon the unique academic Twitterverse.

A WOMAN, AN AVATAR, AND THE ACADEMY

An account of the web-based rise of @AcademicBatgirl is particularly meaningful because she is an academic superhero (read: not "heroine") in two arenas – the academy and the computer-mediated – in which gender plays a significant role. Amid the walls of the Ivory Tower, the gender gap is very real. Full-time male faculty members still outnumber women by nearly 20 percent, and the overall average salary for women in higher education has, since the 1970s, continued to be sustained at significantly below the average for men (Curtis, 2011; Chen & Crown, 2019). Gender inequities also exist in leadership, the division of time spent in the teaching/research/service triumvirate, tenure-track versus non-tenure-track/ adjunct positions, and part-time versus full-time work. For example, gender biases have been identified in the perception of quality in scientific studies (Knobloch-Westerwick, Glynn, & Huge, 2013), and a large-scale analysis revealed that men predominate in first author positions as well as authorship of sole-author papers in the academy (West, Jacquet, King, Correll, & Bergstrom, 2013). These inequities persist internationally (Catalyst, 2015) and are reported by both news outlets and, in a more critical manner, by the feminist, activist tweets posted by @AcademicBatgirl, and discussed in the Results of this chapter.

Figure 2.

Dr Academic Batgirl @A... · 2019-10-23 ∨
Sometimes it's just one of those days in academia when you gotta put on a brave face.

Be kinder than necessary because everyone is fighting their own battle.

ME WALKING INTO WORK

AFTER CRYING IN MY CAR FOR 15 MINUTES

💬 17 🔁 99 ♡ 854 ⬆ ᴵᶦᶦ

Academic Twitter does not necessarily reflect the gender-biased phenomena in the bricks-and-mortar academe. Of the top 25 twitter accounts that "every #Phd should follow" (onlinephdprogram.org), ten are women (nine are men, six are organizations unable to be classified by gender; race and sexual orientation are largely indiscernible given the complexities of online handles). The suggestion that women, in particular, are promoted via Twitter may be a result of the many-to-many nature of this social media tool. While Twitter operates such that individuals emerge as leaders - or helper-mentors - and gain a following, this does not imply that social media embodies the limited one-to-many broadcast model. Marwick & boyd (2010) argue that Twitter users imagine their audiences, and tweet with the "audience" in mind. However, in keeping with arguments by Baym (1999) and Jenkins (2005), Marwick & boyd further suggest that the Twitter audience is not characterized by passive consumption; rather, the audience is both active and engaged, as both individuals and groups work to create their own content. In other words, Twitter users both consume *and* produce. This dynamic allows for connection, dialogue, and clear avenues through which individuals communicate. It is this "networked audience" (Marwick & boyd, 2010) that sets Twitter apart from static blogs or websites, and allows for women, more specifically, to build relationships, share information, and both provide and receive support.

This networked audience often evolves into a sense of community. In their study of word usage on Twitter, Bryden, Funk & Jansen (2013) suggest that Twitter users form online communities. These communities share a specific vocation, hobby, political orientation, or ethnicity and can be characterized by their most significantly used words. Online communities have been similarly identified in discussion groups (Baym, 1999) and gaming (Boellstorff, 2008). Academics are a unique band, and the identification of an online academic community was (and still is) part of my experience in using Twitter.

Figure 3.

I created @AcademicBatgirl after observing the flirtatious humour of @ResearchMark, an online, academic version of Mark Wahlberg; a sexy professor, a clever and suave quantitative scholar. @Research Mark (and @AcademicBatgirl) are by definition internet memes. Contemporary usage of the term "internet meme" encompasses "digital content units with common characteristics, created with awareness of each other, and circulated, imitated, and transformed via the Internet by many users" (Shifman, 2013). This contemporary definition is an evolution of the foundational definition coined by Dawkins (1976): any idea, behaviour, or trend that has the ability to transmit from person to person. In current form and practice, memes can include videos or photos that are copied and varied, or in my case, iconic photographs augmented with humorous text. @ResearchMark makes every attempt to validate (statistical pun intended) women in the academy by being flirtatious ("Hey research girl…") or offering encouragement, oftentimes directed specifically to women. However, I found the flirtatiousness a bit off-putting (really, we *have* to go there?).

Figure 4.

There was no strong female character with an online #AcademicTwitter presence, and with messages more directly relative to women in the academy (minus the flirtation). I could do *that*. And even more so, I *wanted* to do it. I saw this as a liberating opportunity to exercise my digital creativity; studies of online presence have also noted that online creativity is both rewarding (Boellstorff, 2008) and can be helpful to productivity (Pearce, 2009).

@AcademicBatgirl made her online debut on 24 April 2014 by tweeting a photographic meme featuring Batgirl battling an unseen foe (in this case, end-of-term grading) with the caption, "Starting another all night grading sesh. Bam! Pow!" It was by no means an award-winning academic meme (it was woefully boring by my currently advanced standards). Nevertheless, it began @AcademicBatgirl's residency online, and established my presence as an academic meme-maker and helper-mentor on Twitter.

COMMUNITY, CREATIVITY, AND COMEDY

The Scholarly Shared Struggle

So what makes community form on Twitter, and what sustains it? And how do women contribute in particular? While there is contemporary research on the importance and helpfulness of community, as above, there is a dearth of literature on what actually makes online communities evolve and, more importantly, sustain themselves. In my experience, in addition to "finding" one another via the shared struggle, humour is part of what unites and sustains communities via Twitter. I have noted that rather than the ritualistic complaining about budgets or manuscripts, a vibrant sense of humour is particularly important in the academic community. The adage "misery loves company" can only last so long, particularly in an online forum. Though one rarely thinks of humour as a key element of the academic persona, in my experience, it is humour that has made the difference in my presence and sustenance online. Here I offer both observations of how the prosocial value of humour has served my social media presence, and how academics must avoid particular issues, no matter how potentially funny.

Figure 5.

In its function as a symbolic gesture, humour affirms, reinforces, and/or challenges concepts and beliefs within society; because humour is, for the most part, expressed in the public sphere, it is an especially meaningful act or ritual (Case & Lippard, 2009, p. 242). McGhee (1976), for example, noted that one popular definition of "sense of humour" emphasizes the individual's ability to laugh at shortcomings, to see the light side of things, or to laugh at one's own expense. In this respect, according to Stillion & White (1976), women appear to have a better sense of humour than men (p. 206). A sense of humour is particularly helpful in the academic community given the frequency with which scholars receive manuscript rejections, engage in the sometimes tedious drudgery of the research process, and the isolation in which many academics engage in their writing, grading, and course preparation. With a prosocial aim, I made every attempt to create my posts and memes in a gender-neutral manner so that academics from a variety of backgrounds could relate. For example, the following meme identifies the quirky side of academics, and having a laugh at our own expense:

Figure 6.

Dr Academic Batgirl
@AcademicBatgirl

3 things academics never regret:

- Conference attendance based on
location
- Writing (even if it's shit, it's better than
trying to edit a blank page)
- Quality coffee/tea/caffeine over
subpar watery garbage

Decide to live well, scholarly friends.

9:46 AM · 2019-11-03 · Twitter for iPhone

ılı View Tweet activity

243 Retweets **1,835** Likes

Most academics can relate to the attraction of a conference in a lovely (read: warm) location, and surely many have planned their conference-going accordingly. Further, the notion of writing – anything, rather than nothing – is relatable for those of us who must produce as part of our scholarly expectations. Finally, it is well-known that academics are magicians who turn caffeine into words, and the necessity of caffeine suggests that we ought to "live well" and consume quality beverages.

Similarly, humour can be considered a coping mechanism (Hay, 2000, p. 726), whereby fantasy alternatives are presented in response to difficult and sometimes oppressive situations that, in my case, academics endure. Such fantasies offer temporary relief and a sense of camaraderie in that others (presumably, other academics) share their challenges. For example, most people – no matter their occupation – can relate to the "Sunday night scaries," or the feeling of dread and anxiety upon realizing that the weekend is nearly over. To that end, I posted the following meme:

Figure 7.

Dr Academic Batgirl
@AcademicBatgirl

Mine kicks in at about 5pm. Hbu?

4:10 PM · 2019-10-06 · Twitter for iPhone

⑪ View Tweet activity

78 Retweets **534** Likes

While Sunday nights are known for not being "prime time" on social media, the notion that this meme got any play at all speaks to the number of academics on Twitter on a Sunday evening – presumably to catch up on news or to connect with friends or colleagues. The notion of "Sunday night scaries" is well-known amongst educators at all levels, from those teaching pre-K to graduate seminars. In this meme, Academic Batgirl provides support to her colleague in an attempt to assuage his Sunday night blues. Here, Academic Batgirl shows her strength and leadership by attempting to soothe a struggling man.

The internet – and social media in particular – is a particularly important venue in which participatory culture (Jenkins, 2005) permits producers and distributors of humour to express frustration and advice. This "frustration and advice" cycle is an integral element of my presence on Twitter, and the defining characteristic of my contribution to the #AcademicTwitter community. For example, encouragement by way of humour has worked in my aim to unify academics.

By way of example, Academic Batgirl's advice to a seemingly despondent Batman takes on a quasi-chasting tone in this meme. She calls out her colleague relative to having a "languishing manuscript:" an article or book chapter that is long overdue, has been in various stages of draft for anywhere from months to even years, and has no hope of finding the light of day. Batgirl boasts that she discovered the #getyourmanuscriptout hashtag; this hashtag was created by @raulpacheco (2012) to encourage academics to get their manuscripts out the door. This "crowdsourcing" of writing has worked in the academic community; it is a consistent reminder that others are getting their writing done and work is getting finished.

This reminder and discourse can inspire others to do the same. One of the most popular hashtags in the #AcWri (academic writing) community, the #getyourmanuscriptout movement has mobilized academics all over the world to get their manuscripts off the laptop and under review.

Figure 8.

YOU HAVE BEEN BLOCKED: STUDENT SHAMING

While self-deprecating humour can identify the "shared struggle" of life in academe, I strongly suggest that critical humour is best avoided, and most importantly, if it includes students. Although faculty are often exasperated with students not reading the syllabus, for example, I suggest that taking to social media to shame students is a nefarious undertaking. I argue that shaming students – and in particular doing so online and via social media – is detrimental to a positive academic culture. It places both students and faculty in a negative, unsupportive position. This is particularly important given that women more often than men take on the "emotional labour" of assisting students with crises or personal struggles (Guarino 2017).

Students are not unique in being shamed online. Ronson (2015) identifies contemporary cases of online shaming, including the case of Justine Sacco, who posted a racist tweet while en route to Cape Town and lost her job at a New York City public relations firm in 2013 (she arguably also lost her professional future). Jonah Lehrer was outed for splicing pieces from other scholars' work in *Imagine: How Creativity Works* (2012). Some shame scholars (e.g., Murphy & Kiffin-Petersen, 2017) suggest that public shaming could be helpful in that it forces the shamed individual to admit their wrongdoings, make reparations, and conform to social, economic, or cultural norms.

It is nearly impossible to argue, however, that student shaming exhibits any prosocial effects. In some instances, I have seen faculty (either via anonymous accounts or even using their professional profiles), identify students as greedy customers clamoring for attention, calling out students for end of term grade-grubbing, or venting outbursts about students conversing in an overly familiar tone (see, for example, Worthen, 2017). There are posts calling out students for not being able to write, making grammar gaffes, and general lamenting about general student carelessness and laziness (e.g., "I don't always ignore your emails, but when I do it's because the answer is in the syllabus"). These posts get significant attention in the academic community, because even "serious academics" use social media (Willingham, 2016). As a popular meme asks, "Y tho?" Why would faculty want to take to the online forum to shame students, when the student-faculty relationship is one that is (or at least should be) founded on trust, respect, and mentorship?

Figure 9.

For example, most faculty can relate to students not reading the syllabus and/or not following directions. I have dealt with same. I have found that the best way to address this is to meet students where they are in language that speaks to them rather than ridiculing them either on social media or face-to-face. I made the meme above, based on Carly Rae Jepsen's "Call Me Maybe," and it never fails to make students laugh. This meme, rather than chastising students, reaches out to them in a humourous way so that they understand that the syllabus is important. The pop culture references humanizes my approach to the syllabus with a "power-with" rather than a "power-over" attitude. When I project this meme on the first day of class, it serves to meet students with humour and connection.[1]

If (and sadly, when) faculty identify and shame students on social media, I argue that the academic community suffers. For example, Worthen's (2017) piece ridiculed students for communicating with faculty in an overly-casual manner. Faculty responses via social media rushed in, suggesting that the role of professors is to help students to learn, practice professionalism, and to understand how to adjust to new and different social situations; faculty response indicated little patience for Worthen's privilege and impatience. In a culture that promotes learning and critical thinking, particularly at a time in which students are in the important developmental period of emerging adulthood (Arnett, 2000), public, online shaming can be particularly destructive. In truth, faculty are not immune to failing to follow directions; how many of us have submitted a manuscript with the wrong formatting or missed a deadline (multiple times!)? Surely faculty may think twice about casting stones from glass houses.

Regardless of the anecdotal accounts of students who behave badly, taking to social media to shame students is unacceptable. When students are shamed online, the culture in academe has a very real potential to suffer. Creed, Hudson, Okhuysen and Smith-Crowe (2014) suggest that if and when leaders use *episodic shaming* in ways that demonstrate power, emphasize organizational norms, and deter problematic behaviors, this serves as a disincentive for professionals. For students, online episodic shaming by faculty can create a culture of power-over, intimidation, and fear. When this culture is shared amongst faculty and across institutions, a culture of support and academic development is unlikely. In this case, students may be likely to either repeat negative behaviors or simply leave the academy altogether, believing themselves deficient. No matter the bizarre nature of (and potential for water-cooler jokes to ensue from) receiving photos of x-rays to be excused from an exam, for example, faculty have the opportunity to redirect and educate students rather than shame them, particularly online.

CONCLUSION

Becoming part of the broader academic discourse in one's field is an essential part of scholarly growth. However, establishing oneself as part of a community of academics and colleagues is not often accomplished by means of becoming well-known or publishing groundbreaking research (although some exceptions apply, such as @astrokatie, who is a well-recognized astrophysicist who shares her research in accessible ways online). Academic community, particularly online, is about recognizing oneself as part of a group of scholars who are united in frustration, support, and camaraderie. Once this sense of community is established, then it becomes safe, possible, and likely that scholarly interests are exchanged, connections made, and offline relationships emerge. I have seen this happen in my own experience on Twitter whereby I established friendships with authors of similar disciplines, then moved on to collaborating and even coauthoring.

I suggest that social media has tremendous potential to shape and sustain the academic community. Faculty have found a meaningful support system particularly via Twitter, and specifically via the hashtag #AcademicTwitter. The role of women is particularly essential to cultivate, given that female academics are integral to looking after the "academic family" (Guarino 2017). Anonymous accounts are entertaining in their pithy comments about deadlines or stacks of grading, and faculty struggling with grant applications or everyone's worst nightmare, Nasty Reviewer 2, can vent and find a support squad. Academic humor on social media ought to focus on issues such as the neverending battle with grading, frustration with writing deadlines, or downright loathing for learning management systems that inevitably crash – all rather than shaming students for what is very often normal developmental behavior. The academic climate, for both students and faculty, is a precarious one. I suggest that social media, and in particular Twitter, can be a safe space for academics of all levels to gather together via humour and support. And @AcademicBatgirl will help lead the way.

REFERENCES

Arnett, J. J. (2000). *Emerging adulthood: A theory of development Baym, N. K. (1999). Tune in, log on: Soaps, fandom, and online community*. New York: Sage.

Bennett, L., & Folley, S. (2014). A tale of two doctoral students: Social media tools and hybridised identities. *Research in Learning Technology, 22*. doi:10.3402/rlt.v22.23791

Boellstorff, T. (2008). *Coming of age in second life: An anthropologist explores the virtually human*. Princeton: Princeton University Press.

Bryden, J., Funk, S., & Jansen, V. A. A. (2013). Word usage mirrors community structure in the online social network Twitter. *EPJ Data Science, 2*(3), 3. doi:10.1140/epjds15

Butler, J. (1988). Performative acts and gender constitution: An essay in phenomenology and feminist theory. *Theatre Journal, 40*(4), 519–531. doi:10.2307/3207893

Case, C. E., & Lippard, C. (2009). Humorous assaults on patriarchal ideology. *Sociological Inquiry, 79*(2), 240–255. doi:10.1111/j.1475-682X.2009.00282.x

Catalyst. (2015, July 9). *Quick take: Women in academia*. New York: Catalyst. Retrieved from https://www.catalyst.org/knowledge/women-academia

Chen, J. J., & Crown, D. (2019). The gender pay gap in academia: Evidence from Ohio State University. *American Journal of Agricultural Economics, 101*(5), 1337–1352. doi:10.1093/ajae/aaz017

Consalvo, M. (2012). Confronting toxic gamer culture: A challenge for feminist game studies scholars. *Ada: A Journal of Gender. New Media, and Technology, 1*(1). doi:10.7264/N33X84KH

Creed, D., Hudson, B., Okhuysen, G., & Smith-Crowe, K. (2014). Swimming in a sea of shame: Incorporating emotion into explanation of institutional reproduction and change. *Academy of Management Review, 39*(3), 275–301. doi:10.5465/amr.2012.0074

Curtis, J. W. (2011). *Persistent inequity: Gender and academic employment*. Prepared for "New voices in pay equity," American Association of University Professors. Retrieved from https://www.aaup.org/NR/rdonlyres/08E023AB-E6D8-4DBD-99A0-24E5EB73A760/0/persistent_inequity.pdf

Dawkins, R. (1976). *The selfish gene*. Oxford: Oxford University Press.

Dibbell, J. (1999). *My tiny life: Crime and passion in a virtual world*. New York: Henry Holt and Company.

Duggan, M. (2017, July 11). Online harassment 2017. *Pew Research Center*. Retrieved from https://www.pewresearch.org/internet/2017/07/11/online-harassment-2017/

Ferguson, H., & Wheat, K. L. (2015). Early career academic mentoring using Twitter: The case of #ECRchat. *Journal of Higher Education Policy and Management, 37*(1), 3–13. doi:10.1080/1360080X.2014.991533

Flaherty, C. (2015, February 2). Student's comment on female professor's clothes prompts criticism. *Times Higher Education*. Retrieved from https://www.timeshighereducation.com/news/students-comment-on-female-professors-clothes-prompts-criticism/2018283.article

Gannon, K. (2016, August 5). I've got a serious problem with "serious academics." *The Tattooed Prof* [Blog post]. Retrieved from https://www.thetattooedprof.com/2016/08/05/ive-got-a-serious-problem-with-serious-academics/

Green, D. (2015). An antidote to futility: Why academics (and students) should take blogging/social media seriously. *The Impact Blog: London School of Economics and Political Science*. Retrieved from https://blogs.lse.ac.uk/impactofsocialsciences/2015/10/26/why-academics-and-students-should-take-blogging-social-media-seriously/

Guarino, C., & Borden, V. M. H. (2017). Faculty service loads and gender: Are women taking care of the academic family? *Research in Higher Education, 58*(6), 672–694. doi:10.100711162-017-9454-2

Gulliver, K. (2012, May 9). 10 commandments of Twitter for academics. *The Chronicle of Higher Education*. Retrieved from http://chronicle.com/article/10-Commandments-of-Twitter-for/131813/

Hay, J. (2000). Functions of humor in the conversations of men and women. *Journal of Pragmatics, 32*(6), 709–742. doi:10.1016/S0378-2166(99)00069-7

Himelboim, I., McCreery, S., & Smith, M. (2013). Birds of a feather tweet together: Integrating network and content analyses to examine cross-ideology exposure on Twitter. *Journal of Computer-Mediated Communication, 18*(2), 40–60. doi:10.1111/jcc4.12001

Hine, C. (2008). Virtual ethnography: Modes, varieties, affordances. In N. Fielding, R. M. Lee, & G. Blank (Eds.), *The SAGE handbook of online research method* (pp. 257–270). Los Angeles: Sage. doi:10.4135/9780857020055.n14

Jenkins, H. (2005). *Convergence culture*. New York: New York University Press.

Jenson, J., & DeCastell, S. (2013). Tipping points: Marginality, misogyny, and videogames. *Journal of Curriculum Theorizing, 29*(2), 72–85. Retrieved from https://journal.jctonline.org/index.php/jct/article/viewFile/474/pdf

Jurgenson, N. (2009, October 5). Towards theorizing an augmented reality. *Cyborgology: The Society Pages*. Retrieved from https://thesocietypages.org/sociologylens/2009/10/05/towards-theorizing-an-augmented-reality/

Knobloch-Westerwick, S., Glynn, C. J., & Huge, M. (2013). The Matilda effect in science communication: An experiment on gender bias in publication quality perceptions and collaboration interest. *Science Communication, 35*(5), 603–625. doi:10.1177/1075547012472684

Lehrer, J. (2012). *Imagine: How Creativity Works*. Edinburgh: Canongate Books.

Markham, A. (1998). *Life online: Researching real experiences in virtual space*. Walnut Creek, CA: AltaMira Press.

Marwick, A. E., & boyd. (2010). I Tweet honestly, I Tweet passionately: Twitter users, context collapse, and the imagined audience. *New Media & Society, 13*(1), 114–133. doi:10.1177/1461444810365313

Meyers, M. (2013). The war on academic women: Reflections on postfeminism in the neoliberal academy. *The Journal of Communication Inquiry, 37*(4), 274–283. doi:10.1177/0196859913505619

Morris, T. (2010). All a Twitter: A personal and professional guide to social networking with Twitter. Indianapolis, IN: Que.

Murphy, S. A., & Kiffin-Petersen, S. (2017). The exposed self: A multilevel model of shame and ethical behavior. *Journal of Business Ethics*, *141*(4), 657–675. doi:10.100710551-016-3185-8

Murthy, D., Hastings, C. M., & Mawrie, S. A. (2014). The use of social media to foster trust, mentorship, and collaboration in scientific organizations. *Bulletin of Science, Technology & Society*, *34*(5-6), 170–182. doi:10.1177/0270467615582196

Murthy, D., & Lewis, J. P. (2015). Social media, collaboration, and scientific organizations. *The American Behavioral Scientist*, *59*(1), 149–171. doi:10.1177/0002764214540504

National Union of Students. (2015). *Talk about it: NUS Women's Department 2015 survey*. Retrieved from https://d3n8a8pro7vhmx.cloudfront.net/nus/pages/144/attachments/original/1454369041/Talk_about_it_Survey_Report.pdf?1454369041

OnlinePhDProgram.org. (n.d.). *101 Twitter accounts every #PhD should follow*. Retrieved from https://onlinephdprogram.org/twitter-accounts/

Pacheco-Vega, R. (2012). *Using the #ScholarSunday hashtag as a #FollowFriday for academics*. Retrieved from http://www.raulpacheco.org/2012/09/scholarsunday/

Parra, D., Trattner, C., Gomez, D., Hurtado, M., Wen, X., & Lin, Y-R. (2016). Twitter in academic events: a study of temporal usage, communication, sentimental and topical patterns in 16 Computer Science conferences. *Computer Communications, 73*(B), 301-314.

Pearce, C. (2009). *Communities of play: Emergent cultures in multiplayer games and virtual worlds*. Cambridge, MA: MIT Press. doi:10.7551/mitpress/8039.001.0001

Ronson, J. (2015, February 12). How one stupid tweet ruined Justine Sacco's life. *The New York Times*. Retrieved from https://www.nytimes.com/2015/02/15/magazine/how-one-stupid-tweet-ruined-justine-saccos-life.html

Scoble, J. (n.d.) *Twitter for academics*. Retrieved from https://onlineacademic.wordpress.com/social-media-for-academics/twitter-for-academics/

Shifman, L. (2013). *Memes in digital culture*. Cambridge: The MIT Press. doi:10.7551/mitpress/9429.001.0001

Stillion, J. M., & White, H. (1987). Feminist humor: Who appreciates it and why? *Psychology of Women Quarterly*, *11*(2), 219–232. doi:10.1111/j.1471-6402.1987.tb00785.x

Tiidenberg, K. (2014). Bringing sexy back: Reclaiming the body aesthetic via self-shooting. *Cyberpsychology (Brno)*, *8*(1), 3. doi:10.5817/CP2014-1-3

Tiidenberg, K., & Gomez Cruz, E. (2015). Selfies, image and the re-making of the body. *Body & Society*, *21*(4), 1 26. doi:10.1177/1357034X15592465

Veletsianos, G., & Kimmons, R. (2012). Networked participatory scholarship: Emergent techno-cultural pressures toward open and digital scholarship in online networks. *Computers & Education*, *58*(2), 766–774. doi:10.1016/j.compedu.2011.10.001

West, J. D., Jacquet, J., King, M. M., Correll, S. J., & Bergstrom, C. T. (2013). The role of gender in scholarly authorship. *PLoS One*, *8*(7), e66212. doi:10.1371/journal.pone.0066212 PMID:23894278

Willingham, E. (2016, August 6). Yes, serious academics should absolutely use social media. *Forbes.com*. Retrieved from https://www.forbes.com/sites/emilywillingham/2016/08/06/serious-academics-should-use-social-media/#9312c544fb17

Worthen, M. (2017, May 13). U can't talk to ur professor like this. *The New York Times*. Retrieved from https://www.nytimes.com/2017/05/13/opinion/sunday/u-cant-talk-to-ur-professor-like-this.html

ENDNOTE

[1] One Twitter user suggested that this song and its pop culture reference was "too old" for contemporary students. I showed this meme in class as recently as December 2020, and all students recognized the reference. This is an evergreen pop culture reference and I suggest that perhaps the Twitter user suggesting that the meme was outdated is himself "too old."

This research was previously published in Critical Reflections and Politics on Advancing Women in the Academy; pages 33-51, copyright year 2020 by Information Science Reference (an imprint of IGI Global).

Chapter 68
#TextMeetsTech:
Navigating Meaning and Identity through Transliteracy Practice

Katie Schrodt
Middle Tennessee State University, USA

Erin R FitzPatrick
UNC Charlotte, USA

Kim Reddig
University of North Carolina at Charlotte, USA

Emily Paine Smith
Southwest Christian School, USA

Jennifer Grow
Middle Tennessee State University, USA

ABSTRACT

This chapter addresses the need to make time and space for transliteracy practices in the classroom. University pre-service teachers are used as the primary example as the chapter documents how these students made meaning across a range of platforms, while reading the acclaimed young adult novel The Hate U Give. The university course, titled Language and Literacy, focuses on methods of literacy instruction in the classroom. A lesson plan framework is included in the chapter that is especially user friendly for educator preparation classrooms as well as high school and middle school teachers. The chapter explores the experiences of the college students while reading The Hate U Give, while detailing how the students created meaning through a variety of traditional and modern teaching practices.

DOI: 10.4018/978-1-6684-7123-4.ch068

INTRODUCTION

Literacy in the 21st century is ever changing. The nature of literacy today is continually being revised and adapted as humans make meaning across a range of platforms (Leu, Kinzer, Coiro, Castek, & Henry, 2018). This fluid nature calls for students today to be savvy in both traditional and modern literacy practices. The term "transliteracy" has been coined to define the ways that students must navigate through multiple media, moving in and out of a variety of platforms, and mapping meaning through traditional literacy practices that include orality, handwriting, reading books, and writing, as well as new literacies that include visual and social media (Thomas et al., 2007).

While research shows youth are often intensely engaged in a wide range of literacy practices outside of the school setting, schools often lack the same wide range of literacy taught in the curriculum (Bazalgette, & Buckingham, 2013; Bezemer, & Kress, 2008; Lenters, 2016). In recent years, literacy educators have increasingly recognized the importance of addressing resources other than the textbook in the classroom. The textbook is no longer the sole source of learning. Digital media has become the main resource for learning in the classroom (Rowsell, & Walsh, 2011). Multimodality is now essential to the literacy practices of youth in the globalized communications environment (Cope & Kalantzis, 2000; Faigley, Kress, & van Leeuwen, 2002). Teachers are being encouraged to include various digital media to introduce new literacies to help students make connections between learning in the home and school. Multimodality includes two or more modes of literacy such as, linguistic, visual, audio, gestural, and spatial (Mills, 2010). Although written work is still vital, more is needed to provide students with meaningful communication in all aspects of their life. Adolescents today require a collection of multimodal and digital literacies for social purposes: critical inquiry, creativity, and communication (Kress, & Selander, 2012; Walsh, & Walsh, 2010).

As information and disciplinary literacy become more popular, it is important for teachers and students to not view literacy in compartments or pockets. Transliteracy opens up the idea of working *across*. It effectively bridges isolated spheres of literacy practice and allows students to view and practice making literacy meaning in a variety of methods and through a number of different platforms. As one librarian blogged, "[Transliteracy] is using Wikipedia to find keywords for a search in CINAHL. It's reading an academic journal article and then looking up the author's personal blog for more context. It's comparing hashtags to subject headings and Amazon reviews to abstracts. In a sense, the real force behind transliteracy is encompassed in one little word in the definition: *across*" (Wilkinson, 2010, p. 1). As teachers, it is critical for us to help students see those connections between daily "non-traditional" literacy practices and those more traditional ones. These practices can merge together to create deeper meaning and connections in the classroom.

This chapter will address the need to make time and space for transliteracy practices in the classroom, using as an example university pre-service teachers making meaning across a range of platforms, while reading the acclaimed young adult novel, *The Hate U Give* (Thomas, 2017). A lesson plan framework will be discussed in the chapter that is especially user friendly for educator preparation classrooms as well as high school teachers. The chapter will explore the experiences of the college students while reading *The Hate U Give*, while detailing how the students created meaning through a variety of traditional and modern teaching practices.

The students essentially created a modern and modified text set as they read through the novel. Across time, the students collected a group of related texts, adding in non-traditional texts, such as photographs, social media, YouTube videos, and songs that connected to their personal experiences and meaning making with *The Hate U Give*. Text sets expand comprehension, increase vocabulary and background knowledge, and cultivate a social learning environment (Beck, 2014). The remixed "text set" presented in this chapter provides an opportunity for transliteracy practices that helps students layer and access multiple levels of meaning within the book.

BACKGROUND

The experiences represented in this chapter are from an undergraduate literacy methods course for pre-service teachers. Fifteen students took this class as a requirement in their pursuit of becoming elementary school teachers. In this class, teacher candidates gain an understanding of the essential components of effective literacy instruction (phonemic awareness, phonics, fluency, vocabulary, and comprehension) and demonstrate how each component can be taught within meaningful contexts. This course met for 6 hours a week for 15 weeks.

Part of this course includes the personal reading and writing practices of the teacher candidates. The foundation of the class is built on the belief that teachers must view themselves as readers, writers, and critical thinkers in order to best teach reading, writing, and critical thinking to young children (Davis-Duerr, 2015; Karabay, Kuşdemir Kayıran, & Işık, 2015; Parten Gerla, 2010). To better understand the preservice teachers' perceptions of themselves as readers, a short reading survey was conducted at the beginning of the course. Two of the fifteen students identified themselves as current readers, citing they are currently reading a novel for pleasure and regularly read in their free time. A consistent theme from the rest of the students included a love for reading in elementary school that quickly died away once hitting adolescence. One student in particular stated she had never read a novel from cover to cover on her own. With this in mind, regular interaction with modern, high quality young adult and children's literature became a significant goal in the class. The students would be given access to great books that spark discussion and require critical thinking and provided opportunities to think, write, and talk about those books.

The book *The Hate U Give* was selected as a classroom novel based on its award-winning status and multitude of accolades as well as its engaging, thought-provoking content. This book was also chosen for its relevance to true current and historical events, allowing for more room for critical thinking and discussion. The book has also been adapted into a movie, which may serve as a source of reading motivation for students (Lamb, 2018). The movie trailer was played in class as a hook for the students and served as the groundwork for a book talk, selling the students on the worth of the novel and increasing the likelihood of engagement (Fisher & Frey, 2018)

TRANSLITERACY METHODS

Socratic Seminars and Text Sets

Socratic seminar is an inquiry-based discussion method that encourages students to have intentional conversations around a common text (Holden, 2002). Socratic seminars are based on the ideas of Socrates and encourage students to form ideas of their own as well as integrate and collaborate to form new ideas. These seminars set the stage for socially meaningful learning as students learn to listen, ask questions, discuss, form opinions, and create new learning. This traditional teaching practice helps students find their voice through inquiry, discussion-based learning.

In this example, Socratic seminar served as the primary face-to-face discussion for the book *The Hate U Give*. Four Socratic seminars were held across the semester to discuss assigned sections of the text. Traditionally, students come to a Socratic circle with a question to pose to the group as students discuss a common text or theme. In order to make more space for transliteracy practice and movement in and out of traditional and new literacies, each student was asked to come to the seminar with a completed guiding discussion template (See Appendix A). This template served as a scaffold for students as they learned the procedures and dynamics of the seminar. This template helped students layer their thinking about the text, scaffolding them to come to the seminar with a "multimodal text set" of sorts. The text set included the traditional Socratic questions as well as more modern and varied literacies such as a hashtag and a connection to a video, song, current event, or piece of artwork. A text set is a collection of related resources that support a common theme, topic, or issue. These resources can come from different genres, text types, and media. Text sets can help students build content knowledge and vocabulary on a topic, as well as prepare them to continue learning through new texts on the same topic (Cervetti, Wright, & Hwang, 2016).

The first seminar was prefaced with ground rules for listening and speaking. Each participant was given two playing cards to represent the two times they were expected to contribute to the conversation. They could "play their card" when they were ready to speak (Gallagher, 2015).

Hashtags

A hashtag is a word or phrase proceeded by the symbol # that is used on social media platforms to identify, summarize, and categorize topics. A hashtag on social media can identify a keyword or theme of a specific piece of content. The students were asked to use this modern communication method to distill the important information from each section of the reading. Each Socratic seminar ended with everyone going around in a circle and reading off their hashtags. These tags allowed for closure to the seminar that helped summarize the ideas that were discussed as well as aided in comprehension and retention of meaning from the section of reading. The students used this modern communication tool to make meaning, express their feelings, and make connections across texts. *The Hate U Give* hashtag examples from each category can be found in Table 1.

Table 1. Hashtags used in student discussions

Making Meaning	Expressing Feelings	Making Connections
#investigatingorjustifying #dontmove #notanotherstatistic #justiceforkhalil #thekhalilIknow #thuglife #fakeprotests #timetospeakup #lilblackpanther #getyourswirlonbaby #blackfemalewitness	#byehailey #intense #emotional #rollercoaster #pissed #changeofheart #tinybravepartofme	#icantbreathe #handsup #BlackLivesMatter #youwillbefound

Multimedia Connections

At each Socratic seminar, the students were asked to make a connection across media platforms. Students asked themselves if this section of the book made them think of a current event, a song, a video, or a historical event.

Accessing History and Current Events

As an important plot point in the story, Angie Thomas mentions Emmett Till, the 14-year-old African American boy from Chicago whose eyes were gouged out as he was beaten, stripped, shot in the head, and tied to a cotton gin with barbed wire before being dumped into the Tallahatchie River by two white men in Money, Mississippi in 1955. He had been accused of flirting with a white woman. Less than two weeks later an eye witness identified both murderers in court, but in less than an hour, a segregated Southern jury issued a verdict of not guilty. The woman later recanted her story.

The main character in *The Hate U Give*, Starr, posted a disturbing photograph of Till to her Tumblr account. Many students were interested in this section of the text as they began to feel negative feelings toward the character Hailey. Hashtags about Hailey (#byehailey #haileysucks) began to surface in the Socratic seminar conversations. In one seminar, a student brought in a picture of Emmett Till, as well as quotes from Emmett Till's mother, who insisted on an open casket funeral so everyone could see the impact of the horrible things that were done to her son. Many students in the class had not heard of Emmett Till or this significant event in history which sparked a movement in the Civil Rights Era. As the students made meaning across historical documents, they gained a deeper understanding of the feelings Starr and her family might have been having as they continued to face injustice decades after the Civil Rights movement.

In these historical conversations, the title of the book and the word *thug* came up over and over. The history of the word *thug* and what students thought of the word became a topic of conversation. An etymological review of the word shows that throughout history the word *thug* has been used as a general descriptor for a violent person, especially a criminal. Even today, presidents have used it to describe insurgents and rioters. Students debated whether the word *thug* has become a codified slur in and of itself; that is, was the term acceptable in public discourse but covertly carrying the stereotypical, negative connotations inherent in more recognized and eschewed bigoted language? Tupac Shakur brought the word into popular culture and gave it a fresh new twist. Tupac spoke, through his rap music, about THUG LIFE and the unfair treatment of his black brothers and sisters and how that affects everyone. He worked to make it cool and powerful. Since his death in 1996, many people have continued to build on his hopes and writings. The students began to connect Angie Thomas' purpose for naming the book *The Hate U Give* as she chose to give "thug" respect and strength while honoring its definition given by Tupac Shakur. Tupac's words continued as a significant source of conversation as the students began to notice the symbol of Maverick's roses within the novel. Starr's dad Maverick, repeatedly waters his rose garden throughout the book. Despite his efforts the roses seem to be dry and dying. One student stated, "Maverick is continuing to water the dead roses—it is kind of like a symbol for the Carters' life in Garden Heights. They are trying and trying to make it work but things keep happening." A famous Tupac poem titled "The Rose that Grew from Concrete" was discussed as a connection as they deepened their understanding of Starr and her family being those roses.

Black Panther 10-point program was another multimedia connection that accessed history. One student brought in a YouTube video discussing the Black Panther Party and its creation of the ten-point program (History Chapel, 2013). This video explains the ten-point program and contains snippets of speeches given by Black Panther Party leaders as well as real photographs from the time period. This video sparked much discussion as students began to grapple with why they had not heard many positive things about the Black Panther party, but rather associated them only with violence. One student stated, "I felt as if it was always taught to me that Martin Luther King Jr. was good and Malcom X was bad. I am realizing there is more to it than that." Each new historical connection allowed for a new layer of meaning within the book.

At the time of this experience, current events began to mirror some of the events happening in the book. One Socratic seminar included a connection to a shooting of a black man by a white police officer in his own apartment. The student brought in an article as part of the discussion (Jail, 2019). This discussion led to hashtag searches that included some of the most popular and trending hashtags related to the #BlackLivesMatter movement as well as #policebrutality. Some examples included #TamirRice, #handsup, #16times, and #ICantBreathe.

Music and Videos

One of the most moving moments came when a student pulled up a YouTube video of Lin-Manuel Miranda and Ben Platt performing a *Hamilton* and *Dear Evan Hansen* mashup titled *Found / Tonight* (Fierberg, 2018). The lyrics are written out below. The themes of *The Hate U Give* can be directly linked to these lyrics—themes of speaking out, feeling forgotten, telling your story, freedom, rising up, and being "found."

We may not yet have reached our glory
But I will gladly join the fight
And when our children tell their story
They'll tell the story of tonight
They'll tell the story of tonight
Tonight
Have you ever felt like nobody was there?
Have you ever felt forgotten in the middle of nowhere?
Have you ever felt like you could disappear?
Like you could fall, and no one would hear?
Well, let that lonely feeling wash away
All we see is light
'Cause maybe there's a reason to believe you'll be okay
For forever
'Cause when you don't feel strong enough to stand
You can reach, reach out your hand
And oh
Raise a glass to freedom
Something they can never take away
Oh

No matter what they tell you
Someone will come running
To take you home
Raise a glass to all of us
Tomorrow there'll be more of us
Telling the story of tonight
Out of the shadows
The morning is breaking /They'll tell the story of tonight
And all is new
All is new
All is new
It's only a matter of
Time
Even when the dark comes crashing through
When you need a friend to carry you
When you're broken on the ground
You will be found
So let the sun come streaming in
'Cause you'll reach up and you'll rise again
If you only look around
You will be found
And when our children tell their story
You will be found
They'll tell the story of tonight
Whoa
No matter what they tell you
Tomorrow there'll be more of us
Telling the story of tonight
The story of tonight
(Miranda & Platt, 2018).

The students created their own videos through Flipgrid. This website allows students to record and respond to videos in a similar format to Snapchat or Instagram stories; that is, the students can record themselves responding to a particular video, providing a context for a virtual conversation. The video-based discussion topics are organized into a grid fostering user-friendly interaction and facilitating both posts and replies. This platform allowed students to post thoughts and reactions to the text in between Socratic seminar sessions. Students felt compelled to post on Flipgrid when they reached a shocking or significant part in the text. For example, throughout the narrative, tension had been building between the main character Starr and her friend Hailey. In one part of the book, Starr finally punches Hailey. Multiple videos surfaced when this happened with reactions such as, "Starr just straight up punched Hailey in the face. I couldn't be happier. She finally got what's been coming." Another student responded, "Hailey was running her little mouth thinking there would never be any consequences! Find your voice, Starr!" Another significant part of the text inspired deeper thinking, and students considered the multiple sides of the character Iesha. Throughout the book, it seems as though Iesha is not a good mother and does not care for her children. At one point, Iesha puts her own safety and well-being on the line to help her children escape from her abusive boyfriend. At this point, many Flipgrid videos popped up as their perspective of Iesha had changed as the book went on. One student said, "This reminded me of the book *Love* by Matt De La Pena. Love isn't always what we think it is. It shows up in ways we don't always expect. Iesha is a mother. She does love her kids. She sacrificed herself to get Devonte out of harm's way." Another student responded with, "Yes Seven's mom is finally stepping up!" When brought back to the Socratic seminar, students began to speak about the complexity of the characters and situations saying, "Every character has so many layers. I am beginning to understand Kenya more. Khalil and Devante's situations have become more relatable across the book. They both only wanted to help their mothers."

Instagram

At the end of the novel, the students were asked to represent the book through a social media-inspired book review. This assignment asks students to create a #bookstagram photograph for social media that advertises the book and starts a discussion about the meaning of the book. The students curated photographs that contained multiple artifacts to represent themes and important events in the text. The photographs included the cover of the book as well as an impactful quote from the book. Then, students created a caption that gives a book summary and review as well as poses a question for discussion about the book. Lastly, the students were asked to add hashtags and emojis to their post. These photos were posted to Instagram and the students were asked to respond to the photographs and questions online. The Instagram post ended up representing a combination book talk, book review, comprehension assessment, and online Socratic seminar of sorts. See Appendix B for a rubric for the assignment. Examples from other books can be found on www.instagram.com/notasinglestory. If Instagram is unavailable or not an option, the assignment can be adapted by printing the photographs and captions and displaying them in the hallway. Add access to sticky notes and pens for people to make comments.

The students carefully curated their photographs for the Instagram post about *The Hate U Give*, placing items and quotes in the perfect format to represent the meaning they made from the text. Details from two of the photographs are included in Figure 1.

This assignment offers an opportunity for making meaning across a range of platforms as students carefully chose items and other modes of art to curate a photo. The students featured here chose artifacts that represented a continuum of comprehension as students demonstrated the literal meaning of the text—representing characters and plot points—and also, deeper meanings as they applied, analyzed, and created new layers of understanding with the final photograph and caption. Each photograph contained items that represented important characters in the book, including a Fresh Prince DVD to represent Starr and Chris, and a badge to represent the police officer 115.

The collections in the photographs added another layer of complexity when items represented both a character and a significant plot point or served as an abstract artifact of the culture. The hairbrush symbolized Khalil as a character but also pointed toward the significant plot point in which his hairbrush is mistaken for a gun resulting in his murder by Officer 115. The black hoodie and the black bandana also represented Khalil as a character but moved into a deeper theme of judgment and marginalization. The hoodie has historically been a politically charged symbol of systemic racism as many young black kids are labeled as dangerous when wearing a hoodie. Trayvon Martin, the unarmed 17-year-old fatally and famously shot by a neighborhood watch representative, was wearing a similar hoodie. Students elevated the meaning by making connections to real people like Trayvon, and creating a list of victims

Figure 1. Student Instagram photographs

Photograph	Caption
	The Hate U Give by Angie Thomas is an eye opening book that allows the readers to witness the lifestyle of living in a low income African American community, through the lens of a high school student named Starr. Starr's life comes to an unruly halt when she witnesses her childhood best friend, Khalil, get shot by a cop, due to no other reason than the color of his skin, after what was suppose[d] to be a routine traffic stop. Khalil's death follows Starr throughout the book as the community she lives in seeks justice for police brutality, while her white privileged school environment is on the police's side, unaware of who Khalil really is. Starr and her family find themselves in multiple heart-wrenching situations where they see who really supports them and who can't see past the public stereotypes. In the end, despite the protest and the court's decision, Starr decides to never give up and never stop fighting. How will you make a change? #powpow #breakout #wewontforget #notasinglestory
	The Hate U Give, by Angie Thomas, is a must-read for all Americans, especially in our society today. It's a story that resonates with people from all walks of life. The book is the story of a black high school student named Starr who is stuck between two worlds – her affluent, predominately white private school world, and her predominantly black neighborhood that she has lived in her whole life. Starr is the witness of a shooting and it changes her life forever. Her childhood best friend, Khalil, is pulled over by a white police officer and the situation escalates. Khalil is shot and killed. Starr was in the car and saw everything happen. Starr is faced with standing up for justice and at the same time, not wanting to get involved in what will surely be a racially-charged insurgence of hate and anger. She is constantly worried about what other people will think – will her white friends and boyfriend think she's a thug? Will her black friends and neighbors think she sold out? Starr feels different no matter where she is. Starr is brave and resilient. She learns to be honest and to use her voice. The character growth in The Hate U Give is inspiring and will hopefully encourage readers that their voices matter! This book is just as much about a young girl learning to speak up as it is about Americans who are marginalized and oppressed. It's beautifully written and I enjoyed it very much. #THUG #justiceforkhalil Have you ever felt like you didn't fit in, or like you weren't meeting anyone's expectations of you? #notasinglestory

of police shootings. The students purposely burned the edges of the list for a two-fold meaning. First, they said because many people wish to ignore and hide the fact that police brutality exists, metaphorically "burning away" their names and memory. Secondly, it represents a significant plot point at the end of *The Hate U Give*, when a fire is set by a fellow black neighbor in Garden Heights. This brings up a significant conversation about a larger theme in the book of how systematic, institutional bias and prejudice serves to fuel more hatred—raising the stakes and decreasing the likelihood of true resolution for everyone involved. This theme is directly linked to the artifact of Tupac's album. The title of the book is named after lyrics from his work and addresses the topic of systemic racism, marginalization, and using your voice to stand up for what is right. In one of the Instagram pictures, each artifact rests on top of a blood-splattered background. This powerful image of blood being shed matched with the quotes from both photographs is a call for action. Both photographs offer quotes that encourage speaking out. "What is the point of having a voice if you're gonna be silent in the times you shouldn't be?" and "I'll never forget. I'll never give up and I'll never be quiet."

Using multiple technology tools: computers, mobile devices, and tablets, as well as social media outlets, allowed students the ability to create projects that are individualized to their personal experiences. When integrated purposefully, media essentials can be powerful and personalized instructional tools (Rao, & Skouge, 2015). Personalizing students' experiences and incorporating culture into reading activities, allows them to deepen their knowledge and comprehension skills and broaden their transliteracy skills.

CONNECTIONS ACROSS ALL PLATFORMS

The goal and eventuality of this process was to move students beyond a traditional reading assignment to further engage, understand, and spur independent literacy practices beyond the classroom. Students read, applying their own lens to understanding the text, then through traditional discussion in Socratic seminars, students encountered the understandings of others and explored the situatedness of their understandings within a more complex timeline of cultural events. Then, they moved their understandings into a technology-based cooperative discussion and the creation of cultural artifacts representing their understandings onto a responsive global platform. In these ways, literacy was demonstrated as a communicative social practice rather than an act of isolation. Classrooms that are home to rich discussion married to challenging academic discourse and instruction support students in internalizing the knowledge and skills to independently carry out literacy tasks (Applebee, Langer, Nystrand, & Gamoran, 2003).

Intertwining meaning and overlapping methods, such as Socratic seminars and multimedia connections, allow students to develop more meaningful, deeper connections to the text. Social interaction and discourse in the classroom create a context which allows for the psychological and semantic growth necessary to support comprehension (Applebee et al., 2003). Incorporating popular culture into the classroom engages students as they encounter and create a variety of multimedia projects bringing the contemporary world into the classroom and fostering connections between reading, technology, and their lived experience. By participating in Socratic seminars, creating hashtags for social media, and relating the book to historical events, music or songs, the students were able to deepen their understanding.

In *Literature as Exploration*, Rosenblatt espoused a philosophy that outlined the relationship between text and the background information a student brings to that text (Rosenblatt, 1938). She argued that social, psychological, and cultural experiences would create differing meaning using the same text. Rosenblatt believes that reading a text is a unique experience and meaning is derived in the transaction between a text and the well of personal experience. "In the interplay between the book and the personality, failures in sensitivity, misinterpretations, and distorted reactions often have their roots in such influences. The effort to help the student arrive at a more balanced and lucid sense of the work thus involves the parallel effort to help him understand and evaluate his personal emphases" (Rosenblatt, 1995).

One meaning does not exist within a text to be mined out like ore by a reader. Rosenblatt valued all of the meanings derived, but held to Dewey's positions of warranted assertions, to justify her position that some meanings were more appropriately aligned with the text than others. She further asserts that students should be given an opportunity to encounter texts that offer them a means to connect, either socially, culturally, emotionally, or otherwise. Then through the process of reading, they can "live through" the characters' lives and operate in a world outside their own, offering them new experiences to fold into their knowledge (assimilation, accommodation, equilibrium). In her view, the aesthetic response to reading encourages students to live through the experience, allowing them to expand their knowledge and understanding of experiences that they may never encounter in their own day-to-day interactions. In this way, students will have a wider view of society, problem-solving, social responsibility, and duties as citizens in the decision-making process.

In Rosenblatt's view, the reason for education is to produce students who are prepared to become citizens active in the decision-making process of moving our country into the future. She was one of the initial theorists to take a social justice stance asserting that, as educators, we have a responsibility to use student responses to literature to help them realize their potential as citizens of a democratic society, to recognize wrongs that are done to people, and to consider methods for righting those wrongs. She also argued for the training of teachers in fields of social sciences to be prepared to better address the psychological and social implications of human nature that are confronted in good literature.

Meaning is not solely in a text but in the individual, who is deciphering the text (Considine, Horton, & Moorman, 2009; Rosenblatt, 1994). Borsheim, Merritt and Reed (2008), stated that a multiliteracy approach promotes a constructivist philosophy of learning in which students gain comprehension through authentic experiences. In this approach, teachers and students play an active role in constructing knowledge, using language as a tool for communication and meaning making (Vygotsky, 1978). Vygotsky's theory promotes learning contexts in which students play an active role in learning. Roles of the teacher and student are therefore shifted, as a teacher should collaborate with his or her students in order to help facilitate meaning construction in students. Learning, therefore, becomes a reciprocal experience for the students and teacher. This reciprocal learning was evidenced in the Socratic seminars and the ways in which new meaning was created throughout the reading of the book based on the knowledge and ideas of the students. They built off of each other, constructing new meaning together.

LAYERED MEANING IN CHARACTER AND THEME

The university students demonstrated a deep understanding of the The Hate U Give and the complexities of the characters and themes. Throughout the book, complex themes and characters are introduced. In many cases, characters in the book show many different sides of themselves, fighting against their inner identities and histories. Characters such as Iesha caught the attention of the students. At first, Iesha continually demonstrated poor judgement and moral character, but throughout the book the students began to see her differently, not judging her decisions and actions so harshly. Students began to connect impact of systemic racism they have been learning about with Iesha's present levels of performance and understanding. Students began to realize that many of the characters had complex identities and were all still learning and growing – or not. One student posed the question, "What different sides of characters do we get to see in this section?" This question sparked one of the most interesting discussions especially about the characters Chris and Hailey. The students were able to see that although both characters possessed white privilege, Chris was trying to understand both his privilege and the perspective of Starr, while Hailey was not. The students were so frustrated with Hailey they began creating anti-Hailey hashtags throughout the Socratic seminars. Two favorite hashtags were #blockdeletereportHailey and #Haileyiscanceled.

The students demonstrated more complex thinking and a deeper understanding of the characters and themes in the books through the discussion and background knowledge cultivated during the updated Socractic seminars. One student connected the tension that all of the characters have been feeling through this quote: "I love the scenes at Seven's birthday party. I think it's the perfect representation of what the book has been building towards. Starr has all the parts of her world in one place, and it's working out okay. I love how we can see Starr grow to learn how to reconcile all the different parts of who she is."

CLASSROOM ADAPTATIONS

University professors or high school teachers who are looking to create space for transliteracy in their classrooms could start by evaluating their own day to day literacy practices, carefully paying attention to practices that require movement across platforms. One effective prompt for both the professor and the university students is to do a one-week log of all literacy practices used throughout the day. People's day-to-day literacy practices are wide, varied, and important. Daily literacy practices can could include art, literacy for a civic duty, participation in community life, structured and unstructured play, formal schooling, or school like learning practices (Purcell-Gates, Perry & Briseño, 2011).

For example, here is a sample morning routine and its intersection with transliteracy.

A young mother quickly checks the refrigerator for the school lunch menu and decides to pack a lunch for her child since he is allergic to the dairy quesadillas being served. She quickly checks Pinterest for the dairy free lunch ideas she pinned yesterday and decides to make turkey wraps. As she adds some sauce to the wraps, she double checks the label to make sure there is no dairy included. Before the mother zips up the lunch box, she writes a love note on a napkin to tuck inside the lunchbox. A text comes in from the neighbor saying her dog is running in the front yard again. In the interest of time she replies with a quick rolling eye emoji text and rushes out before the dog runs into the street. After corralling the dog, she loads up everyone for school. She plugs her first destination into Google Maps to check the traffic and estimated time to arrival. Before she gets everyone in the car, she opens up the Starbucks app and places her order for pick up.

Have all students bring their log to class to discuss and reflect on the similarities and differences among the class in terms of literacy practices. The group may consider the following questions:

How many literacy practices are demonstrated in this simple, but common, morning routine? Which practices were more traditional? Which ones more modern? Did you or your classmates move seamlessly in and out of these practices? Which kind of practices were most prevalent throughout your week?

Additionally, professors and teachers can evaluate their already existing assignments and ask themselves ways to incorporate modern literacy practices into them.

Is there a way to make this assignment multimodal? Can this assignment be adapted to include some of our daily transliteracy practices from our log?

For example, teachers may require students to link a YouTube video through a QR code and paste it into an article normally read for class. *Could traditional article reflections become multimodal as leaving space for student to respond through art, videos, song, or social media? Could students blog about field experiences or post to Flipgrid throughout the week about stories from the field?* Teachers may also consider bringing the assignments to the students, asking for their help on ways to modernize and engage in new literacies. The possibilities are endless.

The assignments presented in this chapter can easily be adapted for different age groups. One fifth grade class adapted the instagram assignment into shared group work while reading the book *Wild Robot* by Peter Brown. The students used Legos to build a robot model and attached a QR code of a video of a real robot. As a group, the students wrote a review of the book that included a summary without spoilers. The students then curated a photo similar to the Instagram photos of the university students. This photo included the book Wild Robot, the Lego robot, and the QR code. The phone was printed to hang on the wall.

The main idea behind transliteracy is for students to fluidly move across a range of technologies, context, and media. This idea can also be adapted into other subject areas like mathematics. For example, students might work with traditional tools such as manipulatives and mathematical equations, while also accessing online coding platforms and blogging about their trials and errors in the process. In science, students might work in nature, logging their observations in a writer's notebook, and then accessing a live stream of a zoo or a documentary clip from YouTube and then post and discuss their thoughts on Flipgrid. Transliteracy work can be done at any age and subject area.

CONCLUSION

This chapter detailed the many ways this assignment can be used and adapted to encourage students to move in and out of various media to create deeper meaning and become a more effective and motivated learner in the 21st century. The example provides teachers with a framework for creating time and space for students as they make meaning within and beyond traditional forms of literacy. The students in this example are seen using language/orality (discussions, linguistics/word history, Socratic seminars); writing and reading (reflections, visual art, curating an Instagram photograph); and social media (photograph, Instagram comments, hashtags, captions, emojis, Flipgrid). By developing transliteracy skills, students are equipped to participate in global conversations, while also having the tools to contribute to in-person classroom discussions. Not only will students be able to communicate with multiple mediums, but they will develop the ability to move seamlessly through various learning and collaboration methods. Having fluency in a wide array of sharing and communication methods provides students with ownership over their reading experience, deepening their connection to the text. The chapter also addressed the importance of incorporating these practices in the college classroom for preservice teachers.

REFERENCES

Applebee, A., Langer, J., Nystrand, M., & Gamoran, A. (2003). Discussion-based approaches to developing understanding: Classroom instruction and student performance in middle and high school English. *American Educational Research Journal, 40*(3), 685–730. doi:10.3102/00028312040003685

Bazalgette, C., & Buckingham, D. (2013). Literacy, media and multimodality: A critical response. *Literacy, 47*(2), 95–102. doi:10.1111/j.1741-4369.2012.00666.x

Beck, P. (2014). Multigenre text set integration: Motivating reluctant readers through successful experiences with text. *Journal of Reading Education, 40*, 12–19.

Bezemer, J., & Kress, G. (2008). Writing in multimodal texts. *Written Communication, 25*(2), 166–195. doi:10.1177/0741088307313177

Borsheim, C., Merritt, K., & Reed, D. (2008). Beyond technology for technology's sake: Advancing multiliteracies in the twenty-first century. *The Clearing House: A Journal of Educational Strategies, Issues and Ideas, 82*(2), 87–90. doi:10.3200/TCHS.82.2.87-90

Cervetti, G. N., Wright, T. S., & Hwang, H. (2016). Conceptual coherence, comprehension, and vocabulary acquisition: A knowledge effect? *Reading and Writing, 29*(4), 761–779. doi:10.100711145-016-9628-x

Considine, D., Horton, J., & Moorman, G. (2009). Teaching and reaching the millennial generation through media literacy. *Journal of Adolescent & Adult Literacy, 52*(6), 471–481. doi:10.1598/JAAL.52.6.2

Davis-Duerr, J. (2015). Planning on preservice teachers' affective domains of reading. *Journal of Reading Education, 40*(3), 17–22.

Faigley, L., Kress, G., & van Leeuwen, T. (2002). Multimodal discourse: The modes and media of contemporary communication. *College Composition and Communication, 54*(2), 318. doi:10.2307/1512155

Fierberg, R. (2018). *Listen to Lin-Manuel Miranda and Ben Platt perform a Hamilton and Dear Evan Hansen mashup*. Retrieved from http://www.playbill.com/article/listen-to-lin-manuel-miranda-and-ben-platt-perform-a-hamilton-and-dear-evan-hansen-mashup

Fisher, D., & Frey, N. (2018). Raise reading volume through access, choice, discussion, and book talks. *The Reading Teacher, 72*(1), 89–97. doi:10.1002/trtr.1691

Gallagher, K. (2015). *In the best interest of students: Staying true to what works in the ELA classroom*. Portland, ME: Stenhouse.

History, C. (2013, May 29). *Black Panther Party - Ten point program* [Video File]. Retrieved from www.youtube.com/watch?v=T7ChnjalY-0

Holden, J., & Schmit, J. S. (2002). *Inquiry and the literary text: Constructing discussions in the English classroom. In Classroom Practices in Teaching English*. National Council of Teachers of English.

Jail, K. C. (2018). Dallas cop who killed Botham Jean in his apartment has been indicted on murder. *The Cut*. Retrieved from https://www.thecut.com/2018/09/dallas-police-shooting- botham-jean.html

Karabay, A., Kuşdemir Kayıran, B., & Işık, D. (2015). The investigation of pre-service teachers' perceptions about critical reading self-efficacy. *Eurasian Journal of Educational Research, 59*, 227–246.

Kress, G., & Selander, S. (2012). Multimodal design, learning and cultures of recognition. *Internet and Higher Education, 15*(4), 265–268. doi:10.1016/j.iheduc.2011.12.003

Lamb, A. (2018). Digital media Part 2: Energize teen readers with book-film adaptations. *INFOTECH, 46*, 52–57.

Lenters, K. (2016). Riding the lines and overwriting in the margins: Affect and multimodal literacy practices. *Journal of Literacy Research, 48*(3), 280–316. doi:10.1177/1086296X16658982

Leu, D., Kinzer, C., Coiro, J., Castek, J., & Henry, L. (2013). New literacies: A dual-level theory of the changing nature of literacy, instruction, and assessment. In D. E. Alvermann, R. B. Ruddell, & N. J. Unrau (Eds.), *Theoretical models and processes of reading* (pp. 1150–1181). Newark, DE: International Reading Association. doi:10.1598/0710.42

Mills, K. (2010). Shrek meets Vygotsky: Rethinking adolescents' multimodal literacy practices in schools. *Journal of Adolescent & Adult Literacy, 54*(1), 35–45. doi:10.1598/JAAL.54.1.4

Miranda, L., & Platt, B. (2018). *Found/Tonight* [CD]. Warner/Chappell Music, Inc.

Parten Gerla, J. (2010). Madelyn, a preservice teacher becomes a writer. *Southeastern Teacher Education Journal, 3*(1), 131–140.

Purcell-Gates, V., Perry, K., & Briseño, A. (2011). Analyzing literacy practice: Grounded theory to model. *Research in the Teaching of English, 45*(4), 439–458.

Roa, K., & Skouge, J. (2015). Using multimedia technologies to support culturally and linguistically diverse learners and young children with disabilities. In K. L. Heider & M. R. Renck (Eds.), *Educating the young child* (pp. 101–115). Boston, MA: Pearson.

Rosenblatt, L. M. (1994). The transactional theory of reading and writing. In R. B. Ruddell, M. R. Ruddell, & H. Singer (Eds.), *Theoretical models and processes of reading* (pp. 1057–1092). Newark, DE: International Reading Association.

Rowsell, J. & Walsh, M. (2011). Rethinking literacy education in new times: multimodality, multiliteracies, & new literacies. *Brock Education: A Journal of Educational Research and Practice, 21*. doi:10.26522/brocked.v21i1.236

Shakur, T. (1999). *The rose that grew from concrete*. New York: Pocket Books.

Sukovic, S. (2017). *Transliteracy in complex information environments*. Cambridge, MA: Chandos Publishing.

Thomas, A. (2017). *The Hate U Give*. New York, NY: Balzer & Bray/Harperteen.

Thomas, S., Joseph, C., Laccetti, J., Mason, B., Mills, S., & Pullinger, K. (2007). Transliteracy: Crossing divides. First Monday, 12.

Vasudevan, L., Schultz, K., & Bateman, J. (2010). Rethinking composing in a digital age: Authoring literate identities through multimodal storytelling. *Written Communication, 27*(4), 442–468. doi:10.1177/0741088310378217

Vygotsky, L. S. (1978). *Mind and society: The development of higher mental processes.* Cambridge, MA: Harvard University Press.

Walsh, M., & Walsh, M. (2010). Multimodal literacy: What does it mean for classroom practice? *Australian Journal of Language and Literacy, 33*, 211–239. Retrieved from http://search.proquest.com/docview/1496986878/

WilkinsonL. (2010, December 21). Why transliteracy? *Libraries and Transliteracy.* Retrieved from https://librariesandtransliteracy.wordpress.com/2010/12/20/why-transliteracy/

ADDITIONAL READING

Fisher, D., & Frey, N. (2018). Raise reading volume through access, choice, discussion, and book talks. *The Reading Teacher, 72*(1), 89–97. doi:10.1002/trtr.1691

Gallagher, K. (2015). *In the best interest of students: Staying true to what works in the ELA classroom.* Portland, ME: Stenhouse.

Ivey, G., & Johnston, P. (2017). Emerging adolescence in engaged reading communities. *Language Arts, 94*(3), 159–169.

Riddell, R. (2018). *Project Lit: How a Nashville educator turned a class project into a nationwide movement.* Retrieved from https://www.educationdive.com/new/project-lit-how-a-nashville-educator-turned-class-project-into-a-nationw/518766/

Thomas, A. (2017). *The Hate U Give.* New York, NY: Balzer & Bray/Harperteen.

Thomas, S., Joseph, C., Laccetti, J., Mason, B., Mills, S., & Pullinger, K. (2007). Transliteracy: Crossing divides. *First Monday, 12.*

KEY TERMS AND DEFINITIONS

Flipgrid: A social media platform created for educators to use for students to share video clips.

Hashtag: A hashtag is a word or phrase proceeded by the symbol # that is used on social media platforms to identify, summarize, and categorize topics.

The Hate U Give: A best-selling, award-winning young adult novel by Angie Thomas.

Instagram: A social media platform used to share photographs and captions.

Multimedia: Using more than one form of communication or expression such as art, text, social media, video, and audio formats.

Socratic Seminar: Socratic seminar is a discussion strategy that allows students to ask questions and engage in discussion about a common text.

Text Set: A collection of related texts that centralize on one theme or topic.

Transliteracy: Transliteracy references the ability for students to make meaning across multiple literacy platforms, including traditional learning methods like discussion and writing, as well as new literacy methods such as social media and art.

This research was previously published in Participatory Literacy Practices for P-12 Classrooms in the Digital Age; pages 233-251, copyright year 2020 by Information Science Reference (an imprint of IGI Global).

APPENDIX A

Socratic Seminar Template

Be prepared to speak at the seminar with some or all of the information below.

One thinking question to pose to the group:
One part that impacted you:
Vocabulary words to think about:
Favorite quote from this section:
Hashtag this section:
Multimedia Connection (did this book remind you of another book, song, photograph, current event, movie, etc):
Writing craft you noticed from the author:
During discussion write one thing you had not thought of:

APPENDIX B

Instagram Book Assignment

In this assignment, you will post a photograph and book review to the Instagram account called "not-asinglestory." This assignment is inspired by a combination of the following: Goodreads book reviews, Instagram book accounts (#bookstagram #booklover #bookworm), the #weneeddiversebooks movement, and Chimamanda Adichie's TED talk titled "The Danger of a Single Story."

Table 1. Rubric

Potential Points	Guidelines
20	**Photograph** • The book is included in the picture and the book title is clearly seen. • The photograph contains at least two artifacts, items, or scenery that is representative of the story. • The photograph includes an important quote from the book. • The photograph contains imagery or explicit depiction of themes representative of the story.
30	**Instagram Caption** When writing your caption consider the following: • What was the author's purpose in writing the book? Did the author accomplish that purpose? • Who is the target audience for the book? • What do you think is the book's greatest value? What makes it special or worthwhile? • Whose voice is heard in this book? Is anyone's voice silenced? • Is the book interesting? Does it hold your attention? • Would it be a useful addition to a school or public library? • How well does the reader relate to the subject? • Is it easy to understand the ideas? • Overall, did you like the book? Would you recommend it to a friend? • Are there any appropriate emojis that might help express your feelings about this book?
10	**Instagram Caption Question** • Pose a question related to themes or characters in the book. This question should serve as a catalyst for future comments and discussion from your classmates.
10	**Hashtag** • Create two hashtags that are representative of the book overall and would be meaningful to someone who read the book. Hashtags can relate to theme, characters, "inside jokes," etc. • Place the hashtag #notasinglestory at the end of your post.
15	**Comment** • Comment on two other pictures on the account. Comments should go beyond "great photo" and address the content in the caption and the question posed by the reader.
10	**Approval and Posting** • Get approval of your picture and caption by your teacher. • Once the teacher has approved, the Instagram posting can be made on your own Instagram account or class Instagram and tag @notasinglestory • If Instagram is not an option, print the photos and hang them on the wall with sticky notes and pens for comments
5	**Length and Mechanics** • Instagram captions can include up to 2,200 characters, including emoji, and up to 30 hashtags. Choose your words thoughtfully when considering the caption. Conventional grammar is not required as long as the message and intention of the post are clear to the reader.

Chapter 69

An Investigation of Social Networking Sites for Language Learning and the User Experience:
The Case of Busuu and Spanish as a Foreign Language

Miguel Saona-Vallejos
https://orcid.org/0000-0002-1980-6042
University of Central Lancashire, UK

Michael Thomas
https://orcid.org/0000-0001-6451-4439
University of Central Lancashire, UK

ABSTRACT

This chapter investigates the user experience of the language learning platform Busuu as a tool for learning Spanish as a Foreign Language (SFL). Social constructionism has been highlighted by previous research as the theory on which Busuu is based, however, Álvarez concluded that Busuu constitutes an ecological system of nested semiotic spaces where pedagogical elements and principles from different theories of language learning interweave in complementary ways. Following a review of existing research, the chapter analyses data arising from a study involving a mixed group of university students who used the premium version of Busuu for four weeks. Data were collected via pre- and post-tests, a user experience questionnaire, and individual interviews, and were analysed using descriptive statistics and thematic analysis. Findings suggest that Busuu did not fully satisfy the requirements of a social network in terms of ease of participation, communication, and collaboration. Further research is required to explore the implications of usability testing for the design of effective SNSLL.

DOI: 10.4018/978-1-6684-7123-4.ch069

INTRODUCTION

Since the emergence of Web 2.0 applications strategies used by language learners to interact on social networking sites (SNS) have been a topic of growing interest to researchers in second language acquisition (SLA) and teacher education (Lamy & Zourou, 2013; Liu et al., 2015). Lee (2006), for example, argued that the frequency with which language learners use SNS may have a positive impact on their oral proficiency, vocabulary acquisition and syntactic complexity. Moreover, Blattner and Lomicka (2012) suggested that the social interaction that takes place in such environments may help students to develop their pragmatic competence. Lin, Warschauer and Blake (2016) inferred that dedicated social networking sites for language learning (SNSLL), rather than generic social networks such as Facebook, may enable language learners to have their first experience of using their L2 in meaningful conversations with others. While this potential seems promising, several challenges have also been identified in the research, including as Jones (2001) has pointed out, that it may be difficult for SNSLL platforms to engage language learners over a long period of time without teachers or peers to drive the process. Moreover, because the focus is often on social interaction, traditional areas that require in-depth knowledge, such as grammar instruction or pronunciation, may be under-represented in SNSLL course materials.

Founded in 2008 as a social network for language learning, Busuu defines itself as "the world's largest social network for language learning, providing courses in 12 different languages on web and mobile to more than 90 million learners worldwide" (https://www.busuu.com). Busuu promotes itself as a platform that enables learners to train their language skills through self-paced learning units following the Common Framework of Reference (CEFR) from A1 to B2 levels. In 2016, Busuu migrated to a mobile compatible platform and began to attract more research studies (Álvarez, 2016; Vesselinov & Grego, 2016), though its functionality remained quite limited in that language learners could only create a profile, upload content and receive feedback. While Busuu has a significant base of language users, it has attracted limited research to date. This chapter is significant in that it provides an extensive review of the growing body of research on social networks for language learning in order to contextualise Busuu, before investigating original data arising from an empirical study of the SNSLL through the lens of user-experience in order to explore the pedagogical principles underpinning the network's design.

BACKGROUND

In their history of SNS, boyd and Ellison (2008) explained that since 1997, at least 45 SNSs had been created. While some general SNS at that time were used by language learners to practise foreign languages, founded in 2007, Livemocha is commonly regarded as the first dedicated SNSLL of its kind (Brick, 2011a, 2013). This was later followed by Babbel in the same year, Busuu in 2008, and Wespeke in 2010. Table 1 lists social media that are commonly identified to be SNS.

While all of the social media listed in Table 1 are generally considered to be SNSLL, particularly Duolingo and Memrise, none of them offers the *sine qua non* pre-requisite of a social network, namely, the opportunity for learners to engage in full social interaction as defined by Boyd and Ellison (2008).

As Table 2 shows, there were already approximately five different language exchange sites before the creation of Livemocha in 2007. These SNSLL were based on the principle of key-palling (e.g., the use of email to conduct pen-friending relationships) as the concept of an online social network did not exist at the time. The most important SNSLL at the time, SharedTalk, does not exist anymore and the other four (i.e., Interpals, Mixxer, My Language Exchange, Polyglot Club) have not evolved to become recognisable SNSLL.

Table 1. List of commonly identified SNSLL

No.	Website	Foundation	Skills	Levels	Model	Languages	Features
1	Conversation Exchange	2005	R/W/L/S	ND	Free	ND	- F2F exchange - Text, voice, video chat - Conversation topics - Foreign characters
2	Duolingo	2009	R/W/L/S	A1-B1	Free	33	- Written lessons - Gamified skill tree - Experience Points - Timed practice - Rewards - Class Platform - Not SNSLL
3	Lernu	2002	R/W/L/S	ND	Free	39	- Multilingual website - Text chat
4	Lingueo	2007	R/W/L/S	ND	Premium	ND	- Foreign language classes: kids, business, travel & leisure, specific subjects, tests - More a 1.2.1 teachers' platform than an SNSLL
5	Memrise	2010	R/W/L	ND	Freemium	200+	- Learn languages, other academic subjects and Trivia and Pop culture - Based on flashcards - Learners can be followed but no direct interaction with them
6	uTalk	1992	R/W/L/S	A1-B2 (CEFR)	Freemium	140+	- Extensive vocabulary - Measure achievements - Speaking games - Native voices - Educational platform - No chat

Table 2. Language communities: basic data and features

N	Community	Foundation	Skills	Levels	Model	Languages	Features	Users
1	Babbel	2007	R/W/L/S	A1-B2	Freemium	13	- Courses - Text chat - Message boards - Review manager -Certificates	20M
2	bili	2016	R/W/L/S	ND	Premium	ND	- Exchange - Parents' login - Teacher profile	ND
3	Busuu	2008	R/W/L/S	A1-B2	Freemium	12	- Level tests - Lessons - Feedback - Flashcards - Courses - 3 versions	70M
4	English Café	2008 – 04/2012	R/W/L/S	ND	Freemium	1	- Video and audio - Open forums - Create groups	ND

continues on following page

Table 2. Continued

N	Community	Foundation	Skills	Levels	Model	Languages	Features	Users
5	English, baby!	2008	R/W/L/S	ND	Free	1	- Text chat - Free lessons, TV - Forums, Quizzes - User comments	2M
6	HelloLingo	2015	R/W/L/S	ND	Free	ND	- Text chat - Mobile app - Language games	ND
7	HelloTalk	2012	R/W/L/S	ND	Free	100+	- Voice to text - Text to voice - Transliteration - Camera share - Doodle share - Translation - Counter - Free calls - Native chat - Save chat	8M
8	HiNative	2014	R/W/L/S	ND	Free	ND	- Q&A Platform - Pre-established forms - A Lang-8 subsidiary	ND
9	Interpals	1998	R/W	ND	Free	150+	- Text chat - Forums - Travel 'buddies'	3.8M
10	iTalki	2007	R/W/L/S	ND	Freemium	100+	- Teachers site - Discussion boards - Community blog - Notebook - No in-site chat - Mobile app	3M
11	Lang-8	2007	Writing	ND	Freemium	90	- Writing exchange	750K
12	Langademy	2016	R/W/L/S	ND	Freemium	ND	- Exchange time	ND
13	Language for exchange	2009	R/W/L/S	ND	Freemium	115	- Directory of schools - Travel abroad - Open forum -Text/audio/video chat	100K
14	LetsPal	2016	R/W	ND	Freemium?	ND	- Text chat - Blogs, photos	ND
15	LingQ	2007	R/W/L/S	ND	Freemium?	14	- Language library - Words tracking	600K
16	Livemocha	2007 – 04/2016 (Closed by Rosetta Stone)	R/W/L/S	A1-C1	Freemium	38	- Synchronous chat - Lessons - Virtual keyboard - Reward system - Weekly reports	18M
17	Mixxer (Dickinson University)	2005	R/W/L/S	ND	Free	9	- Skype - Group exchanges - Lessons - Blog - Writing correction	ND
18	MyLanguage Exchange	2000 Oct	R/W/L/S	ND	Free	115	- Text chat - Translation - Homestay - Monitored pals - Notepad - Library - Bulletin board - Multi-dictionary -Lesson plan - Timer	3M

continues on following page

Table 2. Continued

N	Community	Foundation	Skills	Levels	Model	Languages	Features	Users
19	Palabea	2007 – 2013	R/W/L/S	ND	Freemium	ND	- Video/voice chat - Marketplace - Forums - Classrooms	ND
20	Pen4Pals	ND	R/W	ND	Free	ND	- Group chats - Open chat - Writing correction - Forums - Open participants	25.6K
21	Penpaland	2015	R/W	ND	Free	ND	- Language exchange - Online chat - Sharing media - Connect with people	ND
22	PlaySay	2008 –2013	R/W/L/S	ND	Freemium	ND	- iPhone game - Text chat - Pronunciation - Facebook practice	ND
23	Polyglotclub	2003	R/W/L/S	ND	Free	ND	- Exchange pals - Face2face events	745K
24	Smalltalk	2005 – 08/2015	R/W/L/S	ND	Free	ND	- Text chat - Mailbox - Public chat rooms - Language games	1.6M
25	Speaky	2015	R/W/L/S	ND	Free	110+	- Text /audio/video chat - Timed exchange - Calendar to set dates	1M
26	Tandem	2015	R/W/L/S	ND	Freemium	8	- Text /audio/video chat - Mobile app - Tutors	3M
27	Tongueout	2012	R/W/L/S	ND	Free	21	- Text /audio/video chat - Public chatroom - Blogs, Photos - Videos, Events, Polls - Android App	ND
28	Triplingo	2011	R/W/L	ND	Premium	14	- Voice-life Translator -Dictionary -Flashcards - Cultural Guide - Calculator.	ND
29	Verbling	2011	R/W/L/S	ND	Freemium	38	- Video chat - Chat rooms by levels	ND
30	Wespeke (Carnegie Mellon University)	2010	R/W/L/S	ACTFL	Freemium	1	- Lessons - Text /audio/video chat - Say it again/slower - Record your voice - Upload pics in chat - Translator - Notepad	5K institutions

Table 2 indicates that after 2007, several new SNS appeared between 2008 and 2011. Four new SNS appeared between 2015 and 2016 to make a total of 30. These Web 2.0 communities, which were explicitly designed for language learning, were categorised into three types according to a typology outlined by Van Dixhoorn, Loiseau, Mangenot, Potolia and Zourou (2010), namely: structured Web 2.0 language learning communities (with lesson content), language exchange sites (without lessons contents), and marketplaces. As can be seen in Table 3, of the 19 communities currently existing only three (15%),

Babbel, Bili, and Busuu, can be considered structured Web 2.0 language learning communities; 63% are merely language exchange sites; while 22% work primarily as marketplaces.

Table 3. SNSLL fulfilling criteria

Communities	Create profile	Add friends	Search for friends	Create a circle of friends	Communicate with friends	Exchange Feedback	Upload content	Peripheral awareness	%
Babbel	✓	✓	✗	✗	✗	✗	✗	✗	25
Bili	✓	✓	✓	✓	✓	✓	✗	✗	75
Busuu	✓	✗	✗	✗	✗	✓	✓	✗	37.5
English, baby!	✓	✓	✗	✗	✓	✗	✓	✗	50
HelloTalk	✓	✓	✓	✗	✓	✓	✓	✗	80
Interpals	✓	✓	✓	✗	✓	✓	✗	✗	70
Lang-8	✓	✓	✓	✓	✗	✓	✓	✓	90
Language for exchange	✓	✓	✓	✗	✓	✓	✗	✗	70
LingQ	✓	✓	✓	✗	✓	✓	✗	✗	70
LetsPal	✓	✓	✓	✗	✓	✓	✓	✗	80
Mixxer	✓	✓	✗	✗	✓	✓	✗	✗	60
MyLanguage Exchange	✓	✓	✓	✗	✓	✓	✗	✗	70
Penpaland	✓	✓	✓	✓	✓	✓	✓	✗	90
Pen4Pals	✓	✓	✓	✗	✓	✓	✓	✗	80
Polyglotclub	✓	✓	✓	✓	✓	✓	✓	✗	90
Speaky	✓	✓	✓	✓	✓	✓	✓	✗	90
Tandem	✓	✓	✓	✓	✓	✓	✓	✗	90
Tongueout	✓	✓	✓	✗	✓	✓	✓	✗	80
Verbling	✓	✓	✓	✓	✓	✓	✓	✗	90

Note: Adapted from boyd and Ilison (2008) and Duffy (2011).

Recent empirical studies on SNSLL have been grounded in and supported by different theoretical frameworks. Most of that research has been framed along socio-cultural and socio-cognitive lines such as sociocultural theory (Álvarez, 2015, 2016; Brick, 2011a; Chwo et al., 2012; Gruba & Clark, 2013; Harrison & Thomas, 2009); activity theory (Malerba, 2015); socio-constructivism (De Azevedo, 2013; Brick, 2013); and social cognitive theory (Harrison & Thomas, 2009; Orsini-Jones et al., 2013). According to Wang and Vásquez (2012), this is due to the shift in CALL from a structural/cognitive approach to one that is more socio-cognitive, which views the computer as a tool that mediates interactions between language learners. This finding further corresponds to current developments of Web technology which has shifted from linking information to linking people, and aims to create more opportunities for greater interaction, in that interaction-based learning is a cornerstone of many socially- oriented approaches to L2 learning involving SNSLL. Most of the interaction on SNSLL takes place through their network functionality and therefore it is important to differentiate between social *network* sites and social *networking* sites, as they are frequently used interchangeably in the literature. For the purposes of this chapter, a *network* implies communicating with people who are already part of an extended social circle. *Networking* refers to relationship initiation, often between strangers.

Focusing on SNSLL, the research literature can be divided into three broad categories: descriptive studies, quantitative studies and qualitative studies (see Table 4).

Table 4. Language learning related topics in empirical research on SNSLL

Research Focus	Study	Number	%
Autonomy	Andriani (2014); Brick (2012); Clark & Gruba (2010); Jee & Park (2009); Lamy & Mangenot (2013); Liaw (2011); Liu et al. (2013); Liu et al. (2015); Malerba (2011); Malerba (2012); Malerba (2015); Orsini-Jones et al. (2013)	12	40%
Collaboration	Andriani (2014); Brick (2011b); Harrison (2013); Lamy & Mangenot (2013); Liu et al. (2013); Liu et al. (2015); Malerba (2011); Stevenson & Liu (2010)	8	26.7%
Motivation	Brick (2011a); Brick (2013); Jee & Park (2009); Kétyi (2015); Liu et al. (2015); Malerba (2011); Malerba (2012); Orsini-Jones et al. (2013)	8	26.7%
Feedback	Andriani (2014); Brick (2011a); Brick (2012); Bündgens-Kosten (2011); De Azevedo (2013); Gruba & Clark (2013); Orsini-Jones et al. (2013)	7	23.3%
Interaction & discourse	Álvarez (2015); Gruba & Clark (2013); Jee & Park (2009); Liu et al. (2015); Malerba (2011); Malerba (2012); Zourou & Lamy (2013)	7	23.3%
Cultural exchange	Álvarez (2015); Harrison & Thomas (2009); Liu et al. (2015); Loiseau, Potolia, & Zourou (2011); Pettes Guikema (2013); Zourou & Loiseau (2013)	6	20%
Informal learning	Brick (2012); Chwo et al. (2012); Kétyi (2015); Lloyd (2012); Malerba (2011); Zourou & Lamy (2013)	6	20%
Community learning	Brick (2013); Bündgens-Kosten (2011); Jee & Park (2009); Liu et al. (2015); Pettes Guikema (2013)	5	16.7%
Exchange (Native / Non-native)	Brick (2011a); Brick (2012); Harrison & Thomas (2009); Jee & Park (2009); Pettes Guikema (2013)	5	16.7%
Formal learning	Brick (2011a); Brick (2012); Bündgens-Kosten (2011); Malerba (2011); Zourou & Lamy (2013)	5	16.7%
Identity	Álvarez (2015); Álvarez (2016); Harrison & Thomas (2009); Malerba (2011); Malerba (2012)	5	16.7%
Peers' assistance / scaffolding	Brick (2011a); Bündgens-Kosten (2011); Malerba (2011); Malerba (2012); Liu et al. (2015)	5	16.7%
Social-constructivist learning	Clark & Gruba (2010); De Azevedo (2013); Harrison (2013); Lloyd (2012); Malerba (2011)	5	16.7%
Authentic materials	Brick (2011a); Brick (2011b); Bündgens-Kosten (2011); Gruba & Clark (2013)	4	13.3%
Engagement	Bündgens-Kosten (2011); Malerba (2012); Liu et al. (2015); Pettes Guikema (2013)	4	13.3%
Negotiation of meaning	Harrison & Thomas (2009); Jee & Park (2009); Malerba (2011); Pettes Guikema (2013)	4	13.3%
Personal Learning Environment (PLE)	Brick (2011a); Brick (2012); Harrison & Thomas (2009); Malerba (2011)	4	13.3%

continues on following page

Table 4. Continued

Research Focus	Study	Number	%
Real life contexts	Clark & Gruba (2010); Liaw (2011); Malerba (2011); Stevenson & Liu (2010)	4	13.3%
Virtual Learning Environment (VLE)	Brick (2011b); De Azevedo (2013); Harrison & Thomas (2009); Malerba (2011); Stevenson & Liu (2010)	4	13.3%
Active learning	Harrison (2013); Malerba (2011); Stevenson & Liu (2010)	3	10%
Basic skills	Andriani (2014); Brick (2011a); Bündgens-Kosten (2011)	3	10%
Communicative experience	Andriani (2014); Brick (2011a); Liaw (2011)	3	10%
Ecology of languages	Álvarez (2015); Álvarez (2016); Clark & Gruba (2010)	3	10%
Effective learning	Brick (2011a); De Azevedo (2013); Kétyi (2015)	3	10%
Grammar exercises	Brick (2011a); Jee & Park (2009); Orsini-Jones et al. (2013)	3	10%
Impression management	Harrison (2013); Harrison & Thomas (2009); Liaw (2011)	3	10%
Learner generated content	Malerba (2011); Loiseau, Potolia, & Zourou (2011); Stevenson & Liu (2010)	3	10%
Tandem learning	Brick (2011b); De Azevedo (2013); Lloyd (2012)	3	10%
TOTAL STUDIES		30	100%

Note: For space reasons, themes that were developed by one or two studies are not included in this table.

A significant list of topics arises from our review of the research on SNSLL, the most significant being autonomy, collaboration and motivation. Descriptive research, primarily, tends to evaluate the main pedagogical features of the SNSLL studied and the role of the learners within the community.

From Table 5 it is evident that Livemocha was the first SNSLL created in the era of Web 2.0, and as a result, it has attracted the most research to date (42.3%). Busuu achieved second place (19.2%), while others such as Lang-8 and Wespeke have attracted fewer studies (3.8%).

Quantitative studies have primarily focused on developing the pedagogical design of SNS communities according to learners' needs. Qualitative studies, on the other hand, frequently combine mixed methods but can be considered mainly interpretive as they focus on topics such as students' perceptions of online communities for L2 learning; affordances and constraints of the platform in relation to pedagogical issues; the role played by learner autonomy; and the thematic analysis of learners' interactive discourse.

Table 6 shows that 30.4% of the empirical research in journals originated in conferences; 17.3% has been published in the Computer-Assisted Language Instruction Consortium (CALICO) journal, and at least 13% have been found on internet repositories.

Table 7 shows the target languages in empirical research on the subject. English (23.3%) is still the language mostly studied when doing research on SNSLL; followed by Spanish (16.7%), which has the same amount as other studies involving multiple languages (16.7%); while French and German share 10% of the research outputs each; Italian, Portuguese and Korean share 6.7% each; and Japanese, Dutch and Russian 3.3% each. Table 7 also shows that at least half of the researchers (50%) prefer to allow the participants of their studies to choose the language they want to practise in SNSLL without indicating the language they have finally focused on.

Table 8 shows the theoretical frameworks of sociocultural theory, socio-constructivism, and Vygotsky's (1978) Zone of Proximal Development as the most cited when researching SNSLL. At least 20% of other research papers in the field do not mention any theoretical framework at all.

Table 5. SNSLL investigated in empirical research

SNSLL	Research	Number	%
Livemocha	Andriani (2014); Brick (2011a); Brick (2011b); Chwo et al. (2012); Clark & Gruba (2010); De Azevedo (2013); Harrison (2013); Harrison & Thomas (2009); Jee & Park (2009); Lloyd (2012); Zourou & Loiseau (2013)	11	42.3%
Livemocha and others	Gruba & Clark (2013); Liu et al. (2013); Loiseau, Potolia, & Zourou (2011); Malerba (2012); Malerba (2015); Orsini-Jones et al. (2013); Stevenson & Liu (2010)	7	26.9%
Busuu and others	Gruba & Clark (2013); Liu et al. (2013); Loiseau, Potolia, & Zourou (2011); Malerba (2012); Malerba (2015); Orsini-Jones et al. (2013)	6	23%
Busuu	Álvarez (2015); Álvarez (2016); Brick (2012); Brick (2013); Kétyi (2015)	5	19.2%
Generic	Lamy & Mangenot (2013); Malerba (2011); Zourou & Lamy (2013)	3	11.5%
Babbel and others	Gruba & Clark (2013); Loiseau, Potolia, & Zourou (2011); Stevenson & Liu (2010)	3	11.5%
English café and others	Liu et al. (2013)	1	3.8%
Italki and others	Liu et al. (2015)	1	3.8%
Lang-8	Bündgens-Kosten (2011)	1	3.8%
Lang-8 and others	Liu et al. (2015)	1	3.8%
LingQ and others	Liu et al. (2015)	1	3.8%
Palabea and others	Stevenson & Liu (2010)	1	3.8%
Polyglotclub and others	Liu et al. (2015)	1	3.8%
Wespeke	Pettes Guikema (2013)	1	3.8%
Not specified	Orsini-Jones et al. (2013)	1	3.8%
TOTAL NUMBER OF SNSLL		**26**	**100%**

Table 9 refers to methodological approaches used in empirical research about SNSLL. It shows that at least 40% of the research has been qualitative in orientation and based on case studies. Only 10% were quantitative studies, of which 6.7% were descriptive, and 3.3%, experimental. Approximately 26.7% followed a mixed-methods approach.

The participants in these studies involved mostly university students (43.3%), while 20% focused on teachers' opinions and 13.3% included the general public. 26.7% of these studies involved no participants. Concerning the duration of the studies, almost half (46.7%) did not define the period of the investigation. 23.3% lasted for at least three months, while 13.3% lasted between one and three months, and only 6.7% lasted for less than a month.

CRITICISMS OF SOCIAL NETWORKING SITES FOR LEARNING LANGUAGES

A frequent criticism of SNSLL relates to learning materials in that their one-size-fits-all approach has led to poor quality (Brick 2011a; Harrison, 2013; Liaw, 2011; Lloyd, 2012). Criticisms have also been levelled at their lack of contextualisation (Álvarez, 2016; Clark & Gruba, 2010; Orsini-Jones et al., 2013), as well as why their language exercises require high levels of memorisation rather than encouraging comprehension and students' critical and analytical skills (Liaw, 2011). Furthermore, SNSLL structured dialogues do not present learners with opportunities for negotiation of meaning, as their speaking exercises do little to help the development of spontaneous communicative skills (Jee & Park, 2009).

Similarly, as it has been argued with respect to some Web 2.0 applications, SNSLL are based primarily on a Web 1.0 pedagogy (Harrison & Thomas, 2009) as the materials revert to behaviourist principles (Álvarez, 2015; Chwo et al., 2012; Clark and Gruba, 2010; Malerba, 2015; Orsini-Jones et al. 2013; Zourou & Loiseau, 2013), leading their users first to motivation, then frustration, and finally demotivation (Brick, 2012; Clark & Gruba, 2010; Orsini-Jones et al., 2013). This cycle is reflected in high levels of user attrition (Lin, et al., 2016; Nielson, 2011; Stevenson & Liu, 2010).

SNSLL also erase the boundaries between peer, co-learner and tutors (Gruba & Clark, 2013), and the value of feedback from peers with low proficiency is questionable (Brick, 2012; Jee & Park, 2009; Liu et al., 2015). Additionally, the artificiality of the sites (Gruba & Clark, 2013) has also been emphasised, in that it could lead to biased or stereotypical representations of culture and identities (Jee & Park, 2009). Other researchers have argued that SNSLL fail to determine clear learning goals (Harrison, 2013); that without a teacher, learners might feel at loss when trying to make sense of the language learned; and thus, experience what Harrison (2013) called "random language learning experiences". Moreover, there may be a tension between the 'formal' aspects of language learning and the 'informal' SNS model (Liaw, 2011), as well as a lack of clear boundaries between their educational and social dimension (Orsini-Jones et al., 2013).

Table 6. Distribution of empirical research about SNSLL in journals

No.	Journal Title	Number	Empirical study
1	Conferences Proceedings	7	Chwo et al. (2012); Clark & Gruba (2010); Kétyi (2015); Loiseau, Potolia, & Zourou (2011); Malerba (2011); Malerba (2012); Malerba (2015)
2	CALICO Journal	4	Jee & Park (2009); Liu et al. (2015); Pettes Guikema (2013); Stevenson & Liu (2010)
3	Internet repositories	3	Andriani (2014); Brick (2013); De Azevedo (2013)
4	ALSIC, Apprentissage des langues est systemes d'information et de Communication.	1	Lloyd (2012)
5	Compass: The Journal of Learning and Teaching at the University of Greenwich	1	Brick (2011a)
6	Computer Assisted Language Learning	1	Álvarez (2015)
7	International Journal of Computer-Assisted Language Learning and Teaching (IJCALLT)	1	Brick (2012)
8	International Journal of Emerging Technologies & Society	1	Harrison & Thomas (2009)
9	International Journal of Virtual and Personal Learning Environments (IJVPLE)	1	Brick, B. (2011b)
10	Language Learning & Technology	1	Liaw (2011)
11	Signo y Pensamiento	1	Álvarez (2016)
12	Studies in Self-Access Learning Journal (SiSAL Journal)	1	Bündgens-Kosten (2011)
	TOTAL	**23**	

Table 7. Target languages investigated in empirical research about SNSLL

Target Language	Study	Number of studies	%
No specified	Brick (2011a); Brick (2011b); Bündgens-Kosten (2011); Harrison (2013); Harrison & Thomas (2009); Lamy & Mangenot (2013); Liaw (2011); Loiseau, Potolia, & Zourou (2011); Malerba (2011); Malerba (2015); Orsini-Jones et al. (2013); Pettes Guikema (2013); Stevenson & Liu (2010); Zourou & Lamy (2013); Zourou & Loiseau (2013)	15	50%
EFL/ESL	Andriani (2013); Chwo et al. (2012); Jee & Park (2009); Kétyi (2015); Liu et al. (2013); Liu et al. (2015); Malerba (2012)	7	23.3%
Spanish/SFL	Gruba & Clark (2013); Kétyi (2015); Malerba (2012); Orsini-Jones et al. (2013); Lloyd (2012)	5	16.7%
Multiple languages	Gruba & Clark (2013); Kétyi (2015); Malerba (2012); Orsini-Jones et al. (2013); Lloyd (2012)	5	16.7%
German	Brick (2012); Brick (2013); Kétyi (2015)	3	10%
French	Álvarez (2015); Álvarez (2016); Lloyd (2012)	3	10%
Italian	Malerba (2012); Kétyi (2015)	2	6.7%
Portuguese	De Azevedo (2013); Lloyd (2012)	2	6.7%
Korean	Clark & Gruba (2010); Gruba & Clark (2013)	2	6.7%
Japanese	Gruba & Clark (2013)	1	3.3%
Dutch	Lloyd (2012)	1	3.3%
Russian	Lloyd (2012)	1	3.3%
TOTAL NUMBER OF STUDIES		**30**	**100%**

In relation to the social aspect of SNSLL, it is evident that it may take time to develop a network of trusted partners and that such groups can only be built upon a trial and error basis (Brick 2011a; Brick, 2012; Harrison & Thomas, 2009). Consequently, without a level of intimacy between users, collaborative learning is likely to encounter difficulties (Gruba & Clark, 2013; Harrison & Thomas, 2009).

In addition to these pedagogical challenges, researchers have also identified a range of other potentially negative aspects of learning online, including cyber-flirting (Brick, 2011b; Harrison, 2013; Lloyd, 2012), Alpha socialisers (Lloyd, 2012), as well as cyberstalking and harassment (Orsini-Jones et al., 2013), which require more sophisticated impression management systems to enable users to set levels of exposure that would put their members at ease about self-disclosure (Cardon, 2008; Liaw, 2011).

In response to these criticisms, Lloyd (2012) pointed out that SNSLL could be considered a convenient, ready-made 'bridge' between classroom-based language learning and the communicative use of L2s students are likely to encounter in real-life situations. Malerba (2011) added that SNS might enhance opportunities for active collaboration in formal L2 learning activities. Likewise, Jee and Park (2009), drew attention to how users need to cultivate learner autonomy, discipline and intrinsic motivation when learning in SNSLL, as there is no pressure brought to bear by the presence of an instructor. Moreover, Álvarez (2016) replied to previous criticisms about the reliance of behaviourist principles and cognitivism, arguing that they also provide other environments where users are required to interact and think of learning as emerging from interaction and co-construction. Then, he also mentioned how SNSLL use other features such as gamification to enliven specific repetitive and monotonous exercises, as well as promote competition through the use of ranking systems and 'friend challenges'. Malerba (2012, 2015) also concluded that formal and informal learning should be compatible and complementary and that the ultimate purpose of learners using SNSLL is to practise language skills, not just socialise (Liu et al., 2013).

Table 8. Theoretical frameworks of the empirical research about SNSLL

Theoretical framework	Study	Number	%
Sociocultural theory	Álvarez (2015); Álvarez (2016); Brick (2011b); Chwo et al. (2012); Gruba & Clark (2013); Harrison & Thomas (2009); Jee & Park (2009); Lamy & Mangenot (2013); Liu et al. (2013); Malerba (2011); Malerba (2012); Malerba (2015); Orsini-Jones et al. (2013); Zourou & Lamy (2013); Zourou & Loiseau (2013)	15	50%
Socio-constructivism	Álvarez (2015); Álvarez (2016); Brick (2012); Clark & Gruba (2010); De Azevedo (2013); Harrison (2013); Harrison & Thomas (2009); Liu et al. (2015); Lloyd (2012); Malerba (2011)	10	33.3%
Vygotsky's ZPD	Gruba & Clark (2013); Harrison (2013); Harrison & Thomas (2009); Jee & Park (2009); Lamy & Mangenot (2013); Malerba (2011); Malerba (2015);	7	23.3%
No identifiable theoretical framework	Andriani (2014); Brick (2011a); Bündgens-Kosten (2011); Kétyi (2015); Liaw (2011); Pettes Guikema (2013)	6	20%
Community of practice	Álvarez (2015); Brick (2013); Zourou & Lamy (2013)	3	10%
Ecologies of learning and teaching	Álvarez (2015); Álvarez (2016); Clark & Gruba (2010);	3	10%
Social interactionism	De Azevedo (2013); Harrison (2013); Harrison & Thomas (2009);	3	10%
More Knowledgeable Other (MKO)	Harrison & Thomas (2009); Jee & Park (2009);	2	6.7%
Social Cognitive Theory	Harrison & Thomas (2009); Orsini-Jones et al. (2013);	2	6.7%
Behaviourism	Álvarez (2016); Loiseau, Potolia, & Zourou (2011)	2	6.7%
Usability Testing	Liu et al. (2015); Stevenson & Liu (2010)	2	6.7%
TOTAL NUMBER OF STUDIES		**30**	**100%**

In their favour, the use of SNSLL is generally considered easy and straightforward, and they work across a range of devices; they can be fun and engaging (Brick, 2013); and they allow learners to personalise learning and increase their autonomy and empowerment (Brick, 2012). Secondly, students may benefit from the authentic language use in a communicative context with native speakers (Brick 2011a; Jee & Park, 2009), something difficult to replicate in the language classroom (Brick, 2011b). Receiving instant feedback from other users, especially more proficient speakers of the target language, is a very important affordance that SNSLL can provide (Brick, 2011; Liu et al., 2013).

In summary, it is clear from the above review that there are still plenty of unanswered questions in the research on SNSLL, such as the proportion of users who have actually completed courses, what kinds of competencies users acquire (e.g., linguistic, pragmatic) and how much proficiency they develop (e.g., basic, intermediate, advanced knowledge), or even more challenging ones, such as the length of time required to achieve proficiency. It is evident that user experience is one of the most significant gaps in the research to date and this will form a central aspect of the research outlined in the next section.

Table 9. Methodological elements used in empirical research about SNSLL

Methodological Issues	Categories		Studies
Research Approach	Qualitative	Case study	Álvarez (2015); Brick (2011b); Brick (2013); Clark & Gruba (2010); De Azevedo (2013); Gruba & Clark (2013); Harrison (2013); Harrison & Thomas (2009); Malerba (2012); Malerba (2015); Orsini-Jones et al. (2013); Zourou & Loiseau (2013)
		Non-case study	Brick (2011a); Bündgens-Kosten (2011); Jee & Park (2009); Lamy & Mangenot (2013); Liaw (2011); Loiseau, Potolia, & Zourou (2011); Zourou & Lamy (2013)
	Quantitative	Descriptive	Brick (2012); Liu et al. (2013)
		Experimental	Kétyi (2015)
	Mixed methods		Andriani (2014); Brick (2012); Chwo et al. (2012); Liu et al. (2013); Liu et al. (2015); Lloyd (2012); Malerba (2011); Stevenson & Liu (2010)
Participants	No participants		Brick (2011a); Bündgens-Kosten (2011); Jee & Park (2009); Lamy & Mangenot (2013); Liaw (2011); Loiseau, Potolia, & Zourou (2011); Zourou & Lamy (2013); Zourou & Loiseau (2013)
	Not specified		Malerba (2011)
	Auto-ethnographic		Álvarez (2015); Clark & Gruba (2010); Gruba & Clark (2013)
	General public		De Azevedo (2013); Malerba (2012); Malerba (2015); Stevenson & Liu (2010)
	University students		Andriani (2014); Brick (2011b); Brick (2012); Brick (2013); Chwo et al. (2012); Harrison (2013); Harrison & Thomas (2009); Kétyi (2015); Liu et al. (2013); Liu et al. (2015); Lloyd (2012); Orsini-Jones et al. (2013); Stevenson & Liu (2010)
	Teachers		Álvarez (2015); Brick (2011a); Brick (2012); Clark & Gruba (2010); Gruba & Clark (2013); Liu et al. (2015)
Sampling	Inexistent. Theoretical Studies		Brick (2011a); Bündgens-Kosten (2011); Jee & Park (2009); Lamy & Mangenot (2013); Liaw (2011); Loiseau, Potolia, & Zourou (2011); Zourou & Lamy (2013); Zourou & Loiseau (2013)
	Not specified		Malerba (2011)
	Convenience sampling		Álvarez (2015); Andriani (2014); Brick (2011b); Brick (2012); Brick (2013); Chwo et al. (2012); Clark & Gruba (2010); Gruba & Clark (2013); Harrison (2013); Harrison & Thomas (2009); Kétyi (2015); Liu et al. (2013); Liu et al. (2015); Lloyd (2012); Orsini-Jones et al. (2013); Stevenson & Liu (2010)
	Purposeful sampling		Malerba (2012)
	Random sampling		De Azevedo (2013); Malerba (2012); Malerba (2015); Stevenson & Liu (2010);
Duration	Not specified		Brick (2011a); Bündgens-Kosten (2011); De Azevedo (2013); Gruba & Clark (2013); Jee & Park (2009); Lamy & Mangenot (2013); Liaw (2011); Liu et al. (2015); Loiseau, Potolia, & Zourou (2011); Malerba (2011); Malerba (2012); Malerba (2015); Zourou & Lamy (2013); Zourou & Loiseau (2013)
	≤ 1 month		Andriani (2014); Stevenson & Liu (2010);
	> 1 month < 3 months		Álvarez (2015); Brick (2013); Kétyi (2015); Lloyd (2012)
	≥ 3 months		Brick (2011b); Brick (2012); Chwo et al. (2012); Harrison (2013); Harrison & Thomas (2009); Liu et al. (2013); Orsini-Jones et al. (2013)

METHODOLOGY

Context and Participants

The participants in this study had access to the premium version of Busuu and, following the platform's own study guide, they were asked to use it daily for a minimum of 10 minutes over four weeks. The participants were not given an upper limit for study time, as the research aimed to reflect the spontaneity that other users of the platform would normally experience. In total, 268 university students from a database of learners who had previously used the online learning platform Rosetta Stone at a language centre in a university in England were invited by email to take part in the study. A total of 14 students agreed to participate, of whom 7 (50%) had a Spanish language proficiency score of CEFR A1 level, 3 (21.42%) were at the A2 level, 2 (14.28%) were at B1, and a further 2 (14.28%) were B2. While the response rate was low, it was nevertheless viable in this context of this mixed methods study. 268 participants are registered with Rosetta Stone, however, the response rate may indicate that a much smaller group of core users interact with the application in a serious way.

Table 10. Demographic data of the participants

Participant	Gender	Age	Nationality	Academic background	Spanish level
pa01	F	49	British	Graduate	B2
pa02	F	20	British	Undergraduate	A2
pa03	F	54	British	Graduate	A1
pa04	F	51	British	Graduate	A2
pa05	F	23	British	Undergraduate	A2
pa06	M	24	British	Undergraduate	A1
pa07	M	47	British	Graduate	B1
pa08	M	23	British	Undergraduate	A2
pa09	M	33	Belarusian	Graduate	A1
pa10	F	18	British	Undergraduate	A2
pa11	F	23	British	Undergraduate	A2
pa12	F	33	Italian	Graduate	B2
pa13	M	44	British	Graduate	B1
pa14	F	21	Greek	Undergraduate	A2

As Table 10 shows, nine were female and five were male and their ages ranged from 18 to 54 years old. Seven participants were graduate students and seven were undergraduates, and nationalities included British (11), Belarusian (1), Italian (1) and Greek (1).

DATA COLLECTION

Based on previous evaluations of other SNSLL (Liu et al., 2015), the data collection tools are presented in Figure 1 and were designed to investigate the principles SNSLL adhere to and observe if there was an evolution in participants' learning performance as a result.

Figure 1. Data collection tools

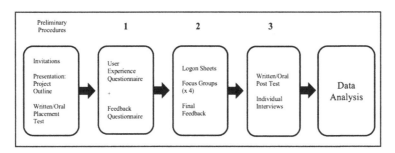

All of the participants were invited to take an online written proficiency test, so their language level could be determined before using the platform. This was important because the results were compared to a post-test that was administered five weeks later, at the end of the main study to measure their learning outcomes. For this purpose, the Rosetta Stone examination, available at the *TellMeMore* campus was used. The participants took the written examination by themselves at home and the results were checked via the Rosetta Stone platform. While enabling the students to take the test at home may be viewed as compromising the efficacy of the test, it is now standard practice for online platforms and teachers and students are increasingly familiar with it. In the context of this research, the added flexibility provided by the online platform was required due to the time constraints placed on the researchers.

For the oral proficiency tests, a 10-item examination was prepared following the Curricular Plan of the *Instituto Cervantes*. An assessment criterion based on the CEFR and Cambridge Assessment Methods was utilised for the moderation of the participants' oral exams by a native Spanish speaking teacher to confirm the reliability of the results.

Based on Liu et al. (2015), participants completed a user experience questionnaire, which consisted of three different types of tasks: exploratory, specific, and open-ended (see Figure 2).

Figure 2. User experience questionnaire

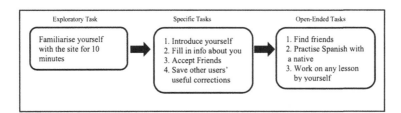

The site feedback questionnaire (based on Liu et al., 2015) was answered immediately after the user experience questionnaire. It offered a Likert scale, anchored in 1 (negative) and 5 (positive), and participants were also allowed to reply with open answers in some cases. The questionnaire was focused on skills, features, and future use and perceptions. The same questionnaire was applied after the participants used Busuu for four weeks to compare if their perceptions of the platform had changed. The participants were asked about the different language skills that could be improved through the use of Busuu to learn Spanish as a Foreign Language (SFL). Additionally, participants were asked if they thought the features present in the platform could help them in their learning of SFL.

The analysis of the data focused on the user experience questionnaire and the pre- and post- website feedback questionnaires. In addition, logon sheets, focus groups, and interviews applied in the research process were also analysed. Based on Brick (2011a), participants were requested to complete a logon sheet online every time they accessed Busuu, immediately after they had finished their practice session. An auto-ethnographic methodology was applied to these documents as participants were asked to describe and interpret their communicative behaviour while connected (Ellis, Adams & Bochner, 2011).

For each session, participants were invited to describe the specific theme practised; what they considered they learnt face-to-face; the means of communication used (message, text chat, voice chat, video chat, any other); a description of what they did and how they did it; mistakes made; what the participants enjoyed or did not enjoy during the session; difficulties during the session; their learning and practising plans for next time; and any specific problems with the platform.

The majority of the participants were able to participate in the four focus groups that took place. The objective of those meetings was to discuss specific topics elicited from the logon sheets as well as the user experience and feedback questionnaires. To further clarify the data from the website feedback questionnaires, logon sheets, and focus groups, participants were invited to participate in semi-structured interviews.

DATA ANALYSIS

The qualitative data collected were analysed through content analysis using NVivo 11. The quantitative data were analysed using IBM-SPSS-Statistics-23.0. As the sample research was small, and there were a limited number of response options, the data obtained were skewed. Hence, it was necessary to apply a nonparametric measure of rank correlation, specifically *Spearman's rho*, which measured the strength of association between two variables.

From the 28 original quantitative variables measured via the pre-site feedback questionnaire, these were doubled to 56 when adding the same number of variables corresponding to the post-site feedback questionnaire. Finally, the ten most relevant features were correlated, always taking pre- and post-written examination variation as a point of reference for all the correlations.

FINDINGS AND DISCUSSION

As the main focus of the analysis of Busuu related to participants' user experience, the five main variables reflecting this process were explored: 1) the features that were found in Busuu; 2) site design; 3) pre- and post-test results; 4) the social aspect of Busuu; and 5) participants' general perception of the Busuu platform.

Features of Busuu

The interview data showed that learning was not participatory in Busuu. On the contrary, while individual learning was encouraged by the platform's layout, it was organised in such a way that was counter to the principles of a community of practice in which learners share goals and are engaged in continuous collaborative and meaningful activity. As Table 11 indicates, the highest division of opinions was related to the usefulness of the learning features found in Busuu. When evaluating the 'friending' feature, 50% of participants agreed that it was not useful in the pre-test, and this increased to 60% in the post-test. Learning was not considered participatory as learners were not able to share their learning processes with other students.

Table 11. Features that can be found in Busuu

Measurable aspect	1		2		3		4		5	
	Pre	Post	Pre	Post	Pre	Post	Pre	Post	Pre	Post
1. Creating a profile	3	2	6	7	5	1	0	0	0	0
2. Friending	7	6	1	0	5	3	1	0	0	1
3. Vocabulary	6	0	2	0	4	2	2	5	0	2
4. Posting	2	2	2	0	3	2	7	5	0	1
5. Receiving feedback	4	0	2	1	3	3	3	4	2	2
6. Giving feedback	6	4	2	2	5	3	1	1	0	0
7. Images	4	2	3	0	4	2	3	4	0	1
8. Corrections and comments	4	2	3	1	3	1	3	3	0	1

Note: the horizontal numbers (1-5) refer to the five-point Likert Scale used in the questionnaire. The scores in each column refer to the raw scores (the numbers of participants choosing these scores in each case). This applies equally to Tables 12 and 14.

Busuu suspended the friending feature when the platform was made compatible with mobile devices, and as a consequence, none of the participants were able to find or accept friends. Therefore, knowledge was individually rather than socially constructed, as there were no peers to create a meaningful learning environment.

Accordingly, as Table 12 shows, the highest number of 'very dissatisfied' users related to the ease of finding contacts with 71.4% of participants. This increased to 85.7% when the dissatisfied replies were also included in the pre-test, and it was also the highest variable for dissatisfaction (70% of participants) for the post-test. Therefore, none of the users expressed being 'satisfied' or 'very satisfied' with this aspect of the site in both cases.

Table 12. Feedback on site design

Measurable aspect	1		2		3		4		5	
	Pre	Post	Pre	Post	Pre	Post	Pre	Post	Pre	Post
1. Ease of finding information	1	0	4	1	5	4	3	4	1	1
2. Quality of learning activities	0	0	2	1	6	3	4	4	2	2
3. Ease of reading texts	0	0	0	1	5	2	4	3	5	4
4. Appearance	0	0	0	1	4	2	5	3	5	4
5. Displaying speed	2	0	1	1	2	1	5	1	4	7
6. Entertainment value	0	0	2	1	6	3	5	4	1	2
7. Overall learning experience	1	0	1	0	6	4	6	5	0	1
8. Instructions for activities	2	0	7	2	3	3	1	3	1	2
9. Ease of moving around	3	1	6	2	3	2	1	3	1	2
10. Ease of finding contacts	10	4	2	3	2	2	0	1	0	0

1= very dissatisfied … 5= very satisfied

PRE- AND POST-TEST RESULTS

Busuu allowed users to create a profile, upload user-generated content, and give and/or receive feedback from peers on spelling, punctuation and grammar. Giving and receiving feedback were also related to learning development as they were shared activities; however, these characteristics meant that only 37.5% of the essential features every SNS should have were evident on the platform, according to the guidelines established by boyd and Ellison (2008) and Duffy (2011). The results in Table 13 show a comparison of the pre- and post-test results and confirms that Busuu favoured individual learning instead of social learning. Only 7.69% of participants, (participant 11) did not experience a positive outcome. 61.54% increased their results by one point. 15.38% increased by two points. 7.69% achieved 2.1 points, and the highest score was obtained by 7.69% of participants, who achieved 3.1 points.

In contrast, the results of the oral tests were not as positive as the increases in scores which were in all cases minimal. None of the participants were able to advance a complete level, and 66.6% remained at the same level of oral competency at the end of the entire process. One reason for this was the lack of native speakers to practise with.

BUSUU'S SOCIAL FEATURES

Participants did not have the opportunity to achieve useful knowledge by engaging in significant language learning activities, as Busuu did not provide opportunities to interact with other learners. When asked for the reasons why participants returned to the site or why they would or would not recommend it, the viewpoints varied between two extremes. One could be synthesised by what participant 14 said: "It is a great app. Although I can only see it as an additional feature. You still need to speak to people and use books". Additionally, participant 3 indicated: "This is supposed to be a social network site to help improve my Spanish. I never found anyone … that I could connect with".

Table 13. Pre- and post-tests results

Participant	Pre-written	Post-written	variation	Pre-oral	Post-oral
pa01	6.6 B2	6.8 B2	0.2	B2	B2
pa02	2.1 A2			A2	
pa03	1.6 A1	4.7 B1	3.1	A1	A1+
pa04	3.5 A2	4.9 B1	1.4	A2	A2+
pa05	2.0 A2	2.4 A2	0.4	A1-	A1
pa06	1.4 A1	2	0.6	A1-	A1-
pa07	5.3 B1	7.4	2.1	B1	B1
pa08	2.1 A2	2.9 A2	0.8	A1	A1
pa09	1.7 A1	2.2 A2	0.5	A1	A1+
pa10	3.9 A2	4.3 B1	0.4	A2+	A2+
pa11	2.7 A2	1.4 A1	-1.3	A1	A1
pa12	7.4 B2	9.2 C1	1.5	B2+	C1
pa13	4.4 B1	5.3 B1	0.9	B1	B1
pa14	3.7 A2	4.3 B1	0.6	A1+	A1+

When asked about what they disliked, 85.71% mentioned the difficulty of navigating the site, and 50% of those specifically identified that it was impossible to contact other language learners. In the post-trial questionnaire, participants were asked about what they liked least. 66.6% of participants mentioned not being able to find "friends"; 55.5% complained about the site not being user-friendly enough; and 33.3% about the grammar contents, which were "not sufficient", "not clear enough", or "difficult to go back to it when needed". Furthermore, 57.14% recommended improvements to its social dimension; participant 12, for example, specifically suggested that "the social aspect of the network should be implemented".

LEARNER PERCEPTIONS OF BUSUU

As learners did not have the opportunity to create a community of learning in Busuu, it was difficult for users to drive their own process of learning. When asked about the likelihood of returning to the site on their own in the pre-test (see Table 14), 71.4% declared they would, while 14.3% had some doubts, and a further 14.3% were neutral. It is important to highlight that none of the participants said that they would not do it; however, this was due to their commitment to take part in the research as some of them explained. In the post-test, the numbers decreased further to 70% who said that they would return, while 30% had some doubts.

Accordingly, when asked if they would recommend Busuu to other users to learn Spanish (Table 14), in the pre-test 42.9% participants expressed neutrality in their opinion. Interestingly, 35.7% said they would not do it, and 21.4% affirmed they would. Figures varied in the post-test: 60% still declared neutrality, 20% said they would not recommend it, and 20% agreed with supporting the site.

Table 14. General perception of the site

Possibilities	1		2		3		4		5	
	Pre	Post	Pre	Post	Pre	Post	Pre	Post	Pre	Post
1. Return to the site	0	0	2	0	2	3	7	6	3	1
2. Recommend the site	2	1	3	1	6	6	2	2	1	0

1= completely disagree … 5= completely agree

DISCUSSION

The study of Busuu outlined above indicates that the SNS satisfies only three of the eight social aspects expected by a social network for language learning (boyd & Ellison, 2008). The language learners in the study were able to create a profile, upload user-generated content, and receive feedback from other users. However, these features were not sufficient to enable them to network and practise the four main skills in Spanish. The backward shift from a social to cognitive approach was evident in the data and goes against the grain of Web 2.0 characteristics, such as ease of participation, communication, information sharing, and collaboration. Therefore, the pre- and post-test results of the study contradicted Vesselinov and Grego's (2016) stance, according to which Busuu users would need an estimated 22.5 hours of study to match the requirements for one college semester of SFL. In this sense, Busuu's language exercises appear to confirm the argument for lack of contextualisation identified by Clark and Gruba (2013) as it relied more on memorisation rather than comprehension (Liaw, 2013) and it was challenging for the learners to find others to learn with (Orsini-Jones et al., 2013).

Moreover, it was evident that there was a tension between the 'formal' aspects of language learning and the 'informal' SNS model (Liaw, 2011) related to Busuu, as well as no boundaries between the educational and social aspects inherent in all SNSLL (Orsini-Jones et al., 2013). Malerba (2012, 2015) focused her research on these aspects and concluded that formal and informal learning should be compatible and complementary and that the ultimate purpose of learners for using SNSLL is to practise language skills (Liu et al., 2013).

Lloyd (2012) had already pointed out this idea when saying that SNSLL could be considered a convenient, ready-made 'bridge' between classroom-based language learning and actual, communicative use of L2s in real-life situations; and Malerba (2011) had added that SNS might enhance opportunities for active collaboration in formal L2 learning activities. So, conversely, some of those very same authors who focused on the negative aspects of SNSLL have also mentioned some favourable options for users.

Arising from the findings on Busuu, course and materials designers may need to consider how the platform can incorporate more authentic language use in a communicative context with native speakers, even in the absence of a teacher's guidance (Brick 2011a; Brick, 2013; Jee & Park, 2009), as this approach may be useful in helping the students to learn foreign languages independently, anywhere and anytime (Andriani, 2014). SNSLL such as Busuu provide learners with the flexibility and variety needed for language learning (Orsini-Jones et al. 2013) but the learners may need more help in creating their own learning environment (Álvarez, 2016; Harrison & Thomas, 2009; Malerba, 2015).

CONCLUSION

Arising from the other studies reviewed above, SNSLL may be useful pedagogical tools for language learners who have different learning preferences (Chwo et al., 2012; Lloyd, 2012). The defining feature of SNSLL is that users with different skills can serve as a 'knowledgeable other' in building a distributed knowledge base for meeting their language needs (Liu et al., 2013). In this chapter we focused, however, on the overlooked area of user experience and SNSLL and found that learners were not able to improve their overall communicative competence in ways previously outlined. While the students' use of the site was relatively easy and straightforward, this was not enough to increase collaboration and collective knowledge-building experiences (Liu et al., 2015). Given the limitations of the study in terms of participants number and duration, it is evident that further longitudinal research is required to explore the pedagogical implications of usability testing for the design of effective SNSLL that are underpinned by constructivist pedagogies, particularly in the area of blended language learning.

REFERENCES

Álvarez, J. A. (2015). Language views on social networking sites for language learning: The case of Busuu. *Computer Assisted Language Learning*, *29*(5), 1–15.

Álvarez, J. A. (2016). Social networking sites for language learning: Examining learning theories in nested semiotic spaces. *Signo y Pensamiento*, *68*(68), 66–84. doi:10.11144/Javeriana.syp35-68.snsl

Andriani, G. (2014). Using Livemocha for independent language learning, a study of students' perception. Paper presented at Sriwijaya University Learning and Education-International Conference 2014, Sriwijaya University, Palembang, May 16-18.

Blattner, G., & Lomicka, L. (2012). Facebook-ing and the social generation: A new era of language learning. *ALSIC, 15*(1). Retrieved https://journals.openedition.org/alsic/2413

Boyd, D., & Ellison, N.B. (2008). Social network sites: Definition, history, and scholarship. *Journal of Computer-Mediated Communication, 13*, 210-230.

Brick, B. (2011a). How effective are web 2.0 language learning sites in facilitating language learning? *Compass: The Journal of Learning and Teaching at the University of Greenwich*, *3*, 57–63.

Brick, B. (2011b). Social networking sites and language learning. *International Journal of Virtual and Personal Learning Environments*, *2*(3), 18–31. doi:10.4018/jvple.2011070102

Brick, B. (2012). The role of social networking sites for language learning in UK higher education: The views of learners and practitioners. *International Journal of Computer-Assisted Language Learning and Teaching*, *2*(3), 35–53. doi:10.4018/ijcallt.2012070103

Brick, B. (2013). Evaluating social networking sites (SNSs) for language learning: An inquiry-based student project. Retrieved from http://coursefinder.coventry.ac.uk.public.freestyleinteractive.co.uk/Global/BES/Active%20Learning/Billy%20Brick.pdf

Bündgens-Kosten, J. (2011). Blogging in the target language: Review of the 'Lang-8' online community. *Studies in Self-Access Learning Journal, 2*(2), 97–99.

Cardon, D. (2008). Le Design de la Visibilité: Un Essai de Typologie du Web 2.0. *Internet Actu.* Retrieved from http://www.internetactu.net/2008/02/01/le-Design-de-la-visibilite-un-essai-de-typologie-du-web-20/

Chwo, G. S.-M., Lin, Y.-S., Chen, P.-J., Lai, G.-W., Liu, H.-C., Ho, C.-C., & Wang, Y.-P. (2012) Engagement with Livemocha® as an informal learning resource - Initial findings from a technology university reading course in central Taiwan. *ICCE 2012. The 20ᵗʰ International Conference on Computers in Education. Proceedings.* 609-613.

Clark, C., & Gruba, P. (2010). The use of social networking sites for foreign language learning: An autoethnographic study of Livemocha. In C.H. Steel, M.J. Keppell, P. Gerbic, & S. Housego (Eds.), Curriculum, technology, & transformation for an unknown future. Proceedings Ascilite, 164-173.

De Azevedo, C. G. (2013). Livemocha: uma rede social de aprendizagem de línguas. Unpublished Masters' Dissertation, Universidade do Minho, Instituto de Educaçao. Retrieved from https://repositorium.sdum.uminho.pt/bitstream/1822/30231/1/Cristiana%20Gracinda%20de%20Azevedo%20Gon%C3%A7alves%20Cerdeira%20Lopes.pdf

Duffy, P. (2011). Facebook or faceblock. Cautionary tales exploring the rise of social networking within tertiary education. In M. Lee, & C. McLoughlin (Eds.), *Web 2.0-based e-learning: Applying social informatics for tertiary teaching* (pp. 284–300). Hershey, PA: IGI Global. doi:10.4018/978-1-60566-294-7.ch015

Gruba, P., & Clark, C. (2013). Formative assessment within social network sites for language learning. In M.-N. Lamy & K. Zourou (Eds.), *Social networking for language education* (pp. 177–193). Basingstoke, UK: Palgrave MacMillan. doi:10.1057/9781137023384_10

Harrison, R. (2013). Profiles in social networking sites for language learning – Livemocha R revisited. In M.-N. Lamy, & K. Zourou (Eds.), *Social networking for language education: New language learning and teaching environments* (pp. 100-116). Basingstoke, UK: Palgrave Macmillan.

Harrison, R., & Thomas, M. (2009). Identity in online communities: Social networking sites and language learning. *International Journal of Emerging Technologies & Society., 7*(2), 109–124.

Jee, M., & Park, M. (2009). Livemocha as an online language-learning community. *CALICO Journal, 26*(2), 448–456. doi:10.1558/cj.v26i2.448-456

Jones, J. (2001). CALL and the responsibilities of teachers and administrators. *ELT Journal, 55*(4), 360–367. doi:10.1093/elt/55.4.360

Kétyi, A. (2015). Practical evaluation of a mobile language learning tool in higher education. In F. Helm, L. Bradley, M. Guarda, & S. Thouësny (Eds), *Critical CALL – Proceedings of the 2015 EUROCALL Conference*, Padova, Italy (pp. 306-311). Dublin, Ireland: Research-publishing.net. 10.14705/rpnet.2015.000350

Lamy, M.-N., & Mangenot, F. (2013). Social media-based language learning: Insights from research and practice. In M.-N. Lamy, & K. Zourou (Eds.), *Social networking for language education: New language learning and teaching environments* (pp. 197–213). Basingstoke, UK: Palgrave MacMillan. doi:10.1057/9781137023384_11

Lamy, M.-N., & Zourou, K. (Eds.). *Social networking for language education: New language learning and teaching environments*. Basingstoke, UK: Palgrave MacMillan. doi:10.1057/9781137023384

Lee, J. S. (2006). Exploring the relationship between electronic literacy and heritage language maintenance. *Language Learning & Technology, 10*(2), 93–113.

Liaw, M.-L. (2011). Review of Livemocha. *Language Learning & Technology, 15*(1), 36–40.

Lin, C.-H., Warschauer, M., & Blake, R. (2016). Language learning through social networks: Perceptions and reality. *Language Learning & Technology, 20*(1), 124–147.

Lloyd, E. (2012). Language learners' 'willingness to communicate' through Livemocha.com. *ALSIC, Apprentissage des langues et systèmes d'information et de Communication.* 15(1): *Médias sociaux et apprentissage des langues: (R)évolution?* Retrieved from http://alsic.revues.org/2415

Malerba, M. L. (2011). Social networking in language learning. In M. Ciastellardi, C. Miranda de Almeida, & C.A. Scolari (Eds.), *McLuhan galaxy Conference. Understanding Media, Today. Conference Proceedings* (pp.142-153).

Malerba, M. L. (2012). L2 Learners' informal online interactions in social network communities. Conference paper. *CALL: Using, learning, knowing.* Gothenburg. Retrieved from http://www.researchgate.net/publication/269243503

Malerba, M. L. (2015). Learner's behaviours and autonomy in and Busuu online communities. Conference paper. Retrieved from http://www.researchgate.net/publication/280730772

Orsini-Jones, M., Brick, B., & Pibworth, L. (2013). Practising language interaction via social networking sites: The expert student's perspective on personalized language learning. In B. Zou, M. Xing, Y. Wang, M. Sun, & C. H. Xiang (Eds.), *Computer-assisted foreign language teaching and learning: Technological advances* (pp. 40–53). Hershey, PA: IGI Global. doi:10.4018/978-1-4666-2821-2.ch003

Pettes Guikema, J. (2013). Software review: WeSpeke. *CALICO Journal, 30*(3), 465–471. doi:10.11139/cj.30.3.465-471

Stevenson, M. P., & Liu, M. (2010). Learning a language with Web 2.0: Exploring the use of social networking features of foreign language learning websites. *CALICO Journal, 27*(2), 233–259. doi:10.11139/cj.27.2.233-259

Van Dixhoorn, L., Loiseau, M., Mangenot, F., Potolia, A., & Zourou, K. (2010). Language learning: Resources and networks. Study operated by the network 'language learning and social media'. Retrieved http://www.elearningeuropa.info/files/LS6/Language_learning-resources_and_networks.pdf

Vesselinov, R., & Grego, J. (2016). *The Busuu efficacy study.* Retrieved from https://www.busuu.com/en/it-works/university-study

Wang, S., & Vasquez, C. (2012). Web 2.0 and second language learning: What does the research tell us? *CALICO Journal, 29*(3), pp. 412-430.

Warschauer, M. (2000). The death of cyberspace and the rebirth of CALL. *English Teachers'. Journal, 53*, 61–67.

Zourou, K., & Loiseau, M. (2013). Bridging design and language interaction and reuse in Livemocha's culture section. In M.-N. Lamy, & K. Zourou (Eds.), *Social networking for language education* (pp. 77–99). Basingstoke, UK: Palgrave Macmillan. doi:10.1057/9781137023384_5

This research was previously published in Recent Developments in Technology-Enhanced and Computer-Assisted Language Learning; pages 72-98, copyright year 2020 by Information Science Reference (an imprint of IGI Global).

APPENDIX

1. Site Feedback Questionnaire
   Please indicate your answers in the table below.

Table 15. Feedback on site design

	VERY UNSATISFIED	NEUTRAL	VERY SATISFIED
1. Ease of finding the information/learning activities	1 2 3 4 5		
2. Quality of information/learning activities	1 2 3 4 5		
3. Ease of reading the text	1 2 3 4 5		
4. Appearance of site, including colours and graphics	1 2 3 4 5		
5. Speed of pages displaying	1 2 3 4 5		
6. Fun, entertainment value	1 2 3 4 5		
7. Overall learning experience	1 2 3 4 5		
8. Ease of understanding the instructions for activities on the site	1 2 3 4 5		
9. Ease of moving around the site without getting lost	1 2 3 4 5		
10. Ease of finding contacts to practise the language with	1 2 3 4 5		

2. Skills
   In your opinion, does this site help you improve the following Spanish skills? Indicate your answers in Table 16.

Table 16.

	VERY UNSATISFIED	NEUTRAL	VERY SATISFIED
1. Speaking	1 2 3 4 5		
2. Listening	1 2 3 4 5		
3. Reading	1 2 3 4 5		
4. Writing	1 2 3 4 5		
5. Grammar	1 2 3 4 5		
6. Pronunciation	1 2 3 4 5		
7. Vocabulary	1 2 3 4 5		
8. Culture	1 2 3 4 5		

3. Features
    Were the following features helpful to you in learning Spanish? Please indicate your answers in the table below:

Table 17.

	Used		Not Useful at all	Neutral	Very Useful
1. Creating/Editing a profile	Yes	No	1 2 3 4 5		
2. Friending Native Speakers			1 2 3 4 5		
3. Reviewing vocabulary			1 2 3 4 5		
4. Posting writings			1 2 3 4 5		
5. Getting feedback from other users			1 2 3 4 5		
6. Giving feedback to other learners			1 2 3 4 5		
7. Watching pictures/videos			1 2 3 4 5		
8. Reading comments other users' posts			1 2 3 4 5		

Did you use any other features during the test session? YES - NO
    If yes, which one? What did you think about these features?

_____
_____
_____

4. Future Use and Perception
    1. How likely are you to return to this site on your own?
        No way 1   2   3   4   5 I'll probably return the next time I sit down at my computer.
        Explain why you are or are not likely to return to this site.

_____
_____
_____

    2. Would you recommend this site to your friends who are learning Spanish?
        No way 1   2   3   4   5 I'll definitely recommend this site.
        Explain why you would or you would not recommend this site.

_____
_____
_____

    3. What do you like best about this site?

_____
_____
_____

4.   What do you like least about this site?

_____

_____

_____

5.   Do you have any recommendations or comments to improve this site?

_____

_____

_____

Chapter 70

Tweets of a Feather Flock Together:
An Analysis of the Impact of Twitter in a Class of Translation

Elena Alcalde Peñalver
University of Alcalá, Alcalá de Henares, Spain

Alexandra Santamaría Urbieta
University of Alcalá, Alcalá de Henares, Spain

ABSTRACT

Nowadays, social networks (SN) are increasingly extended at a professional and personal level, and their use has also been included in educational contexts. In the field of translation and interpretation, in which this proposal is framed, the use of SN seems even more relevant, since working as a freelancer is one of the main professional opportunities of translators and interpreters. This article analyses the impact of Twitter on the learning process of an English class for students of the degree in translation and modern languages in terms of enhancing their communicative competence in English while at the same time increasing their motivation with an approach to professional reality. This analysis was part of a pilot study to examine to what extent the use of this social network could be useful and positive for our students.

INTRODUCTION

Nowadays social networks (from now on SN) are increasingly extended at a professional and personal level, and their use has also been included in educational contexts. In the field of translation and interpretation, in which this proposal is framed, the use of SN seems even more relevant, since working as a freelancer is one of the main professional opportunities of translators and interpreters. For these professionals, marketing strategies to advertise their services is of the utmost importance. In fact, Marking (2017) qualifies freelance translators as "the lifeblood of the language services industry", since although companies have

DOI: 10.4018/978-1-6684-7123-4.ch070

translators on staff, it is always necessary to maintain a contact base of freelance translators who can be specialized in a topic and provide specific solutions that adapt to the client's requirements at a specific time. This same author gives as an example the case of the EU Court of Justice and the European Central Bank, institutions that, despite having translators on staff, have included the hiring of freelancers in their budget. Faced with this situation, SN can be very useful for freelance translators to advertise their services to potential clients. The objective of any marketing activity is undoubtedly communication with current and future clients, and their development (Richardson, Gosnay & Carrol, 2013, p. 15). In this sense, we can affirm that the translation sector has benefited greatly from marketing in SN, since these represent a new means for translators to be known and advertise the services they offer as professionals.

Taking this professional situation into account and also the fact that SN are part of the process of interaction among students, we considered designing a teaching innovation proposal using Twitter in the classroom. The reason for this choice is based on the fact that it promotes professional development (Hitchcok & Young, 2016) and it also helps students extend their personal learning network (Luo, Sickel & Cheng, 2017), as well as feel part of a worldwide community. Moreover, even though there is an increasing number of studies on the use of social media at the university level and their positive impact in terms of promoting informal learning (Abella & Delgado, 2015), cooperative learning (Prestridge, 2014) as well as interaction and scholarly engagement (Dijkmans et al., 2015; Chawinga, 2017), we believe that it is a practical way of linking the academic context of the classroom to the practical reality of the profession from the very first levels of students' translation training.

The aim of this paper is to analyse students' perceptions on the impact of Twitter on their learning process in an English class of the Degree in Translation and Modern Languages in terms of enhancing their communicative competence in English while at the same time increasing their motivation with an approach to professional reality. This analysis was part of a study to examine to what extent the use of this social network could be useful and positive for our students instead of writing learning logs, since this activity was something that students declared that they did not enjoy and thus did not benefit their learning.

The methodology used for the study was qualitative. The research questions (RQ) were adapted to a translation training context based on a previous study conducted in the field of Education (Abellá et al., 2018) but that we considered replicable for ours because of what it aimed at analysing in terms of educational purposes:

RQ1: What perceptions do students have about what they learn using Twitter?
RQ2: Will the use of Twitter promote critical thinking in students using English as a second language?
RQ3: Will the use of Twitter enhance students' motivation?
RQ4: Will the use of Twitter increase students' interest in the translation and interpreting profession?

More specifically these were the research objectives (RO) in line with the above mentioned RQ:

RO1: To analyse students' perceptions about their learning using Twitter in an ELT classroom.
RO2: To promote students' critical thinking skills when using English as a second language.
RO3: To increase students' motivation towards the learning of a second language.
RO4: To determine to what extent the use of this SN could be of interest for the professional future of students who belong to the Degree of Translation.

BACKGROUND

To Tweet or Not to Tweet?

Twitter, though being the youngest of all micro-blogs, is among the top two tools chosen by educators to use in their classrooms (Haythornwaite, 2016), ranked before other popular tools such as Facebook. As previously mentioned, there are a number of studies that focus on the great potential of Twitter in language learning (Chisega-Negrila, 2015; Kumar Sah, 2015; Hattern & Lomicka, 2016), as it takes the teaching and learning process beyond formal lessons (Ebner et al., 2010; Evans, 2014) and it increases motivation, engages students and connects them with the real world (Kumar Sah, 2015, p. 13) and, consequently, with cultural awareness. Digital immediacy, briefness as well as contact with popular culture allow teachers to transform the class and the way students learn, both inside and outside the traditional classroom. Vygotsky (1978) highlighted that interaction is the key to active language learning through the inclusion of socio-cultural situations in the classroom and this is a feature that students can benefit from using this SN. Nicol and McFarlane-Dick (2006) argue that is a way of empowering students by allowing them to be in control of an aspect of their education, "as well as providing them with an increased sense of responsibility in guiding their education towards the course's intended learning outcomes" (Cooke, 2017, p. 257).

However, its popularity and features should not be the imperative to include it in our classroom, as meaningful incorporation of the tool is needed (Tang & Hew, 2017), which is only obtained through comprehensive and critical review. To that end, Tang and Hew's study (2017) dedicated its pages to the analysis of 51 empirical studies of using Twitter in teaching and learning from 2006 to 2015 in different academic fields. Furthermore, Barczyk and Duncan (2011:270) postulate that "if tools [social media] are available to help better engage and educate students, they should be incorporated into the curriculum, not exclusively, but rather, in a supplemental fashion". In summary, including SNs in the curriculum should be done comprehensibly, critically and as a supplementary tool.

Although there are studies that express their concerns when using Twitter with educational purposes, the majority of the research has focused on their advantages and positive learners' perceptions towards its use like, for instance, the simple and user-friendly interface (Ebner et al., 2010; Bahner et al., 2012; Feliz et al., 2013), the mere form of entertainment (Bista, 2015), as well as the increase in motivation and engagement (Kumar Sah, 2015; Yousef Zaidieh, 2012). Others have as well labored the point of future vocational advantages (Mckenzie, 2014). Motivation, being the engine that moves the inclusion of SNs in the classroom, is seen by Yousef Zaidieh (2012: 20) as an opportunity "to attract, motivate and engage students in meaningful communicative practice, content exchange and collaboration". Also, the convenience and flexibility that SNs offer not only in the classroom, but also outside of it, motivates students to successfully complete educational tasks (Yousef Zaidieh, 2012).

As for the negative comments, these include four main concerns: (1) increased workload (McEachern, 2011; Dijkmans et al, 2015; Bexheti et al, 2014), (2) privacy (Popuiu et al, 2012), (3) message length limitations and (4) possible distractions (Tang & Hew, 2017). To this list of drawbacks Tur & Marín (2015: 47) add the overwhelming number of tweets received and the unfamiliarity of students with the application, and the importance to choose the content shown (Voloaca et al, 2011). Since the students of this study were adults, we would neither include the possible distractions nor the non-familiarity with the application as impediments of the use of Twitter with educational purposes. The former because students at these ages are eager to learn through new technologies and, specially, through applications and software which they use every other day at home, on the street or at the library (Jankauskaitė, 2015). As for the latter, students are what we now call digitally friendly, which means they would definitely consider tweeting as part of their daily lives. Nonetheless, before starting the activity students were asked if they had ever used this SN, and although only three of them declared that they had never tweeted before, they were eager to download the application in their phone and start working with it since they were already in other SN that were similar to it. All in all, if Shakespeare lived in today's world, he would for sure decide to tweet it.

Twitter as a Learning and Professional Tool for Prospective Translators

The link between the real life and the digital one is what makes SN a useful and practical tool. As teachers we intend that our students experience what they will have to confront in their future, in our case, as translators and interpreters. Through the use of deadlines, real translation projects, last-minute interpreting jobs and many others, we put students in the shoes of the professionals of tomorrow. This is, indeed, our students' intrinsic motivation, that is, finding the act of learning all the necessary tools and tricks to confront what is ahead of them rewarding itself. The liking of the profession, in most cases, is what moves students towards achieving their goals and as educators we should provide knowledge in the utmost quality and practicality.

Motivation is the key to success and it is an essential condition of learning and a value-based concept (Wlodkowski & Ginsberg, 2017). Effective teachers help students to develop goals, attitudes and beliefs which will sustain a long-term involvement in learning and in their future occupations. Undergraduate students have a strong need to apply what they have learnt and also to feel competent when applying it, due to the fact that they value what they learn. Furthermore, in order to successfully help them we need to do so through an enjoyable manner and we would have made the difficult desirable (Wlodkowski & Ginsberg, 2017, p. 87).

Not only does Twitter help teachers and students interact digitally, but also connect these two to experts of a specific field of study, that is, to worldwide translators (real translators, as students see them). Much has been said about the use of social media to learn languages or, as stated before, to learn about economy, engineering or technology (Tang & Hew, 2017), but there are no previous studies on how to use Twitter to learn about translation. We should also bear in mind the possibility that Twitter offers undergraduate degree students to follow the latest projects of well-known translators and translator's associations, get in touch with future e-workmates or read and learn about translation related topics. All in all, the use of this social network goes far beyond the language learning field and it is extended to its use as a professional and development tool, as well as a way of communicating and keeping in touch with the translator's global community.

According to the blog *Marketing Tips for Translators* (2016) popular hashtags for freelance translation include:

- #xl8 and #t9n (for translation)
- #xl8or (for translator)
- #l10n (for localization)
- #1nt (for interpreting)
- #i18n (for internationalization)
- #g11n (for globalization)

- #translation
- #language

In order to analyse the frequency of use of these hashtags in Twitter, we have decided to study their presence on the Internet during a 7-day period (from April 10th to April 17th, 2018).

Figure 1. The frequency of use translation related hashtags in Twitter between April 10th and April 17th, 2018

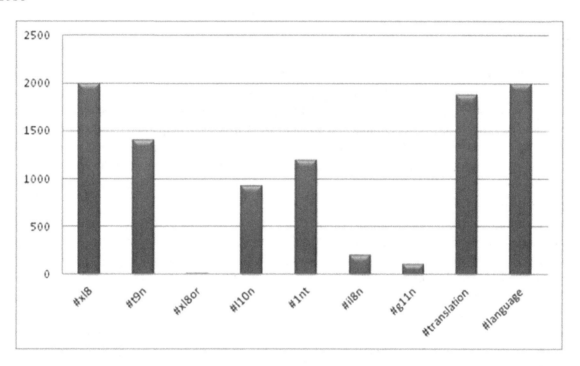

Figure 1 shows how the hashtags #xl8 (1,993 tweets), #language (1,986), #translation (1,878) and #t9n (1,396) are the most popular ones, whereas #xl8or (4) and #g11n (104) the least frequent. These results are coherent, as those which appear in most cases represent more general concepts and cover a wider range of topics, while those focusing on more concrete topics are reduced to fewer tweets or retweets. These figures, although taken as a mere example of the presence of translation related topics in the world of Twitter, give teachers and idea of the number of tweets, retweets, links, images and replies that flood the translation digital world.

In summary, empirical studies evidence that, generally speaking, undergraduate degree students perceive the inclusion of SN in the classroom as favourable. Much has been said about their use in language learning environments, but much more should be said about their use in translation and interpretation studies. Students feel motivated when engaged through significant learning activities and even more when using friendly applications or software which can be used outside the classroom to know more about professionals of the field, about global communities and associations or about the latest news. Moreover, being an active user of SN like Twitter gets the word out of your profession and could help translators build a digital image of themselves. As teachers we focus on helping them acquire the tools to deliver quality translations but forgetting about giving them information and teaching them about ways to be present on SN, which not only will they need to get by in today's world but also to focus on their writing skills.

MAIN FOCUS OF THE ARTICLE

Method

Academic Context

This research study was part of the English 2 course of the Degree in Translation and Modern Languages of the University of Alcalá (Spain). This is a compulsory course of the second semester of the first academic year of the degree and, as indicated in the syllabus, it is designed to give students the necessary language skills in terms of grammar and oral and written skills to help them master their studies in English. In addition, students are expected to achieve greater independence in their language learning with a view toward lifelong learning as English language specialists. At the end of the course, students must have reached a B2.2 level, or higher, according to the Common European Framework (Syllabus of the English II course, 2017).

As part of the continuous assessment process of the course, students were required to submit a learning log every two weeks in which they explained the activities they had completed out of class as part of their personal learning process to continue learning English. This learning log and students' active participation in class accounted for 20% of students' final grade. After two submissions of these logs, they became repetitive and student's writing consisted of merely simple sentences that did not contribute in any way to improve their level of English. When asked about it in class, students expressed lack of motivation when writing the learning log. At this point, we realized that we needed to enhance their after-class learning from a different perspective that would also increase their motivation, and as stated above, Twitter could be a tool to achieve this aim. Thus, we introduced the kind of personalized learning that, according to Maznah and Zher (2013) develops social practices to enable students to become what they are capable of becoming. In this sense students of this degree are going to become professional translators and language professionals but in their first year of studies they are still unaware of the implications of the profession and have no contact with the professional translation market. Twitter could then become a way to introduce this in the classroom.

Description of the Activity

The following instructions were given to students. First of all, they were asked to follow the course account, which was created specifically for this activity: @EnglishTrad. Students were also required to create an account if they did not have one already, and if some of them were concerned about privacy issues they were informed that the account would only be used for professional purposes. For this activity, each week they had to follow five different accounts related to one of the topics that had been established for the course. Once they had done this they needed to quote at least three tweets from three different accounts and write a short opinion about what they thought after reading that tweet. Some examples already done by the professor on the SN were shown to illustrate this.

In addition, each week they were required to interact with at least one of their classmates. They had to tag one of them and ask them a question to raise debate about the assigned translation topic of that week. The activity was conducted for a period of six weeks. For the first four weeks they were assigned a topic and they were given a hashtag for their tweets and a suggested account to help them identify other related accounts. Hashtags were given so that we could identify tweets for our analysis and see if they had been used by other accounts to participate in the discussions (e.g. some students from other classes also tweeted using the hashtag because they were interested in the discussions of one of the topics). It was also a conducting thread to enhance communication among them on a particular topic. Moreover, it was a way to show students hashtags related to the world of translation so that they could continue using them in the future to discover more about the profession. Table 1 includes a summary of the hashtags chosen for the activity.

Table 1. List of topics, weeks of the assignment, hashtags and suggested accounts to follow

Topic and Week	Hashtag	Suggested Account
Translation professionals. Week 1	#xl8people	Henry Liu @interpretaatioo
Translation professional associations. Week 2	#xl8assoc	EST @estrans
News about the profession. Week 3	#xl8news	Slator @slatornews
Translation events. Week 4	#xl8event	CIJITI Conference @CIJITI2018

For week 5, students were supposed to be already familiar with translation events, translation professionals, associations and news about the profession. Therefore, they were required to create a thread in which they had to give their opinion about what they had learned about the field of translation using Twitter. The hashtag they had to use was #xl8opinion. Finally, in week 6 students had to raise debate about topics of their interest using the hashtag #xl8debate.

Sample

As stated before, this was part of a study to analyse if the introduction of Twitter in an English class of a Translation Degree could be beneficial for our students. All students from one class participated in this activity (24 students in total).

Instrument

For this class experiment there was no specific validated survey that had already been designed on the use of Twitter in an English course for translators. However, previous studies had developed instruments that could be adapted for this purpose such as the one used by Halic et al. in 2010. In this case the survey aimed at measuring students' perceptions of blog effectiveness. Abella et al. (2018) also used one adapted from the survey designed by Arquero and Romero-Frías (2013) for the assessment of a closed social network. For this study, we adapted items related to students' perceived learning and adapted the one on critical thinking applied to an English course for translators. We created two more related to students' motivation in the class and their interest in the profession. Each item was rated on a five-point Likert-type scale with five possible answers: (1) strongly agree, (2) agree, (3) neutral, (4) disagree, and (5) strongly disagree (see Table 10 in the Appendix). The survey was validated by three professors that have used this research method before. The aim of the validation process was to state whether the survey was in line with our research objectives and if questions had been clearly formulated. The survey was distributed in a printed version in class to ensure that all students completed it. The descriptive statistical data from the survey was also triangulated with qualitative information obtained from the open questions. This information was selected according to the relevance it presented in relation to the RQ.

Results

Results were analyzed according to the RQ and objectives indicated above. They include descriptive statistical data from the survey as well as some qualitative examples from what students tweeted during the period of completion of the activity. Tables 2, 4, 6 and 8 include the percentages of each of the RQ presented to the students, rated on a five-point scale. Tables 3, 5, 7 and 9, on the other hand, include a sample of the students' tweets recorded during this study.

Table 2 focuses on students' perception about the use of this SN. The objective of this question was to determine whether students found the use of this SN useful for the improvement of their learning experience as a whole.

Table 2. RQ1: What perceptions do students have about what they learn using Twitter?

Statement	Disagree	Neutral	Agree	Strongly Agree
Twitter has helped me to share my knowledge and opinions with other people.		29.2%	33.3%	37.5%
I believe that incorporating Twitter in this course has enhanced my overall learning experience.	8.3%	8.3%	45.8%	37.5%
Using Twitter has enhanced my English language skills.	4.2%	25%	45.8%	25%

The strongly disagree column was deleted since none of the students chose this option. As we can see, students highly agreed that Twitter was a good way to share knowledge and opinions with other people and that it contributed positively towards their learning experience both in terms of overall learning and English language acquisition. Some tweets that we gathered from students also proved the perceptions shown in Table 3.

Generally speaking, and bearing in mind students' tweets, both the overall learning experience and English learning have benefited from the use of this SN. Adjectives like 'interactive, 'easier', 'amazing' 'improved' or 'helpful' and 'enriching' are just the tip of the iceberg of the powerful learning tool that Twitter can grow to be in an ESL classroom.

For this second question, both columns in Table 4 showing disagreement were deleted since they were not chosen by the students. Again, results show that Twitter has been a useful tool to promote critical thinking in students using English as a second language and some of the thoughts students tweeted also supported this finding (see Table 5).

Table 3. Students' tweets to RQ 1

Overall Learning Experience	Students' Tweets
Student 1	I personally found this activity really helpful, interesting and enriching. #xl8opinion So all in all, I'm really happy with this new activity that has indeed been a great experience!! #xl8opinion
Student 2	I think it's necessary to share a thread dedicated to the amazing things I have been learning the past weeks with twitter. #xl8opinion Using a social media platform like Twitter to debate and learn more about the field of translation is amazing. Our generation is tied to technology and seeing it as an opportunity to acquire more knowledge makes this learning process more attractive for young people like us.
Student 3	This activity was easier than writing a learning log where you didn't even know what to say. I think that this was because it was more interactive and it consisted in using a social network that is something really close to us, due to us being so young.
English Learning	
Student 1	And of course, it has been a great way to improve my English and learn new words, rather than writing a "Learning Log" that I wasn't really paying attention to while doing it. #xl8opinion
Student 2	Because of reading articles and writing some opinions about them, my writing and reading skills have improved. Also, because I have read different types of articles I have learned some new vocabulary. #xl8opinion
Student 3	Besides, thanks to this activity I have learned new vocabulary in English and French through some accounts like @inglesaldia or @Les_Machin. #xl8opinion

Table 4. RQ2 – Will the use of Twitter promote critical thinking in students using English as a second language?

Statement	Neutral	Agree	Strongly Agree
Twitter discussions have helped me understand other points of view.	16.7%	70.8%	12.5%
Using Twitter has enabled me to better develop critical and reflexive attitudes towards the translation and interpreting profession.	12.5%	25%	62.5%
Using Twitter has enabled me to better develop critical and reflexive attitudes towards the contents available on the Internet.	16.7%	50%	33.3%
Using Twitter has enabled me to better develop critical and reflexive attitudes towards other students' opinions.	41.7%	45.8%	12.5%

Table 5. Students' tweets to RQ 2

Students' Critical Thinking	Students' Tweets
Student 1	I found incredible seeing the different issues which affect this sector and how its members, the translators, resolve them even helping each other. I was glad to find that some problems are funny, for example, those which *relationed* to the titles translation.
Student 2	These few weeks, during the Twitter project, I think I have learnt lot of curious facts about translation and its methods, mostly things I would not have learnt in class or in a book, things that were interactive, that came easy to the eye, that were interesting and short enough to keep my eighteen years old mind's attention. The article that I found more interesting was the one about what were the most difficult parts of court interpreting; I think it made me feel sorry for court interpreters, Things like that are not taught in a classroom.

These two opinions represent what 22 out 24 students stated about the development of critical thinking when reading about translation related topics, as the activity was able to grasp their attention, as well as create an argued presumption on a given topic. Although it should also be said that this could be extrapolated to any topic, not only those translation-related, due to the fact that what students highlighted was the interesting topics and short pieces of writing from which they could benefit themselves in this SN.

Table 6. RQ3 – Will the use of Twitter enhance students' motivation?

Statement	Disagree	Neutral	Agree	Strongly Agree
Using Twitter has made me feel more involved in the subject than in other traditional classes.	0%	4.2%	58.3%	37.5%
Using Twitter has increased my motivation in this subject.	4.2%	29.2%	37.5%	29.2%
I visit Twitter for professional purposes more than required by the instructor.	20.8%	41.7%	20,8%	16.7%
The activity has helped me feel connected to other students in this course.	8.3%	54.2%	25%	12.5%

As we can observe in the answers from the survey in Table 6, including Twitter as part of the assessment of the class increased students' motivation in the course. However, even though a considerable number of students uses now Twitter for professional purposes more than required by the instructor, a higher percentage was neutral or disagreed about it. The reason behind this may be that students are not currently working and may not still use it for professional purposes. The same applies to feeling connected to other students in the classroom, which could be due to the already existent relationship among them and the strictly professional profile given to the Twitter account. Some qualitative data regarding these statements can be found in Table 7.

Table 7. Students' perception to RQ 3

Students' Motivation	Students' Tweets
Student 1	I have never done something similar in class, but I think it really helps us to see how the real world is. Interacting with people from the translation world makes me want to be a translator more than before. #xl8opinion
Student 2	We had to follow accounts about translation so we can be in touch with the translation field, which I find really interesting. I feel motivated to do this because this is what I want to be in the future.
Student 3	Finally, I enjoyed this activity so much that many times I have been reading because I really was intrigued with the subject, not because I had to do it.
Student 4	I have decided that I will not delete this account, because it is a great work tool and a way of *know* people with my same interests

The last RQ here analysed looks towards the future of our students and their possible careers as translators or interpreters (see Table 8).

Again, statements showing disagreement were deleted since no students chose this option. In this case we can observe that RQ 4 is clearly answered in an affirmative way, since as we can observe in the table more than 50% of students chose the agree or strongly agree options. This is also supported by evidence from some of students' tweets in this regard (see Table 9).

Table 8. RQ4 - Will the use of Twitter increase students' interest in the translation and interpreting profession?

Statement	Neutral	Agree	Strongly Agree
Using Twitter has allowed me to learn about and to use tools which are useful to keep my professional knowledge updated in the future.	4.2%	66.7%	29.2%
Using Twitter has encouraged me to read more information related to the translation and interpreting profession.	4.2%	37.5%	58.3%
Using Twitter has allowed me to get in touch with other translation/interpreting professionals.	8.3%	41.7%	50%
Using Twitter has motivated me to be a translator and/or interpreter.	20.8%	25%	54.2%

Table 9. Students' perception to RQ 4

Learning About the Profession	Students' Tweets
Student 1	This activity has greatly changed my perspective on my university degree and my future, since I have learned tons of new things and also I have found great translators that are passionate about their job. #xl8opinion
Student 2	Never in a million years did I believe that there was so much debate about this field in Twitter. It even has a hashtag! It was a huge surprise for me because the profession of translators has always been unknown and hidden.
Student 3	It has been an eye-opening experience because I never thought of going to Twitter in order to learn about translation. I have learned a lot of things about the translation and interpreting subjects, such as how are translators taken into consideration, where will our names appear when we translate a text in the near future, and where the future of our degree is headed to. #xl8opinion
Student 4	So, this activity has been the perfect way of introducing us to our future profession and to encourage us to keep this going! #xl8opinion

Being this research study, and quoting, 'an eye-opening experience' and a 'perfect way of introducing us to our future profession', it could be said that Twitter is demonstrated to be a useful and enriching tool for both students and teachers. The former get to learn about new ways of getting in touch and keeping in contact with other professionals of the field and reading about the latest trends and pieces of news in the translation and interpreting world. The latter, on the other hand, put into practice a more motivating tool which gets the attention of students and helps assess a closer-to-reality writing piece.

However, we are aware of the limitations of this study. First of all, even though students could freely express negative opinions about the activity in Twitter and even in class where professors always ask about their perceptions of what it is done, and despite the option of showing disagreement in the survey, we believe that the lack of negative statements in it could have misled some of the students' opinions on the topic. Moreover, since it was the first time this SN was incorporated in the classroom, the sample was limited to students of this class. Therefore, as a future research proposal we will continue working with Twitter to have a wider sample and also to include a corpus analysis of what students tweet following the methodology used in a recent study published by Ross & Rivers (2018). This will provide different kind of qualitative data that will contribute to making our study in language learning applied to the translation classroom more useful to the field.

CONCLUSION

As stated in previous studies that we mentioned in our introduction and literature review, this activity was innovative for students since, until the introduction of this SN in the classroom, they had only considered it as a tool for leisure and social interaction. However, and quoting some of the above included opinions, they now see it as a professional tool and as the "perfect way of introducing us to our future profession". Results mainly show that more than half of the students have answered positively towards the use of this SN in the classroom and it is clear that they have understood its importance towards their future as translators, both to share knowledge and to learn and improve their English language.

The promotion of critical thinking and the increase of motivation, towards the subject and the translation and interpreting profession, are the other two main results obtained in this study. As for the first one, 62.5% of students strongly agree on having used Twitter to better develop their critical and reflexive attitude towards translation. As seen in the results, more than 50% of students have stated the development of a more critical attitude towards what they can find on Twitter regarding the translation and interpreting profession. As for the increase of motivation towards the subject, 58.3% of students agree on the fact that the use of this SN has been intrinsically motivating. The change from a learning log to the use of this SN has meant a development towards a significant learning methodology, which has had an effect on the way students perceived the learning of English and the wide possibilities that this SN, which could also be extrapolated to others, offers to their needs as professionals of a foreign language. Regarding the last conclusion obtained, we would highlight, on the one hand, the fact that 66.7% of students agree that its application will be of use to keep their professional knowledge updated in the near future and, on the other hand, that 58.3% of students have, after the use of Twitter in class, read more about the translation and interpreting profession. Finally, to get in touch with other professionals (50%), as well as to feel motivated to be a translator (54.2%) have been two of the most relevant results obtained. We would also like to point that due to the visibility of their tweets on the Internet, as well as the fact that what they wrote would be linked to their profession, students took their time to write meaningful and grammatically and vocabulary enriched and complex sentences.

The use of new technologies in education is increasingly motivating for our students and the results gathered in this study show that sharing and learning are the two main benefits of the inclusion of Twitter for their future lives as translators. The incorporation of social technological tools results in an increase in motivation towards the profession and the subject itself, as students feel closer to what is ahead of them and feel that the *real world* of the translator is represented inside the four walls of a classroom. All in all, we could conclude saying that, through the use of these technological tools we introduce students into their future career and, more importantly, to potential customers, vendors and colleagues. In summary: tweets of a feather, flock together.

REFERENCES

Abella, V., & Delgado, V. (2015). Learning to use Twitter and use Twitter to learn. *Profesorado: Revista de Currículum y Formación del Profesorado*, *19*, 364–378.

Abella, V., Delgado, V., Ausín, V., & Hortigüela, D. (2018). To tweet or not to tweet: Student perceptions of the use of Twitter on an undergraduate degree course. *Innovations in Education and Teaching International*, 1–10. doi:10.1080/14703297.2018.1444503

Arquero, J. L., & Romero-Frías, E. (2013). Using social network sites in Higher Education: An experience in business studies. *Innovations in Education and Teaching International, 50*(3), 238–249. doi:10.1080/14703297.2012.760772

Bahner, D. P., Adkins, E., Donley, C., Nagel, R., & Kman, N. E. (2012). How we use social media to supplement a novel curriculum in medical education. *Medical Teacher, 34*(6), 439–444. doi:10.3109/0142159X.2012.668245 PMID:22449268

Barczyk, C. C., & Duncan, D. G. (2011). Social networking media as a tool for teaching business administration courses. *International Journal of Humanities and Social Science, 1*(17), 267–276.

Bexheti, L. A., Ismaili, B. E., & Cico, B. H. (2014). An Analysis of Social Media Usage in Teaching and Learning: The Case of SEEU. In *2014 International Conference on Circuits, Systems, Signal Processing, Communications and Computers*, Venice (pp. 90-94).

Bista, K. (2015). Is Twitter a pedagogical tool in higher Education? Perspectives of education graduate students. *The Journal of Scholarship of Teaching and Learning, 15*(2), 83. doi:10.14434/josotl.v15i2.12825

Chawinga, W. D. (2017). Taking social media to a university classroom: Teaching and learning using Twitter and blogs. *International Journal of Educational Technology in Higher Education, 14*(3).

Chisega-Negrila, A. M. (2015). Using Social Media for ESL Learning–Twitter Vs. Pinterest. JADLeT. *Journal of Advanced Distributed Learning Technology, 3*(5).

Cooke, S. (2017). Social teaching: Student perspectives on the inclusion of social media in higher education. *Education and Information Technologies, 22*(1), 255–269. doi:10.100710639-015-9444-y

Dijkmans, C., Kerkhof, P., & Beukeboom, C. J. (2015). A stage to engage: Social media use and corporate reputation. *Tourism Management, 47*, 58–67. doi:10.1016/j.tourman.2014.09.005

Ebner, M., Lienhardt, C., Rohs, M., & Meyer, I. (2010). Microblogs in higher education – a chance to facilitate informal and process-oriented learning. *Computers & Education, 55*(1), 92–100. doi:10.1016/j.compedu.2009.12.006

Evans, C. (2014). Twitter for teaching: Can social media be used to enhance the process of learning? *British Journal of Educational Technology, 45*(5), 902–915. doi:10.1111/bjet.12099

Feliz, T., & Feliz, R. (2013). Analysis of the use of Twitter as a learning strategy in master's studies. *Open Learning: The Journal of Open. Distance and E-Learning, 28*(3), 201–215. doi:10.1080/02680513.2013.870029

Finding Clients on Twitter. Tips and Strategies (2016). *Marketing Tips for Translators.* Retrieved from https://marketingtipsfortranslators.com/finding-clients-twitter-tips-strategies/

Halic, O., Lee, D., Paulus, T., & Spence, M. (2010). To blog or not to blog: Student perceptions of blog effectiveness for learning in a college-level course. *Internet and Higher Education*, *13*(4), 206–213. doi:10.1016/j.iheduc.2010.04.001

Hattern, D., & Lomicka, L. (2016). What the Tweets say: A Critical Analysis of Twitter research in language learning from 2009 to 2016. *E-Learning and Digital Media*, *13*(1-2), 5–23. doi:10.1177/2042753016672350

Haythornwaite, C. (2016). *E-learning and new learning cultures and case: Social media in higher education*. The University of Hong Kong.

Hitchcock, L. I., & Young, J. A. (2016). Tweet, Tweet: Using live Twitter chats in social work education. *Social Work Education*, *35*(4), 457–468. doi:10.1080/02615479.2015.1136273

Jankauskaitė, D. (2015). Social Media as a Tool for Improving Teaching and Learning Experience. *Signum Temporis*, *7*(1), 54–59.

Kumar Sah, P. (2015). Let's Tweet to learn English: Using Twitter as a Language Tool in the ESL/EFL Classroom. *Language and Literature*, *2*, 10–17.

Luo, T., Sickel, J., & Cheng, L. (2017). Preservice teachers' participation and perceptions of Twitter live chats as personal learning networks. *TechTrends*, *61*(3), 226–235. doi:10.100711528-016-0137-1

Marking, M. (2017). Reader Polls: How Translation Will Be Paid For and Where to Find Freelance Linguists. Retrieved from https://slator.com/features/reader-polls-how-translation-will-be-paid-for-and-where-to-find-freelance-linguists/

Maznah, R. H., & Zher Ng, H. (2013). Training Academicians to Develop Personalized Learning Environment and Students Engagement (PLEaSE). *International Journal of Virtual and Personal Learning Environments*, *4*(4).

McEachern, R. W. (2011). Experiencing a social network in an organizational context: The facebook intership. *Business Communication Quarterly*, *74*(4), 486–493. doi:10.1177/1080569911423963

Mckenzie, B. A. (2014). Teaching Twitter: Re-enacting the Paris commune and the battle of Stalingrad. *The History Teacher*, *47*(3).

Nicol, D. J., & McFarlane-Dick, D. (2006). Formative assessment and self-regulated learning: A model and seven principles of good feedback practice. *Studies in Higher Education*, *31*(2), 199–218. doi:10.1080/03075070600572090

Popoiu, M.C., Grosseck, G., & Holotescu, C. (2012). What do we know about the use of social media in medical education? *Social and Behavioral Sciences*, *46*, 2262-2266.

Prestridge, S. (2014). A focus on students' use of Twitter - Their interactions with each other, consent and interface. *Active Learning in Higher Education*, *1*(2), 101–115. doi:10.1177/1469787414527394

Richardson, N., Gosnay, M. R., & Carroll, A. (2013). *Guía de acceso rápido al marketing en redes sociales: marketing de alto impacto y bajo costo que sí funcionan*. Buenos Aires: Granica.

Ross, A. S. & Rivers, D. J. (2018). Discursive Deflection: Accusation of "Fake News" and the Spread of Mis- and Disinformation in the Tweets of President Trump. *Social Media + Society*.

Tang, Y., & Hew, K. F. (2017). Using Twitter for Education: Beneficial or Simply a Waste of Time? *Computers & Education, 106*, 97–118. doi:10.1016/j.compedu.2016.12.004

Tur, G., & Marín, V. I. (2015). Enhancing learning with the social media: Student teachers' perceptions on Twitter in a debate activity. *Journal of New Approaches in Educational Research, 4*(1), 46–53. doi:10.7821/naer.2015.1.102

Universidad de Alcalá. (2017). Guía docente de la asignatura Inglés II. Retrieved from http://www.uah.es/export/sites/uah/es/estudios/estudios-oficiales/grados/.galleries/Programas/G791/251009_G791_2017-18.pdf

Voloaca, I. D., Bratu, S., Georgescu, M., Ghencea, F. L., & Voicu, A. (2011). The importance of creativity in advertising, digital technology, and social networking. *Economics, Management, and Financial Markets, V6*, 449–458.

Vygotsky, L. S. (1978). *Mind in Society*. London: Harvard University Press.

Wlodkowski, R., & Ginsberg, M. B. (2017). *Enhancing Adult Motivation to Learn: A Comprehensive Guide for Teaching All Adults*. John Wiley & Sons.

Yousef Zaidieh, A. J. (2012). The Use of Social Networking in Education: Challenges and Opportunities. *World of Computer Science and Information Technology Journal, 2*(1), 18–21.

This research was previously published in the International Journal of Virtual and Personal Learning Environments (IJVPLE), 8(2); pages 10-23, copyright year 2018 by IGI Publishing (an imprint of IGI Global).

APPENDIX

The Survey Instrument

Table 10. RQs

RQ 1: What perceptions do students have about what they learn using Twitter?
Learning perceived by the students during the activity in Twitter Twitter has helped me to share my knowledge and opinions with other people. I believe that incorporating Twitter in this course has enhanced my overall learning experience. My peers' and other people's comments about my tweets and retweets are important. Twitter discussions have helped me understand other points of view. Using Twitter has enhanced my English language skills.
RQ 2: Will the use of Twitter promote critical thinking in students using English as a second language?
Students' critical thinking using Twitter Using Twitter... Has enabled me to better develop critical and reflexive attitudes towards the translation and interpreting profession. Has enabled me to better develop critical and reflexive attitudes towards the contents available on the Internet. Has enabled me to better develop critical and reflexive attitudes towards other students' opinions. Has enabled me to express my opinions and points of view more freely than in class.
RQ 3: Students' motivation in the class
Students' motivation using Twitter Using Twitter has made me feel more involved in the subject than in other traditional classes. Using Twitter has increased my motivation in this subject. Using Twitter has been useful to enhance my English language skills. I visit Twitter for professional purposes more than required by the instructor. The activity has helped me feel connected to other students in this course.
RQ 4: Will the use of Twitter increase students' interest in the translation and interpreting profession?
Students' interest in the translation and interpreting profession Using Twitter has allowed me to learn about and to use tools which are useful to keep my professional knowledge updated in the future. Using Twitter has encouraged me to read more information related to the translation and interpreting profession. Using Twitter has allowed me to get in touch with other translation/interpreting professionals. Using Twitter has motivated me to be a translator and/or interpreter.

Chapter 71

Facebook for Engagement:
Telecollaboration Between Finland and New Zealand in German Language Learning

Kirsi Korkealehto

Häme University of Applied Sciences, Hämeenlinna, Finland & University of Helsinki, Helsinki, Finland

Vera Leier

University of Canterbury, Christchurch, New Zealand

ABSTRACT

This research presents a virtual exchange project between two tertiary institutions in New Zealand and Finland with 26 participants who were intermediate German language students. During the project, the students used a closed Facebook group to post about given topics; the posts combined video, audio, and text that adhered to multimodal meaning-making theory. The theoretical framework was task-based language teaching underpinned by the notion of engagement, social media in language learning, and telecollaboration. Language learning was viewed through a socio-cultural lens. A mixed-methods approach was used to collect data including questionnaires, interviews, and FB-logs. The qualitative data was analysed by content analysis method. The results indicate that the students perceived FB as an applicable tool for community building and they enjoyed the variation it brought to the course. Collaboration, use of communication tools, authenticity, and teachers' support fostered student engagement.

INTRODUCTION

Technology-mediated social networking sites (SNSs), such as Facebook (FB), have become an integral part of students' social and educational lives (Blattner & Fiori, 2011; Espinosa, 2015; Leier, 2017; Picciano, 2009). They are virtual spaces where students can join groups of learners from different countries

DOI: 10.4018/978-1-6684-7123-4.ch071

and backgrounds, thus developing into new global contact zones that have led to the creation of online communities (Kulavuz-Onal & Vasquez, 2018; Oskoz & Gimeno-Sanz, 2020).

These spaces can develop into learning communities that foster engagement when teachers carefully design the learning activities and assignments. The notion of community and learning refers to Dewey's concepts of student-driven learning via engagement, active learning, and collaboration (Fink & Inkelas, 2015). Online communities and interactivity that Web 2.0 facilitates draws attention as discussed by Palloff and Pratt: "Without the support and participation of learning communities, there is no online course" (Palloff & Pratt, 1999, p. 29). Kopp and Hill (2008) continued this line of thinking: "Learning occurs when knowledge is actuated through the process of a learner connecting to and feeding information into a learning community" (p. 1). In this study the instructors created a Facebook group as a learning environment. Two groups of tertiary students of German who live in two opposite parts of the world meet on this platform and work on teacher-designed tasks. The students who knew only little about each other's cultures build a community of learners by conducting tasks which were designed applying the three-layer task design (Ware & O'Dowd, 2008). The final task creating a joint product was the most challenging. The type of telecollaboration between two groups of non-native speakers from remote parts of the world using Facebook as a platform are first getting to know each other and finally creating a joint product is a new and innovative study and a contribution to the CALL literature.

LITERATURE REVIEW

Due to developments in network communication technologies, foreign language learners can extend their face-to-face classroom learning and gain access to other learners globally to learn a target language together, leading to intercultural communication and, consequently, intercultural competency (Byram, 1997). The extant literature references this approach to language learning as telecollaboration (Belz, 2003; Goodwin-Jones, 2019; Hauck & Young, 2008; Kurek & Müller-Hartmann, 2019; O'Dowd, 2011) or virtual exchanges (O'Dowd, 2018; The EVALUATE Group, 2019)

Traditionally, telecollaborations were email exchanges or situated on an institution's learning platform (Belz, 2003; O'Dowd, 2011; Sadler & Dooley, 2016) since technology afforded easier and more affordable communication telecollaboration gained a lot of interest in recent years with studies reporting on telecollaboration initiatives between language students (Oskoz & Gimeno-Sanz, 2020), between language teacher students (Ryshina-Pankova, 2018), but also studies about practices and attitudes towards telecollaboration both of teachers and students (Helm, 2015). Telecollaboration projects are predominantly concerned about intercultural competence, either synchronous communication (Ryshina-Pankova, 2018; van der Zwaard & Bannink, 2019) or asynchronous communication using different social Web-tools (Lee, 2018; Oskoz & Gimeno-Sanz, 2020; Ryshina-Pankova, 2018; van der Zwaard & Bannink, 2019). Oskoz & Gimeno-Sanz studied 24 second language learners in the US and Spain over a period of one semester. The students completed collaborative tasks in groups of 3 or 4 using online tools such as Google +, online forums and Skype. Applying the appraisal framework, Martin & White's (2005) results indicated that students enjoyed creating a close and safe learning environment. Lee (2018) established a Spanish American exchange over one semester using Voicethread, blogs and video chats. The communication was in Spanish and the US learners of Spanish profited of this exchange in particular gaining pragmatic knowledge. Ryshina-Pankova (2018) formed a telecollaboration with 13 teacher students in the US and 13 foreign language teacher students in Germany who communicated via online chat for a period of seven weeks. The topic of their chats was videos on soccer the students had to watch and subsequently discuss with their partners. Van der Zwaard & Bannink (2019) reported on a study between 60 Dutch and Australian students who collaborated for eight weeks on making a digital theatre play using synchronous computer-mediated communication, Skype and instant chat.

The community in a telecollaboration does not form naturally, as in a classroom; the course design is based on communication cues to influence community formation. Language teachers become designers and acquire the necessary skills and competencies themselves before being able to support learner autonomy in Web 2.0 contexts (Fuchs, Snyder, Tung, & Han, 2018; Hauck & Young, 2008; Palfreyman, 2018).

Task design enhances not only intercultural competence but also a sense of community. Beneficial tasks allow discourse to develop interactivity, reciprocity, and interactional balance (Chun, 2011; Ware & O'Dowd, 2008). Chun (2011) explored how online exchanges can play a role in second language learners' development of pragmatic and intercultural competence. She studied the discourse style of advanced learners of the German language and learners of the English language. The exchanges occurred over a period of 10 weeks via an online discussion forum. The task was to discuss specific vocabulary that the instructor had provided. The students wrote about the terms, and then they discussed the vocabulary in a synchronous final chat session. The exchange was mostly successful, with some students failing to contribute. Ware and O'Dowd (2008) conducted a study in which they connected English language students in Chile and Spanish language students in the US to communicate during two 8-week sessions about tasks that the researchers designed. The focus was on giving each other feedback. This asynchronous exchange was partially successful, but the researchers highlighted that tasks are to be designed carefully and adapted to both student groups.

Telecollaboration tasks situated on an SNS are a new and under-researched topic (Blattner & Fiori, 2011; Fuchs, Hauck, & Müller-Hartmann, 2012; Ziegler, 2016). Utilisation of widely accessible and user-friendly SNSs, such as FB, has allowed students to connect with friends worldwide and develop international networks. Furthermore, language learners perceive SNSs as authentic communication platforms. Thus, bringing an SNS into the language classroom to connect German language learners from different parts of the world, creating a collaborative learning environment within the principles of task-based language teaching (TBLT) (Ellis, 2003) and social constructivism (Vygotsky, 1978), seems to be a logical continuation of students' online lives (Boyd, 2014).

A few researchers have used tasks as in TBLT situated on FB in their language classes (Blattner & Fiori, 2011; Leier, 2017; Foogooa & Ferdinand-James, 2017), with one of the first studies using it in a language class and as a part of the overall assessment conducted by Blattner and Fiori (2011). Spanish language learners in the US accessed FB to observe appropriate language usage, especially greetings in specific contexts. The students found that understanding the authentic language was challenging, but the task increased their sociopragmatic awareness. Blattner and Fiori also focused on raising awareness of speech acts on FB to trigger future production: "This sociopragmatic task was chosen to develop communicative competence, which would lead to production" (p. 37). Likewise, Leier (2017) integrated tasks in an FB group as part of the assessment. Her German language students communicated with each other over a period of 12 weeks. The platform enhanced developing a stronger class community and cultivating writing skills in the target language, particularly when applying informal language. Moreover, Foogooa and Ferdinand-James (2017) researched English as a Second Language (ESL) student engagement through two online communication tools: a learning-management system (LMS) and an FB group. Indeed, these tools engaged the students, as they enjoyed the combination more than merely using an LMS.

Engagement Model as a Theoretical Framework

The digital era provides educators with various means to engage students who are studying at institutions of higher education and who have grown up with digital technology. Educational technology and use of socio-digital technologies in learning seem to foster student engagement (Korkealehto & Siklander, 2018). Several studies have researched the relationship between engagement and SNS usage for learning activities in higher education.

A plethora of literature define student engagement from different viewpoints. As we are interested in tasks which lead to engagement, we build our interpretation on the model presented by Lay-Hwa Bowden, Tickle and Naumann (2019). Their model comprises four pillars: behavioural, affective, social and cognitive engagement; they added social engagement to the widely agreed three-part typology (Fredricks, Blumenfeld, & Paris, 2004; Ryu & Lombardi, 2015) in which student engagement includes behavioural, affective, and cognitive components. Behavioural engagement entails participation and involvement in academic activities through time and effort spent on learning activities and interactions with peers and teachers (Kahu, 2013; Kuh, 2009). Affective engagement entails students' emotional reactions to learning (Fredricks et al., 2004), including reactions and attitudes that students have related to teachers, peers, studying, subjects, and school in general. Social engagement relates to the sense of belonging to the learning community (Pekrun & Linnenbrink-Garcia, 2012). In class, social engagement is shown as collaboration and listening to the others. Finally, cognitive engagement entails willingness and motivation to invest effort in comprehending complex ideas and mastering high-level skills (Fredricks et al., 2004). In this study, we address student engagement as a holistic phenomenon including the four abovementioned aspects.

Results of studies on engagement in combination with SNS use are ambivalent. Some studies show that FB, as an SNS, positively affects engagement and learning results (Heiberger & Harper, 2008; Mbodila, Ndebele, & Muhandji, 2014), while others indicate that FB fosters social, rather than cognitive engagement (Wise, Skues, & Williams, 2011) or that it both positively and negatively affects engagement and learning results (Junco, 2012).

In this article, we present findings from a study that involved two groups of German language students: one in Finland, one in New Zealand. The objectives were to offer the students opportunities to connect and to use their target language in an informal environment and get to know students on the other side of the world. Connecting learners studying the same target language enhanced the students' ability to make their German language learning more relevant and to extend their language skills by providing different tasks starting from simple tasks of introduction and ending with the most complex task type to create a shared product with participants from both countries. This final product was presented and it included a comparison of cultural artefacts which enhanced the learners' knowledge base as the students did not know much about each other's countries. The aim of our study is to gain a comprehensive understanding of how telecollaboration designed using TBLT principles and situated on a closed FB group as a learning environment can influence student engagement in a German language course. We proposed the following research questions:

RQ1: *How do students perceive the implementation of the tasks in a FB-group?*
RQ2: *Does task-based language teaching applied in a technology-enhanced environment lead to student engagement in foreign language learning?*

METHODS

Project and Participants

This study investigates a telecollaboration project between two German language classes at institutions of higher education in two countries: Finland and New Zealand. The participants in Finland comprised 12 business administration students at the University of Applied Sciences in Helsinki, the students who were conducting their degree programme in the English language (aged 20–25 years). The telecollaboration project was one part of a five-credit German course, which was the students' second German language course at the University of Applied Sciences. In New Zealand, a group of 14 tertiary students (aged 18–24 years) participated in an intermediate course in the German language. They studied German in addition to their core subjects, which included diverse fields, such as law and engineering. Students' language levels in both countries were B1, according to the Common European Framework of Reference for Languages (CEFR).

The telecollaboration occurred over a period of six weeks, and it was integral to the German language course curricula in both countries and was part of the course assessment. The 26 students conducted five tasks based on the three-layer task design (O'Dowd & Ware, 2009) and posted them on the closed FB group.

The task design included tasks organized into three principal categories (Table 1). The task type one included information exchange tasks, in which the students created videos to introduce themselves and had to find a student with similar interests and comment on their post. In the second post, the students were asked to write about their hometowns, and their families supporting their posts with photos. The task type two entailed comparison and analysis tasks. The students wrote about their mealtimes and favourite foods, using photos to support their posts, and in the fourth post, they presented their favourite clothes shops, using external weblinks and photos. The students from the other country were asked to find similarities and differences before commenting on the FB group. The task type three was a collaborative task i.e., a joint project for both groups. The teachers assigned the students in groups of three or four people from both classes. The students chose their own topics, comparing relevant phenomena from each country. The multimodal meaning-making theory, a model for designing instruction grounded in multiliteracy (Kress & van Leeuwen, 2001; Pegrum, 2009) supported our task design.

The pedagogical tasks were in line with the framework introduced earlier in this study. The tasks prepared for the students focused on meaning and learners were asked to include semantic and pragmatic meaning rather than form. The purpose and goal of the tasks was authentic communication modelled by the real world.

Data and Data Analysis

This research was conducted using a mixed-methods approach to collect quantitative and qualitative data. The total number of the students participating in the telecollaboration project was 26; but only part of the students answered the questionnaires and volunteered to be interviewed. The data comprised 11 participants who completed pre-study questionnaires, 12 who completed post-study questionnaires, and 11 who volunteered to semi-structured interviews, which varied from 10–20 minutes each. The FB log data comprised 138 posts, totalling 4,607 words. The questionnaires were anonymous and not subjected to ethical consent whereas the interviews needed a written consent by the volunteering students.

Table 1. Tasks and Topics of the Exchange

Tasks	Topics
Task type 1: Information exchange	
1. Video: Individual introductions	Make a video that is not longer than three minutes in which you introduce yourself and your hobbies.
2. Photos, weblinks: Local culture and people	Present your hometown and family. The distance partners are required to comment on at least two of the posts.
Task type 2: Comparison and analysis	
3. Photos: Food and eating habits	Write about food in your country, using photos to support your writing. The distance partners are required to compare the information with topics from their own country.
4. Photos, weblinks: clothes and shopping	Present your favourite clothes shop, using external weblinks and photos to support your writing. The distance partners are required to compare the information with topics from their own country.
Task type 3: Collaboration	
5. PowerPoint or video: Present on a given topic in groups of three or four students from both classes.	Compare Christmas, summer holidays, or national holidays between the two countries.

The quantitative data were collected through Google Forms online questionnaires, which were conducted at the beginning and end of the project. The pre-project questionnaire comprised 14 multiple-choice questions, mapping out students' preferences and activities on social media. The post-project questionnaire contained 11 multiple-choice questions and 9 open-ended questions on students' perceptions of the project. In both questionnaires, the multiple-choice questions used a 5-point Likert scale, ranging from 1 (*strongly disagree*) to 5 (*strongly agree*).

The qualitative data included the answers to the semi-structured interview questions conducted after the project and the answers to the open-ended questions in the post-project questionnaire. Five students from Finland and six from New Zealand were interviewed; the Finns by their teacher and the New Zealand students' interviews were conducted by a student teacher. The interviews were done individually face-to-face, audio-recorded and transcribed verbatim. The semi-structured interview responses and the open-ended post-project questionnaire answers were analysed using content analysis method, which provides procedures for rigorous analysis of written data (Flick, 1998; Krippendorff, 2004; Schreier, 2012). Applying qualitative content analysis facilitates describing qualitative data in a systematic way.

Both researchers in this study worked independently, one in Finland and the other in New Zealand; they read and identified common phrases, key themes, and patterns concerning students' perceptions on the FB collaboration and their views on how the online collaboration led to student engagement in foreign language learning. Both researchers analysed independently the data several times for reliability, they identified categories and subcategories which were then discussed and refined. A coding frame was developed, resulting in the following themes:

- Collaboration
- Use of communication tools on FB
- Authentic learning
- Teachers' activities

- Enjoyment

RESULTS

The telecollaboration project in the German language course regarding students' perceptions on collaboration in an online community and the community's ability to foster student engagement showed that the students were engaged in the activity and interested in their group members' posts. In this section, we will describe the activity in the FB group during the study period and then answer the research questions.

Facebook Activity

The students participating in the telecollaboration posted regularly during the six-week period, particularly when they were required to add artefacts. Figure 1 shows the activity for the four tasks applying task type one and two. The final task (task type three) was not included on the chart because the presentations were not required to be posted in the FB group. The FB activity in Figure 1 shows posts, comments, "likes," and "seens" for each post. The "seen" reactions drew the highest numbers for each post. "Seen" is a function only available in a FB group, listing each viewer by name.

The posts, 138 in total, triggered comments Figure 1 such as *"Tolles Video, das Mädchen ist so hübsch"* ("Great video; the girls are so pretty") or questions about the group members' culture: *"Was ist das für eine Mütze?"* ("What type of a hat is that?"). Occasionally, students used the FB group to exchange information about the target language (e.g., "Hey, guys—grammar tips,", as illustrated in Figure 2.

The posts that referred to topics other than the assigned tasks showed that the students perceived the platform as an authentic communication place which was also observed in the way students communicated on FB using a variety of emoticons to enhance their posted content. The students used several emoticons (e.g., smiley face, wave, smiley face with sunglasses, sad face, and surprised face) to create a more emotionally charged environment.

Figure 1. Facebook (FB) activity

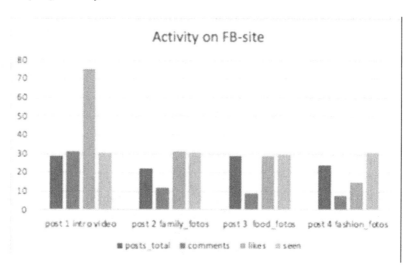

Figure 2. The students' shared information on the target language in FB

The students perceived FB as a platform to communicate with fellow students they had just met online; the results show that most students (80%) perceived the tasks and experiences on the FB site favourably and as meaningful. As shown in the following example one student commented in an interview: "I have learned more about both of our cultures while improving my German". Several students also stated that they gained confidence and found the course content interesting.

Engagement

According to the results, collaboration, use of communication tools, authentic learning, teachers' activity and enjoyment fostered student engagement during the telecollaboration project.

Collaboration. As evident in Figure 3, collaboration fostered engagement. The results ranged from 1 (*strongly disagree*) to 5 (*strongly agree*).

Figure 3. Collaboration fostered engagement

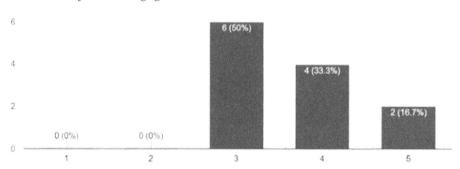

In the following the examples are taken from the interviews and the post-study questionnaire.

Use of communication tools on Facebook. The students were required to comment on each other's posts in all five assignments. According to the FB logs, commenting was used less frequently to develop collaboration compared with the usage of the 'like' function. Nevertheless, one student explained that comments led to a short conversation: "There were, like, some really nice comments. I was actually surprised people were […] because I first thought I am not going to comment, but then people were commenting, and I was answering back… [Laughter]". The student continued: "It motivated, and it was nice that somebody commented and maybe asked something. And you could ask about some other person's life who lives really far away". Hence, the comments sparked real conversation, even if students were initially reluctant to comment or respond to the comments. The students from different countries also noticed that they had common interests, which resulted in genuine conversation: "The girl who's vegan because, like, I'm vegan as well, so we might bond over something". The students were able to communicate meaningfully without being penalized when not applying the correct forms. Therefore, the common ground built with communication tools contributed to engagement, as the students from different countries discovered that they could interrelate. Furthermore, as stated in the previous example, students perceived commenting as a motivator for learning about habits and people from the other side of the world and as a conversation starter. Figure 4 shows how the students had a conversation about their favourite dishes.

Regardless of the number of comments, the students considered themselves engaged. The tasks were designed to be learner-centred which triggered communication and a feeling of belonging to the group. One student noticed that his posts did not trigger any comments, but he still regarded himself as motivated, and the lack of comments did not discourage him. Furthermore, instead of commenting, students simply "liked" each other's posts. They used this feature more frequently than the commenting function. Some students stated that when they noticed that the FB group members liked their posts, it motivated them to communicate more often on FB, especially with the "like" function.

Figure 4. FB conversation on favourite dishes

The students particularly liked and commented on posts with appealing information, such as photos of pets. When asked why so many comments were added to such a post, one student replied: "Must have been the dog".

On FB, the "seen" feature shows the usernames of those who view a post, Thus, this feature revealed the students who had seen any post in the group. The students stated that it contributed to their feelings of belonging, being noticed by other FB group members, even if those members did not leave a comment or push the "like" button. Digital natives perceive this as a way to communicate and receive acknowledgment.

Generally, the data analysis revealed that comments and likes contributed strongly to student engagement in this German language course, even though some students complained that comments on FB can disappear in the stream, and some students forgot to read and respond to their comments.

Authentic learning. Designing age-relevant and appealing topics for the FB tasks initiated to authentic learning. The students enjoyed sharing details and information about their everyday lives, such as hobbies, mealtimes and eating habits, shopping, and the clothes they wear, as can be seen in Figure 5, with a post on eating habits.

The topics stimulated exchanges of authentic personal information because students' questions and comments led to genuine interest and authentic learning about other cultures and students' personal lives. The differences and similarities between the cultural environments of Finland and New Zealand surprised the participants.

Realizing that the German language is an authentic tool for communication fostered engagement and contributed to students' eagerness to learn the language. They appreciated the opportunity to describe and reflect on their everyday lives in multiliteral ways, a task not often done. One student considered these tasks to be valuable practice for his upcoming student exchange period in Berlin. He praised the FB communication as being more practical compared with traditional face-to-face classes: "I don't know if you can really compare it, if you studied those things in class; it was more practical". The student continued: "Someone asked me about what basketball teams I support; I mean, we had quite a good conversation on that".

Figure 5. Eating habits

As seen in the two examples above, students noticed that they could have real life conversations. Using German as a common language with students from another country inspired them, helping to engage them with the course content and motivated them to learn more.

Teachers' activities. The two teachers —one in Finland, the other in New Zealand—were also members of the closed FB group. They were flexible, as evident in the following example: "It was good that you gave us a little bit more time". They also contributed to the group when necessary to maintain the flow of conversation or to inform the students about an upcoming deadline. The students perceived the teachers' availability as positive and necessary, but some would have valued more feedback, especially corrective feedback for their German language production. When asked about potential improvements, one student responded: "Maybe mistakes to point out what we have written, not just ticking off what we've done. If we keep making mistakes, we keep making them". However, students appreciated it when the teachers contributed to the tasks with their own posts or comments. The students mentioned that it was beneficial if the teachers intervened when the students had difficulties in starting the tasks.

Enjoyment. Enjoyment is a vital aspect when stimulating student engagement. The students claimed that the FB tasks added value to the course design and continued that the closed FB group, as a shared platform, provided an enjoyable and safe learning environment that fostered engagement, and contributed positively to their learning experiences.

Figure 6. Enjoyment

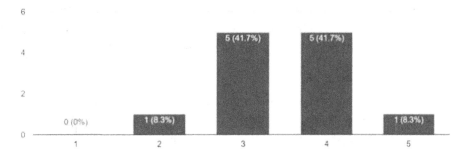

Figure 6 indicates that the students found the telecollaboration project to be fun, at least to some extent; none of them judged the project as being no fun at all. One student appreciated the cultural comparisons: "I've quite enjoyed it because it is quite interesting to see the different cultures between Helsinki and Christchurch". Another student reflected on the novelty that the FB collaboration brought to the language course: "It was definitely different, but I think that was good". Furthermore, some students had not previously used FB as a frequent platform for studying, but they soon became used to it and valued its benefits when compared with traditional teaching. They mentioned that conducting weekly tasks as well as reading and commenting on the posts became a routine for them. According to the results, over 91% of the students considered all five tasks fun. Moreover, the students generally preferred assignments that included photos and written text rather than video recordings. They also viewed the fifth task (the group presentations) as contributing to their enjoyment, even though some of the groups found it challenging to create a group and start the collaborative task.

DISCUSSION

The first research question investigated how the students perceive the implementation of the tasks in a FB-group. According to the results, the students perceived the tasks on the site as meaningful and learner-centred. The students' shared the interest in learning the German language and the interest in each other's cultures, leading to social presence. They enjoyed sharing the photos, which contributed to a deeper understanding of a foreign culture. Despite some reluctance at the beginning to share personal photos and videos, the students gradually developed a feeling of belonging to the group, which coincided with the results from Zepke and Leach (2010).

In our study, the first task was to create a personal video. Considering previous usage of the FB platform it would have been ideal to start with a less revealing task, because videos are authentic but can be intimidating for participants who do not know each other. FB is an extension of users' offline social life. Ellison, Steinfield, and Lampe (2007) concluded that "SNSs help maintain relationships as people move from one offline community to another" (p. 1164). The participants of this study experienced FB as a suitable platform for language learning. De facto, being asked to meet strangers violates the code of the platform and can cause disruptions, but in contrary to previous studies, in our research, the students perceived it motivating to contact strangers. The eagerness to communicate with unknown students from different part of the world triggered a more engaged approach enhancing students' performance in the target language.

In addition to language learning, the students enjoyed gaining authentic and meaningful cultural knowledge as well as connecting with students of German language on the other side of the world. This unique exchange was useful because both learner groups studied the same target language at the same level, and they both experienced the same feelings of limitation. This novel experience of negotiating tasks, talking about and comparing cultural issues required practice and training in the target language and led to reflecting learning.

Research question two was answered by investigating the task design in relation to the engagement of the students. Instead of measuring student engagement objectively, we chose to use students' self-evaluation and subjective feedback. In our opinion, the students' perceptions provided more valuable information on FB's ability to foster engagement. According to the results the telecollaboration in FB led to engagement in terms of five components: collaboration, use of communication tools, enjoyment, authentic learning, and teachers' activities. The students praised FB's ability to promote communication and collaboration which is in line with Irwin, Ball, Desbrow, and Leveritt's (2012) results. FB used as an educational tool offers technology which supports collaboration and communication. In a private FB group, communication is stress free, allowing participants to concentrate on the message without concerns about the correctness of their writing or speaking. In addition, interaction with the teachers and their support contributed not only to behavioural engagement but also to affective and social engagement, as the students experienced a feeling of belonging with the teachers and peers. The students perceived the teachers' actions in the platform as positive, which is consistent with the study by Richardson, Besser, Koehler, Lim, and Strait (2016), who found that instructor presence was important for student success when connecting with foreign students, making each other more approachable, showing concern for their success, and demonstrating expertise. In the present study teachers' comments triggered enhanced participation and helped clarifying assignment guidelines.

Furthermore, the teachers' activities and enhanced engagement sparked by the affordances of the platform demonstrate that the course design was successful. Thus, engagement was reciprocal between the students and teachers. The students constructed collaboratively an authentic learning environment that motivated them to learn and participate more. For example, the students made several attempts making video or audio recordings, trying to produce the perfect version. This indicates persistence and a willingness to focus on quality in learning activities (Fredricks et al., 2004; Kuh, 2009; Schindler et al., 2017). In online learning, enjoyment fosters student engagement (Korkealehto & Siklander, 2018). Similarly, the telecollaboration through the closed FB group added pleasure to the German language course, as the students enjoyed creating their own recordings, videos and written tasks, and they had pleasure in reading, watching, and listening to their peers' products. The students' positive attitude toward the assignments fostered their affective engagement (Schindler et al., 2017).

Contrary to many telecollaboration studies, even though we as teachers are novices to telecollaboration, we managed to include the demanding task type 3 – a joint presentation (Helm, 2015). Unanticipated, the students perceived it enjoyable yet challenging. Being challenged promotes engagement and creates the feeling of progress. In addition, given that the target language in this study was for both groups not the mother tongue German - which is seldomly used in telecollaboration - increases the value of this research. The results encourage language teachers to use telecollaboration with other lingua franca than English. Further, the use of FB as the learning platform for telecollaboration is a novelty. In addition, previous research report difficulties in teacher collaboration, but in our case the teachers collaborated without friction, regardless of the time difference and long distance (Helm, 2015).

According to the students, the five factors, *collaboration, the use of communication tools on FB, authentic learning, teachers' activities,* and *enjoyment* contributed positively to student engagement. These five factors were interdependent; consequently, their combined effect was stronger than one factor would have been on its own. The students perceived the tasks in the closed FB group added value to the course and to their overall learning experiences. The fact that the FB group was closed enhanced students' willingness to share details about their lives. These findings are in line with extant research on student engagement in technologically enhanced learning (Lay-Hwa Bowden et al., 2019).

CONCLUSION

This study described how students from the opposite sides of the globe connected with each other using technology and the common medium of the German language. Although we conducted the project on a small scale, with 26 participants over a short period of time, it was rewarding for students to gain insights into new cultures. Regardless of Finland and New Zealand being in opposite hemispheres with different university schedules and time zones, we found an open six-week block in our teaching schedules that suited both countries. The problems with the time difference were minimized by creating telecollaboration on an asynchronous communication platform.

The time difference and distance created challenges for the teachers, but with flexibility on both sides, a shared understanding developed for this fruitful collaboration. Moreover, the teachers developed their digital and pedagogical knowledge and the ability to facilitate the learning process, providing timely support and feedback. By cooperating the teachers created a comfortable and safe learning environment for their students to learn the language.

In future studies, our objective is to implement online exchange possibilities over an extended duration, preferably with more opportunities for the students to communicate with each other. The students should be offered the opportunity to become acquainted with each other through individual dialogues before advancing to more public SNS platforms.

ACKNOWLEDGMENT

We would like to thank all the students and student teachers who participated in this study. The New Zealand and the Finnish students who volunteered to take part in this study gave written ethical consent.

AUTHOR CONTRIBUTIONS

Both authors contributed equally to the writing and conceptual structure of this manuscript.

REFERENCES

Belz, J. (2003). Linguistic perspectives on the development of intercultural competence in telecollaboration. *Language Learning & Technology*, *7*(2), 68–99.

Blattner, G., & Fiori, M. (2011). Virtual social network communities: An investigation of language learners' development of sociopragmatic awareness and multiliteracy skills. *CALICO Journal*, *29*(1), 24–43.

Boyd, D. (2014). *It's complicated: The social lives of networked teens*. Yale University Press.

Byram, M. (1997). *Teaching and assessing intercultural communicative competence*. Philadelphia, PA: Clevedon.

Chun, D. (2011). Developing intercultural communicative competence through online exchanges. *CALICO Journal*, *28*(2), 392–419. doi:10.11139/cj.28.2.392-419

Ellis, R. (2003). *Task-based language learning and teaching*. Oxford University Press.

Ellison, N., Steinfield, C., & Lampe, C. (2007). The benefits of Facebook "friends": Social capital and college students' use of online social network sites. *Journal of Computer-Mediated Communication*, *12*(4), 1143–1168. doi:10.1111/j.1083-6101.2007.00367.x

Espinosa, L. (2015). The use of Facebook for educational purposes in EFL classrooms. *Theory and Practice in Language Studies*, *5*(11), 2206–2211. doi:10.17507/tpls.0511.03

Fink, J. E., & Inkelas, K. K. (2015). A history of learning communities within American higher education. In M. Benjamin (Ed.), *Learning communities from start to finish: New directions for student services* (pp. 5–15). Jossey-Bass. doi:10.1002s.20113

Flick, U. (1998). *An introduction to qualitative research*. Sage.

Foogooa, R., & Ferdinand-James, D. S. (2017). Use of Facebook for enhancing student engagement in a higher-education-blended engineering course. *Innovative Issues and Approaches in Social Sciences IIAS*, *10*(1), 8–31. doi:10.12959/issn.1855-0541.IIASS-2017-no1-art1

Fredricks, J. A., Blumenfeld, P. C., & Paris, A. H. (2004). School engagement: Potential of the concept, state of the evidence. *Review of Educational Research*, *74*(1), 59–109. doi:10.3102/00346543074001059

Fuchs, C., Hauck, M., & Müller-Hartmann, A. (2012). Promoting learner autonomy through multiliteracy skills development in cross-institutional exchanges. *Language Learning & Technology*, *16*(3), 82–102.

Fuchs, C., Snyder, B., Tung, B., & Han, Y. J. (2018). The multiple roles of the task-design mediator in telecollaboration. *ReCALL*, *29*(3), 239–256. doi:10.1017/S0958344017000088

Goodwin-Jones, R. (2019). Telecollaboration as an approach to developing intercultural communication competence. *Language, Learning & Technology, 23*(3), 8–28.

Hauck, M., & Young, B. (2008). Telecollaboration in multimodal environments: The impact on task design and learner interaction. *Computer Assisted Language Learning*, *21*(2), 87–124. doi:10.1080/09588220801943510

Heiberger, G., & Harper, R. (2008). Have you facebooked Astin lately? Using technology to increase student involvement. *New Directions for Student Services*, *124*(124), 19–35. doi:10.1002s.293

Helm, F. (2015). The practices and challenges of telecollaboration in higher education in Europe. *Language Learning & Technology*, *19*(2), 197–217.

Irwin, C., Ball, L., Desbrow, B., & Leveritt, M. (2012). Students' perceptions of using Facebook as an interactive learning resource at university. *Australasian Journal of Educational Technology*, *28*(7), 1221–1232. doi:10.14742/ajet.798

Junco, R. (2012). The relationship between frequency of Facebook use, participation in Facebook activities, and student engagement. *Computers & Education*, *58*(1), 162–171. doi:10.1016/j.compedu.2011.08.004

Kahu, E. R. (2013). Framing student engagement in higher education. *Studies in Higher Education*, *38*(5), 758–773. doi:10.1080/03075079.2011.598505

Kopp, R., & Hill, A. (2008). Connectivism: Learning theory of the future or vestige of the past? *International Review of Research in Open and Distance Learning*, *9*(3), 1–8. doi:10.19173/irrodl.v9i3.523

Korkealehto, K., & Siklander, P. (2018). Enhancing engagement, enjoyment and learning experiences by gamification on an English course for healthcare students. *SeminarNet, International Journal of Media, Technology, and Lifelong Learning, 14*(1), 13-30. https://journals.hioa.no/index.php/seminar/article/view/2579

Kress, G., & van Leeuwen, T. (2001). *Multimodal discourse: The modes and media of contemporary communication*. Arnold.

Krippendorff, K. (2004). *Content analysis: An introduction to its methodology*. Sage.

Kuh, G. D. (2009). The National Survey of Student Engagement: Conceptual and empirical foundations. *New Directions for Institutional Research*, *141*(141), 5–20. doi:10.1002/ir.283

Kulavuz-Onal, D., & Vasquez, C. (2018). "Thanks, shokran, gracias": Translingual practices in a Facebook group. *Language Learning & Technology*, *22*(1), 240–255.

Kurek, M., & Müller-Hartmann, A. (2019). The formative role of teaching presence in blended virtual exchanges. *Language Learning & Technology*, *23*(3).

Lay-Hwa Bowden, J., Tickle, L., & Naumann, K. (2019). The four pillars of tertiary student engagement and success: A holistic measurement approach. *Studies in Higher Education*. Advance online publication. doi:10.1080/03075079.2019.1672647

Lee, L. (2018). Using Telecollaboration 2.0 to Build Intercultural Communicative Competence: A Spanish-American Exchange. In D. Tafazoli, M. Gomez Parra, & C. Huertas-Abril (Eds.), *Cross-Cultural Perspectives on Technology-Enhanced Language Learning* (pp. 303–321). IGI Global. doi:10.4018/978-1-5225-5463-9.ch017

Leier, V. (2017). Learning language through Facebook. *International Journal of Computer Assisted Language Learning*, *7*(3), 40–57. doi:10.4018/IJCALLT.2017070103

Martin, J. R., & White, P. R. R. (2005). *The language of evaluation: Appraisal in English*. Palgrave. doi:10.1057/9780230511910

Mbodila, M., Ndebele, C., & Muhandji, K. (2014). The effect of social media on students' engagement and collaboration in higher education: A case study of the use of Facebook at a South African university. *Journal of Communication*, *5*(2), 115–125. doi:10.1080/0976691X.2014.11884831

O'Dowd, R., & Ware, P. (2009). Critical issues in telecollaborative task design. *Computer Assisted Language Learning*, *22*(2), 173–188. doi:10.1080/09588220902778369

O'Dowd, R. (2018). Innovations and challenges in using online communication technologies in CLIL. *Theory into Practice*, *57*(3), 1–9. doi:10.1080/00405841.2018.1484039

Oskoz, A., & Gimeno-Sanz, A. (2020). Exploring L2 Learners' engagement and attitude in an intercultural encounter. *Language Learning & Technology*, *24*(1), 187–208.

Palfreyman, D. M. (2018). Learner autonomy and groups. In A. Chik, N. Aoki, & R. Smith (Eds.), *Autonomy in language learning and teaching* (pp. 51–72). Palgrave Pivot. doi:10.1057/978-1-137-52998-5_4

Palloff, R., & Pratt, K. (1999). *Building learning communities in cyberspace: Effective strategies for the online classroom*. Jossey-Bass.

Pegrum, M. (2009). From blogs to bombs: The future of digital technologies in education. Crawley, WA: UWA Publishing.

Pekrun, R., & Linnenbrink-Garcia, L. (2012). Academic emotions and student engagement. In Handbook of research on student engagement (pp. 259-282). Springer Science+Business Media. doi:10.1007/978-1-4614-2018-7_12

Picciano, A. (2009). Blending with purpose: The multimodal model. *Journal of the Research Centre for Educational Technology*, *5*(1), 4–15.

Richardson, J. C., Besser, E. D., Koehler, A. A., Lim, J., & Strait, M. (2016). Instructors' perceptions of instructor presence in online learning environments. *International Review of Research in Open and Distance Learning*, *17*(4), 82–104. doi:10.19173/irrodl.v17i4.2330

Ryshina-Pankova, M. (2018). Discourse moves and intercultural communicative competence in telecollaborative chats. *Language Learning & Technology*, *22*(1), 218–239.

Ryu, S., & Lombardi, D. (2015). Coding classroom interactions for collective and individual engagement. *Educational Psychologist*, *50*(1), 70–83. doi:10.1080/00461520.2014.1001891

Sadler, R., & Dooly, M. (2016). Twelve years of telecollaboration: What we have learnt. *ELT Journal*, *70*(4), 401–413. doi:10.1093/elt/ccw041

Schindler, L., Burkholder, G., Morad, O., & Marsh, C. (2017). Computer-based technology and student engagement: A critical review of the literature. *International Journal of Educational Technology in Higher Education*, *14*(1), 1–28. doi:10.118641239-017-0063-0

Schreier, M. (2012). *Qualitative content analysis in practice*. Sage.

The EVALUATE Group. (2019). Executive summary—The key findings from the EVALUATE European policy experiment project on the impact of virtual exchange on initial teacher education. *Research-Publishing.Net*. doi:10.14705/rpnet.2019.30.9782490057344

Van der Zwaard, R., & Bannink, A. (2019). Toward a comprehensive model of negotiated interaction in computer-mediated communication. *Language Learning & Technology*, *23*(3), 116–135. http://hdl.handle.net/10125/44699

Vygotsky, L. S. (1978). *Mind in society: The development of higher mental processes*. Harvard University Press.

Ware, P., & O'Dowd, R. (2008). Peer feedback on language form in telecollaboration. *Language Learning*, *12*(1), 43–63.

Wise, L., Skues, J., & Williams, B. (2011). *Facebook in higher education promotes social, but not academic, engagement*. Ascilite Conference 2011, Hobart, Australia.

Zepke, N., & Leach, L. (2010). Improving student engagement: Ten proposals for action. *Active Learning in Higher Education*, *11*(3), 167–177. doi:10.1177/1469787410379680

Ziegler, N. (2016). Taking technology to task: Technology-mediated TBLT, performance, and production. *Annual Review of Applied Linguistics*, *36*, 136–163. doi:10.1017/S0267190516000039

This research was previously published in the International Journal of Computer-Assisted Language Learning and Teaching (IJCALLT), 11(1); pages 1-20, copyright year 2021 by IGI Publishing (an imprint of IGI Global).

APPENDIX A

Telecollaboration, Preliminary Questionnaire

This questionnaire focuses on students' experiences and opinions on telecollaboration. Please answer truthfully and carefully to all the questions. The answers will be analysed and the results of this study will be presented at a conference and published as an article. This questionnaire is confidential and anonymous.

1. Your organisation
    Haaga-Helia
    UC
2. Your age
    under 20
    21 - 25
    26 - 30
    30 -
3. Your gender
    male
    female
    other
    prefer not to say
4. Social networks Which of the following (if any) social working sites are you a member?
    Facebook
    Instagram
    WhatsApp
5. If you answered 'other', which ones?

Facebook
6. How many Facebook friends do you have?
    20-60
    60-100
    100-150
    more than 150
7. Do you have FB-friends from other countries than your native country?
    yes
    no
8. If you answered 'yes', how many foreign FB-friends have you got and from which countries do they come from?
9. How do you know your online friends?
    most of them are friends from my real-life
    most of them are friends I have never met in person
    most of my friends I know in real-life and some of them I never met before

10. How often do you check your personal Facebook?
    several times a day
    once a day
    several times a week
    once a week or less frequently
11. Do you post items on you FB wall?
    yes, regularly- almost every day
    yes, sometimes – maybe once a week
    not very often, maybe once a month or less
    never, but I follow the entries of my friends
12. Do you use the 'like' ('gefällt mir') function on FB?
    yes, every time
    yes, sometimes
    no, never
13. Do you use the 'comment' ('kommentieren') function on FB?
    yes, every time
    yes, sometimes
    no, not actively, but I read the comments
    no, and I never read the comments

Facebook Groups

14. Do you work with Facebook group feature in other courses at your university?
    yes
    no
15. If you answered 'yes', which course is it? And is it part of the assessment in the course/courses. Please explain
16. Do you feel that Facebook group used as a platform of your class assessment is:
    intruding into your personal FB life
    doesn't intrude into your personal FB life
17. Do you belong to FB-groups?
    yes
    no
18. If 'yes', how many?
19. If you belong to FB-groups, what type of groups are they?
    hobbies, leisure
    professional
    educational
    other
20. Please, indicate if you answered 'other'

APPENDIX B

Telecollaboration, Post -Questionnaire

Please, fill in after the telecollaboration project

1. Your organisation
    Haaga-Helia
    UC

2. Task 1, video introduction

	Strongly disagree	Disagree	Neutral	Agree	Strongly agree
fostered engagement					
fostered oral language skills					
fostered written language skills					
was fun					

3. Other comments on Task 1
4. Task 2, photos and text on your family and hometown

	Strongly disagree	Disagree	Neutral	Agree	Strongly agree
fostered engagement					
fostered oral language skills					
fostered written language skills					
was fun					

5. Other comments on Task 2
6. Task 3, food & mealtimes

	Strongly disagree	Disagree	Neutral	Agree	Strongly agree
fostered engagement					
fostered oral language skills					
fostered written language skills					
was fun					

7. Other comments on Task 3
8. Task 4, fashion and shopping

	Strongly disagree	Disagree	Neutral	Agree	Strongly agree
fostered engagement					
fostered oral language skills					
fostered written language skills					
was fun					

9. Other comments on Task 4

10. Task 5, joint product

	Strongly disagree	Disagree	Neutral	Agree	Strongly agree
fostered engagement					
fostered oral language skills					
fostered written language skills					
was fun					

11. Other comments on Task 5
12. Collaboration

	Strongly disagree	Disagree	Neutral	Agree	Strongly agree
fostered engagement					
fostered oral language skills					
fostered written language skills					
was fun					

13. Other comments on collaboration
14. Facebook

	Strongly disagree	Disagree	Neutral	Agree	Strongly agree
The teachers were present on Facebook					
Your privacy was disturbed					

15. What would you say you have learned from this exchange?
16. How did you find the tasks?
17. Did you find any of them difficult?
18. Did you find it difficult to create groups with students in the other country?
19. Did you find it difficult to describe your home culture?
20. Which medium did you prefer to create your own post?
    video
    audio
    written
    photo
21. What did you enjoy most about this project?
22. What did you enjoy the least about working in this project?
23. Did you feel that you became part of an online community?
24. Which factors do you think contributed to this feeling?
25. How did you feel about the others' comments on your posts?
26. Do you have any other comments or feedback on this project?

Submit

This content is created by the owner of the form. The data you submit will be sent to the form owner. Never give out your password.

Powered by Microsoft Forms

|

Privacy and cookies

| Terms of use

APPENDIX C

Semi-Structured Interview Questions

1. Could you explain how you perceived this assignment task. Tell us all about it.
2. What are the benefits?
3. What are the drawbacks?
4. Was this project beneficial for learning more German?
5. Did this project motivate you to be interested in the target language?
6. What effect did the comments on your posts have? Did it motivate you or discourage you?
7. Was this project a good tool to connect with another culture?
8. Did you learn about another culture?
9. Did you get more awareness about your own culture?
10. Did you have technical issues, did you have problems?
11. Any issues about Facebook. Did you find it uncomfortable that you did not know the students in the other class in person?
12. How did you find the structure of the assignments?
    a) Did the assignment include too many / not enough tasks?
    b) Were the required lengths of writing or speaking tasks according to your proficiency level?
    c) How did you find the topics?
13. Could you give us feedback? Could you recommend topics for future use? Would you change something about the project or assignments?

Chapter 72

Using Social Media in Education and Using Social Media Strategies in Education and Corporate Organizations in the U.S. and Belarus:
A Practitioner Study

M. Olguta Vilceanu
Rowan University, Glassboro, USA

Suzanne FitzGerald
Rowan University, Glassboro, USA

Jekaterina Yurievna Sadovskaya
School of Business, BSU, Minsk, Belarus

ABSTRACT

Rapid growth of new media technologies allows organizations to communicate with consumers in immediate and interactive ways via blogs and social media websites such as Facebook and Twitter. Consumers, companies, and organizations bypass mass media gatekeepers and engage in direct communication exchanges. This study examines social media efficacy from the perspective of corporate and educational organizations in the United States and Belarus. Using the Delphi method, authors administered iterative surveys to a panel of sixteen experts, seeking consensus points. Access to financial, staff, and technical resources allow corporations to make intensive and effective use of social media. Non-profit and education organizations are interested in ability to relate to stakeholders by low-cost technologies, human interest stories, and personal connections. US organizations valued appropriateness for target audience as the most important factor in evaluating the best use of social media. Belorussian organizations valued effectiveness of the channel itself or ease of use.

DOI: 10.4018/978-1-6684-7123-4.ch072

INTRODUCTION

Today's organizations must engage consumers and stakeholders with interactive rather than one-way communication. Audiences are increasingly interested and engaged in communication with their brands, institutions, and philanthropic causes via social and interactive media. The age of constant communication in a society connected across political, social, geographic, and national borders, demands continuous updates and immediate response to whatever information needs to be addressed by media in general and social media in particular. Responding well and quickly versus responding late, or not responding at all, often makes the difference between a successful or failed message, campaign, or brand. This study explores the field perspective of using social media in education and corporate organizations in Belarus and the U.S. While there is an abundance of research regarding social media in the U.S., from a variety of socioeconomic, technical, and knowledge perspectives, the Belarusian counterpart is under-represented in existing literature. Therefore, most of this study will focus on presenting and interpreting the findings for the Belarus dataset, with the US dataset serving as a counterpart to help readers gain a better understanding on the differences and similarities between strategic use of social media in Belarus.

The field of public relations is intrinsically connected to and through social media channels, such as blogging/microblogging websites, Facebook, and Twitter, as they encourage and facilitate conversation between organizations and their key stakeholders. Whether we call it chatter, buzz, Word-of-Mouth, or viral, extensive communication often commences between information sponsors and consumers on blogging platforms such as WordPress, Blogger, or Tumblr, where campaigns are launched or erupt unexpectedly with comments on blog posts and bloom into bona fide debates among wide audiences across various media channels.

Because consumers can gain access to these channels easily, content morphs instantly from mass communication to individualized communication, thus breaking information barriers between organizations and consumers. Whether social networking is based on user location (FourSquare) or simply willingness to belong to a cultural subgroup (Tumblr and Instagram), multi-way communication makes it possible for messages to be adapted and adopted across media platforms without time restrictions. Of course, this creates new strategic needs for organizations as they redefine their communication to focus on the social media imperatives of information, community, and action (Lovejoy, Waters, & Saxton, 2012).

Historically, it can be argued that mediated communication exchanges started with families gathering around their radios in the early 1900s for news and stories that offered a glimpse into the wider world. Then, cinema and television took this context and built it into the center of social life all around the world, fostering change and exchange in terms of values, customs, events, and ideas. Social media morphed the process by replacing the central role of the communicator who owned (or paid for) the message to be delivered a certain way, with the equivalent of an exchange market for information. Today, audiences receive and access information instantly, and discourse can alter irrevocably by moving the focus of communication away from the originating story and into a direction that may or may not be beneficial to the original storyteller. One way or another, the need for information on topics deemed worthy of consumer attention remains well-supplied by individuals and organization vying for access to voice in a crowded social media space (Qualman, 2010).

The miles of red tape for obtaining an answer to a pressing question about an organization, product, or event are swiftly eliminated by individuals with a stake in using and changing social media to facilitate information exchange. Successful organizations have taken on personal qualities and engage in conversations with individuals, rather than simply disseminating messages via mass media (Dasilva,

Arratibel, & Aierdi, 2013; Safko, 2012). Furthermore, communication does not always originate within the organization, as in the old 'pontification model'; in fact, the availability of social media channels makes it quite easy for angry customers to launch successful campaigns against international corporations, as in the case of the "United Breaks Guitars" incident where an irate customer wrote a song that became the rallying cry of unhappy air travelers from all around the world (over 20 million YouTube views and growing). What might have been considered harmless griping in the old days has considerably more value today, when disgruntled customers, students, or clients take to the web to share their opinions and concerns in rapidly growing forums, also known as the advent of 'viral' communication.

Two-way or multi-way communication models are deeply rooted in the basic principles of marketing and will continue to guide the management of strategic communication for years to come. The need to establish, maintain, and manage relationships with key stakeholders, until they are ready to purchase and re-purchase whatever it is the sellers make available, applies to products (almost anything tangible, from cars to technology and packaged goods), services (e.g., finance, insurance, hospitality, education), ideas (from weight loss to everything Hollywood, and from democracy to religion or extremism), or people (such as political or civic leaders for various movements and positions).

Beyond simple information gathering, social media has emerged as a major contributor to changes in consumer behavior from shopping to lifestyle, risk perceptions and overall expectations of products, organizations, and performance (Mohana & Kata, 2017). Whether engaging in retail or civic engagement behaviors, seeking formal education or performing informal information searches, digital media users embrace multiple roles, choose to belong to multiple communities, and constantly reshape their learning and expectations (Jahnke, 2010).

Previous literature investigated strategic use of social media in a variety of corporate or nonprofit settings, separately. It is obvious that corporate and nonprofit organizations differ in the amount of resources and the magnitude of outcomes they expect from their investment in social media. Furthermore, the differences are augmented by social, economic, and political factors specific not only to the industry sector, but also the country where communication is happening, as well as the size of the organization and the type of audience it serves. Our research questions focused on the strategic roles and value associated with social media, according to two panels of experts representing corporate and educational organizations in the United States and Belarus.

Today's Social Media: US and Belarus

One of the most popular books on social media strategies and tactics (Safko, 2012) built on a survey of business professionals, asking them what they knew about social media and, subsequently, what they wanted to see in a book about social media. The initial survey determined that almost every participant knew social media was going to become important to them, their business, and society in general, even though two-thirds of them could not define the concept of social media. Furthermore, heavy consumption of owned media (corporate sites, media outlet websites) and user-generated content (microblogging, Facebook, Twitter, consumer reviews about company and products) drives the seek-and-share processes as consumers look up information about an organization, brand, or product.

Recent efforts to coalesce a broad yet precise definition for 'social media' refer to internet-based channels facilitating opportunistic interactive communication with and self-presentation to broad and narrow audiences, primarily around the concept of two-way and multi-way communication, often referred to as user-generated content (Carr & Hayes, 2015). Channels are provided and supported by corporate or nonprofit entities, as well as individuals with an interest in self-promoting and possibly managing opinions and perceptions among specific publics. As a consequence, social media often emerge as a locus of communication about social and technical conflicts, opportunities, and developments (Skagebi, 2009). Communication may be synchronous or asynchronous, while the content remains available regardless of users' online or offline status at any given moment. Human and algorithmic-based (automated) facilitators are constantly monitoring and managing communication with key stakeholders–which is the very definition of public relations.

From the perspective of social media affordances and constraints (Bucher & Helmond, 2018), users engage with platform-specific features to generate material artifacts such as posts (text, pictures, audio-video) and reactions (like, block, share, comment)—while aware to various degrees of the limitations of each platform. For example, a study of public relations practitioners from the United States discovered strong connections between effective use of social media, career growth, and 'prestige power'–the professional cache derived from having social media followers (Diga & Kelleher, 2009). One of the main reason behind public relations practitioners' willingness to invest in developing social media capabilities resides in the value of 'user-generated value': most people tend to believe consumer comments over organizations' official postings about the quality of products, services, and relationships rendered (Carr & Hayes, 2015). Similarly, in contexts where use of social media is directed toward activism, social protest, or social transformation, research has found that savvy organizations engage along platform-specific user psycho-demographics and construct communication campaigns that emphasize the independent or alternative characteristics of the information shared within and across targeted groups (Comunello, Mulargia, & Parisi, 2016).

In the US, users have become increasingly more aware of corporate and brand communication strategies and do not hesitate to call out brands when they perceive such targeted communication to be merely opportunistic pandering. For example, when brands used Instagram to cheer the US Supreme Court ruling on same-sex marriage in 2015, consumers were quick to leave negative comments on posts from brands who suddenly posted LGBT-friendly messages in an attempt to promote sales, rather than genuine communication with their consumers (Vilceanu & Novak, 2017). In this case, the same technical feature that allowed brands an opportunity to create content immediately related to a current event (the SCOTUS ruling) also provided users with the capability to generate immediate responses directly to the brands they perceived to be insincere. In the words of one of the forefathers of human-computer interaction design, "when affordances are taken advantage of, the user knows what to do just by looking" (Norman, 1990, p. 9).

In Belarus, the lines between informal communication, public relations, and official propaganda are often undefined. The history of modern public relations is only some 30 years old. Within the former Soviet bloc, Russia was the first to start using PR and the first to offer university degrees in the discipline in the early 1990s. Although the Soviet power/authority originally rejected the notion of public relations, it is somewhat difficult for professionals and the general public to differentiate between PR and propaganda. A clear example of this dilemma is found in the substantial changes triggered by a PR campaign that transitioned President Lukashenko from an undesirable political entity to a seasoned leader worth of international support, in particular from the European Union (Ioffe, 2011). It is difficult for the general population to distinguish between clear communication and effective propaganda, when the same political leader has been elected and re-elected as country president for the past 25 years. While the point of this study is not to embark into a detailed analysis of the political context in Belarus, such details might be relevant for readers who wish to understand the finer nuances of information and statements collected from various practitioners.

Where East vs. West used to be seen in terms of the difference between controlled market, lesser technology, communist countries, and their free-market, technologically-advanced, and capitalist counterparts, the boundaries are consistently more blurred today. While English continues to be the closest equivalent to an international language in much of the world, it is by no means the only option available for the general public to partake into the wonders of modern technology. Vkontakte[1] or VK (Russian for "in contact") is the Russian-language competitor of Facebook, and it was established in 2006 by Pavel Durov, after he graduated from St. Petersburg State University. As of early 2019, VK boasted over 100 million active users, the vast majority of which were registered in Russia (68%), Ukraine (6.6%) and Belarus (4.5%)—and over 2 billion visits per day[2]. VK offers mostly the same capabilities as Facebook: users can instant-message contacts; create groups; share and tag images, audio and video; and play browser-based games.

Most importantly, VK offers four positioning blocks for placing targeted, paid marketplace, and classified advertisements for products, services, and apps. While VK "votes" cannot be converted into actual currency, they do function as an exchange coin within the site, for example buying virtual gifts for a friend (Odnoklassniki https://ok.ru/). Because of VK's popularity in Russian-speaking countries like Belarus, this research might reveal not only insight about Facebook, but also Vkontakte and other similar social media networks. While the use of social media in general is much newer in Belarus and other former Soviet bloc countries than in the United States, the authors wanted to compare perception and usage of this new technology/channel (social media) in these two countries.

Hypotheses

H1: Corporate organizations use social media more extensively than nonprofit educational organizations

Corporate organizations rely on word of mouth communication to gain and retain consumers. Electronic word-of-mouth communication (eWOM) enables consumers to communicate their experience with a product or company. The interactive dialogue capabilities of blogging and microblogging specific to Web 2.0 were incorporated into the corporate legitimacy development discourse (Navarro & Humanes, 2012). Companies have more resources than educational organizations and use them to measure results and thus retain only the most effective social media strategies.

Nonprofit social groups, on the other hand, rely on the internet to mobilize public opinion and generate active support, whether through voting, lobbying, or fundraising. In Turkey, for example, a case study of Ka-der (Association for the Support of Women Candidates) revealed asymmetrical use of various Internet capabilities for internal vs. external communication purposes (Polat & Cagli, 2014). Candidates for political offices negotiate informational trust and openness (Himelboim, Lariscy, Tinkham, & Sweetser, 2012), while most governmental agencies and organizations are poised to take advantage of their social media presence in order to establish and enhance their political credence and potential (Waters & Williams, 2011).

H2: Corporate organizations use Facebook more effectively than educational organizations

Businesses are trying to determine the best way to assess return-on-investment for marketing via social media (Safko, 2012) while managing their reputation across the internet. Corporate organizations encourage consumers to use 'share' and 'like' features, thus helping to promote their name and reputation. The healthcare industry uses Facebook to recruit and interact with patients, offer service promotion/discounts, exchange professional information, and promote positive business reputation (Ahmed et al., 2013). In some countries, the heavy presence of some brands on social networks may turn them into 'consumption prescribers' (Dasilva et al., 2013).

Educational uses of social networking services/applications documented successful emotional appeal mobilization against cyberbullying on Facebook (Alhabash, Kononova, Chiang, & Wise, 2013); patterns of Internet usage among Israeli nonprofit organizations, primarily consisting of organizational blogs and incipient two-way communication functions such as inviting comments and questions on traditional websites read-only (Avidar, 2011); and recruiting research participants (Child, Mentes, Pavlish, & Phillips, 2014). In higher education, libraries are often at the forefront of Facebook usage, in their attempt to maintain relevance and connectedness with the digital generation (Jacobson, 2011).

H3: Educational organizations use Twitter more effectively compared to corporate organizations

Education organizations, like their corporate organization counterparts, rely on engagement and two-way communication. In higher education, consumers (potential and current students), use social media for news and information. Education organizations are increasingly invested into creating social media portals to serve multiple communication needs, from recruitment to advising and facilitating job placement (Pidaparthy, 2011). This is another facet of the dialogical communication process, which relies heavily on two-way listening as well, beyond the ability of everyone included to have a voice in the conversation.

Twitter is more similar to traditional 'information dissemination' models, which makes it easier to adopt into educational organizations. Beyond the ability to broadcast short messages to large groups of followers, Twitter also provides the means to listen to 'chatter' about a particular political candidate or other public entities. In a study of 60 US government organizations, Waters and Williams (2011) discovered that micro-blogging communication (i.e., Twitter) was primarily used to support other public relations efforts by disseminating information to followers, either by posting direct news or by inviting redirects to their own website for news, news releases, and position papers. This strategy provided a means to augment digital communication without requiring any of the substantial additional investment in developing complex multimedia presence specific to Facebook.

METHODS

To determine how corporate and educational organizations in the United States and Belarus use social media, the authors conducted a Delphi study of sixteen experts. Researchers selected four organizations from the corporate sector and four educational organizations in each country. Organizations were selected purposefully, based on their pre-existing usage of social networking services such as Facebook, Twitter, and blogs. Respondents were directly involved in developing/maintaining the electronic/social media presence of their organization.

The Delphi consensus-building method is a systematic, interactive, and qualitative research method that relies on extensive communication with panels of independent experts. The carefully selected experts answer survey questionnaires consisting of close-ended and open-ended questions, in an iterative format. After each round, a study facilitator sends participants an anonymous summary of the previous findings, along with any rationales and comments provided by respondents. Panelists are invited to re-rank factors/answer choices and convey their level of agreement with the previous findings. Then researchers carefully analyze the new set of answers to identify key convergence points within the panel.

Delphi studies are relatively frequently used in public health research, primarily where, in the absence or during the emergence and testing of 'gold standards' it is important to identity and rank-order key stakeholders' opinions and preferences on a variety of topics such as support for development of new drugs and therapies, health leadership initiatives, and health system reforms (Fletcher & Marchildon, 2014). In other fields, authors Keeney, Hasson, and McKenna (2006) reviewed application of the Delphi technique for the purpose of identifying or building consensus on critical issues in business, defense, and education contexts.

Based on a thorough review of pre-existing information, researchers generate a list of factors most likely to play important roles in the decision-making process. Next, one or more panels of experts are invited to rank-order and comment on those factors, within the context of their own company, experience, and expertise, as well as from the perspective of wider environments, such as the private or educational economic sectors. The iterative nature of the investigation allows researchers to fine-tune their framework of reference before the study proceeds with the next steps in the form of traditional surveys or experimental surveys.

In this study, the Delphi technique was used to collect responses from sixteen experts (eight from each country) in a two-step electronic survey. Each of the experts played a significant role in their organization's social media strategy. The questionnaires investigated participants' opinion of social media usage within their organization and industry, and which industry sector uses social media most effectively overall. The entire communication process (Delphi Round 1 questionnaire, summary review, and Delphi Round Two questionnaire) was conducted via email.

Delphi Round 1 - Question Set

1. Which organizational sector do you think makes the overall best use of social media (i.e. Facebook, Twitter, blogs)?
2. Please rank-order the factors you deem most effective in evaluating the best use of social media from 1 to 5, where 1 is 'most effective' and 5 is 'least effective':
   a. Appropriateness for target audience;
   b. Ease of use;
   c. Effectiveness of the channel itself;
   d. Credibility of the channel;
   e. Personal/organizational familiarity with the channel;
3. Which, if any, from the following social media tool does your organizational sector use most effectively: Facebook, Twitter, or blogs?

Delphi Round 2 - Question Set

1. Please review our summary for answers from round one, question one. Rank the degree to which you agree with our findings on a scale of 1 to 8, where 1 means you agree the most and 8 means you agree the least;
2. Please review our summary for answers from round one, question three. Rank the degree to which you agree with our findings as they apply to your sector only.

RESULTS

Delphi Round One, Exploratory Phase

Q1-1. Which organizational sector do you think makes the overall best use of social media (i.e. Facebook, Twitter, Blogs)?

United States. According to corporate respondents in the United States, corporate organizations make the best use of social media, compared to nonprofit educational organizations. Most stated it would make sense that corporations make the most from social media, since a strong presence on Facebook, Twitter and blogs requires time, expertise, and financial resources. One respondent notes that media tactics work best in tandem with traditional media support; it is harder for educational and nonprofit organizations to successfully acquire and maintain popularity in the social media.

Educational respondents in the United States also believe corporations in general and "consumer products in particular" (Respondent #1) make the best use of social media, due to their ability to access the resources necessary to maximize social media results. There certainly are some nonprofit organizations, including government and educational institutions, who do engage social media effectively. Social networking services (such as Facebook) are an incredible platform for "storytelling" and "spreading the word" (Respondent #6). However, a strong presence in social media requires staff, expertise, and financial resources that are more likely to be available to corporate organizations.

Belarus. According to corporate respondents in Belarus, corporate organizations made the best use of social media. At the time of this study, some of the larger companies used social media successfully to complement promotion and advertising in other traditional media. Businesses focused on 'trendy' products targeting younger or 'hip' or status-oriented audiences (e.g., car dealerships, travel agencies, boutique stores, and beauty/spa centers) were also more likely to invest in developing a social media presence. One respondent noted that more and more Belarusian companies in diverse spheres were starting to use social media because of the low entry cost. One hundred percent of corporate respondents agreed that most corporate sectors used Facebook or the Russian-language equivalent Vkontakte; Twitter and blogs were still in their infancy and there were barely any companies using them.

Educational respondents in Belarus agreed that corporate organizations made the best use of social media overall, with the services industry at the forefront of adoption and development. Most educational establishments in Belarus did not use social media. Among educational organizations that did use social media, universities used it more than secondary education institutions, and business and economic schools used it more than medical schools. These findings made sense given the higher likelihood of exposure to social media among young adults; universities' need to meet their audience in the social media realm for networking purposes; and the dependency of business and economic departments on access to electronic professional and individual connections, as well as professional literature.

Q1-2. Please rank-order the factors you deem most effective in evaluating the best use of social media

United States vs. Belarus. The strongest correlation between any two variables for our first round of questionnaires connected respondents' ranking of channel appropriateness for target audience and ease of use. More importantly, appropriateness for target audience placed among top-two attributes for almost all US respondents, a finding that makes sense in a society where information is abundant and multiple sources are competing for respondents' attention.

Ease-of-use is simply not an issue for US respondents (α= -0.612, p<0.05), since tutorials and experts are always a couple of clicks away. Belarus (α= 0.626, p<0.05) is the exact antipode with its government-driven information censorship leading to a considerable dearth of information sources (in Russian or English). Ease-of-use is the most important criterion for communicators who are looking for any available ways to disseminate information quickly and at low entry costs in terms of knowledge and acquisition/maintenance of digital 'real estate' (accounts, domains, etc.).

Aside from this strong (but not surprising) difference in terms of targeting and ease of use, US and Belarus responses were quite similar, with channel credibility and familiarity typically placing mid-rank. Corporate and education responses were also consistent, with the exception of the familiarity with channel attribute. Education respondents prioritized ease of use and familiarity with channel, while corporate respondents were less concerned with these two items, primarily due to the difference in resources and expertise available to the two types of organizations.

Channel effectiveness was most likely to place in top-two position overall (US, Belarus, corporate, and education). The reasons are different though: while corporate respondents are more focused on the ability of social media to back up communication strategies (promotion and advertising) from traditional media, education respondents are more focused on the low entry-cost (if they use social media at all) and the fact that other types of electronic media (official websites) might meet all their current needs.

Another overall finding that was statistically significant (α = -.623, p < 0.05) for our first round contrasted users' prioritizing the importance of channel effectiveness, placing predominantly in top-two, over familiarity with channel, which ranked predominantly in bottom-two (See Table 1, Overall column). The remaining criterion, channel credibility, was somewhat evenly distributed.

Q1-3. Which Social Media Tool Does Your Organizational Sector Use Most Effectively (Facebook, Twitter, Blogs)?

United States. Corporate respondents selected blogs, Twitter, and Facebook as the tools most effectively used. Many of the companies are diversifying into Instagram, Flickr, and so on. Educational respondents selected Facebook and Twitter, for the obvious reason of low entry-cost and also because their customers require a constant stream of communication (information dissemination). Several respondents indicated active blogging or plans to expand into blogging as a way to promote and manage their organizational reputation.

Belarus. Corporate respondents indicated that most for profit organizations use Facebook or Vkontakte (Facebook's Russian-language social media equivalent and main competitor). E-media censorship, however, makes some of the companies less eager to engage actively in social media activities. Consequently, private companies that are perceived to be related to status and fun (car dealerships, consumer goods, travel, and beauty/cosmetics) are most likely to develop a staff and strategy for effective social media presence.

Educational respondents indicated that students prefer to use Vkontakte, whereas educators/universities use primarily official university websites. Both categories use Facebook as a second option.

Table 1. Overall rank-order placement of channel attributes

Attribute Placement	Overall (%)	US (%)	Belarus (%)	Corporate (%)	Education (%)
Target audience					
Top-two	53	86	25	57	50
Middle	13	-	25	14	13
Bottom-two	33	14	50	29	38
Ease of use					
Top-two	27	-	50	14	38
Middle	27	29	25	29	25
Bottom-two	46	71	25	57	38
Effectiveness					
Top-two	67	71	63	86	50
Middle	20	14	25	14	25
Bottom-two	13	14	13	-	25
Credibility					
Top-two	33	29	38	43	25
Middle	40	57	25	43	38
Bottom-two	27	14	38	14	38
Familiarity					
Top-two	20	29	25	-	38
Middle	-	71	75	-	63
Bottom-two	80	-	-	100	-

Delphi Round Two

Open-ended answers from the first round were summarized and submitted for evaluation (anonymously, so respondents were not aware of who had provided each of the items) and rank-ordering. Most comments referred to the entry-cost and level of expertise required to efficiently use social media. On the other hand, most comments also indicated heavy and efficient use of each of the four applications included in the study (Facebook, Twitter, blogs, and organizational websites).

Q2-1. Please review our summary for answers from round one, question one. Rank the degree to which you agree with our findings, from 1 (agree the most) to 8 (agree the least).

The most popular answers (ranked first or second) among our set of respondents pointed at a bimodal (or at least, non-mutually exclusive) distribution. Possibly due to our set of respondents—very experienced in using social media and thus heavily exposed to other organizations and professionals who are heavy users of social media—there is a clear opinion that many of the nonprofits and many of the corporations are not only heavy users of social media, but also effective users.

The least popular answers, on the other hand, were specific to our government and education respondents from Belarus, who were either unable or not allowed to use the full range of social media applications, primarily due to funding and organizational policies. That situation may change substantially as the country continues to balance its political and economic environment between the heavy weight of traditions imposed by its status as a former member of the Soviet bloc, and the lure (and pressure) presented by its increasing level of business interaction with the European Union and the rest of the world.

In terms of correlations between rank-ordering of our open-ended answers from the first round, one of the polarizing arguments included unequivocal opinions about either nonprofits or corporations having the ability to make the best use of social media applications.

Corporate Arguments

- […] best use of social media […] consumer products in particular, [access to] necessary resources to get the max out of social media;
- […] blogs […] allow companies to establish themselves as experts in their area;
- […] most companies are on multiple social media channels;
- […] large companies have the resources […];
- […] most [social] media tactics work best in tandem with […] traditional media/ advertising/ PR […] nonprofits just don't have the money to get the notoriety that those in the corporate sector can;
- Large corporations […] are more likely to have the funding.

Nonprofit Arguments

- […] Facebook […] great way to spread the word about an organization and get people to rally behind […] storytelling;
- […] Charities connect with people on a deeper emotional level than products like soda, clothes, food and entertainment. […] engage with those affected or interested in their mission as well as facilitate connections between volunteers;
- […] use discussion boards and chat rooms to support each other and help promote different organizations;
- [nonprofit] audience can be more emotional than consumers of goods and services, and you risk losing support and donations quickly if you make a wrong decision;
- […] Most nonprofits do not have a large marketing/PR budget […] social media is huge benefit […] it doesn't really cost us anything […] to increase our audience, engage with our followers and spread awareness of our mission through various social media channels;

Q2-2. Please review our summary for answers from round one, question three. Rank the degree to which you agree with our findings as they apply to your sector only.

Corporate respondents from both countries agreed that Facebook was probably the most used social media vehicle (arguably balanced by its Belarusian counterpart, VK). The most common rank-order for social media applications listed Facebook, Twitter and blogs—with the exception of answers from the subset of participants from Belarus, where Twitter was not widely used at the time of this study (it was available, just not yet popular), and blogs were under intense scrutiny by political organizations and government. Also, important to note is the agreement on the importance and relevance of blogs to corporate communication.

Nonprofit respondents believed that Facebook (or Vkontakte) were the tools most used in their sector. Definitive support of all other social media applications (e.g., discussion groups, LinkedIn) was also expressed by most of our nonprofit respondents. On the other hand, there was some disagreement over the best practices in using Twitter (e.g., specific vs. generic hashtags, as well as using Twitter as the only/predominant social media tactic among nonprofit organizations.

DISCUSSION AND FUTURE RESEARCH

The reality of social media in Belarus is challenging today—befitting the turbulent realities reverberating from the multiple crises associated with Russia's political and economic environment, as well as the constant rise of activists and bloggers presenting various and often extreme points of view using various channels Radio Free Europe, World Policy, Committee to Protect Journalists, and Beyondbrics leading to confrontation with authorities. New bloggers will use new channels, and key issues will emerge or disappear in the public discourse.

Our first hypothesis that the corporate sector would make the best use of social media was supported by the Delphi study. All respondents agreed that access to financial, staffing, and technical resources are clear advantages used very successfully by the corporate sector. However, we need to add an important consideration here, supported by a large number of our nonprofit respondents, regarding the ability of some (though not all or even most) of the nonprofit organizations to use all social media very effectively for their goals—in actuality or in principle. While technical skills are constantly improving for professionals across all industry sectors, they are employed within a complex political context.

The Belarusian parliament has established strict restriction over online media communication and blocked several independent news websites (as of Jan. 1, 2015), while at the same time pro-Russian media and blogs are becoming much more active[3]. As of early 2019, the Belarusian parliament was working on increasing governmental control over all news websites and social-media networks. According to Radio Free Europe, this move would officially eliminate freedom of expression in the form of anonymous comments on social-media posts, independent or unregistered online news sites, and home-operated independent news media[4].This development would have major implications for any nonprofit organizations campaigning in Belarus.

The second hypothesis that the corporate sector makes the best use of Facebook was also supported by the Delphi study. Our Belarusian sample indicated that Facebook had serious competition in the Russian-language equivalent Vkontakte. This finding underscores the importance of proximity, relevance, and immediacy among the social media affordances. In a country where Russian counts as the most important international language, VK provides an authentic and original platform, as opposed to the translated version of Facebook. From the perspective of technology affordances, social media provides an interesting example: whereas Facebook users tend to be established adults (age 30-50), using English or Russian to communicate with family and friends, it is also more likely to be used by corporate organizations. On the other hand, Vkontakte users tend to be much younger and less concerned with filters, tracking, and surveillance.

The third hypothesis posited that the educational sector would make the best use of Twitter. There was partial support in that some respondents selected blogs and other applications, Twitter as the most effective social media tool, but only in the United States. However, Twitter is not available or even allowed everywhere—and VK has its own versions for Twitter, Snapchat, Instagram, and all the other mobile social media applications.

Finally, an interesting general finding is that US organizations tended to value appropriateness for target audience as the most important factor in evaluating the best use of social media. Belarusian organizations, on the other hand, valued effectiveness of the channel itself or ease of use as the most important factor. Given the platform integration and freedom of speech considerations presented above, this finding strengthens, rather than undermines, the importance of combining technical skills, platform-specific features, and public relations expertise for communication across all three domains (nonprofit, education, and corporate).

New developments in Belarusian social media including three starting points for future research: first, Instagram has recently become one of the most popular social media in Belarus, since it has allowed for posts including both pictures and videos; second, blogging and vlogging have become very popular with the younger crowd; and third, the economic/trade relations between Belarus and Russia have lost the copacetic veneer and they may trigger changes into the political context as well. Future research should perhaps focus on the use of social media to promote and engage social activism and compare Belarus with other countries in similar situations. The authors recommend expanding this study by using a survey format to gain additional responses. Also, the authors suggest conducting a series of in-depth interviews with social media managers from different corporate and educational entities. The additional quantitative and qualitative techniques will help future researchers to confirm or disconfirm the results of the Delphi study from this research. It would also prove interesting to replicate the Delphi study in five years to determine changes in social media use by organizational type in the USA and across the ocean.

REFERENCES

Ahmed, O., Claydon, L. S., Ribeiro, D. C., Arumugam, A., Higgs, C., & Baxter, G. D. (2013). Social media for physiotherapy clinics: Considerations in creating a Facebook page. *The Physical Therapy Review*, *18*(1), 43–48. doi:10.1179/1743288X12Y.0000000039

Alhabash, S., Park, H., Kononova, A., Chiang, Y., & Wise, K. (2013). Exploring the motivations of Facebook use in Taiwan. *Cyberpsychology, Behavior, and Social Networking*, *15*(6), 304–311. doi:10.1089/cyber.2011.0611 PMID:22703036

Avidar, R. (2011). Israeli public relations and the Internet. *Israel Affairs*, *17*(3), 401–421. doi:10.1080/13537121.2011.584668

Bucher, T., & Helmond, A. (2018). The Affordances of Social Media Platforms. In J. Burgess, A. Marwick, & T. Poell (Eds.), *The SAGE Handbook of Social Media* (pp. 233–253). Sage Publications. doi:10.4135/9781473984066.n14

Carr, T. C., & Hayes, R. A. (2015). Social Media: Defining, Developing, and Divining. *Atlantic Journal of Communication, 23*(1), 46–65. doi:10.1080/15456870.2015.972282

Child, R., Mentes, J., Pavlish, C., & Phillips, L. (2014). Using Facebook and participant information clips to recruit emergency nurses for research. *Nurse Researcher, 21*(6), 16–21. doi:10.7748/nr.21.6.16. e1246 PMID:25059083

Comunello, F., Mulargia, S., & Parisi, L. (2016). The 'proper' way to spread ideas through social media: Exploring the affordances and constraints of different social media platforms as perceived by Italian activists. *The Sociological Review, 64*(3), 515–532. doi:10.1111/1467-954X.12378

Dasilva, P., Arratibel, G., & Aierdi, M. (2013). Companies on Facebook and Twitter: Current situation and communication strategies. *Revista Latina de Comunicacion Social, 068*, 676–695.

Diga, M., & Kelleher, T. (2009). Social media use, perceptions of decision-making power, and public relations roles. *Public Relations Review, 35*(4), 440–442. doi:10.1016/j.pubrev.2009.07.003

Fletcher, A., & Marchildon, G. (2014). Using the Delphi method for qualitative, participatory action research in health leadership. *International Journal of Qualitative Methods, 13*(1), 1–18. doi:10.1177/160940691401300101

Himelboim, I., Lariscy, T. W., Tinkham, S. F., & Sweetser, K. D. (2012). Social media and online political communication: The role of interpersonal informational trust and openness. *Journal of Broadcasting & Electronic Media, 56*(1), 92–115. doi:10.1080/08838151.2011.648682

Ioffe, G. (2011). Belarus and the West: From estrangement to honeymoon. *Journal of Communist Studies and Transition Politics, 27*(2), 217–240. doi:10.1080/13523279.2011.564090

Jacobson, T. (2011). Facebook as a library tool: Perceived vs. actual use. *College & Research Libraries, 72*(1), 79–90. doi:10.5860/crl-88r1

Jahnke, I. (2010). A way out of the information jungle: A longitudinal study about a socio-technical community and informal learning in higher education. *International Journal of Sociotechnology and Knowledge Development, 2*(4), 18–38. doi:10.4018/jskd.2010100102

Keeney, S., Hasson, F., & McKenna, H. (2006). Consulting the oracle: Ten lessons from using the Delphi technique in nursing research. *Journal of Advanced Nursing, 53*(2), 205–212. doi:10.1111/j.1365-2648.2006.03716.x PMID:16422719

Lovejoy, K., Waters, R. D., & Saxton, G. D. (2012). Engaging stakeholders through Twitter: How nonprofit organizations are getting more out of 140 characters or less. *Public Relations Review, 38*(2), 313–318. doi:10.1016/j.pubrev.2012.01.005

Mohana, R., & Katta, R. (2017). Influence of perceived risks on consumers' online purchase behavior: An empirical study. *International Journal of Sociotechnology and Knowledge Development, 9*(3), 38–64. doi:10.4018/IJSKD.2017070103

Navarro, C., & Humanes, M. L. (2012). Corporate blogging in Spanish companies: Design and application of a quality index (ICB). *Comunicación y Sociedad, 25*(2), 117–144.

Norman, D. (1990). *The Design of Everyday Things*. New York: Doubleday Business.

Pidaparthy, U. (2011, Oct. 20). How colleges use, misuse social media to reach students. Retrieved from http://www.cnn.com/2011/10/20/tech/social-media/universities-social-media/

Polat, R. K., & Cagli, E. (2014). New directions for women's political development in Turkey: Exploring the implications of the internet for Ka-der. *Information Polity*, *19*(3,4), 179–194. doi:10.3233/IP-140343

Qualman, E. (2010). *Socialnomics: How social media transforms the way we live and do business*. Hoboken, NJ: Wiley.

Safko, L. (2012). *The social media bible, tactics, tools, and strategies for business success*. Hoboken, NJ: Wiley.

Skagebi, J. (2009). Online friction: Studying sociotechnical conflicts to elicit user experience. *International Journal of Sociotechnology and Knowledge Development*, *1*(2), 62–74. doi:10.4018/jskd.2009040106

Vilceanu, M.O., & Novak, A.N. (2017). Love, Brands, and Marriage: Audience Reception of LGBT Instagram Posts after the 2015 Supreme Court Ruling on Same-sex Marriage. *Ohio Communication Journal, 55*, 146-164.

Waters, R., & Williams, J. (2011). Squawking, tweeting, cooing, and hooting: Analyzing the communication patterns of government agencies on Twitter. *Journal of Public Affairs*, *11*(4), 353–363. doi:10.1002/pa.385

ENDNOTES

[1]   http://www.liveinternet.ru/stat/vkontakte.ru/index.html?avgraph=yes

[2]   http://www.similarweb.com/website/vk.com

[3]   http://belarusdigest.com/story/russian-media-attack-belarus-warning-minsk-21055

[4]   https://www.rferl.org/a/belarus-moves-to-tighten-control-over-online-news-social-media/29177551.html

This research was previously published in the International Journal of Sociotechnology and Knowledge Development (IJSKD), 11(4); pages 20-33, copyright year 2019 by IGI Publishing (an imprint of IGI Global).

Chapter 73

Learner Views of a Facebook Page as a Supportive Digital Pedagogical Tool at a Public South African School in a Grade 12 Business Studies Class

Helgaardt Hannes Meintjes

https://orcid.org/0000-0003-4639-8803

University of South Africa, South Africa & Carolina Akademiese Skool, South Africa

ABSTRACT

Technology is almost indispensable in general life, and it is constantly evolving. Therefore, it is important to determine how these advances can be of benefit in teaching and learning. ICTs and social media for educational purposes is a notion not only fraught with challenges but also offering much-untapped potential. Web 2.0 technologies and electronic teaching aids can be used to greatly advance the transmission of knowledge in the school setting. The investigation at hand attempted to go a step further by showing the potential benefits of incorporating the Grade 12 Business Studies curriculum into a Facebook page to enhance learners' subject knowledge competence. An exploratory mixed-method research design was adopted to describe the implementation of the mentioned Facebook page. The data were collected using a Facebook page and an online open-ended questionnaire. Based on the research, the learners concurred to unequivocally concur that the Facebook page for Business Studies did, in fact, assist and support them in their learning.

INTRODUCTION

Information and communication technologies (ICTs) have penetrated society to the point of becoming almost indispensable to use in general life and to education. Technology is constantly evolving, and it is important to determine how these advances can be of benefit in the teaching and learning landscape.

DOI: 10.4018/978-1-6684-7123-4.ch073

A literature review uncovered several studies that have been conducted on the educational benefits of social media tools for improving student learning in the classroom and beyond. Across the world and more specifically as it stands in South Africa, ICTs and social media for educational purposes is a notion not only fraught with challenges but also offering much-untapped potential. These Web 2.0 technologies and electronic teaching aids can be used to greatly advance the transmission of knowledge in the school setting. Indeed, the investigation at hand attempted to go a step further by showing the potential benefits of incorporating the Grade 12 Business Studies curriculum at a public school in South Africa through a Facebook page to enhance learners' subject knowledge competence and academic performance. An exploratory mixed-method research design was adopted to describe the implementation of the mentioned Facebook page in a Grade 12 Business Studies class at a public school in South Africa. The data were collected using a specifically created Facebook page and an online open-ended questionnaire. The analysis of the data was completed through the extracts from the participants' responses on the Facebook page and according to the questionnaire in table format. A few analysts have concurred that social media applications have the potential to back collaborative learning by upgrading learning execution in both personal information and cluster information. By utilizing social media to interact with classmates, positive connections are set up which can be essential to the creation of learning communities where learners know one another for them to work together and help each other. Based on the research the learners agree to strongly agree that the Facebook page for Business Studies did assist and support them in their learning. Furthermore, the findings revealed the success of the intervention as a supportive teaching strategy, and it suggested that Business Studies teachers should be empowered through receiving training on the use of social media tools in their occupation. Rather than finding themselves restricted to utilize Facebook, teachers can usefully apply Facebook as an instructing apparatus for supporting learners' nonstop learning encounter. To work towards meeting the educational needs of the net generation in South Africa, the integration of web innovations into educational programs is not only fundamental but moreover profoundly advantageous in that these applications increase learners' inspiration to participate in classroom activities and compels them to form more suitable choices when interacting in a virtual environment. In preparation for Facebook to be advantageous as a supportive teaching methodology, all learners must have equal access to the fundamental technology. Further research is needed across other grade levels or at the same grade but at other schools and provinces to gain an enhanced understanding of learners' responses towards Facebook as a supportive teaching tool. A further suggestion for future research would be to investigate the use of social media applications run specifically on smartphones in South Africa as a supportive teaching strategy.

The 21st century has globally propelled the educational environment into a new sphere. It has seen the introduction of various innovative technological advances which have made teaching and learning more interactive. This has led to a need for a more virtual approach to teaching in South Africa. Social media has grown quickly in both personal and academic use and researchers such as Greenhow and Robelia (2009) have conducted studies examining how online environments, computer-based learning and the integration of Web 2.0 tools have improved academic attainment for the new generation of learners. Moreover, for the past decade, we have seen tremendous numbers of new Web developments across the globe. As a matter of fact, Alexander (2006) believes that social media software has surfaced as an important component of the Web 2.0 movement, leading to the rise of blogs, wiki's, trackback, video blogs, podcasting and numerous other social networking tools such as Facebook and MySpace. Because of the development of social networking applications, there has been a growing interest in how social media can be applied as an effective teaching strategy worldwide. Social network communities have undergone rapid and sophisticated development for use in education in recent years (Van Wyk, 2013). Social media applications and ICTs for educational purposes, in particular, supporting students in South Africa, bring both opportunities and challenges to the classroom. These Web 2.0 technologies and electronic teaching aids could be used to great effect to advance education in South African schools. Most schools are adapting Web 2.0 technologies, in particular, to advance their school image on the school's webpage, but it can also be implemented for teaching and learning. The researcher regards it important that learners in South Africa should have the opportunity to collaborate in discussions outside the classroom to come up with possible subject-related solutions that are monitored by the educator who plays an advisory role. The specifically created Facebook page was used to communicate homework, assignments, class discussions and content that supports the subject matter, such as newspaper articles and video clips from YouTube. The research aims to explore how grade 12 learners in South Africa at a public school experience the use of a Facebook page as a supportive teaching and learning strategy in the Business Studies class. The primary research question is: How do learners in South Africa react on the attempts at using a Facebook page as a social media tool to support grade 12 Business Studies learners in enhancing learners' subject knowledge competence?

LITERATURE REVIEW

It is essential to place this study in the context of certain theoretical frameworks to justify the selection of subjects; the variables being studied and the design (McMillan & Schumacher, 2010). It is also important to apply suitable theories to show a logical link between the research question and the methodology. New opportunities and dilemmas have emerged since the world have become a global village and the use of the Internet in teaching and learning. In response to this shift, innovative theories of learning have been created and according to Del Valle García Carreño (2014), teachers are obliged to continue seeking new strategies for their teaching and learning. She also maintains that most learning theories to date have relied on the notion of classroom attendance as well as teaching and evaluation strategies, but the 21st century has given rise to opportunities to explore alternative skills and styles such as e-Learning, e-portfolio and e-blogs, amongst others. Del Valle García Carreño (2014) further points out that modern-day connectivity creates a space for a learning model that recognises the tectonic shift in society and that the field of education has been slow to recognise new learning tools. These observations prompted the researcher to undertake a study in South Africa, looking at the introduction of a Business Studies Facebook page as an additional supportive teaching strategy to connect and integrate a specific group of learners that share the same interests.

According to Johnson and Johnson (2005), Social Interdependence Theory is a classic example of the interaction of theory, research and practice. The underlying principle of this theory is the way that goals are structured and determines how individuals interact, which in turn creates specific outcomes. More than seven decades ago Social Interdependence Theory has been modified, extended, and refined based on the increasing knowledge about, and application of the theory (Johnson & Johnson, 2005). The Social Interdependence Theory was applied during the research to determine how the participants in South Africa interact on the Facebook page that was created by the teacher, who is known as the researcher for this study. The researcher was dependent on the respondents to actively take part in the activities posted on the Facebook page to complete the research and the respondents were depended on the researcher to post subject-related activities and to respond and interact to the online comments and answers that the participants posted.

STUDENT PERCEPTIONS OF HOW SOCIAL MEDIA CAN SUPPORT THEIR LEARNING

In a study carried out in South Africa by Van Wyk (2012) the majority of students indicated that they used Mxit, Facebook, Twitter and SMS as their preferred social media tools for communication. What emerged from students' postings in this study is that social media encouraged collaboration with peers and facilitated platform where they gave their peers support or advice (Van Wyk, 2012). Students argue that social media is characterised as Web 2.0-based e-Learning that emphasises dynamic participation, collaboration and sharing knowledge and ideas (Van Wyk, 2013; Van Wyk, 2014a). Ophus and Abbitt (2009) reported comparable data, indicating that students were mostly supportive of using a social networking system in their education. Likewise, McCarthy (2012) reported supportive attitudes from students for the use of Facebook as an academic tool, highlighting responses indicating Facebook is a platform familiar to students and allows access to academic information on a system that they are constantly engaged with. Furthermore, students' feedback reflected that they found social media a useful learning tool for promoting and supporting the e-Learning experience (Van Wyk, 2013). However, Van Wyk's (2013) findings also revealed, as with Baran's (2010), that many of the students used the social media tools to interact socially rather than using them to discuss or complete subject-related matter (Van Wyk, 2014a). On a more positive note, some students confirmed that the establishment of the social media group enabled them to foster trust between the members and these social media applications provided them with a functional platform on which to communicate with each other and to use for reflection. Despite these possibilities, there are still some students who avoided communication and kept things superficial (Van Wyk, 2012). Gallop (2008) also reported overall positive results with students claiming that they believed technology helped them to learn.

RESEARCH DESIGN AND METHODOLOGY

The interpretive paradigm describes reality as created in that it is based on people's personal experiences of their immediate world. The researcher stance toward reality is inter-subjective and empathic. The social constructivist paradigm sees reality as socially constructed and sees systems of meaning as originating on a social rather than an individual level (Van Wyk & Toale, 2015). This research adopts an exploratory mixed-method design to describe how a Facebook page can be used as a supportive teaching strategy in the Business Studies class at a specific school in South Africa. The motivation for using this is first to explore Grade 12 learner's views and experiences on the Facebook page regarding specific topics the researcher taught over the duration on the Facebook page to enhance their knowledge, skills and attitudes in Business studies. Secondly, an online questionnaire was designed to determine Grade 12 learner's experiences in supporting their learning through a Facebook page. Finally, this pragmatic approach was used through qualitative and quantitative research including extensive literature review to achieve triangulation for the study. Marshall's (1996) study emphasised that the selection of a study sample is a very important step in any research project since it is rarely practical, efficient, or ethical to study entire populations. Marshall (1996) further asserted that sample sizes for qualitative investigations tend to be small and that this adequately answers the research question, which is why the researcher has chosen to use convenience sampling by focusing on the Grade 12 Business Studies learners from Carolina Akademiese Skool. The main sampling strategy was purposeful sampling that consists of convenience sampling. As indicated earlier the researcher created a Facebook page to incorporate into the Grade 12 Business Studies class as a supportive teaching strategy. The Business Studies Facebook page was incorporated over a period of ten weeks according to CAPS. Observations of how the learners used the Facebook page provided the researcher with a clear picture of the types of activities the learners became engaged in. All data was collected as screenshots and the Facebook page is still available on the internet. The researcher compiled the online closed-ended questionnaire and posted the Surveymonkey link on the Facebook page for learners to complete after they already had six weeks of access to the page. The format of an online questionnaire facilitated ease of storage, retrieval, and qualitative analysis. This enabled the researcher to easily export the data and statistics and provided ready access without the need for transcription. Thus, the researcher could refer to the participants' responses effortlessly in the case of needing to verify the data after the analyses had already been completed. Various activities were loaded onto the Facebook page that was related to the subject content and to gather information deemed pertinent to the study. The researcher also prepared additional follow-up questions in case it turned out that inconsistent data was yielded. Informal interviews were also conducted during class time. The informal interviews took the form of an open discussion, and various questions were asked based on the Business Studies class and the teacher teaching Business Studies through a Facebook page as a supportive teaching strategy.

The researcher was cognisant of the obligation to respect the rights, needs, desires and values of the participants. Permission to embark on the research was requested from the Mpumalanga Department of Education in South Africa, the school and the participants. In ensuring ethical soundness of the research, the researcher adhered to certain principles cited by Guba and Lincoln (1994), namely informed consent, an explanation to participants of the voluntary nature of their participation, assurances of safety in participation as well as privacy, confidentiality, anonymity and trust. Ethical clearance (Ref no 2017/07/12/90233522/12/MC) for the study was also requested from the University of South Africa (UNISA).

USING SOCIAL MEDIA IN TEACHING AND LEARNING

As educational institutions like universities, colleges and schools involuntary moved towards online education through various platforms, it is time to rethink the use of social media as a supportive teaching strategy. When it comes to using Facebook in education, opinions differ, particularly concerning the time involved in preparing and conducting educational activities on the social media platform. Furthermore, Van Wyk (2012) stated that blogs as a form of learning enrich students' learning experiences and bring about deeper learning. In addition, Cain (2008) and Gallop (2008) are also strongly of the opinion that web technologies can only enhance learning, with the former stating: "social networking sites such as Facebook provide individuals with a way of maintaining and strengthening social ties, which can be beneficial in both social and academic settings". Undoubtedly, Gallop (2008) emphasised that it is not the use of technology or social media that is essential for effective learning but rather how skilfully it is applied during the learning experience, going on to say that the degree to which learning principles are incorporated into the students' environment determines the effectiveness of the learning tools. Equivalently Van Wyk (2014a) argues that by selecting various social media tools such as blogs or wiki's, educators can create differentiated learning paths that can be combined to create active learning environments to accommodate the student of today. In fact, several studies have demonstrated that these personalised and customised learning environments may be better suited to address the diverse needs of today's generation (Van Wyk, 2014a).

In addition, Fogg-Phillips et al. (n.d.) discussed the huge role that Facebook plays in the lives of millions of students, a fact that many wonders are a good or bad thing. Munoz and Towner (2009) reported that "in addition to the incredible usage rate among students there are some unique features that make it amenable to educational pursuits". These researchers furthermore explain that Facebook "indirectly" creates a learning environment by connecting students. In the same vein, Skerrett (2010) states that "the Facebook event represented an opportunity to hold conversations about gender, male privilege, and more generally hegemonic power structures that circulate throughout social networking sites". Furthermore, Fogg-Phillips et al. (n.d.) also reassert that Facebook has the power to enhance learning inside the classroom and beyond but advise that the interaction between learners in the educational setting must be open, transparent and secure.

Instead of finding themselves opposed to the use of Facebook, teachers can constructively apply Facebook as a teaching tool for supporting students' continuous learning experience. When the curriculum permits for self-directed online learning, learners can learn more than what is taught during class because they can create meaning for themselves beyond the classroom and beyond the teacher's objectives (Fogg-Phillips et al. n.d.). Furthermore, these researchers claim that to incorporate digital learning opportunities into the curriculum meets the needs of the net generation and their digital learning styles, hence enhancing their learning. Thus, teachers need to give serious thought to how best to meet their learners' needs through Web 2.0 and other networking tools (English & Duncan-Howell, 2008). The present learner profiles, referred to as the Net generation or as digital natives, have challenged the 21st century's teaching and learning environment (Van Wyk, 2013; Van Wyk, 2014a). Again, teachers need to be cognisant of how young people connect and interact on the web so that a more appropriate and more inclusive digital experience can be created for them in and outside the classroom. However, teachers also need to be aware that not all learners (especially those in rural areas) have the means to readily access the internet since, as pointed out by Fogg-Phillips et al. (n.d.), the use of a mobile-only to connect to the internet is less than 25 percent in developing countries.

Since millions of students around the world use Facebook regularly and with ease, this entertainment-oriented social media platform lends itself for use as a supportive learning tool (Saikaew, Krutkam, Pattaramanon, Leelathakul, Chaipah, & Chaosakul. 2011). Although there are various tools available for e-Learning, Facebook seems to be one of the most useful because students generally respond to discussions speedily and are comfortable enough in their "space" to share their information and opinions (Saikaew et al. 2011). The work of Baran's (2010) study, which examined Facebook being utilised as a formal instruction environment, noted that: "not all students are ready to embrace the use of social networking tools such as Facebook during formal teaching, learning and assessment". This particular study (Baran, 2010) revealed that certain students are indeed more interested in socialising than in the educational component of the experience. This can be a problem when teachers want to integrate social media applications like Facebook into their curriculum since it could distract students from their subject content as opposed to enhancing their learning. Thus, the planning of Facebook users should be done in such a way as to include the best aspects of the traditional classroom along with the advantages of real-time and mobile learning.

Support of Social Media in Teaching and Learning

It is a known fact that Facebook has given rise to many incongruous discussions and will continue to do so (Boghian, 2013). Several researchers have agreed that social media applications have the potential to support collaborative learning by enhancing learning performance in both individual knowledge and group knowledge (Van Wyk, 2012). Alexander (2006) believes that social media applications appear to be valuable learning tools in a variety of different settings and for a variety of different purposes, from student group learning through to faculty department work and even staff teamwork.

Gallop (2008) cited numerous ways in which social media are used to enhance the learning experience. Social media can:

- Help extend the learning activities outside the classroom;
- Increase opportunities for student-teacher and student-student contact; and
- Encourage students to reflect on their work (Van Wyk, 2012).

Van Wyk (2012) believes that social media is an undervalued and underutilised tool in the learning experience. Moreover, Van Wyk (2014a) posits that by using social media to interact with classmates, positive relationships are established which can be essential to the creation of learning communities where students are known to one another for them to work together and assist each other. Furthermore, Van Wyk (2014a) believes that the dynamic nature of social media tools allows students to actively take part in the learning experience rather than being passive learners. Fogg-Phillips et al. (n.d.) drew attention to the fact that the learners of today are being raised in the "always-on" world of interactive media, the Internet and social media technologies and they have different expectations and learning styles than those from previous generations. By using Facebook in the teaching and learning environment, the learner's role can shift from that of being a passive recipient of knowledge to that of searching and sharing knowledge, i.e. the ubiquitous use of social media gives learners the unprecedented opportunity to create self-organising learning communities (Fisher & Baird, 2006). Moreover, communication with teachers can become more instantaneous since teachers and students can respond much more rapidly via Facebook (Saikaew et al. 2011).

RESULTS

Learner Perceptions of the Use of a Facebook Page as a Supportive Teaching Strategy

To provide further analysis of the use of Facebook as a supportive teaching strategy, learners were presented with 15 questionnaire items for scoring. These items aimed to collect learner opinions about the following: (1) the teacher's sharing of subject-related information; (2) the rate of information sharing via Facebook; (3) the application's potential as communication platform between teacher and learners; (4) the opportunity to communicate with the teacher outside the classroom; (5) the potential it offers for sharing and exchanging files, links, information, polls and videos; (6) the opportunity it presents for group members to learn from each other; (7) boosting learner confidence through the opportunity to ask questions on the page as opposed to during class time; (8) assisting the learner to think more deeply about the subject content; (9) helping learners to make connections between ideas and preparing them for class participation; (10) supporting learners to organise their learning; (11) making the learning process more visible; (12) improving learner interest in Business Studies; (13) promoting understanding of the subject content; (14) potential to boost students' marks; and (15) whether learners thought the Facebook page might distract them from their learning at school.

Table 1. Mean standard deviation, percentages of learner perceptions of the use of a Facebook page as a supportive teaching strategy

Statements	Mean	SD	Strongly Disagree	Disagree	Neutral	Agree	Strongly Agree
1. Educator sharing subject-related information	4.41	0.731	0%	0%	20%	50%	30%
The majority of respondents (50%) agreed to strongly agree (30%) that the educator shared subject-related information on the Facebook page (mean = 4.41; SD = 0.731) with the Grade 12 Business Studies class and 20% indicated a neutral response.							
2. Facebook conveys information quickly	4.68	0.781	0%	0%	10%	60%	30%
The majority of respondents (60%) agreed to strongly agree (30%) that information is rapidly conveyed (mean = 4.68; SD = 0.781) through the Business Studies Facebook page.							
3. Communicating information from the educator to the learner	4.48	0.721	0%	0%	40%	60%	0%
Sixty percent (60%) of the respondents held that the educator communicated information to the learners (mean = 4.48; SD = 0.721) and the minority of 40% had a neutral response.							
4. It creates the opportunity to communicate easily with the educator outside the classroom	4.88	0.789	0%	0%	0%	70%	30%
An overwhelming majority of the respondents (70%) agreed and strongly agreed (30%) that the Facebook page creates (mean = 4.88; SD = 0.789) an opportunity to easily communicate with the educator outside the classroom.							
5. Members of the page can exchange and share files, links, information, polls and videos with one another	4.68	0.781	0%	0%	10%	60%	30%
The majority of the respondents agreed (60%) to strongly agreed (30%) that members of the Facebook page can exchange and share information (mean = 4.68; SD = 0.781) such as files, links, information, polls and videos with one another and merely (10%) were undecided.							
6. Members of the page learn from each other	4.03	0.811	0%	0%	33.33%	33.33%	33.33%
Of the respondents, 33.3% strongly agreed, 33.3% agreed and 33.3% indicated a neutral response (mean = 4.03; SD = 0.811) on the statement that members of the Facebook page learn from each other.							
7. You have more confidence to ask questions on the Facebook page than during class time	4.48	0.731	0%	20%	10%	50%	20%
The respondents had a mixed response in that 50% agreed and 20% strongly agreed that they have more confidence (mean = 4.48; SD = 0.731) to ask questions on the Facebook page than during contact time. The minority (20%) disagreed and a mere 10% were indecisive.							
8. It helped me think more deeply about the subject content of Business Studies	4.78	0.788	0%	0%	30%	70%	0%
The majority of the respondents agreed (70%) that the Facebook page let them think more deeply (mean = 4.78; SD = 0.788) about the Business Studies subject content and 30% had a neutral response.							

continues on following page

Table 1. Continued

Statements	Mean	SD	Strongly Disagree	Disagree	Neutral	Agree	Strongly Agree
9. It helped me to make connections between ideas and prepare myself better for classroom participation	4.55	0.751	0%	0%	50%	50%	0%
Of the respondents, 50% were neutral and 50% agreed that the Facebook page (mean = 4.55; SD = 0.751) helped them to make better connections in the subject and better prepared them for classroom participation.							
10. It supported me and organized my learning in the subject	4.62	0.780	0%	0%	20%	70%	10%
The majority of the respondents agreed (70%) to strongly agreed (10%) that the Facebook page supported them and organized their learning (mean = 4.62; SD = 0.780) in the subject, with 20% being neutral.							
11. Most obviously, the Facebook page supports me by making the learning process more visible	4.68	0.761	0%	0%	30%	50%	20%
The majority of the respondents agreed (50%) to strongly agreed (20%) that the Facebook page supported them (mean = 4.68; SD = 0.761) by making the learning process more visible, and 30% were indecisive.							
12. My interest in Business Studies improved because of the use of the Facebook page	4.28	0.721	0%	0%	30%	40%	30%
The majority of the respondents agreed (40%) to strongly agreed (30%) that use of the Facebook page improved their interest (mean = 4.28; SD = 0.721) in the subject, with the minority (30%) being indecisive.							
13. Facebook as a supportive teaching strategy promotes my understanding of the subject content	3.88	0.981	10%	0%	20%	60%	10%
The majority of the respondents agreed (60%) to strongly agreed (10%) that the Facebook page promoted their understanding of the subject content (mean 3.88; SD = 0.981). In contrast, 10% strongly agreed and 30% provided a neutral response.							
14. Do you think that you and your peers will achieve better results if the Facebook page is integrated into lessons?	4.18	0.701	0%	0%	30%	40%	30%
The majority of the respondents agreed (40%) to strongly agreed (30%) that they would achieve better results (mean 4.18; SD = 0.701) when the Facebook page is incorporated into lessons, with 30% indicating a neutral response.							
15. The Facebook page distracted me from my educational work	3.48	0.981	20%	60%	20%	0%	0%
The majority of the respondents disagreed (60%) to strongly disagreed (20%) that the Facebook page caused a distraction (mean = 3.48; SD = 0.981) with regards to their educational work, and 20% were indecisive.							

Based on the information presented in Table 1, overall Grade 12 learners agreed to strongly agree that the Facebook page for Business Studies did indeed assist and support them in their learning.

Learners' Perceptions of a Facebook Page to Assist and Support Them With Specific Learning Content in Business Studies

Components of the third term Grade 12 Business Studies curriculum according to the CAPS Business Studies document (DoE, 2011:41) were incorporated via the Facebook page as an educational tool, the results of which are described below.

Learners had to follow the above-mentioned link provided on the Facebook post and use it to determine which investment opportunities are the best between shares, unit trusts and exchange-traded funds. The learners did not respond to this activity although it reached at least nine learners on the Facebook page. The teacher thus decided to use the different investment opportunities information in the form of a discussion during class time.

Table 2. Investment Securities

CAPS Topic	Investment Securities
Content in lesson plans:	Different types of investment
Facebook activities by Grade 12 learners:	Comparison between different investment opportunities was shared through a Fin24 (2016) link (screenshot 1). Link to South African retail bonds website (screenshot 2). Other activities included: The Sharenet (2016) link was shared and a share certificate was published.
Assessment:	Article about the Johannesburg Stock Exchange (JSE) was shared. Each learner identified one of the Top 15 listed companies and the type of certificate presented. Learners compared the three different investment opportunities and commented on what they thought was the best investment opportunity and why. Learners used www.rsaretailbonds.gov.za to answer the questions from the Facebook page. One of the CAPS Business Studies recommendations for resources is the Internet and the purpose was to bring practice into the classroom and to make the textbook come alive.

The activity below assisted learners to gain a better understanding of South African retail bonds. The learners had to follow the link that directed them to the official government portal of South African retail bonds which presents up to date information as opposed to the outdated interest rates given in the textbook. The information on the website was also used for the learners' formal assessment research project as prescribed by the CAPS Business Studies document (DoE 2011:42).

Table 3. Investment insurance

CAPS Topic	Investment Insurance
Content in lesson plans:	Compulsory and non-compulsory insurance Over insurance and underinsurance
Facebook activities by Grade 12 learners:	Pictures of compulsory insurance were posted, and learners had to identify them (refer to screenshot 3). Other activities included: Homework revision activity about investment and insurance. Types of insurance for businesses. Distinguish between individual and business insurance. Underinsurance.
Assessment:	According to the Business Studies CAPS document learners must be able to identify and distinguish compulsory insurance. The three different types of compulsory insurances were depicted in the pictures and the learners identified these through comments. The reason why the activities were designed in this format was to support the learners in their processing of the subject content and to prepare them for formal examination.

By adding pictures of the three different types of compulsory insurance in South Africa the learners were able to distinguish these as was seen in their comments identified it on the Facebook page through their comments (see below):

1. Road Accident Fund (RAF);
2. Unemployment Insurance Fund (UIF); and
3. Compensation for Occupational Injuries and Diseases Act (COIDA).

Table 4. Grade 12 Business Studies learners' presentations

CAPS Topic	Presentations
Content in lesson plans:	Verbal and non-verbal presentation
Facebook activities by Grade 12 learners:	All the activities on the Facebook page were used by the teacher in the form of a presentation via a data projector during class time to explain verbal and non-verbal presentation.
Assessment:	The learners identified photographs and written material as forms of non-verbal communication and the explanations by the teacher and videos as forms of verbal communication. According to the CAPS Business Studies document, learners must accurately and concisely identify and distinguish between verbal and non-verbal presentation of a variety of business-related information. The Facebook page created the ideal opportunity to recapitulate the presentation of business information in verbal and non-verbal formats as required by the CAPS Business Studies guideline.

The following topics were incorporated into the lesson plans prescribed by the CAPS Business Studies document (DoE, 2011:41):

- Investment securities:
  - Different types of investment
- Investment insurance:
  - Compulsory and non-compulsory insurance
  - Over insurance and underinsurance
- Presentations:
  - Verbal and non-verbal presentation

Based on the information presented in Table 5, it is evident that the Grade 12 learners agreed to strongly agree that the Business Studies Facebook page assisted and supported them in their learning.

Table 5. Grade 12 Business Studies learners' perception with using a Facebook page to assist and support learning content

Statements	Mean	SD	Strongly Disagree	Disagree	Neutral	Agree	Strongly Agree
1. It helped me to distinguish between assurance and insurance	4.78	0.761	0%	0%	0%	70%	30%
The majority of respondents (70%) agreed to strongly agree (30%) that the Facebook page assisted and helped them (mean = 4.78; SD = 0.761) to distinguish between assurance and insurance in the Grade 12 class.							
2. I understand what compulsory and non-compulsory insurance is	4.54	0.693	0%	0%	10%	40%	50%
The majority of respondents (40%) agreed to strongly agree (50%) that the Facebook page helped them (mean = 4.54; SD = 0.693) to understand what compulsory and non-compulsory insurance is.							

continues on following page

Table 5. Continued

Statements	Mean	SD	Strongly Disagree	Disagree	Neutral	Agree	Strongly Agree
It assisted me to understand the difference between compound and simple interest	4.68	0.781	0%	0%	30%	60%	10%
The majority of respondents (60%) agreed to strongly agree (10%) that the Facebook page helped them (mean = 4.68; SD = 0.781) to understand the difference between compound and simple interest. The minority (30%) were indecisive.							
3. It supported me to understand and calculate over insurance and under insurance	4.68	0.781	0%	0%	30%	60%	10%
The majority of respondents (60%) agreed to strongly agree (10%) that the Facebook page helped them (mean = 4.68; SD = 0.781) to understand and calculate over- and under insurance. The minority (30%) were indecisive.							
4. It helped me to understand why life insurance and retirement annuities are important	3.78	0.661	0%	0%	40%	30%	30%
The majority of respondents (30%) agreed to strongly agree (30%) that the Facebook page helped them (mean = 3.78; SD = 0.661) to understand why life insurance and retirement annuities are important. The minority (40%) were indecisive.							
5. It supported me to understand the extent to which a particular form of ownership can contribute to the success or failure of a business	4.08	0.631	0%	0%	40%	50%	10%
The majority of respondents (50%) agreed to strongly agree (10%) that the Facebook page helped them (mean = 4.08; SD = 0.631) to understand the extent to which a particular form of ownership can contribute to the success or failure of a business. The minority (40%) were indecisive.							
6. It assisted me to be able to understand and distinguish between verbal and non-verbal presentation	4.08	0.721	0%	0%	20%	50%	30%
The majority of respondents (60%) agreed to strongly agree (10%) that the Facebook page helped them (mean = 4.08; SD = 0.721) to understand and distinguish between verbal and non-verbal presentation. The minority (20%) were indecisive.							
7. It empowered me to understand the criteria for a logical and effective presentation	4.18	0.761	0%	0%	30%	50%	20%
The majority of respondents (50%) agreed to strongly agree (20%) that the Facebook page helped them (mean = 4.18; SD = 0.761) to understand the criteria for a logical and effective presentation. The minority (30%) were indecisive.							
8. It supported me to know how to handle and respond to feedback in a non-aggressive and professional manner	3.88	0.561	0%	0%	40%	40%	20%
The majority of respondents (40%) agreed to strongly agree (20%) that the Facebook page supported them (mean = 3.88; SD = 0.561) to know how to handle and respond to feedback in a non-aggressive and professional manner. The minority (40%) were indecisive.							
9. I am pleasantly surprised at how the Business Studies Facebook page assisted and supported my understanding and learning in the subject	4.83	0.861	0%	0%	11.11%	88.89%	0%
The majority of respondents (88.89%) agreed that the Facebook page surprised them (mean = 4.83; SD = 0.861) in terms of how it assisted and supported their understanding and learning in the subject. A marginal percentage (11.11%) were indecisive.							

Scale: SD-Strongly disagree; D-Disagree; N-Neutral; A-Agree; SA-Strongly agree

DISCUSSION OF FINDINGS

It was found in this study that the respondents showed overwhelming positivity towards the social networking tool and further indicated that the Facebook page should indeed be utilised as a supportive teaching strategy. Gallop (2008:74) agrees that "social networking sites such as Facebook provide individuals with a way of maintaining and strengthening social ties, which can be beneficial in both social and academic settings". The literature review yielded several studies which have been conducted on the educational benefits of social media tools in the classroom (Gallop 2008; Van Wyk, 2014b). Furthermore, it emerged from the respondent's comments that subject knowledge was indeed enhanced supported with literature. Some of the comments included in the Facebook entries were as follows: "It gives us a better outlook and perspective towards Business Studies, and additional information and resources regarding our work in the classroom", "Yes because it helps me understand more about the subject", and "My level of understanding within the subject has highly increased. The page has been extremely useful, mentally it has groomed me". The findings of Gallop (2008:75-77) and Van Wyk (2014b) concur with these positive sentiments expressed by the learners, thus confirming that the incorporation of social media into the learning space supports and enhances the e-Learning experience. Moreover, Bute (2013:79) expressed a view pointing at the diversity of tools available in the public sphere for learning, knowledge and information; tools that are improving at a rapid pace. Similarly, Hunter-Brown (2012:19) argued that technology has allowed learners to access much more information than in the past and at a much quicker rate, thus improving subject knowledge. The researcher succeeded in incorporating a Business Studies Facebook page for grade 12 learners to improve their subject knowledge by completing interactive activities on the page as a supportive teaching strategy. Students argue that social media is characterised as Web 2.0-based e-Learning that emphasises dynamic participation, collaboration and sharing knowledge and ideas (Van Wyk, 2013:529; Van Wyk, 2014a:370). The researcher shares the view of Lam (2009:334) that the use of Web 2.0 tools as educational motivators creates a classroom of autonomy, connectedness and active participation, and is also in strong agreement with Lim (2010:73) who remarked on the multifunctionality of a Facebook page in presenting subject content.

In order for Facebook to be beneficial as a supportive teaching strategy in South Africa, all learners must have equal access to the necessary technology. Although the present study found that many learners had limited access to the Internet through not being able to afford data bundles or not being near Wi-Fi hotspots, the researcher purchased data bundles for all participants and made his Wi-Fi router available to them during contact time; an arrangement which is not feasible in the long run. As a consequence, some learners only had limited time to access the Facebook page and were not able to continue their participation outside the classroom environment; thus, constituting a serious obstacle.

CONCLUSION AND RECOMMENDATIONS

In order to work towards meeting the educational needs of net generation learners in South Africa, the integration of web technologies into the curriculum is not only essential but also highly beneficial in that these applications increase learners' motivation to participate in classroom activities and compels them to make more appropriate choices when interacting in a virtual environment. The incorporation of Web 2.0 tools into the educational curriculum holds several possibilities for learners to attain academic success. Teachers must assess the pros and cons of the digital world before deciding on the best tools for use in the curriculum. It is important to be cognizant of the fact that not all learners in South Africa have ready access to the internet, especially those from rural areas. The South African Department of Education must address the poor (or indeed no) access to the Internet in schools for teachers to incorporate ICT successfully. It is recommended that larger sample sizes of teachers, schools and learners must be investigated in South Africa since this will be extremely advantageous to the education system. It is recommended that workshops be offered on how to incorporate Facebook pages as a supportive teaching strategy within the Economics and Business Management field by inviting other educators in South Africa to understand the importance of ICT in education. The researcher suggests that the use of a Facebook page as a supportive teaching strategy should be introduced to various subject clusters. It can also be expanded to the district, provincial and national level to empower all teachers and learners older than 13 years. The researcher recommends that teachers form support teams and motivate local businesses to invest in the teaching of Business Studies at school so that learners can be provided with the necessary equipment for incorporating ICTs. Although the purpose of this study was to explore the use of a Facebook page as a supportive teaching strategy in the grade 12 Business Studies class at a specific school in South Africa, the information that was collected and can be used to grant a small overview of its effectiveness and cannot be generalised to a wider population. Not all learners who indicated that they would participate in the focus group discussion eventually completed the survey. The most apparent need in terms of further research concerns the fact that more research needs to be conducted across all grades of the high school curriculum and using greater sample sizes throughout South Africa.

REFERENCES

Alexander, B. (2006). *Web 2.0. A new wave of innovation for teaching and learning?* https://net.educause.edu/ir/library/pdf/ERM0621.pdf

Boghian, I. (2013). Using Facebook in Teaching. In Social media in higher education – Teaching in Web 2.0. Information Science Reference (IGI Global).

Bryan, A. (2006). Web 2.0: A new wave of innovation for teaching and learning. *EDUCAUSER Review*, *41*(2), 32–44.

Bute, S. J. R. (2013). Integrating Social Media and Traditional Media within the Academic Environment. In Social Media in Higher Education – Teaching in Web 2.0. Information Science Reference (IGI Global).

Cain, J. (2008). Online social networking issues within academia and pharmacy education. *American Journal of Pharmaceutical Education*, *72*(1), 44–54. doi:10.5688/aj720110 PMID:18322572

Del Valle Garcia Carreňo, I. (2014). Theory of Connectivity as an Emergent Solution to Innovative Learning Strategies. *American Journal of Educational Research*, *2*(2), 107–116. doi:10.12691/education-2-2-7

Department of Education. (2011). *National Curriculum Statement. Curriculum and Assessment Policy Statement: Further Education and Training Phase Grades 10 – 12 (Business Studies)*. Government Printers.

English, R., & Duncan-Howell, J. (2008). *MERLOT.org. Facebook© Goes to College: Using Social Networking Tools to Support Students Undertaking Teaching Practicum*. Available at: https://jolt.merlot.org/vol4no4/english_1208.pdf

Fisher, M., & Baird, D. (2006). Making eLearning Work: Utilizing Mobile Technology for Active Exploration, Collaboration, Assessment, and Reflection in Higher Education. *Journal of Educational Technology Systems*, *35*(1), 3–30. doi:10.2190/4T10-RX04-113N-8858

Fletcher, G. (2011). Digital learning-and school reform-now! *The Journal*, *38*(3), 14–16.

Fogg-Phillips, L., Baird, D., & Fogg, B.J. (n.d.). *Facebook for educators*. Academic Press.

Gallop, R. (2008). *Do blogs help students to learn?* http://insight.glos.ac.uk/tli/resources/lathe/documents/issue%202/case%20studies/gallop.pdf

Greenhow, C., & Robelia, B. (2009). Informal learning and identity formation in online social networks. *Learning, Media and Technology, 34*(2), 119–140. doi:10.1080/17439880902923580

Guba, E. G., & Lincoln, Y. S. (1994). Competing paradigms in qualitative research. In N. K. Denzin & Y. S. Lincoln (Eds.), *The handbook of qualitative research.* Sage.

Hall, B. (2006). *Student-centred learning.* http://secondlanguagewriting.com/explorations/Archives/2006/Jul/StudentcenteredLearning.html

Hunter-Brown, S. R. (2012). *Facebook as an instructional tool in the secondary classroom: A case study* [Doctoral thesis, Liberty University. Lynchburg]. https://core.ac.uk/download/pdf/58824655.pdf

Johnson, D. W., & Johnson, R. T. (2005). *New developments in social interdependence theory.* https://www.ncbi.nlm.nih.gov/pubmed/17191373

Lam, P. (2009). Quasi-Experimental research into the effects of an international collaboration project on Hong Kong secondary school students' learning motivation. *International Journal of Learning, 16*(7), 325–337. doi:10.18848/1447-9494/CGP/v16i07/46437

Lim, T. (2010). The use of Facebook for online discussions among distance learners. *Turkish Online Journal of Distance Education, 11*(4), 72–81.

Marshall, M. N. (1996). Sampling for qualitative research. *Family Practice, 13*(6), 522–525. doi:10.1093/fampra/13.6.522 PMID:9023528

McCarthy, J. (2012). International design collaboration and mentoring for tertiary students through Facebook. *Australasian Journal of Educational Technology, 28*(5), 755–775. doi:10.14742/ajet.1383

McMillan, J. H., & Schumacher, S. (2010). *Research in education: evidence-based inquiry* (7th ed.). Pearson.

Munoz, C. L., & Towner, T. L. (2009). Opening Facebook: How to use Facebook in the college classroom. In *Proceedings of Society for Information Technology & Teacher Education International Conference.* Chesapeake, VA: AACE. http://www.editlib.org/p/31031

Ophus, J. D., & Abbitt, J. T. (2009). Exploring the potential perceptions of social networking systems in university courses. *Journal of Online Learning and Teaching, 5*(4), 639–648.

Saikaew, K. R., Krutkam, W., Pattaramanon, R., Leelathakul, N., Chaipah, K., & Chaosakul, A. (2011). *KKU.ac.th. Using Facebook as a supplementary tool for teaching and learning.* https://gear.kku.ac.th/~krunapon/research/pub/usingFB4Learning.pdf

Skerrett, A. (2010). Lolita, Facebook, and the third space of literacy teacher education. *Educational Studies, 46*(1), 67–84. doi:10.1080/00131940903480233

Van Wyk, M. M. (2012). Using blogs as a means of enhancing reflective Teaching Practice in open distance learning ecologies. *African Education Review, 10,* 47–62. https://www.unisa.ac.za/contents/conferences/odl2012/docs/submissions/ODL-010-2012EDITFinal_vanWykM.pdf

Van Wyk, M. M. (2013). Exploring students' perceptions of blogs during teaching practice placements. *Mediterranean Journal of Social Sciences*, *4*(14), 525–533. doi:10.5901/mjss.2013.v4n14p525

Van Wyk, M. M. (2014a). Blogs as an e-learning strategy in supporting economics education students during teaching practice. *Journal of Communication*, *5*(2), 135–143. doi:10.1080/0976691X.2014.11884833

Van Wyk, M. M. (2014b). Using social media in an open distance learning teaching practice course. *Mediterranean Journal of Social Sciences*, *5*(1), 370–377. doi:10.5901/mjss.2014.v5n4p370

Van Wyk, M.M., & Toale, M. (2015). Research design. In O. Chinedu & M. Van Wyk (Eds.), *Educational research: An African approach*. Oxford University Press.

This research was previously published in the International Journal of Smart Education and Urban Society (IJSEUS), 12(2); pages 32-45, copyright year 2021 by IGI Publishing (an imprint of IGI Global).

Chapter 74
Facebook Use, Personality Characteristics and Academic Performance:
A Case Study

Georgia Sapsani
University of Patras, Patras, Greece

Nikolaos Tselios
University of Patras, Patras, Greece

ABSTRACT

The present article examines the relationship between student personality, use of social media and their academic performance and engagement. Specifically, this article examines the relationship of students' Facebook (FB) use and personality characteristics using the Big Five Personality Test. This is focused on (a) student engagement; (b) time spent preparing for class; (c) time spent in co-curricular activities; and (d) academic performance. 204 higher education students participated in the study. Results illustrate that FB time was significantly positively correlated to student engagement and time spent preparing for class. Sharing links activity was positively correlated with student engagement and playing FB games with time spent preparing for class. However, sending private messages and status updates were significantly negatively correlated with student engagement and time spent preparing for class. Also, viewing videos was negatively correlated with time spent in co-curricular activities. Chatting on FB and viewing photos found to be the most popular activities. Moreover, students' extraversion, conscientiousness, openness to experience were positively correlated to student engagement. In addition, extraversion had a positive relationship with time spent in co-curricular activities, although agreeableness had a negative relationship. Implications of the study for the instructors and the students are also discussed.

DOI: 10.4018/978-1-6684-7123-4.ch074

INTRODUCTION

The last few years, an important penetration of the Web 2.0 technologies in different aspects of the socio-economic activities has been observed (Straus et al., 2014, Orfanou, Tselios, & Katsanos, 2015, Katsanos, Tselios, & Xenos, 2012). Junco and Cole-Avent (2008) examined the technologies used by students. Some of these are already been used (e.g. FB) or present the potential to be used to enhance students' learning experience. In specific, the technologies which can be used for educational purposes are the following: social media (such as FB, myspace), blogs, other services that permit the user to create context (i.e. YouTube, Picasaweb), instant messages using FB and myspace, cell phones and virtual worlds (Junco & Cole-Avent, 2008).

Nowadays, social networks such as Facebook, and Twitter constitute a part of the citizens' daily life in the modern societies. According to Junco (2014a, p. 6), social networks are considered as implementations, services and systems that let the user create and share data with other users. Social networks replaced to a great extent, message sending and phone calls. Digital devices are being used especially from youngsters for the use of the social networks which help them communicate with each other almost instantly and with low cost.

Ellison, Steinfield, and Lampe (2007) investigated the relationship between FB use and the formation and preservation of the social capital. They found a strong relation between FB use and the three types of social capital (bridging, bonding, and maintained). Furthermore, they found that FB use interacts with measures of the phycology health, suggesting that is possible to offer bigger advantages for the users that present low self-confidence and satisfaction in life (Ellison, Steinfield, & Lampe, 2007).

Moreover, social networks are extensively used in educational settings (Altanopoulou, Tselios, Katsanos, Georgoutsou, & Panagiotaki, 2015, Lopes, Fidalgo-Neto, & Mota, 2017). However, their ever-increasing use has received some forms of criticism. The claim that the use of social networks in education involves many risks in students' performance is widespread. However, this is mainly attributed to the way students use them and not to their inherent nature (Junco, 2014a). One peril is called "multitasking", namely the execution of many actions at the same time, for instance sending a message to a friend while studying for an examination (Junco, 2014a). Other risks which can lead to lower student performance are using the laptop computer, sending instant messages and carrying out specific actions on FB during the lesson or while completing a learning task (Junco, 2014a). Moreover, Junco and Cotten (2011) found that extensive use of instant messaging had a negative effect on their academic tasks. The risks, which were referred above, may be some of the reasons that some teachers possess the perception that social networks, especially FB, have a detrimental effect on students' academic performance.

To further explore the issue, Junco and Cotten (2012) examined the effect of multitasking on educational results. The aim was to investigate how students interact with the technologies of information and communication (ICT's) and the effect of ICT use on students' GPA (Junco & Cotten, 2012). It was demonstrated that students spend enough time using ICT's, on which they don't search for context related to the modules but use FB, email, instant messages, talk on their cell phones and text, while doing schoolwork (Junco & Cotten, 2012). By using hierarchical regression, it was found that using FB and texting while doing homework were negatively associated with overall college GPA.

In a study conducted by Junco (2014b), a tool was used to record and examine what students actually do when they are using the internet. He gathered data related to their actions by using a data logging tool in students' computer (Junco, 2014b). The results show that students used FB frequently and that many of them regulated their computer use to enhance their academic performance (Junco, 2014b). Thus, negative attitude of some educators towards social networks sometimes originates from the fact that they don't get accustomed to technology and it is not founded on concrete evidence (Junco, 2014a). On the other hand, there are organizations which use social networks to communicate with their students and provide help. Moreover, a lot of instructors use them to inform their students via twitter for opportunities such as available work positions (Junco, 2014a).

FACEBOOK USE AND ACADEMIC PERFORMANCE: LITERATURE REVIEW

Engaging in Facebook use or texting while trying to complete schoolwork may impair students' capacity for cognitive processing and preclude deeper learning (Junco & Cotten, 2012). However, emailing, talking on their cell phones and instant messaging is not correlated with GPA (Junco & Cotten, 2012). They concluded that multitasking isn't an inherent burden on student results but it depends on the type and the aim of ICT's usage, while doing schoolwork. (Junco & Cotten, 2012).

Junco (2012b) examined the relationship between multiple indicators of FB use and academic performance. In specific, by using a hierarchical regression analysis he showed that the relationship between FB time and college grade point average (GPA) is statistically significant, as the followings relationships: frequency of which entered FB and college grade point average, time spend on FB and time spent preparing for class, frequency of which entered FB and time spent preparing for class (Junco, 2012b). It was found that time spend on FB and frequency of which entered FB was negatively related to GPA (Junco, 2012b). Time spend on FB is negatively related to time spent preparing for class (Junco, 2012b). Sharing links and checking up on friends on FB showed to be positively related to GPA, in contrast to status updates which was found negatively related to GPA (Junco, 2012b). Moreover, the use of FB chatting was negatively related to time spent preparing for class (Junco, 2012b). To sum up, using FB for collecting and sharing information offer positive results on students since using the platform for socializing (status updates and chatting, Junco, 2012b).

Junco (2013) examines the frequency of FB use, comparing the time the users reported spending on FB with the time that they really spent. To this end, the participants installed on their computer an application which tracked the time that they really spent on FB (Junco, 2014b). After completing the investigation, the results showed that a high correlation exist between the time that users declared spending on FB and the time that they really spent (Junco, 2013). However, a remarkable difference between these two variables emerged, since the students spend fewer time on FB than the time they reported. The relationship between student engagement and FB use has been also investigated. Student engagement is defined by Astin (1984, p. 518) as "the amount of physical and psychological energy that the student devotes to the academic experience". In a prominent study, Junco (2012a) addressed to a large sample (N = 2368) of students and examined the relationship between frequency of FB use (FBtime and FBcheck) and frequency of participating in FB activities with student engagement, time spent preparing for class and time spent in co-curricular activities.

Frequency of FB use was negatively correlated to engagement scale score. In addition, some of the FB activities such as playing games and checking up on friends were negatively correlated to engagement scale score and some others such as commenting, creating or RSVP (replay please) to events positively related (Junco, 2012a). Furthermore, there was no relationship between the frequency of FB use and time spent preparing for class. On the contrary, a significant negative relationship between FB chat and time spent preparing for class emerged (Junco, 2012a). Moreover, FB time was positively related to time spent participating in co-curricular activities in contrast to FB check which was not related. Some activities (commenting, creating or RSVP to events, viewing photos) had a positive relationship with time spent in co-curricular activities and some others (playing games, checking up on friends, posting photos) negative (Junco, 2012a). To further explore these claims, Junco (2014a) examined a variety of social network activity and its relation to specific facets of students' academic involvements. In specific, he presents studies in which he investigated extensively the relationships between: FB and student engagement, FB and social and academic integration of the student, FB and academic performance, twitter and student engagement, twitter and social and academic integration of the student, twitter and academic performance (Junco, 2014a).

Heiberger & Harper (2008) also examined the relationship between FB use and student engagement. They concluded that FB can be used to increase student engagement and also support first year university students in their transition from school reality to academic life. Yu, Tian, Vogel, and Kwok (2010) examined if the student engagement on FB is positively related to the growth of self-esteem, their satisfaction with university life and the pursuance of tasks in a proficiency level. In all three research questions, a positive correlation was established.

Lastly, Kirschner and Karpinski (2010) examined the relationship between FB use and their self-reported academic performance (college grade point average and the weekly hours spent on studying). The results show that FB users declare to have lower college grade point average and spend fewer hours on studying in comparison to the students who did not use FB (Kirschner & Karpinski, 2010).

OBJECTIVE OF THE STUDY/HYPOTHESES

Understanding of social media behavior is critical to a way forward in computing education. To this end, it would be useful to deeper understand how technology/FB use affects educational outcomes. However, from the studies presented previously, it emerges that the research related to the effect of FB use on student performance, is still at its infancy. Therefore, more studies which examine FB use, students' characteristics and their performance are required. This goal constitutes the core of the rationale of the study.

This paper attempts to extend the framework proposed by Junco (2012a) to examine relation between specific types of FB use and academic performance. To further explore the issue, the students' personality characteristics using the Big Five Personality Test (Goldberg, 1999) and their relation to specific measures of academic activity (Kakaraki, Tselios & Katsanos, 2017) was also examined.

Thus, the study presented in paper examines the relationship between the students' use of social media and personality with their performance and their integration in academic society. In specific, the aim of this study is to examine the relationship of Facebook (FB) use and personality characteristics of the students, using the Big Five Personality Test (Goldberg, 1999) with (a) student engagement, (b) time spent preparing for class, (c) time spent in co-curricular activities and (d) academic performance. In specific, the research questions examined were:

Question 1a (and 1b): Is there a relationship between frequency of Facebook use (and Facebook activities) and student engagement?

Question 2a (and 2b): Is there a relationship between frequency of Facebook use (and Facebook activities) and time spent preparing for class?

Question 3a (and 3b): Is there a relationship between frequency of Facebook use (and Facebook activities) and time spent in co-curricular activities?

Question 4a (and 4b): Is there a relationship between frequency of Facebook use (and Facebook activities) and academic performance?

Question 5: Is there a relationship between Big Five characteristics and student engagement?

Question 6: Is there a relationship between Big Five characteristics and time spent preparing for class?

Question 7: Is there a relationship between Big Five characteristics and time spent in co-curricular activities?

Question 8: Is there a relationship between Big Five characteristics and academic performance?

As mentioned previously, the framework of this study is based on Junco's (2012a) pioneering research. Therefore, the first three research questions are identical and formulated to examine their validity in a different educational environment. The next five research questions constitute an extension of the beforementioned research, while investigating at the same time the relationship between frequency of FB use and academic performance and students' personality characteristics respectively.

The rest of the paper is organized as follows: Firstly, the research method is presented, followed by the presentation and analysis of the results obtained. Subsequently, the obtained results are discussed and compared to the results reported by Junco (2012a). The practical implications of the study are also discussed.

METHODOLOGY

Research Method

The present study constitutes a case study and is categorized to the mixed research example (Cohen, Manion, & Morrison, 2013). In a case study, the researcher pay attention on the characteristics of an individual unit. The goal of this observation is to examine deeply and analyze further these characteristics which constitute the life circle of a unit with the aim of establishing conclusions for the wider environment, in which the unit belongs (Cohen, Manion, & Morrison, 2013, Hoinville & Jowell, 1978). A questionnaire to identify students' demographic data, student engagement, academic performance, FB use and personality was designed.

Participants

The sample comprises students of the Department of Educational Sciences and Early Childhood Education of University of Patras, who attended the laboratory section of three modules (Information and Communication Technology in Education, Introduction to Web Science, Design and Evaluation of Educational Software). Overall, 204 students participated in the study, 198 women, 6 men, aged 18-36 (mean = 20.63, SD = 2.23).

Instruments and Measures

This study used a questionnaire in which students were asked to report demographic data (gender, age, year of study, high school grade point average, high school direction) and data related their academic performance (university grade point average, number of modules which haven't been completed successfully).

As far as the questions about student engagement (Astin, 1984) are concerned, the first 21 questions were taken from Junco's (2012a) study. Questions 1-19 are obtained from the National Survey of Student Engagement (NSSE, Junco 2012a). In specific, questions 1-14 were coded by using a four-point, positively anchored Likert scale, ranging from "Never" to "Very often." For these analyses, "Never" was coded as 1, "Sometimes" as 2, "Often" as 3, and "Very often" as 4. Questions 15–17 were presented as a seven-point, positively anchored Likert scale and were coded with responses 1 or 2 as "1," responses 3 or 4 as "2," responses 5 or 6 as "3," and response 7 as "4". Responses for question 18 were coded 1 for "Very little," 2 for "Some," 3 for "Quite a bit," and 4 for "Very much". Finally, responses for question 19 were coded 1 for "Poor," 2 for "Fair," 3 for "Good," and 4 for "Excellent".

The final score for the 19-item NSSE instrument is an aggregate engagement score (sum of the individual items). In the last two questions, which are related to student engagement, the students were asked to estimate the average amount of time they spent preparing for class (academic engagement) and engaging in co-curricular activities (co-curricular engagement) each week. Answers to these questions were converted to minutes for these analyses (Junco, 2012a, p. 164).

In addition, students were asked to estimate their *FB use*. Specifically, students were asked to estimate their time spent on FB (FB time) as well as how often they checked FB (FB check). They were asked to evaluate average time spent daily and time spent "yesterday," as well as the average number of times they checked FB daily and "yesterday". For FB time, students used a pull-down menu to select the hours and minutes spent using FB and for FB check students were allowed to input an open-ended number. The hours and minutes spent using Facebook were converted to minutes for these analyses.

Students were also asked to estimate the frequency with which they conducted various activities on FB. These 14-items are also taken from (Junco, 2012a) and there are presented in Figure 1. Students were asked how frequently they perform the FB activities when they are on FB. Fb activity items were coded using a five-point, positively anchored Likert scale ranging from "Never" to "Very Frequently (close to 100% of the time)." For these analyses, "Never" was coded as 1, "Rarely (25%)" as 2, "Sometimes (50%)" as 3, "Somewhat frequently (75%)" as 4 and "Very frequently (close to 100% of the time)" as 5.

In the last part of the questionnaire, there are 50 questions of the Big Five Personality Test (Goldberg, 1999). The 50 questions are evenly distributed to 5 personality characteristics, which are the followings: extraversion (sociable), agreeableness (co-operative), conscientiousness (liable), emotional stability (calm) and openness to experience (open-minded). These factors are well-known as Big Five (Goldberg, 1999). This title was not given as a reflection of its inherent glory but to emphasize on the fact that each one of these factors is extremely wide. Therefore, the structure of Big Five is not implying that the differences in personality can be reduced in only five characteristics. On the contrary, these five dimensions depict the personality in a wider level of distraction and each dimension summarize one big number of more specific characteristics of personality (John & Srivastava, 1999). In this study, the Greek version of Big Five was adopted. The questionnaire was created on Google Forms and for the data analysis was used SPSS v20.

Reliability Analysis

Regarding engagement instrument and big five personality test reliability, the Cronbach's alpha estimate for the engagement instrument of NSSE was 0.75 and for the big five personality test was 0.79, which are both considered acceptable. Regarding the engagement instrument validity, for the 19-item engagement scale the total score on the scale was correlated to the number of minutes which students reported spending in co-curricular activities in a typical week (Junco, 2012a). Also, a weak but significant correlation between scores on the engagement instrument and average minutes per week which students reported spending in co-curricular activities (Pearson's r = 0.26, p < 0.01), which is in line to Junco (2012a) findings. Also, the big five personality test validity is being tested and is proved by Goldberg (1999).

Procedure

The study took place from 24/03/2016 to 27/05/2016. The participation in this study was voluntary and there was not an incentive for their participation. The announcement of the questionnaire took place in the courses' laboratory sessions which were mentioned above and in the official Facebook group of the department. The students had to spent approximately 15-20 minutes to complete the questionnaire.

RESULTS

For all research questions, descriptive statistics, appropriate correlations' analysis, statistical significance testing and hierarchical regression took place. Hierarchical regression has been carried out by using five groups of variables: in the first group is included "gender" and "years of study", in the second the variable "FB time", in the third "FB check", in the fourth "the frequency with which they conducted various activities on FB" and in the fifth "the characteristics of big five personality test".

Figure 1. Frequency of use for the 14 measured FB activities

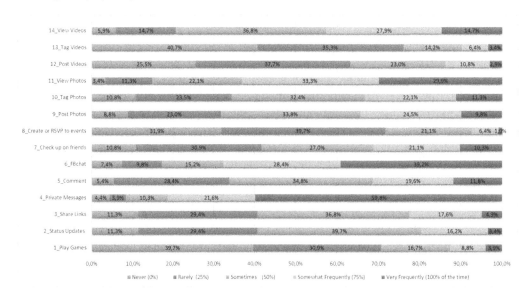

Moreover, the independent variable "FB use" comprised two variables: FB time and FB check. Since FB time and FB time "yesterday" were highly and significantly correlated (Pearson's $r = 0.73$, $p = 0.00$), only FB time was used in the analyses. Furthermore, since FB check and FB check "yesterday" were also highly and significantly correlated (r Pearson $= 0.95$, $p = 0.00$), only FB check was used in the analyses. Also, the independent variable "academic performance" consist of two other variables: university grade point average and number of modules which haven't been completed successfully. The results obtained for each research questions are presented in the following.

As reported previously, most participants (198/204) were females. For the variable "high school direction", 171 (83.8%) were from theoretical direction, 8 (3.9%) from scientific direction and 25 (12.3%) from technological direction. 52 (25.5%) students were at their first year of study, 54 (26.5%) students were at the second year of study, 33 (16.2%) students were at the third year of study, 61 (29.9%) students were at the fourth year of study and the last 4 (2%) students were at their fifth or higher year. Attention was given to include a satisfactory number of participants from each year. The frequency of the 14 FB activities reported by the students is presented in Figure 1.

The aggregated descriptive statistics for the most significant variables of the study are presented in Table 1.

Table 1. Descriptive statistics

	Sample		1st Year		2nd Year		3rd Year		4th Year	
	Mean	**SD**	**Mean**	**SD**	**Mean**	**SD**	**Mean**	**SD**	**Mean**	**SD**
Age	20.63	2.23	19.10	1.59	20.02	2.32	20.97	1.45	21.95	1.59
High school grade point average	17.18	1.20	17.10	1.38	17.14	1.10	17.45	1.02	17.15	1.12
University grade point average	7,08	1,01	6,94	1,71	6,97	0,73	7,44	0,69	7,11	0,46
Number of modules which haven't been passed	3.14	4.15	1.04	1.95	3.24	3.21	2.52	2.36	4.90	5.76
Student Engagement	44.17	7.39	44.75	7.67	44.24	8.15	45.73	6.68	42.84	6.91
Time spent preparing for class (min)	276.24	239.47	220.33	248.64	310.48	205.71	260.24	242.42	282.33	229.39
Time spent in co-curricular activities (min)	127.02	179.76	110.08	166.88	87.89	144.10	144.15	148.83	165.26	218.20
Fb time (min)	255.25	233.39	378.38	319.34	222.50	202.20	223.94	184.88	198.52	154.60
Fb time yesterday (min)	192.18	219.65	300.73	310.92	164.44	145.02	212.88	263.36	119.13	89.24
Fb check	10.67	17.27	14.77	17.05	11.43	26.86	8.55	7.17	7.51	8.13
Fb check yesterday	8.81	16.47	13.04	15.32	9.81	26.76	6.52	5.85	5.69	5.98
1_Play Games	1.06	1.13	1.06	1.13	1.04	.99	1.03	.88	1.10	1.35
2_Status Updates	1.71	.98	2.00	1.12	1.76	.93	1.67	.85	1.51	.92
3_ Share Links	1.75	1.03	1.94	1.26	1.81	.99	1.70	.88	1.59	.92
4_ Private Messages	3.28	1.09	3.50	.87	3.02	1.32	3.33	.92	3.30	1.09

continues on following page

Table 1. Continued

	Sample		1st Year		2nd Year		3rd Year		4th Year	
	Mean	SD	Mean	SD	Mean	SD	Mean	SD	Mean	SD
5_ Comment	2.04	1.08	2.60	1.14	1.70	1.00	2.00	.94	1.89	.97
6_Fb chat	2.82	1.25	3.04	1.24	2.76	1.18	2.76	1.06	2.72	1.39
7_ Check up on friends	1.89	1.17	2.33	1.23	1.83	1.02	2.03	1.07	1.51	1.16
8_ Create or RSVP to events	1.05	.94	1.15	1.02	1.20	.94	.91	.84	.93	.91
9_ Post Photos	2.03	1.11	2.42	1.14	2.00	1.12	1.94	1.09	1.79	1.03
10_ Tag Photos	2.00	1.16	2.27	1.21	1.96	1.10	1.91	1.18	1.85	1.15
11_ View Photos	2.75	1.11	3.17	.92	2.69	1.08	2.94	1.00	2.38	1.20
12_ Post Videos	1.28	1.05	1.62	1.17	1.17	.88	1.48	1.18	1.00	.95
13_ Tag Videos	.97	1.06	1.48	1.31	.74	.81	1.00	1.09	.70	.86
14_ View Videos	2.31	1.08	2.67	1.22	2.20	.92	2.27	.91	2.10	1.08
Extraversion	32.87	6.76	34.69	6.99	33.11	5.67	33.15	5.88	30.77	7.37
Agreeableness	42.90	4.95	41.87	6.71	42.46	4.29	44.67	3.36	43.11	4.30
Conscientiousness	35.46	6.97	35.23	6.39	35.57	7.20	37.06	7.57	34.36	6.93
Emotional Stability	27.73	6.81	26.10	6.61	28.24	7.07	27.33	5.80	28.34	6.76
Openness to Experience	35.60	5.53	35.63	6.05	35.17	5.45	36.52	5.14	35.21	5.47
Total Score of Big Five	174.56	17.46	173.52	17.83	174.56	18.73	178.73	14.51	171.80	16.16

Research Questions

Question 1a (and 1b): Relationship Between Frequency of Facebook Use (and Facebook Activities) and Student Engagement

The relationship between FB time and student engagement was weak and significant ($r = 0.20$, $p = 0.00$). However, the relationship between FB check and student engagement was not significant. Also, only the relationship between sharing links and student engagement was weak and significant ($r = 0.21$, $F = 3.17$, $p = 0.01$).

Hierarchical regression unveiled a significant positive relationship between FB time and student engagement, although there was no relationship between FB check and student engagement. Frequency of sharing links was a positive predictor of student engagement while sending private messages was a negative one.

Question 2a (and 2b): Relationship Between Frequency of Facebook Use (and Facebook Activities) and Time Spent Preparing for Class

The relationship between FB time and time spent preparing for class was weak and significant ($r = 0.14$, $p = 0.04$) but the relationship between FB check and time spent preparing for class was not significant. Moreover, only the relationship between playing games and time spent preparing for class was weak and significant ($r = 0.15$, $F = 3.25$, $p = 0.01$).

Hierarchical regression demonstrated a significant positive relationship between FB time and time spent preparing for class, although there was no relationship between FB check and time spent preparing for class. Frequency of playing games was positively predictive of time spent preparing for class while status updating was negatively predictive.

Question 3a (and 3b): Relationship Between Frequency of Facebook Use (and Facebook Activities) and Time Spent in Co-Curricular Activities

There was no relationship between frequency of FB use and time spent in co-curricular activities. Also, the relationships between sending private messages and time spent in co-curricular activities ($r=-0.12$, $F=2.73$, $p=0.03$) and between viewing videos and time spent in co-curricular activities ($r=-0.27$, $F=4.85$, $p=0.00$) are weak and significant.

Hierarchical regression unveiled no relationship between frequency of FB use and time spent in co-curricular activities. Frequency of viewing videos was negatively predictive of time spent in co-curricular activities.

Question 4a (and 4b): Relationship Between Frequency of Facebook Use (and Facebook Activities) and Academic Performance

The relationship between FB time and academic performance (for both university grade point average and number of modules which haven't been completed successfully) as the relationship between FB check and academic performance (for both university grade point average and number of modules which haven't been completed successfully) was not significant. Also, only the relationship of status updates and university grade point average ($r = -0.14$, $F = 4.65$, $p = 0.00$) is weak and significant. The relationships of playing games ($r = 0.14$, $p = 0.04$), commenting ($r = -0.18$, $p = 0.00$), viewing photos ($r = -0.20$, $p = 0.00$) and posting videos ($r = -0.14$, $p = 0.04$) with number of modules that haven't been completed successfully by the students were all weak and significant.

By using hierarchical regression, there was no relationship between frequency of FB use and university GPA. Frequency of commenting was positively predictive of university GPA while frequency of engaging in FB chat and status updating were negative predictors. Furthermore, there was no relationship between frequency of FB use and number of modules which haven't been completed successfully. Frequency of posting photos and playing games found to be a positive predictor of number of modules which haven't been completed successfully.

Question 5: Relationship Between Big Five Characteristics and Student Engagement

The relationship between extraversion (r = 0.34, p = 0.00), agreeableness (r = 0.15, p = 0.02), conscientiousness (r = 0.23, p = 0.00), openness to experience (r = 0.33, p = 0.00), total score of Big Five (r = 0.39, p = 0.00) and student engagement were weak or medium and significant. The relationship between emotional stability and student engagement was not found significant.

Hierarchical regression, unveiled a significant positive relationship between extraversion, conscientiousness, openness to experience and student engagement.

Question 6: Relationship Between Big Five Characteristics and Time Spent Preparing for Class

The relationship between Big Five characteristics (for each one of them and total score) and time spent preparing for class was not significant. By using hierarchical regression, there was a significant positive relationship between extraversion and time spent preparing for class.

Question 7: Relationship Between Big Five Characteristics and Time Spent in Co-Curricular Activities

Only the relationship between agreeableness and time spent in co-curricular activities (r=-0.19, p=0.00) was found weak and significant. By using hierarchical regression, there was a significant positive relationship between extraversion and time spent in co-curricular activities.

Question 8: Relationship Between Big Five Characteristics and Academic Performance

Only the relationships between openness to experience and university grade point average (r = 0.25, p = 0.00), total score of Big Five and GPA (r = 0.17, p = 0.02) were found to be significant. Moreover, the relationships of conscientiousness (r = -0.30, p = 0.00), total score of Big Five (r = -0.13, p = 0.05) with number of modules which haven't been completed successfully were found to be weak and significant.

Hierarchical regression unveiled a significant positive relationship between openness to experience and university grade point average while there was a significant negative relationship between conscientiousness and number of modules which haven't been completed successfully. The groups of variables that had a significant contribution to student engagement were the characteristics of big five personality test (22%) and FB time (3%). Also, FB time (3%) has a significant contribution on time spent preparing for class.

The frequency with which they conducted activities on FB shows a significant contribution on time spent in co-curricular activities (15%). Moreover, the group of variables that shows a significant contribution on university GPA was the frequency with which they conducted various activities on FB (16%) and the characteristics of big five personality test (8%). Finally, the characteristics of big five personality test (9%) shows a significant contribution on the number of modules which haven't been completed successfully.

DISCUSSION

The results of the current study in contrast with the results reported by Junco (2012a) are presented in Table 2. According to the data obtained sending personal messages, chatting on FB and viewing photos were the most popular activities for all participants. On the contrary, in Junco (2012a, p. 166) the most popular activities were viewing photos, commenting and checking up on friends.

In this study, a positive relationship between FBtime and student engagement was found, although in Junco (2012a) a negative one was found (Table 2). Heiberger and Harper (2008) also found a positive relationship between FBtime and student engagement. The different results may be attributed to different uses of Facebook. Also, the relationship between fbcheck and student engagement was not significant but, in the study conducted by Junco (2012a), it was found to be negative. Furthermore, in the present study sharing links was positively related to student engagement and sending private messages was negatively related. In Junco (2012a), commenting and creating or RSVP to events was positively related to student engagement. Playing games and checking up on friends were negatively related to student engagement.

Fb time (mean = 255,25, SD = 233,39) and fbtime yesterday (mean = 192,18, SD = 219,65) but also FB check (mean = 10,67, SD = 17,27) and FB check yesterday (mean = 8,81, SD = 16,47) seem to be different in relation with the results reported by Junco (2012a, p. 166) for the same variables. This difference is possibly due to the different participants' characteristics of each study as well as the evolution of the Facebook itself and its use during the years.

Table 2. Comparison of the results reported in this study and the study conducted by Junco (2012a). (ns= no significant)

	Student Engagement		Time Spent Preparing for Class		Time Spent in Co-Curricular Activities	
	Current Study	Junco (2012a)	Current Study	Junco (2012a)	Current Study	Junco (2012a)
Fbtime	positive	negative	positive	ns	ns	positive
Fbcheck	ns	negative	ns	ns	ns	ns
Frequency of Facebook activities	Sharing links (positive) Sending private messages (negative)	Commenting & Creating or RSVP to events (positive) Playing games & Checking up on friends (negative)	Playing games (positive) Status Updating (negative)	Fb chatting (negative)	Viewing videos (negative)	Commenting, Creating or RSVP to events & Viewing photos (positive) Playing games, Checking up on friends & Posting photos (negative)

Moreover, in the present study, a positive relationship between FB time and time spent preparing for class was found, although in Junco (2012a) was not found significant. Both in this study and in Junco (2012a) the relationship between FB check and time spent preparing for class was not found significant. Also, in this study, playing games was positive related to time spent preparing for class and status updating was negatively related. In Junco (2012a), the only significant FB activity was FB chatting which was negatively related to time spent preparing for class.

A comparison of the current study and the results reported by Junco (2012a) as far as the relationship between FB time and time spent in co-curricular activities is concerned, unveiled significant differences. The only thing that they have in common was the relationship between FB check and time spent preparing for class and the relationship between FB check and time spent in co-curricular activities, which both were not found significant. In this study, FB time and time spent in co-curricular activities was not found significant, although in Junco (2012a) the same relationship was found positive. The relationship between FB check and time spent in co-curricular activities was not demonstrated significant, both in this study and in the study conducted by Junco (2012a). Lastly, in Junco (2012a), commenting, creating or RSVP to events and viewing photos were positively related to time spent in co-curricular activities and playing games, checking up on friends and posting photos were negatively related. In the present study, the only significant FB activity was the frequency of viewing videos which was negatively related to time spent in co-curricular activities.

As far as the remaining research questions are concerned, for the fourth research question, there was no relationship between FB use and academic performance. Commenting had a positive relationship with university GPA. However, number of status updates and chatting on FB had a negative relationship. Furthermore, playing games and posting photos had a positive relationship with the number of modules which haven't been completed successfully by the students, although commenting, viewing photos and posting videos had a negative relationship.

For the fifth research question, extraversion, agreeableness, conscientiousness, openness to experience and total score of Big Five were positively correlated with student engagement. For the sixth research question, only extraversion had a positive relationship with time spent preparing for class. For the seventh research question, extraversion had a positive relationship with time spent in co-curricular activities, although agreeableness had a negative relationship. Lastly, for the eighth research question, openness to experience and total score of Big Five present a positive relationship with university GPA, even though conscientiousness and total score of Big Five present a negative relationship with the number of modules which haven't been completed successfully.

CONCLUSION

The study reported in this paper examines the relationship between the students' social media use their personality and their performance as well as the integration of the students in academic society. In concordance with the finding reported by Junco (2012a,b) it was found that efforts to draw conclusions on the relationship between *general* Facebook use and academic performance are somewhat superficial, without an attempt to identify, and measure, specific types of use.

The implications of this study are important for all stakeholders, both instructors and the students. Firstly, instructors can use a FB group or a FB page as a place in which their students can express themselves on things that are related to a subject, make a debate or a discussion on a theme, exchange ideas and queries. The results illustrate that the time spent on FB is positively related to student engagement and to time spent preparing for class, and specifically sharing links presents a positive relationship with student engagement and playing games on FB presents a positive relationship with time spent preparing for class. Thus, instructors should design appropriate interventions and encourage their students spend more time on FB group or page by sharing links or playing educational games, which are related to the theme of the module.

Moreover, commenting showed a positive relationship with university GPA and viewing photos and posting videos had a negative relationship with the number of modules which haven't been completed successfully by the students. To have a better GPA and fewer number of modules which haven't been completed successfully, instructors could encourage their student to comment on topics, view more photos and post more videos on FB which are related to a module. Finally, specific students' characteristics extraversion (positive related to student engagement, to time spent preparing for class and to time spent in co-curricular activities), openness to experience (presents a positive relationship with university GPA) and conscientiousness (presents a negative relationship with the number of modules which haven't been successfully completed) could be exploited and cultivated to acquire better educational results. Finally, students could achieve better educational results if their instructor use FB as a part of the module because it is a well-known environment for them and an appropriate tool for education (Junco, 2014a).

The study is not without limitations. Firstly, that it is correlational by nature. Thus, no causal relations could be established. Secondly, the sample cannot be considered as representative. Thirdly, the use of students' self-report measures constitutes a validity threat to the data obtained. More studies in different educational settings and institutions and with more representative samples should be carried out. In addition, the investigation of learners' behavioral intention to use structured educational activities mediated by social networks using technology acceptance models constitutes an additional research goal (Tselios, Daskalakis, & Papadopoulou, 2011, Altanopoulou & Tselios, 2017). Moreover, deeper investigation of the interaction between students' observed activity in other social networks and the learning outcome (Katsanos, Tselios & Avouris, 2010; Tselios & Avouris, 2003; Tselios, Avouris, & Kordaki, 2002) will be also examined.

Nowadays, education is undergoing a profound change. A deeper understanding of social media use is critical to a way forward in computing education. From the results of the current study, it derives that Facebook can have positive effects on student engagement which could increase students' learning performance. Finally, the instructors by taking into consideration the students' personality characteristics could adjust appropriately the designed didactic interventions which is expected to lead to an increased students' engagement.

REFERENCES

Altanopoulou, P., & Tselios, N. (2017). Assessing acceptance toward wiki technology in the context of higher education. *The International Review of Research in Open and Distributed Learning, 18*(6), 127–149. doi:10.19173/irrodl.v18i6.2995

Altanopoulou, P., Tselios, N., Katsanos, C., Georgoutsou, M., & Panagiotaki, A. (2015). Wiki-mediated activities in higher education: Evidence-based analysis of learning effectiveness across three studies. *Journal of Educational Technology & Society, 18*(4), 511–522.

Astin, A. W. (1984). Student involvement: A developmental theory for higher education. *Journal of College Student Personnel, 25*(4), 297–308.

Cohen, L., Manion, L., & Morrison, K. (2013). *Research methods in education.* Routledge.

Ellison, N. B., Steinfield, C., & Lampe, C. (2007). The benefits of Facebook "friends": Social capital and college students' use of online social network sites. *Journal of Computer-Mediated Communication, 12*(4), 1143–1168. doi:10.1111/j.1083-6101.2007.00367.x

Goldberg, L. R. (1999). A broad-bandwidth, public domain, personality inventory measuring the lower-level facets of several five-factor models. *Personality psychology in Europe, 7*(1), 7-28.

Heiberger, G., & Harper, R. (2008). Have you Facebooked Astin lately? Using technology to increase student involvement. *New Directions for Student Services, 2008*(124), 19–35. doi:10.1002s.293

Hoinville, G., & Jowell, R. (1978). *Survey research practice*. London: Heinemann Educational Books.

John, O. P., & Srivastava, S. (1999). The Big Five trait taxonomy: History, measurement, and theoretical perspectives. In Handbook of personality: Theory and research (Vol. 2, pp. 102-138).

Junco, R. (2012a). The relationship between frequency of Facebook use, participation in Facebook activities, and student engagement. *Computers & Education, 58*(1), 162–171. doi:10.1016/j.compedu.2011.08.004

Junco, R. (2012b). Too much face and not enough books: The relationship between multiple indices of Facebook use and academic performance. *Computers in Human Behavior, 28*(1), 187–198. doi:10.1016/j.chb.2011.08.026

Junco, R. (2013). Comparing actual and self-reported measures of Facebook use. *Computers in Human Behavior, 29*(3), 626–631. doi:10.1016/j.chb.2012.11.007

Junco, R. (2014a). *Engaging Students through Social Media: Evidence-Based Practices for Use in Student Affairs*. John Wiley & Sons.

Junco, R. (2014b). iSpy: Seeing what students really do online. *Learning, Media and Technology, 39*(1), 75–89. doi:10.1080/17439884.2013.771782

Junco, R., & Cole-Avent, G. A. (2008). An introduction to technologies commonly used by college students. *New Directions for Student Services, 2008*(124), 3–17. doi:10.1002s.292

Junco, R., & Cotten, S. R. (2011). Perceived academic effects of instant messaging use. *Computers & Education, 56*(2), 370–378. doi:10.1016/j.compedu.2010.08.020

Junco, R., & Cotten, S. R. (2012). No A 4 U: The relationship between multitasking and academic performance. *Computers & Education, 59*(2), 505–514. doi:10.1016/j.compedu.2011.12.023

Kakaraki, S., Tselios, N., & Katsanos, C. (2017). Internet addiction, academic performance and personality traits: A correlational study among female university students. *International Journal of Learning Technology, 12*(2), 151. doi:10.1504/IJLT.2017.086382

Katsanos, C., Tselios, N., & Avouris, N. (2010). Evaluating web site navigability: Validation of a tool-based approach through two eye-tracking studies. *New Review of Hypermedia and Multimedia, 16*(1-2), 195–214. doi:10.1080/13614561003605179

Katsanos, C., Tselios, N., & Xenos, M. (2012). Perceived usability evaluation of learning management systems: a first step towards standardization of the System Usability Scale in Greek. In *Proceedings of the 16th Pan-Hellenic Conference on Informatics, PCI 2012*, Piraeus, Greece, October 5-7 (pp. 302-307). IEEE. 10.1109/PCi.2012.38

Kirschner, P. A., & Karpinski, A. C. (2010). Facebook and academic performance. *Computers in Human Behavior*, *26*(6), 1237–1245. doi:10.1016/j.chb.2010.03.024

Lopes, R. M., Fidalgo-Neto, A. A., & Mota, F. B. (2017). Facebook in educational research: A bibliometric analysis. *Scientometrics*, *111*(3), 1591–1621. doi:10.100711192-017-2294-1

Orfanou, K., Tselios, N., & Katsanos, C. (2015). Perceived usability evaluation of learning management systems: Empirical evaluation of the System Usability Scale. *The International Review of Research in Open and Distributed Learning*, *16*(2), 227–246. doi:10.19173/irrodl.v16i2.1955

Straus, J. R., Williams, R., Shogan, C., & Glassman, M. (2014). Social Media as a Communication Tool in Congress: Evaluating Senate Usage of Twitter in the 113th Congress. In *APSA 2014 Annual Meeting*.

Tselios, N., Avouris, N., & Kordaki, M. (2002). Student Task Modeling in design and evaluation of open problem-solving environments. *Education and Information Technologies*, *7*(1), 19–42. doi:10.1023/A:1015306507126

Tselios, N., Daskalakis, S., & Papadopoulou, M. (2011). Assessing the technology acceptance of a blended learning university course. *Journal of Educational Technology & Society*, *14*(2), 224–235.

Tselios, N. K., & Avouris, N. M. (2003). Cognitive task modeling for system design and evaluation of non-routine task domains. In E. Hollnagel (Ed.), *Handbook of Cognitive Task Design* (pp. 307–332). Amsterdam, The Netherlands: Lawrence Erlbaum.

Yu, A. Y., Tian, S. W., Vogel, D., & Kwok, R. C. W. (2010). Can learning be virtually boosted? An investigation of online social networking impacts. *Computers & Education*, *55*(4), 1494–1503. doi:10.1016/j.compedu.2010.06.015

This research was previously published in the International Journal of Web-Based Learning and Teaching Technologies (IJWLTT), 14(2); pages 1-14, copyright year 2019 by IGI Publishing (an imprint of IGI Global).

Chapter 75
Social Media Use in Academic Libraries:
Applications and Implications in a Developing Country

Goodluck Ifijeh
Covenant University, Nigeria

Julie Ilogho
Covenant University, Nigeria

Juliana Iwu-James
https://orcid.org/0000-0001-5141-1457
Covenant University, Nigeria

Happiness Chijioke Michael-Onuoha
https://orcid.org/0000-0003-2996-6979
Covenant University, Nigeria

Ifeakachuku Osinulu
Covenant University, Nigeria

ABSTRACT

Social media use has become the norm in information services delivery. It holds the unique advantage of delivering service to users through social interaction. This chapter discussed social media use in academic libraries in a developing country: Nigeria. It examined the concept and definition of social media; it also discussed trends in social media usage in libraries. The chapter further outlined the types of social media tools used in libraries. It discussed the peculiar challenges of social media use in Nigeria and proffered solutions.

DOI: 10.4018/978-1-6684-7123-4.ch075

INTRODUCTION

Social media, a term which is sometimes referred to as social media tools, has gained so much popularity over the past few years. In a study, Jacka and Scott (2011) argued that there is no single definition of social media. But some authors have tried to define the term. Social media can be said to be a medium of communication that is virtual, participatory and collaborative. Kaplan, and Haenlein (2010) defined social media as 'a group of internet-integrated applications that build on the ideological and technological foundations of Web 2.0 (the platform) and that allow the creation and exchange of User Generated Content (the ways in which people make use of social media). Social media is an evolution of word of mouth that scaled up by leveraging the persuasiveness of the internet. Its major components are social networking, microblogs, blogs, RSS feeds, widgets, linking and posting, content rating, book marking sites, audio podcasting and video podcasting (Sajithra & Patil, 2013). Social media has been defined as website and applications used for social networking. It is sometimes said to mean the same thing as social network even though some authors have tried to differentiate social media from social network (Hartshorn, 2010). Social media is primarily used to transmit or share information with a broad audience, while social networking is the act of engaging people with common interest to associate together and build relationships through community (Cohen, 2009; Hartshon, 2010). Bedell (2010) opines that social media is a simple system, a communication channel; it is not a location that you visit. Social networking is a two-way communication, where conversations are at the core and through which relationships are developed (Edosomwan et al 2011).

Social media have evolved over the years into what is obtainable presently and in recent times. The use of the telegraph to transmit and receive messages over long distances was the experience in 1792 (Ritholz, 2010) as cited by Edosomwan et al, 2011. Then, in the 1800s, the radio and telephone were used for social interaction (Rimskii, 2011; Wren, 2004). Phone phreaking was a popular term in the 1950s, a term used for the rogue searching of the telephone network. Phreaks were able to hack into corporate unused voice mailboxes to host the first blogs and podcasts (Borders, 2010). During the 1960s, the public saw the advent of email (Borders, 2010). It was originally a method to exchange messages from one computer to another, which are online (Mwangi & Wagoki, 2016). Although, there has been a lot of debates as to whether the email is social media, Sajithra and Ratil (2013) opined that the introduction of Email marked the beginning of the much more collaborative social media years later, even though Edosomwan et al (2011) opined that social media started with the telephone and not computer.

The 1970s witnessed further social media development; Multi-User Domain, a real-time virtual world with role-playing games, interactive fiction, and online chat have since emerged. The process of managing email list was automated and christened LITSERV in the 1980s. Internet Relay Chat (IRC) was introduced in the late 1980s to ease the group discussions in a chat as well as data transfer. The 1990s witnessed the birth of private internet service providers which gave rise to personal websites, discussion groups and chat groups. This brought about the need for online media etiquette standard known as netiquette to serve as a control mechanism. The first social networking site, classmate.com was introduced in the mid-1990s. This was closely followed by the invention of blogs in the 1990s. The need to generate user contents gave rise to Web 2.0 (a term commonly associated with web applications) which was created in the late 1990s; this sprang into the early 2000s.

A web 2.0 site gives its users the free choice to interact or collaborate with each other in a social media dialogue as creators of user-generated content in a virtual community. These include social networking sites, blogs, wikis, video sharing site etc. This was closely followed by Web 3.0 which could be described as an extension of Web 2.0's participatory technologies and social networks into 3D space. This has also evolved into Web 4.0, sometimes referred to as the semantic web. The impact of social media in various fields, including librarianship relies on how well an organization's goals are matched with digital technologies as well as the needs of its target (Sajithra & Ratil, 2013). Kaplan and Haenlein (2010) classified social media into six types: collaborative projects, blogs, content communities, social networking sites, virtual social worlds and virtual game worlds.

Social media can be used by individuals and organizations or institutions as a very powerful tool for disseminating information. The library as an institution employs social medial tools for promoting its services and resources. One of the challenges institutions in the information era face is how to harness the potentials of social media tools and get the best results. Social media can be used in a variety of communication methods broadly summarized as broadcast messages, response to enquiries and then conversation between institution and users. Regardless of the approach taken, there are compelling reasons for libraries to engage with social media. Social media offer librarians a way to reach out to their users who may not have considered the library as a resource for their information needs.

One important question that may be asked is: how are social media tools being used by some major libraries across the world? A 2010 survey by the Society of Chief Librarians in the UK found that internet users trust library staff more than most other providers of online support and information, and public library staff are second only to doctors in terms of the trust placed in them by seekers of information. The core of the work of librarians is information sharing; this survey results suggest librarians are in a unique position to implement and exploit social media to their (and their users) advantage (Canty, 2012).

Social media can give a competitive edge in a time of major technological change and competition from other information channels. Libraries need to demonstrate the value of their proposition. Social media give librarians a way to reach out to their users who may not have considered the library as a resource for their information needs (Islam & K. Tsuji, 2016).

Background

Information and communication technology (ICT) has brought great changes in the way individuals, organizations, society and the world at large conduct their day- to – day activities. ICT has not only made creation and access to information very easy, it has made communication of useful information to any part of the world smarter and seamless. Though there are various definition of ICT, the concept may be described as the various technologies (applications, equipment, devices or tools) deployed in the transmission and communication of information. In this regard, social media can be viewed as ICT networking tools designed for social interaction. Boyd and Ellison (2007) defined social network sites as web-based services that allow individuals to (1) construct a public or semi-public profile within a bounded system, (2) articulate a list of other users with whom they share a connection and (3) view and traverse their list of connections and those made by others within the system. The nature and nomenclature of these connections may vary from site to site. Chu and Du (2013) opined that social networking can encompass almost all collaborative environments employing web 2.0 technologies. The original aim of web 2-0 technologies is collaboration among users. It proffers solutions in the use of the internet for interactive purposes engaging tools like blogs, wikis, RSS (Really Simple Syndication), podcasting, social bookmarking, social networking, feeds, and Google (Churchill 2007 as cited by Chu & Du 2013). Any website designed to allow multiple users to publish content of themselves is a social networking site (SNS). The amazing thing about these websites/tools is that they are free, hence users are allowed to create personal pages with content in diverse forms such as images, texts, music, videos etc. Members of the sites are also able to share web pages with friends, search for friends with similar interests and interact for as long as they so desire leading to establishing long and lasting relationships.

Boyd and Ellison (2007) stated that websites vary in terms of features and membership. In other words not all the websites are all-encompassing. Some websites allow photo/video sharing, others blogging, and private messaging while some others are for content sharing. Wikis, blogs, chat rooms, instant messengers, message boards and social bookmarking are web 2.0 technology applications that have been used to facilitate members' interaction and thus are referred to as social networking tools (Jones & Conceicao 2008 as cited by Chu & Du 2013). Burkhardt (2010) posits that the use of social media is all about sharing, learning, ability to have conversations and give same back.

Current trends from literature show that social media use in developed countries is in a very advanced stage; though social media use in developing countries was initially low, it began to steadily increase due to proliferation of mobile devices and internet (Poushter, Bishop & Chwe, 2018). Poushter, Bishop and Chwe (2018) reported that internet use among 19 developing countries increased to a median of 64% in 2017, compared to the 42% increase witnessed in year 2013 and 2014. The same report revealed that a median of 87% was sustained for 17 developed countries who indicated occasionally using the internet. The trend in developing countries applies also to Nigeria. In 2017, it was reported that about 75% of Nigeria's population use the social media for various purposes (Amaefule, 2017).

A major advantage of social media tools lies in their ability to reach a large number of a targeted population within a very short time. It is not surprising therefore that social media tools have become very useful in disseminating library and information services. The use of social media provides tremendous values to the library. Canty (2012) posits that social media can be powerful information dissemination tools and offer a way for libraries to promote their activities, resources, and services while allowing a two-way dialogue with stakeholders. It is also not enough to have these social media but they must be used to enable users appreciate their values. Palmer (2014) supported this assertion by saying that any value created for an organization through social media comes not from any particular platforms but from how they are used. The potential value of social media for academic libraries was recognized comparatively earlier on with the term 'Library 2.0' (referring to the application of web 2.0 online tools to library functions) being coined by Casey in 2005 (Harinarayana & Raju, 2010; Mahmood & Richardson, 2011; Palmer, 2014). Stuart (2010) notes that libraries use social media platform to make their services public. Libraries also use Web. 2.0 technologies to extend their services to students outside the traditional library buildings (Muhamad & Khalid, 2012; Andrea et al, 2010; Matthews, 2006). The traditional library as it is known, confines library users to a particular place or location, but with the introduction of Web. 2.0 technologies to library operations, it is now possible for users to enjoy library services anywhere in the world. On the international platform, libraries have adopted social media tools in marketing and disseminating information services. For example, libraries in the United States, Canada and countries in Western Europe have since adopted social media tools like Facebook, Youtube, Twitter, Flickr and others in carrying out library and information services with great success (Chu & Du, 2013).

Like every other developing country, the adoption of any ICT-based platform is not without challenges in Nigeria. Social media use by Nigerian libraries have been relatively poor, when compared with trends in developed countries. Though a large number of the Nigerian population including librarians and library users are active on social media platforms through mobile technology devices, libraries as organizations are not well equipped with necessary facilities that will facilitate effective and efficient social media use for information service delivery. However, this does not imply that these services do not exist; the crust of the matter is that social media usage in Nigerian libraries is still at infancy stage when compared with their counterparts in developed countries. A review of literature reveals that academic libraries are in the forefront of social media adoption in the country. Amuda and Adeyinka (2017)'s study revealed that social media networks are widely adopted for the delivery of library services by professional librarians in South-West Nigeria. The most popularly used social media in the region include Facebook, Blog, LinkedIn, Twitter, Myspace, Delicious and Flickr, with Facebook being the most used social media network (Olajide, Otunla & Omotayo, 2017). Respondents in this study affirmed that reference services, communication, dissemination of information and news are the major driving motivation for using social media in their respective academic libraries in South-West Nigeria. In this same region, librarians in federal universities make use of social media for the delivery of library services (Adewoyin, Onouha, & Ikonne, 2017). From the study of the latter, the popular social media network used among librarians in this part of the country include: Facebook, WhatsApp, YouTube and Instant message 39.8% most of the time. Olajide, Otunla and Omotayo (2017) also discovered from their study that libraries loved to use visual social media like YouTube, VIMEO and Pinterest, while social media specifically designed for library (e.g. Library Thing and Ning) were not being used. It was also observed from the study that most libraries maintained one social media platform. Again the investigation revealed that collaboration among libraries using social media was poor. In one study titled "Social Media for Library Outreach and Collaboration by Librarians in Private Universities Libraries in South-South Nigeria (Odiachi & Omorodion, 2018), it was revealed that South–South Nigeria Private Universities prefer to use Facebook, WhatsApp, Twitter, Blogs and LinkedIn and that their level of use is very high compared to other social media tools.

TYPES OF SOCIAL MEDIA USED IN LIBRARIES

There are various types of social media tool used in academic libraries. The different types of social media tools or platforms include but are not limited to Facebook, LinkedIn, Google+. Others include Twitter, Tumblr; the photo sharing include Instagram, Snapchat, Pinterest; the video sharing include YouTube, Facebook live, periscope, Vimeo etc. While some of these platforms are popular among Nigerian Libraries and librarians, others are not.

Colburn and Hanes (2012) and Palmer (2014) affirmed that the use of twitter and Facebook seem to be the most commonly observed social media application for libraries. Winn, Rivosecchi, Bjerke, and Groenendyk (2017) during a study on the 'big four' academic libraries in Montreal stated that during the 2015/2016 academic session, the four libraries used five different social media sites: Facebook, Instagram, Pinterest, Twitter, and YouTube.

For the purpose of expanding knowledge, it is important to discuss some social network platforms and applications relevant to libraries.

Facebook

This is a popular social media tool that can be used to reach library audience/users irrespective of where they are. According to Alexa topsites (1996), Facebook is the most visited website in the world with close to one billion users across the world. There are different types of user account under Facebook. They may seem to be serving different purposes; yet they share the same features. They include profiles, groups, and pages. Aharony (2012) as cited by Palmer (2014) posits that to use Facebook, a library would typically create a Facebook page, while Facebook users have a personal profile that allows them to describe themselves and their interests and through this locate and connect with other users and interest groups. There are diverse ways and methods of using these social media such that users are able to maximize their benefits and are also maximally served. Facebook can be used to provide reference services, share information and broadcast news concerning the library. As at today, Facebook is the number one choice social media used by libraries all over the world, including libraries in developing countries like Nigeria (Vassilakaki & Garoufallou, 2014).

To make use of Facebook, a Facebook account must be consciously created using the link Facebook.com. Palmer (2014) averred that individual users, requests to be 'friends' with other users, and if a request is accepted, this connection allows enhanced interactions between the two-users. Now, all the library need do if they know any Facebook account, is send a friend request to these accounts and wait for the requests to be accepted after which interaction has begun. The interactions also referred to as communication takes place on each user's 'wall'. On the 'walls', messages are sent or posted, and replies are made via comments. Users can also 'like' a post or show other emotional feelings by the use of 'emojis' displayed on the posts. Emojis are small digital images used to express one's emotions or feelings during an electronic communication.

Libraries can take advantage of the Facebook feature called 'newsfeed'. The newsfeed is a part of the Facebook where activities of what user's friends have sent or responded to are harvested. It is the main place where all activities on the page are recorded and this notifies a Facebook user of how his/her post is being appreciated or turned down. So libraries can from newsfeed harvest the way they are being appreciated or know what users think about what is posted about them. Once a Facebook user likes a page or a message is shared, any other message(s) the account user sends subsequently, these 'friends' will automatically be able to view the posts. So for a library, when a Facebook user searches out your social media page, likes or expresses his/herself same friend will receive all library services posts deposited on that library's Facebook wall.

Facebook is a very good platform to market whatever the library does. It helps deliver better customer service, promote your library, and drives traffic to your library website and events. One can also be assured that once the Facebook page remains active with relevant contents post from the library, the audience will grow naturally because they will always stop by to check for new, relevant and educative posts and most likely share same on their walls for their friends to read and when their friends are reached, your audience increases and a community is formed.

According to Chen et al (2012), libraries have reported that both twitter and Facebook are used because the features they provide work in related but different ways. The amazing thing about Facebook and twitter is that both platforms can be linked together in order to increase the total reach of libraries social media contents. Saylor, Schnizer, Alee, and Blumenthal (2011) asserted that it is possible to configure twitter and Facebook to automatically route updates in one system to the other, and this has been reported to be useful for libraries that use both systems concurrently.

Twitter

Twitter is a social media tool for communication. Canty (2012) refers to it as a platform possibly better than other platforms which exemplify the ability to enable a rapid two-way dialogue. He added that library use of twitter suggests it is a popular platform for reaching out to communities. There are various services the library can engage in, using twitter. Canty (2012) listed such as operational issues like Library opening and closing hours; showcasing activities of the library; advertising new additions to the library collections; responding to questions and also giving feedback. The way twitter is used actually varies across libraries. Some may choose to adopt a conversational approach while others could go for a conventional 'top down' broadcast medium.

Dickson and Holley (2010), and Kim and Abbas (2010) asserted that twitter is a particular and rapidly growing microblogging service where users can post quick and frequent short messages (up to 140 characters) called tweets. They explained that these tweets may contain links to other online material such as photos and websites, to their 'followers' who have subscribed to their twitter account. Audience can further be reached by the use of hashtags on twitter. The hashtag becomes active when a program or event publicizes a hashtag for its participants to use in order to participate in the event and to enable them collate their tweets by the use of such named hashtags. One event can have as many participants as possible if the few audience reached 'retweets' the content of the sending account. Palmer (2014) averred that except for the content of tweets from protected accounts, all tweets are effectively broadcast to 'the world' and are publicly discoverable via a search. Twitter can be used in the readers' services section to broadcast messages to users on the arrival of new books, and can be used to send notices to borrowers to return borrowed books and many more services provided by the library.

Flickr

This is a photo sharing site. Pictures of events could be shared here include community development visits and others. It is a great channel to display photographic collections (Canty, 2012). Pictures and library images are posted, and shared for the knowledge of library users.

Pinterest

This social media tool is relatively new. It was founded in 2010 (Canty, 2012). It acts like a virtual pin board. It is used in organizing, sharing, images around themes, hobbies and activities such as social events. Libraries can use Pinterest to publicize events like library week and orientation by displaying images and pictures of previous events.

YouTube

This social media tool is great for demonstrating products. It is used to post videos and sometimes static images.

Videos could be streamed and posted on the library website. The key indicator in YouTube is the number of subscribers (Canty, 2012). The number of subscribers shows how much people like the content and wish to maintain contact with the channel. The YouTube channel can be promoted in such a way that users are urged to subscribe to the channel. This is done by the use of prompts and hints. When the library does this successfully, it indicates better engagement and shows that the library has succeeded in building up following viewers and not random viewers.

Ongoing library events can be captured or recorded in camera and shared for a later view. The video could be on the tour of the library. It could augment for fresh students who usually miss the physical library orientation embarked on during school resumptions. The video will help them to get to know the library and the services made available for all library users. Canty (2012) averred that it is more difficult to post decent quality videos than static images. He added that YouTube could also contain contents like interviews, recorded presentations of full conferences. The library can as well add its university's programme like inaugural lectures, special visits, and if there are Vice Chancellors' visits to the library in various institutions depending on the extent to which such activities are allowed to be on the internet.

Blog

Before now, social media tools such as blogs and wikis were seen as ideal channels to disseminate information about a library and her services. Cooper and May (2009) as cited by Collins and Quan-Haase (2014) recorded that the implementation of a blog at a small academic library in Alabama served as an important tool in reaching out to students regardless of their involvement on campus and previous experience with the library. Blogs are considered relevant social media tool because they can be used to send latest happenings in the library. A survey was carried out by Draper and Marthea (2008) and it was discovered that 265 academic librarians used the blog tool overwhelmingly to market the library services. There are some potential library users who may not be aware of the existing resources and services in the library, these social media applications/tools are used to get them to connect and have access to what is made available.

In summary, a lot of libraries tend to adopt different web 2.0 tools but implementation of those tools in different libraries differs. Some libraries prefer to use blogs and RSS feeds as they are seen as being more popular than being interactive. Others use Facebook and twitter. A study conducted by Xu, Ouyang, and Chu, (2009) on the impact of web 2.0 in 81 University libraries in New York revealed that 34 libraries incorporated one or more web 2.0 applications for various purposes. Many of the web 2.0 tools were used as web-based extensions of traditional library services such as reference, news updates and the like. The tools enable librarians to retain custodianship of information and have authority over user account. (Kim & Abbas 2010).

CHALLENGES OF SOCIAL MEDIA USE IN NIGERIA

A developing country (also called less developed or underdeveloped country) is a sovereign state that is not yet highly industrialized compared with other countries and has a low human development index. These countries are found mainly in Africa, South America and parts of Eastern Europe and Asia. In our contemporary world, developed countries which are geographically located in Europe, North America and parts of Asia are highly industrialized and have an edge in science and technology. They also possess greater levels of wealth, with very stable governance structure. Due to their low level industry, human development and socio-economic bases, developing countries are far behind their developed counterparts in terms of ICT acquisition, accessibility and application. As earlier alluded, most developing countries like Nigeria have peculiar challenges in the execution of ICT-based projects. These challenges also affect social media use. Note that some of the challenges outlined here may also be experienced in developed countries, but the enabling environment and policies provided by the Government in these countries have helped libraries to deal with the issues easily.

The challenges of social media use include the following:

Digital Divide and Lack of Infrastructure

Digital divide maybe defined as a technological gap with regard to access to, use of and impact of information and communication technologies among a group of people either within a country or between two or more countries. The gap between countries is termed global digital divide. It is a disparity in the availability, accessibility and deployment of ICT infrastructure between the industrialized or developed and underdeveloped countries. The concept has gained importance because it carries educational and socio-economic inequality consequences. Ogunsola and Okusaga (2006) posited that the line of demarcation between the developed and developing countries is not income (criteria of wealth) but technology (criteria of skill). Digital divide is anchored on inequalities which the emergence of and access to ICTs have either inherited or widened. Indicators show that there is a significant difference between developed and developing countries in terms of availability, affordability, access and use of ICTs. In its report in 2010, the International Telecommunication Union (ITU) observed that 72% of the population in developed countries are internet users, while just 21% of the population in developing countries are internet users (ITU, 2010). Nigeria falls in the developing countries' bracket.

The digital divide is measured through the digital opportunity index (DOI). DOI is an internationally accepted ICT indicator developed to measure and capture technological divides. The digital opportunity index classifies and measures the divide in three categories – opportunity, infrastructure and utilization. Opportunity encompasses accessibility and affordability. Infrastructure include network indicators and availability of facilities. Utilization relates with ICT usage and quality. Ogege (2010) observed that developing countries like Nigeria had very low scores and performed very poorly in the global digital opportunity index indicator released by the International Telecommunication Union (ITU) in 2005. No developing country appeared in the digital opportunity index first 25 top economies. This implies that developing countries are inherently disadvantaged as far as availability and access to ICT infrastructure and electronic resources are concerned. Consequently, it is more expensive and difficult for academic institutions in developing countries to acquire, access and maintain ICT infrastructure and facilities required to manage electronic resources like e-journals.

Nigeria, like other developing countries does not have basic infrastructure needed as foundation on which to run electronic facilities. Poor electricity supply is a common occurrence in Nigeria. It is common place in the country for individuals and institutions to purchase and maintain power plants due to irregular electricity supply from the national grid. Access to adequate bandwidth to run efficient internet system is also a major challenge. Academic institutions and libraries in Nigeria have a lot of hurdles to cross in terms of infrastructure in their quest for access to electronic resources and platforms including social media networks.

Copyright Violations and Plagiarism

The concept of 'cut and paste' is an old long issue and has grown easier over time. The use of intellectual property of others without permission, copying data and circulating/reposting text, quotes, ideas, music, pictures etc. is a popular culture on social media and has become a great source of worry and concern for copyright violations and plagiarism. Ifijeh (2014) warns that this may pose a challenge to Librarians who are not well knowledgeable in the process of establishing originality of idea/content before making information accessible on social media. Rapier (2015) opines that committing copyright or trademark infringement via social media is oftentimes unintentional. Nevertheless, infringing on copyrights has consequences for the librarian, the library and even their users.

Lack of Authentication

Librarians are not just supporting researchers, they carry out researches too. The issue of gathering content for research purposes on social media is faced with a lot of hurdles. There is need for caution in social media data usage, interpretation and generalization. Bright, Margetts, Hale and Yasseri (2014) in their study about using social media and its role in social research and analysis, reported that data sources from most social media are very difficult to authenticate and interpret in isolation. They blamed the situation on the unmitigated number of social networking sites available, continuous changes in user interface; unreliable information sources. This makes it hard for the librarians or library users to utilize them for research. They further recommended the benchmarking of all social media data be against other sources.

Time Consuming

Librarians already have their hands full with their routine duties of cataloguing and classification, collection development etc.; these duties in themselves are time consuming. Collins and Quan-Haase (2012) and Cvetkovic (2009) assert that social media adoption and use by librarians will significantly consume more time and effort. Creating additional time for constantly responding to chats, postings, updates and the likes can be overwhelming for any librarian. Frustrations may set in when Library users queries are not attended to as at when due.

Inadequate Computer Skills

Users of social media are sometimes faced with technical difficulties that cannot be overlooked. Significant computer skills are required for effective use of social media. Herrick and Burriesci (2009) recognize that social media platforms like Wiki require users to know how to use computer markup languages to edit or modify their inputs. Baro, Idiodi and Godfrey (2012) and Mahmood and Richardson (2013) also observed that librarians needed requisite skills for tagging, bookmarking and incorporating social media into their Public Access Catalog. Ezeani and Igwesi (2012) revealed that lack of awareness and training among the library professionals in Nigeria has drastically contributed to the non-use of social media in the library environment. Thanuskodi (2012) submits that librarians who lack adequate social media skills are oftentimes discouraged from adopting and adapting the technologies. Many librarians, considering their training may not possess needed skill to function effectively in this area .This, as observed by Tyner (2010) has prompted academic libraries to hire persons who possess requisite skills in social data analytics and create job titles like web services Librarian or social media librarian for them.

Identity Fraud

Social media often requires a record of personal data input during profile creation/ new sign ups; as expected, this provides enough identifying information about a user to the public. This has turned social media to a one stop shop for information about subscribers. Identity thieves are known for stealing the real identity of an individual and thereafter, create synthetic identities compiled from elements of the data stolen from a user personal information that social media users have on the social networks, exposing the real owners to different levels of risk. Fear of becoming a victim can stand as an impediment to the adoption of social media by librarians. Facebook has tried to reduce this menace by introducing picture guard and picture watermark which are not foolproof but the trend has been on the increase. Mansfield-Devine (2015) apprises that social media providers are not doing enough to create awareness and protect users against identity theft.

Social Media Distractions

The original intent of joining a network may be for information dissemination, user enquiry, academic purposes etc. but often times there are distractions. Herrick and Burriesci (2009) explains that law librarians and law students are often times faced with distractions. They blame the situation on availability of personal data, games, advertisements, captive debates, interesting updates and pictures which can serve as distractions to the users.

Reduced Productivity

Bryson and Forth (2007) define productivity as the output a worker, firm or country generates per unit of labor and capital inputs. Productivity can be measured based on hours spent on a given task. Leftheriotis and Giannakos (2014) posit that internet connectivity and access is commonplace in today's workplace, whether provided by the organization or the individual. According to them, this is responsible for reduced productivity of employees. They argue that social media is rich in time occupying activities and apps e.g. status updates, gaming, betting, chatting etc., persons may spend time on these things instead of performing tasks that are work-related. In order to curb the huge loss of official resources and maintain productivity level, Aguenza, Al-Kassem, and Som, (2012) reported that many organizations and more than half of U.S. employers reportedly block access to social media at work.

Privacy and Confidentiality Issues

Fernandez (2009) maintain that confidentiality is one of the foundations on which librarianship is built and that libraries are trusted for placing value on privacy. The library is supposed to protect confidentiality of users. The history of internet usage or social networks visited by any user should remain confidential and not revealed for any reason. This privacy right is entrenched in ALA intellectual freedom manual, which describes an information seeker's privacy right as "the right to open inquiry without having the subject of one's interest examined or scrutinized by others" (ALA Office for Intellectual Freedom. American Library Association, 2013). McHone-Chase (2009) observes that the challenge is that libraries do not have a social media policy in their libraries. They do not know what confidentiality policies covers and what it does not cover.

Inadequate Understanding of Data Protection Rights

Signing up to a social network of choice is quite easy but it has been revealed that many SM users do not bother to read the policy details, some have a poor understanding of data protection rights guiding the social networks of their choice. Senthil, Saravanakumar, and Deepa (2016) blames this on a dearth of technical makeovers. The assertion that many social media users are not aware of what violates their rights and those of others is a major concern as expressed by Romansky (2014) who strongly believes that data protection rights is an object of serious discussion. Kosta, Kalloniatis, Mitrou and Gritzalis (2010) decry the incautious attitude with which users reveal personal information on social network sites; they blame this on the lack of awareness and understanding of the potential threats and dangers lurking that may arise as a result of this. Bonneau and Preibusch (2010) outlined the lack of awareness on vague terms of agreement, the unnecessary use of legal jargon, the length and content of formal privacy policies as reasons for inadequate understanding of data protection rights among social media users.

Social Media Addiction

According to Ashwini and Samuel (2012), the need to be connected with friends, family, collaborators, co-workers, and classmates has inadvertently led to increased and extensive use of social media. This has also led to Social media addiction which is a growing social problem. Erfanmanesh and Hossseini (2015) compared social media addiction to addictions to substance like alcohol and drugs.

Emotional and Ergonomic Issues

Hansraj (2014) revealed that Surgeons have discovered that people spend 700 to 1400 hours a year looking down as a result of their mobile phones. Slouching has been revealed by the surgeons to affect the body posture, especially the hands, eyes back and other parts of the body. The Surgeons linked poor body posture to chronic pain, cervical scoliosis, breakdown of cervical tissues, headaches and other neurological problems, depression, constipation, and heart disease

Social Media-Induced Techno Stress

Brooks and Califf (2017) postulate that interacting and alternating between multiple social media platforms and technologies while also trying to complete work related tasks simultaneously for a long period of time usually leads to stress.

Information Overload

Bawden, Holtham and Courtney (1999) describes information overload as occurring when information received becomes a hindrance rather than a help. Social media is plagued by rapidly-expanding number of information feeds. Social media users are inundated by sometimes irrelevant innumerous information, sometimes the same information sent over and over again. When the person is overloaded with information, consequently, this affects the time to effectively process the information, the ability to take decisions, and even the final quality of the decision. (Benselin & Ragsdell, 2016).

Cyberbully

Behind a keyboard or phone, young people and adults are emboldened to bully others. Posting hurtful negative remarks or rumors on social media sites for the world to see. Unlike traditional websites, social media comments cannot really be deleted since third party and others who have access may save and continually have the information. These harmful or hurtful information when released has the potential to affect the health, mental, psychological and social well-being of an individual. Many have committed suicide as a result of this (Garett, Lord, and Young, 2016).

Lack of Awareness and Perceived Usefulness

Baro, Idiodi and Godfrey (2012) also noted that many librarians in developing countries like Nigeria are not aware of social media networks. They opine that so many of them do not know how to use web 2.0s to affect their services. Similarly, De Rosa, Cantrell, Havens, Hawk, Jenkin, Gauder, and Cellentani (2007) discovered that many librarians were avers to social media. They saw it as a distraction.

In the same vien, Charnigo and Barnett-Ellis (2007) reported in their survey of academic librarians attitudes about Facebook, that the majority of librarians studied considered Facebook outside the scope of professional librarianship.

Lack of Cyber Knowledge

According to Christie (2017) cyber security is an intimidating subject for most librarians. And that libraries have had their systems breached and infected with malware through social media. Profile hacking and malwares (viruses, Trojans and worms) are some of the most common challenges posed by cyber attackers on social media. Khan and Bhatti (2012) posit that librarians in developing countries lack adequate cyber knowledge and advice that librarians cannot identify their vulnerability and take steps to clamp down on cyber attackers without adequate cyber knowledge.

Poor Academic Performance

While some researchers (Ahmed & Qazi, 2011; Akanbi & Akanbi, 2014) argue that social media usage has no significant impact on academic performance of students in developing countries like Nigeria, other studies (Paul et al., 2012; Burak, 2012; Rouis et al., 2011; Bányai et al., 2017) revealed a drastic drop of grades/poor academic performance among students as a result of heavy social media usage.

Cost Implications

There are cost implications for purchasing and maintaining needed infrastructure in terms of bandwidth requirements of social media, computers and mobile devices, training staff to be active, steady power supply. Many academic libraries are grappling with budget cuts and may see this as unnecessary expenses.

SOLUTIONS AND RECOMMENDATIONS

Bridging the Digital Divide and Provision of Infrastructure

Bridging the digital divide in any nation requires the commitment of the government at the national, state and local or district level. The government must take ICT acquisition as a top priority. This would require allocation of a substantial amount of the nation's budget on the acquisition of ICT infrastructure and facilities and training. There should be an appropriate fiscal policy and discipline on ICT development on a short and long term basis. The initial step would be to import required facilities. However, on the long run, persons would need to be trained abroad who would return back home as indigenous ICT specialists. The indigenous ICT specialists would help to assemble facilities locally, thus reducing the cost of acquisition. Alternatively, foreign ICT specialists may be invited to help train selected individuals locally. Either way, the objective is to make ICT facilities readily available, accessible and very importantly cheaper to acquire.

One big challenge of developing nations is political instability. There is incessant change of government. Unfortunately, each government comes with its own agenda; thus projects started by a particular government are abandoned by subsequent ones. Therefore, to forestall any hitch on the long term plan for ICT acquisition and training, there is need to formulate and legislate a national ICT policy document. Legislating the ICT policy document would compel any government to implement its stipulated contents at any point in time.

Fortunately, the governments of many developing countries are becoming much more interested in ICT acquisition. A few like India and Malaysia are progressing very fast towards attaining self-dependence status.

Provision of Funds and Eradication of Corruption

As earlier noted, cost implication is a major challenge to social media use in developing countries. The situation has become worse in the face of current global economic recession. Libraries and their parent organizations should begin to look for alternative means of generating funds rather than depending on government subventions and allocations. They should seek funds from corporate bodies, multinationals, philanthropic individuals and donor agencies. In this regard, the Carnegie Corporation and MacArthur Foundation in the United States have contributed immensely to the development of higher institutions and libraries in developing countries in terms of ICT deployment. Institutions and libraries should take advantage of the opportunities provided by these bodies to subscribe to electronic journals, as well as acquire necessary facilities to use them.

Institutions and libraries can also take advantage of consortia platforms to reduce cost of acquiring ICT facilities. Consortium provides opportunities to negotiate for cheaper prices on the basis of number. However, efforts must be made to ensure that such consortia are sustainable on the long run. Furthermore, the alumni base of institutions can also be exploited for better funding. This would require the institutions making appeals to their graduates or alumni to make donations towards projects in their alma mater.

No matter the funds provided, if corruption is not eradicated, no laudable objective can be achieved. Governments at all levels in developing countries should take up the responsibility of fighting and eradicating corruption. Like the example of Nigeria, special anti-corruption agencies should be set up to apprehend and prosecute corrupt officials in both public and private sectors. Severe penalties should be meted on convicts to serve as a deterrent to others.

Awareness Creation and Promotion of Information Literacy Programs

Libraries and librarians should offer effective current awareness service to users, by informing users of innovative services and resources available on the library's social media platforms. Kiscaden (2014) discovered that many library users are not aware of tools available to create their own service. According to him, lack of awareness presents a barrier to adoption of ICT-based services. The onus is still on librarians to make individual users responsible for subscribing to various social media platforms.

For effective current awareness services, the Liaison librarians should be responsible for the development and delivery of professional/ specialized information services to support for faculty staff and students. To be effective, they can do the following:

- **Join Research Cluster:** The library needs to maintain close collaboration with faculty, and students' research cluster to identify areas of need that could be addressed by the librarian. In agreement, Federer (2013) opine that librarians possess the required expertise that researchers can harness to help them create better research output especially: performing database searches, locating materials relevant to their research, providing links to critical information in e-journals and citation assistance.
- **User Education/ Awareness:** Foote and Rupp-Serrano 2010 touting the need for awareness, believe that discoverability is paramount for the usage of e-resources. The library is expected to provide adequate platforms for user education/ awareness campaigns. There are different methods of educating users about new developments and services. Through seminars, workshops, YOU-Tube videos, formal and informal training and retraining for the faculty and students on how to carry out better and efficient online searches. Users need to know what the library has as per content, browser requirements, issues concerning location/ access points. Some libraries create information slides, some send links of their social media platforms to the network of faculty and staff. Creating this awareness will result in increased usage and downloads.

Training Programs for Librarians

Sequel to the challenges earlier discussed, there is need for ICT and social media training programs for librarians. Workshops and seminars on ICT skills acquisition would enhance librarians' use of ICT facilities in general and social media in particular. Training programs would also help address critical social media issues like copyrights, privacy and data protection rights, authentication, identity theft, time management and others. These trainings could be organized and facilitated by libraries, Library Associations, Government and non-Governmental agencies.

FUTURE RESEARCH DIRECTIONS

Global trends indicate that social media platforms are effective tools and channels through which libraries can reach their users. Researches carried out in developing countries like Nigeria show that the adoption of ICT related services including social media have been slow due to ICT challenges peculiar to these nations. These peculiar challenges in developing countries have been perennial; there is a need to properly investigate the remote causes of these challenges, with a view to proffering lasting solutions. Therefore, future research directions should focus on dealing with state of social media usage among librarians and library users, formulation of correct hypotheses to test various variables responsible for usage or non-usage of social media platforms as well as uncover remote challenges and proffer lasting solutions.

CONCLUSION

This chapter has dealt with the emergence and concept of social media and their usage among faculties in Nigeria. The chapter outlined the important roles social media use could play in academic libraries. Challenges militating against social media usage in Nigeria (which are generally peculiar to developing countries) were examined and solutions were proffered.

From the aforementioned discussions in the chapter, it is clear that social media usage have come to stay in academic libraries. Authorities of institutions, libraries and other relevant agencies in Nigeria must of necessity make provisions for the full adoption of social media in order to align with global trends. Libraries and librarians should realize that the world has gone digital; they either adapt to the changing academic environment or they will be sidelined and become irrelevant in the scheme of things. They should take personal responsibility for digital and information literacy and be empowered to take full advantage of the opportunities provided by social media tools.

REFERENCES

Adewoyin, O.O., Onuoha, U.D., & Ikonne, C.N. (2017). *Social Media Use and Service Delivery by Librarians in Federal Universities in South-West, Nigeria.* Retrieved from https://digitalcommons.unl.edu/libphilprac/1641/

Aguenza, B. B., Al-Kassem, A. H., & Som, A. P. (2012). Social Media and Productivity in the Workplace: Challenges and Constraints. *Interdisciplinary Journal of Research in Business, 2*(2), 22–26.

Ahmed, T., & Qazi, F. (2011). A look out for academic impacts of social networking sites: A student based perspective. *African Journal of Business Management, 5*(12), 1–6.

Akanbi, M., & Akanbi, A. (2014). Influence of social media usage on self-image and academic performance among senior secondary school students in Ilorin west Local Government, Kwara State *Int. Res. J. Pure Appl. Phys., 24*, 42–50.

ALA office for Intellectual Freedom. (2010). *Intellectual Freedom Manual* (8th ed.). Chicago: ALA Editions.

Amaefule, E. (2017). *75% of Nigeria's Online Population Use Social Media.* Retrieved from https://punchng.com/75-of-nigerias-online-population-use-social-media-minister/

American Library Association. (2013). *Questions and answers on ethics and social media.* Retrieved from: http://www.ala.org/tools/ethics

Amudaa & Adeyinka. (n.d.). Application of Social Media for Innovative Library Services in South-Western Nigerian University Libraries. *Journal of Balkan Libraries Union.* Retrieved from http://dergipark.gov.tr/download/article-file/399735

Ashwini Veronica, S., & Samuel, A. U. (2012, December). Social Media Addiction among Adolescents with Special Reference to Facebook Addiction. *IOSR Journal of Humanities and Social Science.* Retrieved from www.iosrjournals.org

Bányai, F., Zsila, Á., Király, O., Maraz, A., Elekes, Z., Griffiths, M. D., ... Demetrovics, Z. (2017). Problematic social media use: Results from a large-scale nationally representative adolescent sample. *PLoS One, 12*(1), e0169839. doi:10.1371/journal.pone.0169839 PMID:28068404

Baro, E., Idiodi, E., & Godfrey, V. (2012). Awareness and use of Web 2.0 tools by librarians in university libraries in Nigeria. *OCLC Systems & Services, 29*(3), 170–188. doi:10.1108/OCLC-12-2012-0042

Bawden, D., Holtham, C., & Courtney, N. (1999). *Perspectives on information overload.* Aslib. doi:10.1108/EUM0000000006984

Bedell, J. (2010, September 20). *What is the Difference Between Social Media and Social Networking?* Retrieved December 2, 2010, from http://jasontbedell.com/what-is-the-difference-between-social-media-and-social-networking

Benselin, J. C., & Ragsdell, G. (2016). Information overload: The differences that age makes. *Journal of Librarianship and Information Science, 48*(3), 284–297. doi:10.1177/0961000614566341

Bentenbi. (2010). Towards a Visibility of Algerian Libraries in a Social Media Era. *Cybrarian Journal,* (12), 28. Retrieved from http://www.journal.cybrarians.org/index.php?option=com_content&view=article&id=622:socialmedia&catid=255:09-studies&Itemid=89

Bonneau, J., & Preibusch, S. (2010). The Privacy Jungle:On the Market for Data Protection in Social Networks. In T. Moore, D. Pym, & C. Ioannidis (Eds.), *Economics of Information Security and Privacy.* Boston, MA: Springer. doi:10.1007/978-1-4419-6967-5_8

Borders, B. (2010). *A Brief History of Social Media.* Retrieved from http://socialmediarockstar.com/history-of-social-media

Breeding, M. (2007). Librarians face online social networks. *Computers in Libraries, 27*(8), 30–33. Retrieved from https://librarytechnology.org/repository/item.pl?id=12735

Bright, J., Margetts, H., Hale, S., & Yasseri, T. (2014). *The use of social media for research and analysis: A feasibility study.* Retrieved from https://www.gov.uk/government/publications/use-of-social-media-for-research-and-analysis

Brooks, S., & Califf, C. (2017). Social media-induced techno stress: Its impact on the job performance of it professionals and the moderating role of job characteristics. *Computer Networks, 114,* 143–153. doi:10.1016/j.comnet.2016.08.020

Bryson, A., & Forth, J. (2007). *Productivity and days of the week.* Royal Society for the Encouragement of Arts, Manufactures & Commerce. Retrieved from https://eprints.lse.ac.uk/4963/1/daysoftheweek%28LSEROversion%29.pdf

Burak, L. (2012). Multitasking in the University classroom. *International Journal for the Scholarship of Teaching and Learning, 6*(2), 1–12. doi:10.20429/ijsotl.2012.060208

Buruga, B. A. (2016). *The Use of Mobile Technologies for Social Media-Based Service Delivery at Muni University Library, Uganda.* Retrieved from https://repository.up.ac.za/bitstream/handle/2263/58991/Buruga_Use_2016.pdf?sequence=4

Canty, N. (2012). Social Media in Libraries: It's like, Complicated. *The Journal of Library and International Library and Information Issues*, *23*(2).

Charnigo, L., & Barnett-Ellis, P. (2007). Checking out Facebook.com: The impact of a digital trend on academic libraries. *Information Technology and Libraries*, *26*(1), 23–34. doi:10.6017/ital.v26i1.3286

Christie, P. (2017). Cyber-security - what your library needs to know. *Vable*. Retrieved from https://www.vable.com/blog/cyber-security-what-your-library-needs-to-know

Chu, S., & Du, H. (2013). Social Networking Tools for Academic Libraries. *Journal of Librarianship and Information Science*, *45*(1), 64–75. doi:10.1177/0961000611434361

Cohen, L. S. (2009, April 30). *Is There A Difference Between Social Media And Social Networking?* Retrieved from http://lonscohen.com/blog/2009/04/difference-between-social-media-and-social-networking/

Cvetkovic, M. (2009). Making Web 2.0 work – from 'Librarian Habilis' to 'Librarian Sapiens'. *Computers in Libraries*, *29*(9), 14–17.

Dawson, M., Wright, J., & Omar, M. (2015). Mobile Devices: The Case for Cyber Security. *New Threats and Countermeasures in Digital Crime and Cyber Terrorism*, 8.

De Rosa, C., Cantrell, J., Havens, A., Hawk, J., Jenkins, L., Gauder, B., & Cellentani, D. (2007). Sharing, privacy and trust in our networked world: A report to the OCLC Membership. Dublin, OH: OCLC Online Computer Library Center. *Electronic Journal of Research in Educational Psychology*, *9*(3), 961–994.

Edosomwan, S., Prakasan, S. K., Kouame, D., Watson, J., & Seymour, T. (2011). The History of Social Media and its Impact on Business. *The Journal of Applied Management and Entrepreneurship*, *16*(3), 79–91.

Erfanmanesh, M., & Hossseini, E. (2015). Internet and Social Media Addiction. *Webology, 12*(2), 1–3. Retrieved from https://search.proquest.com/docview/1787761590?accountid=14548%0Ahttps://julac.hosted.exlibrisgroup.com/openurl/HKU_ALMA/SERVICES_PAGE??url_ver=Z39.88-2004&rft_val_fmt=info:ofi/fmt:kev:mtx:journal&genre=unknown&sid=ProQ:ProQ%3Alisa&atitle=Internet+and+Socia

Ezeani, C. N., & Igwesi, U. (2012). Using social media for dynamic library services delivery: the Nigerian experience. *Library Philosophy and Practice*. Retrieved from http://digitalcommons.unl.edu/libphilprac/814

Fernandez, P. (2009). Online Social Networking Sites and Privacy: Revisiting Ethical Considerations for a New Generation of Technology. *Library Philosophy and Practice*, *2009*, 1–9.

Hartshorn, S. (2010). *5 Differences between Social Media and Social Networking*. Retrieved December 1, 2010, from socialmediatoday: http://www.socialmediatoday.com/SMC/194754

Ifijeh, G. (2014). Adoption of digital preservation methods for theses in Nigerian academic libraries: Applications and implications. *The J. of Acad. Lib*, *40*, 399–404.

Information Professionals' Knowledge Sharing Practices in Social Media. A Study of Professionals in Developing Countries. *International Journal of Knowledge Content Development & Technology*, 6(2), 43-66. Retrieved from http://ijkcdt.net/xml/08903/08903.pdf

Islam & Tsuji. (2016). Information Professionals' Knowledge Sharing Practices in Social Media: A Study of Professionals in Developing Countries. *International Journal of Knowledge Content Development & Technology*, 2(6), 43–66. Retrieved from http://ijkcdt.net/_common/do.php?a=full&b=12&bidx=669&aidx=8903

Kaplan, A. M., & Haenlein, M. (2010). Users of the World, Unite! The Challenges and Opportunities of Social Media. *Business Horizons*, 53(1), 59–68. doi:10.1016/j.bushor.2009.09.003

Khan, S. A., & Bhatti, R. (2012). *A review of problems and challenges of library professionals in developing countries including Pakistan.* Retrieved from http://digitalcommons.unl.edu/libphilprac/757/ •

Kiscaden, E. (2014). *Creating a Current Awareness Service Using Yahoo! Pipes and LibGuides Information Technology and Libraries.* Retrieved from https://ejournals.bc.edu/ojs/index.php/ital/article/download/5273/pdf

Kosta, E., Kalloniatis, C., Mitrou, L., & Gritzalis, S. (2010). Data protection issues pertaining to social networking under EU law. *Transforming Government: People, Process and Policy*, 4(2), 193–201. doi:10.1108/17506161011047406

Leftheriotis, I., & Giannakos, M. N. (2014). Using social media for work: Losing your time or improving your work? *Computers in Human Behavior*, 31(1), 134–142. doi:10.1016/j.chb.2013.10.016

Mabweazara, R. M. (2014). *Use of social media tools by library staff at the University of the Western Cape, South Africa and the National University of Science and Technology, Zimbabwe.* Retrieved from http://etd.uwc.ac.za/xmlui/handle/11394/4120

Mahmood, K., & Richardson, J. V. Jr. (2013). Impact of Web 2.0 technologies on academic libraries: A survey of ARL libraries. *The Electronic Library*, 31(4), 508–520. doi:10.1108/EL-04-2011-0068

Maisiri, E., Mupaikwa, E., & Ngwenya, S. (2015). *Strategic Planning for Social Media in Libraries: The Case of Zimbabwe.* Information Science Reference, IGI Global. Retrieved from http://ir.nust.ac.zw/xmlui/bitstream/handle/123456789/515/Strategic%20Planning%20for%20social%20media%20in%20libraries.pdf?sequence=1&isAllowed=y

Mansfield-Devine, S. (2015). Computer Fraud & Security: Editorial. *Computer Fraud and Security, 2015*(6). doi:10.1016/S1361-3723(15)30052-X

McHone-Chase, S. (2009). Privacy and Confidentiality Issues: A Guide for Libraries and their Lawyers. *Reference and User Services Quarterly*, 49(1), 104–105. doi:10.5860/rusq.49n1.104

Mpoelong, D., Totolo, A., & Jibril, L. (2015). *Perception of University of Botswana Librarians on the potential of Web 2.0 Tools (IFLA, WLIC, 2015).* Retrieved from https://www.ifla.org/files/assets/reference-and...services/.../210-mpoeleng-en.doc1.pdf

Mwangi, M. W., & Wagoki, J. (2016). Effect of Social Media on Performance of Advertisement Business in the Mainstream Media in Kenya: A Survey of Leading Media Groups in Kenya. *International Journal of Economics, Commerce and Management United Kingdom, 4*(4), 159. Retrieved from: http://ijecm.co.uk/

Njoroge, G. G., & Kange'the, P. (2013). *University Libraries and Social Media: The Case of the Postmodern Library, Kenyatta University*. Retrieved from http://0277.ch/ojs/index.php/cdrs_0277/article/view/14/53

Odiachi, R. A., & Omorodion, O. (2018). *Use of Social Media for Library Outreach and Collaboration by Librarians in Private Universities Libraries in South-South Nigeria*. Retrieved from https://www.researchgate.net/publication/323782017

Olajide, Otunla, & Omotayo. (2017). How Libraries are Using Social Media: Nigeria Perspective. *International Journal of Digital Library Services, 7*(3). Retrieved from http://www.ijodls.in/uploads/3/6/0/3/3603729/8ijodls3717.pdf

Omorodion, O. (2018). *Librarians' Awareness of Social Media Usage for Informal Scientific Communication in University Libraries in South-south, Nigeria*. Retrieved from https://digitalcommons.unl.edu/cgi/viewcontent.cgi?article=4847&context=libphilprac

Paul, J., Baker, H., & Cochran, J. (2012). Effect of online social networking on student academic performance. *Computers in Human Behavior, 51*(8), 249–255.

Poushter, J., Bishop, C., & Chwe, H. (2017). *Social Media Use Continues to Rise in Developing Countries but Plateaus Across Developed Ones: Digital Divide Remain both within and across Countries*. Retrieved from: http://assets.pewresearch.org/wp-content/uploads/sites/2/2018/06/15135408/Pew-Research-Center_Global-Tech-Social-Media-Use_2018.06.19.pdf

Rapier, R. (2015, June 22). *Fair Use or Misuse? Social Media and Copyright Law*. Retrieved from https://www.ncu.edu/blog/fair-use-or-misuse-social-media-and-copyright-law

Rimskii, V. (2011). The influence of the Internet on active social involvement and the formation and development of identities. *Russian Social Science Review, 52*(1), 79–101. doi:10.1080/10611428.2011.11065416

Ritholz, B. (n.d.). *History of social media*. Retrieved December 05, 2010, Retrieve from http://www.ritholtz.com/blog/2010/12/history-of-social-media/

Romansky, R. (2014). Problems of Privacy and Data Protection in Online Learning Based on the Network Space. In *International Conference on e-Learning'14* (pp. 187–193). Retrieved from http://elearning-conf.eu/docs/cp14/paper-28.pdf

Rouis, S., Limayem, M., & Salehi-Sangari, E. (2011). *Impact of facebook usage on students' academic achievement: Role of self-regulation and trust*. Retrieved from https://eric.ed.gov/?id=EJ960123

Sajithra, K., & Rajindra, P. (2013). Social Media- History and Components. *IOSR Journal of Business Management, 7*(1), 69–74. doi:10.9790/487X-0716974

Scott, P. R., & Jacka, J. (2011). *Auditing Social Media: A Governance and Risk Guide.* Hoboken, NJ: Wiley.

Thanuskodi, S. (2012). Awareness of library 2.0 applications among library and information science professionals at Annamalai University, India. *International Journal of Library Science*, *1*(5), 75–83. doi:10.5923/j.library.20120105.02

Tyner, R. (2010, August 3). Re: Is There a Social Media Librarian In Your Library's Future? [Blog comment]. Retrieved from http://acrlog.org/2010/08/03/is-there-a-social-media-librarian-in-your-l...

Vatter, Z. (2016). *Sing Social Media for Libraries.* Retrieved from http://www.peacelibrarysystem.ab.ca/sites/default/files/images/peacelibrarys ystem/Social%20Media%20for%20Libraries%20-%20Introduction.pdf

Zainuddin. (n.d.). Social Media Promotional Tools: Academic Library. *Journal of Computer Theory and Engineering*, *8*(3), 40 – 46.

Chapter 76
Raising Awareness About Public Archives in East and Southern Africa Through Social Media

Nampombe Saurombe
University of South Africa, South Africa

ABSTRACT

Archives serve as society's collective memory because they provide evidence of the past as well as promoting accountability and transparency of past actions. Appreciation of the archives should therefore result in citizens linking these records with their identity, history, civic duty and cultural heritage. However, research in east and southern Africa seems to indicate that very few citizens are aware of and use the archives. Social media platforms have been utilized to raise awareness about the archival institutions elsewhere. This study sought to find out whether the National Archives in east and southern Africa used social media to raise awareness about archives. The study involved 12 national archives affiliated to the East and Southern Regional Branch of the International Council on Archives (ESARBICA) using a multi-method research strategy. The findings indicated that social media platforms were not a preferred option in outreach strategies, even though they were recognized as useful means to reach online information seekers.

INTRODUCTION

The public archival institutions of east and southern Africa keep precious records and archives that are of immense value to their societies (Ngulube, 2004). Bountouri (2017, p. 51) explains that "archives are and should always be an active part of our culture and society. They document the history of mankind, the financial and legal activities and cultural developments. They have to be open to our society". Despite this fact, the public archival institutions are some of the least known and used cultural institutions in east and southern Africa. (Saurombe & Ngulube, 2018). This calls for more efforts towards raising awareness about the valuable holdings that these institutions keep (Kamatula, Mnkeni-Saurombe & Mosweu, 2013; Venson, Ngoepe & Ngulube, 2014; Ngulube, 2018; Saurombe, 2016; Mnjama, 2018).

DOI: 10.4018/978-1-6684-7123-4.ch076

According to Bountouri (2017), public archival institutions in east and southern Africa should strive to be known and used by the communities they serve. These institutions can start public programming initiatives to make their activities known to the communities. Public programming initiatives refer to activities conducted by archival institutions with the aim of raising awareness about the archives in society (McCausland, 2017; Mnjama, 2018). The literature indicates that a number of public archives from east and southern Africa do conduct public programming initiatives. However, the number of users of these archiving services continues to decrease (Venson, Ngoepe & Ngulube, 2014; Sulej, 2014; Saurombe, 2016; Mnjama, 2018). Garaba (2015) argues that there is a need for change, and this means keeping up with trends to ensure that archival institutions can address the information needs of the communities they serve.

Keeping up with trends in the current information society includes using new technologies (Ngulube, 2004). The use of social media in society, especially by organisations, is becoming a common trend (Hood & Reid, 2018). Lately, more cultural organisations including archives use social media to do outreach and encourage more participation from the public (Theimer, 2011; Bountouri & Giannakopolous, 2014; Liew et al., 2015). Garaba (2015) is of the opinion that social media can enhance public programming initiatives and have a greater impact than traditional outreach methods such as tours in the archives or exhibitions. Bountouri and Giannakopolous (2014, p. 215) in line with Garaba's (2015) argument state that archival services can benefit from using social media because it enables direct contact with archival users. In addition, social media provides archival institutions with the opportunity to improve their services and public image as well as facilitating greater visibility of the archival institution.

A number of archival institutions have successfully used different social media platforms to market their institutions. Hager (2015) and Williamson, Vieira and Williamson (2015) speak of social media platforms such as, Facebook, Twitter, Pinterest, Flickr, HistoryPin and Instagram among others which have been used to engage with their communities on cultural and historical content-related issues and maintain contact with their patrons.

Most accounts on using social media to promote cultural and heritage institutions such as archival repositories, museums and libraries originate from the western hemisphere. In this regard, research from Africa, especially east and southern Africa is scarce, yet social media usage is a worldwide trend. In light of this observation, the interest of this particular chapter lies in the use of social media in public programming initiatives by the National Archives of east and southern Africa.

Overview of the National Archives Affiliated to ESARBICA

The National Archives in east and southern Africa is affiliated to the East and Southern Africa Branch of the International Council on Archives (ESARBICA). The member states of this organisation are Kenya, South Africa, Mozambique, Angola, Malawi, Namibia, Swaziland, Botswana, Zambia, Zimbabwe, Lesotho and Tanzania (ESARBICA, 2014). These archival institutions offer a range of services that are related to these countries' culture, identity and documentary heritage.

These institutions keep and preserve documents of enduring value that are of significance to personal, social, civic, governmental and business-related matters; though they are not commonly known as information providers in many communities (Kamatula, 2011; Ngoepe & Ngulube, 2011; Saurombe, 2016). This was also demonstrated in the choice of the main theme of 23rd ESARBICA Biennial Conference held in Victoria Falls, Zimbabwe in 2015. The conference theme was *Archives uses, abuses and under-utilisation* (ESARBICA, 2015). This proves the need for public archival institutions in this region to seek ways to actively raise awareness about these institutions in east and Southern Africa. Public programming initiatives could significantly contribute towards this goal. Public programming initiatives are often described as actions or activities implemented by archival institutions with the aim of raising awareness about the archives and facilitating access to the archival holdings (McCausland, 2017; Mnjama, 2018). These activities can range from lectures, exhibitions, tours, education programmes, seminars and other activities. These programmes are often planned and designed to address the different needs of the various users of the archives (Saurombe, 2016). As more citizens in east and southern Africa seek information online due to the connectivity made largely possible by mobile networks and mobile devices (Lanerolle, 2013), this study investigated whether National Archives of the ESARBICA region used social media platforms as part of their public programming strategies.

Mabweazara and Zinn (2016, p. 1) describe social media as "powerful technological tools for communication, loosely summed up as technology used for interacting, creating and sharing information all built on the ideological foundations of Web 2.0". Social media is one of the key developments brought about by using the internet. As from 31 December 2017, there were approximately 453,329,534 internet users and 1,942,054, 452 Facebook subscribers in Africa and the number is increasing (Internet World Stats, 2017). Though there are still challenges such as the digital divide in sub-Saharan Africa, it is apparent that more people have access to social media through mobile networks. Lanerolle (2013) reports that the number of people who own mobile phones in Africa surpasses the number of individuals who own computers. Furthermore, these phones are internet capable, which makes it easier to access social media platforms. According to Mutula (2013, p. 3), "…social media is influencing the information landscape significantly with people of all persuasions irrespective of education, social status, age, profession, sex, religion, political orientation adopting and using it in both developed and developing countries…" Social media platforms have made it possible for people to interact, create and share information (Mabweazara & Zinn, 2016, p. 1). Graham (2016, p. 24) asserts that 'sharing' is central to social media, instead of watching, listening or reading, people are encouraged to share ideas, images, information and entertainment with self-selected networks of friends, contacts and personal audiences. There are many forms of social media. These include:

- **Blogs and Micro Blogs:** Wikipedia and Twitter
- **Content Communities:** YouTube, Flickr, Instagram and Pinterest
- **Collaborative Projects:** Wikis
- **Social Networking Sites:** Facebook
- Virtual game worlds

Bountouri (2017, p. 53) states that the common features of social media are:

- They are all interactive Web 2.0 internet-based applications.
- They consist of user-generated content such as posts, comments, photos or videos.
- Users can create service specific profiles for the website or application that are designed and maintained by the social media organisation.
- Social media facilitates the development of online social networks by connecting a user's network with those of other individuals or groups.

Some of the commonly known social media platforms in the ESARBICA region include Facebook, Twitter, Instagram and WhatsApp (Anduvare, 2013; World Wide Worx, 2017). As more archival institutions in the ESARBICA region seek to become well-known among their patrons and potential patrons, perhaps using social media platforms could contribute positively towards this goal.

Promoting Archival Repositories: Can Social Media Platforms Make a Difference in the ESARBICA Region?

National Archives are not commonly known among the citizens in east and southern Africa. The National Archives of the ESARBICA region are encouraged to develop and implement more public programming initiatives in order for their institutions to become more visible and appreciated by their communities (Kamatula, 2011; Venson, Ngoepe & Ngulube, 2014; Garaba, 2015, Saurombe, 2016; Saurombe & Ngulube, 2018). In 2012, the International Council of Archives compiled a document of the 'Principles of Access' (ICA, 2012) The principles state that archival institutions are encouraged to proactively raise awareness about their existence and activities. The use of social media to promote public archival holdings could be considered as a proactive action in this regard. Not much is known regarding the use of social media in raising awareness about National Archives in the ESARBICA region. As more citizens in east and southern Africa get connected to the internet via mobile networks and other means (Mutula, 2013), this study investigated whether the National Archives of the ESARBICA region incorporated social media platforms in their public programming initiatives.

The objective of the study was to explore whether the National Archives of the ESARBICA region used social media to raise awareness about the National Archives. In order to address this objective, the following research questions were developed:

1. Are archivists in the ESARBICA region familiar with social media?
2. Which social media tools are used in the National Archives of the ESARBICA region?
3. For what purposes are these social media tools used for?
4. Are the social media used for outreach programmes?
5. What are the advantages and disadvantages of using social media to market archives in the ESARBICA region?
6. In cases where no social media were used, why not?

SOCIAL MEDIA STRATEGIES: CONNECTING PEOPLE WITH PUBLIC ARCHIVAL REPOSITORIES

Information communication technologies (ICTs) have impacted the different functions of archival management (Roberts, 2008). Roberts (2008, p. 329) explains that digital technology has enabled archival institutions to prepare documentation and find aids, offer reference services, develop collection management systems, distribute and publish information and digitise records. He explains that the digitisation of records made it possible to "preserve the original record, make records more accessible and it serves as a means of security in the event of loss".

Similar to Roberts (2008), Garaba (2010) explains that the proliferation of ICTs hugely impacted how people access information. Garaba (2010) argues that though ICTs have made information more accessible, one still needs to focus on other challenges such as the digital divide that still hampers this development, particularly in Africa.

Jimerson (2011) comments on the impact ICTs had on archival practices, particularly that they eased seeking and retrieval processes. Jimerson (2011) explains that archival institutions of the 21st century compete with other information services such as cultural organisations, libraries and museums. In his article, it is pointed out that these other information services strive to adapt their services with rapid changes such as technological advancements to meet their customers' needs. As a result, there was an increased use of their services as compared to archival institutions. He therefore questions whether archives are moving fast enough. Could these approaches be used to improve public programming activities? To answer this, he advises archives to "enter into the information mainstream, to mould it to our needs, and to be a part of the contemporary process instead of just a passive custodian of the past". More cultural heritage organisations use social media to disseminate information. However, Bountouri and Giannakopolous (2014) and Garaba (2015) report that archival institutions have been slow compared to libraries and museums in integrating social media.

Promoting Archives Through Social Media

Essays in Theimer (2011) provide numerous case studies on how different social media were used by archival institutions to promote access to their holdings. A few are listed below:

- The use of a processing blog at the University of North Carolina to manage the expectations of users of a special photographic collection (Fletcher, 2011). The goal was to let users understand the work that goes into processing a photographic collection before it is made available to users. This initiative was considered as successful as it made their users appreciate what archivists do more. Referring to the number of visits to the blog and the discussions or feedback on the various posts in the blog it meant there was also an increase in the content of the photographic collection. Some of the encountered problems included the amount of time involved in compiling substantive posts for the blog and handling negative comments from readers (Fletcher, 2011).

- Posting of videos on YouTube at Iowa University, enabling access to a collection that was not easily accessible in the past. A special collection of digitised films based on the university, the State of Iowa and the agriculture sector in this region were uploaded on YouTube. Fifty films, which were viewed more than 52,000 times were then uploaded permanently broadening the visibility of this repository. Also, these films led to fruitful partnerships with the local television broadcaster and other cultural organisations. Issues such as minimal time to select and prepare or convert films for uploading, dealing with spam and obscene comments and copyright matters were some of the challenges experienced by this institution (Christian & Zanish-Belcher, 2011).

- The creation of virtual archives in Second Life at Stanford University. This has enabled this institution to teach archival literacy and facilitate browsing on a platform that is seen as more appealing to their student body. This allowed for more interaction in a three dimensional context. The institution received overwhelmingly positive feedback which resulted in virtual seminars, newspaper articles and increased interest in the collection. Similar to the cases above finding time to run the project was a challenge furthermore some of the staff felt that they lacked certain technological expertise that could enhance the project further (Taormina, 2011).

- The University of Alabama used Facebook to raise awareness about their special collections among their student body. Facebook was used to promote lecture series, activities, information about collections and endeavours of this particular repository. This enabled the repository to create a network with other similar institutions as well, to communicate, explore and share information or various matters regarding their collections. Facebook offered the opportunity to communicate with a variety of users, with different political, religious and social inclinations. As a result, the repository had to be mindful whenever posting details related to certain collections in order not to offend some of their patrons. (Lacher-Feldman, 2011).

- Interaction among Jewish women with particular interests, who use the Jewish women's archive, became more feasible with using Twitter. This was seen as positive way of reaching out to a specific audience and encouraging them to interact with the resources in this collection. Posts in this case were on content from the institution's website, questions for the public and success stories. This was seen as an effective means of pushing content to regular and irregular users of the repository. Regarding posting content, this particular repository was of the opinion that posts on Twitter should not only be done by one task assigned person. Including many voices enriched and enhanced the dialogue between them and their users. The challenge here was that, not all their staff were familiar with Twitter and how to use it for outreach (Medina-Smith, 2011).

These accounts outline the planning, implementation and challenges encountered when embarking on using these different social media. Nevertheless, increased interaction, search visits and uses of the holdings are reported as the benefits of using social media in the archives.

Crymble (2010, p. 127) argues that times have changed and more people seek information online. Therefore, it has become a necessity for archivists to find out how their users and potential users seek information online. This should help them to determine which online tools are most suitable (and affordable) to disseminate information to society. Similarly, Garaba (2015, p. 218) emphasises that, "users are voting with their fingers in cyberspace and the community expects its information sources to be available online and increasingly regards anything that is not online as being irrelevant. Other information providers such as libraries and museums have noted the importance of integrating social media in their operational practices. They also view this as a way of linking up with the users of their services and keeping them informed of their services and activities (Liew et al., 2015). These experiences could benefit archival institutions wishing to incorporate social media in their public programming initiatives (Liew et al., 2015). Bountouri (2017, p. 57) explains the following:

Social media is allowing archives to make their institutions more attractive and at the same time broaden its audience especially with younger people who are using social media apps very often. Social media encourages users' active participation and assessment, it also allows archival institutions to collect feedback and indirectly engage the audience in a dialog related to shared content.

Archivists as other information providers should be aware of the information seeking behaviours of their users (Katuu, 2015; Saurombe & Ngulube, 2016). As information technologies rapidly change in the current information society, archivists must be wary of the changing information needs of their users (Garaba, 2015). Though the digital divide is still a reality in Africa, there are a significant number of people online (millennials) whose information preferences should not be overlooked (Garaba, 2015; Saurombe, 2016).

Ethical Concerns on Promoting Archives Through Social Media

Theimer (2011) reminds archivists not to get carried away and forget that technologies such as social media are tools and not goals. In her opinion, archivists should take note of the benefits and limitations and determine which tool will work most favourably in promoting access to the archives. Archivists should also consider the option of using both traditional methods and technology to facilitate access to their holdings. The benefits of applying Web 2.0 tools like social media in promoting access include offering people new ways to connect, access and interact with the archives' holdings. However, it is critical to note limitations such as the digital divide, in case such initiatives disregard the fate of the underclass, sub-literate and minorities. Jimerson (2011, p. 315) also lists the following as limitations of using Web 2.0 tools such as social media:

- Finding a balance between the archivist gatekeeper and the user who wants direct accessibility and control of what they see, when and how.
- The false notion that everything is available on the web. The quest for answers may require one going beyond the web, namely visiting the archive.
- **Technological Obsolescence:** Rapid changes render software, equipment and skills useless within a short period of time.
- Preservation of digitised information can be tricky due to the obsolescence of technologies.
- Privacy concerns.

The use of Web 2.0 tools such as social media to promote archives is a relatively new field of interest. Further research will give more light on how to effectively use these tools to promote access to archival holdings (Fereiro, 2011).

Though social media offers vast opportunities to promote archival institutions (Theimer, 2011; Bountouri & Giannakopolous 2014; Garaba, 2015), it is important to note that the 'sharing' of information could lead to exploitation and misuse of information (Bortree & Distaso, 2014). Organisations such as public archives need to be careful of what they share and how they share this information. Bortree and Distaso (2014, p.158) state that "organisations need to know that social media is not a free for all space but rather an extension of their brand. As such organisations must maintain the same standards online as they do in their traditional communication programmes". In most organisations, there are communication frameworks, guidelines or policies that they adhere to. Similarly, communication via social media networks should be guided by social media policies that the organisation or the public archival institution set in this instance (Bountouri, 2017). According to Wasike (2013, p.9), a social media policy for organisations such as archival institutions will facilitate governance, provide access to vital information, communicate with the public and promote civic participation. The use of standards in a policy creates order for those who adhere to the standards. It will also help the institution to understand the consequences of the improper and irresponsible use of social media. On a similar note, Sinclair (2012, p 76) explains that a social media policy should also clearly point out how the content to be shared by the archives is created and vetted.

The Use of Social Media for Public Programming Initiatives Within ESARBICA

Kamatula, Mnkeni-Saurombe and Mosweu (2013) did a study on promoting documentary heritage by the National Archives of Tanzania, South Africa and Botswana (members of ESARBICA). The findings of this study revealed that social media were not categorically considered as viable means to enhance public programming initiatives. Five years later in 2018, a quick search on Google revealed an active Facebook page for the Botswana National Archives and Records Services, but the National Archives of Tanzania and South Africa still did not use any social media platforms yet.

Sulej (2014) and Dominy (2017) report of the challenges faced by the National Archives of South Africa on promoting archives in South Africa. Their discussions are based on the websites of this institution, social media is not mentioned as part of outreach strategies at this archival institution. The only other ESARBICA member state that had a Facebook page is the Kenya National Archives and Documentation Service.

Perhaps limitations such as the digital divide can be mentioned in this instance (Mutula, 2005, 2008). Mutula (2005) reports that technological related challenges that cause the digital divide in sub-Saharan Africa include inadequate infrastructure, high cost of access, inappropriate or weak policy regimes, inefficient provision of telecommunications networks, financial constraints, ICT awareness, literacy and information skills.

Ten years after Mutula's (2005) account, a report by Facebook (2016) on the state of connectivity worldwide states that though connectivity has improved worldwide, there are still approximately three billion people who are not connected online. According to this report, a significant number of these people is found in sub-Saharan Africa.

Primary barriers to connectivity are availability, affordability, relevance and readiness, which are mainly affected by rurality and remoteness, low incomes, lack of education and low connectivity among peers (Facebook, 2016). In 2015, 190 countries at the United Nations (UN) committed towards 17 sustainable development goals (SDGs). In these SDGs, the UN emphasised the need for universal connectivity. According to the UN (2015), governments should strive to provide universal access to all their citizens as digital technologies and platforms are key enablers in achieving SDGs in 2030. In recent times mobile technology has made web access more affordable in developing countries (World Wide Worx, 2017).

The high cost of data that many people complain about contributed to the digital divide resulting from using high cost equipment such as satellites and other systems. In recent times more affordable infrastructure such as fibre optic cable is used to connect more people online (Mutula, 2008; Facebook 2016). Mutula (2008, p. 480) further explains that, the high cost of connectivity has prompted the establishment of major infrastructure projects across the African continent and between Africa and other continents. Some of these projects include:

- East African Submarine cable system
- SEACOM-carriers project
- Multipurpose community centres
- Common Market for Eastern and Southern Africa (COMESA) Telecommunications projects

These projects have to a certain extent enabled many citizens in east and southern Africa to access and afford internet connectivity and use social media platforms such as Facebook, Twitter and others (Anduvare, 2016). Most likely, as per Garaba's (2015) argument, more people in the ESARBICA region seek information online. Perhaps archival institutions in this region should embrace these social media platforms to improve their visibility in society (Kamatula, Mnkeni-Saurombe & Mosweu, 2013).

RESEARCH PROCEDURE

The study followed a descriptive explanatory design within the positivist paradigm (Babbie, 2011; Neuman, 2014). The study explored whether the National Archives of the ESARBICA region integrated social media in their public programming initiatives to increase their visibility in society. Permission was sought from the ESARBICA Board to collect data from participants of the XXII ESARBICA Biennial Conference that took place in Nairobi, Kenya. The selected participants were the directors of the National Archives, archivists working at the National Archives and selected members of the ESARBICA Board. The researcher was of the opinion that these participants would be able to provide a credible overview about using social media in their public programming initiatives. The Directors of the National Archives were requested to complete a questionnaire, while the selected archivists and ESARBICA board members participated in face to face interviews. Furthermore, the ESARBICA Board provided their 2013-2015 strategic plan and reports from the respective member states that were analysed to determine whether social media integration in public programming initiatives was a part of their strategy. Utilising multiple tools in the research process is also known as methodological triangulation (Ngulube, 2015; Saurombe, 2016). The combination of data collection methods provided both depth and breadth in the findings of the study.

There are many nations that are part of east and southern Africa; however not all of them are active members of ESARBICA. Participants of the study were from 12 consistent members of ESARBICA. The National Archives of Uganda was also present at the conference, though they are not categorised as 'consistent' according to the ESARBICA Board (2013-2015). They were also requested to participate in the study and share details regarding social media use in their institution. Table 1 provides an overview of the participants of the study.

The summary in table 1 indicates that all member states took part in this study, except one member. Nine of 13 (69%) Directors of the National Archives completed the questionnaire while 8 out of 12 (67%) archivists agreed to be interviewed. The national directors of Botswana, Angola, Malawi and Mozambique did not participate in the study. Nevertheless, the information gathered from the national directors, the archivists, ESARBICA board members and the country reports, which were prepared on the different activities (including outreach). The activities that took place in these countries were enough to provide an overview of social media use in the public programming initiatives in the region.

Data analysis of the quantitative data was conducted using Microsoft Excel, resulting in the findings being organised in graphs. The information gathered from the interviews was read and categorised according to themes that emerged from the discussion.

The findings of the study are discussed in the following section.

FINDINGS

This section focuses on the perspectives of archivists from the ESARBICA region, which are on using social media to raise awareness about archives in their communities.

Table 1. Summary of the composition of the participants

Member State	Director Completed Questionnaire	Archivist Interviewed	ESARBICA Board Member Interviewed
Zimbabwe	Yes	Yes	Yes
Botswana	No	Yes	No
South Africa	Yes	No	No
Namibia	Yes	Yes	No
Swaziland	Yes	Yes	No
Lesotho	No	No	No
Tanzania	Yes	Yes	No
Zanzibar	Yes	No	No
Kenya	Yes	Yes	Yes
Uganda	Yes	No	No
Zambia	Yes	No	No
Mozambique	No	Yes	Yes
Malawi	No	Yes	No

The Use of Social Media to Raise Awareness About the Archives

Garaba (2015) and Bountouri (2017) report that archival institutions have a lot to gain from integrating social media in their public programming initiatives. For that reason, the Directors of the National Archives were asked whether they used social media to promote the National Archives. The majority of the National Archives (7 or 78%) did not use social media. Facebook and Twitter were identified as the preferred social media platforms by the two (22%) National Archives that used social media.

The Directors of the National Archives were further asked if they thought that visibility on social media would influence the public's awareness of the National Archives. Four (44%) stated that it would have a positive effect while four (44%) other directors said the opposite.

Even though not all of the National Archives used social media, the Directors of the National Archives were asked if there were any advantages that they knew about using social media. Six (67%) of the participants were of the opinion that social media could help the National Archives to reach a wider audience. Most of the Directors of the National Archives (6 or 67%) agreed that social media could reach more people. Two of the participants went further and explained that social media were more appealing to the youth as well. The fact that most people access social media over their cell phones was pointed out by two (22%) of the participants. When asked about the disadvantages, six (67%) declined to answer, while three of the participants offered the following reasons:

- Social media only reaches the elite.
- It allows distortion and manipulation.
- Some users may introduce petty issues.

Out of the archivists who were interviewed only one mentioned that they used social media to communicate and raise awareness about the archives. Facebook was the social media platform used by this particular repository. Seven of the interviewees indicated that their National Archives had websites, while one did not. This particular National Archives have a link within their governing National Department's website. The archivists shared similar views as the directors regarding the disadvantages of using social media. One participant shared that:

There are a lot of challenges with regard to using social media as a tool of communication, we are talking about issues of privacy, and we are talking about public records. Do you know what to share out to the public, there is also the question of how do you treat those records through social media?

Most participants had personal Facebook accounts. Two of the interviewees mentioned that they did talk about National Archives on their pages; however, this was done in their personal capacities.

Since social media was not integrated into outreach in most of the National Archives of ESARBICA, the interview participants were asked whether they used any other online means to market or raise awareness about their institutions and services. All the archivists highlighted that their National Archives websites were used to market different programmes.

The Directors of the National Archives who did not use social media were asked to give reasons why their National Archives did not do so. The results were as follows:

- There are stringent procedures to be followed considering the fact that we belong to the Ministry of Home Affairs (security ministry).
- Social media are used by people to share issues like politics and social issues.
- Lack of creativity (exposure).
- It is something in the pipeline.
- The archives need to get permission from the department which it falls under, the bureaucracy prevents archives from establishing a Facebook page.
- High staff turnover.
- Financial constraints.

The ESARBICA Board members and the available country reports did not mention the promotion of public archives by using social media.

DISCUSSION

From the findings, it is clear that social media is not effectively integrated in public programming initiatives in the ESARBICA region. The following discussion attempts to highlight the necessity for these repositories to use social media, especially because the number of people with access to internet in the ESARBICA region is increasing.

Social Media as Integral Part of the Information Society: Can the ESARBICA National Archives Ignore Reality?

Holmner and Britz (2013) as well as Kim et al., (2014, p. 29) argue that development in the information society saw the increase of mobile based services over web-based services. This is also reflected in Africa (Mutula, 2008), "with mobile internet in Africa rapidly overtaking fixed internet access" (Stork, Calandro, & Gamage 2014, p. 76). In addition, though there has been an increase in mobile technology and broad band availability, progress in this regard differs from country to country in southern Africa (Holmner & Britz, 2013). Increased accessibility to social media can be attributed to the rapid development of mobile internet platforms; as a result, many people can access information and perform different transactions (Holmner & Britz, 2013). This is also possibly linked to e-governance initiatives and strategies taking place in most African countries (Holmner & Britz, 2013). Onyancha (2010, p. 33) describes e-governance simply as "being online and providing the public with relevant information".

Naidoo (2012, p. 63) further explains that e-governance is a public sector strategy which uses ICTs to improve information and service delivery. Also, e-governance encourages citizen participation in the decision-making processes of the government and as a result, governments become more accountable, transparent and effective. Though many African countries are striving to adopt e-governance strategies, Komba and Ngulube (2012, p. 29) report that there are a number of countries that are still lagging behind. This is because of lack of infrastructure, connectivity challenges, high cost of internet access, illiteracy and other factors. Nevertheless, countries in the ESARBICA region such as Kenya, Tanzania, South Africa, and Namibia are among some of the African countries that are progressing in developing e-government systems (Chaterera, 2012).

Kallberg (2012) explains that many governments are implementing e-governance strategies. However, they complain that archivists have seemingly taken a back seat letting other information professionals perform their important roles. Kallberg (2012) is of the opinion that archivists must acquire the necessary skills and take their rightful position in facilitating access to information in both paper and electronic formats. As more African governments strive to provide information online, the ESARBICA National Archives should also be actively involved in e-governance initiatives. Providing information about their archival holdings and services and their benefits to society could result in public archives acquiring more recognition in government, public and other spheres of society. Consequently, integrating social media strategies in public programming initiatives could form part of these e-government systems.

Social media platforms offer archives an opportunity to facilitate access to information. Theimer (2011) provides examples such as Facebook, Twitter, Wikis and Blogs as social networking services that could be used by archival institutions. Kim et al. (2014, p. 30) agree with the ideas of Theimer (2011) but caution archival institutions to understand that they do not have full control over what is shared due to terms and conditions set by these social networking services. They further highlight that these platforms can also cause problems such as distribution of malware, invasion of privacy, violations of intellectual property rights and other problems.

Wasike (2013), and Hood and Reid (2018) seem to indicate that these challenges can be minimised with using social media policies that govern what is shared, how it is shared and outlining steps of action when such challenges arise. Kim et al., (2014) maintain that due to developments in the field of ICTs, it is possible for organisations to develop their own social networking services via mobile platforms on their own terms. For such reasons, Kim et al. (2014, p. 33) advise archival institutions to develop their own social networking services. This will enable archivists, experts and users to interact within a controlled environment which is safer as compared to public platforms such as Facebook. This could work for the National Archives in the ESARBICA region as people in this region have access to mobile internet (Stork, Calandro, & Gamage, 2014, p. 76). Some of the archivists who participated in this study were concerned about issues such as privacy, but most likely developing a customised archival social network could alleviate their fears on control over information shared online.

Though more archival institutions and libraries are incorporating social media in their operations, Liew et al., (2015) argue that most of it is experimental. In their opinion, there was very little research done on evaluating the use of these platforms and determining their impact on attaining organisational goals. They seem to echo the views of Ngoepe and Ngulube (2011) as well as Fereiro (2011) that more research on using social media is required.

Social Media Strategies as Part of Public Programming Initiatives at the ESARBICA National Archives

The lack of integration of social media in most public programming initiatives in the ESARBICA region is worrying. As indicated in the literature (Mutula, 2008; Ngoepe & Ngulube, 2011; Garaba, 2015; Bountouri & Giannakopoulos, 2014; Bountouri, 2017), there could be a number of factors that have contributed towards these institutions not using social media in their public programming initiatives. According to these authors, some of the factors that may possibly be inhibiting the ESARBICA National Archives from utilising social media include:

- **The Digital Divide:** Lack of network or connectivity
- **Fear of Change:** Most of the managers at the helm of the National Archives are from a generation that find it difficult to keep up with all the current technological changes in the current knowledge economy
- Shrinking budgets
- Lack of manpower to monitor interaction on social media platforms
- Lack of expertise
- Absence of social media policies and knowledge of legal matters with regard to sharing content such as copy right laws

Some of these challenges are similar to those highlighted by the archivists who were interviewed. Nevertheless, they should not prevent archival repositories from having a social media presence. Most of the National Archives indicated that they had websites for their institutions, adopting social media platforms does not have to result in eliminating these websites. Preferably, the social media platforms could be used to generate more interest for the websites. As Garaba (2015) indicated, most information seekers start searching online, archival institutions such as those in ESARBICA should seek ways to reach out to online users and guide them to their holdings. Ngulube (2004) speaks of the challenges archives in the ESARBICA region face about digitising collections. Garaba (2015) confirms that most of the archival holdings in the region are still paper based. In such instances, social media platforms can still be used to inform the public of what is available and how they can be accessed. These social media platforms could also be used to inform the public of the efforts of these institutions towards digitising collections and other initiatives aimed at improving the archives' services. Bountouri and Giannako-polous (2014) also state that social media platforms are great tools for marketing events. On occasions such as commemoration events, national holidays and other cultural-related events the archives can use social media to reach out and inform the public of what they have planned for such occasions and invite them to participate.

Not everyone knows how to seek and use information within archival holdings (Saurombe & Ngulube, 2016), social media platforms could be used to offer simple information literacy training to the public. As more people access information online, the question, therefore, is what role do archival institutions play in empowering people to access information in this environment? According to the United Nations' (2015) SDGs, it is clear that information plays a critical role in people's lives. As more people seek information, especially online information, institutions such as archival repositories, libraries and other information providers should assist people to access information in its various formats. The ESARBICA National Archives should therefore recognise current trends and adopt what is feasible for their repositories and users.

A Social Media Strategy to Raise Awareness About the National Archives in the ESARBICA Region

The National Archives in the ESARBICA region could learn from the experiences of other information providers such as libraries and museums from within the region. Also, they could try to determine how social media platforms could work for their organisations (Saurombe & Ngulube, 2018). King (2015, p. 6) claims that social media has enabled libraries to listen, make connections, get responses and extend their reach into society. Most likely, archival repositories can achieve the same. As the number of online information seekers increases, it is becoming apparent for archival repositories to ensure that their holdings are also easily discoverable and accessible online (Augusyniak & Orzechowski, 2017). Section 2.1 of this chapter outlines some accounts from some repositories that have benefitted from using social media. Examples of social media platforms that are used by archival institutions include (Williamson, Vieira & Williamson, 2015, p. 491):

- **Wordpress and Tumblr:** Detailed written accounts
- **Facebook:** News and events
- **Twitter:** Current awareness service
- **Instagram, Pinterest, Flickr:** Photographs and short videos
- **Linkedin:** Professional information
- **YouTube:** Films and videos

Embarking on such a social media strategy requires proper planning to ensure that the social media strategy is in line with the repository's objectives, policies and the relevant legislation. Proper planning also eases the implementation and evaluation process (Liew et al, 2015).

King (2015, pp. 33-35) offers some key guidelines for starting a social media campaign, they are as follows:

- **Set up a Channel:** Select the best social media platform for your institution, bearing in mind the different types of audiences that you serve. For instance, lengthy posts are not suitable for Twitter, but great for Wordpress or Tumblr.

- **Set Goals:** Determine why the repository needs a social media strategy. Reasons may vary from reaching out to younger audiences, maintaining contact with regular patrons, marketing an event and others.
- **Listen:** – Learn and understand how each social media platform functions.
- **Create a Team:** The accounts in section 2.1 indicate that social media projects require time and creativity. Teamwork will make the project more manageable and provide a holistic overview of the institution by allowing different staff to describe collections or events.
- **Create Content:** The team should plan and decide which content will be shared or promoted on the platform. Some audiences may find it easier to relate to visual content rather than lengthy written accounts. For such reasons, the team may decide to use different platforms to reach out to the different types of users.

Encourage interaction with the public, let the repository ensure that there is always someone at hand to respond to comments or questions.

- **Use Analytics to Measure Success:** Evaluating success is an important aspect of a social media strategy. Social media analytic tools can be used to compile information for reports to determine the effectiveness of the project. These metrics may provide details such as the number of likes, number of followers, number of clicks, number of pages viewed, comments, mentions, messages and other details.

In line with the guidelines by King (2015), the repository should focus on developing a strategy that is suitable for their context. This will require the repository to have sound knowledge of their users to determine which social media platforms will be most appropriate. Furthermore, proper knowledge of the holdings and intellectual property rights is also important or else the repository will struggle in determining what and how to share the content from the archival holdings.

FUTURE RESEARCH DIRECTIONS

Though social media usage has become a common trend in society, not much research has been done with regard to use and its implications on public archival repositories (Liew et al., 2015, Kim et al., 2014). Moreover, not much is known about the integration of social media in public programming initiatives at public archival repositories in Africa. Therefore, as the use of social media in Africa, in this instance east and southern Africa, increases due to factors as the affordability of mobile telephones and internet connectivity, more archival repositories should consider incorporating them in their effort to promote access to their archives. Research that focuses on such initiatives will help archival repositories to determine how best to accomplish this task of adopting social media to promote their holdings effectively and efficiently.

Social media, especially marketing or promoting organisations through social media is an extensive and dynamic topic, it would not be possible for this chapter to exhaust all the factors related to promoting archives through social media. However; it recommends that further research on the following factors could be useful for archivists in east and southern Africa:

- **The Concept of Influencer Marketing:** This is a social media strategy that focuses on how to connect with new users and improve the relationship between the organisations such as archival repositories and their existing users.
- **The Influence of Social Media on Culture and Heritage:** Information on culture and heritage form an integral part of our public archival repositories. Knowledge of how social media influences people's knowledge of their culture and heritage could help archivists to plan, design and implement outreach initiatives that are appropriate for the different target populations they reach out to.
- **Ethical Matters:** Most legislation and policies on communications and records keeping in east and southern Africa countries are vague with regard to social media communication. Perhaps research in this area could lead to the necessary amendments that will help organisations such as public archives to have a clear direction on how to use social media.

CONCLUSION AND RECOMMENDATIONS

Most of the National Archives in the ESARBICA region were reluctant to use social media. Reasons given were linked to inexperience, bureaucracy, budgetary constraints and the lack of expertise to do so. This is a phenomenon that was also discovered by Liew et al., (2015). These researchers in their world wide study (Liew et al., 2015, p. 3) argue that archival institutions were slow to accept social media as a tool that can enhance their operations. Sadly, it also confirms Garaba's (2015) observations that we have "Dodos" in the archives in this particular region as we are not adapting to change and current trends in the present information society; yet other cultural organisations and information service providers have done so despite similar challenges. Though the integration of social media in public programming initiatives has many benefits (Bountouri & Giannakoplous, 2014; Bountouri, 2017), archivists must be wary that they are just tools (Jimerson, 2011). These tools if not used wisely they can harm the institution rather than promote it. Policies and legislation on social media or online information will help to govern what, how and when information can be shared (Sinclair, 2012; Wasike, 2013).

The Directors of the National Archives and the archivists did acknowledge that social media could help reach out to more people, particularly young people. These views are similar to those of Garaba (2015) and Bountouri (2017). The National Archives of the ESARBICA region could benefit from using social media as more citizens in this region get access to the internet and seek for information online (Mutula, 2008; Facebook, 2016; World Wide Worx, 2017). In view of that, this study suggests a number of recommendations that can encourage using social media in public programming efforts by the National Archives in the ESARBICA region:

- Garaba (2015), Holmner and Britz (2013) and Onyancha (2010) report on the increased use of web-based services in sub-Saharan Africa; due to this fact, the National Archives of the ESARBICA region are advised to rope in social media to improve their visibility online. The archival holdings do not necessarily need to be online, but rather social media platforms such as Facebook or others could be used to inform the public of what is available and services offered at a particular archival service.
- Shrinking budgets are a reality that most archival institutions are faced with (Bountouri, 2017). Bountouri (2017, p. 51) advises that social media platforms offer archival institutions a platform

to communicate how the budget was spent to meet their needs. This may further help to advocate for more funding from authorities or donors who would like to contribute towards effective and efficient archival services. Bountouri (2017) also explains that social media sites are more cost effective than regular websites that demand constant attention and maintenance from within the organisation. Social media sites are maintained by the social media organisation.

Advocacy is a skill that may be helpful in this regard, as it will enable the National Archives to request for support and justify the return on investment for provided support. Support could come in terms of funds, expertise, training and other means that will make applying social media possible in public programming initiatives.

- There is a common adage that says 'the only constant thing in the world is change.' In line of the views of Garaba (2015), archivists in the ESARBICA region will need to update their skills and training so that they can address the information needs of their online social media users. Archivists should seek for opportunities to learn more about using social media in raising awareness about the archives. This could be done through a number, of avenues such as attending conferences on related issues and following blogs or online discussions of other information professionals involved in promoting their institutions. In addition, this could be done by participating in workshops, joining professional groups involved in marketing archives or other information providers, and referring to literature based on social media in the archives and other avenues.
- The National Archives should investigate the needs of their users on a regular basis. Information gathered from such research could further justify the integration of social media into public programming initiatives (Duff et al., 2008; Saurombe & Ngulube, 2016).
- Liew et al., (2015) report that institutions such as libraries and museums seem to have successfully embedded social media in their marketing operations. Perhaps, archivists could learn from the experiences of these professionals. Collaboration initiatives could lead to join projects and on the task training, such initiatives are cost effective and are more favourable than expensive training programmes (Saurombe & Ngulube, 2018).
- To avoid problems regarding copy right and intellectual property rights, the National Archives are advised to develop social media policies that will govern what, how and when information will be shared (Wasike, 2013).

The National Archives of the ESARBICA region should strive to address the information needs of the increasing number of online information seekers in this region. It may be a daunting task, nevertheless it is important that they remember that their mandate is to serve all their citizens regardless of their different socio-economic backgrounds. The National Archives of the ESARBICA region should consider integrating social media in their public programming strategies or the risk being redundant in an ever-changing information society.

REFERENCES

Anduvare, E. M. (2013). Networking as a new way of sharing and communicating information. *Innovation: Journal of Appropriate Librarianship and Information Work in Southern Africa*, *47*, 84–99.

Babbie, E. (2011). The basics of social research (6th ed.). Wadsworth: Cengage.

Bortree, D. S., & Distaso, M. W. (2014). *Ethical practise of social media in public relations*. New York: Routledge.

Bountouri, L. (2017). *Archives in the digital age: Standards, policies and tools*. Cambridge, MA: Chandos.

Bountouri, L., & Giannakopolous, B. (2014). The use of social media in archives. *Procedia, 147*, 510–517.

Chaterera, F. (2012). Towards harnessing e-government adoption in Zimbabwe. *Mousaion, 30*(1), 92–107.

Christian, M. A., & Zanish-Belcher, T. (2011). Broadcast yourself: Putting Iowa State University's history on You Tube. In K. Theimer (Ed.), *A different kind of web: New connections between archives and our users* (pp. 33–41). Chicago, IL: SAA.

Crymble, A. (2010). An analysis of Twitter and Facebook use by the archival community. *Archivaria, 70*, 125–151.

Dominy, G. (2017). The effects of an administrative and policy vacuum on access to archives in South Africa. *Archival Science, 17*(4), 393–408. doi:10.100710502-017-9282-3

Duff, W. M., Dryden, J., Limkilde, C., Cherry, J., & Bogomazova, E. (2008). Archivists' views of user based evaluation: Benefits, barriers and requirements. *The American Archivist, 71*(Spring/Summer), 144–166. doi:10.17723/aarc.71.1.y70837374478t146

ESARBICA. (2014). *Members*. Retrieved from http://www.esarbica.com/board_members.html

ESARBICA. (2015). Archives uses, abuses and underutilisation. In *23rd Biennial Conference*, Victoria Falls, Zimbabwe.

ESARBICA Board. (2013). *Country reports- ESARBICA Board Meeting 4 June 2013*. Nairobi, Kenya: Safari Park Hotel.

ESARBICA Board. (2013). (pp. 2013–2015). Nairobi, Kenya: Strategic Plan.

Facebook. (2016). Using data to move towards a more inclusive internet. Retrieved from https://newsroom.fb.com/news/2017/02/state-of-connectivity-2016-using-data-to-move-towards-a-more-inclusive-internet/

Ferreiro, D. S. (2011). Foreword. In K. Theimer (Ed.), *A different kind of web: new connections between archives and our users* (pp. ix–xvii). Chicago: SAA.

Fletcher, S. J. (2011). A view to a view to Hugh: reflections on the creation of a processing Blog. In K. Theimer (Ed.), *A different kind of web: new connections between archives and our users* (pp. 22–32). Chicago, IL: SAA.

Garaba, F. (2010). *An investigation into the management of the records and archives of former liberation movements in east and southern Africa held by national and private archival institutions*. Unpublished doctoral thesis, University of Kwa-Zulu Natal, Pietermaritzburg.

Garaba, F. (2015). Dodos in the archives: Re- branding the archival profession to meet the challenges of the 21st Century within ESARBICA. *Architectural Record, 36*(2), 216–225. doi:10.1080/23257962.2015.1030609

Graham, M. (2016). *Social media: Communication, sharing and visibility*. New York: Routledge.

Hager, D. (2015). To like or not to like: Understanding and maximising the utility of archival outreach on Facebook. *The American Archivist, 78*(1), 18–37. doi:10.17723/0360-9081.78.1.18

Holmner, M., & Britz, J. J. (2013). When the last mile becomes the longest mile: A critical reflection on Africa's ability to become part of the global knowledge society. *Innovation: Journal of Appropriate Librarianship and Information Work in Southern Africa, 46*, 117–134.

Hood, C., & Reid, P. (2018). Social media as a vehicle for user engagement with local history: A case study in the North East of Scotland. *The Journal of Documentation, 74*(4), 741–762. doi:10.1108/JD-12-2017-0167

International Council of Archives (ICA). (2012). *Principles of access to archives*. Retrieved on 10 May 2018, from http://www.ica.org/13619/toolkits-guides-manualsand-guidelines/draft principles-of-access-to-archives.html

Internet World Stats. 2017. Internet users. Retrieved from www.internetworldstats.com

Jimerson, R. C. (2011). Archives 101 in a 2.0 world: the continuing need for parallel systems. In K. Theimer (Ed.), *A different kind of web: New connections between archives and our users* (pp. 304–333). Chicago: SAA.

Kallberg, M. (2012). Archives 2.0: Redefining the archivist's profession in the digital age. *Records Management Journal, 22*(2), 98–115. doi:10.1108/09565691211268162

Kamatula, G. (2011). Marketing and public programming in records and archives at the Tanzanian Records and Archives Management Department. *Journal of the South African Society of Archivists, 44*, 74–89.

Kamatula, G., Mnkeni-Saurombe, N., & Mosweu, O. (2013). The role of archives in the promotion of documentary national heritage in Tanzania, South Africa and Botswana. *ESARBICA Journal, 32*, 109–127.

Katuu, S. (2015). User studies and user education programmes in archival institutions. *Aslib, 67*, 442–457.

Kim, Y., Kang, K. H., Kim, E., & Kim, G. (2014). Archival information services based on social networking services in a mobile environment: A case study of South Korea. *Library Hi Tech, 32*(1), 28–49. doi:10.1108/LHT-03-2013-0039

King, D. L. (2015). *Managing your library's social media channels*. Chicago: ALA.

Komba, M. M., & Ngulube, P. (2012). Factors for e-government adoption: Lessons from selected African countries. *Mousaion, 30*(1), 24–32.

Lanerolle, I. (2013). The rise of social media in Africa. African Media Online. Retrieved from http://O-hdl.handle.net/oasis.unisa.ac.za/10520/ejc141573

Lasher-Feldman, J. (2011). Making friends and fans: using Facebook for special collection outreach. In K. Theimer (Ed.), *A different kind of web: New connections between archives and our users* (pp. 54–64). Chicago: SAA.

Liew, C. L., King, V., & Oliver, G. (2015). Social media in archives and libraries: A snapshot of planning, evaluation and preservation decisions. *PDTandC*, *44*(1), 3–11.

Mabweazara, R. M., & Zinn, S. (2016). Assessing the appropriation of social media by academic librarians in South Africa and Zimbabwe. *SAJLIS*, *82*(1), 1–12.

McCausland, S. (2017). Archival public programming. In H. MacNeil & T. Eastwood (Eds.), *Currents of archival thinking* (2nd ed., pp. 225–244). Santa Barbara, CA: ABC-CLI.

Medina-Smith, A. (2011). Going where the users are: The Jewish women's Archive and its use of Twitter. In K. Theimer (Ed.), *A different kind of web: New connections between archives and our users* (pp. 65–74). Chicago, IL: SAA.

Mnjama, N. (2018). Archival access and public programming. In P. Ngulube (Ed.), *Heritage management and preservation* (pp. 47–68). Hershey, PA: IGI Global. doi:10.4018/978-1-5225-3137-1.ch003

Mutula, S. (2005). Peculiarities of the digital divide in sub-Saharan Africa. *Program*, *39*(2), 122–138. Retrieved on26May2018. doi:10.1108/00330330510595706

Mutula, S. (2008). Digital divide and economic development: Case study of sub-Saharan Africa. *The Electronic Library*, *26*(4), 468–489. doi:10.1108/02640470810893738

Mutula, S. (2013). Editorial-Ethical dimension of social media in the information Society. *Innovation: Journal of Appropriate Librarianship and Information Work in Southern Africa*, *47*, 3–7.

Naidoo, G. (2012). Implementation of e-government in South Africa – Successes and challenges: The way forward. *International Journal of Advances in Computing and Management*, *1*(1), 62–66.

Neuman, W. L. (2014). *Social research methods: Qualitative and quantitative approaches (7th ed.).* Harlow: Pearson.

Ngoepe, M., & Ngulube, P. (2011). Assessing the extent to which the National Archives and Records Service of South Africa has fulfilled its mandate of taking the archives to the people. *Innovation: Journal of Appropriate Librarianship and Information Work in Southern Africa*, *42*, 3–22.

Ngulube, P. (2004). Implications of technological advances for access to the cultural heritage of selected countries in sub-Saharan Africa. *Government Information Quarterly*, *21*(2), 143–155. doi:10.1016/j.giq.2004.01.003

Ngulube, P. (2015). Trends in research methodological procedures used in knowledge management studies. *African Journal of Library Archives and Information Science*, *25*(2), 125–143.

Ngulube, P. (2018). Using action research to develop a public programming strategy for heritage assets, with an example from South Africa. In P. Ngulube (Ed.), *Handbook of research on heritage management and preservation* (pp. 69–95). Hershey, PA: IGI Global. doi:10.4018/978-1-5225-3137-1.ch004

Onyancha, O. B. (2010). E-governance and e-governments in Africa: A webometrician's perception of the challenges, trends and issues. *Mousaion*, *28*(2), 32–63.

Roberts, D. (2008). Using computers. In J. Bettington, K. Eberhard, R. Loo, & C. Smith (Eds.), *Keeping archives* (pp. 321–348). Canberra: Australian Society of Archivists.

Saurombe, N. (2016). *Public programming of public archives in ESARBICA: towards an integrative and inclusive framework*. Unpublished doctoral thesis, University of South Africa, Pretoria.

Saurombe, N., & Ngulube, P. (2016). Perceptions of user studies as a foundation for public programming activities by archivists from east and southern Africa. *ESARBICA Journal, 35,* 29–45.

Saurombe, N., & Ngulube, P. (2018). To collaborate or not to collaborate, that is the question: Raising the profile of public archives in east and southern Africa. *Information Development, 34*(2), 162–181. doi:10.1177/0266666916684181

Sinclair, J. M. (2012). *The interactive archives: Social media and outreach*. Unpublished Masters dissertation, University of Manitoba/Winnipeg, Manitoba.

Stork, C., Calandro, E., & Gamage, R. (2013). The future of broadband in Africa. Retrieved from https://ssrn.com/abstract=2363781

Sulej, Z. (2014). Access to archives in South Africa in the first 20 years of democracy: Is there transformation or deformation? *ESARBICA Journal, 33,* 13–35.

Taormina, M. (2011). The virtual archives: Using Second Life to facilitate browsing and archival literacy. In K. Theimer (Ed.), *A different kind of web: New connections between archives and our users* (pp. 42–53). Chicago, IL: SAA.

Theimer, K. (2011). Building a community of supporters: the role of new technologies in advocacy. In L. Hackman (Ed.), *Many happy returns: Advocacy and the development of archives* (pp. 337–356). Chicago, IL: SAA.

Theimer, K. (2014). Introduction. In K. Theimer (Ed.), *Outreach: Innovative practices for archives and special collection* (pp. vii–xii). Lanham, MD: Rowman & Littlefield Publishers.

United Nations. (2015). *Sustainable Development Goals*. Retrieved from https://www.un.org/sustainabledevelopment/sustainable-development-goals/

Venson, S. L., Ngoepe, M., & Ngulube, P. (2014). The role of public archives in national development in the East and Southern Africa Regional Branch of the International Council on Archives. *Innovation: Journal of Appropriate Librarianship and Information Work, 48,* 46–68.

Wasike, J. (2013). Social media ethical issues: Role of a librarian. *Library Hi Tech News, 30*(1), 8–16. doi:10.1108/07419051311320922

Williamson, F., Vieira, S., & Williamson, T. (2015). Marketing finding aids on social media: What worked and what didn't work. *The American Archivist, 78*(2), 488–513. doi:10.17723/0360-9081.78.2.488

World Wide Worx. (2017). *Report - Internet access in South Africa*. Johannesburg: World Wide Worx.

KEY TERMS AND DEFINITIONS

Digital Divide: Economic and social inequality resulting from access to, use of, or impact of information and communication technologies in society.

Promotion: Making the content of archives more widely known and accessible to users.

This research was previously published in the Handbook of Research on Advocacy, Promotion, and Public Programming for Memory Institutions; pages 160-181, copyright year 2019 by Information Science Reference (an imprint of IGI Global).

Chapter 77
Social Media Strategies and Students' Satisfaction at Egyptian Universities

Nasser Fathi Easa
Alexandria University, Alexandria, Egypt

ABSTRACT

This article aims to investigate the impact of social media strategies on student satisfaction at Egyptian universities. The research employed four social media strategies (the Predictive Practitioner, Creative Experimenter, Social Media Champion and Social Media Transformer). A survey was posted to students Facebook groups in different universities. 530 students from the universities of Alexandria, Tanta Damanhour, Kafrelsheikh, Damietta, and Suez responded to the survey. It was noted that Facebook was the most common social media platform used. The Predictive Practitioner, Creative Experimenter, and Social Media Champion strategies were not clearly implemented, as opposed to the Social Media Transformer. It was noted that there was a lack of satisfaction of students with the information reliability, responsiveness and privacy faculties unusually posted on Facebook. It has been found that the four social media strategies account for positively influencing student satisfaction at Egyptian universities.

INTRODUCTION

The concept 'Web 2.0' was first introduced in 2004 to the O'Reilly Media Web 2.0, leading the evolution of social media (Graham, 2005; Kaplan & Haenlein, 2010). Social media platforms utilize a Web 2.0 format, which provides the users with a dynamic setting for personal interaction wherever they can interact with similarly minded people, as opposed to a Web 1.0 format wherever the user may be a passive recipient (Bennett & Glasgow, 2009; Chandran, 2016; Schroeder, 2014).

Social media may be considered as a style of electronic or on-line communication where a shared content will be manipulated or created by the users themselves (Donelle & Booth, 2012; Hamm et al., 2013). Examples of common social media channels/platforms include blogs, social networking sites

DOI: 10.4018/978-1-6684-7123-4.ch077

(Facebook), microblogs (Twitter), wikis or collaborative information projects (Wikipedia), and content communities (YouTube) (Risiling et al., 2017).

Through further understanding of who may be engaged in the use of social media, a lot of thought can be given to what types of activities are most typical on these platforms. To understand the enormity of the volume of information flow that typifies each day in the digital realm, the numbers are reported in 60 increments. The statistical reports have explained these "every minute of every day" usage examples: Twitter users produced around 347,000 tweets; Facebook users liked around 4.1 million posts; YouTube users uploaded 400 hrs of new videos; Instagram users post around 1.7 million images and like around 2.4 million posts; Dropbox users uploaded around 830,000 new files. This reflects that their sharp focus on information being exchanged through the social media sites (Novillo-Ortiz & Hernández-Pérez, 2017).

Governments and international institutions consider social media as an important tool to communicate with others and also use it for a better response in international crises (Comlekc & Guney, 2016). In business, social media applications create new opportunities for organizations to collaborate in new ways with their business partner, customers, and suppliers and to improve their internal operations (Culnan et al., 2010). For organizations, the social media provide opportunities to actively engage with consumers & employees and build relationships (Abeza et. al., 2013; Williams & Chinn, 2010). Social media allows organizations to share content, facilitate interaction and build community with customers (Achen, 2016; Smith, 2013). Employees also communicate through social media sites and contribute to the organization's reputation and image. The role of internal communication expands in the direction of getting feedback from within the organization (Ng & Wang, 2013). Internally, social media can also contribute to the community development, improvement of communication processes, promotion of values and organizational culture, facilitation of information flow, and stimulation of creativity (Ng & Wang, 2013).

Social media is used by a wide variety of organizations ranging from very small businesses to Fortune 500. However, the business value derived from social media continues to cause challenges for many organizations. McKinsey published in 2009 the results of a worldwide survey of nearly 1,700 executives to investigate their companies' use of social media platforms. The results indicated that 64% use social media platforms internally, 56% to work with customers, and nearly 40% to communicate with suppliers or external partners. However, about one-third of users reported that their social media applications did not provide measurable benefits (Culnan et al., 2010). In a similar study of executives by Barnes and Mattson (2009), 52% reported they were using social media as an effective tool in their organization. When asked if their company used social media "to communicate with other companies like vendors, suppliers or partners," they found that "social networking was the most widely used with 34% reporting they employed these tools" (Remidez & Jones, 2012).

Research shows that social media has recently penetrated almost all types of organizations. Higher education institutions have not been left behind but have been adopters of this global phenomenon (Chugh, 2017). According to ProQuest's dissertation and theses database, the use of social media in education represents only 5% of all research done on social media (Chris, 2014). Social media enables educational institutions to provide information about changes to policies, new research programme, job vacancies, events, institutional news and alumni engagement. To attract more students, social media provides a perfect platform to highlight research and teaching staff, new courses, and campus facilities (Chugh, 2017). Some colleges and universities also use social media as a tool for recruiting students.

One of the major challenges of higher education to develop social media as a platform for marketing is the lack of a clear model and the process for constructing and delivering the university's marketing, especially since universities rely so heavily on faculty governance (Chapleo, 2007). One of the most common questions being discussed among those managing social media for institutions is: who at the faculty is responsible for a social media strategy in the first place? This lack of responsibility has certainly increased the apprehension of higher education stakeholders about embracing social media as a platform for marketing to reach a potentially large and engaged audience (Peruta et al., 2013). Therefore, the challenge for institutions is whether they will be able to make their structures harmonized and flexible to integrate social media into their communication policy (Ng & Wang, 2013).

Egypt, along with other countries, has witnessed a massive growth in the use of social media networks. Facebook, in particular, played a vital role in the Egyptian revolution of 2011 (Gaber & Wrights, 2014). Statistics show that the number of social media users, mainly Facebook, has reached 15 million, with a penetration of nearly 16% of the population, of which more than 73% are between the ages of 15 and 29 (Dubai School of Government, 2013).

In Egypt, internet users have increased to about 54.6% of the population in 2015, compared to 35.6% in 2012. The use of computer technology and the widespread dominance of the internet has attracted many people, and particularly university students (Saied et.al. 2016). The majority of students reported that they had internet access (85.8%) at home, mostly via mobile phones (92.4%). Facebook is the most frequently used social media application by Egyptian students (93%), while other social media such as Twitter, WhatsApp, Skype were less frequently used. The habitual use of Facebook late at night was reported by 26.9% of Egyptian students (Saied et al., 2016).

This research aims to investigate the impact of social media strategies employed by Egyptian universities on their students' satisfaction.

LITERATURE REVIEW

Despite the importance of getting a social media strategy (Agostino, 2013; Effing et al., 2011; Hanna et al., 2011; Wilson et al., 2011), the literature hardly mentions the development of social media strategies. A social media strategy is "a corporate plan or policy to provide directions regarding social media practices in order to achieve business opportunities, reduce risks, and deal with the unregulated personal use of employees" (Effing et al., 2011, p. 7). Social media should be connected to the business strategy. There are three different approaches to the social media strategy: content approaches, strategy developing frameworks and generic strategies (Kersbergen, 2013; Werder, et al., 2014).

Content Approaches

Content approaches offer practical advice on the way to behave on social media. Kaplan and Haenlein (2010) gave ten points on the use of social media as an organization: they suggest that an organization may carefully select their channels, and if multiple channels are used, all of them may be aligned. Social media should be connected to the whole organization and should be accessible to all. Kaplan & Haenlein (2010) also address social media behavior and suggest that an organization have to be active, humble, interesting, professional and honest. Therefore, Kaplan & Heinlein (2010) revealed that it is crucial for organizations to possess a strategy that is accessible to different forms of social media. De Swaan Arons et al. (2014) added that both managers and marketers should be responsible for managing social media. Successful implementation strategies require four elements. Firstly, coordination between the relevant departments to market the use of social media. Secondly, address the risk management issues up front. Thirdly, develop procedures to process unstructured transactions. Finally, consider lessons for implementing the internal social media applications (Culnan et al., 2010; Effing, 2013).

In general, companies received full credit for engagement, if resources were allotted to managing an ongoing presence and the brand participated with the social media channel (Ashle & Tuten, 2015). The most powerful social media strategies focused closely on particular stages in the social media interaction channel, which indicated high levels of consumer and employee engagement (Klautzsch, 2017). The contents of social media need to be kept fresh and relevant by using an appropriate internal change management plan to handle any possible resistance to change (Brown, 2010).

Social media content needs to be relevant for the stakeholders to engage (Effing & Spi, 2016). Four forms of engagement with social media were identified: Firstly, adversarial engagement uses social media space to provide equal opportunities to all positions or interests on an issue. Secondly, information exchange uses the social media space to provide regular updates through text and visual media to communicate the status of group planning or program development and implementation. Thirdly, civil society engagement uses the social media space to provide interest groups and communities to share information relevant to or of possible concern to stakeholders, who are interested in the policy, program, or infrastructure project. Lastly, collaborative engagement uses the social media aspect to provide stakeholders with an equal chance to contribute ideas, as well as responses to those ideas and questions (Bryer, 2013).

Although these suggestions by Ashle and Tuten (2015); Effing and Spi (2016); Kaplan and Haenlein (2010); Klautzsch (2017) cannot be seen as a strategy, they are useful as guidelines for a more advanced social media strategy.

Strategy Developing Frameworks

There are three distinguished stages for social media strategy development: Initiation, Diffusion and Maturity Stages (Kersbergen, 2013, Werder et al., 2014). In the initiation stage the first key element for a social media strategy is to decide on the platform choice (Facebook, LinkedIn, Twitter to deliver "high quality postings" and to find high quality personnel. The second key element is to define the target audience (Berthon et al., 2012). During the diffusion stage organizations have to pay attention to the main element of monitoring, which is necessary to introduce insights that can help to gain future resources (Mergel & Bretschneider, 2013). During the maturity stage organizations should develop a social media activity plan. Some of the aims for activity planning are increasing the number of followers, increasing the interactivity and increasing the reach. Klang and Nolin (2011) described both planning and monitoring as important factors of the social media strategy (Effing & Spi, 2016).

Kietzman et al. (2011) presented a different social media strategy-developing framework using seven elements: identity, conversations, sharing, presence, relationship, reputation and groups. When using this framework, organizations need to keep in mind four major considerations: cognize, congruity, curate and chase. The cognize reveals an organization should recognize and consider the social media landscape. Congruity means developing a strategy that is connected to the business goals of the organization and different social media applications. The curate stands for acting act as curator on social media interactions with a clear view of when to participate in online conversations. The chase stands for the never-ending pursue of information about social media activities, and the evaluation of social media practices (Kersbergen, 2013; Kietzman et al., 2011).

According to Mergel and Bretschneider (2013), the social media usage can be evolved in three stages. In the first stage, organizations, on an informal basis, experiment with social media. This occurs outside of the approved technology use and policies. In the second stage, organizations acknowledge the need for regulations and norms for the social media use. In the third stage, organizations develop a clear guide for accepted behavior, interaction types, and the new forms of communication that are formalized in the social media strategies (Mergel & Brenschneider, 2013).

Korzeniowski (2015) and Piskorski (2011) added that to manage a social media strategy, companies should follow three steps. Firstly, permission push – where the company provides a form through community and social media to reach and influence engaged customers with relevant information. Secondly, permission pull – where the company, through the use of and its web-site and mobile applications, draws customers closer to the engagement point, which then moves to fulfillment once appropriateness and relevance have been established. Finally, permission direct – where the company communicates with individual customers through SMS or email (Durkin et al., 2013). The social media strategy should mainly focus on networking and customer relation management (Korzeniowski, 2015; Piskorski, 2011).

Generic Strategies

Generic social media strategies set a direction for detailed strategic planning (Kersbergen, 2013). Wilson et al. (2011) and Munar (2012) addressed generic social media strategies. First, Wilson et al. (2011) analyzed the social media strategies across 1100 organizations and interviewed 70 executives who managed social media. They found that an experimental approach to social media strategies was rarely successful. Therefore, companies should employ an integrated approach to social media efforts that results in the desired outcome (Chandran, 2016; Wilson et al., 2011).

Wilson et al. (2011) suggested then four different types of social media strategies that organizations can adopt. These four strategies and can move from one to another.

The first is the "Predictive Practitioner" where a business allocates social media groups to specific departments with well-defined goals behind these groups (Mizrachi & Sellitto, 2015). This approach encloses usage to a certain area, such as customer service. The approach works well for organizations seeking to deliver measurable results and established tools and to avoid uncertainty (Kersbergen, 2013). Or, the strategy can be restricted to R&D where organizations try to get customers involved in that specific area. Potential customers, for example, can be asked what kind of features they would like to see on new products. Via social media, organizations can also ask for new ideas and designs for products. Every social media group, in this strategy, has its own target and business objectives.

The second strategy is the "Creative Experimenter," where an organization needs to learn and improve by practicing social media applications (Mizrachi & Sellitto, 2015). This strategy embrace uncertainty, In contrast to the strategy of predictive practitioner. Creative experimenters use small-scale tests to find out methods to improve distinct practices and functions. For example, organizations do so by interacting with customers on social media platforms such as Twitter and Facebook (Kersbergen, 2013; Wilson et al., 2011).

The third strategy is having a "Social Media Champion," where a dedicated social media department or group with a clear policy of social media administers and runs social media activities (Mizrachi & Sellitto, 2015). It may depend on collaboration across multiple levels and functions and include potential external parties. Wilson et al., (2011) added that this strategy also involves large initiatives, which are designed for predictable outcomes.

The final strategy is the "Social Media Transformer," which focuses on how a social media platform can transform the business (Mizrachi & Sellitto, 2015; Wilson et al., 2011). The strategy enables a large-scale interaction that involve external stakeholders, allowing an organization to improve the way of doing business (Wilson, et al., 2011).

Munar (2012) presented another three generic strategies namely: mimetic, advertising and analytic. The mimetic strategy copies the culture and style of social network sites for the organization's own site, like techniques that help to share photos, videos and experiences (Munar, 2012). The advertising strategy adopts more traditional ways to use a social media. This strategy is bases only on making use of advertisements and sending information on social media sites. The analytic strategy analyzes that already available on the web. The logic of the strategy is risks and trends can be predicted if the content have been analyzed, classified and evaluated by (Munar, 2012).

The four strategies of Wilson et al. (2011) are widely approved by academics and practitioners and have been recommended for adaptation (Durkin et al., 2013; Effing & Spi, 2016; Kersbergen, 2013; Mizrachi & Sellitto, 2015). However, there is no study (to the best of author knowledge) attempted to relate the four social media strategies to the students' satisfaction at the higher education sector. Therefore, the current research investigates first, to what extent Egyptian universities employ the four social media strategies introduced by Wilson, et.al. (2011). The research then investigates the extent to which students are satisfied with the content released through social media, their received feedback for inquiries and complains, and the extent to which their privacy and connectivity are protected. Finally, the research investigates the impact of the four social media strategies on the students' satisfaction.

RESEARCH METHODOLOGY

In order to investigate the relationship between Social media strategies and Students' satisfaction at Egyptian universities, the following hypothesis will be tested:

H 1: Social media strategies positively influence students' satisfaction at Egyptian Universities

This hypothesis will be testing through the following sub- hypotheses:

H1.1: Predictive Practitioner strategies positively influences students' satisfaction at Egyptian Universities.
H1.2: Creative Experimenter Strategy positively influences students' satisfaction at Egyptian Universities.
H1.3: Social media champion Strategy positively influence students' satisfaction at Egyptian Universities
H1.4: Social media Transformer Strategy positively influences students' satisfaction at Egyptian Universities.

The research hypothesis and its sub-hypotheses are showed in the following research model.

An online survey (monkey survey) was distributed to students' Facebook groups at different universities. The researcher received 530 responses of which 55% were from Alexandria University (Faculty of Commerce 23.5%, Faculty of Education 12%, Faculty of Art 10.5%, and Faculty of Tourism and Hotels 9.5%). The rest of respondents (45%) were from the Faculties of Commerce from different universities; Damanhour 11%, Tanta 10%, Kafrelsheikh 8.5%, Damietta 8%, and Suez 7%. More than half of the respondents were female students (55%).

Figure 1. Research model

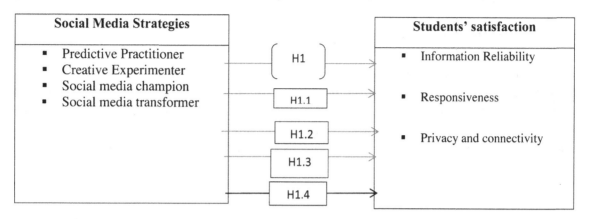

To examine the use of social media strategies, the study employed the four social media strategies: Predictive Practitioner, Creative Experimenter, Social Media Champion and Social Media Transformer (see Appendix -1), introduced by Wilson et al. (2011). Responses were on a five-point scale (ranging from 1 = strongly disagree to 5 = to strongly agree). The results from an exploratory factor analysis indicated that all four items loaded onto factors with an eigenvalue of 6.63 and explained 61.3% of the variability. Cronbach's alpha for this measure was 0.82 for predictive practitioner, 0.78 for creative experimenter, 0.86 for social media champion, and 0.68 for social media transformer. To examine students' satisfaction, the study employed the three factors; Information reliability, Responsiveness, and Privacy & Connectivity (see Appendix -1) used by Khan, et.al. (2017). Responses were on a five-point scale (ranging from strongly disagree to strongly agree). The results from the exploratory factor analysis indicated that all three items loaded onto one factor with an eigenvalue of 2.73 and explained 58.3% of the variability. Cronbach's alpha for this measure was 79%.

The multiple regression analysis was used to investigate the impact of social media strategies on Students' satisfaction. To maintain the statistical power of the multiple regression findings, the minimum sample size may be 50 and preferably 100 (Field, 2009, p. 222; Hair et al., 2010, p. 175). In this research, therefore, the total of 530 responses were used for each independent variable to meet the standard required.

RESEARCH FINDINGS

It was noted that Facebook was the most common social media platform used in Egyptian universities. Respondents gave 93% for Facebook, 3% for YouTube, 1% for Twitter, and 3% for others. Respondents also confirmed that universities mainly uploaded their posts in the form of photos & texts (83%), followed by links (28%) and documents or files (20%). The posting only a text or a photo was rarely used (14%, 7% accordingly). About 45% of posts were news, events or announcements. However, less importance was given to educational materials and advertisements (15% each) and 11% for others.

The Use of the Four Social Media Strategies

Predictive Practitioner

The predictive practitioner strategy was not clearly implemented. More than half of the students confirmed that each of the Facebook groups belonged to a specific functional group or department (61%), the content of each Facebook group was clear (53%). However, less than half of them (44%) agreed that there was little or no cross-functional coordination among the Facebook groups. About 40% of the students disagreed that each Facebook group either had a clear business objective or knew its own target audience clearly.

Creative Experimenter

About 58% of the students agreed that the faculty encouraged them to actively provide insights and feedback on videos and pictures as well as comments to blog posts. 65% of respondents agreed that the faculty usually used its Facebook groups to explore their opinions and suggestions on certain topics. However, 60% of students disagreed that each Facebook group had it unique style of postings and responses. Around half of them (46%) were not in agreement that each Facebook group enabled engagement and gave feedback to their posts.

Social Media Champion

About half of the students noticed that there was homogeneity and coordination between the faculty Facebook groups (56%), and that the faculties regularly developed their Facebook groups (56%). However, they did not agree that the faculties provided clear polices and guidelines for using the Facebook groups (51%). About two-thirds of them (62%) disagreed that their faculties published regular reports on their Facebook groups' achievements, their number of followers, or the number of complaints received and solved.

Social Media Transformer

It was noted that the social media transformer strategy was widely used by Egyptian universities. The majority of students agreed that there were a lot of posts about how each faculty responded to surprises and emerging trends (83%) and how Facebook groups targeted students, internal staff, and interested external bodies e.g. companies, society (74%). 61% of the students confirmed that the Facebook groups typically represented multiple departments and about 37% of them agreed that sometimes they faced technical problems to access Facebook groups.

Students' Satisfaction

Information Reliability

It was noted that there was a lack of satisfaction of students with the information reliability faculties unusually posted on Facebook. 48% of respondents were unsatisfied and 30% were undecided. The respondents confirmed that it was rare that faculties posted important information on social media (59.5%), but there were lots of posts of news, events and announcements. Around half of the respondents (44%) agreed that the information posted on social media was regularly updated. More than half of the respondents (57%) confirmed that they frequently accessed the posts, and also that the content of theses posts was ethically acceptable. Around one third of respondents (49%) agreed that they found contradictable information posted by the same department on social media. Only half of them (46%) trusted the posted information. About 45% of respondents explained that there was a lack of guidance and instructions provided to access the posted links. Also, 42% of students asserted that the social media team had the ability to resolve any technical problems related to open posted links, videos or documents.

Responsiveness

Regarding the faculty's responsiveness to any inquires on the social media channel, half of the students agreed that they could easily lodge their complaints and suggestions to the faculty through social media sites. However, only a small number of respondents had positive feedback to their considerations. Around 20% of students confirmed that they did not receive immediate acknowledgement that their concerns were received. Responses usually came late and sometimes were ambiguous and not fully understandable, they were not persuasive and not supported by enough evidence. Moreover, only one third of students confirmed that their problem raised through social media got resolved favorably, and responses to complaints /suggestions were shared on SM. 31% of student agreed that whenever they approached the faculty through social media, proper advice was given for taking further action.

Privacy and Connectivity

About 44% of the students confirmed that they were fearful of giving negative feedback on a post to the faculty. They confirmed that it was possible that the faculty blocked their social media account for giving negative feedback. Also, half of the students (50%) confirmed that they usually received unknown messages from outsiders other than the faculty when they responded to posts.

Social Media Strategies and Students' Satisfaction

The following table explains the findings of the multiple regression analysis

To limit the multicollinearity between the independent variables, the VIF values should be above 10 (Hair et al., 2010). The table above shows that VIF values were around 4.00 for all the variables. The multicollinearity between the variables was not pointed and the results of regression, accordingly, were meaningful.

The regression analysis indicates that the variances of the four social media strategies account for .196 of the total variances in the student satisfaction at Egyptian universities. As depicted in Table (1), the overall results of the regression model are significant at P value = .000 which indicates that the results of regression are statistically significant. The ranking of the beta (B) values in Table (1) also indicates that the Predictive practitioner variable has the highest value (.482), followed by Social media champion (.237), Creative experimenter (.181), and Social media transformer (.018), all significant at P < .05. This suggests that variances in the Predictive practitioner strategy account for the largest proportion of variances in students' satisfaction, followed by the social media champion, creative experimenter, and social media transformer combination, respectively. The table also showed a positive sign of B value for each independent variable, concluding that each of the social media strategies positively influenced students' satisfaction. The positive sign of B, as shown in Table (1), indicates that the four social media strategies positively influence the students' satisfaction. Accordingly, all hypotheses are accepted.

Table 1. The outputs of multiple regression analysis

	Unstandardized Coefficient		Standardized Coefficient	T-value	Sig. (P)	VIF
	B	Std. Error	Beta			
(Constant)	.387	.167		2.310	.024*	
Predictive practitioner	.451	.122	.482	3.702	.000*	4.560
Creative experimenter	.150	.103	.181	1.459	.041*	4.124
Social media champion	.235	.110	.237	2.126	.037*	3.348
Social media transformer	.016	.110	.018	.144	.016*	4.059
Prediction Accuracy	R= .454; R^2 = .206; Adjusted R^2 = .196					
Significance	F= 49.891; P value= .000; No. 530					

Independent variables are social media strategies (Predictive practitioner, Creative experimenter, Social media champion, and Social media transformer). The dependent variable is the effective use of social media.

* Significant at 0.05.

DISCUSSION AND CONCLUSION

The research findings indicate that there is a lack of satisfaction in students on the information which faculties usually post on Facebook. There are many reasons like information reliability, responsiveness, privacy and connectivity. The findings also explain that the four social media strategies of Wilson, et al. (2011) contribute about 20% to the change in students' satisfaction level. Within the research scope therefore, faculties should implement the four social media strategies effectively in order to increase the students' level of satisfaction.

The predictive practitioner strategy was not clearly implemented. Each of the Facebook groups of a faculty should belong clearly to a specific functional group or department with a clear content for each of them. In addition, faculties should establish cross-functional coordination among Facebook groups to avoid contradictory information. Each Facebook group should have clear business objectives and know clearly its own target audience. For example, the public relations Facebook group should focus on events relevant to external communities, while the students' affairs group should focus on lectures, exams and events relevant to students. The students' activities group should focus on activities related to students. Each Facebook group should have regular content review requirements. Faculties can also measure the impact of each Facebook group with existing metrics. Facebook groups should pay more attention to educational posts and less attention to news, events and announcements.

Each Facebook group should also provide training for its social media team on written communication, effective content, how to respond for comments and inquiries effectively and timely. Responses should be unambiguous and fully understandable, more persuasive and supported by enough evidence. Online and interpersonal communication skills, flexibility, creativity, and risk awareness are required skills for employees who design a Facebook group, or are involved in representing an organization online. Other skills are also required such as: project planning management, social media sites technical knowledge and monitoring tools, and analytical and problem-solving abilities (Schroeder, 2014). Organizational systems should also be concerned with compensation and performance management to promote the right types of behaviors and attitudes for successful social media use (Harold, 2014).

Faculties need more practice to enhance the creative experimenter strategy. Faculties should give more encouragement to students to provide insight and feedback on videos and pictures, and comment on blog posts. Each Facebook group has to have it unique style of postings and responses. Each Facebook group should pay more attention to students' engagement and giving feedback to their posts. Faculties should enable engagement, listen and learn from the resulting conversations. Students should ensure that their negative feedback on posts does not affect them negatively or that their account will be blocked. In order to limit the negative effects of unfavorable comments, the social media strategy should include a content plan. Meaningful content is necessary to create disseminating viral effects that help to spread the business message across a social media channel (Mizrachi & Sellitto, 2015).

For the social media champion, faculties should keep homogeneity and coordination in their Facebook groups. A faculty may have specific leaders and a centralized group dedicated to managing and coordinating Facebook groups across departments or functions. All groups should be continuously developed and updated. Faculties should provide clear polices and guidelines for the users of their Facebook groups. Faculties also need to publish regular reports on their Facebook groups' achievements, the number of followers and the number of complaints received and solved. Each Facebook group should share best practice and lessons learned from other groups throughout the faculty. It is recommended to encourage executive champions and other promoters, including external influencers, to stimulate and participate in faculties' Facebook groups.

The social media transformer strategy was clearly implemented. However, faculties may need to pay more attention to limit the technical problems of downloading files, send feedback or even access the Facebook groups. Each faculty should also have centralized groups dedicated to thinking about how the social media platform can inform the faculty's culture and business strategy in light of emerging trends.

Successful social media strategies need to have an integrated approach comprising factors from both positivism and negativism (Klautzsch, 2017). On the one side, the strategy should exploit the upside of social media such as the faculty benefits. On the other hand, the strategy should limit the downside by reducing the attacks of social media towards the faculty (Berthon et al., 2012; Effing, 2013; Klang & Nolin, 2011; Thackeray et al., 2008).

Finally, the research findings indicate that not enough concern was directed towards educational posts, only 15%, with more space given to news, events and announcements. Therefore, universities need to work to employ social media in the learning and teaching process. Social media provides a unique stage for interaction amongst students and teachers and amongst students themselves. Through social media, students find it easy as well as convenient to communicate, access information, and to provide information. In recent years academics have been expanding their social media usage to offer after-hours support for students, deliver and host lectures, disseminate information and engage in discussions (Chugh, 2017). However, universities need to ensure that there is a high-quality technical infrastructure in place to facilitate these (Harold, 2014). As Facebook is currently the most common social media platform used at Egyptian universities, it is therefore recommended to employ other platforms e.g. YouTube, Twitter, and others in increasing measure.

Research Limitations and Further Research

This research only considered the public Egyptian universities. It is recommended to conduct further research on social media strategies in private/foreign universities such as the American University of Cairo, the German University of Cairo, and the British University of Egypt to investigate the difference between public and private /foreign universities in Egypt. Other public universities may also be included. This research employed quantitative methods to investigate the research aims and objectives. Using qualitative methods, such as in depths interviews, may provide a better understanding of the research topic. The findings also revealed that the four social media strategies of Wilson et al. (2011) contribute only about 20% to the change of students' satisfaction levels. Therefore, further research is required to investigate the other factors that might affect students' satisfaction.

REFERENCES

Abeza, G., O'Reilly, N., & Reid, I. (2013). Relationship marketing and social media in sport. *International Journal of Sport Communication*, *6*(2), 120–142. doi:10.1123/ijsc.6.2.120

Achen, R. (2016). Examining the influence of Facebook fans, content, and engagement on business outcomes in the National Basketball Association. *Journal of Social Media for Organizations*, *5*(1), 1–15.

Agostino, D. (2013). Using social media to engage citizens: A study of Italian municipalities. *Public Relations Review*, *39*(3), 232–234. doi:10.1016/j.pubrev.2013.02.009

Ashle, Ch., & Tuten, T. (2015). Creative strategies in social media marketing: An exploratory study of branded social content and consumer engagement. *Psychology and Marketing*, *32*(1), 15–27. doi:10.1002/mar.20761

Barnes, N., & Mattson, E. (2009). Social media in the 2009 Inc. 500: New tools & new trends. Master New Media. Retrieved from http://www.masternewmedia.org/social-media-research-and-trends-do-top-brands-adopt-and-use-socialmedia

Bennett, G., & Glasgow, R. (2009). The delivery of public health interventions via the internet: Actualizing their potential. *Annual Review of Public Health*, *30*(1), 273–292. doi:10.1146/annurev.publhealth.031308.100235 PMID:19296777

Berthon, P., Pitt, L., Plangger, K., & Shapiro, D. (2012). Marketing meets Web 2.0, social media, and creative consumers: Implications for international marketing strategy. *Business Horizons*, *55*(3), 261–271. doi:10.1016/j.bushor.2012.01.007

Bottles, K., & Sherlock, T. (2011). Who should manage your social media strategy? *Physician Executive*, *37*(2), 68–72. PMID:21465899

Brown, E. (2010). *How implementing social media strategies (the right way) attracts customer loyalty*. Unpublished master thesis, American University, Washington, D.C.

Bryer, T. (2013). Designing social media strategies for effective citizen engagement: A case example and model. A Publication of the National Civic League.

Chandran, D. (2016). Social media and HIV/AIDS: Implications for social work education. *Social Work Education, 35*(3), 333–343. doi:10.1080/02615479.2016.1154659

Chris, P. (2014). Social Media: Major Topics in Dissertation Research. *Education, 135*(3).

Chugh, R. (2017). The Role and Use of Social Media in Higher Education. *The Higher Education Review.* Retrieved from https://www.thehighereducationreview.com/opinion/in-my-view/the-role-and-use-of-social-media-in-higher-education-fid-38.html

Comlekce, F., & Guney, S. (2016). Social media strategies of the European Union bodies: A comparison with Turkey's experience. *Gaziantep University Journal of Social Sciences, 15*(4), 1119–1130. doi:10.21547/jss.265501

Culnan, M., McHugh, P., & Zubillaga, J. (2010). How large U.S. companies can use Twitter and other social media to gain business value. *MIS Quarterly Executive, 9*(4), 243–259.

De Swaan Arons, M., van den Driest, F., & Weed, K. (2014). The ultimate marketing machine. *Harvard Business Review, 92*(7), 54–63.

Donelle, L., & Booth, R. (2012). Health tweets: An exploration of health promotion on twitter. *Online Journal of Issues in Nursing, 17*, 4. PMID:23036060

Dubai School of Government. (2013). Transforming Education in the Arab World: Breaking Barriers in the Age of Social Learning (5th ed.). Arab Social Media Report.

Durkin, M., McGowan, P., & McKeown, N. (2013). Exploring social media adoption in small to medium-sized enterprises in Ireland. *Journal of Small Business and Enterprise Development, 20*(4), 716–734. doi:10.1108/JSBED-08-2012-0094

Effing, R. (2013). Social media strategy design. In *2nd Scientific Conference Information Science In an Age of Change*, Warsaw, Poland.

Effing, R., Hillegersberg, J., & Huibers, T. (2011). Social media and political participation: Are Facebook, Twitter and YouTube democratizing our political systems? In *Electronic Participation, Third IFIP WG 8.5 International Conference*, Delft, Netherlands.

Effing, R., & Spi, T. (2016). The social strategy cone: Towards a framework for evaluating social media strategies. *International Journal of Information Management, 36*(1), 1–8. doi:10.1016/j.ijinfomgt.2015.07.009

Gaber, H., & Wright, L. (2014). Fast-food advertising in social media: A case study on Facebook in Egypt. *Journal of Business and Retail Management Research, 9*(1), 52–63.

GrahamP. (2005). Web 2.0. Retrieved from http://www.paulgraham.com/web20.html

Hamm, M., Chisholm, A., Shulhan, J., Milne, A., Scott, S., Given, L., & Hartling, L. (2013). Social media use among patients and caregivers: A scoping review. *BMJ Open, 3*(5), 1–9. doi:10.1136/bmjopen-2013-002819 PMID:23667163

Hanna, R., Rohm, A., & Crittenden, V. (2011). We're all connected: The power of the social media ecosystem. *Business Horizons, 54*(3), 265–273. doi:10.1016/j.bushor.2011.01.007

Harold, S. (2014). Social media in business strategy: The learning and development implications. *Development and Learning in Organizations: An International Journal, 28*(6), 12–15.

Hoffman, D. L., & Fodor, M. (2010). Can you measure the ROI of your social media marketing? *MIT Sloan Management Review, 52*(1), 40–49.

He, X., & Pedraza-Jiménez, R. (2015). Chinese social media strategies: Communication key features from a business perspective. *El Profesional de la Información, 24*(2), 200–209. doi:10.3145/epi.2015.mar.14

Kaplan, A., & Haenlein, M. (2010). Users of the world, unite! The challenges and opportunities of social media. *Business Horizons, 53*(1), 59–68. doi:10.1016/j.bushor.2009.09.003

Kersbergen, R. (2013*). Use social media to your advantage: The validation of the Social Media Strategy Design framework in the municipality of Enscheda.* Unpublished master thesis, Uuiversiteit Twente, Netherlands.

Kietzmann, J., Hermkens, K., McCarthy, I., & Silvestre, B. (2011). Social media? Get serious! Understanding the functional building blocks of social media. *Business Horizons, 54*(1), 241–251. doi:10.1016/j.bushor.2011.01.005

Klang, M., & Nolin, J. (2011). Disciplining social media: An analysis of social media policies in 26 Swedish municipalities. *First Monday, 16*(8), 1–18. doi:10.5210/fm.v16i8.3490

Klautzsch, E. (2017). *Social media performance management leveraging social interactions along the customer journey.* Unpublished PhD thesis, University of St. Gallen, School of Management, Germany.

Korzeniowskiki, P. (2015). Enterprises love from passive to active: social media strategies. *Customer Relationship Management Magazine,* 20-23.

Mattias, R., & Ivaylo, Y. (2017). *Building an online presence - A new social media strategy framework for startups.* Unpublished master thesis, Lund University, Sweden.

Mergel, I., & Bretschneider, S. (2013). A three-stage adoption process for social media use in government. *Public Administration Review, 73*(3), 390–400. doi:10.1111/puar.12021

Mizrachi, I., & Sellitto, C. (2015). Building a Facebook strategy: Some insights from Australian Accommodation Small Tourism Enterprises (STEs). *Journal of Quality Assurance in Hospitality & Tourism, 16*(1), 63–79. doi:10.1080/1528008X.2015.966297

Munar, A. (2012). Social media strategies and destination management. *Scandinavian Journal of Hospitality and Tourism, 12*(2), 101–120. doi:10.1080/15022250.2012.679047

Ng, C., & Wang, W. (2013). Best practices in managing social media for business. *Paper presented at the International Conference on Information Systems (ICIS),* Milan, Italy, Dec 15- 18.

Novillo-Ortiz, D., & Hernández-Pérez, T. (2017). Social media in public health: An analysis of national health authorities and leading causes of death in Spanish-speaking Latin American and Caribbean countries. *BMC Medical Informatics and Decision Making, 17*(16), 1–12. PMID:28158986

Piskorski, M. (2011). Social strategies that work. *Harvard Business Review, 89*(11), 116–122. PMID:22111430

Peruta, A., Ryan, W., & Engelsman, R. (2013). Social Media Branding Strategies for Higher Education: Comparing Facebook pages and Web Sites. *International Journal of Technology, Knowledge and Society*, *9*(1), 11–23. doi:10.18848/1832-3669/CGP/v09i01/56326

Remidez, H., & Jones, N. (2012). Developing a model for social media in project management communications. *International Journal of Business and Social Science*, *3*(3), 33–36.

Risling, T., Risling, D., & Holtslander, L. (2017). Creating a social media assessment tool for family nursing. *Journal of Family Nursing*, *23*(1), 13–33. doi:10.1177/1074840716681071 PMID:28795937

Saied, S., Elsabagh, H., & El-Afandy, A. (2016). Internet and Facebook addiction among Egyptian and Malaysian medical students: A comparative study, Tanta University, Egypt. *International Journal of Community Medicine and Public Health*, *3*(5), 1288–1297. doi:10.18203/2394-6040.ijcmph20161400

Schroeder, H. (2014). Social media in business strategy: The learning and development implications. *Development and Learning in Organizations: An International Journal*, *28*(6), 12–15.

Smith, S. (2013). Conceptualising and evaluating experiences with brands on Facebook. *International Journal of Market Research*, *55*(3), 357–374. doi:10.2501/IJMR-2013-034

Thackeray, R., Neiger, B. L., Hanson, C. L., & McKenzie, J. F. (2008). Enhancing promotional strategies within social marketing programs: Use of Web 2.0 social media. *Health Promotion Practice*, *9*(4), 338–343. doi:10.1177/1524839908325335 PMID:18936268

Werder, K., Helms, R., & Jansen, S. (2014). Social media for success: A strategic framework. In *18th Pacific Asia Conference on Information Systems PACIS 2014*, Chengdu, China, June 24-28.

Williams, J., & Chinn, S. J. (2010). Meeting relationship-marketing goals through social media: A conceptual model for sport marketers. *International Journal of Sport Communication*, *3*(4), 422–437. doi:10.1123/ijsc.3.4.422

Wilson, H., Guinan, P., Parise, S., & Weinberg, B. (2011). What's Your Social Media Strategy? *Harvard Business Review*, *89*(7-8), 23–25.

This research was previously published in the International Journal of Customer Relationship Marketing and Management (IJCRMM), 10(1); pages 1-16, copyright year 2019 by IGI Publishing (an imprint of IGI Global).

APPENDIX 1- RESEARCH SURVEY

Personal Information
Faculty & University:
Gender:
Part 1:

    1. Out of %100, rate the Kind of social media mainly your faculty use for its posts:

Social media	Facebook	Twitter	YouTube	Skype	Others (Please mention)
% of use					

    2. Out of %100, rate the form of posts:

Form	Photo	Text	Both photo and text	Link	Documents (file)	Videos	Others (Please mention)
% of use							

    3. Out of %100, rate the post types:

Type	News	Events	Advertisements	Announcements	Educational posts	Others (Please mention)
% of use						

Part 2: Students' Satisfaction

Please indicate to what extend do you agree with the followings:

Activities	Strongly Disagree	Disagree	Neutral	Agree	Strongly Agree
Information Reliability					
1. I am satisfied with the information posted by the company/ faculty through Social media					
2. Important information for me are easily obtained through social media					
3. The company/faculty regularly updates the information through Social media					
4. Social media team have the ability to resolve any technical problem related to open posted links, videos or documents.					
5. Guides and instructions are provided (if necessary) to access posted links, videos or documents					
6. Frequent access to social media is available					
7. I am usually trust posted information					
8. the content of posts is ethically accepted.					
9. Sometimes find contradictable information posted from the same department/ different departments					
Responsiveness					
10. Lodging complains & suggestions to my company through social media is easy					
11.suggestions & complaints through social media are received, and acknowledgement is issued immediately					
12. Receive response to complaints and suggestions sent through social media in reasonable time					
13. Whenever, I approach my company through social media, proper advices are given for taking up any action.					
14. Responses I received is simple language and fully understandable.					
15. Responses regarding my complaints and suggestion are persuasive and are usually supported by evidence.					
16. My problem appraised through social media got resolved favorably.					
17. Responses to complaints /suggestions of all consumers are shared in SM by the company.					
Privacy & Connectivity					
18. I have fear of making a negative feedback on my company/faculty on its post.					
19. I receive unknown messages from outsiders other than my company/faculty due to acting to posts.					
20. It is possible that the company/faculty blocked my social media account for negative feedback.					

Any additional comments...

Part 3: Social media strategies

    Please indicate to what extend do you agree with the followings:

Predictive Practitioner	Strongly Disagree	Disagree	Natural	Agree	Strongly Agree
1-Each of Facebook group is owned by a specific functional group or department.					
2. There is little or no cross-functional coordination among Facebook groups					
3. Each Facebook group has clear business objectives.					
4. The content of each Facebook group is clear					
5. Each Facebook group knows clearly its own audience target.					
Creative Experimenter					
5-Each Facebook group has it unique style of posting and responsiveness.					
6-Each Facebook group enables engagement and giving feedback to their					
7-The faculty usually use its Facebook groups know our opinions and suggestion on certain topics					
8-The faculty encouraged us to actively provide our insights, feedback, on videos, pictures, and comments to blog posts.					
Social Media Champion					
9-We notice a homogenous and coordination between the faculty Facebook groups.					
10-The faculty provides clear polices and guidelines for using it Facebook groups use.					
11-The faculty regularly developed its Facebook groups					
12-The faculty publishes regular reports on its Facebook groups' achievements, no. of followers, no. of complains received and solved, etc.					
13-We notice a homogenous and coordination between the faculty Facebook groups.					
Social Media Transformer					
14- Facebook groups target students, internal staff, and interested external bodies e.g. companies, society, etc.					
15-Sometimes, we face technical problems to access Facebook groups.					
16-The faculty Facebook groups typically represent multiple departments.					
17-There are many posts about how our faculty is in light of surprises and emerging trends.					

Any additional comments...

Index

C

F

G

Ensure Quality Research is Introduced to the Academic Community

Become an Evaluator for IGI Global Authored Book Projects

Premier Reference Source

Stabilizing Currency and Preserving Economic Sovereignty Using the Grondona System

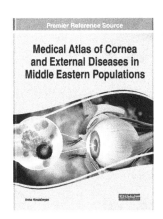

Premier Reference Source

Medical Atlas of Cornea and External Diseases in Middle Eastern Populations

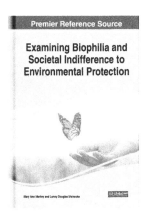

Premier Reference Source

Examining Biophilia and Societal Indifference to Environmental Protection

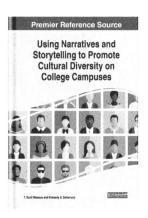

Premier Reference Source

Using Narratives and Storytelling to Promote Cultural Diversity on College Campuses

The overall success of an authored book project is dependent on quality and timely manuscript evaluations.

Applications and Inquiries may be sent to:
development@igi-global.com

Applicants must have a doctorate (or equivalent degree) as well as publishing, research, and reviewing experience. Authored Book Evaluators are appointed for one-year terms and are expected to complete at least three evaluations per term. Upon successful completion of this term, evaluators can be considered for an additional term.

If you have a colleague that may be interested in this opportunity, we encourage you to share this information with them.

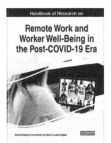

Are You Ready to
Publish Your Research ?

IGI Global
PUBLISHER of TIMELY KNOWLEDGE

IGI Global offers book authorship and editorship opportunities across 11 subject areas, including business, computer science, education, science and engineering, social sciences, and more!

Benefits of Publishing with IGI Global:

- Free one-on-one editorial and promotional support.
- Expedited publishing timelines that can take your book from start to finish in less than one (1) year.
- Choose from a variety of formats, including Edited and Authored References, Handbooks of Research, Encyclopedias, and Research Insights.
- Utilize IGI Global's eEditorial Discovery® submission system in support of conducting the submission and double-blind peer review process.
- IGI Global maintains a strict adherence to ethical practices due in part to our full membership with the Committee on Publication Ethics (COPE).
- Indexing potential in prestigious indices such as Scopus®, Web of Science™, PsycINFO®, and ERIC – Education Resources Information Center.
- Ability to connect your ORCID iD to your IGI Global publications.
- Earn honorariums and royalties on your full book publications as well as complimentary copies and exclusive discounts.

Join Your Colleagues from Prestigious Institutions, Including:

Australian National University

Massachusetts Institute of Technology

JOHNS HOPKINS
UNIVERSITY

HARVARD
UNIVERSITY

COLUMBIA UNIVERSITY
IN THE CITY OF NEW YORK

Learn More at: www.igi-global.com/publish

or Contact IGI Global's Aquisitions Team at: acquisition@igi-global.com

Printed in the United States
by Baker & Taylor Publisher Services